US Air Force
AIR POWER DIRECTORY

US Air Force
AIR POWER DIRECTORY

Editor: David Donald

Aerospace Publishing London
Airtime Publishing USA

Published by
Aerospace Publishing Ltd
179 Dalling Road
London W6 0ES
UK

Copyright © 1992 Aerospace
Publishing Ltd

First published 1992
Reprinted 1994

Aerospace ISBN 1 874023 25 5
                (hardback)
                1 874023 57 3
                (softback)
Airtime ISBN   1-880588-01-3
                (hardback)
                1-880588-16-1
                (softback)

Published under licence in USA and
Canada by AIRtime Publishing Inc.,
10 Bay Street, Westport,
CT 06880, USA

Distributed in the UK,
Commonwealth and Europe by
Airlife Publishing Ltd
101 Longden Road
Shrewsbury SY3 9EB
UK
Telephone: 0743 235651
Fax: 0743 232944

Publisher: Stan Morse
Editor: David Donald
Production Editor: Karen Leverington
Picture Researcher and
    Editorial Assistant: Tim Senior
Design: Barry Savage
        Robert Hewson
Authors: Bob Archer
         Chris Chant
         David Donald
         Robert F. Dorr
         Lindsay Peacock
Artists: Chris Davey
         Grant Race
         John Weal
Typesetting: SX Composing Ltd

Printed in Singapore

The publishers gratefully acknowledge
the assistance given by the units of the
US Air Force, Air National Guard and
Air Force Reserve, and aviation
corporations, who have generously
helped with this publication.

World Air Power Journal is a
registered trademark in the
United States of America of
AIRtime Publishing Inc.

World Air Power Journal is
published quarterly and is available
by subscription and from many
fine book and hobby stores.

**SUBSCRIPTION AND BACK
NUMBERS:**

UK and World (except USA and
Canada) write to:
Aerospace Publishing Ltd
FREEPOST
PO Box 2822
London
W6 0BR, UK

(No stamp required if posted
within the UK)

USA and Canada, write to:
AIRtime Publishing Inc.
Subscription Dept
10 Bay Street
Westport
CT 06880, USA

Regular phone number:
(203) 266-3580
Toll-free order number in USA:
1 800 359-3003

Prevailing subscription rates are as
follows:
Softbound edition for 1 year:
    $58.00
Softbound edition for 2 years:
    $108.00
Softbound back numbers (subject
to availability) are $17.95 each for
delivery within mainland USA,
Alaska and Hawaii. Canadian and
overseas prices available upon
request. American Express,
Discover Card, MasterCard and
Visa accepted. When ordering
please include your card number,
expiration date and signature.

Publisher, North America:
    Mel Williams
Subscription Director:
    Linda DeAngelis
Retail Sales Director:
    Jill Brooks
Charter Member Services
Manager:
    Janie Munroe

US Air Force
AIR POWER DIRECTORY

CONTENTS

USAF ORGANIZATION AND DEPLOYMENT

The United States Air Force (USAF) is the world's most powerful air arm. Even after dramatic reductions in equipment and personnel, it maintains an impressive strategic bomber and missile force. More important in these changing times, the USAF is the only air force capable of rapidly deploying combat-ready assets to any location in the world, and is increasing its potential to fight in Third World trouble spots – in recognition that American interests in the 1990s will be threatened more by brushfire wars than from the independent nation-states of the dismantled Soviet Union. It remains the only air force with global airlift capability.

In the post-Desert Storm era, the USAF has undergone its most fundamental changes since it became an independent service in 1947. The changes were rapid, and have had a strong impact on every aspect of air operations – aircraft, missions, units and people. Some of the change reflects a fundamental decision to reduce the size of US armed forces to their lowest level since before World War II, not just because the Cold War ended but, in part, due to the budget deficit crisis which drives American policy. Continuing changes affect not the USAF's size but its shape: the strengthening of home-based expeditionary, composite task groups of fighters, fighter-bombers, attack aircraft and tankers which will substitute for the costly, traditional approach of garrisoning aircraft and people overseas. Only a few principal airbases and combat wings now remain on foreign soil in Europe and Korea. Most, now, are being revamped to go to war from American soil.

Though whittled in size from 36 to 26 tactical wings, from 570,000 to 400,000 personnel, and being reshaped in ways that are no less than traumatic, the hi-tech USAF of B-1B, F-117, F-15, F-16, C-17 and other aircraft types remains second to none in its competence for what a sign in the Pentagon describes as its official mission: TO FLY AND FIGHT.

Not since General Curtis E. LeMay, and perhaps not ever, has a single person left such an imprint on the USAF as General Merrill (Tony) McPeak, its chief of staff during the 1991 war with Iraq and during post-war restructuring.

LeMay led the bomber offensive against Germany and Japan, shaped the Strategic Air Command (SAC) which was the showcase of USAF policy and purpose during the Cold War, and held the top job during Vietnam. Because of him, the USAF was led by 'bomber generals' from 1945 into the 1970s. McPeak made it clear that the USAF of the 1990s is to be run by fighter pilots. McPeak demanded imaginative thinking at all levels of the service, and made it clear that nothing would be allowed to stand in the way of a leaner, 'smarter' force.

Although not destined to see through all of the changes he began, McPeak was the driving force for reductions, innovations and changes. The chief of staff presided over the dismantling of tradition-honored Strategic Air Command, Tactical Air Command and Military Airlift Command. To replace SAC, TAC and MAC, McPeak laid the foundation for new Air Combat and Air Mobility Commands. McPeak even introduced a new uniform.

Never before has so much changed, so rapidly. But the United States Air Force has been through nine decades of development and change, and has evolved over time in cadence with changes in the world around it.

History

The modern-day USAF traces its roots to the Aeronautical Division of the US Army's Signal Corps, established on 1 August 1907. Its first aircraft was a Wright Flyer. On 18 July 1914, the name was changed to Aviation Section, still within the Signal Corps, and remained so well into World War I when, on 20 May 1918, it became the US Army Air Service. The first US-trained American Expeditionary Forces air ace was Captain Edward V. Rickenbacker, who, by the end of the conflict, became the leading Air Service ace with 26.33 aerial victories.

Between wars another change of name occurred, when today's USAF was renamed the US Army Air Corps on 2 July 1926. Prior to America's entry into World War II, yet another renaming took place on 20 June 1941 and the Air Corps became US Army Air Forces (USAAF).

The wartime USAAF, fed by the giant industrial

Opposite: Air power personified: a pair of USAF Eagles exudes power and aggressiveness. Despite recent advances in the CIS and elsewhere, the F-15 is rightly regarded as the world's premier service fighter, and is the yardstick by which all others are measured.

Below: The label 'flying gas-station' seems more than appropriate as this KC-135Q uses a mass of lights to direct an F-117 during a radio-silent refueling. The F-117 is the undisputed king of the night skies – the only operational aircraft to be able to regularly penetrate air defenses undetected.

Organization

Right: Its port side bristling with guns and sensors, a Lockheed AC-130H gunship cruises at medium altitude, hunting for targets. The new-look Air Force places great emphasis on Special Operations, and has recently put all its SOF assets into a separate command to maximize their effect by streamlining the chain of command.

Far right: Many in the Air Force see the Lockheed/Boeing/General Dynamics F-22 as one of the most vital programs currently being undertaken by the service. By combining stealth with agility, performance and new weapons, the F-22 will be able to continue the tradition set by the F-15 as the world's top fighter.

machine of the American heartland, eventually had nearly 60,000 warplanes and reached its peak strength of 2,372,292 personnel in 1944. The B-17 Flying Fortress, B-29 Superfortress and P-51 Mustang were among the best-known warplanes and played vital roles in defeating the Axis. A Superfortress brought the dawn of the atomic age with the 6 August 1945 bombing of Hiroshima.

In a period of upheaval very much like today's, the years after VJ Day brought dramatic changes in the US defense establishment, including transformation of the USAAF into an independent United States Air Force on 18 September 1947. By this time, two of the newly-independent USAF's best-known components, Strategic Air Command (SAC) and Tactical Air Command (TAC), had been established and were in operation.

The Cold War presented new challenges when the USAF's transports (the term airlift was not in use then) became the backbone of the 1948 Berlin Airlift, supplying that city during a Soviet blockade which was eventually broken. The USAF fielded the Boeing B-47 Stratojet bomber in time to coincide with the 1949 explosion of the Soviet Union's first atomic bomb. Commanded and shaped by the 'bomber generals' who had led the strategic campaigns of World War II, the USAF abruptly found itself fighting not against a Soviet nuclear threat but, rather, on the Korean peninsula.

The 'police action' in Korea (1950-53) produced the first jet-versus-jet battles, established the North American F-86 Sabre as a world standard bearer, and added 40 more air aces to the USAF's hundreds from the world wars.

During the mid-1950s, the USAF reached the pinnacle of its strength, with more than 2,000 B-47s equipping SAC and being joined by the Boeing B-52 Stratofortress and Convair B-58 Hustler. A 'century series' of supersonic fighters was introduced, beginning with the North

American F-100 Super Sabre. It was an era of fiery tension between the world's two superpowers, enflamed by the introduction of the first ICBMs (intercontinental ballistic missiles) in the 1960s.

But it was war in Vietnam (1960-73) which occupied the US Air Force during a period of domestic as well as political turmoil. Curiously, tactical fighter-bombers were carrying out what had previously been called strategic bombing missions, to Hanoi and environs, while B-52s were striking Viet Cong guerrillas in South Vietnam. The Republic F-105 Thunderchief and McDonnell F-4 Phantom joined the roster of USAF classic aircraft and the helicopter became, finally, an integral part of the force. The USAF's Sikorsky HH-53B/C Super Jolly Greens, among other types, pulled off very successful combat rescues.

Like all wars, Vietnam brought changes. Never defeated in battle, the American military emerged from Vietnam in disrepute and plagued with internal strife. The shift from the national conscription (which had been in effect from 1940 to 1975) to an all-volunteer force, at the time it happened, reflected public scorn for the profession of arms; within the service, it was a time of racial conflict and drug problems. While this low ebb was being reversed, it happened very quietly that generals with tactical experience – fighter pilots – began to run the Air Force. The difficult years of the middle to late 1970s were also a time of successes, when the USAF forged ahead with some of the highly proven items employed today: the F-117 'Stealth Fighter', the F-15 and F-16 series, the AMRAAM missile. Social change, plus a 'hard line' towards drugs and intolerance, brought a higher caliber of recruit into the USAF's 'shade 84' blue. By the 1990s the USAF was the best-educated and most highly motivated force it had ever been, not merely equipped with hi-tech items but almost entirely free of drugs, crime, violence, racism and discrimination. The best-trained officers, NCOs (noncommissioned officers) and enlisted personnel ever carried on the USAF's rosters found themselves confronting the 1990s (after defeating Saddam Hussein) with no worry except whether they, themselves, might have a career left when the current 'downsizing' ended.

Integral to the force of the 1990s was the Reserve com-

Below: The most futuristic shape yet to have taken to the air publicly is the Northrop B-2, an advanced strategic bomber. With the global situation having removed much of the nuclear threat to the United States, procurement of no more than 20 of these hugely expensive aircraft can be justified.

Aircraft

A date for the end of the Cold War, if one must be chosen, may as well have been 28 January 1992 when President Bush announced that the B-2 'Stealth Bomber' – the result of an exceedingly ambitious 'black' program at the outer edge of technological capabilities – would not be further developed. Just 18 months earlier, Pentagon planning had looked to an Air Force with no fewer than 132 B-2s (and growth to 40 tactical wings rather than a cutback to 26 or fewer). The B-2s were to be backed up by 95 B-1B penetrators and perhaps 100 surviving B-52H bombers in the stand-off role. Advanced missiles, among them the AGM-129A ACM (Advanced Cruise Missile), were part of plans for the 1990s and remain so, but today's strategic force is down to fewer than 200 long-range bombers, and ACM procurement was cut back sharply.

The Lockheed F-22 Rapier ATF (Advanced Tactical Fighter) was developed to supplant the F-15C Eagle. Even in a time of tight dollars and 'downsized' forces, 500 F-22s are wanted, but in early 1992 no assurance existed beyond an FSD (full-scale development) fleet of nine single-seat F-22As, two two-seat F-22Bs, and two test vehicles.

ponent. In fact, about 50 per cent of the USAF's fighter strength will come from the Air National Guard and Air Force Reserve under a scenario envisaged in 1992.

Above: It takes a lot to make the KC-135 tanker look like a small airplane, but the C-5 Galaxy transport manages with ease. Both types are examples of the disparate support fleet that maximizes the effect of the combat warplanes.

Below: The USAF's most numerous aircraft is the F-16, which serves in a variety of fighter roles. This pair is from the Florida Air National Guard which, along with other strategically-placed ANG units, flies the ADF (Air Defense Fighter) variant on interception duties to protect the United States.

Above: The General Dynamics F-16C has been and will continue to be the backbone of the USAF. The reliance placed on it during the Gulf War underlined the need for a versatile combat aircraft. The program to find a Fighting Falcon replacement is slowly getting underway, but it will be well into the next century before the F-16's reign is ended.

Center right: Recipient of Europe's first F-15E Strike Eagle was Lakenheath's 48th Fighter Wing, who are trading in their F-111Fs for the new Eagles. With the end of the Cold War, and the threat of war in Europe fast receding, the F-15E will happily fill the shoes of the deep-strike F-111s.

Two hundred and ten C-17 airlifters were once planned, a total officially reduced to 120 but possibly likely to end up even smaller. Many of the recent USAF aircraft programs have been subject to criticism, but few as pointedly as the C-17 (where the cost of getting the first example into the sky would have paid for 50 Lockheed C-5B Galaxies). More rigorous control over development of new items of equipment is a part of the changing 1990s.

The USAF had once planned a special operations force of 55 Bell/Boeing CV-22 Ospreys. This plan is unlikely to be resurrected and the USAF's helicopter fleet, like the bulk of its fighter force, will be strongly in need of service-life extension efforts in the 1990s. Virtually every principal aircraft in service – B-1B, F-117, F-15, F-16, MH-53J and others – will need upgrading as a compensation for new airplanes unlikely to be purchased.

The final major aircraft purchases of the century are trainers, including the T-1A Jayhawk TTTS (Tanker Transport Trainer System), JPATS (Joint Primary Air Trainer System) and EFS (Enhanced Flight Screener). Like all USAF programs from the purchase of nuts and bolts to the acquisition of hi-tech missiles, these programs will be eyeballed far more closely than in the past.

Units

Perhaps the most difficult change to keep track of (and to document in this volume) is the change in nomenclature of Air Force units. F-16s and A-10s once belonged to Tactical Fighter Squadrons, C-141s and C-5s belonged to Military Airlift Squadrons, and so on. No longer. Virtually every unit in the USAF has changed the adjectives which describe its mission.

What has *not* changed is the terminology used by the service to name its formations. Using terms which date to the 1930s (and to simplify, somewhat, a complex topic) USAF formations are named as follows:

A **flight** is the smallest formation, usually consisting of a dozen or fewer people or, typically, of four aircraft. The typical flight leader would be a captain. Letter designations are used: A Flight, B Flight, etc, rendered in phonetics as Alpha Flight, Bravo Flight, etc.

A **squadron** is made up of several flights (typically four), usually a couple of hundred people, and from eight (C-141B) to 24 (F-16C) airplanes. A squadron is commanded by a lieutenant colonel or, infrequently, a major. Number designations apply, one or two digits for the regular Air Force (7th Fighter Squadron), 100s series for the Air National Guard (121st Fighter Squadron), 200s series unused (except for the 210th RQS, Alaska ANG), and 301 onward for the regular Air Force again.

A **group** is made up of squadrons. The group was mostly omitted in recent years but will become increasingly important in the restructured 1990s.

A **wing** is made up of several squadrons (typically three

B-52s and KC-135 tankers always shared bases while under SAC control. This is set to continue with the new 'mixed-wing' policies now being implemented. The B-52s, with their place in any future USAF bombing force assured, are now largely training for conventional missions.

or four) and, after recent changes, now encompasses not merely flying operations but support activities as well, with a single wing having responsibility for a single base. Under this arrangement, most wings will now be commanded by a brigadier general rather than, as in the past, a colonel.

These formations in the past have reported to numbered air forces (8th Air Force) or to Air Divisions (315th Air Division) on the chain of command leading to the top of their 'majcom' (major command), such as Air Mobility Command. After recent changes, most Air Divisions were eliminated. A wing commander in Air Combat Command is now much closer to dealing directly with the four-star general in charge of the command.

People changes

To many airmen (the term for all people, regardless of gender or rank, in the USAF) the 'people changes' of the 1990s include the USAF decision to deny NCO status and the title 'sergeant' to people in pay grade E-4 – who have now been relegated to 'senior airman'. To an Air Mobility Command aeromedical evacuation specialist on a Lockheed C-141B StarLifter, such a seemingly innocuous change can be murder: flying red-eye missions attending to the injured and ill in the back of the bouncing metal tube that is a C-141B fuselage, coping with time-zone changes, flight-line food, discomfiting layovers, and the 'Airlift Big Eye' (it's time to sleep and your eyes won't close); a low-

Above: Three F-15C Eagles of the 128th Fighter Squadron, GA ANG. The Air National Guard faces a much expanded role in the future, as evidenced by the deployment of several units in the front line of Operation Desert Storm.

ranking enlisted person might be excused for wondering if the paycheck will ever suffice, or the promotions come, to make a tough job seem rewarding. Many in the middle enlisted ranks, ranging from F-16 crew chiefs to 'rehabbed' B-52 tail gunners (their job was eliminated on hours' notice on 1 October 1991) are keenly motivated to press on with the careers they launched in the heady, free-spending 1980s. Increasingly, they have to accomplish tasks with fewer people and coax satisfactory performance out of ageing equipment and airplanes, while facing tough choices about livelihood, family and future.

For officers, questions arise about retention, promotion and opportunity. Newly trained fighter pilots are now being 'banked' (placed behind desks with the prospect of flying jobs two to three years in the future), a significant morale issue. In 1985, a good officer could reach the rank of colonel (O-6) in a 20-year career and perhaps command a wing. Today, this officer will retire as a lieutenant colonel and never command anything larger than a squadron.

Turmoil, upheaval, even revolution, are words in no way too strong to characterize the changes that at every level which have impacted on the USAF's missions, units and people. If General McPeak's plans persist, even the tra-

Right: For many years the US Air Force has seen the importance of electronic warfare, and remains in the forefront of technology within the discipline. Protection of strike forces by airborne platforms is vital to minimizing losses, this task being entrusted to the EF-111A Raven – known more informally as the 'Spark Vark'.

ditional uniform will be gone, replaced by a uniform so radically different that the first airmen to wear it feel disoriented, resembling nothing if not the bridge crew of the 'Enterprise' in *Star Trek: The Next Generation*.

The bottom line is that the USAF is now moving to reach its smallest size since it became an independent service, and will focus on rapid deployment of home-garrisoned forces rather than keeping up costly installations overseas. It is still possible today to do a walk-through inspection of an Air Force squadron and see posters bearing a traditional slogan of the recent past: THE MISSION OF THE UNITED STATES AIR FORCE IS TO FLY AND FIGHT, AND DON'T YOU EVER FORGET IT. Though other traditions – SAC, TAC, MAC, some familiar aircraft, some personnel accoutrements – are gone, the motto is still valid in the final decade of the 20th century.

National command structure

The National Command Authority (NCA) is the 'chain of command' under which the USAF flies in peacetime and fights in war. Unlike the USAF itself, the NCA has not been restructured. It is rooted in the principle that policy decisions are made by civilian leaders.

Key figure in this national chain of command is the CINC, pronounced 'sink,' the Commander-in-Chief of any of the Joint-Service unified and specified commands. A celebrity-class CINC in recent years was US Army General H. Norman Schwarzkopf, who headed US Central Command responsible for the Middle East. A CINC is a four-star general or admiral: except for the Chairman of the Joint Chiefs of Staff, he is the highest-ranking officer to command combat forces.

Most CINCS have geographic purview, an example being the CINC of US European Command at Stuttgart, Germany, who heads up American forces in the European theater (this officer wears another 'hat' as NATO commander). A few CINCs have functional responsibility, an example being the CINC of US Strategic Command, or Stratcom, at Offutt AFB, Nebraska, who commands all strategic bomber, missile and submarine nuclear forces.

This NCA 'chain of command' runs downward from the President, in his role as Commander-in-Chief, to the Secretary of Defense, to the Chairman of the Joint Chiefs of Staff, to the CINCs. Unlike many nations, the United States does not have a general staff. The Chairman is the *only* officer above the CINC. Other Washington brass, including the Air Force Chief of Staff, hold advisory roles and command no combat forces – though they wield enormous influence.

Air Force command structure

When the USAF's command structure was reorganized in 1992, publicists wrote a glitzy sentence to sum it up: "Air Force people building the world's most respected air and space force, with global power and reach for America." Translated into English, 'power' is Air Combat Command while 'reach' is Air Mobility Command – these being two of the USAF's three principal components:

Air Combat Command (ACC), at Langley AFB, Virginia, is responsible for warplanes (with few exceptions) ranging from B-2s to F-16s. ACC is a 'holding' command: it carries out realistic warfighting preparation but in actual conflict would turn its resources over to the CINC of a unified or specified command.

It works this way: ACC 'owns' fighters, fighter-bombers and assault transports in a composite wing, but would turn them over to the CINC of US Central Command if they were deployed to fight in the Middle East. ACC 'owns' B-2s, B-1Bs and B-52s, but would turn them over to the CINC of US Strategic Command if they were employed in an actual nuclear conflict. Turnover is easy because the people remain the same; the officer who carries out his USAF role by commanding ACC's 9th Air Force, for example, also has a second duty in his Joint-Service role as Commander of US Central Command's Air Forces (CENTAF).

ACC was formed on 1 June 1992 from combat assets of the former SAC and TAC, in recognition that the distinction between 'strategic' and 'tactical' air power was artificial. Thus, ACC trains for B-2 'strategic' missions *and*

for expeditionary deployment to Third World locations by OA-10s, A-10s and C-130Hs of a 'tactical' composite wing.

Air Mobility Command (AMC) at Scott AFB, Illinois, is responsible for airlift and most inflight-refueling tanker operations. Also formed on 1 June 1992 by merging airlift forces of the former Military Airlift Command with most SAC tankers, AMC is responsible for C-17s, C-5Bs, KC-135s and other globe-spanning combat support aircraft.

Air Force Materiel Command (AFMC) at Wright-Patterson AFB, Ohio, is responsible for developing, acquiring, delivering and sustaining USAF weapons systems. Formed 1 July 1992, AFMC employs integrated weapons systems management for 'cradle to grave' management of USAF aircraft and other systems. While the other commands break down into numbered air forces, AFMC is broken into centers, such as the Aeronautical Systems Center (formerly ASD, Aeronautical Systems Division) at Wright-Patterson AFB.

At home, other USAF components also include Air Training Command (ATC) and AF Special Operations Command (AFSOC). Abroad, the USAF operates US Air Forces in Europe (USAFE), and Pacific Air Forces (PACAF).

Above: Designed for the close air support role, the A-10 'Warthog' has always been the subject of hot debate between those who claimed it was too vulnerable and those who point to its achievements (notably recently in Operation Desert Storm). Many have been re-roled for forward air control.

Below: The days of nuclear alert may have passed, but strategic bomber crews never take their jobs any less seriously. A large fleet of B-1B bombers forms the main airborne element of the US nuclear deterrent, backed up by cruise missile-launching B-52s.

WARFIGHTING ROLES

The United States Air Force is the most powerful air arm in the world, equipped largely with state-of-the-art aircraft and weapons which are available in sizeable quantities. In an era of defense budget stringency, the USAF is attempting to maintain its premier position by having fewer, more sophisticated aircraft, and by utilizing them more efficiently. This chapter reviews, role by role, the aircraft types currently in service with the US Air Force, and those being procured or under development to replace them. Finally, the manner in which the various systems would be brought to bear as a single, cohesive force is examined, illustrating how the US Air Force may expect to go to war if called upon to do so in the next few years.

When the US Air Force entered the 1990s, the service had never been more uncertain about the nature of the threats it would face during the decade. Dramatic upheavals in the Soviet Union and Eastern Europe had radically altered the political temperature of superpower relations and, with the end of the Warsaw Pact, the concept of a fierce conflict involving nuclear weapons on the European Central Front seemed virtually impossible. Yet, on paper the arsenal still maintained by the new Commonwealth of Independent States (CIS) could not be ignored, and the failed military coup in August 1991 would give the Pentagon further cause for alarm.

Just a few months previously the US Air Force had been involved in a swift and bloody conflict to oust Saddam Hussein from Kuwait. The successes of the Gulf War were achieved largely by air power, and the key factors had proved to be 'smart' technology, rapid deployment and excellent training for personnel at all levels. The message to the Pentagon from both the Middle East and Moscow was that while there was a great peace 'dividend' to be gained from the final thawing of any remnants of the Cold War, the huge potential for armed conflict remained in the world. Considerable budget cuts were likely, and money would have to be spent wisely on weapon systems that

would be of maximum effectiveness in a wide variety of combat scenarios.

By 1992 the US Air Force had set out its stall for the rest of the decade: a slimmer, leaner force with a considerable cut in personnel, unit and aircraft numbers. Gone are the days of huge interceptor forces to meet the Soviet bomber threat; gone is the vast organization of Strategic Air Command, whose principle *raison d'être* was to stand ready to wage all-out nuclear war at a moment's notice; gone are the massive tactical forces in Europe who waited for the first tanks to come crashing through the border from the East.

In their place is a far more flexible force, able to respond to many varying threats coming from any direction and in any part of the globe. The nature of wing structures is moving away from the single-type concept with the introduction of 'composite wings', with several aircraft types attached in order to provide a self-contained rapid projection force tailored to a specific threat. Traditional single-type wings are having their roles widened to spread their capabilities across a greater number of scenarios. With the budget axe swinging on Capitol Hill, many famous units are being disbanded.

Budgetary concerns are being felt strongly in the Pentagon, and procurement of expensive weapon systems to meet the projected threats of the future is being met with more political opposition than ever before. How many of the prestigious procurement programs will survive the decade remains to be seen. In order to understand the implications of the sweeping changes under way within the US Air Force organization, one must examine, role by role, the aircraft it currently uses and has procured, and the way in which it expects to use them.

Strategic bombers

Since the days of the Eighth Air Force in Europe, the strategic bomber has been the king of the US Air Force fleet. Vast armadas of large aircraft have been maintained to crush major enemies in all-out nuclear war. Their very existence can be seen as the primary defense against any such conflict, for any aggression against the United States would prompt the infliction of total destruction upon one's

Above: As a type, the B-52 is set for years' more service, but the days of the B-52G are numbered. Currently these are assigned to a mixture of conventional and nuclear missions, the latter involving the carriage of 12 AGM-86B cruise missiles in clutches of six under each wing. In the Gulf War, the new AGM-86C version was used, this featuring a conventional warhead.

Far left: Currently shouldering the main nuclear deterrent burden is the Rockwell B-1B, the only nuclear bomber type assigned to missions involving the penetration of hostile airspace.

Opposite page: The way ahead for the USAF lies with sophisticated weapon systems that employ the latest in technology, such as the Lockheed F-117. Adopting such systems may be costly at the acquisition stage, but proves remarkably cost-effective in terms of low aircraft loss rates and high percentage kill capability against key targets.

Northrop B-2

In his 1992 State of the Union speech, President Bush announced that production of the B-2 bomber would be cut to 20 operational aircraft and one test airframe (AV-2). Depicted here is the third prototype (AV-3), shown after joining the flight test program with the 6510th Test Squadron at Edwards.

Flight control
Control is effected by surfaces along the trailing edge of the wing, controlled by a quadruplex fly-by-wire system. The outer surfaces are split to act as 'drag rudders' or airbrakes.

Weapons
The B-2 has two bomb bays, located side-by-side in the central body. Each can accommodate a Common Strategic Rotary Launcher for the carriage of eight nuclear weapons each.

Refueling
The aircraft's unrefueled range of over 7,200 miles can be extended to over 11,500 miles with just one refueling. The receptacle is mounted on the spine.

Still surrounded by mystique long after many of its capabilities have been made public, the F-117 is undoubtedly the most talked-about military aircraft of the last decade. Here an example displays the retractable bomb pylons which extend down from the internal weapons bays.

own nation. Today the current incarnation of that force still has a part to play, but the idea of a nuclear deterrent is seen by many as obsolete in the current political climate.

Three basic roles are flown by the strategic bomber force: penetration, stand-off missile launch and conventional tasks. The nuclear penetration role is the most dangerous, and calls for the most sophisticated aircraft – today, that role is entrusted to the Rockwell B-1B. Optimized for low-level attack, the B-1B carries a load of free-fall bombs and short-range missiles to attack key targets that may be well hidden or mobile. More obvious and fixed targets are earmarked for attack by air-launched cruise missiles, as carried by the Boeing B-52G and B-52H. These are launched from considerable stand-off distances, thereby releasing the elderly Boeing bombers from the suicidal task of penetrating sophisticated defense networks. Finally, some B-52Gs are assigned to the conventional bombing role, the 1991 Gulf War proving that the old dinosaurs could still play an important role in a conventional war if the air defenses could be sufficiently weakened to allow direct overflights of the target by these highly vulnerable platforms.

Looming on the horizon is the Northrop B-2, its stealthy planform allowing it to penetrate air defenses with far greater ability than the B-1B currently assigned to the role. However, the B-2 is the most expensive aircraft ever built, and it seems highly likely that only a handful will ever serve with the US Air Force, if the program survives at all. Some 'cascading' would occur within the strategic bomber fleet if the B-2 is acquired for the penetration role – B-1Bs would be relegated to cruise missile carriers while B-52Hs would replace B-52Gs on conventional missions. Highlighting the new-found flexibility of US airpower, both B-1Bs and B-2s have awesome conventional bombing capabilities themselves.

Strategic nuclear bombers at present only constitute one-third of the US deterrent 'triad', the other two-thirds being the submarine-launched ballistic missiles of the US Navy, and the nuclear missiles operated by the Air Force. The latter were the hardest-hit by the INF Treaty, the USAF having to destroy all of its ground-launched cruise missiles. This leaves it with a still-sizeable ICBM force consisting of silo-launched Minuteman and Peace-

Powerplant
Power comes from four General Electric F118-GE-110 turbofans, buried in pairs within the wing structure and each producing 19,000 lb (84.5 kN) thrust. The intakes are set well back from the leading edge and highly serrated to avoid giving a strong radar return.

Cockpit
The B-2 is intended for two-man operation, the right-hand co-pilot/ weapon system officer being the mission commander. Provision is made for a third crew member if one is required.

Exhausts
The engines exhaust into a wide trough on the upper surface of the wing. The hot air is blown across a wide area of carbon-coated surface, which dissipates the heat and reduces infra-red signature.

Radar
The B-2's primary attack sensor is the Hughes APQ-181 LPI (Low Probability of Intercept) radar. This can detect targets with very short and highly-directed beams, thus making the chance of a ground intercept by passive receivers highly unlikely.

keeper missiles, but these are prime candidates for being bargained away in superpower arms restriction talks. As with the bombers, the missiles are expensive to acquire and maintain, and new procurement in the current world political climate seems highly unlikely.

Strike/attack aircraft

As the Cold War has thawed, and the importance of SAC's bomber fleet waned, so the strike/attack aircraft has emerged as the most important offensive tool in most combat scenarios, a fact graphically illustrated during the Gulf War when sophisticated strike platforms accounted for most of the destruction dealt out to Iraqi forces.

At the sophisticated end of the range, the US Air Force currently has three aircraft types: the F-117, F-111F and F-15E. All share the capability to employ precision-guided munitions, which, though expensive to procure, possess such accuracy that they are often far more cost-effective than conventional ordnance. In fact, such an argument has led the US Air Force to favor the high-technology approach to most of its tactical requirements rather than spend its money on larger forces.

Lockheed's F-117 'Stealth Fighter' is the undeniable current 'star' of the US Air Force following its superb achievements in the Gulf War. Blessed with the ability to penetrate air defenses unseen, its weapon system allows the delivery of ordnance with unerring accuracy. Only one wing is equipped with the type, but its abilities are such that it has great application to many different combat scenarios.

For many years the backbone of the USAF's interdiction force, the General Dynamics F-111 'Aardvark' is now taking second place to the F-15E and F-117. F-111F veterans of the Libya raid and Gulf War are returning from their UK base to Cannon AFB, where they will oust the F-111D (illustrated) from service. The night attack capability of the F-111F, with its Pave Tack target acquisition/ designation pod, is outstanding, although the aircraft may now be considered as more vulnerable in hostile airspace than the F-117 or F-15E.

Warfighting Roles

Although not publicly stated, it seems certain that the aircraft could be employed in the tactical nuclear role for which the F-111 and F-15E are currently used.

Much overlooked in the Gulf War was the contribution made by the General Dynamics F-111. In its F-111F form (with Pave Tack target acquisition/designation pod), the elderly 'Aardvark' is still fully capable of operating in a dense threat environment, with a combat range and payload half-again greater than the newer F-15E, which is largely taking its place. The McDonnell Douglas F-15E is a two-seat Eagle fighter fully missionized for the strike/attack role but retaining the phenomenal air-to-air capabilities of its progenitor.

Here, at last, is an aircraft made for the 1990s USAF. In many ways the first 'complete warplane', the F-15E represents the state of the art in strike technology, combining the extraordinary powers of the APG-70 radar with a full night/adverse weather kit which includes infra-red and terrain-following radar. Laser designation ensures accuracy when using precision-guided munitions, and the many pylons can accommodate virtually every item of ordnance in the USAF inventory, allowing the F-15E to perform battlefield or interdiction missions with equal ease. And yet, it is still an Eagle, and with bombs gone and fuel tanks punched off the F-15E can outfight most opposition. No doubt at a later date roles such as reconnaissance and defense suppression could be added.

Such multi-role versatility is seen by many in the Air Force as the key to an effective force in the days of stringent budgets. It also accounts for the fact that the most numerous aircraft in the inventory is a true multi-role performer: the General Dynamics F-16. Initially, the F-16 was seen as a lightweight fighter, but in USAF service it is primarily an attack aircraft, armed with conventional ordnance, but with an outstanding and regularly practiced air-to-air ability if required. Later versions mirror the trend towards sophistication by adding night/adverse weather capability and better weapons. Although not able to carry as much as far as an F-15E, or deliver with the same accuracy, the F-16 in its own right is a potent warplane able to perform many different missions. At a purchase cost considerably below the big McDonnell Douglas fighter, it is no wonder that so many are in service, and its future development is inextricably linked with the USAF's future plans.

As for other attackers, the Vought A-7 Corsair II is now almost out of Air National Guard service and its replacement, the Fairchild A-10A, is also on the way out. A specialist anti-armor platform, the A-10 put up a good show in the Gulf War, but it is considered vulnerable in the close air support mission, and is intended for eventual replacement by a missionized F-16C. The A-10 still plays an important part in the USAF's make-up, and several have been re-roled to perform the forward air control mission, a task incidentally also performed by F-16s in the Gulf War.

Procurement for the strike/attack fleet is in abeyance, perhaps pending the outcome of the still-secret development of ultra-stealthy aircraft, which is believed to be ongoing. An F-16 follow-on is required for the next century, and the success of the F-117 and F-15E would suggest that a stealthy and highly potent strike platform will certainly be required. In addition to stealthiness, rapid deployment capability and ease of maintenance, the ability to perform a multitude of roles without compromising any of them will be paramount in the procurement plans of any new aircraft.

Fighters

It is perhaps the first role of any air force to protect its home nation from attack, and the US Air Force still maintains a strong defense at home, although it is a shadow of its former self during the time when a separate Command

was required to control the assigned assets. Today the job is entrusted to First Air Force of Air Combat Command, which, apart from a single Eagle squadron which protects Iceland, is now bereft of aircraft. Instead, it is an administrative command controlling the various assets which can still defend the United States.

Air Combat Command still has many fighter units, but these are all primarily concerned with battlefield duties rather than interception. Instead, the US interceptor force is now concentrated in the Air National Guard organization. Two aircraft types are flown, the F-15 and the F-16 ADF. F-15s serve with a West Coast and an East Coast

Guard unit, bolstered by several units across the nation flying the ADF version of the F-16, tailored to the interceptor role with Sparrow missile capability, searchlight and long-range communications. Another Guard unit also flies the F-15 in defense of the Hawaiian islands.

By far the greatest number of USAF fighters are flown by the 'tactical' units which have battlefield tasks. These include active-duty, Air Force Reserve and Air National Guard units based within the United States, and active-duty units based overseas. The standard equipment is the F-15 Eagle, which can perform the whole spectrum of fighter activities, including intercepts, sweeps, escorts and

Above: The F-16 Fighting Falcon is the USAF's bread-and-butter aircraft. In Desert Storm, lack of PGM capability made the type ineffective in the medium-level bombing rope.

Thrust vectoring
Two-dimensional thrust vectoring nozzles are fitted to the F-22, improving its take-off performance and pitch rate during maneuvering. An afterburner is incorporated for maneuvering and acceleration, although the design can easily cruise subsonically without it.

combat air patrols. As has been noted elsewhere, the F-16 is a potent backup to the Eagle force, notably for air combat immediately over the battlefield where engagements would largely be undertaken at close-in ranges and in multi-bogey 'furballs', and where the F-16's excellent agility would be of the greatest advantage.

SRAAMs
Short missile bays on the side of the intake trunks house the four short-range air-to-air missiles, which are ejected sideways on launching. The AIM-9 Sidewinder will be used, perhaps in a new AIM-9X version tailored to the F-22.

Flight control
In order to meet the performance and low-observable goals, the F-22 has a fly-by-wire system. This controls the actions of leading-edge flaps, ailerons, all-moving tailplanes, rudders, vectoring nozzles and airbrake.

Lockheed
YF-22 Rapier

Winner of a hard-fought battle with the Northrop/McDonnell Douglas YF-23 to form the basis of the USAF's Advanced Tactical Fighter program, the YF-22 is a skillful blend of performance, agility and stealthiness. Intended as a replacement for the F-15 Eagle, the production Rapier will differ significantly in detail from the two prototype YF-22s, and faces an equally hard battle against cost-cutting politicians who are worried by the high cost of the program and growing weight of the aircraft.

Radar
The F-22's radar has long range and high resolution for the early detection of opposing aircraft. Combined with the aircraft's own stealthiness, the low signature from the radar allows the F-22 to approach its quarry closely without being detected.

McDonnell's mighty Eagle is still arguably the world's best fighter, but the performance and radar capability of aircraft such as the Sukhoi Su-27 have considerably eroded and may even have surpassed the Eagle's supremacy. Consequently, the US Air Force is well advanced along the path to providing a successor in the form of the Lockheed/Boeing/General Dynamics F-22 Rapier. Again, the F-22 is a big, yet highly maneuverable, aircraft with outstanding BVR (beyond visual range) kill capability and all-round prowess far in advance of anything else flying today. Again, however, it is a costly program, and politicians argue that the turmoil in the CIS may mean that the F-22 never has to face aircraft that require the level of technology woven into the design.

The F-22 is another program facing complete cancellation, but it should be stressed that achieving air superiority/supremacy in any battle is the most important prerequisite for a victory on the ground, a fact graphically illustrated in the war against Iraq. If the F-22 is cancelled, then upgrades to the F-15 are the most likely option, rather than a completely new design.

Reconnaissance and control

Fighters, bombers and attack aircraft represent the main defense/offense 'teams' of the US Air Force, but a multitude of aircraft are in use to maximize their effectiveness. For years the leader in the field, the United States operates a varied and highly capable reconnaissance fleet, but one which again faces a considerable change in the light of reduced force levels and doctrinal changes.

Two basic reconnaissance missions are outlined in USAF doctrine: strategic and tactical. The first produces intelligence data necessary for formulating national policy, while the latter produces data necessary for commanders in battle. By the nature of intelligence-gathering and the use to which the data is put, aircraft types designed for stra-

Apart from an F-15 squadron based on each coast, the defense of the US is now entrusted to the F-16 ADF, an F-16A missionized for the interception role with Sparrow/AMRAAM capability and long-range communications. ANG units are placed at strategic locations around the periphery of the country, these machines being from Texas's 147th FG.

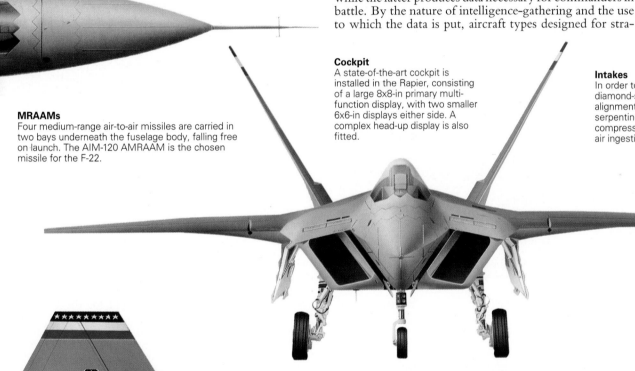

MRAAMs
Four medium-range air-to-air missiles are carried in two bays underneath the fuselage body, falling free on launch. The AIM-120 AMRAAM is the chosen missile for the F-22.

Cockpit
A state-of-the-art cockpit is installed in the Rapier, consisting of a large 8x8-in primary multi-function display, with two smaller 6x6-in displays either side. A complex head-up display is also fitted.

Intakes
In order to preserve 'stealthiness', the diamond-shaped intakes follow the same alignments as the fuselage, and have serpentine ducts to shield the engine compressor faces. A pronounced lip aids air ingestion at high angles of attack.

F-15 Eagles are the mainstay of the USAF's fighter force, serving principally with battlefield air superiority units. These units are based in Europe, Iceland, Alaska and Japan for theater support, and in the CONUS for rapid deployment duties.

Powerplant
Engine manufacturers General Electric and Pratt & Whitney fought a battle to power the F-22, and the latter's F119-PW-100 engine was declared the winner. This powerplant is in the 35,000-lb (135-kN) thrust class.

tegic reconnaissance purposes can provide outstanding tactical intelligence, and vice versa.

Since the withdrawal from service of the Lockheed SR-71, the US Air Force is without the services of a high-speed, high-altitude, air-breathing reconnaissance platform, although again rumors emanating from the California/Nevada desert suggest that secret high-speed aircraft are under development, and may even be in service, to provide capability in this arena in advance of that possible with the SR-71.

Currently, the 9th Wing has the Lockheed U-2R in service, this aircraft being able to fly for long durations at high altitudes with a multi-sensor suite to provide continuous intelligence. Chief among its sensors is a long-range stand-off radar which can produce high-resolution imagery of enemy forces in both peacetime and war. Also carried are communications intelligence receivers for eavesdropping and emitter locators to precisely monitor the whereabouts of hostile radars. The aircraft retains the ability to carry optical sensors for conventional photography.

Another important reconnaissance fleet is that of the Boeing RC-135s, which collects signals intelligence of all kinds, specialities being the individual and intimate classification of radars, notably those of air defense networks.

Intelligence is normally gathered from friendly or international airspace during long sorties that take the RC-135s to many parts of the globe. Three specialist RC-135s are employed in Alaska to monitor ICBM tests of other nations.

Both RC-135 and U-2R are of great use during time of tension or war, but are normally considered as strategic platforms. In the tactical arena, where the standard method of intelligence gathering is with fast- and low-flying jets flying over individual targets, the US Air Force relies on the McDonnell Douglas RF-4C Phantom, although the age and limitations of the basic airframe mean that it is fast approaching retirement. The RF-4C still uses traditional film and optical sensors for most of its intelligence gathering, but the current trend is towards video and infra-red imagery, as evidenced by the European Tornado reconnaissance variants which have dispensed with film altogether. Accordingly, a new tactical reconnaissance system is under development for the US Air Force, to be carried in podded form by F-16s.

Providing intelligence of a completely different form, but within the tactical framework, are two of the US Air Force's most important assets: the Boeing E-3 AWACS and E-8 J-STARS. Both are based on the 707 airliner airframe, and both perform similar functions, i.e. airborne control of friendly assets. The E-3 monitors all aircraft flying within the range of its large rotating radar, while itself staying well away from the battle. Coupled with IFF interrogators, the radar gives onboard operators a complete picture of the air battle, and allows them to vector friendly fighters towards enemy aircraft and position them in the most advantageous position for attack. It can also steer friendly aircraft around hostile fighters.

J-STARS does for the land battle what the AWACS does for the air fighting. Its powerful radar gives a complete picture of ground movements, and again onboard controllers can provide warning and vectoring information to friendly ground units. It has the added ability to provide excellent target information to attack aircraft. J-STARS is not yet in service, but its performance in the Gulf War while still under development has convinced many that it is a high-cost program that the United States can ill afford to be without.

Combat support

Reconnaissance and control assets are just two of many disciplines that the US Air Force undertakes in order for its main force to operate to maximum effect. Other aircraft are similarly employed on other tasks, including those dedicated to defense suppression, airborne command and control, tanking and rescue.

Closely allied to most tactical operations are the defense suppression aircraft, which fly in the strike package to protect it from surface-to-air defenses. Despite most tactical aircraft carrying their own electronic countermeasures, the use of dedicated electronic warfare platforms is employed to complete the disruption of enemy air defense systems. For the US Air Force, the General Dynamics/Grumman EF-111A Raven is the chosen vehicle, a version of the F-111 bomber with delicate receivers to detect enemy radars, and powerful jammers to then deceive or negate their signals. Since it is based on the F-111, the Raven is particularly good in the strike escort role as it has the performance and avionics to accompany strike aircraft into the target area. It retains the ability to provide jamming from stand-off orbits. Providing a different kind of stand-off jamming is the EC-130H Compass Call, which can jam communications networks.

Similarly, the USAF's main anti-radar weapon can accompany, or often precede, attack forces. This is the McDonnell Douglas F-4G, a 'Wild Weasel' version of the trusty Phantom, with sensitive radar homing and warning system and missiles which home on the signals from hostile radars. Whereas the EF-111A interferes with the ability of radars to provide the right information for the defense network, the F-4G presents a hard-kill option.

EF-111As and EC-130Hs are fairly recent conversions, and their continued use for some years is assured. However, the F-4Gs are now old, and the future is less rosy. Already in Europe the US Air Force deploys the F-16 in a defense suppression role, working alongside the F-4G to act as the shooter in a hunter-killer pair. Further development could see the F-16 become the main defense suppression platform for the service in years to come, while the F-15E may also prove to have the right credentials for the job.

A small fleet of USAF aircraft has a command and control task. Boeing EC-135s are on charge to carry battle commanders aloft during times of tension or war, but this job was largely to continue the chain of command during a nuclear exchange. As such a conflict is deemed consider-

Above: Suppression of enemy air defenses is a key role in today's Air Force, protecting attack aircraft from SAMs. The fin-tip fairing on the EF-111A Raven contains receivers to locate and analyze enemy radars: the underfuselage canoe fairing houses jamming equipment.

Left: Vital to any combat operation is the use of tanker aircraft such as this Boeing KC-135E. Not only does the tanker extend the range of attack aircraft by topping off their tanks prior to entering hostile airspace, it also extends the endurance of fighters flying CAP missions and surveillance aircraft on patrol.

Lockheed MC-130H Combat Talon II

Developed to augment and eventually replace the MC-130E Combat Talon I aircraft of the Special Operations wings, the MC-130H is entering service with the 8th SOS at Hurlburt Field. Despite some development problems, causing a delay in delivery, the MC-130H brings considerably enhanced capability to the night/adverse weather covert operations mission. Its primary role is the infiltration and support of special forces operating behind enemy lines, and its impressive sensors allow it to fly at low level in all weathers.

Defensive avionics
The MC-130 is exceptionally well protected, its suite including ALQ-8 ECM pods, ALR-69 radar warning receiver, ALQ-172 detector/jammer, WJ-1840 signals detector, AAR-44 launch warning receiver, QRC-8402 IR jammer and chaff/flare dispensers.

Powerplant
The MC-130H is powered by four Allison T56-A-15 turboprops, each developing 4,508 shp (3362 kW). Each engine drives a Hamilton Standard 54H60 four-bladed constant-speed propeller.

Radar
The enlarged nose radome of the MC-130H houses an Emerson Electric APQ-170 ground-mapping/weather/terrain-following radar. This system can 'look into the turn' to provide terrain-avoidance information as the aircraft maneuvers through hilly or mountainous areas.

Fuel tanks
Six integral wing tanks hold a capacity of 6,960 US gal (26344 liters), to which are usually added two 1,360-US gal (5146-liter) underwing tanks. The MC-130 can also carry hose-drum units for refueling special forces helicopters in flight.

Far right: Making a dramatic rise in capability in recent years is the USAF's Special Operations force, which was heavily involved in operations inside Iraq and Kuwait prior to and during the main ground offensive. Here USAF MH-53Js line up for an operation during Desert Storm.

Crew
The MC-130H is flown by a basic crew of five, consisting of two pilots, navigator, electronic warfare officer and loadmaster. The EWO is accommodated on the flight deck, instead of in a pallet-mounted station as in the MC-130E.

Color scheme
For their primary night low-level role, the MC-130H fleet is finished in the 'European One' or 'lizard' camouflage, consisting of two shades of dark green and one of gray. This aircraft carries the 'ED' tailcodes of the 6510th Test Wing, with whom it underwent trials with the 6518th Test Squadron.

FLIR
A retractable FLIR pod provides the crew with imagery in bad light conditions. Allied to commands from the terrain-following radar, this allows safe flight at very low level, necessary to penetrate hostile airspace without being detected.

Rear ramp
The ramp opens in flight for the air-dropping of equipment, while side doors are used for paratroops. A minor role for the MC-130 is the dropping of BLU-82 'Big Blue' bombs from the rear ramp.

ably less likely in the current climate, the alert status of the EC-135s is being eroded dramatically. Another control post asset is the EC-130E ABCCC version of the Hercules, which acts as an on-scene command post for tactical aircraft.

Completing the combat support force are the tankers. Inflight refueling of combat aircraft allows the US Air Force to project its power to any point on the globe, and is vital to the ability of its aircraft (which are being increasingly based within the United States itself) to deploy overseas at short notice. Combat operations can be conducted across far greater ranges than are possible without tanker support.

A massive fleet of Boeing KC-135 Stratotankers is augmented by the McDonnell Douglas KC-10 Extender, and the operations of both are increasingly being interwoven with tactical aircraft to provide greater flexibility of response to any crisis that may arise. The KC-10s are relatively new, but the KC-135s are anything but, and are the subject of a major updating program that replaces old 1950s-vintage turbojets with modern turbofans to increase the aircraft's effectiveness and reduce operating costs.

Special Operations

With limited conflicts becoming more widespread, and the rise in importance of unconventional warfare methods, it is no surprise that the US Air Force has a large and ever-growing Special Operations fleet. This group has also assumed the responsibility for combat rescue of downed aircrew, a major consideration in wartime with a dramatic effect in both morale and cost terms.

Helicopters and Hercules sum up the Special Operations fleet, equipped as it is with the Sikorsky MH-53 and MH-60 for rotary-wing operations, and several special C-130 variants for a variety of tasks. The most spectacular of these are the AC-130 gunships, presently comprising AC-130A (Reserve) and AC-130H (active-duty). In the near future the active-duty gunship unit will welcome the AC-130U into its ranks, passing its current aircraft on to the Reserve. MC-130s are also in service, these being dedicated to Special Operations roles involving the covert infil/exfil of commando teams and their equipment, psy-war leaflet dropping or even use as makeshift bombers. New MC-130H aircraft are entering service to increase the force's effectiveness. Two further Hercules variants are in

Above: Lockheed products dominate the current transport fleet, including the C-130 Hercules and C-141 StarLifter. The giant C-5 Galaxy is used for the heaviest tasks, which often involves the shipment of tanks and helicopters.

Above left: A new shape for the transport fleet is the McDonnell Douglas C-17, which is being procured to replace the elderly C-141 StarLifters.

use: the HC-130 for the support (including refueling) of rescue helicopters, and the EC-130E, a handful of which fly with an Air National Guard unit on psychological warfare and related tasks.

Sophisticated avionics allow the MC-130, MH-53 and MH-60 to operate in all weathers and at very low level, necessary for their chosen roles. In addition to their Special Operations roles, the AC-130s are often called upon to act in a more conventional tactical manner, supporting troops-in-contact over a lightly defended battlefield.

Transport

While a plethora of aircraft types provide staff transport and liaison, the main transport effort is handled by three Lockheed products. The C-130 is the standard in-theater transport, blessed with short- and rough-field capability. It is also used on longer-range work when required, augmenting the main fleet of C-5 Galaxies and C-141 Star-Lifters. KC-135 and KC-10 tankers also have an additional transport role.

Re-equipment for the transport fleet centers on the McDonnell Douglas C-17 intra-theater airlifter, intended to replace the elderly StarLifter. This was originally to have featured rough-field capability to allow the delivery of materiel directly into the battlefield, but this has been deleted on cost-saving grounds. Even with the C-17 in service, the US Air Force will have to rely on a C-130-class aircraft to move supplies into forward positions. The Hercules itself is an old design, but one which is still capable of performing more than adequately in its role. In the future a replacement may be sought, but an update of the existing design seems more likely.

Training

In order to provide aircrew for its massive fleet, the US Air Force has a large and well-organized training effort. At present, potential fliers are graded during a short course on the Cessna T-41 before progressing to the basic phase, accomplished using the Cessna T-37, followed by the advanced phase using the Northrop T-38. A major re-equipment plan is under way, introducing four new types to replace the three current designs. To begin with, the Enhanced Flight Screening program seeks a new light aircraft to replace the T-41s. For the basic phase, the USAF has the JPATS program which will bear fruit in the late 1990s for a T-37 replacement. A considerable list of contenders has already been drawn up, including both turboprop- and jet-powered designs.

For the advanced phase, the stream will split into two tracks: the Bomber/Fighter Training System which will continue with T-38s until a suitable successor can be found later in the decade, and the Tanker/Transport Training System for pilots destined for the large aircraft fleets. Due to a shortfall in T-38 capacity, the TTTS was the first requirement to be filled to relieve the problem, the Beech T-1 Jayhawk being the chosen vehicle.

The USAF at war

With this vast array of weaponry at its disposal, with aircraft types tailored to meet a wide variety of roles, how then does the US Air Force intend fighting a battle? Of course, each battle and each enemy would have its own peculiarities, but peacetime planning centers on certain tactical concepts that can be adapted to meet all potential scenarios. Such planning also mirrors changes to potential threats during peacetime, and requires a constant vigil by reconnaissance aircraft and other intelligence-gathering platforms to keep abreast of military advances in nations likely to be future enemies of the United States.

Indeed, the reconnaissance effort is the first and last act of any war, preceding and following any actual conflict by some considerable time. As has been mentioned, during times of peace strategic reconnaissance aircraft are in constant action to monitor military changes in potentially hostile nations. If tensions rise, the reconnaissance effort is stepped up so that aircraft such as the U-2R and RC-135 may be in action around the clock to prevent any surprises occurring and to compile an accurate order of battle of the opposing side.

As relations worsen, so attention turns to individual potential targets, plotting their positions as precisely as possible so that they can be accurately attacked should the need arise. Immediately before a shooting match appears likely the traditional tactical reconnaissance types may be used to provide detailed imagery of certain targets,

A continual flow of intelligence is vital to the successful execution of an air campaign. Aircraft such as the Lockheed U-2R maintain a continuous surveillance effort with radar, electronic and other sensors. On highly sensitive missions, the Senior Span satellite communications equipment can be carried in a dorsal fairing, thus allowing the data which is gathered by the U-2's sensors to be transmitted in near real-time back to command posts in the United States.

although obtaining such intelligence would be seen as an open escalation of hostilities. Throughout any action that may follow, both strategic and tactical reconnaissance aircraft would fly to maintain the flow of information to the US command, with targeting and post-strike intelligence becoming of prime importance. Communications and electronic intelligence gathering, a valuable peacetime exercise, would assume new importance as US forces attempted to break down defense networks and divine the intentions of the enemy.

Another force active before any actual fighting occurred would be the fighters, which would begin mounting combat air patrols to secure friendly airspace and deter any aggression by air. E-3 Sentries would stand round-the-clock watches of enemy airspace to detect any impending attack, and the E-8 J-STARS may be brought in to monitor ground forces across the border.

Modern all-out warfare can be broadly split into two classifications: conventional (maybe with chemical, biological and some tactical nuclear weapons), and full nuclear war. The latter is increasingly unlikely in the more enlightened climate of recent years, but the strategic bomber and missile crews stand ready for the unthinkable. For the bombers, an all-out assault would involve B-1Bs penetrating the defenses to deliver free-fall and short-range weapons, while B-52s would launch cruise missiles from safe distances, leaving the weapons themselves to thread their way through to their targets. ICBMs would be launched against larger preprogrammed targets such as airfield and industrial complexes, their accuracy being less than the air-launched weapons.

If the hypothetical war went down the conventional route, the first exercise for the US Air Force would be to render its enemy's air defense network unusable. This rolling back is absolutely vital to any air actions which may follow, as demonstrated by the Gulf War. Key nodal points of the network would have been singled out for attack in the first wave, which would likely be the job of the F-117s. Using tanker support as far as friendly airspace would allow, they would set off singly into hostile airspace and attack the control centers of the air defenses, denying the enemy any centralized control of the network. Using their low-observables technology, the F-117s would create maximum surprise.

Following behind would be the main thrust of the counter-air forces. Defense suppression aircraft would attempt to punch holes through the front line of defenses using missiles (F-4G) and jamming (EF-111A) to knock out SAM radars, and so create a safe corridor through which strike aircraft could flow. F-111s, F-15Es and further F-117s would be used to take out additional air defense sites and other vital strategic targets. The anti-airfield mission would be important to hinder the ability of the opposing air force to launch aircraft against this first wave of attacks. Any that did manage to take off would be engaged by F-15s flying as either escorts with the main strike forces or on

Above: Regular exercises on varying scales ensure that USAF units can work together effectively in combat situations. These exercises also involve friendly foreign air arms, as evidenced by the NATO E-3 Sentry.

Above left: Linchpin of the air battle is the E-3 AWACS, which controls air assets from a stand-off orbit. Its main tasks are twofold: to detect, monitor and warn of enemy air activity; and to ensure deconfliction among friendly forces.

Above: Standard fighter Phantoms have passed from service, but two special variants remain, the F-4G 'Wild Weasel' and the RF-4C tactical reconnaissance platform. Here an example of the latter from the Idaho ANG approaches a tanker for refueling.

Above right: Not only do USAF units have to work together for maximum effect, their activities may also involve aircraft from other services. This Desert Storm operation involved a Washington ANG KC-135E providing fuel for carrier-based F/A-18 Hornets on a bombing mission. The KC-135 has an add-on drogue which attaches to the standard boom for refueling Navy, Marine or foreign aircraft.

sweeps in particular sectors to 'sanitize' them of enemy air activity.

This rolling back of an air defense system is an ongoing task, and in the longer term requires considerable destruction of airfields and equipment to prevent facilities being repaired and brought back on line. In the Gulf War a sustained campaign of hardened shelter take-downs was required to prevent the Iraqi air force ever becoming a threat. In a Central European conflict, the tactical nuclear weapon was considered as the most effective anti-airfield weapon, but would have led to a dangerous reduction in the all-out nuclear war threshold.

A constant effort against the air defenses and major strategic installations results in a considerably weakened enemy, leaving the main forces to concentrate on other targets. Sophisticated strike aircraft can be engaged against more traditional interdiction targets such as railyards, bridges and stores areas to prevent the enemy troops at the front from gaining supplies, while less potent attack platforms such as the F-16 can be brought to bear in large numbers in the battlefield arena. As air superiority is gained, and hopefully turned into complete air supremacy, even systems such as conventionally-armed B-52s can be used to soften up the enemy's ground forces.

This softening-up process is intended to reduce the enemy's forces to a point where a land battle is virtually assured of success, and where friendly casualties will be kept to a minimum. Towards the end of the process, as happened over Iraq, the deep-strike aircraft may have run out of suitable interdiction targets and will be used to deplete the enemy in the battlefield itself, turning their sophisticated systems to going after tanks and artillery.

With the opposing land forces suitably weakened, a ground offensive can begin. Here the Air Force is com-

mitted to maintaining the successes it has already achieved, i.e. keeping air defense and strategic targets from being repaired, but also supporting the land forces in the field. Traditional close air support is available from A-10s and F-16s, but may also involve AC-130 gunships, B-52s and the deep-strike aircraft. In a land war the role of the forward air controller becomes important so that targets can be identified and attacked by an on-scene controller with intimate knowledge of the battle at that particular point in time. Individual kill-boxes are assigned to formations of attack aircraft, so that they can work the area with their own FAC for maximum effectiveness.

Throughout the conflict, combat support forces would be vital to the overall effort. E-3s and E-8s would provide the 'big picture' of both air and ground battles, supplying a stream of vectoring and targeting information to friendly aircraft and to deconflict various strike forces. The importance of the defense suppression team would not diminish after the first attack: their missiles and jammers would keep up an incessant barrage against the remnants of the air defenses. Fighter forces would be extremely busy, not only sweeping and escorting, but also keeping friendly airspace clean with CAPs and protecting high-value assets such as the AWACS and J-STARS. Tankers would accompany most strike packages, not only to give the aircraft enough fuel for their forays into hostile airspace, but also to provide emergency fuel if they return damaged or short of fuel. Rescue crews would stand ever-ready to selflessly fly into enemy territory to save downed airmen, while other Special Forces aircrew would fly shadowy missions, mostly at night, to support the unconventional warfare effort.

USAF attack operations usually use the strike package concept, which uses a mixed force of aircraft types. In addition to the main force of attack aircraft, be they F-111s or F-16s, support aircraft such as EF-111 jammers, F-4G HARM shooters and F-15 fighters will be part of the formation, all supported by a large group of tankers. The strike package is arranged so that the attack aircraft are afforded the easiest and safest passage through to the target, with defense suppression aircraft and fighters forging ahead to clear the area.

Aircraft such as the F-117 have a fair degree of autonomy built into their operations, and indeed the use of support such as jammers may even lessen their effectiveness, as jamming itself gives the enemy an idea that an attack is imminent. F-117s are designed to operate alone in 'bad guy' territory, although it is possible that a secret TR-3A support aircraft operates with them to provide detailed targeting information. F-15Es, on the other hand, may still require jamming support, but the fighter escorts can often be left to other tasks as the 'E' itself is a superb fighter. F-15E crews train to fight their way through to a target

Left: Despite the attentions of defense suppression aircraft, the strike/attack force would still have to face considerable air defenses, notably smaller AAA and infra-red-guided SAMs. To counter the latter, all tactical aircraft are provided with flares which lure the missile away from the aircraft by providing a far more inviting heat source.

themselves, without having to call on additional support.

By introducing sophisticated attack aircraft with the potential for autonomous operations, the Air Force is reducing the need for the support aircraft, which can be turned to other tasks. A gradual shift to these 'smarter' types could result in a decrease in costs of keeping the service at the required level of capability by reducing the numbers of aircraft needed. Certainly the cost-effectiveness of precision-guided munitions launched from high-value strike aircraft was graphically illustrated in the Gulf War.

This is how the USAF would go to war in a major conflict. In such a scenario it would also have to work closely with not only other US services, but also with the air arms of allied nations. To this end the US Air Force regularly exercises with all friendly forces, and equipment standardization is widespread to ensure the minimum of confusion. Again, the Gulf War was a perfect example of how the operations of other services can be neatly grafted into the overall USAF master plan, thereby maximizing the potential of the new skills brought to the combined force by other air arms.

An idea of the scale of major combat operations can be gained by this Desert Storm refueling scene, with 28 F-16s visible tanking from four KC-135s. To this group must be added the F-15 fighter top cover, EF-111 and F-4G defense suppression, and various stand-off support systems.

Cessna

A-37 Dragonfly

The **A-37 Dragonfly** is a small, low-cost combat aircraft employed in recent years for the FAC (forward air control) mission. Developed from the proven T-37 trainer, A-37s were used in the COIN (counter-insurgency) air-to-ground role but have now been re-assigned to the FAC mission under the designation **OA-37B**.

The aircraft is a conventional, all-metal, twin-jet monoplane with a single functional crew seat (at left) and a second crew position (at right) which is normally not used, both in side-by-side ejection seats beneath a single broad clamshell canopy. The OA-37B is configured with two small engines in the wing roots with nozzles at the trailing edge. Tricycle landing gear is low and wide-tracked. The horizontal tail of the aircraft is mounted above the fuselage about one-third of the way up the fin to assure that the airstream flowing past it is undisturbed by jet exhaust.

The OA-37B has manual controls with electric trim, hydraulic slotted flaps, and hydraulic landing gear. Its strengthened wing has eight underwing hardpoints for a variety of bombs and rockets, and a GAU-2B/A 7.62-mm Minigun in the fuselage. The OA-37B is powered by two 2,850-lb (1293-kg) thrust General Electric J85-GE-17A turbojet engines.

History of the OA-37B begins with the **T-37** jet trainer, itself dating to the mid-1950s. The **XT-37** prototype (54-0716) first flew on 12 October 1954, and the first **T-37A** (54-2729) on 27 September 1955. Five hundred and thirty-four T-37As were followed in November 1959 by the **T-37B** with more powerful engines. The **T-37C**, with armament and wing hardpoints for ordnance, was exported but not adopted by the USAF.

Efforts to adopt the basic T-37 design for an air-to-ground combat mission began in 1958 when the US Army evaluated three T-37s at Fort Ord, California. Soon thereafter, the Army looked at the Fiat G91, Douglas A4D-2 Skyhawk and Northrop N.156 fighters, but never overcame the legal bar to the Army operating fixed-wing combat aircraft.

The USAF tried its own version with the **YAT-37D**. Two T-37 trainers were modified on the production line to result in the YAT-37D armed version of the trainer, which first flew on 22 October 1963. With crew armor, strengthened wings, J85 engines (replacing J69s on the trainer), and hardpoints for ordnance, the YAT-37D was exhaustively tested but not evaluated.

During the Vietnam War, efforts to find a combat role for the basic T-37 resumed. The USAF on 2 May 1967 began to fly the **A-37A Dragonfly**, a converted T-37B, for close air support and Special Operations missions. Thirty-nine A-37As (briefly known, in the planning stage, as **AT-37D**s) with de-rated J85s were built by converting T-37Bs on the production line. Some were assigned to the South Vietnamese Air Force.

The **A-37B** which followed in January 1967 was virtually a new aircraft, weighing nearly twice as much as a T-37 trainer. A total of 577 A-37Bs was built.

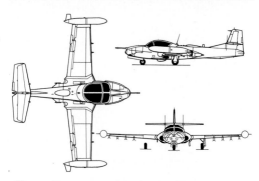

Above: Based on the Cessna T-37 primary jet trainer, the OA-37B Dragonfly is now primarily employed on forward air control duties, although it is nearing the end of its USAF career.

MISSION PROFILE

Armament options: internal 7.62-mm GAU-2B/A Minigun in nose forward firing position with maximum of 618 rounds; 10 wing hardpoints for the carriage of most stores in US inventory, including conventional low-drag and retarded bombs, cluster-bomb units, napalm bombs and rocket pods, plus wingtip fuel tanks; ferry configuration with four underwing and two wingtip drop-tanks

Close air support: on a typical CAS mission the A-37 flies to a radius of 400 miles (643 km) to be on station for one hour with 618 rounds of ammunition for the GAU-2B/A, two BLU-23B napalm bombs, two 2.75-in rocket tubes, and two wingtip drop-tanks

Forward air control: OA-37B FAC (forward air control) aircraft flies to a radius of about 475 miles (764 km) with token or no ordnance for the purpose of directing fighter-bombers to their targets

USAF VARIANTS AND SERIALS

OA-37B: Following the withdrawal of the A-37B in the ground-attack role, the type was adapted to conduct forward air control duties to replace the O-2 Skymaster. Over 100 A-37Bs were redesignated to OA-37B configuration, although very few remain in service.

GOA-37B: Two retired OA-37Bs have been allocated to the Inter-American Air Forces Academy (IAAFA) as ground instruction airframes to teach technical skills to students from Central and Latin American countries. 69-6375; 73-1098

NOA-37B: At least two OA-37Bs were allocated to permanent test duties with the Air Force Flight Test Center at Edwards AFB, with the prefix N assigned. 70-1310; 73-1090

Below: This Dragonfly survives as a GOA-37B ground instructional airframe with the IAAFA. Flying examples still serve at Edwards AFB.

SPECIFICATION

Cessna OA-37B

Wing: span over tip-tanks 35 ft 10.5 in (10.93 m); aspect ratio 6.2; area 183.9 sq ft (17.09 m²)
Fuselage and tail: length excluding probe 29 ft 3.5 in (8.93 m); height 8 ft 10.5 in (2.70 m); tailplane span 13 ft 11.25 in (4.25 m); wheel base 7 ft 10 in (2.39 m)
Powerplant: two General Electric J85-GE-17A each rated at 2,850 lb (12.68 kN) dry thrust
Weights: basic empty 6,211 lb (2817 kg); empty equipped 5,843 lb (2650 kg); maximum take-off 14,000 lb (6350 kg)
Fuel and load: internal fuel 3,307 lb (1500 kg); external fuel up to four 100-US gal (378-liter) drop-tanks; maximum ordnance 4,100 lb (1860 kg)
Speed: maximum level speed at 16,000 ft (4875 m) 507 mph (816 km/h); maximum cruising speed at 25,000 ft (7620 m) 489 mph (787 km/h)
Range: with maximum internal and external fuel at 25,000 ft (7620 m) 1,012 miles (1628 km); range with a 4,100-lb (1860-kg) warload 460 miles (740 km)
Performance: maximum rate of climb at sea level 6,990 ft (2130 m) per minute; service ceiling 41,765 ft (12730 m); take-off distance 2,030 ft (619 m) to 50 ft (15 m); landing distance 6,600 ft (2012 m) from 50 ft (15 m)

USAF OPERATORS

Air Force Materiel Command (AFMC)

6520th TW	6512th TS	'ED'	Edwards AFB, CA	OA-37B, NOA-37B

Air Combat Command (ACC)

IAAFA	nil	nil	Homestead AFB, FL	GOA-37B

Air National Guard (ANG)

182nd FG	169th FS	'IL'	Gtr Peoria Apt, IL	OA-37B

Vought
A-7

The **A-7** attack aircraft remains in service with a few Air National Guard squadrons. The Air Force did not adopt the popular 'Corsair II' nickname given to the aircraft in its US Navy versions. Single-seat **A-7D** and two-seat **A-7K** aircraft were scheduled to be replaced by other aircraft types in ANG service by the end of 1993.

The A-7 is a straightforward, shoulder-wing aircraft with swept flight surfaces, provision for inflight refueling, and narrow-track tricycle landing gear. ANG airplanes retain the folding wings and arrester hook employed on Navy versions, but have self-starter units, and improved avionics system with a continuous-solution NWDS (navigation and weapon delivery system) which is still considered very accurate more than two decades after it was designed. The A-7 gives substantial range, endurance and load-carrying capability to the CAS (close air support) and BAI (battlefield area interdiction) missions.

The A-7 was developed in 1964-65 and first flew on 27 September 1965. **A-7A**, **A-7B**, **A-7C**, **TA-7C** and **A-7E** versions served with the US Navy. **A-7H** and **TA-7H** airplanes were delivered to Greece. **A-7P** aircraft went to Portugal. Versions which were never built included the **KA-7F** tanker for the US Navy and a simplified **A-7G** proposed to Switzerland.

The A-7D is armed with a single M61A1 Vulcan 20-mm cannon, routinely carries two AIM-7L Sidewinder missiles on forward-fuselage hardpoints, and can handle up to 15,000 lb (6804 kg) of air-to-surface missiles, bombs, cluster bombs, rockets, or gun pods on six underwing ordnance stations. The pilot sits far forward on the fuselage in a McDonnell Douglas Escapac ejection seat, and has a HUD (head-up display) to assist in flight maneuvering and weapons delivery.

Below: Based at Des Moines, Iowa, this brace of A-7D Corsair IIs displays the current camouflage scheme worn by the 'SLUF'. Once a stalwart of the ANG, the A-7D is now being phased out from the inventory and should be entirely replaced by the end of 1993.

The A-7D was adopted by the USAF in the late 1960s, its first A-7D (67-14584) flying on 26 September 1968. Late in the Southeast Asia conflict, the A-7D went into combat in October 1972. Four hundred and fifty-nine A-7Ds were delivered, powered by a 14,250-lb (63.39-kN) thrust Allison TF41-A-1 turbofan engine based upon the Rolls-Royce Spey.

In 1977, the USAF began retrofitting its A-7D fleet with Automated Maneuver Flaps (AMF) to improve the aircraft's performance at high angles of attack and to counter its tendency to 'depart' when nose-high. On 383 A-7Ds, the Pave Penny system, or TISL (Target Indicator System Laser), was added to a chin protuberance and slaved to the HUD, improving target acquisition and bombing accuracy. In 1987-88, some 48 A-7Ds and eight A-7Ks were modified to carry the LANA (low-altitude navigation and attack) system, which introduced a new forward-looking infra-red, automatic terrain-following capability, and wide-angle HUD. A Singer tactical

mission computer is to be installed on non-LANA-modified A-7Ds. The 162nd Tactical Fighter Group at Tucson, the RTU (replacement training unit) for the type, has evaluated a single-piece windshield which offers increased visibility and improved protection against birdstrikes.

Final operational version was the two-seat A-7K, which never served with the active-duty USAF but went directly to the ANG. The first A-7K (73-1008), which made its maiden flight in January 1981, was a conversion of an existing A-7D, while a further 30 airplanes were delivered in this series.

The USAF evaluated two **YA-7F** aircraft (the second time the F suffix was used) in 1989-91. The two YA-7F airframes introduced new, afterburning engines and avionics systems. Though these aircraft accumulated 316.1 flight hours in 183 sorties between November 1989 and January 1991, the USAF decided not to authorize production. The two YA-7F airframes (70-1039; 71-0344) have since been retired from flying status.

The last A-7D/K airplanes to leave inventory will be those with ANG units at Rickenbacker (Ohio), Des Moines (Iowa), Tulsa (Oklahoma) and Springfield (Ohio).

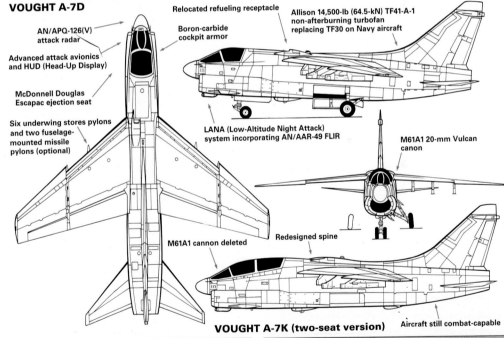

VOUGHT A-7D

AN/APQ-126(V) attack radar

Advanced attack avionics and HUD (Head-Up Display)

McDonnell Douglas Escapac ejection seat

Six underwing stores pylons and two fuselage-mounted missile pylons (optional)

Relocated refueling receptacle

Boron-carbide cockpit armor

Allison 14,500-lb (64.5-kN) TF41-A-1 non-afterburning turbofan replacing TF30 on Navy aircraft

LANA (Low-Altitude Night Attack) system incorporating AN/AAR-49 FLIR

M61A1 20-mm Vulcan canon

M61A1 cannon deleted

Redesigned spine

VOUGHT A-7K (two-seat version)

Aircraft still combat-capable

Above: For a while it looked as though a large number of ANG A-7Ds would be upgraded to A-7F standard with afterburning engines and revised avionics equipment. After testing two modified aircraft, the proposal was shelved.

MISSION PROFILE

Armament options: internal M61A1 Vulcan 20-mm cannon with maximum of 1,000 rounds; two fuselage and six wing hardpoints for the carriage of most stores in US inventory, including conventional low-drag and retarded bombs, cluster-bomb units, gun and rocket pods; defensive stores include AN/ALQ-119 or -131 ECM pod, AIM-9L/M Sidewinder missile (one on each fuselage station), AN/ALE-39 chaff dispenser; typical ferry configuration with two or four drop-tanks

Close air support/battlefield area interdiction: on a CAS, BAI, or combined CAS/BAI mission the A-7D flies to a radius of 460 miles (740 km) to be on station for 1-2 hours with 1,000 rounds of ammunition for the M61A1, two wing drop-tanks on inboard hardpoints (stations 3 and 4), and six to 12 Mk 82 500-lb (227-kg) bombs (total of 12 on two double MERs or six on two TERs on mid-wing hardpoints, stations 2 and 5), with outboard wing hardpoints (stations 1 and 6) normally not used; for dedicated anti-armor work the load-out would be two wing drop-tanks and eight Mk 20 Rockeye CBUs on two mid-wing hardpoints (stations 2 and 5), with outboard wing hardpoints not used; ECM pod may be carried

USAF VARIANTS AND SERIALS

A-7D: The basic version of the Corsair II was the A-7D, with 459 being ordered between 1967 and 1975 for service with TAC. The majority were transferred to the ANG, although they are in the process of being replaced by the F-16.
67-14582 to 67-14586; 68-8220 to 68-8231; 69-6188 to 69-6244; 70-0929 to 70-1056; 71-0292 to 71-0379; 72-0169 to 72-0265; 73-0992 to 73-1015; 74-1737 to 74-1760; 75-0386 to 75-0409

A-7K: Following the evaluation of a two-seat A-7K modified from A-7D 73-1008, 30 production versions were ordered during 1979, 1980 and 1981 for the ANG. 79-0460 to 79-0471; 80-0284 to 80-0295; 81-0072 to 81-0077

GA-7D: At least two GA-7Ds have been allocated to ground instruction duties with the Lowry Technical Training Center.
69-6188; 74-1746

YA-7D: The first three aircraft from the initial batch were allocated the designation YA-7D to indicate service test without modification.
67-14582; 67-14583; 67-14584

YA-7F: Two A-7D aircraft modified by LTV for the close air support role. Following an evaluation, the project was cancelled with the two YA-7Fs placed in storage.
70-1039; 71-0344

SPECIFICATION

Vought A-7D
Wing: span unfolded 38 ft 9 in (11.81 m) and folded 23 ft 9 in (7.24 m); aspect ratio 4; area 375 sq ft (34.83 m²)
Fuselage and tail: length 46 ft 1.5 in (14.06 m); height 16 ft 0.75 in (4.90 m); tailplane span 18 ft 1.5 in (5.52 m); wheel base 18 ft 1.5 in (4.83 m)
Powerplant: one Allison TF41-A-1 rated at 14,500 lb (64.5 kN) dry thrust
Weights: basic empty 19,127 lb (8676 kg); operating empty 19,915 lb (9033 kg); maximum take-off 42,000 lb (19050 kg)
Fuel and load: internal fuel 9,263 lb (4202 kg); external fuel up to four 300-US gal (1136-liter) drop-tanks; maximum ordnance theoretically 20,000 lb (9072 kg) but practically 15,000 lb (6804 kg); maximum ordnance with maximum internal fuel 9,500 lb (4309 kg)
Speed: maximum level speed 'clean' at sea level 698 mph (1123 km/h); maximum speed at 5,000 ft (1525 m) 646 mph (1040 km/h) with 12 Mk 82 bombs or 685 mph (1102 km/h) after dropping bombs
Range: ferry range 2,281 miles (3671 km) with internal fuel and 2,861 miles (4604 km) with internal and external fuel; combat radius 715 miles (1151 km) on a hi-lo-hi mission

Performance: maximum rate of climb at sea level 15,000 ft (4572 m) per minute; service ceiling 42,000 ft (12800 m); take-off distance 5,600 ft (1705 m) at maximum take-off weight

Vought A-7K
generally similar to the A-7D except in the following particulars:
Fuselage and tail: length 48 ft 11.5 in (14.92 m)

Above: The smoke-blackened gun port of the 20-mm M61A1 Vulcan cannon is clearly visible in this study of an A-7D of the Ohio Air National Guard at Rickenbacker. This unit is due to convert to the KC-135R during 1993.

USAF OPERATORS

Air Force Materiel Command (AFMC)

6510th TW	6512th TS	'ED'	Edwards AFB, CA	A-7K

Air Training Command (ATC)

3400th TTW	Lowry TTC		Lowry AFB, CO	GA-7D

Air National Guard (ANG)

121st FW	166th FS	'OH'	Rickenbacker ANGB, OH	A-7D/K
				to convert to KC-135R in 1993
132nd FW	124th FS	'IA'	Des Moines MAP, IA	A-7D/K
				to convert to F-16C in 1993
140th FW	120th FS	'CO'	Buckley ANGB, CO	A-7D/K
				converted to F-16C late 1991
112th FG	146th FS	'PT'	Gtr Pittsburgh IAP, PA	A-7D/K
				converted to KC-135E late 1991
114th FG	175th FS	'SD'	Joe Foss Fd, Sioux Falls, SD	A-7D/K
				converted to F-16C late 1991
138th FG	125th FS	'OK'	Tulsa IAP, OK	A-7D/K
				to convert to F-16C in 1993
150th FG	188th FS	nil	Kirtland AFB, NM	A-7D/K
				converting to F-16C in 1992
156th FG	198th FS	'PR'	San Juan IAP, PR	A-7D
				converting to F-16A in 1992
162nd FG	152nd FS	'AZ'	Tucson IAP, AZ	A-7D
	195th FS	'AZ'	Tucson IAP, AZ	A-7K
				converted to F-16A mid/late 1991
178th FG	162nd FS	'OH'	Springfield-Beckley MAP, OH	A-7D/K
				to convert to F-16C in 1993
180th FG	112th FS	'OH'	Toledo Express Apt, OH	A-7D/K
				converting to F-16C in 1992
185th FG	174th FS	'HA'	Sioux Gateway Apt, Sioux City, IA	A-7D/K
				converting to F-16C in 1992
192nd FG	149th FS	'VA'	Byrd IAP, Richmond, VA	A-7D/K
				converted to F-16C late 1991

Fairchild Republic
A-10 Thunderbolt II

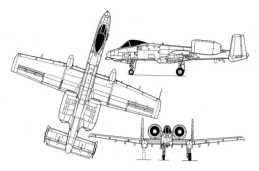

The **A-10 Thunderbolt II**, or 'Warthog', proved its worth as an anti-tank aircraft in Operation Desert Storm but faces an uncertain future in the USAF of the 1990s.

The A-10 is uniquely dedicated to a single mission – killing tanks. Its secondary role is CAS (close air support). In its anti-armor guise, the A-10 may be the only warplane of its era influenced by plans for Europe and Korea, rather than by combat in Vietnam. The armored threat posed by the Warsaw Pact (which has since been dismantled) and by North Korea (which still presents a threat) inspired the A-10. Regarded by some as too slow for a modern battlefield, the A-10 relies on maneuverability, armor and systems redundancy, rather than speed, to minimize vulnerability to ground fire.

In 1967, the USAF originated its A-X program for a new CAS warplane with anti-armor capability. The A-X was expected to be lethal against main battle tanks, tough and survivable, but still subsonic, in spite of an old fighter pilots' maxim that 'speed is life'.

Prototype awards were issued for the Northrop A-9A and Fairchild **A-10A**, the latter becoming the USAF's A-X choice on 18 January 1973. Counting six DT&E (development, test and evaluation) aircraft, the USAF made plans to acquire 733 A-10As.

First flight of the A-10A was made on 10 May 1972. The first production aircraft flew in February 1975. After developmental workups at Edwards AFB, California, and Eglin AFB, Florida, in 1976, Tactical Air Command (TAC) received its first A-10s for follow-on test and evaluation (FOT&E) at Davis-Monthan AFB, Arizona. The latter became the location of the first operational squadron, the 333rd Tactical Fighter Training Squadron, part of the 355th Tactical Fighter Training Wing, which equipped with the A-10 beginning in April 1976. Early developmental efforts were marred by the 3 June 1977 crash of an A-10 (75-0294) at the Paris air show.

The A-10 – a compromise between weapons-carrying capability and affordable cost – was designed to use numerous major parts, including flaps, main landing gears and movable tail surfaces (interchangeable, left/right) and internal systems which were easy to maintain and redundant, thereby enabling the aircraft to survive if some parts were shot away. Locating the twin General Electric TF34-GE-100 turbofan engines (similar to those on the S-3 Viking ASW aircraft) atop the rear fuselage reduces infra-red signature and makes the A-10 relatively easy to fly on one engine. The A-10A's cannon is the most powerful (in muzzle velocity) ever installed on a tactical warplane, firing milk bottle-sized rounds at rates hydraulically controlled at 2,100 or 4,200 rounds per minute.

The 19 ft 10½ in (6.06 m) long General Electric GAU-8/A cannon – a seven-barreled, rotating Gatling design, driven by the A-10's two hydraulic systems and fed with ammunition from a tub behind the cockpit – weighs only 620 lb (281 kg). A full load of API (armor piercing/incendiary) ammunition adds 2,066 lb (937 kg). The heaviest round employed by the cannon, API weighs 1.65 lb (0.75 kg) per round despite its aluminum casing. A 0.94-lb (0.43-kg) projectile leaves the barrel with a muzzle velocity of 3,240 ft (988 m) per second. The API round has a warhead of depleted uranium capable of penetrating any Soviet tank, including the T-80 series.

In addition to the cannon – which can disable a main battle tank from a distance of 21,600 ft (6584 m) – the A-10A has proved potent against main battle tanks with the infra-red-imaging version of the AGM-65 Maverick missile.

The single-seat A-10A is intended to operate with as little support equipment as possible, from crude FOLs (forward operating locations) where facilities are sparse. Larger than most tactical attack aircraft, the A-10 uses a HUD (head-up display), Have Quick secure UHF (ultra-high frequency) radio, and both TACAN and inertial navigation to assist the busy pilot. Enhancing bombing accuracy of the aircraft is the Pave Penny laser guidance pod hanging from an off-center right pylon beneath the cockpit. This system requires laser illumination (normally from the ground) of the target, the pilot's attention being attracted by a HUD symbol on the illuminated target.

The A-10 'Warthog' is well-armored for protection of pilot and systems. Armor plate adds 2,900 lb (1315 kg) to the aircraft's weight. The pilot is shielded by a bulletproof windscreen and encircled by a titanium armor 'bath tub' which weighs 1,200 lb (544 kg) and varies in thickness up to 1½ in (3.8 cm). Coupled with the thick skin and innards of the aircraft, this armor is rated as adequate defense against a 23-mm cannon round.

Above: Designed primarily for the tank-busting task, the A-10A Thunderbolt II is an immensely rugged but decidedly unattractive machine built around the massive GAU-8/A 30-mm cannon.

Tests with a two-seat night/adverse-weather variant designated **YA-10B** (but usually called the **N/AW A-10**) did not lead to production of the A-10B variant, and the two-seat demonstrator airframe has long since been put to pasture. Production of the single-seat A-10A ended in 1983 with the 713th aircraft.

In the late 1980s the A-10 was selected for the fast FAC (forward air control) mission. This move was accomplished partly to generate a replacement for ageing OV-10 Broncos and OA-37B Dragonflys, but it also reflected the Air Force's internal difficulty with the A-10: the service had long wanted a version of the F-16 Fighting Falcon for CAS/BAI (close air support/battlefield area interdiction) and welcomed a chance to shunt the A-10 to other duties. Externally unmodified, the fast FAC **OA-10** came into existence and now operates with several units.

Below: An ECM pod, Pave Penny laser-guidance pod, AGM-65 Maverick ASM and rocket launcher pod are all carried beneath the fuselage and wings of this pair of lightly-armed A-10A Thunderbolts. In addition to the mission of eliminating enemy armored fighting vehicles, the 'Warthog' has been assigned to FAC duty as the OA-10A since the late 1980s.

USAF Aircraft

Right: Gases pour from the muzzle of the 30-mm cannon of an A-10A Thunderbolt during a live-firing training exercise at a weapons range in the USA. Although designed for use against AFVs such as main battle tanks, the A-10A's gun was used in an air-to-air mode during the Gulf War and claimed two helicopter victims.

The A-10 was designed for a European or Korean scenario. At the height of its career, more than 100 served with the 81st Tactical Fighter Wing at RAF Bentwaters-Woodbridge, UK, forming no fewer than six squadrons, which frequently deployed to five FOLs in West Germany. In 1988, two of the 81st's squadrons were transferred to the 10th TFW at RAF Alconbury, UK. This unit participated in Desert Storm before being deactivated in 1992. The 81st will continue to support post-Desert Storm activities until its deactivation in 1993. A-10s remain at Osan AB, RoK, where armored threat to US forces persists in the post-Cold War era. OA-10s also serve at Eielson AFB, Alaska.

The homely, rugged A-10 had been designed to support US Army ground troops in daylight. But in the 1980s, US forces gradually shifted to the concept of an AirLand battle – or 'joint' battle employing close co-operation between the services – in which much of the fighting would be conducted at night, to exploit US technology. The simple and straightforward A-10, which had been built without a terrain-avoidance radar (and rejected by the USAF in its night/adverse-weather version) now seemed out of date. Still, the A-10 rehearsed night desert warfare at the NTC (National Training Center), Fort Irwin, California. At NTC, pilots flew in dust and haze against tanks in very realistic practice fighting.

Plans were well advanced to phase out the A-10 when the warplane was granted a reprieve for Operation Desert Shield, the Middle East buildup which followed Iraq's invasion of Kuwait on 2 August 1990. Typical of deployments made during Desert Shield was that of the 23rd Tactical Fighter Wing, England AFB, Louisiana, whose pilots made a 13.1-hour overnight flight to Spain, refueled immediately, and flew another 10 hours to King Fahd Airport, Saudi Arabia, with eight air-to-air refuelings.

The A-10 force deployed to the Saudi desert included the 23rd TFW; the 354th TFW from Myrtle Beach AFB, South Carolina; and one squadron (511th TFS) from the 10th TFW at Alconbury, UK. In addition, the Air Force Reserve's 706th TFS from New Orleans, Louisiana, and the 23rd TASS with OA-10As from Davis-Monthan AFB, Arizona, participated in the buildup and the conflict.

The USAF deployed 144 A-10s to the war zone. During the January-February 1991 fighting, when air superiority was quickly gained, A-10s were used in innovative fashion in various roles. A daytime tank killer, the A-10 also became a daytime 'Scud' hunter in Western Iraq, suppressed enemy air defenses, attacked early warning radars, and even shot down two helicopters with its cannon – the only air-to-air victories accomplished with guns. While the A-10 flew almost 8,100 combat sorties, it maintained a mission-capable rate of 95.7 per cent.

MISSION PROFILE

Armament options: the A-10 is built around a single 30-mm GAU-8/A Avenger cannon in the nose, depressed 2° with the bulk of the weapon offset slightly to port so that the firing barrel is always on the centerline, and with a maximum capacity of 1,350 rounds; cannon rounds are high explosive or armor piercing, the latter having a dense depleted uranium core; the gun has two selectable rates of fire, 2,100 or 4,200 rpm; three fuselage and eight wing hardpoints (one fuselage station usually not employed) for the carriage of most stores in US inventory, including conventional low-drag and retarded bombs, cluster-bomb units, and AGM-65 Maverick missile; US-based A-10s carry the AN/ALQ-119 ECM pod while those stationed overseas carry the AN/ALQ-131 ECM; one outboard wing station is usually reserved for the ECM pod, the other for two AIM-9L/M Sidewinder missiles; ferry configuration is with one or two wing drop-tanks

Close air support and anti-armor: on a typical CAS mission the A-10 flies to a radius of 475 miles (764 km) with 1,350 rounds of ammunition for the GAU-8/A, two AGM-65 Maverick air-to-ground missiles (on LAU-117 rails on stations 3 and 9), AN/ALQ-131 ECM pod, and two AIM-9M Sidewinders (stations 8 and 11)

Forward air control: the OA-10 dedicated forward air control (FAC) aircraft also has a combat radius of 475 miles (764 km) with 1,350 rounds of ammunition for the GAU-8/A and a full ordnance load; in practice, the USAF does not want the OA-10 carrying full ordnance; with a lighter load of just two rocket pods and Sidewinders, radius of the OA-10 increases to around 885 km (550 miles)

USAF VARIANTS AND SERIALS

A-10A: A total of six pre-production and 707 production A-10As were ordered between 1975 and 1982 for tactical squadrons in the USA, Europe and the Pacific, as well as the Reserves.
73-1664 to 73-1669; 75-0258 to 75-0309; 76-0512 to 76-0554; 77-0177 to 77-0276; 78-0582 to 78-0725; 79-0082 to 79-0225; 80-0140 to 80-0283; 81-0939 to 81-0998; 82-0646 to 82-0665

YA-10A: The two prototype Thunderbolt IIs were assigned the designation YA-10A as they undertook service tests with both the manufacturer and Air Force Systems Command. Six pre-production aircraft were also allocated this designation.
71-1369 to 71-1370; 73-1664 to 73-1669

OA-10A: The prefix O was applied to numerous A-10As which were redesignated for Forward Air Control (FAC) duties. The OA-10A refers to the mission as no external modification was carried out and there are no visible means to distinguish this version from the basic Thunderbolt II.
Dozens of A-10As redesignated without modification

YA-10B: The first pre-production A-10A was converted to YA-10B configuration as the proposed two-seat trainer version. Following an evaluation by the manufacturer and the Air Force, the project was abandoned and the sole YA-10B placed on display at Edwards AFB.
73-1664

A-10B: The designation was assigned to the production versions of the two-seat Thunderbolt II, although none was built after evaluating the prototype.

GYA-10A/GA-10A: The prefix G, indicating ground instructional airframe, was assigned to the fourth and fifth aircraft built following their transfer to the Sheppard Technical Training Center and to a pair of ex-TAC A-10As employed by ATC TTC.
73-1665; 73-1666 (GY); 75-0260; 76-0518 (G)

SPECIFICATION

Fairchild Republic A-10A
Wing: span 57 ft 6 in (17.53 m); aspect ratio 6.54; area 506.0 sq ft (47.01 m²)
Fuselage and tail: length 53 ft 4 in (16.26 m); height 14 ft 8 in (4.47 m); tailplane span 18 ft 10 in (5.74 m); wheel base 17 ft 8.75 in (5.40 m)
Powerplant: two General Electric TF34-GE-100 each rated at 9,065 lb (40.3 kN) dry thrust
Weights: basic empty 21,541 lb (9771 kg); operating empty 24,959 lb (11321 kg); maximum take-off 50,000 lb (22680 kg); forward airstrip armed 32,771 lb (14865 kg)
Fuel and load: internal fuel 10,700 lb (4853 kg); external fuel up to three 600-US gal (2271-liter) drop-tanks; maximum ordnance 16,000 lb (7250 kg); maximum ordnance with full internal fuel 14,341 lb (6505 kg)
Speed: never-exceed speed 518 mph (834 km/h); maximum level speed 'clean' at sea level 439 mph (706 km/h); cruising speed at sea level 345 mph (555 km/h)
Range: ferry range 2,454 miles (3949 km); deep strike combat radius 621 miles (1000 km); CAS combat radius with 1.7-hour loiter 288 miles (463 km)
Performance: maximum rate of climb at sea level 6,000 ft (1828 m) per minute; take-off distance 4,000 ft (1220 m) at maximum take-off weight, 1,450 ft (442 m) at forward strip weight; landing distance 2,000 ft (610 m) at maximum weight, 1,300 ft (396 m) at forward strip weight

USAF OPERATORS

Air Force Materiel Command (AFMC)

3246th TW	3247th TS	'ET'	Eglin AFB, FL	A-10A

Air Training Command (ATC)

3400th TTW	Lowry TTC		Lowry AFB, CO	GA-10A
3700th TTW	Sheppard TTC		Sheppard AFB, TX	GA-10A, GYA-10A

Pacific Air Forces (PACAF)

51st FW	19th FS	'OS'	Osan AB, RoK	OA-10A
343rd Wg	11th TASS	'AK'	Eielson AFB, AK	OA-10A

Air Combat Command (ACC)

23rd FW	74th FS	'EL'	England AFB, LA	A-10A
	76th FS	'EL'	England AFB, LA	A-10A

Note: 76th FS inactivated November 1991, but is resurrecting as part of 23rd Wg at Pope with tail code 'FT'

33rd FW	?	'EG'	Eglin AFB, FL	OA/A-10A by late 1992

Weapons
The A-10 can carry a wide variety of stores. This aircraft carries six cluster bombs and two AGM-65 Maverick anti-tank missiles.

Configuration
The A-10 was designed for maximum survivability. The engines are positioned so that they are masked from heat-seeking missiles by the fins as much as possible.

57th FW	A-10 FWS	'WA'	Nellis AFB, NV	A-10A
354th FW	353rd FS	'MB'	Myrtle Beach AFB, SC	A-10A
	355th FS	'MB'	Myrtle Beach AFB, SC	A-10A
	356th FS	'MB'	Myrtle Beach AFB, SC	A-10A
355th FW	354th FS	'NF'	Davis-Monthan AFB, AZ	OA-10A
	357th FS	'DM'	Davis-Monthan AFB, AZ	A-10A
	358th FS	'DM'	Davis-Monthan AFB, AZ	A-10A
507th ACW	21st FS	'SF'	Shaw AFB, SC	OA/A-10A
	33rd FS	'NF'	Shaw AFB, SC	OA-10A
AWC	4485th TS	'OT'	Eglin AFB, FL	A-10A

United States Air Forces in Europe (USAFE)

81st TFW	78th TFS	'WR'	RAF Woodbridge, UK	A-10A
	91st TFS	'WR'	RAF Woodbridge, UK	A-10A
	92nd TFS	'WR'	RAF Bentwaters, UK	A-10A
	510th TFS	'WR'	RAF Bentwaters, UK	A-10A

Air National Guard (ANG)

128th FW	176th FS	'WI'	Truax Field, Madison, WI	A-10A
103rd FG	118th FS	'CT'	Bradley ANGB, CT	A-10A
104th FG	131rd FS	'MA'	Barnes MAP, MA	A-10A
110th FG	172nd FS	'BC'	WK Kellogg RAP, MI	OA-10A
111th FG	103rd FS	'PA'	NAS Willow Grove, PA	OA-10A
175th FG	104th FS	'MD'	Glenn L. Martin State Apt, Baltimore, MD	A-10A
			To gain six OA-10As in late 1992	

Air Force Reserve (AFRes)

442nd FW	303rd FS	'KC'	Richards Gebaur AFB, MO	A-10A
			To gain six OA-10As in mid-1992	
917th FW	46th FS	'BD'	Barksdale AFB, LA	A-10A
	47th FS	'BD'	Barksdale AFB, LA	A-10A
			47th FS to add 12 OA-10As in early 1993	
926th FG	706th FS	'NO'	NAS New Orleans, LA	A-10A
930th FG	45th FS	'IN'	Grissom AFB, IN	A-10A

Self-defense
The outer pylons are usually used for self-defense stores, in this case twin AIM-9M Sidewinder missiles (port) and ECM pod (ALQ-119) starboard.

Gun
Much of the forward fuselage houses the massive Avenger cannon. Up to 1,350 rounds can be carried in an internal armored tank.

Fairchild A-10A Thunderbolt II

Known universally as the 'Warthog', the A-10A is used for the anti-armor/close air support role. In addition to its active-duty users, it equips six Air National Guard and four Air Force Reserve units. Many aircraft are being re-roled as OA-10As for the forward air control task.

Above: Stationed at Bradley ANGB, Connecticut, the 118th FS is one of half a dozen Air Guard units that operate the 'Warthog'.

Markings
This aircraft is shown in the markings of the Reserve's 706th TFS, 926th TFG, as it appeared during service in Desert Storm. The nose badge shows a shrimp throwing a lightning bolt, alluding to the basing of the aircraft at New Orleans. The unit scored one helicopter kill during the war.

Boeing
B-52 Stratofortress

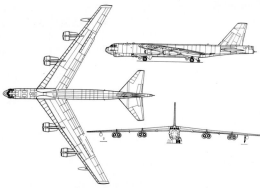

Longest-serving USAF warplane in history, the **B-52 Stratofortress** is known to crews as the 'BUFF', for 'Big Ugly Fat Fucker'. Designed for trans-polar nuclear warfare with the Soviet Union, the B-52 has both nuclear and conventional duties today.

The B-52 was employed in combat as a conventional bomber in Vietnam (1965-73) and in the Persian Gulf (1991). **B-52A**, **B**, **C**, **D**, **E** and **F** models had all been retired by the mid-1980s, but the **B-52G** and **H** soldiered on, as the largest part of the manned bomber portion of the American strategic triad. The 'BUFF' continues to have a major role as a much-reorganized US Air Force trims itself from 36 to 26 combat wings, and a new US Strategic Command takes over all long-range American nuclear forces.

XB-52 and **YB-52** prototypes (49-0230/0231) were built in secrecy and the YB-52 flew first at Seattle. The B-52 resembled a B-47 Stratojet with its 35° swept wing, podded engines, and 'bicycle' undercarriage.

Fuel capacity was greater than in any previous production aircraft at 38,865 US gal (147121 liters) with drop-tanks. Powerplants were eight Pratt & Whitney YJ57-P-3 axial-flow turbojets, delivering 8,700 lb (3946 kg) of thrust each and podded in pairs on four underwing pylons. The gigantic fin, with only its trailing edge hinged to form a rudder, made the bomber's height 48 ft 3⅔ in (14.72 m) and could be folded to permit the bomber to enter standard hangars. The B-52 did not rotate on take-off but, rather, popped aloft, its wing set at an incidence of 8° for a flyaway with the fuselage horizontal. On landing, the B-52 employed a 44-ft (13.41-m) braking parachute, stowed in a compartment in the rear fuselage.

The B-52 changed little during its 10-year production run. Three B-52As (52-0001/0003) were followed by 23 B-52Bs, which entered service with SAC's 93rd Bomb Wing, Castle AFB, California, on 29 June 1955. Twenty-seven **RB-52Bs** came next. B-52Bs and RB-52Bs were eventually modified to B-52C standard, in addition to 35 new B-52Cs introduced from March 1956. These retained reconnaissance capability but not an R prefix.

The B-52D, of which 170 were built, was first flown on 14 May 1956. One hundred B-52Es followed, and 89 B-52Fs were manufactured, beginning in February 1959.

Boeing produced 193 B-52G aircraft at Wichita. The B-52G introduced a shorter vertical tail and numerous internal changes, including a new integral-tank wing with internal fuel capacity increased to 46,576 US gal (176309 liters) and with external drop-tanks reduced in volume to 700 US gal (2650 liters) each. The weight of the aircraft was increased to 488,000 lb (221357 kg). The B-52G was designed for the GAM-87A Sky Bolt, an air-launched ballistic missile which underwent extensive Anglo-American design and development work before being cancelled. Its bomb bay was also configured to carry four ADM-20A Quail decoy missiles. B-52Gs also

carried two North American GAM-77 (AGM-28) Hound Dog inertial-guidance stand-off weapons. Later, the B-52G was modified to carry 20 AGM-69A SRAMs (short-range attack missile) or ALCMs (air-launched cruise missile).

Where earlier models had a manned tail gun position, the B-52G had its gunner relocated in the main crew compartment and operating his guns via the AN/ASG-15 fire control system. Armament of four .50-caliber (12.7-mm) machine guns in the tail was retained.

The USAF ordered 102 B-52H aircraft in 1960-61, taking first delivery on 30 September 1960. With the short vertical fin of the B-52G, the H model was powered by eight 17,000-lb (7711-kg) thrust Pratt & Whitney TF33-P-1 or -3 turbofan engines, developed from the familiar J57 but without the latter's water-injection feature. Gross weight of the B-52H went up to 505,000 lb (229068 kg) for take-off and a maximum of 566,000 lb (256738 kg) after inflight refueling. Tail armament of the B-52H was again remotely operated but now comprised a single T-171 (later M61A1) 20-mm Vulcan cannon. The B-52H, like the G model, was configured to carry Sky Bolt, Quail, Hound Dog, SRAM and ALCM. The last B-52H was delivered to the USAF on 26 October 1962, ending production of 744 Stratofortresses.

In 1972, a program commenced to reconfigure most B-52s with an electronics suite to assist in low-level terrain following, a suite which includes EVS (electro-optical viewing system), a low-light television, and FLIR. In 1976 came the Rivet Ace program to update ECM equipment aboard the aircraft, enhancing the capability of the B-52 to take on enemy radars while flying in the head-on mode.

Today's SIOP-assigned B-52G and B-52H aircraft carry B61 and B83 nuclear bombs. Standard load is a 'clip' of four B61s, which can accommodate a variety of nuclear warheads – these being 'maximum-drogued' bombs designed to be severely retarded during a low-level drop to enable the 'BUFF' crew to get away. Also retarded by parachute when dropped, the B83 is a one- to two-megaton thermonuclear bomb which is 12 ft (3.65 m) long, 18 in (0.45 m) in diameter, and weighs 2,400 lb (1089 kg).

The B-52G and B-52H fly missions today with a crew of five – the pilot or aircraft commander (AC), co-pilot, electronic warfare officer (EWO), navigator and radar navigator (RN). In an economy move, the aerial gunner crew position was eliminated on 1 October 1991.

First successful test-firing of an ALCM from a B-52 was accomplished on 5 March 1976. On 25 March 1980, the USAF chose the Boeing AGM-86B over the competing General Dynamics AGM-109 Tomahawk. The AGM-86, conceived as a second-generation decoy, became a nuclear delivery vehicle and made it possible for a 'BUFF' to attack a target from a distance as great as 1,550 miles

Above: Known unofficially as the 'Cadillac', the turbofan-powered B-52H was the final model of the Stratofortress to be produced, featuring superior unrefueled range characteristics when compared with the B-52G.

(2494 km). Powered by a 600-lb (272-kg) thrust Williams F107-101 turbojet, eight ALCMs can be carried on an internal rotary launcher in the B-52G and H, and 12 more on underwing pylons. The first operational AGM-86B was placed in service in January 1981. Subsequently, the USAF has developed the AGM-129A Advanced ALCM, to be carried by the B-52H (but not the B-52G).

The AGM-129A, also called ACM (advanced cruise missile), is 21 ft (6.5 m) long, powered by a 900-lb (4.0-kN) thrust Williams F112 turbojet engine, and combines low-observable features with low-altitude maneuvering to evade air defenses *en route* to its target. The AGM-129A was designed to be effective at a stand-off distance of 2,000 miles (3218 km). Displayed publicly in June 1991, the AGM-129A was expected to be carried on operational B-52Hs in the same manner as its predecessor.

At the outset of the 1990s, the USAF's position was that the B-52H would continue for a number of years in the stand-off role, while the B-1B remained the US's primary penetrator and the B-2 would begin to join the force in the mid-1990s. The B-2 remains a highly visible target for cost-cutting reductions.

During Operation Desert Storm, B-52G Stratofortresses served in provisional bomb wings and mounted combat missions from Diego Garcia; Jeddah, Saudi Arabia; Moron, Spain; and Fairford, England. B-52Gs flew 1,624 missions, dropped over 72,000 weapons, and delivered over 25,700 tons (23.32 million kg) of munitions on area targets in the Kuwait theater of operations and on airfields, industrial targets, troop concentrations and storage areas in Iraq. Gulf War B-52Gs had a mission-capable rate of over 81 per cent, or two per cent higher than the peacetime rate. B-52Gs also launched conventional-warhead AGM-86C cruise missiles.

Rapid changes affecting the B-52 force included the 27 September 1991 announcement of plans to create a US Strategic Command (and of an end of nuclear alert by B-52s and other bombers), which seemed to overtake earlier USAF plans to place SAC aircraft into an Air Combat Command. Some B-52s were expected to join one or more composite 'intervention' wings. Today's force numbers 254 B-52 bombers (159 B-52G and 95 B-52H).

Left: Various bumps and bulges associated with mission avionics protrude from the nose sections of these 2nd Wing B-52Gs at Barksdale AFB. Both also display examples of the nose art which has become such a common feature on SAC bombers and tankers in recent years.

Below: The drooping wings visible on this B-52G indicate that it is fully-fueled and ready to launch on a training mission from Barksdale. In present service, the B-52G can fulfil nuclear and conventional bombing tasks.

Bottom: B-52Gs like this 2nd Wing machine were responsible for delivering more than one-third of all the ordnance deposited by USAF aircraft during the Gulf War of 1991.

37

Top: A dozen M117 750-lb general-purpose 'iron bombs' are carried on each of the two underwing racks which can be seen on this B-52G, getting airborne from Fairford, England, with the usual cloud of smoke generated by eight J57 turbojet engines working at full bore.

Above: In addition to featuring TF33 turbofans, the B-52H also embodied a different defensive armament arrangement, relying on a single M61A1 Vulcan 20-mm cannon in place of the quartet of 0.5-in machine guns fitted to earlier members of the Stratofortress family.

MISSION PROFILE

Armament options: four 0.5-in (12.7-mm) machine guns (B-52G) or one 20-mm M61A1 cannon with 1,242 rounds (B-52H) fitted, but tail gun installation not used and tail-gunner crew position not filled in current operations; internal bomb bay and inboard wing pylons with provision for AGM-69A SRAM-A (short-range attack missile) not used in current operations; AGM-86B ALCM (air-launched cruise missile) (B-52H only) AGM-129A ACM (Advanced ALCM); (B-52G/H) B61 or B83 nuclear bombs; provision for a variety of conventional bombs and AGM-142A Have Nap precision attack missiles

Strategic bombardment: on a nuclear mission, the B-52 would employ air refueling but could have a range up to 8,000 miles (12875 km) unrefueled with eight AGM-86B ALCM (air-launched cruise missiles) internally

plus six on each of two wing pylons to total 20 missiles launched 1,500 miles (2414 km) from target; or (B-52H only) up to 20 AGM-129A ACM (Advanced ALCM); or (B-52G/H) 'clip' of four B61 700-lb (318-kg) or B83 2,400-lb (1089-kg) maximum-drogued nuclear bombs

Theater/conventional bombardment: on a conventional mission, the B-52 would employ air refueling but could have a radius up to 3,800 miles (6115 km) unrefueled with (non-ALCM B-52G and B-52H) up to 27 internal and up to nine Mk 84 2,000-lb (907-kg) bombs externally on each of two inboard wing pylons with stub pylons and HSAB (heavy stores adapter beam) to total 45 bombs; 27 750-lb (340-kg) M117 or 1,000-lb (454-kg) Mk 83 bombs in internal bay plus 12 on inboard 'Hound Dog' wing pylon with MERs to total 51 bombs; AGM-142A Have Nap TV-guided precision missile carried externally provides 50-mile (80-km) stand-off capability with 1,975-lb (896-kg) high-explosive warhead; AGM-86C conventional cruise missiles available

USAF VARIANTS AND SERIALS

B-52G: 193 B-52Gs were ordered at the end of the 1950s with the majority still operational, although these are gradually being retired. A host of additional sensors has altered the nose profile considerably.
57-6468 to 57-6520; 58-0158 to 58-0258; 59-2564 to 59-2602

GB-52G: Surplus B-52Gs have begun to join Air Training Command as ground instructional airframes, including three with the Sheppard TTC.
57-6469; 58-0200; 59-2578

B-52H: The most distinguishable feature to differentiate the B-52H from its predecessors is the fitment of TF33 turbofan engines in place of the J57 turbojets, and a six-barreled 20-mm rotary cannon instead of the four 0.5-in guns. One hundred and two B-52Hs were obtained during 1960 and 1961 with all, except a handful lost in accidents, remaining operational.
60-0001 to 60-0062; 61-0001 to 61-0040

GB-52D/GB-52F: Although long since retired from operational duty a single B-52D and a pair of B-52Fs are still used by the two major Technical Training Centers.
56-0589 (D); 57-0048; 57-0071 (F)

SPECIFICATION

Boeing B-52H
Wing: span 185 ft 0 in (56.39 m); area 4,000.0 sq ft (371.6 m²)
Fuselage and tail: length 160 ft 10.9 in (49.05 m); height 40 ft 8 in (12.40 m); tailplane span 55 ft 7.5 in (16.95 m); wheel base 50 ft 3 in (15.48 m)
Powerplant: eight Pratt & Whitney TF33-P-3 each rated at 17,000 lb (75.62 kN) dry thrust
Weight: maximum take-off more than 505,000 lb (229068 kg)
Fuel and load: internal fuel 299,434 lb (135823 kg); external fuel up to 9,114 lb (4134 kg) in two 700-US gal (2650-liter) underwing tanks; maximum ordnance about 50,000 lb (22680 kg)
Speed: maximum level speed 'clean' at high altitude 595 mph (957 km/h); cruising speed at high altitude 509 mph (819 km/h); penetration speed at low altitude between 405 and 420 mph (652 and 676 km/h)
Range: maximum range on internal fuel more than 10,000 miles (16093 km)
Performance: service ceiling 55,000 ft (16764 m); take-off distance 9,500 ft (2896 m)

Boeing B-52G
generally similar to the B-52H except in the following particulars:
Powerplant: eight Pratt & Whitney J57-P-43WB each rated at 13,750 lb (61.16 kN) dry thrust
Weight: maximum take-off more than 488,000 lb (221357 kg)
Range: maximum range on internal fuel 7,500 miles (12070 km)
Performance: service ceiling 12190 m (40,000 ft)

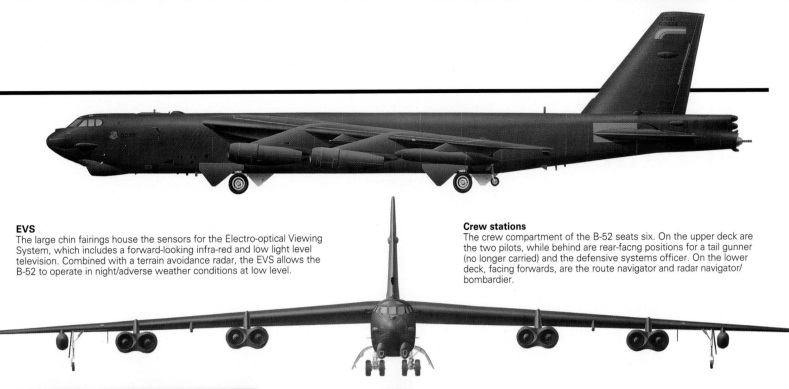

EVS
The large chin fairings house the sensors for the Electro-optical Viewing System, which includes a forward-looking infra-red and low light level television. Combined with a terrain avoidance radar, the EVS allows the B-52 to operate in night/adverse weather conditions at low level.

Crew stations
The crew compartment of the B-52 seats six. On the upper deck are the two pilots, while behind are rear-facng positions for a tail gunner (no longer carried) and the defensive systems officer. On the lower deck, facing forwards, are the route navigator and radar navigator/bombardier.

USAF OPERATORS

Air Force Materiel Command (AFMC)

6510th TW	6519th TS	'ED'	Edwards AFB, CA	B-52G/H

Air Training Command

3400th TTW	Lowry TTC		Lowry AFB, CO	GB-52F
3700th TTW	Sheppard TTC		Sheppard AFB, TX	GB-52D/F/G

Air Combat Command (ACC)

2nd Wg	62nd BS		Barksdale AFB, LA	B-52G
	596th BS		Barksdale AFB, LA	B-52G

Boeing B-52H Stratofortress

The B-52H is a more capable aircraft than the G model, its TF33 turbofans providing much better range/payload performance. Four wings fly this model, at present being mainly concerned with the carriage of AGM-86 air-launched cruise missiles. However, their duties will increasingly involve conventional weapons in the coming years as they assume this role from B-52Gs.

Powerplant
The H model is powered by eight of the Pratt & Whitney TF33-P-3 turbofans, each producing 17,000 lb (75.65 kN) thrust. The use of turbofans not only increases operational range to around 10,000 miles (16090 km) but also reduces internal noise considerably.

Fuel
Fuel is held in tanks in the wings and fuselage, augmented by 700-US gal (2650-liter) external tanks. Total capacity is 48,030 US gal (181813 liters).

Bomb bay
The massive bomb bay can accommodate up to 12 B61 or B83 free-fall bombs, or 12 AGM-86 cruise missiles on a rotary launcher. Many alternative conventional loads exist.

Markings
This B-52H sports the recently-adopted all-over gray camouflage. It wears the rainbow markings of the 410th Wing, which resides at K. I. Sawyer AFB.

Undercarriage
The B-52 has a unique undercarriage arrangement that incorporates four twin-wheel units along the main fuselage to support the weight, and small outrigger wheels to prevent damage to the wings. The main wheels can swivel so that the aircraft can 'crab' when taking off in crosswinds.

5th Wg	23rd BS	Minot AFB, ND	B-52H
7th Wg	9th BS	Carswell AFB, TX	B-52H
	20th BS	Carswell AFB, TX	B-52H
42nd Wg	69th BS	Loring AFB, ME	B-52G
92nd Wg	325th BS	Fairchild AFB, WA	B-52H
93rd Wg	328th BS	Castle AFB, CA	B-52G
	329th CCTS	Castle AFB, CA	B-52G
97th Wg	340th BS	Eaker AFB, AR	B-52G
			Inactivating late 1992
379th Wg	524th BS	Wurtsmith AFB, MI	B-52G
410th Wg	644th BS	K. I. Sawyer AFB, MI	B-52H
416th Wg	668th BS	Griffiss AFB, NY	B-52G

All SAC wings changed designation on 1 October 1991 with the elimination of the identifying pre-fix letters, e.g. 2nd Bombardment Wing (2nd BW) became 2nd Wing (2nd Wg). Some B-52s are to be assigned to new composite wings.

Rockwell
B-1 Lancer

The **B-1B Lancer** was developed as the principal manned bomber for the United States' strategic triad. In the 1980s, the B-1B enjoyed high priority even though USAF plans focused not solely on the B-1B but also on the B-2A 'Stealth Bomber', then a 'black' program.

The B-1B has been controversial. Its AN/ALQ-161 defensive electronics system has required frequent modifications. The USAF grounded the B-1B on 15 December 1990 following two catastrophic engine failures within a three-month period. In all, the B-1B has been grounded half a dozen times.

The B-1B can lay claim to being the first stealthy bomber, ahead of the B-2A, since its fuselage blends into the variable-geometry wing to create a low-drag configuration. Heart of the B-1B's structure is its massive titanium wing carry-through box which lies across the center of the fuselage. At each end is a hinge fitting for the swing-wing. The wing is kept at its least degree of sweep, 15°, for handling on the ground and during take-off. Flaps can be activated only when the wing is swept less than 20°. The maximum sweep is 67° 30' when the B-1B is in high-speed flight at high altitude.

The bomber's wing carry-through structure supports the main undercarriage. Fore and aft of this structure are intermediate fuselage sections, to which are affixed the rear fuselage and empennage and the nose section/crew compartment.

The B-1B has been reported to have a radar cross section (RCS) only one-fourth that of a B-52. Much use is made of radar-absorbent materials throughout the bomber's key components. Unlike the B-52, the B-1B was designed to go into combat at low altitude.

The four men aboard a B-1B sit in Douglas-designed, Weber-built ACES II (Advanced Concept Ejection Seats) which have zero-speed, zero-altitude capability. Parachute and individual oxygen supply are stowed aboard the seat itself.

The B-1B is powered by four 30,000-lb (136.92-kN) thrust General Electric F101-GE-102 turbofan engines. Its variable-geometry, or 'swing', wing helps the B-1B get aloft from an alert pad faster than the B-52.

Pilot and co-pilot of the B-1B are side-by-side and have an instrument panel which includes a mixture of digital and analog instruments and several cathode ray tubes. Both fly-by-wire and mechanical flight control systems are used, the former connected to the pilot's station and the latter to the co-pilot's. A reversionary link ties the two together if one fails. The B-1B is flown much like a fighter, using stick and rudder pedals, though it has no HUD (head-up display) and needs none for its low-level, terrain-following bomb mission.

The third and fourth crewmen, OSO and DSO (offensive and defensive systems operators), also sit side-by-side behind the pilots and face forwards, although they do not have much of a view outside the aircraft. The former is a navigator: his job is to get the aircraft to the target and to release the ordnance at

the right time. The latter operates the AN/ALQ-161 system. This system is largely automatic, detecting hostile emissions through receivers placed strategically around the aircraft and analyzing and prioritizing them before instructing jammers to obliterate or confuse them. The DSO monitors the system on two graphic displays, showing threats with alphanumeric labels. Another display gives tabulated information on threats.

On the ground, the B-1B is boarded by climbing a retractable ladder up through a hatch, reaching a cabin with far more room for its crew than the interior of the B-52. The B-1B provides a chemical toilet and a miniature gal-

ley with microwave oven. There is a full-sized jump seat, as compared with the B-52's half-sized jump seat, for an IP (instructor pilot).

While making a low-level penetration in enemy territory, the B-1B crew flies 'zipped up', shielded from thermonuclear flash blindness by thermal blast curtains into which are placed six portholes equipped with PLZT (polarized lead zirconium titanate), reducing external light to 0.003 of its original intensity when exposed to a sudden burst of light.

The Reagan administration announced in September 1981 its intention to put 100 B-1Bs into SAC inventory. On 4 September 1984, the first B-1B (82-0001) was rolled out at Rock-

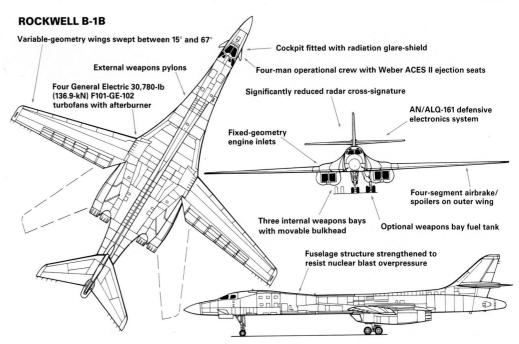

ROCKWELL B-1B

Variable-geometry wings swept between 15° and 67°

External weapons pylons

Four General Electric 30,780-lb (136.9-kN) F101-GE-102 turbofans with afterburner

Cockpit fitted with radiation glare-shield

Four-man operational crew with Weber ACES II ejection seats

Significantly reduced radar cross-signature

AN/ALQ-161 defensive electronics system

Fixed-geometry engine inlets

Four-segment airbrake/spoilers on outer wing

Three internal weapons bays with movable bulkhead

Optional weapons bay fuel tank

Fuselage structure strengthened to resist nuclear blast overpressure

Above: Cancelled by Carter and resurrected by Reagan, 100 examples of the Rockwell B-1 Lancer were delivered to Strategic Air Command during the latter half of the 1980s. Most of these remain active with four wings, fulfilling the strategic nuclear deterrent mission.

well's Palmdale, California, plant. The manufacturer later made something of the fact that the B-1B was well ahead of the similar Soviet Tu-160 ('Blackjack'). 82-0001, nicknamed 'Leader of the Fleet', made its first flight on 18 October 1984. This first ship was also one of two B-1Bs (with 83-0065) to wear the nickname 'Star of Abilene' (a Texas city near Dyess).

The first B-1B was delivered at Offutt AFB, Nebraska, on 27 July 1985. The first 29 B-1Bs were assigned to the 96th Bomb Wing at Dyess AFB, Texas. This excluded the ninth B-1B which went to Edwards AFB, California, for test work, where two B-1Bs are operated by Air Force Materiel Command. IOC (initial operating capability) was attained in July 1986.

Given uncertainty that the B-2A 'Stealth Bomber' will ever serve in more than token numbers, the B-1B's job as a strategic penetrator is likely to be secure well into the 21st century.

In the 'expeditionary' US Air Force of the 1990s, where 24-hour nuclear alert has been discontinued, the B-1B's conventional bombing capability may receive greater currency; indeed, one aircraft is currently being modified as a testbed for evaluations of conventional ordnance. The B-1B is also suitable for maritime surveillance and could be fitted (with minimal changes) with aerial mines or AGM-84 Harpoon anti-shipping missiles. The aircraft is capable of carrying the AGM-129A ACM (advanced cruise missile) although the USAF has no plans, at present, to so equip it. Tests had begun with the AGM-131A SRAM II, but development of this missile was cancelled in late 1991. The conventional capability is also to be exploited more in the future.

Above: Ellsworth AFB, South Dakota, is presently home to the pair of B-1B squadrons which forms the cutting edge of the 28th Wing, one of whose Lancers is seen flying over the hangar complex set aside for the bomber fleet.

Left: Configured for landing, with wings fully spread and gear and flaps down, a B-1B Lancer of the 319th Wing at Grand Forks banks slightly as it swoops towards the runway.

Below: 'Spectre' returns to Ellsworth and is guided to its parking spot at the conclusion of a day/night training mission, sorties of this type invariably including a radar bomb scoring run as well as extended periods of time at low level and at least one inflight refueling.

MISSION PROFILE

Armament options: internal bomb bay with three sections each having one gravity weapon launcher or SRAM launcher; alternatively, CSRL (common strategic rotary launcher) in center bay only; provision for up to a maximum of 125,000 lb (56699 kg) of ordnance, including AGM-69A SRAM-A (short-range attack missile) not used in current operations; AGM-86B ALCM (air-launched cruise missile); B61 or B83 nuclear bombs; limited provision for ordnance carried externally including AGM-69A SRAM-A or AGM-86B ALCM not used in routine operations

Strategic bombardment: on a nuclear mission, the B-1B would employ air refueling but could have a range up to 7,455 miles (11998 km) unrefueled with up to eight AGM-86B ALCM or eight AGM-69A SRAM-A attack missiles on each of three rotary launchers to total 24 missiles (SRAM-A not used in current operations); up to 28 B61 700-lb (318-kg) or B83 2,400-lb (1089-kg) nuclear bombs

Theater/conventional bombardment: the B-1B was not assigned conventional bombing duties in late 1991 but plans were being considered for conventional bomb trials using one airframe in 1992 or 1993; the B-1B would carry up to 84 500-lb (227-kg) Mk 82 conventional bombs

USAF VARIANTS AND SERIALS

B-1B: One hundred B-1Bs were ordered for SAC between 1982 and 1986 with both production and test aircraft assigned the same designation.
82-0001; 83-0065 to 83-0071; 84-0049 to 84-0058; 85-0059 to 85-0092; 86-0093 to 86-0140

GB-1A: One of four B-1As built, 74-0160 is employed by the Lowry TTC as a ground instruction trainer.

Right: An almost perfect plan view of a B-1B with wings at the maximum sweep angle for high-speed cruise. Low-level penetration is normally accomplished at heights of around 200 ft.

Below: A development B-1 lays down a stick of conventional retarded bombs during trials from Edwards AFB while observers watch and film the drop from F-4 and F-111 'chase' aircraft.

SPECIFICATION

Rockwell B-1B

Wing: span 136 ft 8.5 in (41.67 m) spread and 78 ft 2.5 in (23.84 m) swept; area 1,950.0 sq ft (181.16 m²)
Fuselage and tail: length 147 ft 0 in (44.81 m); height 34 ft 10 in (10.62 m); tailplane span 44 ft 10 in (13.67 m); wheel base 57 ft 6 in (17.53 m)
Powerplant: four General Electric F101-GE-102 each rated at 14,600 lb (64.94 kN) dry and 30,780 lb (136.92 kN) afterburning thrusts
Weights: empty equipped 192,000 lb (87091 kg); maximum take-off 477,000 lb (216367 kg)
Fuel and load: internal fuel 195,000 lb (88452 kg); maximum ordnance 75,000 lb (34020 kg) carried internally and 59,000 lb (26762 kg) carried externally
Speed: maximum level speed 'clean' at high altitude about 825 mph (1328 km/h); penetration speed at about 200 ft (61 m) more than 600 mph (965 km/h)
Range: maximum range on internal fuel about 7,455 miles (12000 km)
Performance: service ceiling more than 50,000 ft (15240 m)

USAF OPERATORS

Air Force Materiel Command (AFMC)

6510th TW	6512th TS	'ED'	Edwards AFB, CA	B-1B

Air Training Command (ATC)

3400th TTW	Lowry TTC		Lowry AFB, CO	GB-1A

Air Combat Command (ACC)

28th Wg	37th BS		Ellsworth AFB, SD	B-1B
	77th BS		Ellsworth AFB, SD	B-1B
96th Wg	337th BS		Dyess AFB, TX	B-1B
	338th BS		Dyess AFB, TX	B-1B
319th Wg	46th BS		Grand Forks AFB, ND	B-1B
384th Wg	28th BS		McConnell AFB, KS	B-1B

All SAC wings changed designation on 1 October 1991 with the elimination of the identifying prefix letters, e.g. 28th Bombardment Wing (28th BW) became 28th Wing (28th Wg).

Northrop
B-2

The **B-2** flying-wing 'Stealth Bomber' was designed to penetrate Soviet air defenses and to attack strategic targets – allegedly including relocatable targets, such as rail-garrisoned ICBMs – with nuclear bombs and stand-off weapons. In the early 1990s, while drastically reducing its overall strength, the USAF continued to assign top priority to fielding 20 B-2s in one bombardment wing.

The B-2 began as a 'black' program, known in its infancy as Project Senior C. J. and later as the ATB (Advanced Technology Bomber) before ever being acknowledged in public.

In the early days of the ATB program, many Air Force leaders believed that the service's top priority was the B-1B bomber, also funded during the free-spending Reagan years (1981-89). Only a handful of officials knew of the B-2 project. To them, the B-1B was an 'interim' weapon.

The B-2 was once scheduled to make its first flight in December 1987. Its existence was publicly disclosed that year and in April 1988 the USAF released an artist's rendering of the B-2 bomber, then nearing completion at Northrop's government-owned Plant 42 in Palmdale, California. The first B-2 (82-1066) was unveiled at Palmdale on 22 November 1988.

First flight of the number one **B-2A** (82-1066), known as **AV-1** or **Air Vehicle One**, took place at Palmdale, California, on 17 July 1989 with Northrop's Bruce Hinds and Colonel Richard S. Cough on board. The second ship flew on 19 October 1990. Test flying to evaluate low observables (LO), or stealth technology, began on 30 October 1990.

The B-2 is powered by four 19,000-lb (84.52-kN) thrust General Electric F118-GE-110 non-afterburning turbofan engines mounted in pairs inside the wing adjacent to the crew/payload area with both inlets and exhausts atop the aircraft to help shield them from infra-red detection from below.

The crew/payload section of the aircraft, which is as close as the B-2 comes to having a fuselage, starts aft of the apex of the wing, ends short of the wing trailing edge, and is smoothly blended on the upper surfaces of the wing. The crew compartment provides side-by-side seating for two crew members, both of whom will be pilots (not navigator or radar-navigator/bombardier) on operational airplanes, seated in Douglas-designed, Weber-built ACES II (Advanced Concept Ejection Seats) which have zero-speed, zero-altitude capability and eject vertically. Plans to include a third crew member have been dropped although a jump seat (non-ejection) is provided for an instructor/observer.

One strong argument for the B-2 bomber is its flexibility. Unlike an ICBM, the B-2 can be 'flushed' – that is, deployed in an airborne alert pattern or even started towards its target but still able to be recalled. Unlike a submarine-launched ballistic missile, it can be extremely accurate against mobile targets, including Soviet rail-garrison ICBMs.

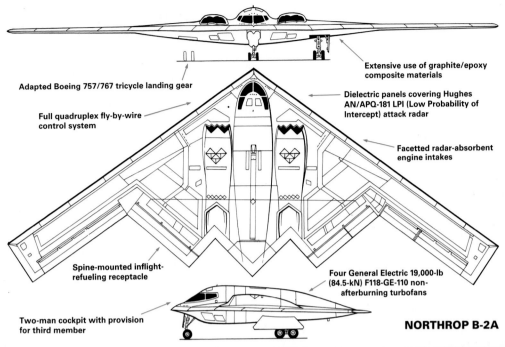

Adapted Boeing 757/767 tricycle landing gear

Full quadruplex fly-by-wire control system

Extensive use of graphite/epoxy composite materials

Dielectric panels covering Hughes AN/APQ-181 LPI (Low Probability of Intercept) attack radar

Facetted radar-absorbent engine intakes

Spine-mounted inflight-refueling receptacle

Four General Electric 19,000-lb (84.5-kN) F118-GE-110 non-afterburning turbofans

Two-man cockpit with provision for third member

NORTHROP B-2A

USAF officers claim that the B-2's radar-eluding qualities mean that it would not have to quickly dash in and out of enemy airspace like other bombers. Instead, a B-2 could get updates from reconnaissance satellites on positions of mobile targets and avoid being shot down while the two-man crew looked for the targets. To verify targets at the last moment, the B-2 will briefly turn on a special radar that spotlights only a small area, and then attack with nuclear bombs. The B-2 reportedly will be equipped with an electronic warfare system, developed secretly and referred to as the ZSR-2, which emits 'minuscule amounts' when employed to deceive a defensive radar system.

Even without emitting much electronic energy, the B-2 may not be as stealthy as its supporters assert. The B-2 is difficult to detect – at least, in time for an effective defense – by the high-frequency radars used in fire-control

Above: The shadow on the desert floor provides a clear idea of the B-2's bizarre shape as it prepares to land at Edwards AFB.

Below: Rapprochement between East and West and a desire to balance the budget seem certain to result in Northrop's B-2 only being deployed in minimal numbers, if at all.

systems today. The USAF claims confidence that the B-2 is equally difficult to detect by lower-frequency, long-range search radars. The question persists as to whether the B-2 is vulnerable to ultra-wide-band radars that may become operational, if technical hurdles can be overcome, by the late 1990s.

Although it gives the appearance of being relatively small for a strategic warplane with a global mission, the B-2 exceeds the B-52G/H and B-1B in its capacity to carry nuclear ordnance over long distances to reach a defended target. The B-2 will have a range of 5,400 nm (6,214 miles; 10000 km) when carrying a 24,000-lb (10886-kg) load of up to 16 B61 or B83 bombs on two internally-carried CSRLs (common strategic rotary launchers). It is also reported that operational B-2s will carry a stand-off weapon designed for this aircraft which, as recently as September 1991, remained secret – name and designation unknown.

Meanwhile, in a dramatic shift of emphasis, the Air Staff began publicizing the B-2's potential as a conventional bomber, drawing from the Gulf War and the success of the stealthy F-117A over Baghdad. In June 1991, the USAF staged a display of the B-2 for Congressmen (along with the F-117A, YF-22 and AGM-129A) at Andrews AFB, Maryland, and argued that the B-2 could "deliver [a] massive conventional payload to any point on the planet within hours." Briefings indicated that two B-2s (each carrying eight large penetrating weapons) could flatten an Iraqi chemical munitions bunker such as the type which had absorbed 50 F-117A sorties.

If the B-2 survives efforts to cut the program, flight testing of the B-2 was scheduled to continue through 1991-95, with critical RCS (radar cross section) evaluations in 1993. The USAF expected to achieve IOC (initial operating capability) in the B-2 with the 509th Bomb Wing at Whiteman AFB, Missouri, by late 1995.

Below: Seen over the western desert near its test base at Edwards AFB, California, the B-2A prototype is the latest manifestation of the Northrop company's predilection for flying wing designs. Like its predecessors, it is unlikely to attain USAF quantity production.

MISSION PROFILE

Armament options: internal bomb bay capable of accommodating B61 700-lb (318-kg) or B83 2,400-lb (1089-kg) nuclear bombs; or possibly a stand-off weapon reportedly designed for this aircraft which the USAF has not identified by designation or type

Strategic bombardment: on a nuclear mission, the B-2 would employ air refueling but has a range of 5,400 nm (6,214 miles; 10000 km) unrefueled when carrying a 24,000-lb (10890-kg) load of up to 16 B61 or B83 bombs on two internally-carried CSRLs

Theater/conventional bombardment: the B-2 was not designed to perform conventional bombing duties but was expected to be tested and adopted for the conventional bombing role if production and procurement plans permit; details of conventional bombload under consideration have not been disclosed

USAF VARIANTS AND SERIALS

B-2A: To date, only three B-2As have been completed with a further 12 in production, although funds have not been made available for all of these. The designation B-2A is the only identity allocated, as the majority of test airframes will become operational later in their careers.
82-1066 to 82-1071; plus additional contracts

Below: Only three examples of the B-2A have so far been completed, the third specimen seen here moments before touch-down.

SPECIFICATION

Northrop B-2A
Wing: span 172 ft 0 in (52.43 m); area more than 5,000.0 sq ft (464.50 m²)
Fuselage and tail: length 69 ft 0 in (21.03 m); height 17 ft 0 in (5.18 m)
Powerplant: four General Electric F118-GE-110 each rated at 19,000 lb (84.52 kN) dry thrust
Weights: empty between 100,000 and 110,000 lb (45360 and 49896 kg); normal take-off 371,330 lb (168435 kg); maximum take-off 400,000 lb (181440 kg)
Fuel and load: internal fuel between 180,000 and 200,000 lb (81648 and 90720 kg); maximum ordnance 50,000 lb (22680 kg)
Speed: maximum level speed at high altitude about 475 mph (764 km/h)
Range: with a 37,300-lb (16919-kg) warload comprising eight SRAMs and eight B83 bombs 7,255 miles (11675 km) with internal fuel on a hi-hi-hi mission or 5,067 miles (8154 km) on a hi-lo-hi mission with 1,152 miles (1853 km) at low level; range more than 11,515 miles (18532 km) with one aerial refueling
Performance: service ceiling 50,000 ft (15240 m)

USAF OPERATORS

Air Force Materiel Command (AFMC)

6510th TW	6510th TS	Edwards AFB, CA	B-2A

Air Combat Command (ACC)

509th Wg	?	Whiteman AFB, MO	to receive the B-2A by 1995

Lockheed
C-130 Hercules

TRANSPORT

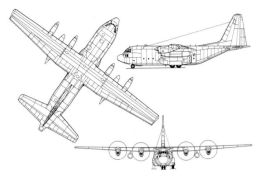

The **C-130 Hercules** is the backbone of the USAF's tactical airlift force at home and abroad. Already in production longer than any aircraft in history, the C-130 is still being purchased in small numbers for assignment to Air Force Reserve units. No other aircraft fills the Hercules' unique role of hauling personnel, vehicles, equipment and supplies within the United States, or within a combat theater.

The C-130 is an all-purpose transport for every mission except the strategic airlift job performed by the larger C-141B and C-5. Included in its transport duties is the airdrop mission, delivering airborne forces to an LZ (landing zone) in combat. The USAF has about 160 **C-130E**s equipped with AWADS (Adverse Weather Aerial Delivery System) to aid in navigation during low-level airdrop operations and about 380 aircrews qualified in the airdrop mission. A substantial number of these will be assigned to the composite wing at Pope AFB, North Carolina, to support the US Army's 82nd Airborne Division at adjacent Fort Bragg.

The C-130 Hercules was first flown in the form of a **YC-130** prototype on 23 August 1954. The C-130 design is based on a high wing, unobstructed cargo compartment, 'roll on/off' ramp, palletized cargo floor, and flat level floor at truck-bed height above the ground.

This configuration, since copied widely, owes its origin to large transport gliders of World War II, especially the Leister CG-10, and to the postwar glider which preceded the twin-engined C-123 Provider, the only previous USAF transport with this layout. The C-130 introduced the Allison T56 turboprop engine, which evolved into the 4,900-shp (3653-kW) T56-A-15 powerplant found today on production **C-130H**s and other upgraded variants. The Hercules, thus, was a mix of the right ingredients at the right time: its pragmatic configuration, substantial power and capability to make rough-field landings or low-level LAPES (Low-Altitude Parachute Extraction System) maneuvers, and to supply deliveries to a combat zone, have made the C-130 not just a successful workhorse, but a valuable contributor – in the airlift role – to combat actions in Vietnam, Grenada, Panama and the Persian Gulf. The proven design led to spinoffs for gunship, rescue, tanker, drone-controller, reconnaissance and other missions.

USAF versions of the C-130 no longer in inventory include **YC-130**, **C-130A**, **C-130A-II**, **JC-130A**, **RC-130A**, **TC-130A**, **JC-130B**, **RC-130B**, **VC-130B**, **WC-130B**, **AC-130E**, **DC-130E**, **JC-130E**, **NC-130E**, **DC-130H**, **JC-130H**, and **RC-130S**.

The oldest version of the Hercules in widespread use in the early 1990s is the **C-130B**, which introduced engine improvements, increased internal fuel capacity, and Hamilton Standard Model 54H60-91 13-ft 6-in (4.17-m) four-bladed hydromatic propellers. These aircraft now equip mostly Air National Guard units. After 123 were delivered for USAF use (and 33 to foreign customers, beginning the Hercules' long career serving some 55 other air forces), production shifted to the C-130E, from 1961.

The C-130E, of which 377 went to the USAF (and 109 to other users) is powered by T56-A-7 engines with increased power to improve take-off performance in hot weather or from airfields at high altitude. The E model also benefits from an internal fuel capacity increased from 6,870 US gal (20006 liters) to 6,960 US gal (26347 liters) to stretch the 'legs' of this tactical transport on longer, trans-oceanic missions. Maximum take-off weight went up from 124,200 lb (56337 kg) in the C-130A to 175,000 lb (79380 kg). The E model also introduced larger external underwing tanks.

The current basic transport, the C-130H, was first delivered in April 1975 and is powered by improved T56-A-15 engines. The power-plants and a number of other features introduced in the H model, including improved brakes and strengthened center-wing design, have been retrofitted to earlier Hercules. Some C-130H transports can be fitted internally for medical evacuation duties.

The **C-130D** Hercules was a ski-equipped version for operations in Arctic climes. Of 13 airplanes which once held this designation, six were later re-named **C-130D-6** on removal of their skis. Though the ski C-130Ds never were assigned an L prefix (for 'winterized'), they

Above: The classic Lockheed Hercules has formed the backbone of the tactical airlift fleet for many years. This is a C-130E.

were replaced by four **LC-130H** ski-equipped airplanes in 1984.

The C-130 Hercules has played a role in every American conflict since the aircraft's inception in 1956. During Operation Desert Storm, C-130s moved substantial numbers of troops but did not carry out any airdrops. In the intra-theater tactical airlift role, some 145 C-130s in the Persian Gulf (assisted by a few C-21A Learjets) carried out 52,300 sorties and carried 514,600 passengers and 490 million lb (222 million kg) of cargo. During the ground campaign, C-130s flew over 500 sorties per day. C-130s in the Persian Gulf also flew some 170 medical evacuation sorties.

Continuing production of the C-130H will permit the Air National Guard to gradually dispose of its ageing C-130Bs and create an all

Below: With engines running in readiness for a prompt departure, four C-130Es from the 374th Airlift Wing are boarded by soldiers of the US Army's South Korean garrison prior to departing for a paradropping exercise.

USAF Aircraft

C-130E/H force. While the merit of the aircraft is indisputable (the 2,000th built was scheduled for delivery in May 1992), it would be unrealistic not to note that the C-130 is manufactured in the home constituency of Senator Sam Nunn (D-GA), Chairman of the Senate Armed Services Committee. The USAF is unlikely, however, to commit in the 1990s to a much-improved, hi-tech variant of the C-130, currently known by the unofficial appellation **C-130J**. The Military Airlift Command has no other aircraft type in mind as a C-130 replacement, and new-build Hercules will almost certainly still be reaching USAF components in the next century.

MISSION PROFILE

Configuration options: the C-130E/H aircraft can be configured for cargo, paratroopers, combat troops, hospital litter patients, or combinations of all of these; the C-130E is usually employed for air drops of troops or equipment and some C-130Es are employed for LAPES (low-altitude parachute extraction system) delivery of heavy cargoes; the C-130H is not usually employed in airdrop operations but otherwise performs the full range of cargo, troop and medical evacuation duties

Theater/tactical airlift: with a maximum payload of 38,702 lb (17555 kg) (C-130E) or 43,400 lb (19686 kg) (C-130H), the Hercules can carry various combinations of cargo to a range of 1,428 miles (2298 km) with a 45-minute fuel reserve and make a tactical landing on an unprepared airstrip using 4,880 ft (1487 m) of landing roll; typical cargo includes five HMMWV tactical vehicles, five 8,818-lb (4000-kg) rectangular palletized freight containers, or three Land Rover vehicles and two trailers

Airborne operations: the C-130E carries 64 fully-equipped paratroopers to a radius of up to 710 miles (1142 km) for a combat air drop with an approach to the DZ (drop zone) at 300 ft (91 m) altitude and actual drop at 500 ft (152 m) with a 45-minute fuel reserve; two C-130E wings are equipped with AWADS (Adverse Weather Aerial Delivery System) to aid in formation flight during low-level airdrop operations

Strategic airlift: normally not assigned strategic airlift duties except when self-deploying to an overseas theater, C-130E/H aircraft can carry typical cargo or troop loads to a range of 1,864 miles (3000 km)

USAF VARIANTS AND SERIALS

(Note: conversions presented are those aircraft which are currently operational and do not include losses, export sales of former USAF C-130s, or those withdrawn from service.)

Original construction designations
YC-130: The two prototype Hercules were allocated the designation YC-130 to determine service test, but without the suffix A to indicate the first version of the type. The two aircraft were constructed with the 'roman nose' which lacked the weather radar fitted to later models and were without underwing tanks.
53-3396 and 53-3397

C-130A: The initial production version with 190 examples built. The first 27 aircraft featured the 'roman nose' although the majority were retrofitted with the conventional radome. Powered by Allison T56-A-1A engines with three-bladed propellers, and fitted with two 450-US gal (1703-liter) underwing tanks positioned outboard of the engines.
53-3129 to 53-3135; 54-1621 to 54-1640; 55-0001 to 55-0048; 56-0468 to 56-0551; 57-0452 to 57-0483

C-130D: Twelve C-130As were fitted with ski/wheel combination and provision for jet-assisted take-off (JATO) bottles for duties in the Arctic. Six subsequently operated with the skis removed as C-130D-6.
57-0484 to 57-0495

DC-130A: A pair of C-130As was modified for drone director duties with an extended radar nose and four underwing pylons to air launch unmanned drones. Initially allocated designation GC-130A, but later changed to DC-130A. Others converted subsequently to DC-130A standard with only one remaining in USAF service. 57-0496 and 0497 are currently operated by a civilian contractor on behalf of the US Navy.
57-0496 and 57-10497

RC-130A: Fifteen C-130As constructed for the photo-mapping role with geodetic surveying equipment and cameras installed in the fuselage. Following the abandonment of the role the 15 aircraft were converted to C-130A standard for conventional airlift duties.
57-0510 to 57-0524

C-130B: The C-130B was the development of its predecessor with Allison T56-A-7 engines driving four-bladed propellers, but lacking underwing tanks, as additional fuel capacity was installed in the wing centre-section. One hundred and thirty-three were ordered between 1957 and 1962, including aircraft modified to C-130B-II, JC-130B, NC-130B and WC-130B configuration, although none of these types remains operational.
57-0525 to 57-0529; 58-0711 to 58-0758; 59-1524 to 59-1537; 59-5957; 60-0293 to 60-0310; 61-0948 to 61-0972; 61-2634 to 61-2649; 62-3487; 62-3492 to 62-3496

C-130E: The third basic version was designed to extend the range of the Hercules, being powered by the same Allison T56-A-7s as the C-130B but with two 1,360-US gal (5148-liter) underwing tanks installed between the engines. Three-hundred and eighty-eight were obtained between 1961 and 1972 with a limited number of conversions, most of which are still current and are detailed under the appropriate section.
61-2358 to 61-2373; 62-1784 to 62-1866; 63-7764 to 63-7899; 63-9810 to 63-9817; 64-0495 to 64-0572; 64-17680 to 64-17681; 64-18240; 68-10934 to 68-10951; 69-6566 to 69-6583; 70-1259 to 70-1276; 72-1288 to 72-1299

C-130H: The fourth and final development of the Hercules to date, and the most prolific version worldwide, is still in production for the US Air Force, Navy, Marine Corps and many overseas customers. It features the Allison T56-A-15 engines, and a pair of 1,360-US gal (5148-liter) underwing tanks installed between the engines as an option. Numerous specialist versions were produced while others were modified from airlift examples, details presented below. More than 200 have been delivered to USAF, including a pair of former US Coast Guard HC-130Hs demodified for the airlift role with MAC. Forty-eight airlift versions were added to the budget at the end of 1991. Some later production versions are fitted with the Long-Range Air Navigation (LORAN) system identifiable by a pair of parallel rails mounted above the rear fuselage.
67-7183 to 67-7184; 73-1580 to 73-1588; 73-1590; 73-1592; 73-1594 to 73-1595; 73-1597 to 73-1598; 74-1658 to 74-1693; 74-2061 to 74-2072; 74-2130 to 74-2134; 78-0806 to 78-0813; 79-0473 to 79-0480; 80-0320 to 80-0326; 80-0332; 81-0626 to 81-0631; 82-0054 to 82-0061; 83-0486 to 83-0489; 84-0204 to 84-0213; 85-0035 to 85-0042; 85-1361 to 85-1368; 86-0410 to 86-0415; 86-0418 to 86-0419; 86-1391 to 86-1398; 87-9281 to 87-9288; 88-1301 to 88-1308; 88-4401 to 88-4408; 89-1051 to 89-1056; 89-1181 to 89-1188; 89-9101 to 89-9106; 90-1057 to 90-1058; 90-1791 to 90-1798; 90-9107 to 90-9108; plus additional contracts

LC-130H: Four ski/wheel-equipped LC-130Hs were purchased in 1983 for the New York ANG, to replace the C-130D.
83-0490 to 83-0493

Above: Smoke drifting from blazing oil wells blackens the sky in the background of this view of a C-130E Hercules from the 314th Airlift Wing at Kuwait International Airport soon after the conclusion of the Gulf War.

Right: Support of Distant Early Warning Line facilities in the Arctic is the principal role of the ski-equipped LC-130H, four examples of which were purchased for service with the NY ANG.

Conversion designations
GC-130A: Three C-130As have been retired from flying duty and transferred to Air Training Command for ground instruction duties gaining the designation GC-130A. No modification or conversion work is carried out for the change of designation.
55-0037; 56-0517; 57-0471

GC-130B: At least two retired C-130Bs have joined ATC to become airframes for technical trade training.
58-0727; 58-0740

GC-130D: Three retired C-130Ds have been assigned to ATC as training airframes at technical training centers.
57-0486; 57-0489; 57-0490

C-130H: The reduction in the weather reconnaissance requirement has permitted eight WC-130Hs to be converted to conventional airlifters with the removal of internal equipment.
64-14866; 65-0964; 65-0967; 65-0969; 65-0972; 65-0976; 65-0977; 65-0985

Left: Skimming just a few feet above the ground while its load is deposited, a C-130E performs a Low Altitude Parachute Extraction System (LAPES) delivery, just one of a number of ways in which cargo can be air-dropped.

Below: Forest fires in California have resulted in the C-130Es of the Air National Guard unit at Point Mugu being configured to operate with the Modular Airborne Fire-Fighting System, seen here during an air display demonstration.

SPECIFICATION

Lockheed C-130H

Wing: span 132 ft 7 in (40.41 m); aspect ratio 10.09; area 1,745.0 sq ft (162.12 m²)

Fuselage and tail: length 97 ft 9 in (29.79 m); height 38 ft 3 in (11.66 m); tailplane span 52 ft 8 in (16.05 m); wheel base 32 ft 0.75 in (9.77 m)

Powerplant: four Allison T56-A-15 each rated at 4,508 ehp (3362 kW)

Weights: operating empty 75,743 lb (34357 kg); normal take-off 155,000 lb (70308 kg); maximum take-off 175,000 lb (79380 kg)

Fuel and load: internal fuel 45,240 lb (20520 kg); external fuel up to 17,680 lb (8020 kg) in two 1,360-US gal (5148-liter) underwing tanks; maximum payload 42,673 lb (19356 kg)

Speed: maximum cruising speed 374 mph (602 km/h); economical cruising speed 345 mph (556 km/h)

Range: with maximum fuel and a 15,611-lb (7081-kg) payload 4,894 miles (7876 km); range with maximum payload 2,356 miles (3791 km)

Performance: maximum rate of climb at sea level 1,900 ft (579 m) per minute; service ceiling 33,000 ft (10058 m) at 130,000 lb (58967 kg); take-off distance 5,160 ft (1573 m) to 50 ft (15 m); landing distance 1,700 ft (518 m) at 130,000 lb (58967 kg)

Lockheed C-130A

generally similar to the C-130H except in the following particulars:

Powerplant: four Allison T56-A-1A or -9 each rated at 3,750 ehp (2796 kW)

Weights: operating empty 59,328 lb (26911 kg); normal take-off 108,000 lb (48988 kg); maximum take-off 102,000 lb (46266 kg) in early aircraft, rising to 124,200 lb (56336 kg) in later aircraft

Fuel and load: internal fuel 5,050 US gal (19116 liters); external fuel up to two 450-US gal (1703-liter) underwing tanks

Speed: maximum speed at 20,400 ft (6220 m) 383 mph (616 km/h); economical cruising speed 328 mph (528 km/h)

Range: ferry range 3,215 miles (5175 km); range with 35,000-lb (15876-kg) payload 2,090 miles (3365 km)

Performance: maximum rate of climb at sea level 2,570 ft (783 m) per minute; service ceiling 41,300 ft (12590 m)

Lockheed C-130B

generally similar to the C-130H except in the following particulars:

Powerplant: four Allison T56-A-7 each rated at 4,050 ehp (3020 kW)

Weight: maximum take-off 135,000 lb (61235 kg)

Fuel and load: internal fuel 6,870 US gal (20006 liters); maximum payload 45,000 lb (20412 kg)

Speed: maximum speed at 20,400 ft (6220 m) 383 mph (616 km/h); economical cruising speed 328 mph (528 km/h)

Range: ferry range 3,215 miles (5175 km); range with a 35,000-lb (15876-kg) payload 2,090 miles (3365 km)

Performance: maximum rate of climb at sea level 2,570 ft (783 m) per minute; service ceiling 41,300 ft (12590 m)

Lockheed C-130E

generally similar to the C-130H except in the following particulars:

Powerplant: four Allison T56-A-7A each rated at 4,050 ehp (3020 kW)

Weights: empty 72,892 lb (33064 kg); normal take-off 155,000 lb (70307 kg); maximum take-off 175,000 lb (79380 kg)

Fuel and load: maximum payload 38,702 lb (17555 kg)

Speed: maximum speed at 25,000 ft (7620 m) 384 mph (618 km/h); cruising speed 340 mph (547 km/h)

Range: with maximum payload 2,420 miles (3895 km)

Performance: maximum rate of climb at sea level 1,830 ft (558 m) per minute; service ceiling 23,000 ft (7010 m)

USAF OPERATORS

Air Force Materiel Command (AFMC)

Warner Robins ALC		Robins AFB, GA	C-130E
3246th TW	3247th TS	Eglin AFB, FL	NC-130A
6510th TW	6518th TS	'ED' Edwards AFB, CA	MC-130H, AC-130U
6545th TG	6514th TS	Hill AFB, UT	C-130B, DC-130A, HC-130H, NC-130H

Air Training Command (ATC)

3700th TTW	Sheppard TTC	Sheppard AFB, TX	GC-130A/D
IAAFA		Homestead AFB, FL	GC-130A/B

Air Mobility Command (AMC)

314th AW	16th AS	Little Rock AFB, AR	C-130E
	50th AS	Little Rock AFB, AR	C-130E
	61st AS	Little Rock AFB, AR	C-130E
	62nd AS	Little Rock AFB, AR	C-130E
317th AW	39th AS	Pope AFB, NC	C-130E
	40th AS	Pope AFB, NC	C-130E
	41st AS	Pope AFB, NC	C-130E
374th AW	345th AS	Yokota AB, Japan	C-130E/H
435th AW	37th AS	Rhein Main AB, Germany	C-130E
463rd AW	772nd AS	Dyess AFB, TX	C-130H
	773rd AS	Dyess AFB, TX	C-130H
542nd CTW	1551st ATS	Kirtland AFB, NM	HC-130P
61st AG	310th AS	Howard AFB, Canal Zone	C-130H

616th AG	17th AS	Elmendorf AFB, AK	C-130H (to PACAF)
nil	71st ARS	Patrick AFB, FL	HC-130N/P

Air Force Special Operations Command (AFSOC)

1st SOW	8th SOS	Hurlburt Field, FL	C-130E, MC-130E/H
	9th SOS	Eglin AFB, FL	HC-130N/P
	16th SOS	Hurlburt Field, FL	AC-130H
39th SOW	7th SOS	Rhein Main AB, Germany	C-130E, MC-130E
	67th SOS	RAF Woodbridge, UK	HC-130N/P
353rd SOW	1st SOS	Kadena AB, Okinawa	C-130E, MC-130E
	17th SOS	Kadena AB, Okinawa	HC-130H/N/P

Air Combat Command (ACC)

28th AD	7th ACCS	Keesler AFB, MS	EC-130E
	41st ECS	Davis-Monthan AFB, AZ	EC-130H

Air National Guard (ANG)

118th AW	105th AS	Nashville Metro Apt, TN	C-130H
123rd AW	165th AS	Standiford Fd, Louisville, KY	C-130B
133rd AW	109th AS	Minneapolis St Paul IAP, MN	C-130E
136th AW	181st AS	NAS Dallas, TX	C-130H
137th AW	185th AS	Will Rogers World Apt, Oklahoma City, OK	C-130H
146th AW	115th AS	NAS Point Mugu, CA	C-130E
106th RQG	102nd RQS	Suffolk County Apt, NY	HC-130H/P
109th AG	139th AS	Schenectady Cty Apt, NY	C-130H, LC-130H
129th RQG	129th RQS	NAS Moffett Field, CA	HC-130H/P
130th AG	130th AS	Yeager Apt, Charleston, WV	C-130H
135th TAG	135th TAS	Glenn L. Martin State Apt, Baltimore, MD	C-130E
139th AG	180th AS	Rosecrans MAP, St Joseph, MO	C-130H
143rd AG	143rd AS	Quonset Point State Apt, RI	C-130E
145th AG	156th AS	Charlotte/Douglas IAP, NC	C-130B
153rd AG	187th AS	Cheyenne MAP, WY	C-130B
164th AG	155th AS	Memphis IAP, TN	C-130A
165th AG	158th AS	Savannah IAP, GA	C-130H
166th AG	142nd AS	Gtr Wilmington Apt, DE	C-130H
167th AG	167th AS	Shepherd Fd, Martinsburg, WV	C-130E
176th CG	144th AS	Anchorage IAP, AK	C-130H
	210th RQS	Anchorage IAP, AK	HC-130H
179th AG	164th AS	Mansfield Lahm Apt, OH	C-130B
189th AG	154th AS	Little Rock AFB, AR	C-130E
193rd SOG	193rd SOS	Harrisburg IAP, PA	EC-130E

Air National Guard – Operational Support Aircraft (ANG-OSA)

127th FW	107th FS	Selfridge ANGB, MI	C-130B
128th FW	176th FS	Truax Fd, Madison, WI	C-130B
119th FG	178th FS	Hector Fd, Fargo, ND	C-130B
120th FG	186th FS	Great Falls IAP, MT	C-130B
125th FG	159th FS	Jacksonville IAP, FL	C-130B
150th TG	188th TS	Kirtland AFB, NM	C-130B
154th CG	199th FS	Hickam AFB, HI	C-130H
159th FG	122nd FS	NAS New Orleans, LA	C-130H
162nd FG	152nd FS	Tucson IAP, AZ	C-130B
169th FG	157th FS	McEntire ANGB, SC	C-130H
187th FG	160th FS	Dannelly Fd, Montgomery, AL	C-130H

Air Force Reserve (AFRes)

94th AW	700th AS	Dobbins AFB, GA	C-130H
302nd AW	731st AS	Peterson AFB, CO	C-130B
403rd AW	815th AS	Keesler AFB, MS	C-130H, WC-130E/H
440th AW	95th AS	Gen Mitchell Fd, Milwaukee, WI	C-130H
907th AG	356th AS	Rickenbacker ANGB, OH	C-130H
908th AG	357th AS	Maxwell AFB, AL	C-130H
910th AG	757th AS	Youngstown MAP, OH	C-130H
911th AG	758th AS	Gtr Pittsburgh IAP, PA	C-130H
913th AG	327th AS	NAS Willow Grove, PA	C-130E
919th SOG	711th SOS	Duke Field, FL	AC-130A, C-130A
914th AG	328th AS	Niagara Falls IAP, NY	C-130E
927th AG	63rd AS	Selfridge ANGB, MI	C-130E
928th AG	64th AS	Chicago-O'Hare IAP, IL	C-130H
934th AG	96th AS	Minneapolis St Paul IAP, MN	C-130E
939th ARG	301st ARS	Homestead AFB, FL	HC-130H/N/P
	304th ARS	Portland IAP, OR	HC-130H/P
	305th ARS	Selfridge ANGB, MI	HC-130H/N/P
943rd AG	303rd AS	March AFB, CA	C-130B

USAF Aircraft

SPECIAL MISSIONS AIRCRAFT

The C-130 Hercules transport has proved to be the ideal platform for a range of special missions which include airborne command post, electronic warfare, weather reconnaissance, special operations, electronic warfare, gunship and air rescue.

The **EC-130E Hercules** ABCCC (Airborne Battlefield Command and Control Center) aircraft has the special task of providing an airborne command post for a battlefield commander in a combat theater. Despite being re-engined with the T56-A-15, the designation EC-130E has been retained, rather than EC-130H. The aircraft (with the new engines and inflight refueling capability) carry out this 'flying headquarters' job using two interior configurations. The 1970-vintage ABCCC II capsule uses manual plotting boards and grease pencils, while the recent ABCCC III uses computer-generated text and graphics and a digital switching system.

The electronic warfare mission is another special function of some C-130 Hercules, which are also designated EC-130E and EC-130H. These aircraft are assigned to stand-off jamming and electronic warfare and to Sigint (signals intelligence) collection. EC-130E Coronet Solo II aircraft are charged with an electronic surveillance mission while other C-130Es are employed for signals intelligence collection. Sixteen EC-130H Compass Call aircraft with blisters on the rear fuselage and ventral antennas are employed for communications jamming.

For weather-reconnaissance duties, the USAF has been well served by **WC-130E** and **WC-130H** special versions of the Hercules, though both were expected to be withdrawn in the 1990s as the USAF curtails its activities in this field.

The gunship **AC-130 Spectre** has perhaps the most dangerous and interesting mission among Hercules variants. The sturdy airframe, range and potential extended loiter time offered by the basic C-130 design make it ideal to exploit the simple principle that an airplane in a pylon turn can continuously employ guns against a fixed target on the ground. **AC-130A Spectres** were being phased out of the Air Force Reserve in the early 1990s while **AC-130H Spectre** gunships were operated by for the active-duty force.

AC-130A models, usually armed with two 7.62-mm guns, two 20-mm M61 cannon and two Bofors 40-mm clip-fed cannon, equipped the Air Force Reserve's 711th Special Operations Squadron at Duke Field on the Eglin military reservation, Florida. A few of these played a key role in Operation Just Cause (December 1989) when they carried out night missions against headquarters of Panama's elite Puma battalion and PDF (Panamanian Defense Forces). These AC-130As were to be replaced in 1993 by **AC-130H**s from the active-duty force at nearby Hurlburt Field when the latter converts to the Rockwell-modified **AC-130U**.

The AC-130H Spectre is the stalwart of the USAF's gunship force. Powered by the improved T56-A-15 engines associated with the H model and equipped for air-to-air refueling, the AC-130H was optimized for night operations and crew comfort, with a 'war room' housing FLIR (forward-looking infra-red), LLLTV (low light level television), electronic warfare and 'Black Crow' consoles – the latter being a device to detect radiation signals from vehicle ignition systems. While the gunship mission remains constant, the sensor suite of the AC-130H has been updated repeatedly. The current airplanes, referred to as **AC-130H (SOF-1)**, were converted from the now-defunct AC-130E, their armament consisting of two 20-mm M61 cannons with 3,000 rounds (capable of 2,200 shots/minute) on fixed gun mounts, one L-60 40-mm Bofors cannon with 256 rounds (with a rate of fire of 100 shots/minute), plus one M102 105-mm howitzer.

USAF 16th SOS AC-130Hs flew night combat missions in Grenada (1983), Panama (1989), and the Persian Gulf (1991). Unopposed in Grenada and Panama, they demonstrated how effective a gunship can be against ground troops and installations in a permissive environment. The loss of AC-130H Spectre 69-6567 in combat in the Persian Gulf on 31 January 1991, with 14 killed, was the costliest aircraft loss of Operation Desert Storm.

The USAF intends to equip the 16th SOS with 12 AC-130U gunships over the 1990s, relegating the AC-130H to the Reserves and retiring the AC-130A. The AC-130U is being converted by Rockwell from new-build H model airframes. The U model retains T56-A-15 engines and has one L-60 40-mm Bofors cannon and one M102 105-mm howitzer. The H model's two M61 cannons have been replaced with a single 25-mm GAU-12 cannon with 3,000 rounds on trainable, rather than fixed, gun mounts (firing rate 1,800 shots/minute) with a stand-off range of 12,000 ft (3658 m) as compared with 9,000 ft (2743 m) for the earlier 20-mm weapon. The first AC-130U reached test status at Edwards AFB, California, in September 1991 and the second was scheduled for rollout in May 1992. The vulnerability of any gunship to man-portable SAMs, even when operating as planned during nocturnal hours, has led the USAF to keep its active-force gunship fleet very small – nine AC-130H (SOF-1)s in 1991, 12 AC-130Us by 1998 – with the intent of employing them in Third World conflicts.

The special operations mission assigned to some **MC-130** Hercules aircraft makes these close cousins of the AC-130 series and equal participants in the close-knit special operations forces community (combined, in May 1990, into Air Force Special Operations Command).

Fourteen **MC-130E** conversions equipped with T56-A-15 engines, air-to-air refueling receptacle and equipment support Seal, Green Beret or Delta Force special-operations troops behind enemy lines. These aircraft carried American commandos in the attempt to rescue hostages in Tehran in April 1980.

The 'special ops' E models are gradually to be replaced by **MC-130H Combat Talon** airplanes, which in turn will give way to **MC-130H Combat Talon II** aircraft to be converted by the IBM Corporation. The latter program was about 24 months behind schedule in early 1992.

Armament
Arranged on the port side of the fuselage are two 20-mm Vulcan cannon (forward), two 7.62-mm Miniguns (midships) and two 40-mm Bofors cannon (aft). The active-duty AC-130H replaces one of the 40-mm weapons with a 105-mm howitzer.

Self-defense
To protect itself from ground-launched missiles, the AC-130 carries ECM pods on the inboard pylons, and chaff/flare dispensers on the outboard pylons. An observer watches for groundfire from the rear ramp.

Above: One of a number of specialized versions developed for use by the Air Rescue Service, the HC-130N is still primarily concerned with rescue and recovery duties even though it now flies with Special Operations Squadrons.

Above: One of the more distinctively modified versions of the Hercules family is the EC-130E 'Rivet Rider', which was used extensively during the Gulf War on airborne broadcasting duties to demoralize Iraqi ground forces.

For air rescue, the **HC-130H** version of the Hercules was delivered with Cook Aerial Trackers (ARD-17) in a 'hump' above the forward fuselage to locate satellite capsules during re-entry from orbit and with rescue kits for long-range recovery missions. The **HC-130N** was fielded for rescue and for recovery of space capsules. The **HC-130P** combined the rescue and recovery configuration and added a tanker mission, having under-wing refueling drogue pods previously developed for the US Marines' **KC-130F** and used primarily to refuel rescue and special-operations helicopters.

Lockheed AC-130A Spectre

The AC-130A aircraft of the 711th SOS are the oldest Hercules still in operational service, and are shortly to be replaced by the later AC-130H when these are handed down from the active-duty unit. Specialist roles of the gunships are night interdiction work, special forces support and close air support.

Left: Airborne Battlefield Command and Control tasks are allocated to the EC-130E, which houses a removable battle staff module in its hold. It also features prominent scoops on the forward fuselage to help cool the electronic suite.

Sensors
In order to locate its targets, the AC-130 employs FLIR, LLLTV, beacon tracking radar and ignition detector. A searchlight is also fitted in the rear fuselage. The pilot is provided with a HUD-style sight in the cockpit window.

MISSION PROFILE

Armament options (AC-130A/H/U): two 7.62-mm guns, two 20-mm M61A1 Vulcan cannon and two L-60 Bofors 40-mm clip-fed cannon (AC-130A); two 20-mm M61A1 Vulcan cannon with up to 3,000 rounds, one L-60 40-mm Bofors cannon with up to 256 rounds and one M102 105-mm howitzer with 100 rounds (AC-130H SOF-1); one 25-mm GAU-12 cannon with up to 3,000 rounds, one L-60 40-mm Bofors cannon with up to 256 rounds and one M102 105-mm howitzer with up to 100 rounds (AC-130U). **(MC-130E):** normally not armed, the MC-130E can carry a 15,000-lb (6803-kg) bomb

Battlefield area interdiction (AC-130): normally employed at night only, the AC-130 Spectre gunship can fly with maximum ammunition load to a radius of about 760 miles (1223 km) with loiter of two hours in target area plus 45 minutes fuel reserve to carry out air-to-ground interdiction, deploying its armament from a low pylon turn over the target; **(MC-130):** on a BAI mission for psychological impact on enemy troops, the MC-130E can fly to a radius of about 760 miles (1223 km) and drop one 15,000-lb (6803 kg) BLU-82 bomb followed by a drop of up to 2,000 lb (907 kg) of psychological warfare leaflets

Special operations: for its primary purpose of inserting/extracting/supporting special operations forces from behind enemy lines, the MC-130E/H employs terrain-following radar, special avionics and low-level flight techniques; can be refueled in flight but is able to fly to a radius of about 600 miles (966 km) unrefueled on a medium-lo profile with up to one-third of its run-in at 300 ft (92 m) altitude and actual airdrop/insertion at 500 ft (152 m) altitude, typically of a team of three to seven Special Forces, SEAL, Delta Force or allied special operations commandos; the MC-130E/H is also employed to support special operations forces with clandestine pinpoint airdrop of high-value supplies; the MC-130E was designed to use a Fulton STAR (surface-to-air recovery) nose personnel recovery yoke intended to snatch people or payloads from the ground, not employed in routine operations; under certain conditions, the MC-130E/H can land on rough surfaces behind enemy lines to extract special operations forces

Combat rescue: on a rescue or combat rescue mission, the extended-range HC-130H/N/P Hercules can operate up to a radius of 860 miles (1384 km) to loiter for up to 2 hours with a 45-minute fuel reserve to direct rescue operations and airdrop rescue kits and survival equipment; the HC-130H was designed to employ the Fulton STAR nose personnel recovery yoke to snatch people or payloads from the ground but does not employ this system in usual operations

Satellite recovery: extended-range HC-130H and HC-130N Hercules aircraft can operate up to a radius of 860 miles (1384 km) to loiter for up to 2 hours with a 45-minute fuel reserve in order to employ Cook Aerial Trackers (ARD-17) to locate satellite capsules during re-entry from orbit, and is equipped with rescue kits for long-range recovery missions; the similar HC-130N was fielded for rescue work and for recovery of re-entering space satellite capsules

Aerial refueling: the HC-130P employs underwing refueling drogue pods previously developed for the US Marines KC-130F and to refuel rescue and special operations helicopters

USAF VARIANTS AND SERIALS

Original construction designations
HC-130H: The first version of the C-130H obtained for the Air Force was the HC-130H, with 43 ordered in 1964 and 1965 for the air rescue and recovery role. Distinguishable by the giant aerial tracking radar housed in a radome atop the forward fuselage and the Fulton recovery system mounted on a modified nose cone. A further two former Coast Guard HC-130Hs were transferred to Air Force charge, although they have yet to become operational.
64-14852 to 64-14866; 65-0962 to 65-0987; 65-0989 to 65-0990; 67-7185; 72-1302

HC-130H(N): Three C-130H airframes were ordered as HC-130H(N) for the Alaskan ANG with very few external changes between these and the original HC-130H, apart from the installation of the latest high-speed refueling pods and additional fuel tanks in the fuselage.
88-2101 and 88-2102; 90-2103

MC-130H: The increasing importance of special operations resulted in the development of the MC-130H 'Combat Talon II' as a replacement for the MC-130E 'Combat Talon I'. A revised nose cone houses a multi-mode radar to enhance low-level navigation, terrain following and avoidance, while defensive equipment includes an infra-red detection system, chaff/flare dispensers, a tailcone-mounted radar warning receiver, and a missile launch warning receiver. Twenty-four aircraft have been funded.
83-1212; 84-0475 to 84-0476; 85-0011 to 85-0012; 86-1699; 87-0023 to 87-0024; 87-0125 to 87-0127; 88-0191 to 88-0195; 88-0264; 88-1803; 89-0280 to 89-0283; plus two

HC-130N: Fifteen H models were constructed as HC-130N standard for the air rescue role with a pair of underwing flight-refueling pods, but without the Fulton recovery system.
69-5819 to 69-5833

HC-130P: Twenty H models were built as HC-130P configuration with the addition of a pair of underwing flight-refueling pods and retaining the Fulton system.
65-0988; 65-0991 to 65-0994; 66-0211 to 66-0225

AC-130U: Fourteen advanced gunship versions of the Hercules have been funded with the prototype aircraft under development. The basic C-130H airframes are equipped with the latest state-of-the-art target acquisition and fire control systems controlling the weaponry fitted to the port side.
87-0128; 89-0509 to 89-0514; 90-0164 to 90-0167; plus three aircraft

Conversion designations

AC-130A: Eighteen C-130As and JC-130As were modified to AC-130A standard with the fitment of four cannon and a pair of Miniguns to the port side, together with tracking systems and radar. Ten remain operational with the Reserves.
53-3129; 54-1623; 54-1628; 54-1630; 55-0011; 55-0014; 55-0029; 55-0046; 56-0469; 56-0509

DC-130A: A small number of C-130As were converted to DC-130A standard later in their career although only two of these remain operational. One is assigned to Flight Systems Inc. on behalf of the US Navy, while the other is the sole DC-130A with the Air Force, conducting drone tests with the 6514th TS.
56-0514; 57-0461

NC-130A: Fewer than half a dozen C-130As have been designated NC-130A to signify assignment to permanent testing, with just one remaining in this role. The aircraft has featured a variety of modifications including test equipment installed in a fairing above the forward fuselage, although in recent years these have been removed as test work has required the carriage of retractable sensors.
55-0022

NC-130B: A single NC-130B is assigned to NASA for ongoing tests connected with the earth survey program. The aircraft has an enlarged radome, additional windows and several antenna-attachment mountings. The Hercules remains the property of the Air Force although bailed to NASA.
58-0712

EC-130E (ABCCC)/(CL)/(RR): Three distinct versions of the EC-130E are currently operated, including seven ABCCC aircraft assigned to ACC which contain a removable battle staff module. Surprisingly, the fitment of T56-A-15 engines has not resulted in a change of designation to EC-130H. The other versions are the EC-130E (CL) Comfy Levi and (RR) Rivet Rider, which are operated by the Pennsylvania ANG for psychological warfare duties. The Rivet Riders feature a large blade antenna on the leading edge of the fin along with another curved antenna beneath the wings outboard of the engines. Underwing pods and a rear fuselage pod contain trailing wire antennas. The Comfy Levi versions externally resemble basic airlifters but are believed to have an Elint role.

Above: The revised contours of the nose radome on this aircraft identify it as a 'Combat Talon II' MC-130H derivative, 24 examples of which are being obtained for special operations.

Above: Communications jamming is the primary role allocated to the EC-130H 'Compass Call' as portrayed here by an aircraft from the 41st ECS at Davis-Monthan AFB, Arizona.

62-1791; 62-1818; 62-1825; 62-1832; 62-1836; 62-1857; 62-1863 (ABCCC); 63-7815; 63-7816; 63-7828; 63-9816 (CL); 63-7773; 63-7783; 63-7869; 63-9817 (RR)

MC-130E (Rivet Clamp)/(Rivet Swap)/(Rivet Yank): Three distinct versions of this model of Hercules exist, consisting of the MC-130E (Rivet Clamp), (Rivet Swap) and (Rivet Yank). Nine aircraft are of the Rivet Clamp version fitted with the Fulton recovery yoke together with an infra-red detection system, chaff/flare dispensers, and a tailcone-mounted radar warning receiver. In addition these aircraft retain the T56-A-7 engines. Three aircraft identified as Rivet Yank are similarly configured but lack the Fulton system and have T56-A-15 engines fitted, while the two Rivet Swap Hercules are powered by T56-A-7 engines and appear to be systems evaluation aircraft, as they lack all the external defensive equipment and have no internal ECM consoles.
64-0523; 64-0551; 64-0555; 64-0559; 64-0561; 64-0562; 64-0566; 64-0567; 64-0568 (Rivet Clamp); 62-1843; 63-7785; 64-0565 (Rivet Swap); 64-0571; 64-0572 (Rivet Yank)

WC-130E: Six aircraft were modified as WC-130Es to conduct weather reconnaissance and hurricane tracking, with an air scoop mounted on the lower forward fuselage to help cool onboard equipment.
61-2360; 61-2365; 61-2366; 64-0552; 64-0553; 64-0554

Above: USAF special operations forces also use the MC-130E version of the Hercules, although these 'Combat Talon Is' are slated to give way to the more advanced MC-130H in due course.

SPECIFICATION

Lockheed HC-130H

Wing: span 132 ft 7 in (40.41 m); aspect ratio 10.09; area 1,745.0 sq ft (162.12 m²)

Fuselage and tail: length 98 ft 9 in (30.10 m) with recovery system folded and 106 ft 4 in (32.41 m) with recovery system spread; height 38 ft 3 in (11.66 m); tailplane span 52 ft 8 in (16.05 m); wheel base 32 ft 0.75 in (9.77 m)

Powerplant: four Allison T56-A-15 each rated at 4,508 ehp (3362 kW)

Weights: basic empty 72,611 lb (32936 kg); maximum take-off 155,000 lb (70307 kg); maximum overload take-off 175,000 lb (79379 kg)

Fuel and load: internal fuel 6,960 US gal (26344 liters); external fuel up to two 1,360-US gal (5146-liter) drop-tanks; maximum payload 43,811 lb (19872 kg)

Speed: maximum speed at 30,000 ft (9145 m) 374 mph (602 km/h); maximum cruising speed 366 mph (589 km/h); economical cruising speed 345 mph (556 km/h)

Range: with maximum internal and external fuel and a 20,000-lb (9072-kg) payload 5,135 miles (8264 km); range with maximum payload 2,356 miles (3792 km)

Performance: maximum rate of climb at sea level 1,820 ft (555 m) per minute; service ceiling 33,000 ft (10060 m); take-off distance 5,160 ft (1573 m) to 50 ft (15 m) at maximum take-off weight; landing distance 2,430 ft (741 m) from 50 ft (15 m) at 100,000 lb (45360 kg)

Lockheed AC-130E

generally similar to the C-130E except in the following particulars:

Weight: empty 72,892 lb (33063 kg)

Speed: maximum speed at 30,000 ft (9145 m) 380 mph (612 km/h); cruising speed 368 mph (592 km/h)

Range: endurance 5 hours 0 minutes

Performance: maximum rate of climb at sea level 1,830 ft (558 m) per minute

Lockheed EC-130E

generally similar to the C-130E except in the following particulars:

Weights: empty 72,892 lb (33063 kg); maximum payload 45,000 lb (20412 kg)

Speed: maximum speed at 30,000 ft (9145 m) 380 mph (612 km/h); cruising speed 368 mph (592 km/h)

Range: 4,700 miles (7564 km)

Performance: maximum rate of climb at sea level 1,830 ft (558 m) per minute

Lockheed MC-130E

generally similar to the C-130E except in the following particulars:

Weight: empty 72,892 lb (33063 kg)

Speed: maximum speed 366 mph (589 km/h); speed for personnel airdrop at 50 ft (15 m) 144 mph (232 km/h)

Range: 2,300 miles (3701 km)

Performance: maximum rate of climb at sea level 1,600 ft (488 m) per minute

USAF OPERATORS

Operators of special missions C-130s will be found under Transport operators.

AC-130H: Eleven C-130Es were modified to AC-130E standard and later upgraded to AC-130H configuration with the fitment of T56-A-15 engines, plus three cannon and a howitzer on the port side, together with numerous sensors. Ten were operational at the start of 1991 with one lost during Operation Desert Storm.
69-6567; 69-6568; 69-6569; 69-6570; 69-6572; 69-6573; 69-6574; 69-6574; 69-6576; 69-6577

EC-130H: Four HC-130H and 12 C-130H aircraft were modified to EC-130H 'Compass Call' standard to conduct communications jamming with antennas housed in a pair of blister fairings fitted to the rear fuselage, and a host of cables connected to a gantry suspended beneath the tail.
64-14859; 64-14862; 65-0962; 65-0989; 73-1580; 73-1581; 73-1583; 73-1584; 73-1585; 73-1586; 73-1587; 73-1588; 73-1590; 73-1592; 73-1594; 73-1595

NC-130H: A single HC-130H was modified for drone test work with the designation DC-130H applied, although this was changed more recently to NC-130H. The aircraft was fitted with four underwing pylons to

Above: Updating of the special operations fleet of gunships will lead to deployment of the new AC-130U as a replacement for the AC-130H. This is the prototype AC-130U.

accommodate drones, and an extended nose housing a modified radar.
65-0979

WC-130H: Six of the 15 aircraft converted to WC-130H standard retain this configuration to perform weather reconnaissance duties.
64-14861; 65-0963; 65-0966; 65-0968; 65-0980; 65-0984

HC-130P: Twelve HC-130Hs were converted to HC-130P standard with the addition of underwing air-refueling pods.
64-14853; 64-14854; 64-14856; 64-14858; 64-14860; 64-14863; 64-14864; 64-14865; 65-0971; 65-0973; 65-0975; 65-0987

Boeing
KC-135 Stratotanker

Derived from Boeing's famous Model 367-80 prototype, the **KC-135 Stratotanker** was built in prodigious quantities between 1956 and 1965, 732 of the basic **KC-135A** tanker version being delivered to Strategic Air Command, with a further 88 transport and special variants making up the grand **C-135** total of 820.

'Dash Eighty' first flew on 15 July 1954, a company-funded prototype for both a jet transport and a jet tanker. In the latter role the aircraft would be fitted with a Boeing Flying Boom under the rear fuselage, as used on the same company's KB-50 and KC-97 piston-engined tankers. In September 1955 the USAF ordered the type as the KC-135A, realizing the need for a fast tanker to support the large fleets of sleek bombers it then had in service or in production. 'Dash Eighty' flew with a test re-fueling boom early in its trials, and a production model, the 717, was derived from the prototype, this differing little outwardly from 'Dash Eighty' but featuring a wider fuselage and numerous detail changes.

55-3118 was the first KC-135A, named 'City of Renton', and it took to the air for the first time on 31 August 1956, with 'Dix' Loesch and 'Tex' Johnston at the controls. An accelerated flight test program ensued, which revealed no immediate flaws, and the first service example was handed over to the 93rd Air Refueling Squadron, 93rd Bomb Wing, on 28 June 1957. The flyaway unit cost was $3,670,000 per copy. Only one major modification was introduced during the entire 732-aircraft production run, this fitting a taller vertical fin and powered controls from the 583rd aircraft onwards (and subsequent retrofitting to the earlier aircraft) to cure take-off stability and control authority problems, while a noticeable minor 'mod' was the fitment of circumferential straps around the rear fuselage to cure cracking associated with shock waves from the

jet engines. With so few production changes and the continued use of the aircraft today, the KC-135 represents one of the most cost-effective military aircraft production runs in history.

Boeing's advanced large aircraft construction technology was brought to the fore in the KC-135. A pressurized fuselage consisted of two circular lobes mounted on top of each other, with the fuselage side crease faired over. This gave a large unobstructed cabin for the carriage of freight or up to 80 passengers, and a large underfloor area for fuel tanks. Together with those in the wings, these added up to 22 tanks in total, with a sophisticated pumping system to move fuel around within the airframe to maintain center of gravity and provide fuel for the boom. Boeing bomber technology was evident in the slender swept wing, which mounted four Pratt & Whitney J57 turbojets in slim pods. In the current era of re-engined aircraft, the J57-powered machines are nostalgically referred to as 'stovepipe' models.

Fifty-six of the baseline production tankers were designated **KC-135Q**, these featuring extra navigation and communications equipment for the dedicated support of the Lockheed SR-71A strategic reconnaissance aircraft, which used high-flashpoint JP-7 fuel. With the SR-71 out of service, the KC-135Qs have reverted to normal tanker duties, although they are often used to support the activities of the Lockheed F-117A. 9th Wing KC-135Qs are being re-engined with F108s, and having air-refueling receptacles added, being redesignated **KC-135T** in the process. Along with the current **KC-135R(RT)** aircraft they will become more involved with the support of 'stealth' aircraft.

Other tanker variants were the **C-135F**, of which 12 were purchased by France for support of the Mirage IV nuclear bomber fleet. Four

tankers are **KC-135D** aircraft, these being surplus **RC-135A** aircraft converted for the tanker mission. Finally a handful of aircraft have the RT suffix attached to their designation, these being ex-test, -reconnaissance or -command post aircraft that have reverted to tanker duties but retained the refueling receptacle with which they were fitted for their special duties.

In service, the KC-135A proved an excellent, safe and reliable aircraft. At first tasked with support of the nuclear bomber fleet, its duties rapidly widened to encompass support of transports and tactical aircraft. It served with distinction during the long Vietnam War, where the climate resulted in many take-offs at high weights in hot and humid conditions. Many years of operating in widely disparate climates and regularly at high weights took its toll on the fleet, and in the mid-1970s a rejuvenation program was initiated.

First was a reskinning program to replace the lower wing and extend the fatigue life of each aircraft by 27,000 hours, begun in 1975. Second was a major re-engining program, which followed two paths to replace the uneconomic, elderly and environment-unfriendly J57 turbojets. The first path resulted in the **KC-135E** for the Air National Guard and Air Force Reserve tanker squadrons. The USAF bought large numbers of surplus Model 707 airliners, and raided them for their widespan tailplanes and JT3D turbofans (TF33 in military parlance), which were fitted to all 163 Reservist KC-135s. Greater power and reverse thrust increased the level of safety margin dramatically, while improving mission versatility. At the same time some special mission aircraft were also refitted under the 'E' program.

Far more radical was the updating of the active-duty fleet to **KC-135R** standard. After a protracted series of re-engining studies, Boeing announced the new program in 1980, and flew the first KC-135R (then designated **KC-135RE**) on 4 August 1982. The 'R' update involves the fitment of CFM International CFM56 (military designation F108) high bypass ratio turbofans of 22,000 lb (97.86 kN) thrust, which offer significantly improved fuel burn figures over the J57s. An auxiliary power unit is fitted in the port rear fuselage to provide autonomous operating capability at austere airfields, and numerous other modifications were made to enhance the effectiveness of the tanker. KC-135Rs can carry more fuel (203,289 lb; 92211 kg) than the KC-135A, and take it a lot further. Shorter runways can be used, while the effect on noise and air pollution is dramatic.

In April 1990 the 200th KC-135R conversion was delivered, and modification of the active-duty tanker fleet is continuing at a slow rate. In 1992 over 500 KC-135s were in service, of which over half were KC-135Rs. Over one hundred KC-135Es were in service with the Air National Guard, while a further 30 E models were in Air Force Reserve service.

While overall force numbers may decrease, the KC-135 has many years of service left, as there are no plans to replace the type. Update programs will continue to keep the old Boeing forever young, such as the fitment of drogue refueling pods to the wingtips of some

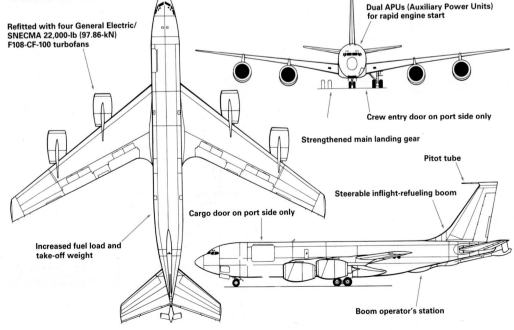

BOEING KC-135R

Refitted with four General Electric/SNECMA 22,000-lb (97.86-kN) F108-CF-100 turbofans

Dual APUs (Auxiliary Power Units) for rapid engine start

Crew entry door on port side only

Strengthened main landing gear

Pitot tube

Steerable inflight-refueling boom

Cargo door on port side only

Increased fuel load and take-off weight

Boom operator's station

Top: 'Stovepipe'-engined KC-135Q Stratotankers like this 380th Wing machine were employed for support of the SR-71A but have reverted to more conventional tanker tasks since the 'Blackbird' was retired from service in 1990.

Above: Re-engining of the Stratotanker fleet as the KC-135R continues and over 250 examples of this long-serving tanker have now been modified for service with SAC. This example is one of a few fitted as KC-135R(RT)s with refueling receptacles.

KC-135Rs to facilitate the refueling of Navy, Marine Corps and foreign receivers. A splendid performance in the 1991 Gulf War continued to enhance the reputation of the type some 37 years after 'Dash Eighty' first took to the air.

C-135 SPECIAL VARIANTS

At an early date in its career, the KC-135 Stratotanker was recognized as an ideal vehicle for many tasks other than tanking. Basic tankers were often used as transports, and this role became an important one for the C-135 in subsequent years. The good cabin capacity, high speed and long range of the type were attractive to the Military Air Transport Service (later Military Airlift Command), which ordered 45 C-135 aircraft that lacked refueling equipment. The first 15 were **C-135A**s with J57 engines, but the rest of the batch were **C-135B**s fitted with TF33 turbofans and wide-span tailplanes from the outset.

Procured mainly as a stopgap, the C-135 transport served with distinction until the C-141B StarLifter entered service, at which time many of the transports were made available for conversion to special duties. Several of these C-135s are retained in service, mostly for staff transport duties.

A large, clear cabin and excellent range/payload performance were the main requirements of many special missions, most of which are electronic in nature. Various KC-135As were removed from the tanker fleet and employed on electronic tests or for command post and reconnaissance missions. Of the multitude of special mission aircraft, only three variants were built as such. The first was the KC-135B, which again had TF33 engines fitted on the line. These were fitted with extra communications equipment for the 'Looking Glass' mission, which involved providing a 24-hour airborne alert with a general on board to take command of SAC's nuclear assets in the event

of a nuclear exchange. The KC-135Bs were redesignated **EC-135C** on entering service, and replaced modified KC-135As that had been flying the command post mission since 3 February 1961.

EC-135Cs were the first of the airborne command post family, which has grown to encompass many C-135 airframes. **EC-135H, J, P** and **Y** conversions are all essentially similar, and were procured for theater and command support. The EC-135J was procured to fulfil the National Emergency Airborne Command Post role now flown by the Boeing E-4B. Further EC-135 aircraft are assigned to radio relay duties, as were a handful of KC-135A 'Combat Lightning' modifications. In the long service compiled by the EC-135s, they have received many modifications to enhance their effectiveness, the latest being a satellite communications hump being evaluated for the EC-135C fleet.

Strategic reconnaissance has been a major task for the C-135 since the early 1960s, when modified KC-135As began flying with electronic recording equipment on the classified 'Iron Lung' and 'Briar Patch' projects. Similarly the **KC-135A-II** began operations under the 'Office Boy' codename and a **JKC-135A** under the 'Nancy Rae' codename in the early 1960s, their efforts being aimed at monitoring Soviet ICBM tests.

'Office Boy' aircraft were redesignated as the **RC-135D**, while 'Nancy Rae' became the **RC-135S**, leading to a small but important reconnaissance fleet which has been based in Alaska. Today the mission is flown by a pair of **RC-135S** Cobra Ball aircraft, and a single **RC-135X** Cobra Eye, all fitted with receivers to intercept downlinked telemetry data from foreign ICBM tests, and optical instruments to photograph re-entry vehicles. Their use is vital not only to intelligence regarding military advances in the ICBM field, but also for verification of treaty compliance.

The second special mission aircraft built as such was the **RC-135B**, which again featured TF33 engines. Ten were delivered, and immediately sent to Martin for fitment with a complex electronic reconnaissance suite. Redesignated **RC-135C**, the 10 aircraft were put to work on general signals intelligence gathering work of national importance, flying close to target nations to 'vacuum' up any electronic signal the sensitive receivers could pick up. Further modification resulted in eight becoming **RC-135V**s, characterized by large cheek fairings housing side-facing sensors and a 'thimble' nose, and two **RC-135U**s with even larger cheek fairings and 'towel rail' antennas on the forward fuselage, although the latter were removed in 1991/92.

RC-135Us and Vs today serve with the 55th Wing, the Air Force's premier Sigint gathering unit. They have been joined by six **RC-135W**s, which are essentially similar to the RC-135V, but were derived from the earlier **RC-135M** conversion of surplus C-135B transports. Both the Alaskan and 55th Wing reconnaissance fleets are supported by a dedicated training aircraft in the form of the **TC-135S** and **TC-135W**, respectively. These have no reconnaissance capability but do have refueling receptacles and 'thimble' noses fitted to simulate the mission aircraft.

The RC-135 fleet is scheduled for re-engining with F108s, and is to be swelled by the addition of three more converted aircraft. Photographic survey was the role for the third new-build special mission variant, although this only covered four aircraft. Built as RC-135As, these featured sliding panels in the lower fuselage which covered a battery of downward-facing cameras. They were converted back to tanker status and redesignated **KC-135D**. The **WC-135B** designation covered 10 surplus C-135B transports converted for the weather reconnaissance mission, of which six still serve with the 55th Weather Reconnaissance Squadron.

Other C-135 specials have been produced for various test and trial missions. Under various designations a sizeable fleet of space tracking aircraft was assembled to take part in the Apollo mission, all featuring a giant bulbous nose radome housing a steerable antenna for tracking spacecraft and receiving telemetry data. Four surviving aircraft, designated **EC-135E**, continue to fly a similar mission, using their onboard equipment and antenna for support of missile tests.

C-135 and KC-135 aircraft with the 'J' and 'N' prefix have been widely used for a multitude of equipment and system trials throughout the aircraft's career. Today the N-prefixed survivors are as busy as ever, providing an airborne platform for whatever system the USAF wants evaluated.

MISSION PROFILE

Boeing KC-135 Stratotanker

Inflight refueling: The primary mission of the KC-135 is as a tanker. Mission profiles are varied to match the requirements of the customers, but usually involve a straight-line escort, with the tanker flying in loose formation with the receiver, supplying fuel when needed, or a racetrack orbit at a predetermined point. Here receivers are vectored into the tanker pattern where a point-parallel rendezvous is undertaken, the tanker and receiver flying on opposing tracks but offset by a mile or two. When the two are the correct distance apart, the tanker performs a 180° turn to roll out a mile or two in front of the receivers, which then approach for refueling. Some tankers are on strip alert, partially prepared for flight so that they can be rapidly launched to provide fuel in an emergency. For refueling non-Air Force aircraft, the KC-135 can be rapidly fitted with a short hose-and-drogue which attaches to the end of the flying boom

Fighter deployment: tankers are often used to shepherd tactical aircraft on long deployments, supplying fuel, communications and navigation *en route*; the capacious cabin of the KC-135 is often used to carry ground crew and spare parts for the deploying aircraft

Transport: a large cargo door in the forward port fuselage admits cargo; alternatively, up to 80 seats can be fitted for passenger/troop transport

Boeing C-135 special variants

Transport: the 89th Airlift Wing maintains a small fleet of C-135Bs for staff and VIP transport tasks; these aircraft remain windowless but are fitted with passenger interiors

Command support: two KC-135E and a single C-135A were flown by the 55th Wing in support of Strategic Air Command activities, providing staff transport for high-ranking officers from Offutt; the CSA fleet was deactivated in early 1992

Signals intelligence gathering: the 55th Wing flies three RC-135 variants on regular missions in international or friendly airspace to monitor military advances in potentially hostile nations; aircraft have a wide variety of sensors that record, locate and analyze a complete range of signals, specific disciplines including communications intelligence (Comint), electronic intelligence (Elint – the classification of radars) and radiation intelligence (Radint – gathering signals from non-emitting sources such as power lines or dormant radars); two RC-135Us, eight RC-135Vs and six RC-135Ws are employed on these global missions, which often involve long-duration, refueled sorties; missions are regularly flown from the 55th Wing base at Offutt and detachments at Souda Bay on Crete, Eielson in Alaska and Mildenhall in England, with other deployments occasionally undertaken such as Riyadh in Saudi Arabia to monitor Iraq and other Middle East nations

Telemetry intelligence gathering: two RC-135S Cobra Ball aircraft and the single RC-135X Cobra Eye were based with the 6th Wing in Alaska to monitor ICBM tests in the Far East; aircraft have various sensors to intercept telemetry data being downlinked from the test missiles and high-resolution optical sensors to photograph the re-entry vehicles; RC-135s launch and fly a racetrack orbit in the approximate landing area of the re-entry vehicles; missions are launched from Shemya but the Telint fleet is now headquartered at Offutt instead of Eielson

Reconnaissance training: a single TC-135S flew with the 6th Wing (now 55th Wing) to provide aircrew training for the RC-135S/X crews, while a single TC-135W performs a similar function for the 55th Wing; both are fitted with refueling receptacles for tanking practice; a secondary wing support and transport role is also undertaken

Command post: a sizeable fleet of EC-135 aircraft is used for command post duties, the majority (EC-135C) flying with the 2nd ACCS of the 55th Wing from Offutt AFB and providing the basis for Strategic Command's Post Attack Command and Control System (PACCS); until recently, 24-hour airborne coverage was maintained, one EC-135 being airborne at all times with a general on board who could take control of ACC's nuclear forces (primarily the ICBMs) in the event of a nuclear attack on land-based command and control systems – the airborne alert has since been relaxed, but EC-135Cs remain on ground alert for a similar function, a full communications suite allowing the aircraft to keep in contact with nuclear installations and other airborne command posts; further EC-135 variants (H, J, P and Y) are assigned to theater or command support, providing a similar airborne command post function for the respective commanders, although these are in the process of withdrawal

Radio relay: a secondary role within PACCS is the provision of EC-135A, G and L radio relay aircraft, which help maintain communications links with far-flung SAC assets; the EC-135G has an additional missile launch control facility

Fighter deployment: a pair of EC-135K aircraft is assigned to the specialist duty of providing communications and navigation support to tactical fighters deploying overseas; both are fitted with comprehensive communications suites, but lack the refueling boom

Range instrumentation: a small number of EC-135E aircraft are flown by Air Force Materiel Command in support of missile and space programs; these feature a giant bulbous nose housing the world's largest steerable airborne antenna, which receives telemetry data downlinked from missiles under test, the information then being downlinked to ground stations

Tests and trials: a fleet of C-135s under the NC-135A, NKC-135A, C-135B and NKC-135E designations fly missions for Air Force Materiel Command on a wide variety of tests and trials, including refueling tests for new aircraft, 'Star Wars' programs, zero-*g* training and numerous systems trials for other aircraft types

Weather reconnaissance: six WC-135B aircraft are flown for global weather reconnaissance and meteorological research duties, fitted with an open-ended cylindrical particulate sampler on the fuselage sides

USAF VARIANTS AND SERIALS

(Note: conversions presented are those aircraft which are currently operational and do not include losses or those withdrawn from service.)

Original construction designations

C-135A: Fifteen C-135A transport aircraft were ordered in 1960 and 1961 for MATS, being essentially similar to the KC-135A but lacking the flying boom. A further three were converted from KC-135As while on the production line, although these have since returned to tanker duties.
60-0369 to 60-0378; 61-0326 to 61-0330

KC-135A: The main production version of the tanker with 732 ordered between 1955 and 1964. Many aircraft were modified to perform specialist roles with a change of designation, while most remaining tankers have been the subject of a re-engining program.
55-3118 to 55-3146; 56-3591 to 56-3658; 57-1418 to 57-1514; 57-2589 to 57-2609; 58-0001 to 58-0130; 59-1443 to 59-1523; 60-0313 to 60-0368; 61-0261 to 61-0325; 62-3497 to 62-3580; 63-7976 to 63-8045; 63-8871 to 63-8888; 64-14828 to 64-14840

C-135B: Thirty C-135Bs purchased in 1961 and 1962 which were similar to the C-135A but with the J57 turbojets replaced by TF33 turbofan engines.
61-0331 to 61-0332; 61-2662 to 61-2674; 62-4125 to 62-4139

KC-135B: Seventeen KC-135Bs ordered in 1962 and 1963 with TF33 engines instead of the J57 turbojets. Equipped as airborne command posts and designated EC-135C with three later converted to EC-135J standard.
62-3581 to 62-2385; 63-8046 to 63-8057

RC-135A: Four RC-135As were constructed for the photo-mapping role with geodetic surveying equipment internally and cameras installed in the nose. The aircraft were converted to tankers when the surveying role ceased, becoming KC-135Ds and retaining this designation when re-engined with TF33s.
63-8058 to 63-8061

RC-135B: Ten TF33-engined aircraft were ordered to perform strategic reconnaissance duties, although they were redesignated as RC-135C before delivery.
63-9792; 64-14841 to 64-14849

Conversion designations

EC-135A: Five KC-135As were modified as airborne launch control centers as part of the backup system between SAC HQ and the ICBMs located in their silos. Various antennas were fitted to the fuselage and wing tips.
61-0262; 61-0278; 61-0287; 61-0289; 61-0297

GNC-135A: A single testbed NC-135A was retired from active service and transferred to ATC for ground instruction duties.
60-0369

GNKC-135A: A former test NKC-135A was transferred to ATC as a ground instruction trainer, although the Air Force Museum wishes to acquire the aircraft and its period with the Air Training Command may be short-lived.
55-3124

NC-135A: A single NC-135A remains in service from three originally assigned this designation, serials 60-0369 to 60-0371, performing a variety of test work.
60-0371

NKC-135A: More than a dozen tanker aircraft were assigned to an assortment of test duties at AFSC and contractors' establishments, although only six retain the NKC-135A designation. At least one of these is employed as a staff transport.
55-3119; 55-3120; 55-3122; 55-3127; 55-3128; 55-3131

WC-135B: Ten C-135Bs were converted to WC-135B standard to perform weather reconnaissance while on transoceanic flights. An air scoop was mounted on both sides of the central fuselage to help reduce the temperature of electronic equipment installed. Seven retain this designation.
61-2665 to 61-2667; 61-2670; 61-2672 to 61-2674

Above: The 'triangle-K' motif on the tail of this KC-135A identifies it as being assigned to the 379th Wing's 920th Air Refueling Squadron at Wurtsmith AFB, Michigan.

Below: Over 150 Stratotankers have been brought to KC-135E configuration through a process of re-engining with TF33 turbofans, for service in ANG and AFRes tanker units.

C-135C: Three WC-135Bs were converted to the VIP role with the installation of extensive communications equipment and plush internal fittings. All three are painted gloss white with highly polished natural metal underside.
61-2668; 61-2669; 61-2671

EC-135C: Thirteen EC-135Cs are operated as airborne command posts /airborne launch control centers with antennas fitted to upper and lower surfaces of the fuselage and the wingtips. One aircraft has been fitted with MILSTARS communications housed in a large radome aft of the cockpit.
62-3581 to 62-3583; 62-3585; 63-8046 to 63-8054

KC-135D: The four RC-135As were allocated the designation KC-135D when they were converted to the tanker role with the fitment of a flying boom and associated equipment. They have retained this designation despite being re-engined from J57s to TF33 turbofans.
63-8058 to 63-8061

C-135E: Three C-135A aircraft were converted to C-135E standard with the replacement of the inefficient J57 engines with TF33s. Two are employed as flying testbeds while the third is a VIP transport for the Commander of US Space Command.
60-0372; 60-0375; 60-0376

EC-135E: The four survivors of eight aircraft converted to EC-135N standard to track satellites with a huge steerable radar housed in a giant radar nose. The reduction in the requirement and the fitting of TF33 engines resulted in the designation EC-135E being allocated.
60-0374; 61-0326; 61-0329; 61-0330

KC-135E: More than 150 KC-135As changed designation to KC-135E following the change of powerplant from J57 to TF33 turbofans.
55-3141; 55-3143; 55-3145; 55-3146; 56-3593; 56-3604; 56-3606; 56-3607; 56-3609; 56-3611; 56-3612; 56-3622; 56-3623; 56-3626; 56-3630; 56-3631; 56-3638; 56-3640; 56-3641; 56-3643; 56-3645; 56-3648; 56-3650; 56-3654; 56-3658; 57-1421; 57-1422; 57-1423; 57-1425; 57-1426; 57-1428; 57-1429; 57-1431; 57-1433; 57-1434; 57-1436; 57-1438; 57-1441; 57-1443; 57-1445; 57-1447; 57-1448; 57-1450; 57-1451; 57-1452; 57-1455; 57-1458; 57-1460; 57-1463; 57-1464; 57-1465; 57-1468; 57-1471; 57-1475; 57-1478; 57-1479; 57-1480; 57-1482; 57-1484; 57-1485; 57-1491; 57-1492; 57-1494; 57-1495; 57-1496; 57-1497; 57-1501; 57-1503; 57-1504; 57-1505; 57-1507; 57-1509; 57-1510; 57-1511; 57-1512; 57-2589; 57-2594; 57-2595; 57-2598; 57-2600; 57-2603; 57-2604; 57-2606; 57-2607; 57-2608; 58-0003; 58-0005; 58-0006; 58-0008; 58-0012; 58-0013; 58-0014; 58-0017; 58-0020; 58-0024; 58-0032; 58-0037; 58-0040; 58-0041; 58-0043; 58-0044; 58-0052; 58-0053; 58-0057; 58-0058; 58-0064; 58-0067; 58-0068; 58-0078; 58-0080; 58-0082; 58-0085; 58-0087; 58-0090; 58-0096; 58-0107; 58-0108; 58-0111; 58-0115; 58-0116; 59-1445; 59-1447; 59-1448; 59-1450; 59-1451; 59-1452; 59-1456; 59-1457; 59-1473; 59-1477; 59-1479; 59-1484; 59-1485; 59-1487; 59-1489; 59-1493; 59-1496; 59-1497; 59-1499; 59-1503; 59-1505; 59-1506; 59-1509; 59-1514; 59-1516; 59-1519; 60-0316; 60-0327; 61-0268; 61-0270; 61-0271; 61-0280; 61-0281; 61-0303; 62-3566

Above: One of the rarest tanker derivatives is the KC-135D, this designation being allocated to the quartet of photo-mapping RC-135As after they were stripped of survey equipment and used for inflight refueling instead. Originally, they retained J57 engines but they have since been given TF33 turbofans and assigned to the Alaska ANG tanker unit at Eielson.

Left: Widespread deployment of the KC-135R has resulted in it becoming a common sight with the tanker task force that operates from Mildenhall in support of USAFE. For many years, this had relied on rotational aircraft from bases in the continental USA but aircraft are now permanently assigned to the 100th Air Refueling Wing. This KC-135R is from the 92nd Wing at Fairchild.

NKC-135E: Two test NKC-135A aircraft changed designation to NKC-135E following the fitment of TF33 turbofans.
55-3132; 55-3135

EC-135G: Four KC-135As were fitted with various antennas on the fuselage and wingtips to act as airborne launch control centers/relay platforms between SAC HQ and silo-housed ICBMs.
62-3570; 62-3579; 63-7994; 63-8001

EC-135H: Four KC-135As were converted as airborne command posts for the operations in Europe. Fitted with TF33 turbofan engines, they retained the EC-135H designation. As with other command posts the aircraft sport various antennas and wingtip probes. A fifth EC-135H was changed to EC-135P standard. All were withdrawn by early 1992.
61-0282; 61-0285; 61-0286; 61-0291

EC-135J: Three EC-135Js employed as the National Emergency Airborne Command Post (NEACP) mission were replaced by the introduction of the E-4 into service. The EC-135Js were transferred to the Commander of Pacific Air Forces and were joined by a fourth aircraft, which was formerly an EC-135C. All were fitted with fuselage antennas and wingtip probes.
62-3584; 63-8055 to 63-8057

EC-135K: A pair of KC-135As was modified as airborne relay aircraft to shepherd deploying cells of fighter aircraft on intercontinental flights. Aircraft were fitted with wingtip probes.
55-3118; 59-1518

EC-135L: Yet another version modified as airborne communications relay platforms between the ICBM silos and SAC HQ, with various antennas fitted to the fuselage and wingtips.
61-0261; 61-0263; 61-0269; 61-0279; 61-0283

EC-135P: An NKC-135A, two KC-135As and an EC-135H were modified to airborne command post duties for the Commander Tactical Air Command, having served originally in a similar role for the Commander of PACAF.
55-3129; 58-0019; 58-0022; 61-0274

KC-135Q: Fifty-six KC-135Qs were assigned the exclusive role of refueling the SR-71A with tanks containing the special JP-7 fuel. Appropriate communications equipment was fitted to the tankers for compatibility with the SR-71.
58-0042; 58-0045; 58-0046; 58-0047; 58-0049; 58-0050; 58-0054; 58-0055; 58-0060; 58-0061; 58-0062; 58-0065; 58-0069; 58-0071; 58-0072; 58-0074; 58-0077; 58-0084; 58-0086; 58-0088; 58-0089; 58-0094; 58-0095; 58-0099; 58-0103; 58-0112; 58-0117; 58-0125; 58-0129; 59-1460; 59-1462; 59-1464; 59-1467; 59-1468; 59-1470; 59-1471; 59-1474; 59-1480; 59-1490; 59-1504; 59-1510; 59-1512; 59-1513; 59-1520; 59-1523; 60-0335; 60-0336; 60-0337; 60-0339; 60-0342; 60-0343; 60-0344; 60-0345; 60-0346

KC-135R: The majority of the AMC fleet of KC-135As is being modified to KC-135R standard with the fitment of General Electric/SNECMA F108-CF-100 engines and a host of internal improvements. More than 250 have completed modification.
57-1418; 57-1419; 57-1427; 57-1430; 57-1437; 57-1439; 57-1440; 57-1454; 57-1456; 57-1461; 57-1462; 57-1469; 57-1470; 57-1472; 57-1473; 57-1483; 57-1486; 57-1487; 57-1488; 57-1493; 57-1499; 57-1502; 57-1506; 57-1508; 57-1514; 57-2597; 57-2599; 57-2605; 58-0001; 58-0004; 58-0009; 58-0010; 58-0011; 58-0015; 58-0016; 58-0018; 58-0021; 58-0023; 58-0027; 58-0030; 58-0035; 58-0038; 58-0051; 58-0056; 58-0059; 58-0073; 58-0076; 58-0079; 58-0083; 58-0093; 58-0098; 58-0100; 58-0104; 58-0109; 58-0120; 58-0122; 58-0123; 58-0124; 58-0126; 58-0130; 59-1444; 59-1446; 59-1453; 59-1455; 59-1458; 59-1459; 59-1461; 59-1463; 59-1466; 59-1469; 59-1472; 59-1475; 59-1476; 59-1478; 59-1482; 59-1483; 59-1492; 59-1495; 59-1498; 59-1511; 59-1515; 59-1517; 59-1521; 60-0313; 60-0314; 60-0315; 60-0321; 60-0322; 60-0323; 60-0324; 60-0329; 60-0331; 60-0333; 60-0334; 60-0341; 60-0347; 60-0353; 60-0356; 60-0357; 60-0359; 60-0360; 60-0362; 60-0364; 60-0365; 60-0366; 60-0367; 61-0264; 61-0272; 61-0275; 61-0276; 61-0277; 61-0290; 61-0292; 61-0293; 61-0294; 61-0295; 61-0298; 61-0299; 61-0300; 61-0302; 61-0304; 61-0305; 61-0306; 61-0307; 61-0308; 61-0309; 61-0310; 61-0311; 61-0312; 61-0313;

Above: Optical and radar sensors are among the equipment fitted to the pair of RC-135S 'Cobra Ball' aircraft that presently operate from Shemya AB at the tip of the Aleutian chain.

Above: Most of the major USAF agencies operated airborne command posts in order to ensure that a survivable means of exercising control over combat forces exists. This particular specimen was assigned to the 1st Wing on behalf of TAC.

61-0314; 61-0315; 61-0317; 61-0318; 61-0321; 61-0323; 61-0324; 62-3499; 62-3500; 62-3504; 62-3506; 62-3507; 62-3508; 62-3510; 62-3511; 62-3513; 62-3514; 62-3515; 62-3516; 62-3518; 62-3519; 62-3521; 62-3523; 62-3524; 62-3530; 62-3531; 62-3533; 62-3534; 62-3537; 62-3540; 62-3541; 62-3542; 62-3543; 62-3544; 62-3545; 62-3546; 62-3547; 62-3548; 62-3549; 62-3550; 62-3551; 62-3552; 62-3553; 62-3554; 62-3555; 62-3556; 62-3557; 62-3558; 62-3561; 62-3564; 62-3565; 62-3568; 62-3569; 62-3571; 62-3572; 62-3573; 62-3574; 62-3575; 62-3577; 62-3580; 63-7976; 63-7977; 63-7978; 63-7979; 63-7980; 63-7981; 63-7984; 63-7985; 63-7988; 63-7991; 63-7992; 63-7993; 63-7995; 63-7996; 63-7997; 63-7999; 63-8002; 63-8003; 63-8004; 63-8006; 63-8007; 63-8008; 63-8011; 63-8013; 63-8015; 63-8020; 63-8021; 63-8023; 63-8024; 63-8025; 63-8028; 63-8029; 63-8030; 63-8032; 63-8033; 63-8036; 63-8037; 63-8038; 63-8039; 63-8040; 63-8041; 63-8871; 63-8872; 63-8876; 63-8880; 63-8883; 63-8884; 63-8885; 64-14828; 64-14829; 64-14830; 64-14831; 64-14832; 64-14834; 64-14835; 64-14840

RC-135S: Two C-135Bs were converted to RC-135S Cobra Ball standard with an elongated radar nose and optical equipment behind windows on the starboard side. An additional aircraft was converted following the loss of one of the originals.
61-2662; 61-2663

TC-135S: A former test aircraft was modified as the sole TC-135S to enable Cobra Ball aircrew to perform training flights without using precious flying hours in the actual reconnaissance examples. The TC-135S is believed to have fake modifications to enable flight characteristics to be maintained.
62-4133

Below: SAC's 55th Wing operates a large fleet of EC-135C command posts from Offutt, one of which has MILSTAR communications equipment in a prominent dorsal fairing.

RC-135U: A pair of RC-135Cs was extensively modified as RC-135U Combat Sent with a large dielectric panel on either side of the nose and a host of sensors and defensive modifications to the fuselage and wingtips.
64-14847; 64-14849

RC-135V: Eight RC-135Cs were converted to RC-135V Rivet Joint standard with a long thimble nose and a dielectric panel on either side of the nose, plus various other modifications including an array of large aerials suspended beneath the center of the fuselage.
63-9792; 64-14841 to 64-14846; 64-14848

RC-135W: Six RC-135Ms were upgraded to RC-135W Rivet Joint configuration, which is essentially similar to the RC-135V but with a lengthened dielectric panel extending partially over the crew entry door.
62-4131; 62-4132; 62-4134; 62-4135; 62-4138; 62-4139

TC-135W: The introduction of the TC-135S trainer produced sufficient savings in flight time of operational aircraft to encourage the conversion of a TC-135W. Modifications are believed to be similar to that of the TC-135S.
62-4129

RC-135X: The sole Cobra Eye reconnaissance aircraft is similar to the RC-135S but features the latest sensor equipment.
62-4128

Above: Specializing in strategic reconnaissance duties, the RC-135Vs of the 55th Wing range far and wide in the search for intelligence and are frequently to be seen at Mildenhall, England.

Right: Another reconnaissance derivative is the RC-135U of the 55th Wing, although the unique 'towel rail' antennas have now been removed.

EC-135Y: An NKC-135A and an EC-135N were modified to EC-135Y standard for VIP duties by the Commander US Central Command with the usual communications antennas and wingtip probes. 55-3125; 61-0327

SPECIFICATION

Boeing KC-135A
Wing: span 130 ft 10 in (39.88 m); area 2,433.0 sq ft (226.03 m²)
Fuselage and tail: length 136 ft 3 in (41.53 m); height 41 ft 8 in (12.70 m); tailplane span 40 ft 3 in (12.27 m); wheel base 46 ft 7 in (14.20 m)
Powerplant: four Pratt & Whitney J57-P-59W each rated at 13,750 lb (61.16 kN) dry thrust
Weights: operating empty 106,306 lb (48220 kg); maximum take-off 316,000 lb (143335 kg)
Fuel and load: internal fuel 189,702 lb (86047 kg); maximum payload 83,000 lb (37650 kg)
Speed: maximum level speed at high altitude 610 mph (982 km/h); cruising speed at 35,000 ft (10675 m) 532 mph (856 km/h)
Range: ferry range 9,200 miles (14806 km); radius to offload 24,000 lb (10886 kg) of fuel 3,450 miles (5552 km), or to offload 120,000 lb (54432 kg) of fuel 1,150 miles (1850 km)

Performance: maximum rate of climb at sea level 393 m (1,290 ft) per minute; service ceiling 45,000 ft (13715 m); typical take-off distance 10,700 ft (3260 m) increasing to 14,000 ft (4270 m) under 'hot and high' conditions

Boeing KC-135E
generally similar to the KC-135A except in the following particulars:
Powerplant: four Pratt & Whitney JT3D-3B each rated at 18,000 lb (80.07 kN) dry thrust

Boeing KC-135R
generally similar to the KC-135A except in the following particulars:
Powerplant: four CFM International F108-CF-100 each rated at 22,000 lb (97.86 kN) dry thrust
Weight: maximum take-off 322,500 lb (146284 kg)
Fuel and load: internal fuel 203,288 lb (92212 kg)
Range: radius to offload 150 per cent more fuel than the KC-135A 2,875 miles (4627 km)

Boeing EC-135C
Wing: span 130 ft 10 in (39.88 m); area 2,433.0 sq ft (226.03 m²)
Fuselage and tail: length 136 ft 3 in (41.53 m); height 41 ft 8 in (12.70 m); tailplane span 45 ft 3 in (13.79 m); wheel base 45 ft 8 in (13.92 m)
Powerplant: four Pratt & Whitney TF33-P-9 each rated at 18,000 lb (80.07 kN) dry thrust

Weights: basic empty 102,300 lb (46403 kg); maximum take-off 299,000 lb (135626 kg)
Fuel and load: internal fuel 189,702 lb (86047 kg)
Speed: maximum level speed at 25,000 ft (7620 m) 616 mph (991 km/h); cruising speed at 35,000 ft (106701 m) 560 mph (901 km/h)
Range: ferry range 5,655 miles (9100 km); operational radius 2,675 miles (4305 km)
Performance: service ceiling 40,600 ft (12375 m)

Boeing EC-135A
generally similar to the EC-135C except in the following particulars:
Powerplant: four Pratt & Whitney J57-P-59W each rated at 13,750 lb (61.16 kN) dry thrust
Weights: basic empty 98,466 lb (44664 kg); maximum take-off 297,000 lb (134717 kg)
Speed: maximum level speed at 30,000 ft (9145 m) 585 mph (941 km/h); cruising speed between 30,500 and 40,000 ft (9300 and 12190 m) 430 mph (853 km/h)
Performance: maximum rate of climb at sea level 2,000 ft (610 m); service ceiling 40,000 ft (12190 m)

Boeing RC-135C
generally similar to the EC-135C except in the following particulars:
Fuselage and tail: length 128 ft 7.3 in (39.20 m)
Weight: maximum take-off 275,500 lb (124967 kg)

USAF Aircraft

Right: Employed on long-range weather research duties on a global basis, a total of 10 former MAC C-135Bs was converted into WC-135B standard for operation by the Air Weather Service. Only about half are still active in this role. All of those that are presently assigned to the 55th Weather Reconnaissance Squadron which operates from McClellan AFB, California, as part of the Military Airlift Command.

Below: Following replacement in MAC service by the Lockheed C-141 StarLifter, several C-135As were passed on to Air Force Systems Command for use as flying testbeds. Most of these are still active with the 4950th Test Wing at Wright-Patterson AFB, Ohio. The NC-135A shown here is typical and functions as the 'Argus' photo-documentation platform, as indicated by photo-reference marks.

USAF OPERATORS

Air Force Materiel Command (AFMC)

4950th TW	4951st TS	Wright-Patterson AFB, OH	C-135A/E, NKC-135A/E, NC-135A, EC-135E
	det 1	Andrews AFB, MD	C-135C

Air Training Command (ATC)

3700th TTW	Sheppard TTC	Sheppard AFB, TX	GNC/ GNKC-135A

US Central Command (US CENTCOM)

det	HQ CENTCOM	Robins AFB, GA	EC-135Y

Air Mobility Command (AMC)

89th AW	1st AS	Andrews AFB, MD	C-135B
	det 1	Hickam AFB, HI	C-135C
608th AG	58th AS	Ramstein AB, Germany	C-135B
nil	55th WRS	McClellan AFB, CA	WC-135B
2nd Wg	71st ARS	Barksdale AFB, LA	KC-135A/Q
5th Wg	906th ARS	Minot AFB, ND	KC-135A
7th Wg	7th ARS	Carswell AFB, TX	KC-135A
9th Wg	349th ARS	Beale AFB, CA	KC-135Q
	350th ARS	Beale AFB, CA	KC-135Q
19th Wg	99th ARS	Robins AFB, GA	KC-135, EC-135Y
	912th ARS	Robins AFB, GA	KC-135R
28th Wg	28th ARS	Ellsworth AFB, SD	KC-135R
	4th ACCS	Ellsworth AFB, SD	EC-135A/C/G/L
42nd Wg	42nd ARS	Loring AFB, ME	KC-135R
	407th ARS	Loring AFB, ME	KC-135R

92nd Wg	43rd ARS	Fairchild AFB, WA	KC-135R
	92nd ARS	Fairchild AFB, WA	KC-135R
93rd Wg	93rd ARS	Castle AFB, CA	KC-135A/R
	924th ARS	Castle AFB, CA	KC-135A/R
96th Wg	917th ARS	Dyess AFB, TX	KC-135A
97th Wg	97th ARS	Eaker AFB, AR	KC-135A
301st Wg	91st ARS	Malmstrom AFB, MT	KC-135R
305th Wg	70th ARS	Grissom AFB, IN	KC-135R, EC-135G/L
	305th ARS	Grissom AFB, IN	KC-135R
319th Wg	905th ARS	Grand Forks AFB, ND	KC-135R
340th Wg	11th ARS	Altus AFB, OK	KC-135R
	306th ARS	Altus AFB, OK	KC-135R
376th Wg	909th ARS	Kadena AB, Okinawa	KC-135A
379th Wg	920th ARS	Wurtsmith AFB, MI	KC-135A
380th Wg	310th ARS	Plattsburgh AFB, NY	KC-135A/Q
	380th ARS	Plattsburgh AFB, NY	KC-135A/Q
384th Wg	384th ARS	McConnell AFB, KS	KC-135R
410th Wg	46th ARS	K. I. Sawyer AFB, MI	KC-135A
	307th ARS	K. I. Sawyer AFB, MI	KC-135A
416th Wg	41st ARS	Griffiss AFB, NY	KC-135R

Air Combat Command (ACC)

28th AD	8th TDCS	Tinker AFB, OK	C-135E, EC-135K
55th Wg	2nd ACCS	Offutt AFB, NE	EC-135C
	24th SRS	Offutt AFB, NE	RC-135S/X, TC-135S
	38th SRS	Offutt AFB, NE	C-135A, NKC-135A
	343rd SRS	Offutt AFB, NE	KC-135E, RC-135U/V/W, TC-135W

Pacific Air Forces (PACAF)

15th ABW	9th ACCS	Hickam AFB, HI	EC-135J
18th Wg	906th ARS	Kadena AB, Okinawa	KC-135R

United States Air Forces in Europe (USAFE)

100th ARW	?	RAF Mildenhall, UK	KC-135R

Air National Guard (ANG)

101st ARW	132nd ARS	Bangor ANGB, ME	KC-135E
126th ARW	108th ARS	Chicago-O'Hare IAP, IL	KC-135E
141st ARW	116th ARS	Fairchild AFB, WA	KC-135E
171st ARW	147th ARS	Gtr Pittsburgh IAP, PA	KC-135E
128th ARG	126th ARS	Gen Mitchell Fd, Milwaukee, WI	KC-135E
134th ARG	151st ARS	McGhee Tyson Apt, Knoxville, TN	KC-135E
151st ARG	191st ARS	Salt Lake City IAP, UT	KC-135E
157th ARG	133rd ARS	Pease AFB, NH	KC-135E
160th ARG	145th ARS	Rickenbacker ANGB, OH	KC-135E
161st ARG	197th ARS	Sky Harbor IAP, Phoenix, AZ	KC-135E
168th ARS	168th ARS	Eielson AFB, AK	KC-135D/E
170th ARG	150th ARS	McGuire AFB, NJ	KC-135E
190th ARG	117th ARS	Forbes Fd, KS	KC-135E

Air Force Reserve (AFRes)

434th ARW	72nd ARS	Grissom AFB, IN	KC-135E
452nd ARW	336th ARS	March AFB, CA	KC-135E
940th ARG	314th ARS	Mather AFB, CA	KC-135E

Boeing
C-137/C-18

Boeing's Model 707 was the standard long-range airliner during the 1960s and early 1970s, sales of civil models reaching 916 aircraft. Like the KC-135 tanker, the Model 707 was derived from the 367-80 prototype, but differed in fuselage diameter from both the other aircraft, and is considered to be a different aircraft from the tanker.

USAF operation of the Model 707 began on 3 May 1959 when the first of three 707-153s was delivered (military designation **VC-137A**). These were powered by J57 turbojets, and were fitted with a 22-passenger VIP interior and extra communications equipment. The initial operator was the 1298th Air Transport Squadron, 1254th Air Transport Wing. The aircraft were re-engined with TF33 turbofans to become **VC-137B**s (707-153B), and remain in service with the 89th Airlift Wing on general VIP transport duties.

On 9 October 1962 the USAF received **VC-137C** 62-6000, outfitted specially for Presidential transport duties. The aircraft had the company designation 707-353B, and it featured the longer fuselage of the Intercontinental version. On 9 August 1972 VC-137C 72-7000 was received, this being a newer 707-353B which took over the 'Air Force One' duties. The original aircraft kept the Presidential scheme, and was retained as a second aircraft to carry the Presidential staff.

The 'V' prefix was dropped from the designation, and in 1985 two further 707-300s were taken on charge as C-137Cs to bolster the 89th Airlift Wing VIP fleet. Both original C-137Cs reverted to general duties when the two VC-25A (Model 747) aircraft were received to take over Presidential transport duties.

During late 1991 US SOUTHCOM received an EC-137E. E-Systems Inc. modified the aircraft with a number of communications antennas above the fuselage.

In 1981 the USAF acquired eight ex-American Airlines 707-323s for use by the 4950th Test Wing under the **C-18** designation. Four were modified as **EC-18B** Advanced Range Instrumentation Aircraft, with an equipment fit similar to that of the EC-135E aircraft already in service. These feature a bulbous nose with steerable tracking/telemetry receiving antenna, other receivers and provision for a mission crew of 16 to 24. A sonobuoy missile impact location system is under development for the aircraft. The first conversion flew in February 1985, and entered service the following January.

Two more C-18s were modified to **EC-18D** standard, these featuring APG-63 radar (as fitted to early F-15 models), weather radar and telemetry receivers for use as Cruise Missile Mission Control Aircraft (CMMCA). In conjunction with the EC-135Es, EC-18Bs and special Navy P-3 Orion variants, these provide airborne tracking and receiving stations for a wide variety of US missile tests.

Of the remaining two 707s procured in this batch, one has been broken up, and one retains the C-18A designation for use as a general trials aircraft, transport or crew trainer.

Above: Used for many years as 'Air Force One' whenever the President was aboard, the second of two C-137Cs has recently been relegated to more general VIP transport duties following the receipt of a pair of Boeing VC-25As.

Above: The C-137 is a VIP-outfitted Boeing 707.

Below: Four of the eight ex-American Airlines Boeing 707-323s obtained in 1981 are being used as advanced range instrumentation EC-18Bs.

MISSION PROFILE

Staff transport: seven C-137 aircraft are used by the 89th Airlift Wing for global VIP transport duties in connection with the government

Range instrumentation: the four EC-18B aircraft are used for range instrumentation duties, augmented by the remaining EC-135Es; aircraft have a large steerable antenna in a bulbous nose for the tracking of space vehicles and missiles, and the receipt of downlinked telemetry data, which is then relayed to ground- or sea-based stations; the two EC-18Ds have specialist equipment, including APG-63 radar, for the tracking of low-flying cruise missiles during tests

USAF VARIANTS AND SERIALS

Boeing C-137
VC-137A: Three Boeing 707-153s were ordered in 1958 for transportation of the President, Vice President and senior aides, with the designation VC-137A. The designation was changed to VC-137B when the three were re-engined with TF33 powerplants, although the V prefix was removed from all VIP types during the late 1970s.
58-6970 to 58-6972

C-137C: A new Air Force One was ordered in 1962 as a VC-137C based on the Boeing 707-353C, and was followed by another VC-137C in 1972, although both changed their designation to C-137C in the late 1970s. A further pair of C-137Cs was added to the fleet during the late 1980s, although these were not for Presidential use.
62-6000; 72-7000; 85-6973; 85-6974

EC-137E: one Boeing 707-355C was modified for the Commander US SOUTHCOM.
19417

Boeing C-18
C-18A: Eight former American Airlines Boeing 707-320 airliners were acquired in 1981, although only two retain this designation and one of these was broken up for spares at Greenville, Texas.
81-0897; 81-0898

EC-18B: Four were modified as Advanced Range Instrumentation Aircraft (ARIA) with the addition of a large steerable antenna in a huge bulbous nose and a probe antenna on each wingtip. A small black oval dome is positioned atop the forward fuselage.
81-0891; 81-0892; 81-0894; 81-0896

EC-18D: Two C-18As are being converted as Cruise Missile Mission Control Aircraft with the fitment of an AN/APG-63 surveillance radar and a telemetry receiver.
81-0893; 81-0895

SPECIFICATION

Boeing C-137C
Wing: span 145 ft 9 in (44.42 m); area 3,010.0 sq ft (279.63 m²)
Fuselage and tail: length 152 ft 11 in (46.61 m); height 42 ft 5 in (12.93 m); tailplane span 42 ft 5 in (13.95 m); wheel base 59 ft 0 in (17.98 m)
Powerplant: four Pratt & Whitney TF33 (JT3D-3) each rated at 18,000 lb (80.07 kN) dry thrust
Weight: maximum take-off 327,000 lb (148325 kg)
Fuel and load: internal fuel 23,855 US gal (90299 liters); maximum payload 51,615 lb (23413 kg)
Speed: maximum level speed at high altitude 627 mph (1010 km/h); maximum cruising speed at 25,000 ft (7620 m) 600 mph (966 km/h); economical cruising speed at optimum altitude 550 mph (886 km/h)
Range: maximum range 7,610 miles (12247 km)
Performance: maximum rate of climb at sea level 3,550 ft (1082 m) per minute; service ceiling 42,000 ft (12800 m); take-off distance 10,350 ft (3155 m) to 35 ft (10.7 m); landing distance 5,930 ft (1807 m) from 50 ft (15 m)

Boeing EC-18B
Wing: span 145 ft 9 in (44.42 m); area 3,050.0 sq ft (283.35 m²)
Fuselage and tail: length 152 ft 11 in (46.61 m); height 42 ft 5 in (12.93 m); tailplane span 42 ft 5 in (13.95 m); wheel base 59 ft 0 in (17.98 m)
Powerplant: four Pratt & Whitney TF33 (JT3D-3) each rated at 18,000 lb (80.07 kN) dry thrust
Weight: maximum take-off 327,000 lb (148325 kg)
Fuel and load: internal fuel 23,855 US gal (90299 liters)
Speed: maximum level speed at high altitude 627 mph (1010 km/h); maximum cruising speed at 25,000 ft (7620 m) 600 mph (966 km/h); economical cruising speed at optimum altitude 550 mph (886 km/h)
Range: maximum range 7,610 miles (12247 km)
Performance: maximum rate of climb at sea level 3,550 ft (1082 m) per minute; service ceiling 42,000 ft (12800 m); take-off distance 10,350 ft (3155 m) to 35 ft (10.7 m); landing distance 5,930 ft (1807 m) from 50 ft (15 m)

USAF OPERATORS

Air Mobility Command (AMC)

89th AW	1st AS	Andrews AFB, MD	C-137B/C

Air Force Materiel Command (AFMC)

4950th TW	unknown	Wright-Patterson AFB, OH	C-18A, EC-18B/D

Air Force Southern Command (AF South Com)

det	HQ SOUTHCOM	Robins AFB, GA	EC-137E

Lockheed
C-141 StarLifter

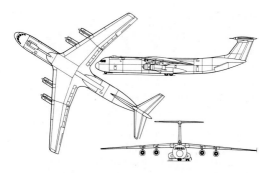

In March 1961, Lockheed's Model 300 design won an Air Force competition for a new transport, essentially a jet-powered version of the C-130 Hercules which retained the latter's body cross-section of 10 ft × 9 ft (3.05 m × 2.74 m). First flown on 17 December 1963, the **C-141A** had its wing swept back at just 23° (quarter chord), which permitted good low-speed operating characteristics in the airfield pattern. The C-141A is powered by four 21,000-lb (93.41-kN) thrust Pratt & Whitney TF33-PW-7 turbofan engines.

The C-141 has an all-weather landing system, pressurized cabin, and crew station. Since rollers in the cargo compartment floor allow quick and easy cargo pallet loading, the C-141 can be quickly modified to perform about 30 different missions. When palletized cargo is not being carried, the rollers can be turned over to leave a smooth, flat surface for loading vehicles.

The first operational C-141A, delivered to Tinker AFB, Oklahoma, in October 1964, began squadron operations in April 1965. The C-141A StarLifter became a familiar sight at airbases in Southeast Asia, hauling men and equipment for the Vietnam War effort. Some C-141As (and later **C-141B**s) were modified to carry the LGM-30 Minuteman intercontinental ballistic missile in its special container, up to a total weight of 92,000 lb (41731 kg). Otherwise, normal payload for the A model was usually listed as 70,847 lb (32136 kg), a fully loaded aircraft weighing 316,600 lb (143610 kg).

The four **NC-141A**s are operated by the 4950th Test Wing, Wright-Patterson AFB, Ohio, as test aircraft, one of them as an Advanced Radar Test Bed (ARTB) airborne laboratories to test sensors in a simulated ECM (electronic countermeasures) environment.

Early on, MAC's hard-working loadmasters saw the obvious, even if designers had missed it – the C-141A could carry more weight than its internal dimensions permitted. The idea of 'stretching' the StarLifter took hold.

In the 1970s, Lockheed won an ambitious contract to overhaul MAC's entire C-141 fleet by lengthening the craft and adding an inflight-refueling receptacle. Under this program, all existing airframes – with the exception of the four C-141A test ships operated by Air Force Systems Command – were rebuilt to C-141B standard. A little-known fact is that the first C-141B (66-0186, personal aircraft of the Commander-in-Chief of MAC/US Transportation Command) was lengthened using a different process than the 269 C-141Bs which followed, producing a 'one of a kind' StarLifter which has doors and windows in different locations

than all the others. The 'stretch' increased cargo capacity by some 30 per cent.

The first production C-141B was delivered in December 1979 and the 'rebuild' program was completed on 30 June 1982. One way to measure the 'stretching' program is to see it as providing MAC with the equivalent of 90 additional airplanes.

The C-141B can carry a variety of palletized loads including most types of vehicles, with the exception of main battle tanks. Up to 166 palletized airline-style seats can be installed. When canvas, side-facing seats are used instead, 205 passengers or 168 fully-equipped paratroopers can be carried. For medical evacuation, the C-141B can carry 103 litter patients or 113 ambulatory patients, or a combination of the two.

C-141Bs have played an essential role in all combat and combat support operations carried out during their service. In Operation Nickel Grass, the emergency airlift of arms and equipment to Israel during the October War (1973), C-141Bs handled a major portion of the 136.6 million ton-miles flown. During Operation Urgent Fury in Grenada (October 1983) and

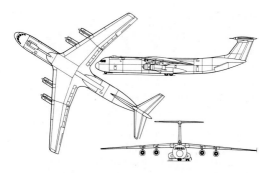

Above: An inflight-refueling receptacle and a fuselage 'stretch' were the main features of the reworked C-141B StarLifter.

Operation Just Cause in Panama (December 1989), StarLifters dropped paratroopers in combat, including the 2,000-man drop on Omar Torrijos Airport near Panama City on 20 December 1989, which was the largest airborne assault since World War II. More importantly, together with the C-5A/B Galaxy (and soon the C-17A), StarLifters have served

Below: The familiar but unphotogenic 'lizard' camouflage of the past decade is at last giving way to a much more attractive light gray color scheme, which is modeled here by a C-141B from the 60th Airlift Wing at Travis AFB.

Right: Remanufacturing of MAC's fleet of 270 StarLifters into C-141B configuration greatly enhanced productivity and provided the command with the equivalent of an extra 90 aircraft for a relatively modest cost.

Cabin
The central fuselage of the C-141B forms a giant compartment for cargo carriage, or for various other uses. Seating can be admitted for a secondary trooping role, while large numbers of stretchers can be carried in the aeromedical evacuation role.

Fuel
The StarLifter's fuel is carried in integral tanks within the wing structure, between the main spars. Total capacity is 23,592 US gal (89305 liters), which gives a maximum payload range of 2,935 miles (4725 km).

as a vital tool of US policy for a variety of duties, including returning prisoners of war from Vietnam (1973) and hostages from Tehran (1981). Since 1974, StarLifters staging from Christchurch, New Zealand, have maintained

Undercarriage
The eight-wheel main undercarriage is housed in fairings on either side of the lower fuselage, leaving the cabin unobstructed. The wide footprint of the tires allows the C-141 to operate from badly-prepared strips, although it does not have full rough-field capability.

Refueling receptacle
At the same time as the C-141B conversion program was stretching the StarLifter's fuselage, a refueling receptacle was added in a characteristic humped fairing above the flight deck. This gives the StarLifter true global airlift capability.

a perfect safety record in hauling people, equipment and supplies for Operation Deep Freeze, the resupply of scientific research teams on the Antarctic shelf. In December 1984, as part of Ethiopian famine relief efforts, two C-141Bs carried tents, water tanks, blankets and 64,000 lb (29030 kg) of foodstuffs to Sudan, where famine victims had taken refuge. When earthquakes caused catastrophic loss of life in Soviet Armenia in 1987, MAC's larger C-5 Galaxy could not land at airfields near the disaster but C-141Bs were able to 'shuttle' in from the West, bringing humani-

Doors
The fuselage has entry doors front and rear, with several emergency escape hatches in the ceiling of the cabin/hold. The rear doors are used rather than the rear ramp for paratroop dropping.

Lockheed C-141B StarLifter

Six wings of Air Mobility Command fly the stretched C-141B on general airlift duties. The fleet is vital to the USAF's requirement to supply US forces overseas, and to provide a means of rapidly deploying forces to trouble spots at a moment's notice. Indeed, the C-141 is the main vehicle used by 82nd Airborne Division troops for long-range paradrop insertions.

Rear ramp
A major feature of the C-141 is the rear door assembly, which features two large clamshell doors and a rear ramp. The ramp allows bulky material to be loaded and unloaded with ease, and also allows the air-dropping of large items, which are extracted using a drogue chute.

tarian supplies. The C-141B-equipped 63rd MAW from Norton AFB, CA, was the winner in the MAC Airlift Rodeo exercise held at Pope AFB, NC, in March 1990.

The moment of glory for the MAC strategic airlift fleet's C-141B and C-5A/B aircraft was Operation Desert Shield (August 1990-January 1991), the abrupt movement of unprecedented numbers of people and tonnages of equipment to Saudi Arabia and other Middle East locations. Strategic airlifters (C-141Bs and C-5s, plus C-130E/Hs and KC-10As when self-deploying) flew 20,500 missions, carried 534,000 passengers, and hauled 542,000 tons (491.7 million kg) of cargo. In all, 4.65 billion ton-miles were moved, as compared with 697.5 million during the 65-week Berlin Airlift or 136.6 million during Nickel Grass. MAC C-141B crews, including Air National Guardsmen and Reservists, worked under extraordinarily difficult conditions making the 10-hour haul from Stateside bases to staging points in Europe, followed by another 10-hour trip to the Persian Gulf.

The US Air Force planned to replace many of its C-141Bs with the C-17, but the C-17 program suffered repeated delays in the 1980s. These delays, coupled with new requirements which had C-141Bs operating at lower altitudes than planned (a number of the aircraft are dedicated to special operations missions) have resulted in the ageing of the C-141B fleet becoming a major concern in the 1990s. The C-141B was projected for a lifetime of 45,000 flight hours following its conversion. This figure may have to be reduced, since low-level flying for special operations missions and paradrops has produced wear and tear (wing cracks and other fatigue problems) at a far higher rate than an ordinary transport. Before the added strain of Operation Desert Shield, in June 1990, the 'high hour' C-141B with 38,958 flight hours was aircraft 63-8075, the 'Golden Bear', stationed at Travis AFB; the 'low hour' ship was 67-0166, at Altus AFB, with 14,184 hours.

The first C-141B unit scheduled to convert to the C-17 was the 17th AS/437th AW at Charleston AFB, no earlier than 1994. As the C-17 becomes operational, C-141Bs are scheduled to join Air National Guard units at Rickenbacker ANGB and Nashville airport. With the purchase of the C-17 reduced from 210 airframes to 120 in a 1990 decision, and in spite of the fatigue problem, the USAF had no plans in the early 1990s to retire any of its Star-Lifter fleet.

Above: A lizard-camouflaged C-141B StarLifter of the 63rd Airlift Wing touches down at Osan, South Korea, at the end of a trans-Pacific trip from Norton AFB, California.

MISSION PROFILE

Configuration options: the cargo compartment in the C-141B fuselage has an internal volume of 6,368 cu ft (180.3 m³) and floor provision for 13 standard cargo pallets; the C-141B can be configured for cargo, paratroopers, combat troops, hospital litter patients, or combinations of all of these, and can be employed for air drops of troops or equipment

Strategic airlift (personnel): to the extent possible, the USAF employs the C-5A/B for equipment and the C-141B for personnel; 166 passengers can be transported in palletized airline-style seats; 205 passengers or 168 fully-equipped paratroopers can be carried using canvas, side-facing seats

Strategic airlift (equipment): with a typical payload of 70,847 lb (32135 kg) and maximum payload of 90,880 lb (41220 kg), on a strategic airlift mission the C-141B would employ air refueling but could have a range up to 6,390 miles (10280 km) unrefueled with a two-hour fuel reserve; in addition to cargoes ranging from medical supplies to fuel, the C-141B can carry such heavy equipment items as a single M551 Sheridan tank, five HMMWV tactical vehicles or an AH-1 Cobra helicopter (although usual practice is to transport such items on the C-5A/B); one C-141B squadron (6th AS/438th AW, McGuire AFB, NJ) transports all nuclear weapons for the USAF

Airborne operations: the C-141B carries 168 paratroopers to a radius of up to 3,660 miles (3890 km) or further with air refueling; a combat air drop is made with an approach to the DZ (drop zone) at medium altitude of 2,000 ft (609 m); some C-141B crews and aircraft are dedicated to special operations airdrop insertions with run-in to DZ (drop zone) at 300 ft (91 m) altitude and actual drop at 500 ft (152 m)

Medical evacuation: on a medevac/ambulance mission, the C-141B would have a range up to 6,500 miles (10460 km) unrefueled with a two-hour fuel reserve; carry 103 litter patients, 113 ambulatory patients, or a combination of the two

USAF VARIANTS AND SERIALS

C-141A: 284 C-141A StarLifters were ordered between 1961 and 1967, with four of the first five assigned to test purposes while the remainder were operated by MATS/MAC.
61-2775 to 61-2779; 63-8075 to 63-8090; 64-0609 to 64-0653; 65-0216 to 65-0281; 65-9397 to 65-9414; 66-0126 to 66-0209; 66-7944 to 66-7959; 67-0001 to 67-0031; 67-0164 to 67-0166

NC-141A: The four test aircraft have frequently been referred to as NC-141As, although this is believed to be an unofficial title.
61-2775 to 61-2777; 61-2779

C-141B: All C-141As were converted to C-141B standard apart from the four NC-141As, and 63-8077, 64-0641, 65-0274, 65-0281, 65-94078, 66-0127, 67-0006, 67-0008 and 67-0030 which were all lost in accidents.

Above: Although fatigue is beginning to cause concern, there are no plans to withdraw any of the C-141Bs that continue to give good service with six AMC airlift wings.

SPECIFICATION

Lockheed C-141B
Wing: span 159 ft 11 in (48.74 m); area 3,228.0 sq ft (299.88 m²)
Fuselage and tail: length 168 ft 3.5 in (51.29 m); height 39 ft 3 in (11.96 m); wheel base 66 ft 4 in (20.22 m)
Powerplant: four Pratt & Whitney TF33-P-7 rated at 21,000 lb (93.41 kN) dry thrust
Weights: operating empty 148,120 lb (67186 kg); maximum take-off 343,000 lb (155580 kg)
Fuel and load: internal fuel 23,592 US gal (89305 liters); maximum payload 90,880 lb (41222 kg) at 2.25g and 70,605 lb (32026 kg) at 2.5g
Speed: maximum cruising speed at high altitude 566 mph (910 km/h); long-range cruising speed at high altitude 495 mph (796 km/h)
Range: ferry 6,390 miles (10280 km); with maximum payload 2,935 miles (4725 km)
Performance: maximum rate of climb at sea level 2,920 ft (890 m) per minute; service ceiling 41,600 ft (12680 m); take-off distance 5,800 ft (1768 m) to 50 ft (15 m); landing distance 3,700 ft (1128 m) from 50 ft (15 m) at normal landing weight

USAF OPERATORS

Air Force Materiel Command (AFMC)

4950th TW	4951st TS	Wright-Patterson AFB, OH	NC-141A

Air Mobility Command (AMC)

60th AW	7th AS	Travis AFB, CA	C-141B
	86th AS	Travis AFB, CA	C-141B
62nd AW	4th AS	McChord AFB, WA	C-141B
	8th AS	McChord AFB, WA	C-141B
	36th AS	McChord AFB, WA	C-141B
63rd AW	14th AS	Norton AFB, CA	C-141B
	15th AS	Norton AFB, CA	C-141B
	53rd AS	Norton AFB, CA	C-141B
437th AW	17th AS	Charleston AFB, SC	C-141B
	20th AS	Charleston AFB, SC	C-141B
	41st AS	Charleston AFB, SC	C-141B
	76th AS	Charleston AFB, SC	C-141B
438th AW	6th AS	McGuire AFB, NJ	C-141B
	18th AS	McGuire AFB, NJ	C-141B
	30th AS	McGuire AFB, NJ	C-141B
443rd AW	57th AS	Altus AFB, OK	C-141B

Air National Guard (ANG)

172nd AG	183rd AS	Allen C. Thompson Fd, Jackson, MS	C-141B

Air Force Reserve (AFRes)

459th AW	756th AS	Andrews AFB, MD	C-141B

Lockheed
C-5 Galaxy

The **C-5A/B Galaxy** is the largest USAF aircraft and the heavyweight of US strategic airlift – operated by active, Reserve and Air National Guard units for the Air Mobility Command (AMC) in June 1992.

Some 126 Galaxy transports are in inventory, divided between 76 surviving C-5As (of 81) manufactured over 1966-70 and all 50 C-5Bs (known in the design stage as **C-5N**s) built in a second batch between 1984 and 1986.

The C-5A/B Galaxy is a conventional high-wing, T-tailed transport resembling a fattened C-141B StarLifter with underslung engine nacelles and main undercarriage retracting into pods on the sides of the center fuselage. In fact, the Galaxy is twice the size of a StarLifter, can carry more cargo in terms of both bulk and weight, and flies faster, hastening an overseas deployment.

Four 43,000-lb (191.27-kN) thrust General Electric TF39-GE-1C turbofan engines hang under the Galaxy's 222-ft 8½-in (67.88-m) wings, each engine large enough for a man or woman to stand inside their intakes. Each engine has the power of a dozen steam locomotives.

The value of the C-5A/B for rapid deployment of large or heavy items of equipment has been demonstrated repeatedly. Key to the Galaxy's mission is its cavernous interior and 'roll on/roll off' capability provided by access to the vast cargo bay at both front and rear. Uniquely, the Galaxy has an upward-lifting visor nose which can be raised above the cockpit for loading/unloading and permits the aircraft to be taxied with the door open. Standard clamshell doors accommodate loading/unloading at the rear of the aircraft.

The Galaxy's primary mission is to carry equipment and vehicles, although it can be configured for up to 363 passengers (73 on upper rear deck, 290 in main compartment). The lower deck, not routinely used for passengers – but able to be so configured with palletized seat rows to accommodate 290 – is 19 ft (5.79 m) wide and 121 ft 1½ in (36.88 m) long. Height of this vast interior ranges from 9 ft 6 in (2.90 m) beneath the wing box to 13 ft 6 in (4.11 m) in the aft section. This section can handle an M1 Abrams main battle tank, four M551 Sheridan light tanks, or a CH-47 Chinook medium transport helicopter. The upper deck houses the flight crew of five (pilot, co-pilot, flight engineer, two loadmasters), a 15-man crew relief compartment with bunks, and, in a separate compartment behind the wing carry-through section, rearward-facing seats for 73 passengers. With unrefueled range of 6,469 miles (10411 km), the Galaxy provides the most ton-miles at the fastest speed of any American airlifter.

Although not usually assigned airdrop duties, the C-5A/B Galaxy can be employed to drop airborne troopers and their equipment. At Pope AFB, North Carolina, on 7 June 1989, a C-5B dropped four M551 Sheridan tanks (each lowered to earth by eight G-11 parachutes) and 73 troopers for a world record of 190,346 lb (86341 kg).

The C-5 has its origins in a 1963 USAF CX-HLS (Cargo Experimental–Heavy Logistics System) requirement aimed at permitting global deployment of heavy items of military hardware, including vehicles and armor. MAC – known prior to 1 January 1966 as the Military Air Transport Service (MATS) – wanted a capability to carry 250,000 lb (113400 kg) over 3,000 miles (4828 km) without air-to-air refueling.

After a 30 June 1968 maiden flight, the first operational C-5A reached MAC on 17 December 1969 and the last was delivered in May 1973. Early in the aircraft's career, a problem with wing cracks delayed IOC (initial operating capability) until a redesign of ailerons solved the problem. The C-5A also foundered, initially, on cost overruns exposed by Washington analyst Ernest Fitzgerald. Critics also recall the crash on 4 April 1975 of a C-5A Galaxy (68-0218) evacuating orphans from Saigon in Operation Baby Lift, which killed 206 (of 382 aboard) and would have taken more lives but for the airmanship of pilot Captain Dennis Traylor. Early controversy notwithstanding, since the C-5A fleet was upgraded with strengthened wings and the C-5B came on line (an inflight-refueling receptacle now being standard), the aircraft has had a positive image.

Delivery of the C-5B version began in January 1985, the latter dispensing with the C-5A's complex crosswind main landing gear (though both versions have a 28-wheel main undercarriage) and introducing improved AFCS (automated flight control system) and MADAR II (malfunction detection and analysis and recording system).

RTU (replacement training unit) for the C-5A/B is the 443rd Airlift Wing at Altus AFB, Oklahoma. The aircraft serves with four active, two Reserve, and one Air National Guard squadrons.

Known to crews as 'FRED', for Fantastic Ridiculous Economic Disaster, the C-5 has served admirably – and economically – in airlifts supporting US operations in Vietnam, Israel during the October War of 1973, and the Desert Shield/Storm effort of 1990-91.

During Operation Desert Shield, C-5s flew 42 per cent of cargo and 18.6 per cent of passenger missions, in an effort which exceeded the tonnage of the 65-week Berlin Airlift in 17 days and totalled 15,800 missions with

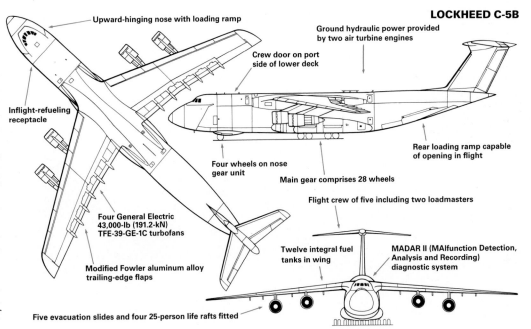

LOCKHEED C-5B

Upward-hinging nose with loading ramp

Ground hydraulic power provided by two air turbine engines

Crew door on port side of lower deck

Inflight-refueling receptacle

Four wheels on nose gear unit

Main gear comprises 28 wheels

Rear loading ramp capable of opening in flight

Flight crew of five including two loadmasters

Four General Electric 43,000-lb (191.2-kN) TFE-39-GE-1C turbofans

Twelve integral fuel tanks in wing

MADAR II (MAlfunction Detection, Analysis and Recording) diagnostic system

Modified Fowler aluminum alloy trailing-edge flaps

Five evacuation slides and four 25-person life rafts fitted

USAF Aircraft

498,900 passengers. One C-5A Galaxy (68-0228) of the 60th MAW (Travis) crewed by Reservists of the 433rd MAW (Kelly) crashed at Ramstein, Germany, 29 August 1990, the only transport lost in the airlift – and only the fifth Galaxy loss ever. Lacking the fatigue problem of its C-141B stablemate, the Galaxy has no scheduled replacement and will be in service at least to 2010.

MISSION PROFILE

Configuration options: the C-5A/B can be configured to carry 290 personnel but normally carries cargo in its main (lower) cargo deck with a volume of 34,795 cu ft (985.29 m³); in addition, the C-5A/B always seats 73 personnel in rearward-facing airline-style seats in the upper aft deck which has a volume of 6,020 cu ft (170.46 m³) located above the main cargo compartment

Strategic airlift (equipment): to the extent possible, the USAF employs the C-5A/B for equipment and the C-141B for personnel; with a maximum payload of 261,000 lb (118387 kg), typically reduced, the C-5A/B would employ air refueling but could have a range up to 3,434 miles (5526 km) with five per cent fuel reserve plus 30-minute loiter for a strategic (transoceanic) airlift mission; typical loads include two M1A1 Abrams main battle tanks, one M1A1 Abrams and two M2 Bradley fighting vehicles, four M551 Sheridan light tanks plus one HMMWV tactical vehicle, 16 ¾-ton trucks, 10 LAV-25s (light armored vehicles), or a CH-47 Chinook medium transport helicopter

Strategic airlift (personnel): for strategic airlift carrying personnel and using palletized seats in its cargo compartment, the C-5A/B would employ air refueling but could have a range of about 3,000 miles (4828 km) unrefueled with five per cent fuel reserve plus 30-minute loiter to carry 363 personnel to an overseas destination

Airborne operations: the C-5A/B is not usually employed for airborne operations but some crews are qualified and the aircraft can be so employed; on a short-range mission, the C-5A/B can match its 1989 feat of dropping four M551 Sheridan tanks and 73 troopers for a total of 190,346 lb (86341 kg); in normal airborne operations, the C-5A/B can deploy to a range of about 3,000 miles (4828 km) unrefueled with five per cent fuel reserve plus 30-minute loiter to drop one M551 Sheridan or up to 338 paratroopers

Above: Strategic airlift is the raison d'être of the C-5 Galaxy, which is equally at ease in moving either men or materiel across prodigious distances. Its ability to receive fuel in flight gives it true global reach and also eliminates dependence upon intermediate staging posts, in the process boosting mobility.

USAF VARIANTS AND SERIALS

C-5A: Eighty-one C-5A models were obtained between 1966 and 1970 with just five lost to accidents. Thirty remain in front-line service while the remainder are operated by the Reserves.
66-8303 to 66-8307; 67-0167 to 67-0174; 68-0211 to 68-0228; 69-0001 to 69-0027; 70-0445 to 70-0467

C-5B: The anticipated shortfall in airlift capability saw the purchase of 50 C-5Bs between 1983 and 1987. The only external difference between the C-5B and the earlier version is a small vertical blade aerial atop the fuselage aft of the wingroot, which is swept back on the C-5A.
83-1285; 84-0059 to 84-0062; 85-0001 to 85-0010; 86-0011 to 86-0026; 87-0027 to 87-0045

SPECIFICATION

Lockheed C-5B
Wing: span 222 ft 8.5 in (67.88 m); aspect ratio 7.75; area 6,200.0 sq ft (576.0 m²)
Fuselage and tail: length 247 ft 10 in (75.54 m); height 65 ft 1.5 in (19.85 m); tailplane span 68 ft 8.5 in (20.94 m); wheel base 72 ft 11 in (22.22 m)

Powerplant: four General Electric TF39-GE-1C rated at 43,000 lb (191.27 kN) dry thrust
Weights: operating empty 374,000 lb (169643 kg); maximum take-off 837,000 lb (379657 kg)
Fuel and load: internal fuel 332,500 lb (150815 kg); maximum payload 261,000 lb (118387 kg)
Speed: never-exceed Mach 0.85; maximum level speed at 25,000 ft (7620 m) 571 mph (919 km/h); maximum cruising speed at 25,000 ft (7620 m) between 552 and 564 mph (888 and 908 km/h)
Range: with maximum fuel 6,469 miles (10411 km); with maximum payload 3,434 miles (5526 km)
Peformance: maximum rate of climb at sea level 1,725 ft (525 m) per minute; service ceiling 35,750 ft (10895 m) at a weight of 615,000 lb (278960 kg); take-off distance 9,800 ft (2987 m) to 50 ft (15 m); landing distance 3,820 ft (1164 m) from 50 ft (15 m) at maximum weight

USAF OPERATORS

Air Mobility Command (AMC)

60th AW	22nd AS	Travis AFB, CA	C-5A/B
	75th AS	Travis AFB, CA	C-5A/B
436th AW	3rd AS	Dover AFB, DE	C-5A/B
	9th AS	Dover AFB, DE	C-5A/B

Air National Guard (ANG)

105th AG	137th AS	Stewart ANGB, NY	C-5A

Air Force Reserve (AFRes)

433rd AW	68th AS	Kelly AFB, TX	C-5A
439th AW	337th AS	Westover AFB, MA	C-5A

One of an increasing number of aircraft that have been reinstated in production, 50 examples of the C-5B version were built by Lockheed and delivered to MAC in the mid-1980s. Apart from a different antenna behind the wing, they cannot be distinguished from the older C-5A model.

McDonnell Douglas
C-9 Nightingale

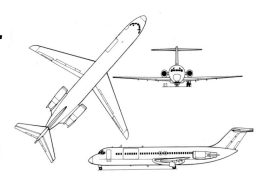

The **C-9A Nightingale** is the USAF's off-the-shelf version of the Douglas DC-9-32F airliner used for aeromedical evacuation duties. The **C-9C** version, originally designated **VC-9C**, is for special missions or VIP transport. The Military Airlift Command, which became Air Mobility Command in June 1992, has 20 C-9As (of 21 delivered) and all three C-9C aircraft purchased. **C-9B** and **C-9K** versions have gone, respectively, to the US Navy and to Kuwait.

The commercial DC-9 short/medium-range airliner, first flown on 25 February 1965, offered a pragmatic design with proven performance to fit the USAF's need for intra-theater or tactical aeromedical missions. The first example of the DC-9-30, from which the military transport was developed, flew on 1 August 1966. A low-wing transport with wings and empennage swept at 24° and engines mounted astride the rear fuselage, the C-9A offers the capability of transporting a load of patients over some 1,430 miles (2300 km) at economical operating and maintenance costs.

Both USAF C-9 versions are powered by two 14,500-lb (64.5-kN) thrust Pratt & Whitney JT8D-9 turbofan engines. The C-9A, uniquely identified as a tactical hospital aircraft by a red cross on its tail, has three entrances: two with special hydraulic stairways and the third, with a cargo door measuring 6 ft 9 in × 11 ft 4 in (2.06 × 3.4 m), on the left-hand side with a hydraulic elevator for loading stretcher patients. These make loading of the aircraft independent of ground facilities.

Flight crew consists of two pilots with crew chief or loadmaster flying on some missions. On aeromedical missions, the C-9A Nightingale can accommodate 40 litter patients or 40 seated ambulatory patients, plus two nurses and three aeromedical technicians.

The USAF's first C-9A (67-22583) was rolled out on 17 June 1968, flew on 8 August 1968, and was delivered two days later. The 21st and last machine was delivered in February 1973. Nightingales serve primarily on routine medical missions but have sometimes been given special tasks, including transporting released US hostages from Tehran to Wiesbaden, Germany, in January 1981.

C-9A Nightingales have been assigned to the 375th Aeromedical Airlift Wing at Scott AFB, Illinois; the 55th Aeromedical Airlift Squadron in Germany; and the 20th Aeromedical Airlift Squadron in the Philippines. One C-9A (71-0876), nominally assigned to the 55th AAS for hospital duties, is actually configured as a VIP transport for the Supreme Allied Commander at NATO Headquarters and is normally based at Chièvres, Belgium. One C-9A (67-22586) was lost in a mishap at Scott Field on 16 September 1971.

The special-configuration VC-9C (redesignated C-9C in 1977) was ordered in December 1973 and delivered beginning in 1975. C-9C VIP transports are among several types operated by the 89th Airlift Wing at Andrews AFB, Maryland.

MISSION PROFILE

Configuration options: the C-9A is configured for the aeromedical mission and has hydraulic stairways and elevator to load hospital litter patients; the C-9C (and one C-9A) are configured for the special air missions, or VIP transport role

Medical evacuation: carrying 30 to 40 litter patients, more than 40 ambulatory patients, or a combination of the two, together with up to five physicians, nurses or medical corpsmen, the C-9A can take off from an airfield runway of 6,800 ft (2073 m) or greater length, operate to a range of 1,725 miles (2776 km), and land on a runway of 4,920 ft (1500 m) or greater length

Special air missions (SAM) airlift: usually carrying one principal VIP plus staff, the C-9C is configured up front with a couch plus two first-class seats facing to the rear and one forward-facing first-class swivel seat for the VIP principal, plus 39 more first-class seats behind the principal for a total of 42 passengers, plus a crew of 11 (pilot, co-pilot, flight mechanic, four flight attendants and four security police); the C-9C can operate with a maximum take-off weight of 110,000 lb (49895 kg) to a range of 1,725 miles (2776 kg)

USAF VARIANTS AND SERIALS

C-9A: Twenty-one C-9As were purchased to perform aeromedical airlift, replacing the C-131A in the USA, Pacific and Europe. Apart from one of the Europe-based aircraft which is operated in the VIP role by the Supreme Allied Commander Europe (SACEUR) from Chièvres, Belgium, all sport a red cross on the fin. 67-22583 to 67-22586; 68-8932 to 68-8935; 68-10958 to 68-10961; 71-0874 to 71-0882

C-9C: Three C-9Cs were acquired in 1973 for VIP duties, joining a mixed fleet at Andrews AFB. These three aircraft are painted in a striking blue and white livery and are specially configured to transport high-ranking military personnel and government figures. 73-1681 to 73-1683

Below: A Yokota, Japan-based C-9A Nightingale of the 20th AAS awaits a fresh load of patients at Hong Kong's Kai Tak airport.

Above: Essentially based on the commercial DC-9 Series 32F, the C-9A Nightingale is primarily used for aeromedical evacuation tasks and operates with units in the USA, Far East and Europe.

SPECIFICATION

McDonnell Douglas C-9A

Wing: span 93 ft 5 in (28.47 m); aspect ratio 8.71; area 1,000.7 sq ft (92.97 m²)
Fuselage and tail: length 119 ft 3.5 in (36.37 m); height 27 ft 6 in (8.38 m); tailplane span 36 ft 10.25 in (11.23 m); wheel base 53 ft 2.5 in (16.22 m)
Powerplant: two Pratt & Whitney JT8D-9 each rated at 14,500 lb (64.5 kN) dry thrust
Weights: manufacturer's empty 57,190 lb (25940 kg); maximum take-off 121,000 lb (54885 kg)
Fuel and load: internal fuel 3,679 US gal (13925 liters); maximum payload 31,125 lb (14118 kg)
Speed: never-exceed 618 mph (995 km/h); maximum cruising speed at 25,000 ft (7620 m) 564 mph (907 km/h); long-range cruising speed between 30,000 and 35,000 ft (9145 and 10675 m) 510 mph (821 km/h)
Range: ferry range 2,280 miles (3669 km); range at long-range cruising speed at 30,000 ft (9145 m) 1,923 miles (3095 km); range with full accommodation 1,484 miles (2388 km)
Performance: maximum rate of climb at sea level 2,900 ft (885 m) per minute; service ceiling 6,800 ft (2073 m); take-off distance 7,400 ft (2255 m) to 35 ft (10.7 m); landing distance 4,720 ft (1440 m) from 50 ft (15 m)

USAF OPERATORS

Air Mobility Command (AMC)

89th AW	1st AS	Andrews AFB, MD	C-9C
374th AW	20th AAS	Yokota AB, Japan	C-9A
375th AW	11th AAS	Scott AFB, IL	C-9A
435th AW	55th AAS	Rhein Main AB, Germany	C-9A
	det	Chièvres AB, Belgium	C-9A

McDonnell Douglas

C-10 Extender

The **KC-10A Extender** tanker/transport, an off-the-shelf version of the DC-10-30CF airliner, was acquired to fill the USAF's need – identified during Operation Nickel Grass, the US airlift to Israel during the October War of 1973 – for a dual-role ATCA (Advanced Tanker/Cargo Aircraft). The US emphasis on rapid deployment of forces in the late 1970s coincided with development of this long-range transport able to haul people and equipment while also functioning as a tanker. In the 1990s, the KC-10 fleet will help the USAF field an expeditionary force to deploy rapidly from US bases to Third World trouble spots.

The KC-10 is a genuine strategic asset with its capability to carry a full payload of 169,409 lb (76843 kg) over a range of 4,370 miles (7033 km), and its facility to be refueled in flight. The value of this tanker/transport is demonstrated when a fighter deploys overseas, with the KC-10 carrying support equipment and personnel while also refueling the fighters *en route*.

For the tanker role, the lower section of the KC-10A fuselage is fitted with bladder fuel cells increasing maximum usable fuel to 54,455 US gal (206134 liters). A boom operator's station is located beneath the rear fuselage where, instead of assuming the prone position as on the KC-135, he or she sits in an aft-facing crew seat. A McDonnell Douglas AARB (Advanced Aerial Refueling Boom) is located on the centerline of the fuselage, with a refueling hose reel unit installed adjacently. This arrangement has permitted single-point refueling of USAF aircraft (with the boom) or US Navy/Marine aircraft (with the hose) on the same mission. Following the heavy demand on tanker assets demonstrated during Operation Desert Storm, the USAF in 1991 announced plans to equip its KC-10 fleet with refueling units on each wing to permit refueling of three aircraft at a time. Prior to the war with Iraq, the 60th and final KC-10 had been fitted with a Flight Refuelling Ltd Mk 32B hose drum pod beneath each wingtip to convert it into a three-point tanker, and underwent lengthy evaluations using this configuration.

For its equally important transport role, the KC-10 has an 8-ft 6-in × 11-ft 8-in (2.59-m × 3.56-m) upwards-hinged cargo door on the port side of the fuselage, able to handle most fighter unit support equipment. Powered rollers and winches are installed in the cargo compartment, which has reinforced main deck flooring for palletized loads. While it cannot be loaded/unloaded from ground level like C-130, C-141 and C-5 airlifters, the KC-10 can accommodate up to 25 463L pallets or mixed loads, which typically might include 75 people in airline-style seats and up to 17 cargo pallets. Total usable cargo space exceeds 12,000 cu ft (340 m³).

The KC-10 is powered by three 52,500-lb (233.53-kN) thrust General Electric CF6-50C2 turbofans. One of the engines is mounted at the base of the tail above the aft fuselage, the other two on pylons beneath the wings.

The USAF announced its choice of the KC-10A in preference to a possible Boeing 747 version on 19 December 1977. First flight of the KC-10A took place on 12 July 1980, and the first air refueling on 30 October 1980, with a C-5 as the receiver aircraft. The first KC-10A was delivered to the USAF on 17 March 1981. During a six-month operational assessment from May 1981, a KC-10A accompanied eight Air National Guard A-7D aircraft from Tulsa, Oklahoma, to RAF Wittering, England. In addition to furnishing 190,000 lb (86184 kg) of fuel to the A-7Ds while in flight, the KC-10 also carried support personnel and ground equipment, demonstrating its dual-role function on this single sortie.

Another memorable achievement occurred in September 1982 when seven KC-10As rendezvoused with 20 MAC C-141B StarLifters near Goose Bay, Labrador, and dispensed 65,000 lb (29484 kg) of fuel to each. The C-141Bs then flew non-stop across the Atlantic to West Germany where they airdropped paratroopers before returning to the US, where another fuel transfer was achieved off the East Coast some 14 hours after the initial contact. KC-10A Extenders were used similarly when 82nd Airborne Division paratroopers embarked from Fort Bragg, North Carolina, made the parachute assault on Panama's Tocumen Airport during Operation Just Cause in December 1989.

KC-10A Extenders supported the massive airlift to the Persian Gulf during Operation Desert Shield in 1990. During Operation Desert Storm (1991), 46 KC-10As were located in the combat zone and flew about 20 per cent of the 4,967 sorties which refueled aircraft heading into combat.

The KC-10A has been officially credited with the best safety record of any USAF aircraft. One aircraft (82-0190) was lost in a ramp fire at Barksdale AFB, Louisiana, on 17 September 1987.

In its first major change as the USAF shifted to its expeditionary concept in the 1990s, KC-10s were assigned to the 4th Wing at Seymour Johnson AFB, North Carolina, to serve directly with, and deploy with, the wing's F-15E Strike Eagles, to position a tactical force at a foreign airfield halfway around the world on very short notice.

Normal crew of the KC-10A is four – pilot, co-pilot, flight engineer and boom operator. INS (inertial navigation systems) make a navigator unnecessary. The KC-10A is not intended to support strategic bombers during a nuclear war and, unlike the KC-135, does not have thermal blast curtains or shielding against electromagnetic pulse. KC-10A aircraft have been based at Barksdale AFB, Louisiana; March AFB, California; and Seymour Johnson AFB, North Carolina. The 60th aircraft was delivered on 29 November 1988.

Below: Configured for dual tanker/transport tasks, a total of 60 KC-10A Extenders entered service with the USAF during the 1980s. All but one are still in use today. Here, a KC-10A furnishes fuel to an F-117A 'Stealth Fighter' from the 37th Wing over the western USA.

Left: Camouflage battle dress gives the KC-10A a decidedly sinister appearance when viewed from above but was appropriate during the Gulf War, when no fewer than 46 of the 59 Extenders on US charge were deployed to the war zone in support of coalition air power.

Above: Loading the KC-10A Extender is facilitated by a large freight door and by a roller-bed floor to the cabin.

Below: The undercarriage retraction cycle has just begun on this KC-10A from the 2nd Wing at Barksdale AFB, Louisiana. Crews for the KC-10A are also provided by AFRes units as part of the long-running 'associate' scheme.

McDONNELL DOUGLAS KC-10A

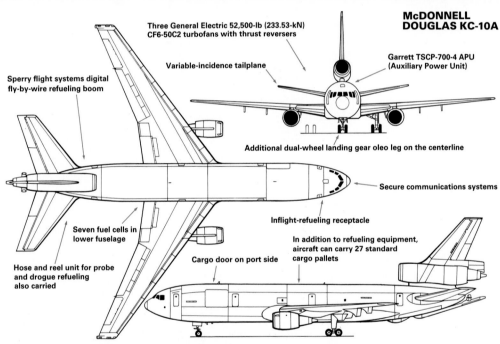

Three General Electric 52,500-lb (233.53-kN) CF6-50C2 turbofans with thrust reversers

Variable-incidence tailplane

Garrett TSCP-700-4 APU (Auxiliary Power Unit)

Sperry flight systems digital fly-by-wire refueling boom

Additional dual-wheel landing gear oleo leg on the centerline

Secure communications systems

Seven fuel cells in lower fuselage

Inflight-refueling receptacle

Hose and reel unit for probe and drogue refueling also carried

Cargo door on port side

In addition to refueling equipment, aircraft can carry 27 standard cargo pallets

MISSION PROFILE

Configuration options: the KC-10 is configured as a dual-role transport/tanker for rapid strategic deployment of personnel and equipment and to air refuel other aircraft during deployment; for transport, the KC-10 employs side loading through an 8-ft 6-in × 11-ft 8-in (2.59-m × 3.56-m) cargo door to accommodate most types of cargo and USAF 463L palletized containers or passenger seats; to air refuel other aircraft, the KC-10 is configured with seven bladder fuel cells in the lower fuselage beneath the cargo/passenger area, interconnected with the aircraft's own fuel system and creating total capacity of 238,236 lb (108062 kg) of fuel

Strategic airlift (rapid deployment, tanker/ transport): on a typical rapid deployment mission, a KC-10 would support and air refuel a four- to eight-ship flight of fighter aircraft, transport fighter maintenance and administrative personnel and equipment, and deploy overseas receiving air refueling *en route*; carrying up to a maximum of 25 pallets with access from both sides of the cargo compartment or 27 pallets with a single aisle on the starboard side (containing cargo or palletized airline-style seats with typically up to 24 seats and cargo in the remaining compartment space), the KC-10 can deploy with a full or partial fuel

load, receive air refueling, or operate unrefueled to a range of about 12875 km (8,000 miles)

Air refueling (tanker): when carrying out the air-refueling mission only, the KC-10 can deliver 200,000 lb (90720 kg) of fuel to one or more receiver aircraft 2,200 miles (3540 km) from its home base and return to base; as of late 1991, only one KC-10 was configured to refuel three aircraft at a time, all others being configured to employ both flying boom and probe- and drogue-systems for single-point refueling; the USAF was considering modifying the remaining fleet of 59 KC-10As to three-point refueling capability

USAF VARIANTS AND SERIALS

KC-10A: Sixty KC-10As were ordered between 1979 and 1987, with all operational apart from one lost in a ground accident. The sixtieth Extender built was fitted with detachable wingtip refueling pods enabling it to be a three-point tanker, although no change in designation was made.
79-0433 to 79-0434; 79-1710 to 79-1713; 79-1946 to 79-1951; 82-0190 to 82-0193; 83-0075 to 83-0082; 84-0185 to 84-0192; 85-0027 to 85-0034; 86-0027 to 86-0038; 87-0117 to 87-0124

SPECIFICATION

McDonnell Douglas KC-10A
Wing: span 155 ft 4 in (47.34 m); aspect ratio 6.8; area 3,861.0 sq ft (358.7 m²)
Fuselage and tail: length 181 ft 7 in (55.35 m); height 58 ft 1 in (17.70 m); tailplane span 71 ft 2 in (21.69 m); wheel base 72 ft 5 in (22.07 m)
Powerplant: three General Electric CF6-50C2 each rated at 52,500 lb (233.53 kN) dry thrust
Weights: operating empty 240,065 lb (108891 kg) as a tanker, and 244,630 lb (110962 kg) as a cargo transport; maximum take-off 590,000 lb (267620 kg)
Fuel and load: internal fuel 356,065 lb (161508 kg); maximum payload 169,409 lb (76843 kg) of cargo
Speed: never-exceed Mach 0.95; maximum level speed at 25,000 ft (7620 m) 610 mph (982 km/h); cruising speed at 30,000 ft (9145 m) 564 mph (908 km/h)
Range: ferry range 11,500 miles (18507 km); maximum range with maximum payload 4,370 miles (7032 km)
Performance: maximum rate of climb at sea level 2,900 ft (884 m) per minute; service ceiling 33,400 ft (10180 m); take-off field length 10,400 ft (3170 m) at maximum take-off weight; landing field length 6,130 ft (1868 m) at maximum landing weight

USAF OPERATORS

Air Mobility Command (AMC)

2nd Wg	32nd ARS	Barksdale AFB, LA	KC-10A
22nd Wg	6th ARS	March AFB, CA	KC-10A
	9th ARS	March AFB, CA	KC-10A

KC-10s are being assigned to other USAF overseas or composite wings, such as that at Mountain Home AFB.

Air Combat Command (ACC)

4th Wg	344th ARS	'SJ'	Seymour Johnson AFB, NC	KC-10A
	911th ARS	'SJ'	Seymour Johnson AFB, NC	KC-10A

Beech
C-12

The **C-12**, a military version of the Beech Super King Air 200, serves the USAF in the OSA (operational support airlift) mission, supporting attachés assigned to overseas embassies. The USAF operates **C-12A**, **C-12D** and **C-12F** versions, which have only minor differences. The Beech 1900, a different aircraft type, has been assigned the designation **C-12J**.

The low-wing, tricycle-gear, T-tailed C-12 is a straightforward aircraft. In its various guises, the type has proved versatile and durable.

The C-12A (Super King Air A200) was first acquired to fill the USAF's 1975 CX-X requirement for a utility transport for air attachés at embassies abroad. The first civil King Air had flown on 20 January 1964 and the name came to refer to a family of similar airplanes. The USAF had operated its sole VC-6B (King Air C90) VIP transport with some success from January 1975 until its retirement in February 1985. The USAF's first C-12A (73-1205) was delivered in September 1975.

The USAF first ordered 30 C-12A models, which replaced C-117Ds and C-131s at embassies around the world. Procurement of one attrition replacement brought the C-12A total to 31. Of these, 29 remain in service. C-12A airplanes are powered by two 750-shp (559-kW) Pratt & Whitney Canada PT6A-38 turboprop engines.

The C-12D (Super King Air B200), the second USAF version, offered minor improvements. The USAF's six C-12Ds (83-0494/0499) are fitted with a 4-ft 4-in (1.32-m) cargo door, high flotation landing gear and provision for wingtip tanks, and have followed the original batch of C-12As in being assigned to overseas embassies.

The C-12F (Super King Air B200C), the USAF's definitive version, has uprated 850-shp (634-kW) Pratt & Whitney Canada PT6A-42 engines with four-bladed metal propellers. It also has weather radar, an autopilot, tactical air navigation system, and HF, VHF and UHF radios. As with other versions, the crew of the C-12F is two pilots, and the aircraft has provision for up to eight passengers or 2,647 lb (1201 kg) of cargo. Additionally, the C-12F, which has the same cargo door as the C-12D, can be configured to support medical evacuation litters. The first C-12F was delivered to the USAF in 1984 to replace the CT-39 Sabreliner. Forty C-12Fs are in service.

The C-12J (Beech 1900C) is a different aircraft type configured for 19 passengers. The USAF acquired six C-12J aircraft for Air National Guard units to replace C-131s in the 'hack' role.

Eleven versions of the C-12 (Super King Air) series are operated by other services: the US Navy/Marine Corps have the **UC-12B**, **UC-12F** and **UC-12M**. The US Army has assigned the name **Huron** to its **C-12A**, **C-12C**, **C-12D**, **RC-12D**, **UC-12D**, **RC-12G**, **RC-12K** and **C-12L**.

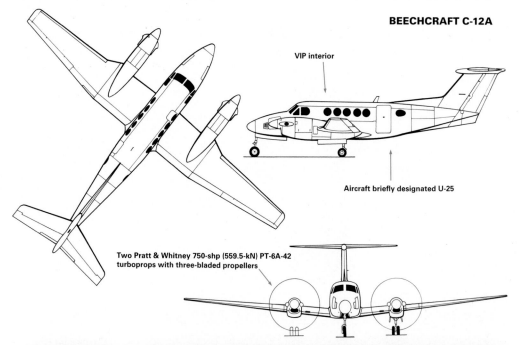

BEECHCRAFT C-12A

VIP interior

Aircraft briefly designated U-25

Two Pratt & Whitney 750-shp (559.5-kN) PT-6A-42 turboprops with three-bladed propellers

MISSION PROFILE

Configuration options: the C-12 (except C-12J) is configured with cargo door and eight standard passenger seats which can be removed for cargo or two litter patients; the C-12J is configured with forward and rear carry-on baggage lockers, cargo door, and 19 single-passenger seats in two single rows on each side of a center aisle

Operational support airlift (OSA): carrying eight passengers or more than 2,300 lb (1043 kg) of cargo, the C-12 (except C-12J) can carry out an OSA mission to a maximum range of 2,262 miles (3641 km) at maximum cruise power with 45-minute fuel reserve

Medical evacuation: although not routinely used for this purpose, the C-12 (except C-12J) has the capability to carry two hospital litter patients and an attendant to its maximum range of 2,262 miles (3641 km) at maximum cruise power with 45-minute fuel reserve

Mission support transport (C-12J): carrying up to 19 passengers, the C-12J can carry out a mission support transport flight; range with 10 passengers is 1,806 miles (2907 km) at maximum cruise power with 45-minute fuel reserve

USAF VARIANTS AND SERIALS

C-12A: Thirty King Air 200s were obtained in 1973 and 1976 to support attaché and military assistance advisory missions at US embassies worldwide. One aircraft was expelled from South Africa for allegedly conducting intelligence gathering while performing routine duties, and was replaced by the one-off 76-3239.
73-1205 to 73-1218; 76-0158 to 76-0173; 76-3239

C-12D: Six C-12Ds were added to the embassy flights in 1983, these being essentially similar to the C-12A model but with the addition of a cargo door.
83-0494 to 83-0499

C-12F: Forty Super King Air B200Cs were leased in 1984 but were later purchased outright for MAC use in the USA, Europe and the Pacific. A further six were ordered during the same year as support aircraft for the Air National Guard.
84-0143 to 84-0182; 84-0484 to 84-0489

C-12J: Six examples of the elongated C-12J Super King Air 1900C joined the ANG in 1986, these being capable of carrying 19 passengers, unlike the smaller versions which can only accommodate eight.
86-0078 to 86-0083

SPECIFICATION

Beech C-12F
Wing: span 54 ft 6 in (16.61 m); aspect ratio 9.8; area 303.0 sq ft (28.15 m²)
Fuselage and tail: length 43 ft 9 in (13.34 m); height 15 ft 0 in (4.57 m); tailplane span 18 ft 5 in (5.61 m); wheel base 14 ft 11.5 in (4.56 m)
Powerplant: two Pratt & Whitney Canada PT6A-42 each rated at 650 shp (634 kW)
Weights: operating empty 8,060 lb (3656 kg); maximum take-off 12,500 lb (5670 kg)
Fuel and load: internal fuel 3,645 lb (1653 kg); maximum payload 2,647 lb (1201 kg)
Speed: maximum level speed at 25,000 ft (7620 m) 339 mph (545 km/h); maximum cruising speed at 25,000 ft (7620 m) 336 mph (536 km/h); economical cruising speed at 25,000 ft (7620 m) 325 mph (523 km/h)
Range: range with maximum fuel at 35,000 ft (10670 m) 2,263 miles (3641 km)
Performance: maximum rate of climb at sea level 2,450 ft (747 m) per minute; service ceiling more than 35,000 ft (10670 m); take-off distance 2,579 ft (786 m) to 50 ft (15 m); landing distance 2,074 ft (632 m) from 50 ft (15 m) with propeller reversal

Beech C-12A
generally similar to the C-12F except in the following particulars:
Powerplant: two Pratt & Whitney Canada PT6A-38 each rated at 750 shp (559 kW)
Weights: empty 7,334 lb (3327 kg)
Fuel and load: internal fuel 3,540 lb (1606 kg); maximum payload more than 2,300 lb (1043 kg)

Left: Fundamentally equivalent to the Super King Air B200C, the C-12F was originally flown by MAC under the terms of a lease arrangement; however, all 40 of the aircraft involved were later purchased outright and are now active in the USA, Europe and the Far East.

Right: A C-12F of the Kadena-based 13th AS taxis for take-off. Missions undertaken by the C-12F include conventional communications and liaison tasks but it may also be employed as a medical evacuation platform and can carry two litter patients and an attendant.

Below: Acquired specifically for operational support tasks with the Air National Guard, the C-12J is merely a Beech 1900C in military use, six examples having been purchased in 1986 to replace Convair C-131s as 'hack' aircraft. In the normal course of events, the C-12J is able to accommodate up to 19 passengers.

Speed: maximum level speed at 14,000 ft (4265 m) 299 mph (481 km/h); maximum cruising speed at 30,000 ft (9145 m) 272 mph (438 km/h)
Range: range at maximum cruising speed 1,824 miles (2935 km)
Performance: service ceiling 30,900 ft (9420 m); take-off distance 2,850 ft (869 m) to 50 ft (15 m); landing distance 2,514 ft (766 m) from 50 ft (15 m)

Beech C-12D
generally similar to the C-12A except in the following particulars:
Powerplant: two Pratt & Whitney Canada PT6A-41 each rated at 850 shp (634 kW)

Beech C-12J
generally similar to the C-12F except in the following particulars:
Fuselage and tail: length 57 ft 10 in (17.63 m); height 14 ft 11 in (4.55 m); tailplane span 18 ft 6 in (5.64 m); wheel base 23 ft 10 in (7.26 m)
Powerplant: two Pratt & Whitney Canada PT6A-65B each rated at 1,100 shp (820 kW)
Weights: typical empty 9,100 lb (4128 kg); maximum take-off 16,600 lb (7530 kg)
Fuel and load: internal fuel 4,470 lb (2027 kg); maximum baggage 1,910 lb (866 kg)
Speed: maximum cruising speed at 25,000 ft (7620 m) 292 mph (471 km/h)
Range: range with 15 passengers at high-speed cruising power 1,481 miles (2383 km)
Performance: maximum rate of climb at sea level 2,330 ft (710 m) per minute; service ceiling more than 25,000 ft (7620 m); take-off distance 3,250 ft (991 m) to 50 ft (15 m); landing distance 2,540 ft (774 m) from 50 ft (15 m)

USAF OPERATORS

Air Mobility Command (AMC)

89th AW	1st AS	Andrews AFB, MD	C-12A
375th AW	1375th AS	Scott AFB, IL	C-12F
	1400th AS	Norton AFB, CA	C-12F
	det 3 1400th AS	Nellis AFB, NV	C-12F
	det 2 1401st AS	Wright-Patterson AFB, OH	C-12F
	1402nd AS	Andrews AFB, MD	C-12F
603rd ASG	13th AS	Kadena AB, Okinawa	C-12F
608th AG	58th AS	Ramstein AB, Germany	C-12F
611th ASG	det 3 1403rd AS	Osan AB, RoK	C-12F
616th AG	det 1	Elmendorf AFB, AK	C-12F
624th ASG	det 1 1403rd AS	Andersen AFB, Gam	C-12F
US Military Training Mission		Dhahran AB, Saudi Arabia	

US Embassy Flights under AMC control

Embassy Flight	Abidjan AP, Ivory Coast	C-12A
Embassy Flight	Ankara AP, Turkey	C-12A
Embassy Flight	Athens AP, Greece	C-12A
Embassy Flight	Bangkok AP, Thailand	C-12A
Embassy Flight	Brasilia AP, Brasil	C-12A
Embassy Flight	Buenos Aires AP, Argentina	C-12A
Embassy Flight	Canberra AP, Australia	C-12A
Embassy Flight	Djakarta AP, Indonesia	C-12A
Embassy Flight	Islamabad AP, Pakistan	C-12A/D
Embassy Flight	Khartoum AP, Sudan	C-12A
Embassy Flight	Kinshasa AP, Zaïre	C-12A
Embassy Flight	La Paz AP, Bolivia	C-12D
Embassy Flight	Madrid Barajas AP, Spain	C-12A
Embassy Flight	Manila AP, Philippines	C-12A
Embassy Flight	Mexico City AP, Mexico	C-12D
Embassy Flight	Mogadishu AP, Somalia	C-12D
Embassy Flight	Monrovia AP, Liberia	C-12D
Embassy Flight	Pretoria AP, South Africa	C-12A
Embassy Flight	Quito AP, Ecuador	C-12D
Embassy Flight	Rabat AP, Morocco	C-12A
Embassy Flight	Riyadh AP, Saudi Arabia	C-12A
Embassy Flight	Tegucigalpa AP, Honduras	C-12A

Air National Guard – Operational Support Aircraft (ANG-OSA)

102nd FW	101st FS	Otis ANGB, MA	C-12J
123rd AW	165th AS	Standiford Fd, Louisville, KY	C-12F
131st FW	110th FS	Lambert Fd, St Louis, MO	C-12F
132nd FW	124th FS	Des Moines MAP, IA	C-12J
141st ARW	116h ARS	Fairchild AFB, WA	C-12J
103rd FG	118th FS	Bradley ANGB, CT	C-12J
109th AG	139th AS	Schenectady Cty Apt, NY	C-12J
114th FG	175th FS	Joe Foss Fd, Sioux Falls, SD	C-12F
152nd RG	192nd RS	Reno-Cannon IAP, NV	C-12J
155th RG	173rd RS	Lincoln MAP, NV	C-12F
158th FG	134th FS	Burlington IAP, VT	C-12J
184th FG	161st FS	McConnell AFB, KS	C-12J
188th FG	184th FS	Fort Smith MAP, AR	C-12F

McDonnell Douglas
C-17

The **C-17** was developed as the USAF's next-generation cargo airlifter for Military Airlift Command (now Air Mobility Command). The C-17 will carry out the long-range strategic airlift mission, joining the C-141B and C-5A/B in this role, but also be capable of delivering troops and equipment near the front lines in a combat zone, using thrust reversers to land on unimproved runways as short as 3,000 ft (914 m). The C-17 was also developed with the LAPES (Low-Altitude Parachute Extraction System) delivery capability found on the C-130 and C-141B. Design of the C-17 included coordination with the US Army and Marine Corps over the size and bulk of items of military hardware to be transported, including armor items, some of which cannot be effectively airlifted by C-130, C-141B or C-5A/B.

The C-17, intended to replace those C-141B StarLifters with highest-hour airframes, was to be the first four-engined airlifter to have a two-member flight cabin crew – the pilots' duties facilitated by an EFCS (electronic flight control system) and integrated mission computer. The EFCS was to employ all-digital FBW (fly-by-wire) flight controls. Its short-field landing capability is based on powered lift using an externally-blown flap principle, directed-flow thrust reversers, and avionics for the air crew, including the first HUD (head-up display) in a transport. Remaining members of the four-person crew are a flight engineer and a loadmaster.

The C-17 is a high-wing, T-tailed aircraft with a rear loading ramp. Wing and tail surfaces are swept 25° and winglets protrude from the wing tips to enhance fuel efficiency. The C-17's ground-level, roll-on/off ramp is located at the rear of the fuselage. A 68 ft 1½ in (20.76 m) long cargo compartment with powered rollers accommodates up to 18 standard 463L pallets. Typical cargo loads can include two armored personnel carriers, a five-ton truck and a Jeep; or four UH-60 Black Hawk helicopters; or two AH-64 Apache and three OH-58 Kiowa helicopters. Fifty-four people can be accommodated in permanently-installed sidewall seats.

Power is provided by four 41,700-lb (185.49-kW) thrust Pratt & Whitney F117-PW-100 (civil PW2040) engines, also used on commercial airliners such as some Boeing 757s.

The C-17 dates from February 1980 when the USAF issued a draft RFP (request for proposals) for a C-X transport able to perform strategic airlift and to land close to the battlefield. Design features of aircraft proposals from three manufacturers drew on experience in the 1970s with the experimental Boeing YC-14 and McDonnell YC-15 transports. C-X proposals by Boeing and Lockheed lost out when Douglas was selected in August 1981·to build the C-X; the C-17 designation was assigned the following month.

The C-17 program was sidetracked in February 1982 when the USAF decided to purchase 50 C-5B Galaxy and 44 KC-10A Extender aircraft (the latter subsequently in-

creased to 60) and purposely delayed development of the C-17, which until then had been scheduled to enter service in 1987. The USAF's AMP (Airlift Master Plan) of 29 September 1983 re-established the development schedule and scale of the C-17 effort.

A full-scale fuselage mock-up, including cargo compartment and flight deck, met with favorable USAF reception. During 11-20 September 1984 a cargo-loading test, using active-duty Air Force loadmasters and users from the Army and Marine Corps, handled 11 load combinations successfully.

The AMP schedule originally called for a first flight in August 1990, but subsequently incurred additional delays. Once the C-17 program was restored, fabrication of the first airframe (87-0025) began in November 1987. The aircraft is manufactured by Douglas, with LTV in Dallas, Texas, supplying C-17 engine nacelles, UARRSI (universal aerial refueling

receptacle slipway installation), and tail sections.

The USAF's planned purchase of 210 C-17s was reduced to 120 as a result of Defense Secretary Dick Cheney's MAR (Major Aircraft Review) in March 1990. Given the cost of the program and the magnitude of force reductions scheduled for the mid-1990s, it appeared likely that the final C-17 purchase would be reduced even further.

Assembly of the first aircraft was completed in December 1990. The C-17 made its first flight on 15 September 1991, from the manufacturer's Long Beach, California, facility to Edwards Air Force Base where developmental testing was to begin. The C-17 flight test program by Edwards' 6510th Test Wing was expected eventually to use five aircraft, of which four were to later become operational with AMC. Ten C-17s were under assembly in late 1991, including two non-flying ground-test

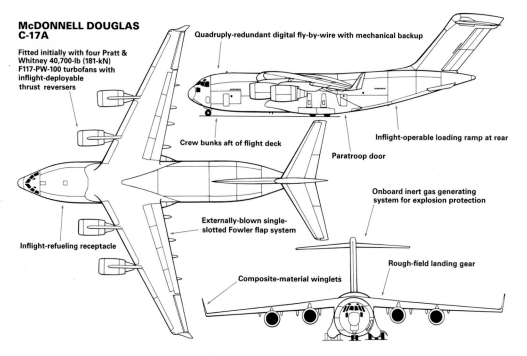

McDONNELL DOUGLAS C-17A

Quadruply-redundant digital fly-by-wire with mechanical backup

Fitted initially with four Pratt & Whitney 40,700-lb (181-kN) F117-PW-100 turbofans with inflight-deployable thrust reversers

Crew bunks aft of flight deck

Inflight-operable loading ramp at rear

Paratroop door

Onboard inert gas generating system for explosion protection

Externally-blown single-slotted Fowler flap system

Inflight-refueling receptacle

Rough-field landing gear

Composite-material winglets

Shown here getting airborne for a test flight during the early part of the trials program, the McDonnell Douglas C-17 is presently set to join the airlift forces with effect from late 1992, although an initial operating capability is not expected until 1994.

airframes, the prototype, and the first seven production aeroplanes.

Dictated by a now-obsolete northern European scenario, the C-17 mission concept, with its emphasis on delivering material directly to the battlefield, has been the subject of much review by Air Staff personnel in the early 1990s. While the need for the C-17 in the strategic airlift role was demonstrated by Operation Desert Shield (1990), when airlift resources were strained to the limit, the C-17's high cost ($342 million per aircraft) makes it unlikely that the USAF would routinely risk landing the aircraft close to enemy forces.

The first C-17 is scheduled to be delivered to AMC in late 1992, with IOC (initial operating capability) by the 17th Airlift Squadron, 437th Airlift Wing, Charleston AFB, SC, in 1994. Under the MAR-revised plan, the 120th and final aircraft is to be delivered in June 2001.

Douglas has proposed a number of applications for the C-17 airframe in which the USAF has some interest, although no formal statement of need has been set forth. One of these is an EC-17 worldwide airborne command post to replace EC-135 Stratotankers now serving in this role.

MISSION PROFILE

Configuration options: the C-17 aircraft can be configured for cargo, paratroopers, combat troops, hospital litter patients, or combinations of all of these; the C-17 is intended for strategic airlift and delivery of cargoes by landing on unimproved runways close to the battlefield, but can be employed for LAPES (low-altitude parachute extraction system) delivery of cargo; ramp of the C-17 is part of its cargo-bearing floor space

Strategic airlift: for the strategic airlift mission, the C-17 would employ air refueling but could fly to a range up to 6,100 miles (9817 km) unrefueled with up to 202 personnel (10 seating pallets for 10 passengers each plus 48 passengers in sets of back-to-back seats carried on board but not permanently installed, plus 54 passengers on permanently-installed sidewall seats); or cargo of up to 18 USAF 463L pallets (including four on ramp) with a maximum payload of 172,200 lb (78108 kg); unlike other strategic airlifters, the C-17 is designed to land with up to 167,000 lb (75750 kg) of personnel or cargo on unimproved airfields 3,000 ft

Below: The prototype C-17 flew for the first time on 15 September 1991 and is now at Edwards AFB, California, for development testing under AFMC auspices. Bottom: Although it is smaller, the C-17's hold is sufficiently roomy to allow it to accommodate some heavy items of armor which even the truly massive Lockheed Galaxy is unable to take.

(914 m) in length. Typical cargo loads could include: two 2.5-ton trucks with trailers, two 5-ton trucks and two 5-ton wreckers; two M2 Bradley fighting vehicles, two Jeeps with trailers, and two 5-ton 8×8 trucks with trailers; four UH-60 Black Hawk helicopters; three AH-1S Cobra and three OH-58 Kiowa helicopters

Airborne operations: the C-17 can carry 202 paratroopers or various heavy cargoes to a radius of about 3,400 miles (5471 km) or further with air refueling for a combat air drop with an approach to the DZ (drop zone) at medium altitude of 2,000 ft (609 m); some C-17 crews and aircraft are expected to be dedicated to special operations airdrop insertions with run-in to DZ at 300 ft (91 m) altitude and actual drop at 500 ft (152 m); or for LAPES of up to 11 USAF 463L pallets (including two on ramp)

Medical evacuation: on a medical evacuation mission, the C-17 can employ air refueling but can fly to a range up to 6,100 miles (9817 km) unrefueled with up to 48 hospital litters, 102 ambulatory patients and medical attendants

Above: Displaying the 'ED' tail code letters of the 6510th Test Wing, the prototype C-17 flies over the sun-baked desert as it prepares for a landing at Edwards AFB. At its height, the test program is eventually expected to require the services of five aircraft, four of which should eventually attain operational service with USAF airlift-dedicated units.

USAF VARIANTS AND SERIALS

C-17A: A total of 120 C-17As is planned for MAC, with the first aircraft fitted with a long nose probe to conduct flight tests.
87-0025; 88-0265; 88-0266; 89-1189 to 89-1192

SPECIFICATION

McDonnell Douglas C-17A
Wing: span 165 ft 0 in (50.29 m) and 171 ft 3 in (52.20 m) between winglet tips; aspect ratio 7.16; area 3,800.0 sq ft (353.02 m²)
Fuselage and tail: length 174 ft 0 in (53.04 m); height 55 ft 1 in (16.79 m)
Powerplant: four Pratt & Whitney F117-P-100 each rated at 41,700 lb (185.49 kN) dry thrust
Weights: operating empty 269,000 lb (122016 kg); maximum take-off 580,000 lb (263,083 kg)
Fuel and load: maximum payload 172,200 lb (78108 kg) at a 2.25-g load factor declining to 158,500 lb (71895 kg) on a heavy logistics mission at the same load factor, and to 129,200 lb (58605 kg) for an inter-theater logistics mission at a 2.5-g load factor
Speed: maximum cruising speed at low altitude 403 mph (648 km/h); airdrop speed at sea level between 132 and 288 mph (213 and 463 km/h)
Range: ferry range with maximum fuel and no payload 5,412 miles (8710 km); range with a 124,000-lb (56245-kg) payload 3,225 miles (5190 km) or with a 167,000-lb (75750-kg) payload 2,765 miles (4445 km); radius with 81,100-lb (36786-kg) payload 575 miles (925 km) or with a 124,800-lb (54245-kg) payload 2,190 miles (3520 km)
Performance: service ceiling 45,000 ft (13715 m); take-off field length with a 167,000-lb (75750-kg) payload 7,500 ft (2286 m); landing field length with a 167,000-lb (75750-kg) payload 3,000 ft (915 m) using thrust reversal

USAF OPERATORS

Air Force Materiel Command (AFMC)

6510th TW	6517th TS	'ED'	Edwards AFB, CA	C-17A

Gulfstream Aerospace
C-20 Gulfstream III

C-20 Gulfstream III transports are employed by USAF's Air Mobility Command, for OSA (operational support airlift), or intra-theater transport (**C-20A**); for SAM (special air missions), or VIP airlift (**C-20B**); and for war readiness alert (**C-20C**). These typify aircraft acquired off-the-shelf to accommodate USAF needs.

The low-wing Gulfstream III, with swept wing and tail surfaces and engines mounted in pods at the rear fuselage, makes use of a supercritical wing with NASA Whitcomb wingtip winglets for fuel efficiency. Power for the C-20A/B/C is provided by two 11,400-lb (50.71-kN) Rolls-Royce F113-RR-100 (Spey Mk 511-8) turbofan engines.

The C-20 operates with a crew of five and is configured to carry 14-18 passengers to a maximum range of 4,718 miles (7592 km). The C-20B provides the SAM (special air missions) fleet, charged with transporting Cabinet heads, Congressmen and other VIPs, with intercontinental 'legs' and the ability to operate from short runways. In an unusual piece of legislation, one C-20B airframe is dedicated to fly the Speaker of the House of Representatives.

The Gulfstream series of civil and military executive aircraft was developed by Grumman but taken over by the Savannah, Georgia-based Gulfstream firm on 1 September 1978. The first Gulfstream III (later acquired as the C-20A/B/C) made its first flight on 2 December 1979.

The C-20A was selected as a fuel-efficient replacement for the fleet of 11 C-140B JetStars which had become increasingly costly to operate and maintain and were retired in the early 1980s. In September 1983, three C-20As were delivered to the 89th Military Airlift Wing, Andrews AFB, Maryland, under a lease/purchase agreement, and were subsequently purchased in November 1984. The three C-20As (83-0500/0502) were shifted from the SAM to the OSA mission and transferred to Ramstein AB, Germany. Subsequent aircraft in the series are stationed with the renamed 89th Airlift Wing's 1st Airlift Squadron at Andrews.

The C-20B, with advanced mission communications equipment and revised interior, was the subject of an order for eight additional aircraft in 1986. One was leased, then purchased, together with the C-20As. A contract in January 1986 brought production of the C-20B variant to seven airplanes (86-0200/0206).

The C-20C version, of which three (85-0049/0050 and 86-0403) serve at Andrews, is an emergency war order aircraft designed to move high-ranking personnel quickly in the event of nuclear conflict, and carries hardened, strategic communications equipment.

The **C-20D** and **C-20E** are US Navy and US Army versions, respectively, of the Gulfstream transport.

The **C-20F** is the very different and improved Gulfstream IV variant, also for the SAM role. The C-20F is to be powered by Rolls-Royce Tay Mk 610 turbofans which provide a 15-per cent improvement in specific fuel consumption over the Spey. The C-20F/Gulfstream IV variant has increased speed and range and can accommodate up to 27 passengers. The USAF has ordered, but has not accepted delivery of, the C-20F. One C-20F with option for two more was authorized and appropriated in 1990 funds, and subsequently moved to 1992, although actual delivery of the first airframe has been delayed by an ongoing dispute over funding details. As the FY 1992 budget was being approved, payment for these C-20Fs was still in the budget; a formal need for seven C-20Fs had been enunciated by the USAF, but the dispute had not been resolved and the aircraft was not close to flying.

The USAF argues that since the original 11 JetStars were replaced with only seven C-20Bs, the C-20F is much needed in the SAM role, especially with political reforms around the world increasing the tasking for transport of government officials.

During Operation Desert Shield/Storm, Andrews-based C-20Bs flew 600 hours and 250,000 nm (287,703 miles/463000 km) on missions into the Middle East. One aircraft was used regularly by field commander General H. Norman Schwarzkopf.

MISSION PROFILE

Configuration options: C-20s are configured for up to 14 passengers and five crew members

Operational support airlift (C-20A): carrying up to 14 passengers, the C-20A can fly to a range of about 4,100 miles (6598 km)

Special air missions (SAM) (C-20B): for the SAM role, C-20Bs have several internal configurations, all of which provide first-class seating to a principal (VIP passenger) and up to eight passengers to operate to its range of about 4,100 miles (6598 km)

War readiness alert (C-20C): under the highly classified COG (continuity of government) program, apparently as part of the PSSS (presidential successor support system), the C-20C would operate with minimal navigation aids to pick up government leaders

Below: A total of 13 examples of the Gulfstream Aerospace Gulfstream III has been obtained in three basic variants for service with the USAF. Missions undertaken include operational support activity, VIP airlift and emergency war order support. The example shown here is the first of seven C-20Bs obtained for VIP taskings.

USAF VARIANTS AND SERIALS

C-20A: Three C-20As were ordered in 1983 for VIP duties at Andrews AFB, but were subsequently transferred to Europe when replaced by the seven C-20B models. Painted in the blue and white scheme, they are fitted for personnel transportation. 83-0500 to 83-0502

C-20B: The seven C-20Bs were similar to the A model but featured advanced communications equipment and a revised interior. 86-0200 to 86-0206

C-20C: The three C-20Cs are special missions aircraft which, although painted in the same color scheme as the C-20B models, are not normally employed in the VIP role as they transport senior military personnel. 85-0049 to 85-0050; 86-0403

SPECIFICATION

Gulfstream Aerospace C-20B
Wing: span 77 ft 10 in (23.72 m); area 934.6 sq ft (86.82 m²)
Fuselage and tail: length 83 ft 1 in (25.32 m); height 24 ft 4.5 in (7.43 m)
Powerplant: two Rolls-Royce Spey Mk 511-8 rated at 11,400 lb (50.7 kN) dry thrust
Weights: manufacturer's empty 32,300 lb (14651 kg); operating empty 38,000 lb (17236 kg); maximum take-off 68,200 lb (30936 kg)
Fuel and load: internal fuel 28,300 lb (12836 kg); typical payload 1,600 lb (726 kg)
Speed: maximum cruising speed at 30,000 ft (9145 m) 576 mph (928 km/h); long-range cruising speed at 30,000 ft (9145 m) 508 mph (818 km/h)
Range: maximum range 4,721 miles (7598 km); typical range 4,200 miles (6760 km)
Performance: maximum rate of climb at sea level 3,800 ft (1158 m) per minute; maximum operating altitude 45,000 ft (13715 m); balanced take-off field length 5,700 ft (1738 m); landing distance 3,400 m (1040 m)

USAF OPERATORS

Air Mobility Command (AMC)

| 89th AW | 1st AS | Andrews AFB, MD | C-20B/C |
| 608th AG | 58th AS | Ramstein AB, Germany | C-20A |

Above: Although the interior configuration can and does vary, the three current versions of the C-20 are all fundamentally similar to the commercial Gulfstream III executive jet.

Learjet
C-21

Left: *Acquired under the terms of a leasing arrangement in 1984-85, the 80 C-21As were off-the-shelf examples of the Learjet 35A.*

Below: *Although the majority of the USAF's C-21 Learjets are operated from various locations in the continental USA, modest quantities are also stationed overseas, the example seen here being one of a handful assigned to USAFE support.*

The **C-21A Learjet 35A** is the USAF's twin-turbofan OSA (operational support airlift) transport used for cargo and passenger airlift within the United States and during intra-theater operations. The C-21A is also capable of transporting litters during medical evacuations. The airplane was one of a number of smaller types operated by active-duty and ANG (Air National Guard) components of MAC (Military Airlift Command), most elements of which have been absorbed into a new Air Mobility Command in June 1992.

Some 79 C-21As are in the active force (of 80 built), while four serve with the ANG.

An off-the-shelf version of the well-known, low-wing, T-tailed executive jet aircraft, the C-21A operates with two pilots. The aircraft is equipped with autopilot, color weather radar, TACAN (tactical air navigation) system, HF, VHF and UHF radios, and an automatic navigation system. Four CRTs (cathode ray tubes) display essential information to the pilots.

On a typical mission, a C-21A can haul six passengers over a distance of 1,900 miles (3058 km), cruising at 508 mph (818 km/h) at a typical altitude of 40,000 ft (12192 km). As an example of routine use, the aircraft typically might carry Pentagon officials to meetings 880 miles (1416 km) away at AMC Headquarters, Scott AFB, Illinois, enabling them to complete the round trip and do nearly a full day's business in one day.

The C-21A is powered by two 3,500-lb (1588-kg) thrust Garrett TFE-731-2-2B turbofan engines. The engines are pod-mounted on the side of the rear fuselage. The C-21A performs very responsively, not unlike a fighter aircraft.

The low wings are swept back very slightly and have hydraulically actuated, single-slotted flaps. The C-21A has retractable tricycle landing gear, single steerable nose gear, and multiple-disc hydraulic brakes.

The design philosophy behind the Learjet dictated a damage-tolerant structure that would exceed the stringent structural requirements for a commercial airliner. The Learjet's fuselage is constructed around a main keel beam in the cabin section. The frames are the natural round shape of a pressurized vessel. Close proximity of the stringers is typical for a damage-tolerant structure. The builder calls this a 'fail safe fuselage': failure of a single structural member will not cause a catastrophic situation since the structural member located nearby is capable of absorbing the additional load.

A two-piece, clamshell door is located on the left side of the cabin. Steps are built into the lower door to facilitate entry into the aircraft. When the door is closed, 10 large steel pins secure the door in vault-like fashion, making it an integral part of the cabin structure when under pressurization.

The C-21A Learjet owes its origins to the corporate transport developed by Bill Lear, based upon Switzerland's FFA P-16 jet fighter, in the early 1960s. The first civil Learjet was flown on 7 October 1963.

The first three C-21As were delivered to Scott AFB, Illinois, for use by the 375th Aeromedical Airlift Wing on 6 April 1984. Delivery of 80 C-21A Learjets (84-0063/0142) was completed in October 1985 and the aircraft, initially obtained under lease, were later purchased. Later, four more C-21As (86-0374/0377) were obtained for Air National Guard operations. One C-21A (84-0121) was lost in a mishap at Maxwell AFB, Alabama, on 14 January 1987. USAF documents assert that in their first three years of operation, C-21As accumulated 190,000 flight hours and 210,000 landings while maintaining a 96-per cent mission capability rate. The manufacturer was unsuccessful in proposing a derivative of the C-21A for the USAF's TTTS (Tanker Transport Trainer System), the multi-engined trainer mission subsequently chosen for the Beech T-1A Jayhawk.

The USAF keeps its C-21As in small detachments at more than a dozen locations. During Operation Desert Shield/Storm, C-21As performed a vital role in intra-theater airlift of personnel and were employed to carry processed reconnaissance films from air bases to the coalition's headquarters in Riyadh, Saudi Arabia.

USAF VARIANTS AND SERIALS

C-21A: Eighty C-21As were leased by MAC for worldwide communications and VIP transportation, and like the C-12Fs were eventually purchased. Four more were acquired in 1986 for the ANG.
84-0063 to 84-0142; 86-0374 to 86-0377

SPECIFICATION

Learjet C-21A
Wing: span over tip tanks 39 ft 6 in (12.04 m); aspect ratio 5.7; area 253.3 sq ft (23.53 m²)
Fuselage and tail: length 48 ft 8 in (14.83 m); height 12 ft 3 in (3.73 m); tailplane span 14 ft 8 in (4.47 m); wheel base 20 ft 2 in (6.15 m)
Powerplant: two Garrett TFE731-2-2B each rated at 3,500 lb (15 kN) dry thrust
Weights: empty equipped 9,838 lb (4462 kg); maximum take-off 18,300 lb (8301 kg)
Fuel and load: internal fuel 931 US gal (3524 liters); maximum payload 3,500 lb (1588 kg)
Speed: never-exceed Mach 0.83; maximum level speed at 25,000 ft (7620 m) 542 mph (872 km/h); maximum cruising speed at 41,000 ft (12495 m) 529 mph (851 km/h); economical cruising speed at 45,000 ft (13715 m) 481 mph (774 km/h)
Range: range with four passengers 2,570 miles (4136 km)
Performance: maximum rate of climb at sea level 4,339 ft (1322 m) per minute; service ceiling 45,000 ft (13715 m); balanced take-off field length at 18,300 lb (8301 kg) 4,972 ft (1515 m); landing distance 3,075 ft (937 m) at maximum weight

MISSION PROFILE

Configuration options: the C-21A is configured to carry six passengers (seven when using a sideways jump seat aft of the flight crew) in first-class seats plus 40 cu ft (1.13 m³) or about 800 lb (362 kg) of baggage/cargo in its 322-cu ft (9.12-m³) passenger cabin

Operational support airlift (OSA): carrying up to seven passengers (usually fewer), the C-21A Learjet can cruise at 529 mph (851 km/h), fly to a maximum range of 2,567 miles (4131 km) and land on a runway 3,075 ft (937 m) in length, with 45-minute fuel reserve

Medical evacuation: although not routinely used for this purpose, the C-21A can carry two hospital litter patients and an attendant to its maximum range of 2,567 miles (4131 km) at normal cruise power with 45-minute fuel reserve

High-value utility duties: because a maximum speed of 529 mph (851 km/h) makes it one of the fastest USAF aircraft capable of carrying up to seven people or miscellaneous very light cargoes, the C-21A has been employed for high-value specialized tasks – for example, intra-theater transport of urgently-needed reconnaissance imagery from a tactical reconnaissance airfield to a headquarters

USAF OPERATORS

Air Force Materiel Command (AFMC)

4950th TW	det 1	Andrews AFB, MD	C-21A

Air Mobility Command (AMC)

374th AW	1403rd AS	Yokota AB, Japan	C-21A
375th AW	1375th AS	Scott AFB, Il	C-21A
	1400th AS	Norton AFB, CA	C-21A
	det 1 1400th AS	McClellan AFB, CA	C-21A
	det 2 1400th AS	Randolph AFB, TX	C-21A
	det 1 1401st AS	Offutt AFB, NE	C-21A
	det 2 1401st AS	Wright-Patterson AFB, OH	C-21A
	det 3 1401st AS	Barksdale AFB, LA	C-21A
	det 4 1401st AS	Peterson AFB, CO	C-21A
	1402nd AS	Andrews AFB, MD	C-21A
	det 1 1402nd AS	Langley AFB, VA	C-21A
	det 3 1402nd AS	Maxwell AFB, AL	C-21A
	det 4 1402nd AS	Eglin AFB, FL	C-21A
61st AG	310th AS	Howard AFB, Canal Zone	C-21A
606th AG	58th AS	Ramstein AB, Germany	C-21A
HQ USECOM	7005th ABS	Stuttgart Echterdingen AP, Germany	C-21A

Air National Guard (ANG)

det 1	121st FS	Andrews AFB, MD	C-21A

USAF Aircraft

Boeing
C-22

The **C-22**, a Boeing 727 formerly operated by commercial airlines, is the medium-range transport operated by the Air National Guard and the National Guard Bureau.

The low-wing, tricycle-gear Boeing transport has a proven configuration with swept wings and T-tail, and three aft-mounted engines, one on each side of the rear fuselage and the third in the tail cone. The unique arrangement of leading-edge devices and trailing-edge flaps permits operation from relatively short paved runways in Third World locations.

The C-22 fuselage had two heated and pressurized baggage compartments located on the right side forward and aft of the wheel well providing 425 cu ft (12.03 m³) of cargo space. The fuselage also incorporates a forward entry door and hydraulically opened integral aft stairs in the tail cone.

The flight controls consist of a hydraulically-powered dual elevator control system with control tab assist during manual reversion. Hydraulically-powered rudders utilize two main systems with a standby system for the lower rudder. The tricycle landing gear consists of a dual-wheel nose gear, left and right dual wheel main gear, and a retractable tail-skid for protection from damage in case of overrotation.

Flight crew consists of two pilots and a flight engineer and three to four attendants for passenger service. The avionics package includes two VHF and one UHF radios, radar altimeters, and dual INS (inertial navigation systems).

On a typical mission, a C-22 can carry 90 passengers or a maximum of 32,336 lb (14667 kg) of cargo over a distance of 1,900 miles (3058 km), cruising at 540 mph (870 km/h). With a full fuel load and 50 passengers, range of the aircraft is 2,900 miles (4667 km). As an example of routine use, the aircraft typically carries military teams, bands and conference groups.

Power is provided by three 14,500-lb (64.5-kN) thrust Pratt & Whitney JT8D-7 turbofan engine in the C-22 variant.

The sole **C-22A** (84-0193) is a Boeing 727-030 operated by US Southern Command. Intended for the Commander-in-Chief, it is maintained and operated by the 310th Airlift Squadron, 61st Airlift Group, at Howard AFB, Panama. Before joining the military, the aircraft was operated by the Federal Aviation Administration.

Four **C-22Bs** (83-4610, 4612, 4615, 4616) are Boeing 727-035s belonging to Detachment 1, DC ANG at Andrews AFB, Maryland. These are former National Airlines/Pan American World Airways transports.

The sole **C-22C** (83-4618) is a 'stretched' Boeing 727-200, flown by Headquarters, US Central Command, from Andrews AFB.

Conversion of these ex-airliners began in 1985. The DC Air National Guard converted to the C-22B from the T-43A (Boeing 737) between September 1985 and April 1987.

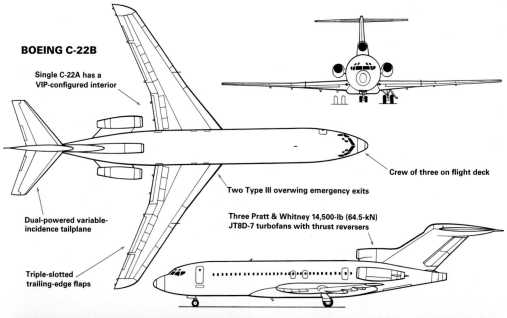

BOEING C-22B

Single C-22A has a VIP-configured interior

Crew of three on flight deck

Two Type III overwing emergency exits

Dual-powered variable-incidence tailplane

Three Pratt & Whitney 14,500-lb (64.5-kN) JT8D-7 turbofans with thrust reversers

Triple-slotted trailing-edge flaps

Above: Obtained during the mid-1980s, the four C-22Bs are all allocated to Detachment One of the District of Columbia ANG at Andrews AFB, an outfit that operates them on behalf of National Guard Bureau headquarters elements.

C-22C: A single Boeing 727-200 was given the designation C-22C, and is believed to be ex-Singapore Airlines. 83-4618

MISSION PROFILE

Configuration options: the sole C-22A is configured as a VIP transport for US Southern Command's CINC (Commander-in-Chief); the four C-22Bs are configured for 89 passengers (24 leather cushion seats, two across each side in six rows in the first-class forward cabin; and 66 tweed fabric seats (one not used), three across each side in 11 rows in the rear cabin) all in rearward-facing, airline-style seats; internal configuration of the C-22C has not been disclosed; in practice, none of the C-22A/B aircraft is converted to cargo hauling

Airlift: usually assigned to carry high-visibility groups such as military bands, sports teams, and conference participants, the C-22B carries up to 89 passengers; with 50 passengers, the C-22B flies at a maximum cruise speed of 480 kt and maximum cruising altitude of 42,000 ft (12801m) to its normal range of 2,500 nm (2,877 miles/4630 km) with 45-minute fuel reserve

CINC support: the sole C-22A carries a military field commander and staff of up to 60 personnel, plus inflight work area and communications, at its maximum cruise speed of 480 kt at 42,000 ft (12801 m) to its normal range of 2,500 nm (2,877 miles/4630 km) with 45-minute fuel reserve

USAF VARIANTS AND SERIALS

C-22A: Former Federal Aviation Agency (FAA) Boeing 727-030 was allocated the designation C-22A. 84-0193

C-22B: Four Boeing 727-035s, formerly operated by National Airlines and Pan American World Airways, were assigned to the Air Force as C-22Bs. 83-4610; 83-4612; 83-4615; 83-4616

SPECIFICATION

Boeing C-22
Wing: span 108 ft 0 in (32.92 m); aspect ratio 7.67; area 1,700 sq ft (157.9 m²)
Fuselage and tail: length 133 ft 2 in (40.59 m); height 34 ft 0 in (10.36 m); tailplane span 35 ft 9 in (10.90 m); wheelbase 53 ft 3 in (16.23 m)
Powerplant: three Pratt & Whitney JT8D-1 turbofans rated at 14,000 lb (62.3 kN) thrust
Weights: basic empty 81,920 lb (37158 kg); operating empty 85,664 lb (38857 kg); maximum take-off 160,000 lb (72575 kg)
Fuel and load: internal fuel 7,174 US gal (27158 liters); maximum payload 32,336 lb (14667 kg)
Speed: maximum level at 22,300 ft (6800 m) 630 mph (1014 km/h); maximum cruising at 19,000 ft (5800 m) 605 mph (974 km/h)
Range: with maximum fuel 2,690 miles (4330 km); with maximum payload 2,050 miles (3300 km)
Performance: rate of climb at sea level 3,150 ft (960 m) per minute; service ceiling 37,400 ft (11400 m); take-off run 4,950 ft (1510 m); landing distance from 50 ft (15 m) 1,800 ft (549 m)

USAF OPERATORS

Air Mobility Command (AMC)

61st AG	310th AS	Howard AFB, Canal Zone	C-22A

Air National Guard (ANG)

det 1	121st FS	Andrews AFB, MD	C-22B

US Central Command (US CENTCOM)

det 14	HQ CENTCOM	Andrews AFB, MD	C-22C

Shorts
C-23 Sherpa

The USAF operates three **C-23A Sherpas** at its TPS (Test Pilots School) at Edwards AFB, California. These aircraft train student test pilots in fixed-wing stalls and handling techniques, and perform a general utility mission as TPS 'hacks'. This trio of Sherpas is what remains of 18 C-23As purchased in 1982-83 for intra-theater airlift in Europe.

The **Sherpa 330** regional airliner was developed from the Shorts SC.7 Skyvan for civil passenger and cargo carriers. The high-winged, twin-tail C-23A appealed to the USAF as an economical and pragmatic transport for tactical items such as jet engines, radar sets, and ordnance. The C-23A is an all-freight airlifter with a 6 ft 6 in (1.98 m) square cabin section running through an impeded cargo hold 29 ft (8.84 m) in length. The box-shaped fuselage of the aircraft can be loaded through a large forward freight door, a full-width hydraulically-operated rear ramp door, and removable roller conveyors.

Two pilots comprise the crew of the C-23A, which was built to a requirement for operations without a flight engineer or loadmaster. The aircraft can carry up to 7,000 lb (3175 kg) of cargo including four LD3 palletized containers. Among cargoes are engines up to and including the size of the J79 and F100. Range on a typical mission with full cargo is 700 miles (1127 km) when cruising at 202 mph (325 km/h) at 10,000 ft (3048 m).

The C-23A is powered by two 1,198-shp (893-kW) Pratt & Whitney Canada T101-CP-100 turboprop engines.

The C-23A Sherpa dates to 1982 when USAFE (US Air Forces in Europe) sought a suitable, cost-effective cargo hauler for its EDSA (European Distribution System Aircraft) program. EDSA was centered at Zweibrücken, Germany, with main warehousing facilities at RAF Kemble, England, and Torrejon AB, Spain, and serviced some 20 USAFE bases, primarily with supplies and parts for tactical jet fighter maintenance units.

The first civil Sherpa made its maiden flight on 22 August 1974. The first C-23A flew on 23 December 1982. The 18 C-23As (83-0512/0513, 84-0458/0473) were delivered between November 1984 and December 1985. A contract option for 48 further Sherpas was not acted upon. The aircraft were operated by the 10th Military Airlift Squadron at Zweibrücken.

After five years of successful operation, at the end of 1990 the USAFE dismantled EDSA and disestablished the 10th MAS. C-23A operations in Europe ceased on 31 October 1990. The last C-23As departed Europe on 14 November 1990.

Fifteen of the 18 C-23As were transferred, eight to the US Army and seven to the US Forestry Service. The three C-23As still in the USAF (83-0512/0513, 84-0458) were relocated in 1990 to Edwards AFB.

The **C-23B** designation is assigned to a US Army National Guard variant. The Army also operates four Sherpa 330s.

Originally acquired for USAFE's EDSA (European Distribution System Aircraft) concept and used by the 10th MAS, all but three of the 18 C-23As were disposed of in 1990. Today, the survivors are flown by the 6510th TW from Edwards AFB.

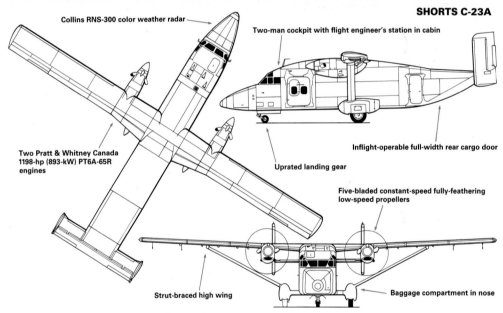

SHORTS C-23A

Collins RNS-300 color weather radar

Two-man cockpit with flight engineer's station in cabin

Two Pratt & Whitney Canada 1198-hp (893-kW) PT6A-65R engines

Inflight-operable full-width rear cargo door

Uprated landing gear

Five-bladed constant-speed fully-feathering low-speed propellers

Strut-braced high wing

Baggage compartment in nose

MISSION PROFILE

No longer employed in the EDSA program for which it was purchased, the three C-23As in USAF inventory train test pilots in handling and flight techniques, including fixed-wing stalls and handling techniques, and are also employed as general utility aircraft

USAF VARIANTS AND SERIALS

C-23A: Eighteen C-23As were obtained to conduct the delivery of urgent cargo and spare parts in Europe, although they were withdrawn and flown to the USA for service with the Air Force, Army and Forestry Service. 83-0512 to 83-0513; 84-0458 to 84-0473

(**Note:** only 83-0512, 83-0513 and 84-0458 remain on USAF charge, as the remaining 15 were transferred to the US Army and US Forestry Service during 1990.)

SPECIFICATION

Shorts C-23A
Wing: span 74 ft 8 in (22.76 m); area 453.0 sq ft (42.08 m²)

Fuselage and tail: length 58 ft 0.5 in (17.69 m); height 16 ft 3 in (4.95 m); tailplane span 18 ft 7.75 in (5.68 m); wheel base 20 ft 2 in (6.15 m)
Powerplant: two Pratt & Whitney Canada T101-CP-100 each rated at 1,198 shp (893 kW)
Weights: empty equipped 14,727 lb (6680 kg); maximum take-off 22,900 lb (19387 kg)
Fuel and load: internal fuel 4,480 lb (2032 kg); maximum payload 7,000 lb (3175 kg)
Speed: maximum cruising speed at 10,000 ft (3050 m) at 21,000 lb (9526 kg) 218 mph (352 km/h); economical cruising speed at 10,000 ft (3050 m) at 21,000 lb (9526 kg) 181 mph (291 km/h)
Range: range 770 miles (1239 km) with a 5,000-lb (2268-kg) payload, and 225 miles (362 km) with a 7,000-lb (3175-kg) payload
Performance: maximum rate of climb at sea level 1,180 ft (360 m) per minute; service ceiling 20,000 ft (6095 m); take-off distance 3,420 ft (1042 m); landing distance 3,650 ft (1113 m) at maximum weight

USAF OPERATORS

Air Force Materiel Command (AFMC)

6510th TW	6512th TS	nil	Edwards AFB, CA	C-23

Boeing
C-25

The **VC-25** designation has been assigned to the USAF's primary Presidential aircraft, a specially-equipped Boeing 747-200B. The term 'Air Force One', properly applies only when the President is on board.

Two **VC-25As** are assigned to the 89th Airlift Wing at Andrews AFB, Maryland. Initially the two aircraft are believed to have been allocated their serials in FY 1986, but they have FY 1982 and FY 1992 (82-8000; 92-9000) respectively, following on from the two C-137Cs.

The VC-25A can carry the President and his staff, with 70 passengers and 23 crew members, a distance of 7,140 miles (11490 km) without air refueling. The crew includes 10 flight personnel for redundancy, three communications specialists, and 10 flight attendants.

On a typical mission, the VC-25A cruises at 560 mph (901 km/h) at 35,000 ft (10,668 m). The VC-25A is equipped with the Bendix Aerospace EFIS-10 electronic flight instrument system. The specification for the aircraft included a requirement to operate in all climates, year-round. When refueled in flight, the VC-25A's flight endurance is limited only by its oil lubricant and meets a requirement to allow flight for a full week. Thus, the VC-25A can serve as an emergency war order aircraft to carry the President or others in the national command authority (NCA) during a nuclear conflict.

Contrary to conventional expectations, use of the VC-25A to replace the C-137C (Boeing 707-320B/C) as the President's aircraft does not reduce the number of the world's airports to which the President has access. The VC-25A, under some circumstances, depending on fuel load, can take off in 35 per cent less runway than its predecessor, and it meets more stringent noise requirements.

The proven Boeing 747 low-wing, four-engined jet transport has been enhanced, in the case of the VC-25A, with prestige accommodations including 85 telephones, 19 television monitors, 11 videocassette players, and secure voice and facsimile equipment, to say nothing of an airborne equivalent of the White House's Oval Office, a senior staff room, and a conference/dining room. The Presidential stateroom has twin beds, twin sinks, dressing table, and a shower in the lavatory.

Separate accommodations are provided for guests, senior staff, Secret Service and security personnel and members of the news media. Two galleys together can serve 100 meals at one sitting. Six lavatories are available for passengers. A separate rest area and a mini-galley are provided for the crew. Another area is outfitted with medical equipment.

The aircraft has built-in airstairs and baggage loader systems. The two airstairs, located fore and aft on the left side, allow entry to the aircraft without a 'jetway' or portable stairway. The baggage loader is a conveyor-type system to load luggage and other small cargo.

The VC-25A is powered by four 56,750-lb (252.44-kN) thrust General Electric F103-GE-180 (CF6-80C-2B1) turbofan engines.

Above: Delivered in 1990, two Boeing 747s were obtained as replacements for the C-137C in the presidential transport role, these being given the designation VC-25A in USAF service.

Above: Although externally similar to the purely commercial Boeing 747, the VC-25A features many detail changes to suit it to its specialised mission of VVIP transportation.

The VC-25A resulted from longstanding plans to provide the US' chief executive with a newer and more capable aircraft to replace the C-137C (Boeing 707) which has been in use since 1961.

The familiar Boeing 747, which first flew on 9 February 1969 and has amassed millions of hours in commercial airline service, was an obvious choice. Boeing was awarded the $250-million contract for the Presidential aircraft in June 1987, beating out McDonnell Douglas which had offered a version of the DC-10 jet airliner. Delivery of the two VC-25As fell more than two years behind schedule, partly because of technical difficulties in 'hardening' the aircraft against EMP (electromagnetic pulse) and other effects of nuclear blast. First flight of the VC-25A was made on 26 January 1990 at Wichita, Kansas.

The first aircraft (82-8000) was delivered to the 89th Military Airlift Wing (now the 89th Airlift Wing) on 30 September 1990. The second VC-25A (92-9000) was delivered on 30 December 1990. The first operational mission of the first aircraft took place on 6 September 1990, taking President George Bush to Topeka, Kansas, and Tallahassee, Florida. The following day, the VC-25A made its first overseas trip, taking Bush to Helsinki, Finland.

MISSION PROFILE

Configuration options: the VC-25A is configured for long-range special air missions (SAM) transport for the President of the United States; the aircraft is shielded against EMP and carries MCS (mission communications system), three operators, and provision for worldwide secure communication; normal accommodation is for up to 70 passengers and 23 crew members; the VC-25A's 4,000 sq ft (372 m²) of interior floor space includes an executive office ('flying Oval Office'), conference/dining room, Presidential quarters, an office area for senior staff members, an office for staff which can be converted to a medical facility, work and rest areas for staff, media representatives and spare crew, and two galleys each able to provide food for 50 people; lower lobes of the aircraft fuselage feature preparation facilities for substantial amounts of food (up to 2,000 meals), and mission-related equipment

Special air missions (SAM) airlift: the VC-25A can carry the President and his staff, up to 70 passengers and 23 crew members, and cruises typically at 560 mph (901 km/h); the VC-25A can receive air refueling but typically can fly unrefueled to a range of 7,140 miles (11490 km)

USAF VARIANTS AND SERIALS

VC-25A: The two VC-25As were ordered as the new 'Air Force One' replacing the C-137C.
82-8000; 92-9000

SPECIFICATION

Boeing VC-25A
Wing: span 195 ft 8 in (59.64 m); aspect ratio 7.0; area 5,500.0 sq ft (510.95 m²)
Fuselage and tail: length 231 ft 10 in (70.66 m); height 63 ft 5 in (19.33 m); tailplane span 72 ft 9 in (22.17 m); wheel base 84 ft 0 in (25.60 m)
Powerplant: four General Electric F103-GE-102 (CF6-80C2B1) each rated at 56,750 lb (252.4 kN) dry thrust
Weight: long-range mission take-off 803,700 lb (364552 kg)
Fuel and load: internal fuel 53,611 US gal (202940 liters); maximum structural payload 145,700 lb (66088 kg)
Speed: maximum level speed at 30,000 ft (9145 m) at 700,000 lb (317515 kg) 610 mph (981 km/h)
Range: range on internal fuel 7,140 miles (11490 km)
Performance: cruise ceiling 45,000 ft (13715 m); take-off distance 10,100 ft (3079 m) to 35 ft (10.7 m); landing field length 6,370 ft (1942 m) at 585,000 lb (265350 kg)

USAF OPERATORS

Air Mobility Command (AMC)

89th AW	1st AS	Andrews AFB, MD	VC-25A

Fairchild Swearingen
C-26 Metro

The **C-26 Metro** is a feeder airliner, purchased off-the-shelf for Air National Guard transport work.

The low-wing, 19-passenger, twin-engined transport is used primarily to move personnel. The aircraft has a fairly conventional structure. The wings incorporate double-slotted trailing-edge flaps; the fuselage is a fail-safe light-alloy structure of circular cross-section stressed to provide pressurization. The tail unit has all-swept surfaces and a large dorsal fin. The landing gear is of retractable tricycle-type with twin wheels on each unit.

Jokingly dubbed a product of the 'San Antonio Sewer Tube Company' because its fuselage so resembles a pipe, the C-26 Metro is configured with 19 high-back passenger seats, movable structural bulkhead, galley/refreshment center, and lavatory. With a crew of two pilots, the aircraft can be configured as an air ambulance or for cargo missions.

On a typical mission, the **C-26A** handles a payload of 19 passengers totaling 3,780 lb (1715 kg) with a range of 662 miles (1065 km). The C-26A cruises at 320 mph (515 km/h). The aircraft has sea level cabin pressurization to 16,800 ft (5120 m). Maximum gross take-off weight is 14,500 lb (6577 kg).

Most C-26As are powered by two 1,119-shp (834-kW) Garrett TPE331-12UAR turboprop engines driving McCauley aluminum propellers. These are more fuel efficient and more powerful than the -11 engines initially employed.

The C-26A owes its lineage to the civil Swearingen Metro (taken over by Fairchild), which first flew on 26 August 1969. Military service began with a March 1988 order for six C-26A airplanes (later increased to 13) for the ANGOSTA (Air National Guard Operational Support Transport Aircraft) role. To win this order, Fairchild overcame competition from the Beech Model 1900C and British Aerospace Super Jetstream 31.

The first C-26As replaced C-131s in scattered Guard units around the continental US. The first 13 aircraft were delivered with TPE331-11 engines but are to be upgraded with the -12UAR powerplant while in service. This original C-26A batch, delivery of which was completed in 1990, was based on the San Antonio, Texas, manufacturer's Model SA-227-AC Metro 3 commuter airliner.

In early 1991, the USAF issued a $235-million contract to Fairchild to produce 53 more C-26As with the -12UAR engine. These were to satisfy the Pentagon's MSAANG (Mission Support Aircraft for the Air National Guard) requirement, with the result that Guard units in all 50 states will operate identical transports. The second batch of C-26s was to replace C-130A/B Hercules and C-7A/B Caribou transports in tactical ANG units. The second batch of C-26As is known to the manufacturer as the Metro 23 and is virtually identical to feeder airliners later sold to Air Mexico and other civil operators.

The designation **C-26B** has been assigned to

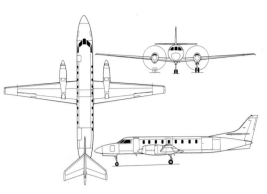

Above: One of a number of types purchased off-the-shelf in recent times, the Swearingen Metro, as the C-26A, performs communication and transport duties for a number of ANG units.

US Army National Guard Metros, including two among the initial 13 (87-1000/1001) which went to Army Guard units in Colorado and Virginia.

The one-off **UC-26C** Metro, assigned to the ANG's 147th Fighter Interceptor Group at Ellington Field, Texas, was modified in 1991 for the drug interdiction role. The UC-26C is equipped with APG-66 air intercept radar like that employed on the F-16 Fighting Falcon, video camera, special communications gear, and FLIR (forward-looking infra-red). In August 1991, it began a four- to five-month series of tests flying anti-drug missions, day and night. They were expected to result in ANG requirements for a law enforcement aircraft. Since one of its main functions was to act as an airborne data link, some observers felt the UC-26C was overequipped for the job, with more items of costly equipment than needed.

In its transport role, the C-26A has not been received with uniform enthusiasm by crews, many of them accustomed to the roomier C-131 Samaritan. An ANG pilot confirms that the C-26 is routinely flown with four of the 19 passenger seats removed.

MISSION PROFILE

Configuration options: the C-26 (except UC-26C) is configured to carry 19 passengers; it can be configured as an air ambulance for medical evacuation missions; the sole UC-26C is configured with nose AN/APG-66 air intercept radar, video camera, special communications gear, and FLIR (forward-looking infra-red)

Airlift: the C-26A can carry up to 19 passengers or 4,800 lb (2214 kg) of baggage/light cargo or a combination of the two; with 19 passengers averaging 662 lb (1065 kg) each and cruising at 320 mph (515 km/h), the C-26A can fly to a range of 662 miles (1065 km); with 10 passengers still averaging 215 lb (97 kg) and still cruising at 320 mph (515 km/h), range of the C-26A increases

Drug interdiction: the sole UC-26C on a drug interdiction mission at medium altitude cruising at 310 mph (498 km/h) can operate to (or loiter over) a radius of about 500 miles (804 km)

USAF VARIANTS AND SERIALS

C-26A: A contract for 10 C-26As in 1988 was followed by another placed in 1989, with an eventual requirement for more than 50 aircraft.
88-0450 to 88-0459; 89-0460; plus other contracts

UC-26C: A single Metro was modified for drug interdiction duties.
89-1471

SPECIFICATION

Fairchild Swearingen C-26A
Wing: span 57 ft 0 in (17.37 m); aspect ratio 10.5; area 309.0 sq ft (28.71 m²)
Fuselage and tail: length 59 ft 4.25 in (18.09 m); height 16 ft 8 in (5.08 m); tailplane span 15 ft 11.5 in (4.86 m); wheel base 19 ft 1.5 in (5.83 m)
Powerplant: two Garrett TPE331-12UAR each rated at 1,119 shp (834 kW) dry and 1,100 shp (820 kW) wet
Weights: operating empty 9,180 lb (4164 kg); maximum take-off 14,500 lb (6577 kg)
Fuel and load: internal fuel 4,342 lb (1969 kg); maximum payload 4,880 lb (2214 kg)
Speed: maximum cruising speed at 15,000 ft (475 m) at 12,500 lb (5670 kg) 320 mph (515 km/h)
Range: maximum range with 19 passengers 662 miles (1065 km)
Performance: maximum rate of climb at sea level 2,370 ft (722 m) per minute; service ceiling 27,500 ft (8380 m); take-off distance 3,250 ft (991 m) to 50 ft (15 m); landing distance 2,450 ft (747 m) from 50 ft (15 m)

USAF OPERATORS

Air National Guard – Operational Support Aircraft (ANG-OSA)

108th FW	141st FS	McGuire AFB, NJ	C-26A
121st FW	166th FS	Rickenbacker ANGB, OH	C-26A
122nd FW	163rd FS	Fort Wayne MPA, IN	C-26A
144th FW	194th FS	Fresno AT, CA	C-26A
111th FG	103rd FS	NAS Willow Grove, PA	C-26A
124th RG	190th RS	Boise AT, ID	C-26A
142nd FG	123rd FS	Portland IAP, OR	C-26A
147th FG	111th FS	Ellington ANGB, TX	UC-26C
182nd FG	169th FS	Gtr Peoria Apt, IL	C-26A
186th RG	153rd RS	Key Field, Meridian, MS	C-26A
192nd FG	149th FS	Richmond IAP, VA	C-26A

If present plans are adhered to, the C-26A will become the standard Air National Guard mission support aircraft. Procurement seems certain to eventually exceed the 50 mark, even though it is far from popular with its crews.

USAF Aircraft

Chrysler/Alenia
C-27

Selected on 20 August 1990, the Chrysler/Alenia C-27 is being purchased specifically for the US Southern Command and as many as 18 examples may eventually be operated from Howard AFB.

The **C-27** is a twin-engined transport serving as an RRITA (Rapid Response Intra-Theater Airlifter) with US Southern Command in Latin America. The aircraft is an Italian-designed Alenia G222 modified by Chrysler in Waco, Texas.

In carrying out its mission, the C-27A is expected to operate from 1,800-ft (549-m) unpaved runways, carry 10,200 lb (4267 kg) or 34 passengers, cruise at 230 mph (370 km/h) with a 300-nm (346-mile/556-km) radius, and operate from an austere forward base for 30 days.

The fuselage of the transport is an all-metal fail-safe structure, the underside of which forms a loading ramp. The C-27A can be configured for up to 19,841 lb (9000 kg) of cargo, 24 paratroopers or 34 combat-equipped troops, 24 litters with four medical attendants, or a variety of wheeled vehicles. The C-27A is capable of making parachute airdrops of personnel and equipment. The aircraft, modified with Third World environs in mind, can be reconfigured by one maintenance worker for another type of mission within one hour.

The C-27A is powered by two 3,400-shp (2535-kW) General Electric T64-GE-P4D turboprop engines.

The basic G222 aircraft, whose builder has been named Fiat, Aeritalia, and (today) Alenia, dates from 1962 when Italian forces were seeking a cost-effective replacement for the C-119 Flying Boxcar. The first G222 made its maiden flight on 18 July 1970.

The USAF's requirement for the C-27A was defined in 1987. The aircraft is operated by AMC for US Southern Command (Southcom), which has responsibility for American combat operations in Central and South America, including anti-drug efforts in Colombia and Peru. Southcom wanted a transport to airlift troops and cargo to remote, unimproved airstrips in support of LIC (low-intensity conflict). The aircraft was viewed as filling a gap in size between the CH-47 Chinook and C-130 Hercules.

When the C-27 RFP (request for proposals) was issued in March 1990, six aircraft types were offered by their builders – G222, British Aerospace 780 Andover, Bromon BR-2000, CASA CN.235, de Havilland Canada DHC-5D Buffalo, Snow & Associates SA-210-TA. All but the G222 and CASA CN.235 dropped out when the USAF required each bidder to provide an aircraft for evaluation during source selection.

Fly-off competition between the G222 and CASA CN.235 was held in June 1990 at Wright-Patterson AFB, Ohio, when crews from Military Airlift Command and from Air Force Systems Command's 4950th Test Wing flew about six sorties with each aircraft, including a night flight and a heavy-cargo mission. On 20 August 1990, the US Air Force chose the G222. An initial order for five aircraft led to a fleet of 10 C-27As, stationed at Howard AFB, Panama, to support US Southern Command in Latin America.

The first C-27A was delivered on 20 August 1991. IOC (initial operating capability) was achieved with acceptance of the third aircraft on 16 October 1991. The 10th and final C-27A was scheduled to be delivered on 31 December 1992. The manufacturer has proposed some minor ECPs (enhanced change proposals) which would result in modest improvements to avionics and instrumentation. Chrysler also has a $5.5-million contract for logistics support.

Ninety-five G222s serve elsewhere. Countries which have purchased the G222 in military form include Italy, Argentina, the Congo, Dubai, Guatemala, Nigeria, Somalia, Venezuela and Yemen.

MISSION PROFILE

Configuration options: the C-27A has cargo/passenger floor area of 276.4 sq ft (25.68 m²) and internal volume of 2,048 cu ft (58. m³) and can be configured to carry a maximum cargo payload of 19,841 lb (9000 kg) or a typical cargo payload of 10,200 lb (4627 kg) or 34 passengers

Rapid response intra-theater airlift (RRITA): on a representative airlift mission, the C-27A operates from an austere, forward 1,800-ft (549-m) unpaved runway, carries typically 10,200 lb (4627-kg) or up to 34 passengers, and cruises at 230 mph (370 km/h) to a 300-nm (345-mile/556-km) radius

Airborne operations: the C-27 is not intended for airborne operations in USAF service, but has the capability to airdrop up to 34 paratroopers at a typical mission radius of 300 nm (345 miles/556 km)

USAF VARIANTS AND SERIALS

C-27A: Five C-27As have been budgeted with 1990 funds, with an order for a further five aircraft, plus options.
90-1070 to 90-0172; plus other contracts

SPECIFICATION

Chrysler/Alenia C-27A
Wing: span 94 ft 2 in (28.70 m); aspect ratio 10.0; area 882.6 sq ft (82.00 m²)
Fuselage and tail: length 74 ft 5.5 in (2.70 m); height 32 ft 1.75 in (9.80 m); tailplane span 40 ft 8.25 in (12.40 m); wheel base 20 ft 5.25 in (6.23 m)
Powerplant: two General Electric T64-GE-P4D each flat-rated at 3,400 shp (2535 kW)
Weights: basic empty 32,165 lb (14590 kg); empty equipped 33,951 lb (15400 kg); maximum take-off 61,728 lb (28000 kg)
Fuel and load: internal fuel 20,723 lb (9400 kg); maximum payload 19,841 lb (9000 kg)
Speed: maximum level speed at 15,000 ft (4575 m) 336 mph (540 km/h); long-range cruising speed at 19,685 ft (6000 m) 273 mph (439 km/h)
Range: ferry range 2,879 miles (4633 km); range with maximum payload 852 miles (1371 km)
Performance: maximum rate of climb at sea level 1,705 ft (520 m) per minute; service ceiling 25,000 ft (7620 m); take-off distance 3,280 ft (1000 m) to 50 ft (15 m); landing distance 2,543 ft (775 m) from 50 ft (15 m)

USAF OPERATORS

Air Mobility Command (AMC)

61st AG	310th AS	Howard AFB, Canal Zone	C-27A

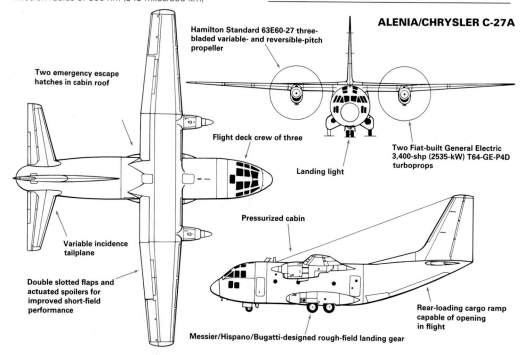

ALENIA/CHRYSLER C-27A

Two emergency escape hatches in cabin roof

Hamilton Standard 63E60-27 three-bladed variable- and reversible-pitch propeller

Flight deck crew of three

Two Fiat-built General Electric 3,400-shp (2535-kW) T64-GE-P4D turboprops

Landing light

Pressurized cabin

Variable incidence tailplane

Double slotted flaps and actuated spoilers for improved short-field performance

Rear-loading cargo ramp capable of opening in flight

Messier/Hispano/Bugatti-designed rough-field landing gear

CASA
C.212

The **CASA C.212** is used in small numbers by the USAF. No military designation has been assigned. Two CASA **C.212-200** aircraft (90-0168/0169) were on strength for some time at Pope AFB, North Carolina, as low-cost utility vehicles for parachute training. In mid-1991, after Operation Desert Storm, they were dispatched to the Persian Gulf region.

Built by the well-known Spanish manufacturer Construcciones Aeronautics SA, the CASA C.212 prototype flew on 26 March 1971. The aircraft is powered by two Garrett TPE-331-10R-513C engines rated at 900 shp (671 kW) with Dowty Rotol propellers.

The CASA **C.212-300** is a conventional, high-wing, twin-engined light hauler and STOL (short take-off/landing) utility transport, with the capability to operate from unprepared airstrips 1,837 ft (560 m) in length. Flight crew consists of two pilots. Passenger capacity is 24. Features which make the aircraft attractive to the USAF include hydraulic rear cargo ramp, quick-change passenger/cargo interior, very effective freon air conditioning system and an airline-type lavatory. The CASA C.212-300 is extremely fuel efficient, burning about 600 lb (272 kg) per hour.

When using the CASA C.212-300 to provide regular parachute training to the 82nd Airborne Division at Fort Bragg adjacent to Pope AFB, at an economical cost of around $230 per hour, the USAF was able to free C-130E Hercules and C-141B StarLifter aircraft for other duties. It is not clear, however, whether this is the purpose for which the USAF's Aviocars were originally obtained, or whether its purchase was limited to the four publicly identified airframes. The use of CASA C.212s by the US Army's Intelligence and Security Command (INSCOM) suggests that the USAF airplanes may have been initially employed for intelligence work and reassigned to Pope only after their original purpose was fulfilled. INSCOM obtained at least three CASA C.212s, one of which (88-3210) crashed at NAS Patuxent River, Maryland, on 1 December 1989.

One CASA C.212-300 is operated by the US Coast Guard, and a dozen or so CASA C.212-200s were operated on a civilian contract basis by Evergreen Helicopters, Inc. at Howard AFB, Panama, to support US Southern Command – a mission which was taken over in 1992 by the Chrysler/Alenia C-27A.

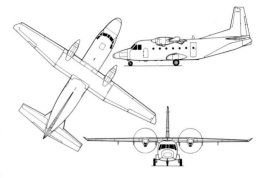

Above: Unusual in that it lacks a US military designation, at least four examples of the CASA C.212 have been operated by the Air Force, with tasks including low-cost parachute training at Pope AFB, North Carolina. During Desert Storm two aircraft were also dispatched.

MISSION PROFILE

Configuration options: the CASA C.212 offers optional configurations for up to 18 paratroopers or 24 passengers, or about 5,952 lb (2700 kg) of cargo

Tactical airlift (equipment): the CASA C.212 typically would perform intra-theater airlift of personnel or equipment with an operating radius of around 480 miles (772 km); the USAF has not disclosed the precise mission of the CASA C.212s in its inventory, but it is believed they are performing routine 'hack' duties

USAF VARIANTS AND SERIALS

CASA C.212: As far as is known, no Air Force designation has been allocated to the four Air Force CASA C.212s, and they are simply referred to by their Spanish identity.
87-0158 and 87-0159; 90-0168 and 90-0169

SPECIFICATION

CASA C.212 Series 300
Wing: span 66 ft 6.5 in (20.28 m); aspect ratio 10; area 441.33 sq ft (41.00 m²)
Fuselage and tail: length 53 ft 1.75 in (16.20 m); height 20 ft 8 in (6.30 m); tailplane span 27 ft 6.75 in (8.40 m); wheel base 18 ft 2.5 in (5.55 m)

Powerplant: two Garrett TPE-331-10R-513C each rated at 900 shp (671 kW)
Weights: basic empty 8,333 lb (3780 kg); empty equipped, cargo 9,700 lb (4400 kg); maximum take-off 17,637 lb (8000 kg)
Fuel and load: internal fuel 3,527 lb (1600 kg); external fuel up to 1,764 lb (800 kg) in two 132-US gal (500-liter) underwing tanks; maximum payload 5,952 lb (2700 kg)
Speed: maximum operating speed 230 mph (370 km/h); maximum cruising speed at 10,000 ft (3050 m) 220 mph (354 km/h); economical cruising speed at 10,000 ft (3050 m) 186 mph (300 km/h)
Range: maximum range with maximum fuel at 10,000 ft (3050 m) 1,007 miles (1620 km); range at economical cruising speed with maximum fuel 1,125 miles (1811 km)
Performance: maximum rate of climb at sea level 1,630 ft (497 m) per minute; service ceiling 26,000 ft (7925 m); take-off distance 1,837 ft (560 m) to 50 ft (15 m); landing distance 1,703 ft (519 m) without propeller reversal

USAF OPERATORS

No unit details are known, other than that the first pair was stationed at Pope AFB, NC, during April 1989, probably with the USAF Airlift Center, while the second pair was flown from the USA to the Middle East in July 1991.

Boeing
E-3 Sentry

The **E-3 Sentry** is the USAF's AWACS (airborne warning and control system) platform, used to detect and monitor an enemy's air activity and to direct fighters in engagements. More than just a flying radar station, AWACS operates as a mobile, airborne C^3I (command, control, communications and intelligence) headquarters, capable of high- or low-level surveillance of air vehicles over all types of terrain. In a broader sense, AWACS is a national asset – able to be dispatched as gunboats once were, to make a show of force in distant locations without being as provocative as ordnance-toting warplanes. The E-3 aircraft is a version of the Boeing 707-320B airliner.

The heart of the AWACS system is its Westinghouse AN/APY-2 (upgraded from AN/APY-1) Overland Downlook Radar

Right: Based on the commercial Boeing 707-320B airliner, the E-3 Sentry is able to perform a host of missions associated with airborne early warning and control. A total of 34 aircraft was delivered to Tactical Air Command.

E-3 Sentry (continued)

(ODR) which, with other sensors and instrumentation, is mounted in a saucer-like rotodome carried on two 11-ft (3.35-m) struts above the rear fuselage. The deep circular rotodome is some 30 ft (9.14 m) in diameter, weighs 3,395 lb (1540 kg) and is canted 2.5° downward. The dome rotates six times per minute during an operational mission.

The radar, which relies on this disc-like dome is, itself, housed in a large part of the fuselage just aft of the wing, both below and above the floor. Radar signals, and received echoes, travel up or down the two rotodome struts. The main radar antenna is a beam 30 ft (9.14 m) long and 6 ft (1.83 m) high.

The basic 707 airframe owes some of its heritage to the B-47 Stratojet bomber developed by the USAF in the late 1940s. It retains the distinctive wing of the jet bomber, swept back 35°, and the underslung mounting of the bomber's jet engines in nacelles, carried on cantilever underwing pylons. The 707 aircraft, with the addition of rotodome, internal crew stations and strengthened landing gear, has proved ideal for the AWACS mission.

During actual operations, an E-3C Sentry AWACS aircraft – which has an unrefueled endurance of 11 hours – routinely refuels and stays aloft for up to 18 hours, carrying a crew of 20 consisting of pilot (aircraft commander), co-pilot, navigator, flight engineer and 16 AWACS mission specialists. The rear-cabin crew is under a mission crew commander, typically a major or lieutenant colonel, and includes weapons controllers, radar operators and communications specialists.

Cruising at 510 mph (860 km/h) and limited to a modest service ceiling of 29,000 ft (8840 m), AWACS can protect itself by detecting aerial threats and vectoring fighters while remaining some distance away. The radar is capable of tracking simultaneously up to 600 low-flying aircraft to a radius of 292 miles (470 km).

The USAF is pursuing an MSIP (Multi-Stage Improvement Program) aimed at upgrading all **E-3B** and **E-3C** aircraft in inventory with upgraded JTIDS (Joint Tactical Information Distribution System) for digital communications including TADIL-J (Tactical Digital Information Link-Joint), Quick Look ESM system to detect signals from hostile targets, and GPS (global positioning system) navigation. A radar upgrade is also expected in the mid-1990s. These enhancements will permit AWACS aircraft to detect smaller targets such as cruise missiles.

The epoch-setting Boeing 367-80, which led to the subsequent 717 (KC-135) and 707 (C-137/C-18/E-3) series, made its first flight on 15 July 1954. While military orders for the KC-135 tanker were clearly a factor in facilitating airline purchases of the civil 707, the military did not use a version of the 707 itself until the prototype for the AWACS series, then designated **EC-137D** (71-1407), flew on 5 February 1972. The first **E-3A** Sentry (73-1675) made its maiden flight on 31 October 1975 (aircraft 73-1674 having been retained by Boeing for developmental work) and the first operational E-3A was delivered to the 552nd Airborne Warning and Control Wing, Tinker

AFB, Oklahoma, on 24 March 1977.

E-3s assumed a continental US air-defense role in January 1979 when NORAD personnel began augmenting Tactical Air Command crews on missions flown from Tinker. Following brief proof-of-concept deployments to Europe, the first operational use of AWACS was the joint US-Korean Team Spirit exercise in March 1979. The US field commander in Korea, General Richard Stillwell, noted in an after-action report that AWACS 'wrought a miracle' in improving his ability to keep track of air movements in a hostile North Korea.

The 960th, 961st and 962nd Air Control Squadrons of the 552nd ACW have subsequently been stationed at Keflavik, Iceland; Kadena AB, Japan; and Elmendorf AFB, Alaska. The 963rd, 964th, 965th and 966th ACS are home-based at Tinker, the last-named being the RTU for the E-3 type. Initially formed as detachments, the squadrons were formed in the late 1970s and comprise flight crews and mission crews for up to as many as 10 aircraft. The 961st and 962nd ACS have been transferred from TAC to PACAF, joining the 3rd and 18th Wings as the first Sentries to be reassigned from Stateside control.

The success of the Korean operation led to a request from Saudi Arabia for an AWACS deployment. A two-month deployment in 1979-80 was followed by a formal arrangement under which American AWACS aircraft have deployed to Saudi Arabia on a regular basis ever since. The first permanent stationing of a detachment was at Keflavik in mid-1979. AWACS aircraft were involved in the unsuccessful attempt to rescue American hostages from Iran in April 1980. Frequent deployments have been made to numerous other locations around the world and AWACS aircraft have been involved in all American combat operations in Grenada (1983), Lebanon (1983) and Panama (1989).

The regular 'Elf One' deployments of American E-3 Sentry AWACS aircraft to Saudi Arabia over more than a decade made 552nd AW&CW personnel among the

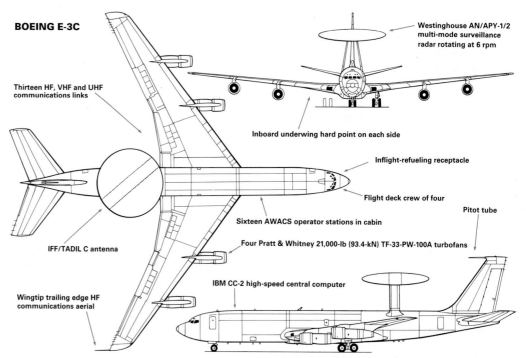

BOEING E-3C

Westinghouse AN/APY-1/2 multi-mode surveillance radar rotating at 6 rpm

Thirteen HF, VHF and UHF communications links

Inboard underwing hard point on each side

Inflight-refueling receptacle

Flight deck crew of four

Pitot tube

Sixteen AWACS operator stations in cabin

Four Pratt & Whitney 21,000-lb (93.4-kN) TF-33-PW-100A turbofans

IFF/TADIL C antenna

IBM CC-2 high-speed central computer

Wingtip trailing edge HF communications aerial

Below: Portrayed over the inhospitable Alaskan landscape, this Boeing E-3 Sentry is one of the small number of aircraft which are permanently stationed at Elmendorf AFB to monitor airspace over the 'roof of the USA'. Crews and aircraft are assigned to the 962nd AW&CS.

USAF's most experienced in the region. During Operation Desert Storm, American AWACS platforms flew four continuous orbits to control over 3,000 sorties a day while maintaining a mission-capable rate of 98 per cent, nine per cent higher than in peacetime. The USAF was especially pleased that in spite of the numerous air forces and languages involved in the coalition, not one instance of friendly air-to-air fratricide occurred. Saudi AWACS also operated during the conflict, but it was an American AWACS vector which positioned the Saudi F-15C Eagle pilot to shoot down two Iraqi Mirage F1s on 24 January 1991. Likewise, the AWACS platform had a role in most of the 39 air-to-air kills scored by American fighter pilots. A USAF after-action report rated AWACS an 'invaluable asset' in pinpointing aerial targets and identifying hostile threats.

The 22 E-3A and two EC-137D airplanes, collectively termed 'core' aircraft when they were standardized in the late 1970s, were subsequently upgraded to E-3B standard. Improvements include advanced computer capabilities, anti-jam communications, a modest maritime surveillance capability, additional radios and five more display consoles. The 552nd AW&CW took delivery of the first E-3B in July 1984.

Nine E-3C Sentry aircraft, beginning with

Above: Originally built as an E-3A, the Sentry depicted here on final approach to Nellis AFB has been upgraded to E-3B standard and features enhanced equipment, allowing it to perform some maritime surveillance tasks. Other improvements included anti-jam communications equipment.

Right: One Sentry receives a fresh load of fuel in readiness for a routine mission, while in the background another machine gets airborne. With internal fuel, the E-3 can remain aloft for up to 11 hours, although inflight refueling does significantly extend patrol duration.

E-3 Sentry (continued)

80-0137, introduced slightly larger crew capacity and improvements in internal systems.

E-3A 'standard' (as distinguished from 'core') versions have been delivered to Saudi Arabia and NATO, the Saudis also acquiring **KE-3A** tankers. **E-3D** aircraft have been delivered to the Royal Air Force. The designation **E-3E** has not been used. **E-3F** models are operated by France.

Production of all versions of the Boeing 707 is scheduled to end in 1992 following delivery of the final French E-3F aircraft. The USAF has lost none of its E-3 Sentries in mishaps.

MISSION PROFILE

Airborne control: cruising at around 29,000 ft (8840 m), the E-3 usually flies racetrack orbits to maintain a constant sector coverage; mission endurance is usually 11 hours unrefueled or 18 hours with one tanking; at 1,000 miles (1609 km) from base, an unrefueled sortie gives six hours on patrol; radar operates in five modes, which can be interleaved or changed during different sectors of the radar's scan – modes are PDNES (pulse-Doppler non-elevation scan) which gives maximum full detection range but no elevation detail, PDES (pulse-Doppler elevation scan) which reduces range but provides target elevation data, BTH (beyond-the-horizon) which does not employ Doppler but gives great range, and Maritime for sea surface search; in pulse-Doppler mode radar detects airborne targets (including cruise missiles) down to tree-top height; controllers monitor and vector friendly aircraft to intercept targets, or steer them away from hostile air threats; system also used for general air traffic control and battle management, ensuring maximum deconfliction of friendly aircraft

Command post: onboard communications equipment makes the E-3 able to converse with most friendly forces and can act as an airborne command post; a commander can control the air battle from the E-3 if required

Search and rescue: operating in Maritime radar mode the E-3 can be used to detect vessels at sea and co-ordinate rescue efforts

USAF VARIANTS AND SERIALS

Original construction designations
E-3A: The first two aircraft were allocated the designation EC-137D although this was changed to E-3A shortly after the maiden flight of the first aircraft. Twenty-five E-3As were purchased between 1971 and 1979.
71-1407 to 71-1408; 73-1674 to 73-1675; 75-0556 to 75-0560; 76-1604 to 76-1607; 77-0351 to 77-0356; 78-0576 to 78-0578; 79-0001 to 79-0003

E-3C: Nine E-3Cs were ordered between 1980 and 1983, equipped for maritime as well as overland operations.
80-0137 to 80-0139; 81-0004 to 81-0005; 82-0006 to 82-0007; 83-0008 to 83-0009

Conversion designations
E-3B: All 25 of the E-3As were upgraded to E-3B standard with the addition of equipment to enable them to operate in the maritime role.
71-1407 to 71-1408; 73-1674 to 73-1675; 75-0556 to 75-0560; 76-1604 to 76-1607; 77-0351 to 77-0356; 78-0576 to 78-0578; 79-0001 to 79-0003

E-3C: The Boeing Company has retained for ongoing development the third aircraft, which has been upgraded to E-3C standard. The designation JE-3A has also been reported for this aircraft, although this is probably unofficial.
73-1674

SPECIFICATION

Boeing E-3C
Wing: span 145 ft 9 in (44.42 m); aspect ratio 7.056; area 3,050.0 sq ft (283.35 m²)
Fuselage and tail: length 152 ft 11 in (46.61 m); height 41 ft 9 in (12.73 m); tailplane span 45 ft 9 in (13.95 m); wheel base 59 ft 0 in (17.98 m)
Powerplant: four Pratt & Whitney TF33-P-100/100A each rated at 21,000 lb (93.4 kN) dry thrust
Weights: operating empty 171,950 lb (77996 kg); maximum take-off 325,000 lb (147420 kg)

Above: Half a dozen Boeing E-3 Sentries occupy part of the extensive flight line at their home base at Tinker AFB, Oklahoma. From here, E-3s regularly deploy to overseas locations.

Below: Dominated by display consoles and their associated keyboards, the Sentry cabin is quite literally packed with millions of dollars worth of sophisticated electronic kit.

Fuel and load: internal 23,987 US gal (90800 liters)
Speed: never-exceed speed Mach 0.95; maximum level speed at high altitude 530 mph (853 km/h)
Range: radius for a 6-hour patrol without refueling 1,000 miles (1609 km); endurance without refueling more than 11 hours
Performance: operating ceiling 29,000 ft (8840 m)

USAF OPERATORS

Air Combat Command (ACC)

552nd ACW	960th ACS		NAF Keflavik, Iceland	E-3B/C
	963rd ACS		Tinker AFB, OK	E-3B/C
	964th ACS		Tinker AFB, OK	E-3B/C
	965th ACS		Tinker AFB, OK	E-3B/C
	966th ACS		Tinker AFB, OK	E-3B/C

Pacific Air Forces (PACAF)

3rd Wg	962nd ACS	'AK'	Elmendorf AFB, AK	E-3C
18th Wg	961st ACS	'ZZ'	Kadena AB, Okinawa	E-3B/C

Boeing
E-4

The **E-4B**, a variant of the Boeing 747B airliner, is operated by the USAF as its AABNCP (Advanced Airborne National Command Post). Its purpose is to provide an aerial platform and command center for the US leadership in the event of nuclear war. Dubbed the 'Doomsday Plane' in popular jargon, the aircraft is kept in readiness to carry the President, or others in the chain of leadership known as the NCA (national command authority), during the initial hours or days of a general conflict. During an attack on US soil, some leaders would be taken to an underground command post in Virginia while others would go aboard the E-4B to direct American forces.

Four E-4Bs are assigned to the 1st Airborne Command & Control Squadron, part of the 55th Wing at Offutt AFB, Nebraska. The practice of keeping a detachment with one E-4B on alert at Andrews AFB, Maryland, a short helicopter trip from the White House, was discontinued in the late 1980s.

The E-4B's flight crew of aircraft commander (pilot), co-pilot, navigator and flight engineer is doubled for redundancy, and the aircraft has a special navigation station and crew rest area.

The E-4B uses the size and bulk of the familiar 747B airliner fuselage to accommodate the President (in his role as Commander-in-Chief of US forces) and key members of his battle staff on its 4,620 sq ft (429 m²) main deck, partitioned into five operating compartments. These are the flight crew section, NCA area (roughly a flying equivalent of the White House Situation Room), a conference room, battle staff area, and C³I (command, control,

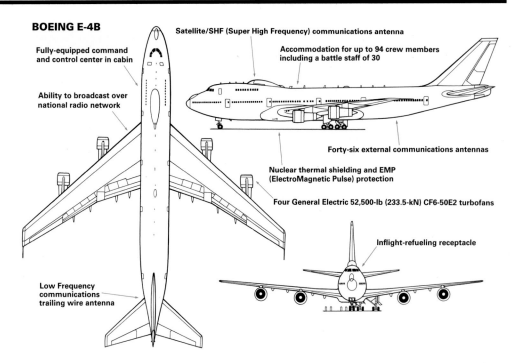

BOEING E-4B

Satellite/SHF (Super High Frequency) communications antenna

Fully-equipped command and control center in cabin

Ability to broadcast over national radio network

Low Frequency communications trailing wire antenna

Accommodation for up to 94 crew members including a battle staff of 30

Forty-six external communications antennas

Nuclear thermal shielding and EMP (ElectroMagnetic Pulse) protection

Four General Electric 52,500-lb (233.5-kN) CF6-50E2 turbofans

Inflight-refueling receptacle

communications and intelligence) area. This main deck is 185 ft (56.4 m) in length, with a maximum width of 19 ft 6 in (5.94 m). A second deck provides a rest area for mission personnel.

This 'war readiness aircraft' is equipped with nuclear thermal shielding, hardening against EMP (electromagnetic pulse), LF/VLF (low frequency/very low frequency) radios, and extensive satellite communications equipment. Included is equipment to tie into commercial telephone and radio networks to broadcast emergency messages to the general population. The current E-4B also has an SHF (super high frequency) system with antennas housed in a distinctive dorsal blister. Every compo-

nent of the aircraft, including engines, avionics and wiring, has been optimized for maximum flight duration.

On its awesome mission, the E-4B cruises typically at 580 mph (933 km/h), is refueled in flight, and meets a requirement to be capable of staying aloft for 72 hours. In actual war, even this duration could be extended to a full week. Like the Presidential VC-25A, which is the other Boeing 747 derivative in the inventory, the E-4B's sustainability aloft is limited only by oil lubricant of its engines. Power is provided by four 52,500-lb (233.53-kN) thrust General Electric F103-PW-100 (CF6-50-E2) turbofan engines.

*Above: Serving as the **NEACP** (National Emergency Airborne Command Post), the E-4 was the first version of the commercial Boeing 747 to enter the **USAF** inventory and one example is never far away whenever the President travels overseas. A complex and comprehensive communications suite is a key feature of the E-4 equipment.*

Left: Entering service in the mid-1970s, the first three aircraft were built as E-4As, only to be brought up to E-4B configuration several years later, when they had been augmented by a fourth aircraft that was delivered as an E-4B. The most noticeable difference between the two versions concerns the dorsal antenna bulge that was introduced by the E-4B.

E-4 (continued)

Today, the E-4 mission is identified as NEACP (National Emergency Airborne Command Post), inevitably pronounced 'kneecap' by those who work on the aircraft.

The E-4 was developed to meet a requirement known as 481B for an airborne national command center. On 28 February 1973 a contract was awarded to Boeing for two **E-4A** airframes, with a third following soon after. The E-4A made its first flight without mission equipment on 13 June 1973. The sophisticated internal fit was added by E-Systems and the first E-4A was delivered in late 1974.

The E-4B version, with improved accommodations, upgraded engines and SHF system, commenced with delivery of the fourth airplane in the series on 21 December 1979. This first E-4B entered service in December 1980, and the three remaining aircraft were subsequently upgraded to E-4B standard. Early plans for a total fleet of six aircraft were eventually reduced to four.

Despite the thawing of the Cold War, the USAF is expected to maintain its fleet of four E-4Bs (73-1676/1677; 74-0787; 75-0125), which has accumulated an impressive safety record in more than a decade of operation.

MISSION PROFILE

Configuration options: the E-4 is configured as an AABNCP (Advanced Airborne National Command Post); its upper deck serves as a crew rest area; the main deck holds the President (as Commander-in-Chief of US forces) and his battle staff in five compartments: the flight crew section, the NCA (National Command Authority) work area, a conference room, battle staff, and C³I (command, control, communications and intelligence) area; the aircraft is shielded against EMP

Advanced airborne national command post (AABNCP): the E-4B cruises typically at 580 mph (933 km/h) at 32,000 ft (9754 m), is refueled in flight, and meets a requirement to stay aloft for 72 hours; in a nuclear war, this duration could be extended to a full week, the E-4B's sustainability aloft being limited only by oil lubricant of its engines

USAF VARIANTS AND SERIALS

E-4A: Three aircraft were obtained during the mid-1970s as E-4As, although these were upgraded to E-4B standard not long after delivery. 73-1676 and 73-1677; 74-0787

E-4B: The single E-4B was ordered in 1975 with a huge satellite communications antenna mounted in a large radome aft of the cockpit. The three E-4As were subsequently modified to this standard. 75-0125

SPECIFICATION

Boeing E-4B
Wing: span 195 ft 8 in (59.64 m); aspect ratio 6.96; area 5,500.0 sq ft (510.95 m²)
Fuselage and tail: length 231 ft 4 in (70.51 m); height 63 ft 5 in (19.33 m); tailplane span 72 ft 9 in (22.17 m); wheel base 84 ft 0 in (25.60 m)
Powerplant: four General Electric F103-GE-100 rated at 52,500 lb (233.53 kN) thrust
Weight: maximum take-off 800,000 lb (362874 kg)
Fuel and load: internal fuel 331,565 lb (150395 kg)
Speed: maximum level speed at 30,000 ft (9145 m) 602 mph (969 km/h)
Range: ferry range 7,830 miles (12600 km); mission endurance without inflight refueling 12 hours, and with inflight refueling 72 hours
Performance: cruise ceiling 45,000 ft (13715 m); take-off distance less than 10,820 ft (3298 m) to 35 ft (10.7 m); landing field length 6,920 ft (2109 m) at maximum weight

USAF OPERATORS

Air Combat Command (ACC)

55th Wg	1st ACCS	Offutt AFB, NE	E-4B

The unit was designated 55th SRW until 1 October 1991, when the prefix letters were removed.

Grumman/Boeing
E-8 J-STARS

The Boeing/Grumman **E-8A** is an airborne command post outfitted for the J-STARS (Joint Surveillance Target Attack Radar System) mission, a joint USAF/US Army program for a battlefield management system that will detect, locate, track and classify enemy ground formations at long range.

Conceived for a Western European scenario, Joint STARS was rushed into use during Operation Desert Storm and was successful in directing fighter-bombers to attack Iraqi tanks and other targets detected by the E-8A's radar system. Like the USAF's C-18 and E-3 series, the E-8A is a version of the Boeing 707-320B airliner.

The two prototypes, both previously-used 707s converted by Grumman, are equipped with a Norden multi-mode SLAR (side-looking airborne radar) located in a 25-ft (7.62-m) 'canoe' faired into the belly of the aircraft. This radar functions in SAR (synthetic aperture radar) mode out to a range of 160 miles (257 km) to detect and pinpoint stationary objects such as parked tanks. The radar alternates between SAR and Doppler modes to locate and track slow-moving targets. The mission crew aboard the E-8A then directs attacks on the targets using the real-time JTIDS (Joint Tactical Information Distribution System). The flight crew of four consists of pilot (aircraft commander), co-pilot, navigator and flight engineer. Mission crew of the E-8A typically is 17, headed by a mission crew commander, typically a lieutenant colonel or colonel. The mixed USAF/US Army mission crew occupies 15 operations/control stations, and two operations/communications positions, using consoles that display color-coded images of enemy terrain and of wheeled and tracked vehicles moving in the region.

For actual operations, an E-8A Joint STARS aircraft has an unrefueled endurance of about 12 hours, although typical missions are shorter. The first two airframes have not been modified for air refueling, although the capability is being considered for later production machines. Cruising at about 500 mph (804 km/h), the E-8A Joint STARS aircraft maintain continuous C³I (command, control, communications and intelligence) operations and monitor hundreds of ground targets at a time. The E-8A carries no weapons or defensive systems and is customarily escorted by F-15 Eagles flying HVACAP (high-value asset, combat air patrol) escort.

Right: A converted Boeing 707, the E-8A is employed for battlefield surveillance and management and has a Norden multi-mode SLAR as its primary sensor system.

Below: The second E-8A development aircraft is shown here complete with a civil registration that was applied during contractor trials work conducted from Melbourne, Florida.

The E-8A is powered by four 19,000-lb (84.52-kN) thrust Pratt & Whitney JT3D-7 turbofan engines almost identical to the military TF33 turbofans employed by other 717/707 variants.

Development of the E-8A Joint STARS system began when the first airframe (86-0416) was delivered in August 1987 to the Grumman facility at Melbourne, Florida. The second machine (86-0417) followed in December 1988. The maiden flight of the first machine after being fully configured for the Joint STARS mission took place in December 1988.

A third airframe was expected to fly in late 1991 in the intended Joint STARS production standard and to be the first of 20 **E-8B** airplanes procured through the 1990s.

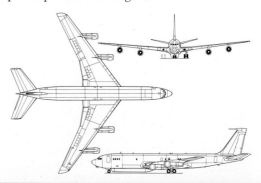

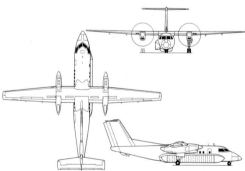

Trials of the system were carried out in Europe in the autumn of 1990, where the aircraft simulated operations in a NATO/Warsaw Pact conflict of the kind for which it had been developed. Though the thawing of the Cold War has diluted its original purpose, the Joint STARS system proved itself adaptable to Third World conflicts during Operation Desert Storm and was given a new lease of life.

The two E-8A prototypes and crews of the 4411th Joint STARS Squadron were pulled from the partly-completed DT&E (Developmental Test and Evaluation) program and sent to the Persian Gulf well in advance of any planned operational use of the system. They flew 54 missions and logged 535 hours locating, identifying and targeting assembly areas, POL (petroleum oil lubricant) sites, 'Scud' launch areas and missiles, convoys, trucks, tanks, and even SAM (surface-to-air missile) sites. Coupled with F-111s, F-15Es and F-16s, Joint STARS enhanced the 'kill box' approach to air interdiction to destroy Iraqi equipment in the KTO (Kuwait Theater of Operations). A USAF after-action report noted that "Joint STARS denied the enemy its night sanctuary and kept continual pressure on ground troops in the KTO."

MISSION PROFILE

Stand-off surveillance: from racetrack orbit the E-8 uses the Norden radar to peer sideways in three modes to build up a complete picture of all ground movements within its search sector; radar modes are WAS/MTI (wide-area surveillance/moving target indicator) which provides visual data on all vehicles moving within a large sector, providing an overall picture of the battlefield, SSM (sector search mode) which is similar to WAS/MTI but on a much smaller scale and highly useful for the individual targeting of vehicles, and SAR (synthetic aperture radar) which creates a bird's-eye radar picture at a range of up to 160 miles (257 km); secondary functions include a history replay mode which runs the accumulated images in fast-forward so that overall trends can be spotted, and a velocity threshold function which eliminates fast-moving vehicles such as cars; computer-generated cartographic information can be overlaid on the screen

Battle control: using information gleaned from the system, the E-8 crew can direct friendly forces via direct communications links; threatened ground forces can be steered away from danger or offensive formations directed to attack; helicopters and close support aircraft can be given precise target information

Stand-off reconnaissance: using the SAR mode the E-8 can be used as a reconnaissance tool to provide clear radar imagery of fixed positions such as airfields and military installations

USAF VARIANTS AND SERIALS

E-8A: A pair of Boeing 707-320 airframes was modified to E-8A standard to evaluate the Norden multimode side-looking radar antenna and associated equipment for the Joint STARS role. Both were allocated civilian identities while under development with Grumman and military serials during Operation Desert Storm. 86-0416 and 86-0417 (allocated N770JS and N8411)

YE-8B: The third aircraft has been allocated the designation YE-8B and will serve as the pre-production aircraft.
88-0322; plus other contracts

Above: Both of the E-8A testbeds are shown at Grumman's Melbourne facility, from where they were hastily deployed to the Gulf region during Operation Desert Storm. Data generated by the radar sensor was of great value in identifying and engaging Iraqi ground forces.

SPECIFICATION

Grumman/Boeing E-8A
Wing: span 145 ft 9 in (44.42 m); area 3,050.0 sq ft (283.35 m²)
Fuselage and tail: length 152 ft 11 in (46.61 m); height 42 ft 5 in (12.93 m); tailplane span 45 ft 9 in (13.95 m); wheel base 59 ft 0 in (17.98 m)
Powerplant: four Pratt & Whitney JT3D-7 each rated at 19,000 lb (84.52kN) dry thrust
Weight: maximum take-off 333,600 lb (151315 kg)
Fuel and load: internal fuel 159,560 lb (72375 kg); maximum theoretical payload 96,126 lb (43603 kg)
Speed: maximum cruising speed at 25,000 ft (7620 m) 605 mph (973 km/h); long-range cruising speed at 35,000 ft (10670 m) 534 mph (860 km/h)
Range: with maximum fuel 5,760 miles (9270 km)
Performance: maximum rate of climb at sea level 4,000 ft (1219 m) per minute; service ceiling 39,000 ft (11890 m)

USAF OPERATORS

Grumman AC		Melbourne, FL	E-8A, YE-8B

Boeing Canada
E-9 Dash 8

The **E-9** is a de Havilland Canada Dash 8 aircraft used for missile telemetry relay work by the USAF's Air Defense Weapons Center at Tyndall AFB, Florida.

The **E-9A** is employed for low-altitude, OTH (over-the-horizon) radar monitoring of air-to-air missile firings and for range clearance, including detecting vessels which intrude into the Gulf Test Range during missile work.

The aircraft operates with a crew of three, consisting of pilot (aircraft commander), co-pilot and systems operator. On a typical mission, the E-9A cruises at 300 mph (483 km/h) and stays aloft for up to five hours, usually operating at 15,000 ft (4572 m).

The high-wing, twin-turboprop E-9A is a Dash 8 100 series aircraft built by Boeing Canada (de Havilland) and modified by Sierra Research Division of LTV with installation of AN/APS-128D sea surveillance radar in a ventral radome and a five-beam, phased-array telemetry antenna in a distinctive 'cheek' radome on the right-hand side of the aircraft. This 75-sq ft (6.97-m²) antenna is capable of automatically detecting, tracking and relaying data simultaneously from five distinct sources traveling at speeds of Mach 5.0 or more.

The USAF's telemetry and range clearance effort is the only American military use of the Dash 8.

MISSION PROFILE

Test relay: during missile tests the E-9A acts as a relay platform for telemetry data, voice communications and drone/fighter control inputs

Range surveillance: performed simultaneously with relay duties is radar surveillance; provides monitoring of missile launches and spots vessels which may inadvertently enter the test area

USAF VARIANTS AND SERIALS

E-9A: The two Dash 8Ms were ordered during the late 1980s with a sensor suite including a steerable phased-array radar mounted in a fuselage pod on the starboard side.
No military serials allocated, with aircraft displaying civilian identities N801AP and N802AP

SPECIFICATION

Boeing Canada E-9A
Wing: span 85 ft 0 in (25.91 m); aspect ratio 12.4; area 585.0 sq ft (54.35 m²)
Fuselage and tail: length 73 ft 0 in (22.25 m); height 24 ft 7 in (7.49 m); tailplane span 26 ft 0 in (7.92 m); wheel base 26 ft 1 in (7.95 m)
Powerplant: two Pratt & Whitney Canada PW120A each rated at 2,000 shp (1491 kW)
Weight: maximum take-off 34,500 lb (15650 kg)
Fuel and load: internal fuel 5,678 lb (2576 kg) or optionally 10,244 lb (4646 kg); maximum payload 9,849 lb (4467 kg)
Speed: maximum cruising speed at 20,000 ft (6095 m) 305 mph (492 km/h)
Range: with 6,000-lb (2722-kg) payload 1,370 miles (2205 km); range with maximum payload 633 miles (1019 km)
Performance: maximum rate of climb at sea level 1,560 ft (475 m) per minute; certificated ceiling 25,000 ft (7620 m); take-off distance 3,150 ft (960 m); landing distance 2,979 ft (908 m)

USAF OPERATORS

Air Combat Command (ACC)

475th WEG	82nd TATS	Tyndall AFB, FL	E-9A

Above: Based on the commercial Dash 8, the E-9A is instantly identifiable by virtue of having a distinctive side-looking phased-array radar on the starboard fuselage adjacent to the cabin.

Below: Operated from Tyndall AFB, Florida, the two E-9As are used for relaying telemetry data and monitoring range areas during live missile firing exercises over the Gulf of Mexico.

General Dynamics/Grumman
F-111/EF-111 Raven

The **F-111**, unofficially known as the 'Aardvark', is a long-range, all-weather interdiction/strike warplane capable of navigating at low level to reach deep targets and deliver ordnance. The F-111 evolved over nearly two decades, after a misguided attempt to make it an all-purpose fighter. Although bearing a fighter designation, the aircraft is decidedly a bomber with limited air-to-air capability, the distinct **F-111D** being more effective for air combat than other versions. The **EF-111A Raven** is an electronic warfare version.

Basic features of the F-111 include a variable-sweep or 'swing' wing (the first in production in the world) with extremes of 16° and 72.5°, side-by-side seating for a crew of two (pilot and weapons systems officer), large main gears with low-pressure tires for no-flare landings on soft strips, and great fuel capacity (typically 5,022 US gal or 19010 liters) permitting an unrefueled range of 2,484 miles (3998 m).

Although now advanced in years, the F-111 retains considerable airframe life and is in some respects superior for air-to-ground work to the F-15E Strike Eagle which will replace it in some units. The USAF is expected to place some F-111s in storage, to assign some to one or more composite wings being formed in the early 1990s, and to consolidate the bulk of the F-111 force at Cannon AFB, New Mexico, with the **F-111F** version expected to remain in service longest as the size of the force is reduced.

The F-111F is equipped with all-weather AN/AVQ-26 Pave Tack infra-red targeting designator/reader carried in a pod-mounted turret. The F-111F can track and designate ground targets for laser, infra-red and electro-optical bombs. The F-111F typically carries an AN/ALQ-131(V) ECM (electronic countermeasures) pod; its ordnance load can include GBU-10, GBU-12, GBU-15, GBU-24, GBU-28, AGM-130 and other precision-guided munitions. The F-111F carries up to 31,500 lb (14228 kg) of conventional ordnance and has nuclear capability. The internal M61A1 Vulcan 0.79-in (20-mm) cannon includes the largest ammunition capacity ever carried by a fighter, up to 2,084 rounds but is rarely fitted.

The F-111F can make a terrain-following, low-level run against a target at a speed of around 700 mph (1126 km/h), or Mach 0.91 at sea level. The F-111F is powered by two 25,100-lb (11.65 kN) thrust Pratt & Whitney TF30-P-100 turbofan engines.

The F-111 resulted from the TFX (Tactical Fighter, Experimental) requirement of 1961, an attempt to create a multi-purpose fighter for both the USAF and US Navy. The prototype **F-111A** (63-9768) first flew on 21 December 1964. Though the Navy **F-111B** was eventually dropped, General Dynamics manufactured 562 F-111s, 532 for the USAF (including 17 research and development aeroplanes), six Navy craft, and 24 **F-111C**s for Australia.

The F-111A was introduced to Tactical Air Command in June 1967 with deliveries to the 474th Tactical Fighter Wing at Nellis AFB,

Nevada. In March 1968, the A model began a premature, and ultimately unsuccessful deployment to Vietnam. A second combat deployment in 1972-73 was more effective.

The **F-111E** was the second production version, retaining most of the features of the F-111A but introducing larger engine inlet ducts (intended for the improved TF30-P-100 engine which did not arrive until the F-111F model) and an improved version of the original TF30 engine. The first F-111Es reached the 20th Tactical Fighter Wing at RAF Upper Heyford in Britain on 12 September 1970.

The out-of-sequence **F-111D** entered service with the 27th Tactical Fighter Wing at Cannon AFB, New Mexico, in October 1971. The D model introduced a very different 'Mark II' avionics system and other unique features, including HUD (head-up display) for both crewmen. Considered superior to other 'Aardvark' variants, as well as being the only version which might perform well in air-to-air combat, the F-111D with its different systems never fully realized its capabilities and was used from the mid-1980s onward in the operational conversion training role. Plans for an **RF-111D** reconnaissance version did not materialize.

The F-111F introduced the TF30-P-100 engine. The TF30, while reliable and cost-effective, had always delivered insufficient power. The new engine did nothing less than transform the performance of the 'Aardvark', increasing the thrust-to-weight ratio from 0.39 in the A model to 0.53 in the F.

The F-111F joined the 347th Tactical Fighter Wing at Mountain Home AFB, Idaho, in February 1972. The F models stayed at Mountain Home with the 366th TFW and sent

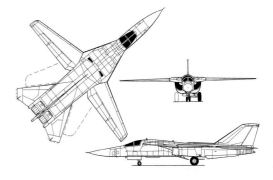

Above: Once known as 'McNamara's Folly', the General Dynamics F-111 was the first variable geometry warplane to attain operational status when it joined TAC in June 1967.

a detachment to Korea during a period of heightened tensions in 1976. In March 1977, the F-111F force was reassigned and relocated to RAF Lakenheath in the UK. F-111Fs spearheaded Operation Eldorado Canyon, the strikes against Libya in April 1986.

The wing deployed for Operation Desert Storm and subsequently returned to Lakenheath. During Desert Storm, the 48th TFW deployed 66 F-111Fs to Taif, Saudi Arabia, which was also temporary home to some EF-111As from both USAF squadrons. The 20th TFW fielded 22 F-111Es and five EF-111As which operated with the 7440th Composite Wing at Incirlik, Turkey. The Saudi-based F-111Fs attacked key military production facilities including chemical, biological and nuclear sites, airfields, bunkers, and portions of Iraq's integrated air-defense system. In over 4,000 sorties, the 84 deployed F-111s had a mission-capable rate of over 85 per cent, or eight per cent higher than peacetime rates. In what became known as 'tank plinking', F-111s were credited with over 1,500 verified armor kills. F-111s were used for precision bombing of the

Left: A brace of F-111Es from the 20th Fighter Wing at RAF Upper Heyford and an EF-111A Raven formate with a KC-135E of the Utah Air National Guard prior to taking on fuel in flight. The F-111E was committed to combat during Desert Storm, but during 1992 the aircraft returned to the United States for service with the 27th FW. At about the same time, a squadron of EF-111As at the same base also returned to the USA, while the Lakenheath-based F-111Fs of the 48th Fighter Wing are giving way to F-15E Strike Eagles.

Below: Retirement of the FB-111A from two SAC medium bomb wings was expected to lead to most being transferred to TAC's 27th Wing at Cannon, New Mexico, as F-111Gs. However, defense cutbacks in the USA have resulted in a change of plan and only sufficient aircraft to equip one squadron were handed on.

Above: Displaying the insignia of the Mountain Home-based 366th Fighter Wing, the F-111A shown here is now mainly used for training crews for the 'Aardvark' force and is being retired in view of plans to reduce the size of that force in the fairly immediate future.

Left: Carrying a clutch of four GBU-10 LGBs, an F-111F of the 48th Fighter Wing flies over its home base at RAF Lakenheath, England. Other key features which are shown to advantage in this view are the AN/AVQ-26 Pave Tack targeting pod beneath the forward fuselage and an AN/ALQ-131 electronic countermeasures pod nestling between the ventral fins at the rear.

Above: Other weapons which can be carried and delivered by the F-111F include the GBU-15, two examples of this glide bomb being toted by this 'Aardvark'. Although it looks similar to an ECM pod, the object beneath the forward fuselage is actually an AXX-14 datalink pod.

F-111/EF-111 Raven (continued)

oil-pumping facility used to disgorge oil into the Persian Gulf. In the final hours of the war, two GBU-28 4,700-lb (2132-kg) 'bunker busting' bombs were dropped in combat on a bunker complex at Al Taji air base near Baghdad. This unusually heavy bomb, based on the standard GBU-27, had been developed to kill senior Iraqi military commanders ensconced in bunkers as deep as 10 ft (30.48 m). One bomb missed its target, but the second

Below: A total of 96 examples of the F-111D saw service with Tactical Air Command, introducing improved avionics equipment and a more powerful engine when it entered the inventory in 1971. A single acquisition-round AIM-9 Sidewinder heat-seeking air-to-air missile is carried by this F-111D, which displays the unit insignia and fin code letter combination of the 27th Fighter Wing at Cannon AFB, New Mexico.

Above: The legend on the vertical tail surfaces of this F-111F identifies it as being assigned to the commanding officer of the 492nd TFS, one of four squadrons operating from RAF Lakenheath as part of the 48th Wing. Shock diamonds may be clearly seen in the afterburner plume, as this aircraft cleans up moments after take-off.

scored a direct hit during a mission conducted on the final evening of the war. One EF-111A scored an unofficial 'kill' by maneuvering a pursuing Iraqi fighter into the ground; another EF-111A was lost in combat.

In 1992, the 48th TFW was scheduled to begin converting from four squadrons of F-111F 'Aardvarks' to two squadrons of F-15E Strike Eagles.

The analog avionics on all 84 surviving F-111F aircraft are being replaced by digital-based systems by Rockwell in the Pacer Strike

program. The upgrade will include a ring laser gyroscope, Standard Inertial Navigation Unit, GPS (global positioning system) receiver, and cockpit multifunction displays. Flight tests of the upgraded F-111F were scheduled for early 1992.

The **FB-111A** strategic variant of the 'Aardvark' entered service in October 1969. The 'FB' was operated by the 380th Bomb Wing at Plattsburgh AFB, New York, and the 509th Bomb Wing at Pease AFB, New Hampshire, and was capable of employing AGM-69 SRAM (Short-Range Attack Missiles) and other nuclear weapons. When the FB-111A was retired in July 1991 after more than two decades as an integral part of Strategic Air Command's long-range force, plans for 59 FB-111As to be transferred to tactical forces were scaled down. Only one squadron at Cannon AFB has received these aircraft, redesignated **F-111G**, with the remainder of the FB-111A force going into storage.

The designation **FB-111H** was assigned to a planned strategic bomber intended for an interim role after the B-1A bomber was cancelled by President Carter in 1977. As events unfolded, the B-1B bomber was fielded instead and the FB-111H was not proceeded with.

Out of sequence in order of designation was the **F-111K** for Great Britain, a program which was well advanced when it was cancelled in January 1967. The F-111 production run ended in September 1976.

The EF-111A Raven, or 'Spark Vark', is a Grumman conversion of the A model to a dedicated tactical jamming system and electronic warfare aircraft. The conversion entailed installation of the AN/ALQ-99E tactical jamming package, with inflight adaptable antennas, digital jamming, and isolated active and passive ECM systems. A distinctive feature is the fin-cap cone of the EF-111A which accommodates 370 lb (168 kg) of pod structure loaded with 583 lb (264 kg) of electronic equipment including AN/ALR-23 infra-red warning system.

The USAF is expected to move ahead with a SIP (service improvement program) developed by Grumman to boost the reliability and performance of the EF-111A's electronic warfare suite to cope with the increasingly sophisticated enemy radars developed and fielded by the 1990s. These first hardware upgrades since the Raven was fielded in 1984 will increase the number of emitters the EF-111A's AN/ALQ-99E suite can handle and the speed with which the system copes with threats. Plans for all 41 surviving EF-111As to be upgraded may have to be scaled down due to funding constraints of the 1990s.

MISSION PROFILE

Armament options: provision for internal M61A1 20-mm cannon mounted in internal weapons bay with 2,084 rounds; eight ordnance hardpoints (stations 1 and 8 not normally used) for the carriage of most stores in US inventory, including nuclear bombs, conventional low-drag and retarded bombs, cluster-bomb units, and GBU-15 glide bomb; future weapons are to include AGM-130 powered stand-off bomb and AGM-137 TSSAM; defensive stores include AN/ALQ-119(V) or AN/ALQ-131(V) ECM pod; (F-111F) AN/AVQ-26 Pave Tack infra-red targeting designator/reader carried in pod-mounted device

Radar
The giant nose radome houses a powerful attack radar which allows precise bombing. The F-111F model adds electro-optical sensors in the form of the Pave Tack pod, giving the F model exceptional precision-guided munition capability.

Nuclear strike: on a nuclear strike mission, the F-111F would refuel in flight but can fly to a combat radius of about 800 miles (1287 km) unrefueled with two B61 or B83 nuclear bombs and one 600-US gal (2271-liter) fuel tank on left or right belly pylon (not both)

Interdiction/strike: on a hi-lo-hi interdiction, the F-111 would refuel in flight but can fly to a combat radius (with low-level high-speed dash of 100 miles/161 km) of about 650 miles (1046 km) unrefueled with six Mk 82 500-lb (227-kg) general-purpose bombs, or four M117D/R 750-lb (340-kg) bombs, or four GBU-12 500-lb (227-kg) laser-guided bombs, all external; internal payload to similar radius could include two 2,000-lb (907-kg) Mk 84 bombs in internal weapons bay and one 60-US gal (2271-liter) fuel tank on left or right belly pylon (not both)

Electronic warfare (EF-111A): on a barrier stand-off jamming mission, the EF-111A would refuel in flight but can fly at high altitude to a combat radius of about 600 miles (965 km) unrefueled to loiter in racetrack orbit short of the FEBA (forward edge of battle area) for two and one-half hours; on a penetration escort mission, the EF-111A would refuel in flight but can fly at high altitude to a combat radius of about 800 miles (1287 km) unrefueled to escort strike aircraft to and from target

USAF VARIANTS AND SERIALS

Original construction designations
F-111A: The initial production model, 17 pre-production versions and 10 production aircraft were employed in the development role. These were followed by 131 service aircraft ordered in 1966 and 1967.
63-9766 to 63-9782; 65-5701 to 65-5710; 66-0011 to 66-0058; 67-0032 to 67-0114

F-111D: The F-111D was a development of the F-111A but featured improved avionics and larger engines, with 96 ordered in 1968.
68-0085 to 68-0180

F-111E: The F-111E was basically an F-111A but with modified air intakes to improve engine performance, with 94 ordered in 1967 and 1968.
67-0115 to 67-0124; 68-0001 to 68-0084

F-111F: The F-111F was the ultimate development of the basic F-111A, with uprated engines and simplified avionics. One hundred and six were ordered between 1970 and 1974.
70-2362 to 70-2419; 71-0883 to 71-0894; 72-1441 to 72-1452; 73-0707 to 73-0718; 74-0177 to 74-0188

FB-111A: Seventy-six FB-111As were ordered for SAC between 1967 and 1969. Changes included a larger wing span and a modified ordnance release system compatible with nuclear weapons.
67-0159 to 67-0163; 67-7192 to 67-7196; 68-0239 to 68-0292; 69-6503 to 69-6514

Conversion designations
F-111G: Former SAC FB-111As were allocated the designation F-111G upon transfer to TAC. The aircraft were fitted with a conventional weapons release

Defensive avionics
All F-111 models are liberally supplied with warning receivers, aimed both at radars (wing glove leading edges and tail bullets) and infra-red (fin tip bullet). Chaff and flare dispensers are standard, and electronic jamming pods are carried externally.

Wing
The F-111G differs from other current USAF variants by having a longer-span wing for extended range. This, however, affects the low-level ride of the aircraft.

Weapons options
When serving with SAC, the F-111Gs (then known as FB-111As) carried the AGM-69 SRAM as their primary weapon, carrying two internally. On transferral to TAC they were wired for conventional ordnance, this normally comprising 'iron' or cluster bombs. This aircraft has MERs loaded with a total of 24 Mk 82 LDGP bombs.

Cockpit
Instead of having individual ejection seats, the crew sit in a capsule, which in emergency is severed completely from the rest of the aircraft. Parachutes stabilize and slow its descent, and after landing it forms a survival shelter.

General Dynamics F-111G

The USAF's 'Aardvark' force is undergoing a major rationalization, with USAFE aircraft returning to Cannon, replacing F-111Ds and Gs with the 27th Fighter Wing. The F-111G only serves with one squadron within the wing, and is primarily used for training purposes.

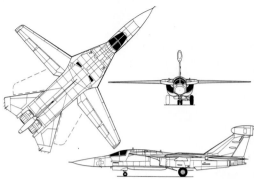

Above: Developed from the original production model, the EF-111A Raven is optimized to fulfil the electronic warfare mission and was subject to extensive modification for this role.

F-111/EF-111 Raven (continued)

system as the only modification. The original plan was for some 60 aircraft to be included, although cutbacks have resulted in this number being reduced to 30.
67-0162; 67-0163; 67-7193; 67-7194; 67-7196; 68-0240; 68-0241; 68-0244; 68-0252; 68-0255; 68-0257; 68-0260; 68-0264; 68-0265; 68-0272; 68-0273; 68-0276; 68-0277; 68-0281; 68-0282; 68-0284; 68-0289; 69-6503; 69-6504; 69-6506; 69-6508; 69-6509; 69-6510; 69-6512; 69-6514

EF-111A: Forty-two F-111As were modified to the defense suppression role with the fitment of powerful processor/jammer equipment installed in the weapons bay and in a special fintip-mounted fairing.
66-0013; 66-0014; 66-0015; 66-0016; 66-0018; 66-0019; 66-0020; 66-0021; 66-0023; 66-0027; 66-0028; 66-0030; 66-0031; 66-0033; 66-0035; 66-0036; 66-0037; 66-0038; 66-0039; 66-0041; 66-0044; 66-0046; 66-0047; 66-0048; 66-0049; 66-0050; 66-0051; 66-0055; 66-0056; 66-0057; 67-0032; 67-0033; 67-0034; 67-0035; 67-0037; 67-0038; 67-0039; 67-0041; 67-0042; 67-0044; 67-0048; 67-0052

GF-111A: Nine retired F-111As have been allocated to Air Training Command to teach technical trade training.
63-9768; 63-9772; 63-9775; 66-0012; 67-0046; 67-0047; 67-0051; 67-0056; 67-0057

YF-111A: Two aircraft from the cancelled F-111K order for the RAF were redesignated as YF-111As to conduct research and development.
67-0149 and 67-0150

YFB-111A: A single pre-production F-111A was modified to FB-111A status and assigned the Y prefix to indicate service test. The aircraft eventually served with NASA.
63-9783

SPECIFICATION

General Dynamics F-111F
Wing: span 63 ft 0 in (19.20 m) spread and (31 ft 11.4 in (9.74 m swept); area 525.0 sq ft (48.77 m²) spread and 657.3 sq ft (61.07 m²) spread
Fuselage and tail: length 73 ft 6 in (22.40 m); height 17 ft 1.4 in (5.22 m)
Powerplant: two Pratt & Whitney TF30-P-100 each rated at 25,000 lb (111.65 kN) afterburning thrust
Weights: operating empty 47,481 lb (21537 kg); maximum take-off 100,000 (45359 kg)
Fuel and load: internal fuel 5,025 US gal (19021 liters); external fuel up to four 600-US gal (2271-liter) drop tanks; maximum ordnance 31,500 lb (14228 kg)
Speed: maximum level speed 'clean' at 36,000 ft (10975 m) 1,650 mph (2655 km/h); cruising speed at high altitude 571 mph (919 km/h)
Range: maximum range with full internal fuel more than 2,925 miles (4707 km)
Performance: service ceiling 60.000 ft (18290 m); take-off distance to 50 ft (15 m) 3,120 ft (950 m); landing distance less than 3,000 ft (915 m)

General Dynamics F-111A and F-111E
generally similar to the F-111F except in the following particulars:
Powerplant: two Pratt & Whitney TF30-P-3 each

Above: Presently operated by just two squadrons of the USAF, the EF-111A Raven incorporates the ALQ-99E tactical jamming system which evolved from the package of equipment developed for the Navy's EA-6B Prowler.

rated at 18,500 lb (82.29 kN) afterburning thrust
Weights: operating empty 46,172 lb (20943 kg); maximum take-off 91,300 lb (41414 kg)
Fuel and load: internal fuel 5,033 US gal (19052 liters)

Grumman EF-111A
generally similar to the F-111A except in the following particulars:
Fuselage and tail: unit length 76 ft 0 in (23.16 m); height 20 ft 0 in (6.10 m)
Powerplant: two Pratt & Whitney TF30-P-3 each rated at 18,500 lb (82.29 kN) afterburning thrust
Weights: operating empty 55,275 lb (25072 kg); normal take-off 70,000 lb (31752 kg); maximum take-off 88,948 lb (4046 kg)
Fuel and load: internal fuel 32,493 lb (14739 kg)
Speed: maximum speed at high altitude 1,412 mph (2272 km/h); maximum combat speed 1,377 mph (2216 km/h); average speed in combat area 584 mpg (940 km/h)
Range: combat radius 929 miles (1495 km); unrefueled endurance more than 4 hours 0 minutes
Performance: maximum rate of climb at sea level 3,300 ft (1006 m) per minute; service ceiling 45,000 ft (13715 m)

General Dynamics F-111D
generally similar to the F-111F except in the following particulars:
Powerplant: two Pratt & Whitney TF30-P-9 each rated at 20,640 lb (91.81 kN) afterburning thrust
Weights: operating empty 46,631 lb (21151 kg)
Fuel and load: internal fuel 5,033 US gal (19052 liters)

General Dynamics FB-111A
generally similar to the F-111F except in the following particulars:
Wing: span 70 ft 0 in (21.34 m) spread and 33 ft 11.5 in (10.35 m swept); area 550.0 sq ft (51.10 m²) spread
Fuselage and tail: length 75 ft 7 in (23.04 m); height 17 ft 1.4 in (5.22 m)
Powerplant: two Pratt & Whitney TF30-P-7 each rated at 20,230 lb (90.52 kN) afterburning thrust
Weights: operating empty 47,980 lb (21763 kg); maximum take-off 119,243 lb (58044 kg)
Fuel and load: internal fuel 5,612 US gal (21243 liters) with bomb bay tanks; external fuel up to six 600-US gal (2271-liter) drop tanks; maximum ordnance 37,500 lb (17010 kg)

USAF OPERATORS

Air Force Materiel Command (AFMC)

Sacramento ALC		'SM'	McClellan AFB, CA	F-111A/ D/E, EF-111A
3246th TW	3247th TS	'ET'	Eglin AFB, FL	F-111E

Air Training Command (ATC)

3400th TTW	Lowry TTC		Lowry AFB, CO	GF-111A
3700th TTW	Sheppard TTC		Sheppard AFB, TX	GF-111A

Air Combat Command (ACC)

27th FW	428th FTS	'CC'	Cannon AFB, NM	F-111G*
	522nd FS	'CC'	Cannon AFB, NM	F-111D**
	523rd FS	'CC'	Cannon AFB, NM	F-111D**
	524th FTS	'CC'	Cannon AFB, NM	F-111**D
57th FW	431st TES	'WA'	McClellan AFB, CA	F-111A/D/ E/F/G
366th FW	389th FTS	'MO'	Mountain Home AFB, ID	F-111A***
	390th ECS	'MO'	Mountain Home AFB, ID	EF-111A***
	391st FTS	'MO'	Mountain Home AFB, ID	F-111A***

United States Air Forces in Europe (USAFE)

20th FW	42nd ECS	'UH'	RAF Upper Heyford, UK	EF-111A to 27th Fighter Wing
	55th FS	'UH'	RAF Upper Heyford, UK	F-111E***
	77th FS	'UH'	RAF Upper Heyford, UK	F-111E***
	79th FS	'UH'	RAF Upper Heyford, UK	F-111E***
48th FW	492nd FS	'LN'	RAF Lakenheath, UK	F-111F****
	493rd FS	'LN'	RAF Lakenheath, UK	F-111F
	494th FS	'LN'	RAF Lakenheath, UK	F-111F****
	495th FS	'LN'	RAF Lakenheath, UK	F-111F
	(495th FS inactivated in December 1991, with the 493rd FS due to follow in 1992)			

* to receive F-111E
** to receive F-111F
*** to deactivate
**** to receive F-15E

Lockheed
F-117 Night Hawk

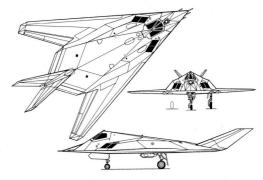

The **F-117 Night Hawk** or 'Black Jet', popularly called the 'Stealth Fighter', is actually a strike aircraft and is the first operational warplane to employ LO (low observables), or stealth, technology to reduce its vulnerability to radar detection. Though called a fighter, the F-117 is not intended for air-to-air combat. Its purpose is to deliver ordnance in a dense threat environment against targets of extremely high value. The F-117 emerged from a 'black' program where it was developed in conditions of unprecedented secrecy.

The mission of the F-117 is unique: to attack small, well-protected targets which are, in Pentagon jargon, highly leveraged, i.e., their destruction will damage an enemy out of proportion to their intrinsic value. A typical assignment would be to 'decapitate' an enemy's C^3I (command, control, communications and intelligence) structure by attacking it by surprise with precision-guided bombs. Other F-117 targets might be nuclear storage sites, critical bridges and tunnels, or key leadership headquarters.

All 57 of the USAF's **F-117A** aircraft belong to the 49th Fighter Wing, which was previously the 49th Fighter Wing before its move in 1992 from Tonopah Test Range Air Field, Nevada, to Holloman AFB, New Mexico. F-117As have been employed in combat in Panama (1989) and in Operation Desert Storm (1991).

The wedge-shaped, V-tailed F-117A (leading edge sweep of 67.5°) employs radar absorbent composite materials on its external surfaces. In addition, it has angular features which contribute to low-observable characteristics by reducing the RCS (radar cross section) of the aircraft. Use of radar absorbent materials should make the aircraft appear dim to a radar while the angular shape should cause it to 'glitter' irregularly as its aspect angle varies.

The angular shape results from a technique known as faceting, which applies computer technology to aircraft design and, in this instance, produced radical use of 'chisel-edge' leading surfaces and sharp fuselage angles, eliminating curved surfaces in order to diffuse radar returns. The skin panels of the airframe are divided into many small, perfectly flat surfaces, which reflect at a variety of angles all signals from probing hostile ground or airborne radars.

The stealth qualities of the aircraft are enhanced by engine exhaust nozzles located atop the fuselage along the wing root just ahead of the tail surfaces. The exhaust bleeds over the aft fuselage to screen the heat emissions from detection below.

The pilot of the F-117A sits on an ACES 2 ejection seat in a small cockpit which features a windshield arrangement with a separate panel in front and two different-sized windows on each side. The pilot has a conventional HUD

Above: One of the most distinctive and elusive items of hardware to be found in today's USAF inventory is Lockheed's F-117A Night Hawk, more familiarly known as the 'Stealth Fighter'.

(head-up display) for basic flight information and infra-red imagery, with an up-front control panel beneath it for radio and display mode selections. On the main panel, standard MFDs (multifunction displays) are installed either side of a large monochrome CRT screen. Four protruding spikes on the aircraft's nose are air data probes for air speed and altitude sensing. The F-117A has quadruple redundant fly-by-wire flight controls. The F-117A is powered by two General Electric F404-GE-F1D2 engines without afterburners. These engines give the aircraft a low noise signature and produce no visible exhaust.

Below: An F-117A of the 37th Fighter Wing flies over Half Dome Mountain in Yosemite National Park during a daylight mission from its base at Tonopah. 'Stealth Fighters' like this played a major role in the aerial onslaught against Iraq, when they invariably operated by night.

F-117A Night Hawk (continued)

The F-117A's primary weapon is the LGB, one type being the GBU-27 employed solely by this aircraft and developed from the Mk 84 series of 2,000-lb (907-kg) weapons.

The F-117A can be carried on board C-5A/B Galaxy airlifters with its wings removed, as the USAF intended the F-117A to be readily deployed to trouble spots. Maintenance can be performed out of vans, not buildings, and the vans can be moved overseas aboard C-130, C-141B or C-5A/B transports.

During the 1970s, low observables technology was studied in great secrecy by DARPA (the Defense Advanced Research Projects Agency) and the USAF with a goal no less ambitious than to alter aerial warfare by producing a warplane invisible to radar. As many as six manufacturers were involved, Lockheed only belatedly. The competition for what became the Have Blue flying prototype narrowed down to Northrop and Lockheed. Two small twin-engined prototypes emerged from Lockheed Advanced Development Projects, the 'Skunk Works', in Burbank, California. In 1977, control of these Have Blue proof-of-concept aircraft was shifted from DARPA to the USAF as a black (special access) project, known only to those with clearance. Test flights of Have Blue aircraft were followed by Project Senior Trend which produced the similar but larger F-117A.

In 1978, a decision was made to proceed with FSD (full-scale development) and low-level production, making use of numerous components from other aircraft types to minimize cost and potential risk. Lockheed used F-16 flight control computers, F-18 cockpit displays, and C-130 environmental systems. First flight was on 18 June 1981, only 31 months later. The 4450th Tactical Group (redesignated 37th TFW in October 1989, 37th FW in October 1991, and 49th FW in January 1992) reached IOC (initial operating capability) in the F-117A on 26 October 1983. The 59th and last F-117A was delivered on 12 July 1990. Two F-117As have been lost in mishaps.

Operating under the tightest security, the aircraft flew almost eight years before its presence was publicly acknowledged. During this period, F-117As were restricted mostly to night flying in order to maintain secrecy. The USAF released limited information and a poor quality photograph in November 1988. This permitted the aircraft to operate in daylight and facilitated its integration into operational planning and exercises.

Flying was initially conducted at Groom Lake, Nevada, and later at Tonopah. To maintain secrecy in its early years, the F-117A was operated out of the remote Tonopah base at night and usually stayed within the large restricted airspace connected with nearby Nellis AFB.

During Operation Just Cause in December 1989, two F-117As flew non-stop from Nevada with air refueling to attack the Rio Hato barracks in Panama using GBU-27 2,000-lb (907-kg) bombs. The accuracy of the attack has been the subject of some debate – one bomb appears to have been aimed in the wrong place – but the F-117A and its systems worked as intended.

Above: Inflight refueling was a vital factor in allowing the F-117A to fly non-stop from its base at Tonopah to Rio Hato on the type's first exposure to the hazards of combat during Operation Just Cause, and also played a noteworthy part in the campaign to liberate Kuwait.

Below: A trio of 'Black Jets' awaits pilots at Khamis Mushait Air Base in Saudi Arabia during Desert Storm. Flying alone and under a cloak of darkness, F-117As completed a total of 1,271 combat sorties against high-value targets at no cost to themselves.

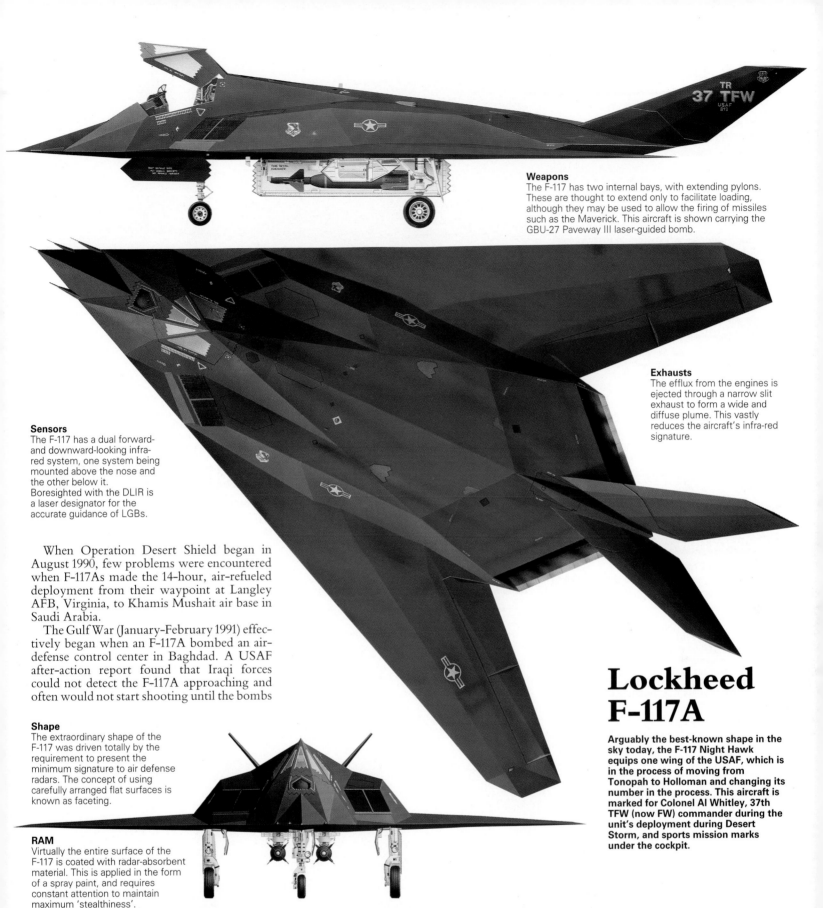

Weapons
The F-117 has two internal bays, with extending pylons. These are thought to extend only to facilitate loading, although they may be used to allow the firing of missiles such as the Maverick. This aircraft is shown carrying the GBU-27 Paveway III laser-guided bomb.

Exhausts
The efflux from the engines is ejected through a narrow slit exhaust to form a wide and diffuse plume. This vastly reduces the aircraft's infra-red signature.

Sensors
The F-117 has a dual forward- and downward-looking infra-red system, one system being mounted above the nose and the other below it. Boresighted with the DLIR is a laser designator for the accurate guidance of LGBs.

Shape
The extraordinary shape of the F-117 was driven totally by the requirement to present the minimum signature to air defense radars. The concept of using carefully arranged flat surfaces is known as faceting.

RAM
Virtually the entire surface of the F-117 is coated with radar-absorbent material. This is applied in the form of a spray paint, and requires constant attention to maintain maximum 'stealthiness'.

Lockheed F-117A

Arguably the best-known shape in the sky today, the F-117 Night Hawk equips one wing of the USAF, which is in the process of moving from Tonopah to Holloman and changing its number in the process. This aircraft is marked for Colonel Al Whitley, 37th TFW (now FW) commander during the unit's deployment during Desert Storm, and sports mission marks under the cockpit.

When Operation Desert Shield began in August 1990, few problems were encountered when F-117As made the 14-hour, air-refueled deployment from their waypoint at Langley AFB, Virginia, to Khamis Mushait air base in Saudi Arabia.

The Gulf War (January-February 1991) effectively began when an F-117A bombed an air-defense control center in Baghdad. A USAF after-action report found that Iraqi forces could not detect the F-117A approaching and often would not start shooting until the bombs exploded. The USAF concluded that the F-117A had demonstrated its ability to cruise to the target at around 580 mph (933 km/h) or about Mach 0.81, identify the target before surface threats became active, and hit it with precision. During Operation Desert Storm, the F-117A's first-generation 'stealth' properties enabled it to fly 1,271 combat sorties in the 42-day war without losses.

The USAF is pursuing OCIP (Offensive Capability Improvement Program) modifications to eventually upgrade all F-117As to increase the pilot's situational awareness. Lockheed is converting F-117As to the OCIP configuration at a rate of one per month. The OCIP modification, aimed at developing a more 'man-efficient' cockpit, includes two-color CRT multifunction displays, digital moving map, and liquid crystal display to be used as a data entry panel to communicate with the avionics system. Also to be added are auto throttles which control the F-117A in altitude, latitude and longitude and determine the time at which the aircraft arrives at specific waypoints or targets. An automatic recovery system is included that can be activated by the pilot in bad weather to return the F-117A to 'wings level' attitude.

The full force of 57 OCIP-modified F-117As was expected to be operational in all three squadrons of the 49th FW by late 1992. The wing's first squadron, its RTU (replacement training unit), was scheduled to acquire its 13th aircraft in mid-1992 and to be declared operational in the new version, although full squadron strength is 18 aircraft. Conversion to the improved F-117A will then be repeated for the wing's two other squadrons, the three units being the 7th, 8th and 9th Fighter Squadrons.

F-1117A Night Hawk (continued)

MISSION PROFILE

Armament options: provision for internal ordnance only; for the carriage of most stores in US inventory, including conventional low-drag and retarded bombs, and cluster-bomb units; GBU-27 Paveway III laser-guided bomb designed for this aircraft was developed from Mk 84 2,000-lb (907-kg) bomb

HVA (high value asset) strike: on an HVA strike against a highly leveraged target, the F-117 would refuel in flight but can fly at high altitude to a combat radius of about 900 miles (1448 km) unrefueled, cruising at around 580 mph (933 km/h) or about Mach 0.81; flies to a radius of about 460 miles (740 km) with one BLU-109/GBU-27 2,000-lb (907-kg) bomb.

USAF VARIANTS AND SERIALS

YF-117A: Two prototype aircraft are believed to have been allocated FY1979 serials even though the first example was lost in 1978!
79?-10780 to 79?-10781

F-117A: Four full-scale development aircraft were followed by 58 production versions ordered in small batches between 1980 and 1988.
79-10782 to 79-10784; 79-0782 to ??-0785; 80-0786 to 80-0791; ??-0792; 81-0793 to 81-0798; 82-0799 to 82-0806; 83-0807 to 83-0808; 84-0809 to 84-0812; 84-0824 to 84-0828; 85-0813 to 85-0820; 85-0829 to 85-0836; 86-0821 to 86-0823; 86-0837 to 86-0840; 88-0841 to 88-0843

(**Note:** the F-117As carry only the last three of the serial externally.)

SPECIFICATION

Lockheed F-117A
Wing: span 42 ft 4 in (13.20 m); area about 1,140.0 sq ft (105.9 m²)

Above: Four of the 37th Fighter Wing's F-117As that were deployed to Saudi Arabia for Desert Storm taxi in at Nellis AFB, Nevada, bringing to a close a spectacularly successful chapter in the continuing saga of Lockheed's celebrated 'Black Jet'. Other returning aircraft evaded public attention by proceeding directly to home base at Tonopah Test Range Airfield.

Fuselage and tail: length 65 ft 11 in (20.08 m); height 12 ft 5 in (3.78 m)
Powerplant: two General Electric F404-GE-F1D2 each rated at 10,800 lb (48.04 kN) dry thrust
Weights: empty about 30,000 lb (13608 kg); maximum take-off 52,500 lb (23814 kg)
Fuel and load: maximum ordnance 4,000 lb (1814 kg)
Speed: maximum level speed 'clean' at high altitude possibly more than Mach 1; normal maximum operating speed at optimum altitude Mach 0.9
Range: combat radius about 500 miles (805 km)

USAF OPERATORS

Air Force Materiel Command (AFMC)

3246th TW	3247th TS	'ET'	Eglin AFB, FL	F-117A
6510th TW	6512th TS	'ED'	Edwards AFB, CA	F-117A

Air Combat Command (ACC)

49th FW	7th FS	'HO'	Holloman AFB, NM	F-117A
	8th FS	'HO'	Holloman AFB, NM	F-117A
	9th FS	'HO'	Holloman AFB, NM	F-117A

Situated in one of the more remote parts of the state of Nevada, conveniently close to the huge Nellis range complex, Tonopah was almost ideal for ensuring that the secrecy surrounding the 'Stealth Fighter' wasn't compromised. Here, two F-117As pose near Tonopah's control tower.

McDonnell Douglas
F-4 Phantom

The **F-4 Phantom**, arguably the world's most effective multi-role fighter in the 1960s, has enjoyed enormous staying power and remains in service in modest numbers. The last **F-4E** unit in the Air National Guard (ANG) was expected to be retired in 1992. **F-4G** 'Wild Weasel' aircraft were scheduled to remain in service until 1995.

The F-4 design is characterized by its two-seat, twin-engined configuration, upturned wingtips, anhedral tailplane and downturned nose. The F-4E spent much of its service life as a multi-role fighter for air-to-air combat and close support/interdiction missions. Outclassed by newer fighters such as the F-15, which has further-reaching radar and better maneuverability, the last E model Phantoms remaining in ANG service were assigned the air-to-ground role.

The E model is equipped with Westinghouse AN/APQ-120 solid-state radar fire control system, which is smaller than the radar on earlier variants. An M61A1 20-mm Vulcan cannon is fitted internally, with an improved fire-control system and increased fuel capacity. The F-4E employs AIM-7 Sparrow and AIM-9 Sidewinder air-to-air missiles, AGM-65 Maverick TV-guided air-to-ground missiles, and a range of guided and unguided bombs.

On a typical mission, the F-4E Phantom carries 6,000 lb (2721 kg) of ordnance out to a combat radius of 650 miles (1046 km) on a hi-lo-hi profile, with air refueling *en route* to target and the sortie lasting about three and one-half hours. The crew (pilot and weapon system officer) has a clear division of labor – the latter being responsible for navigation and serving as an extra pair of eyes and ears to relieve the pilot of some busy tasks. The huge load-carrying capacity of the Phantom is rarely exploited in practical situations: its maximum payload of up to 16,000 lb (7258 kg) of ordnance is effective only at much shorter distance.

In 1991, the USAF retired its final F-4Es. These were the last F-4Es in the active-duty force and were also the only Phantoms (and the only aircraft other than the F-111F) equipped with the AN/AVQ-26 Pave Tack pod-mounted infra-red targeting designator/reader. Pave Tack-capable F-4Es had been assigned to Clark AB, Philippines.

The F-4G 'Wild Weasel' is a modified F-4E with its cannon replaced by an AN/APR-47 electronic warfare suite for the active SEAD (suppression of enemy air defense) mission, which means striking or otherwise neutralizing SAM-related air defense radars. The F-4G carries AGM-88A/B/C HARM (high-speed anti-radiation missiles). It can operate with other F-4Gs or serve as a hunter to direct fighter-bombers such as the F-16 in hunter-killer teamwork. A typical F-4G mission against an enemy's SAM sites lasts for about four hours, the aircraft refueling *en route* and cruising at around 660 mph (1062 km/h) or Mach 0.90 at 30,000 ft (9144 m). In the F-4G, the second crew member is an EWO (electronic warfare officer) who navigates, assists with communication and sets up the attack on SAM radars.

The F-4E and F-4G are powered by two 17,900-lb (8119-kg) thrust afterburning Pratt & Whitney J79-GE-17A turbojet engines.

When its configuration was decided upon in the design stages in 1954-57, the Phantom was unorthodox in offering a two-man crew, twin-engines, and (prior to the F-4E) all-missile armament for air-to-air combat. The first Phantom flew on 27 May 1958. The aircraft was developed by the US Navy and joined the USAF only belatedly in 1962. **F-4A, F-4B, F-4G, F-4J, F-4N** and **F-4S** were Navy/Marine Corps versions of the Phantom, while **RF-4E, F-4F, F-4K** and **F-4M** are foreign variants. **F-4C** (originally F-110A) and **F-4D** models served with the USAF in Vietnam and into the late 1980s, and have since been retired from USAF/ANG inventory. The **RF-4C** (originally RF-110A) reconnaissance version is treated separately.

The F-4E model resulted from experience gained in early air-to-air engagements over North Vietnam and was the only Phantom version to incorporate an internal gun. The first F-4E (66-0284) flew on 30 June 1967. The E model entered service in 1968 and reached the Vietnam combat zone in November of that year. The F-4E became the most numerous version of the Phantom and, in its prime, was widely used by the USAF and ANG. Eight hundred and thirty-one were manufactured for American use while a further 566 were built for Germany, Greece, Iran, Israel, Japan and Turkey. Now out-performed by a new generation of fighters, the F-4E is obsolescent and increasingly expensive to operate.

The first F-4G 'Wild Weasel' (69-7254) flew on 6 December 1975. One hundred and sixteen were converted from E models for the SEAD or SAM-suppression roles. The F-4G reached IOC with the 37th TFW at George AFB, California, in October 1978 and subsequently served at Spangdahlem, Germany, and Clark AB, Philippines.

During Operation Desert Storm, RF-4Cs and F-4Gs operated with the 35th Tactical Fighter Wing (Provisional) from Sheikh Isa air base, Bahrain, while RF-4Cs, F-4Es and F-4Gs flew with the 7440th Composite Wing at Incirlik AB, Turkey. The Pave Tack-equipped F-4Es deployed from the Philippines and, operating with the 7440th, flew a small number of combat sorties. F-4G 'Wild Weasels' led early attacks against the Iraqi air defense network and flew throughout the conflict, one aircraft being lost in a combat-related mishap.

McDONNELL DOUGLAS F-4G

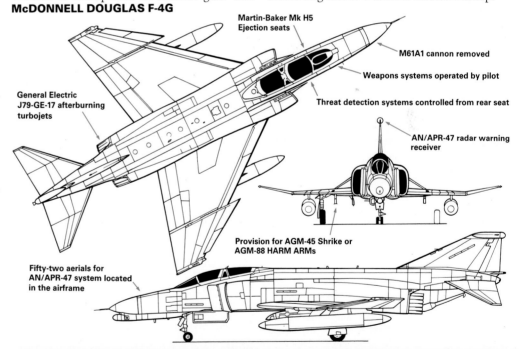

Martin-Baker Mk H5 Ejection seats

M61A1 cannon removed

Weapons systems operated by pilot

Threat detection systems controlled from rear seat

AN/APR-47 radar warning receiver

Provision for AGM-45 Shrike or AGM-88 HARM ARMs

General Electric J79-GE-17 afterburning turbojets

Fifty-two aerials for AN/APR-47 system located in the airframe

Carrying special markings for the commander of the 831st Air Division, this F-4E Phantom II was from the training organization at George AFB.

USAF Aircraft

F-4 Phantom (continued)

MISSION PROFILE

Armament options: (F-4E) internal M61A1 Vulcan 20-mm cannon with 639 rounds; provision for four AIM-7M Sparrow radar-guided missiles or three AIM-7Ms and one ECM pod in underfuselage wells; provision for up to four AIM-9M Sidewinder infra-red air-to-air missiles astride inboard wing pylons; one fuselage and eight wing hardpoints for the carriage of most stores in US inventory, including conventional low-drag and retarded bombs, cluster-bomb units, SUU-23/A gun and LAU-10A or LAU-3A/A rocket pods; some F-4Es able to accommodate AN/AVQ-26 Pave Tack laser designator/fire control system; (F-4G) one fuselage and four wing hardpoints, normally employed to carry centerline fuel tank and up to four AGM-45 Shrike or AGM-88A HARM (high-speed anti-radiation missiles)

Close air support/battlefield area interdiction: on a CAS, BAI or combined CAS/BAI mission the F-4E would refuel in flight but can fly to a radius of about 500 miles (805 km) unrefueled to be on station for 45 minutes with 639 rounds of ammunition for the M61A1, four AIM-7M in centerline wells, two AIM-9M on inboard pylons, centerline drop-tank, and six to eight Mk 83 750-lb (340-kg) bombs; ECM pod would replace one AIM-7M on one aircraft in a flight of four

Combat air patrol: for escort or combat air patrol in the solely air-to-air mission, the F-4E would refuel in flight but can cruise at medium to high altitude to a radius of about 700 miles (1127 km) unrefueled to be on station for 45 minutes with 639 rounds of ammunition for the M61A1, four AIM-7M in centerline wells, two to four AIM-9M on inboard pylons, and a centerline drop-tank; ECM pod would replace one AIM-7M on one aircraft in a flight of four

SEAD (suppression of enemy air defenses): on a SEAD mission against air defense radars, the F-4G would refuel in flight but can cruise at medium to high altitude to a radius of about 740 miles (1191 km) unrefueled from medium altitude with four AGM-45 Shrike or four AGM-88 HARM, or to a radius of about 900 miles (1448 km) with centerline drop-tank, two wing drop-tanks on outboard stations and two AGM-45 or two AGM-88 on inboard pylons

USAF VARIANTS AND SERIALS

Original construction designations

F-4C: Five hundred and eighty-five F-4Cs were obtained for the Air Force, including three purchased in 1962 which were modified to other basic versions. These were similar to the US Naval F-4B but with uprated engines and provision for inflight refueling with the flying boom method. Surplus aircraft were supplied to Spain.
62-12199 to 62-12201; 63-7407 to 63-7713; 64-0654 to 64-0928

F-4D: The second basic version for the Air Force, with 793 ordered between 1964 and 1966, was similar to the F-4C but with a modified radar housed in an enlarged radome. Surplus aircraft were supplied to South Korea.
64-0929 to 64-0980; 65-0580 to 65-0801; 66-0226 to 66-0283; 66-7455 to 66-7774; 66-8685 to 66-8825

F-4E: Improved version of the F-4D with uprated engines, a smaller diameter radar and a 20-mm rotary cannon mounted beneath the nose. Included in the 1,003 presented in the batches below were some 150 transferred to Israel, while many surplus aircraft were supplied to Egypt, Greece, Israel and Turkey. Others were sold to Iran but these were in separate batches.
66-0284 to 66-0382; 67-0208 to 67-0398; 68-0303 to 68-0547; 69-0236 to 69-0307; 69-7201 to 69-7303; 69-7546 to 69-7589; 71-0224 to 71-0247; 71-1070 to 71-1093; 71-1391 to 71-1402; 72-0121 to 72-0144; 72-0157 to 72-0168; 72-1476 to 72-1499; 73-1157 to 73-1204; 74-0643 to 74-0666; 74-1038 to 74-1061; 74-1620 to 74-1653; 75-0628 to 75-0637

Conversion designations

F-4G: One hundred and sixteen F-4Es were modified to F-4G standard for the 'Wild Weasel' role, with the nose cannon replaced by electronic warfare equipment.

Top: AGM-88A HARM air-to-surface anti-radiation missiles figure among the armament carried by a pair of F-4G 'Wild Weasels' from George AFB's 35th Fighter Wing.

Above: Defense suppression assets within USAFE are assigned to the 52nd FW which is based at Spangdahlem, Germany. F-4Gs and F-16Cs are operated in 'hunter-killer' pairs.

A small number of attrition replacements were converted recently.
69-0236 to 69-0248; 69-0250 to 69-0255; 69-0257 to 69-0259; 69-0261; 69-0263; 69-0265; 69-0267; 69-0269 to 69-0275; 69-0277; 69-0279 to 69-0281; 69-0283 to 69-0286; 69-0291 to 69-0293; 69-0297; 69-0304; 69-0306 and 69-0307; 69-7201 and 69-7202; 69-7204 to 69-7220; 69-7223; 69-7228; 69-7231 to 69-7236; 69-7251; 69-7253; 69-7254; 69-7256 to 69-7260; 69-7262 and 69-7263; 69-7267 and 69-7268; 69-7270; 69-7272; 69-7286 to 69-7291; 69-7293; 69-7295; 69-7297 and 69-7298; 69-7300 to 69-7303; 69-7546; 69-7550; 69-7556; 69-7558; 69-7560 and 69-7561; 69-7566; 69-7571 and 69-7572; 69-7574; 69-7579 to 69-7584; 69-7586 to 69-7588

GF-4C: At least a dozen retired F-4Cs have been transferred to Air Training Command to become technical training airframes, with the designation GF-4C.
63-7413; 63-7417; 63-7434; 63-7487; 63-7491; 63-7507; 63-7588; 63-7657; 63-7702; 64-0658; 64-0772; 64-0889

NF-4C: A pair of NF-4Cs is assigned to the permanent test role conducting weapons tests and chase plane duties.
63-7407; 63-7654

GF-4D: Surplus F-4Ds have been allocated to ATC to teach technical training as GF-4Ds.
65-0585; 65-0735; 66-7500; 66-7518

NF-4E: Three NF-4Es remain in service from more than a dozen employed by AFSC for permanent testing of weapon systems.
66-0284; 66-0329; 66-0384

GF-4E: At least three GF-4Es are employed in the ground training role with ATC.
66-0368; 67-0249; 68-0366

YF-4E: An F-4D was modified to YF-4E standard with the fitment of a 20-mm cannon beneath the nose.
65-0713

SPECIFICATION

McDonnell Douglas F-4E
Wing: span 38 ft 7.5 in (11.77 m); aspect ratio 2.82; area 530.0 sq ft (49.24 m²)

Fuselage and tail: length 63 ft 0 in (19.20 m); height 16 ft 5.5 in (5.02 m); tailplane span 17 ft 11.5 in (5.47 m); wheel base 23 ft 4.5 in (7.12 m)
Powerplant: two General Electric J79-GE-17A each rated at 11,810 lb (52.5 kN) dry and 17,900 lb (79.6 kN) afterburning thrust
Weights: basic empty 30328 lb (13757 kg); mission empty 31,853 lb (14448 kg); combat take-off 41,487 lb (18818 kg); maximum take-off 61,795 lb (28030 kg)
Fuel and load: internal fuel 12,290 lb (5575 kg); external fuel up to 8,830 lb (4005 kg) in one 600-US gal (2271-liter) and two 370-US gal (1401-liter) drop-tanks; maximum ordnance about 16,000 lb (7258 kg)
Speed: maximum level speed 'clean' at 36,000 ft (10975 m) 1,430 mph (2301 km/h); cruising speed at maximum take-off weight 571 mph (919 km/h)
Range: ferry range 1,978 miles (3184 km); defensive counter-air combat radius 494 miles (795 km); interdiction combat radius 712 miles (1145 km); air interception combat radius 786 miles (1266 km)
Performance: maximum rate of climb at sea level 9,340 ft (2847 m) per minute; service ceiling 58,750 ft (17905 m); take-off distance 4,390 ft (1338 m) at maximum take-off weight, 3,180 ft (969 m) at a weight of 53,814 lb (24410 kg); landing distance 3,780 ft (1152 m) at maximum landing weight, 3,520 ft (1073 m) at a weight of 35,134 lb (15937 kg)

USAF OPERATORS

Air Force Materiel Command (AFMC)

3246th TW	3247th TS	'ET'	Eglin AFB, FL	F-4D/E
6510th TW	6512th TS	'ED'	Edwards AFB, CA	NF-4C/E, YF-4E

Air Training Command (ATC)

3700th TTW	Sheppard TTC	Sheppard AFB, TX	GF-4C/D/E

United States Air Forces in Europe (USAFE)

52nd TFW	81st FS	'SP'	Spangdahlem AB, Germany	F-4G

Air National Guard (ANG)

108th FW	141st FS	'NJ'	McGuire AFB, NJ,	F-4G
124th FG/RG	190th FS		Boise Air Terminal, ID	F-4G
152nd FG/RG	192nd FG		Reno-Cannon IAP, NV	F-4G

McDonnell Douglas
RF-4C Phantom

The **RF-4C Phantom** is the USAF's only dedicated tactical reconnaissance aircraft and is expected to remain in service until 1997 with Air National Guard squadrons.

Although the USAF wants to turn over the reconnaissance mission to an F-16R Fighting Falcon with centerline reconnaissance pod (probably a conversion of F-16 airplanes already in inventory), funding for the latter aircraft appeared elusive in the early to mid-1990s. The USAF places great importance on battlefield and rear-area tactical reconnaissance and would like to retain a capability like that which the RF-4C has afforded since the Vietnam era.

The RF-4C is an unarmed multisensor reconnaissance aircraft now employed for day operations, and is expected to be the last version of the Phantom to be phased out of active and ANG squadrons. Optical cameras and infra-red sensors are housed in a modified nose which increases the length of the aircraft by 33 in (0.85 m) compared to the fighter version. The RF-4C is powered by two 17,000-lb (7710-kg) thrust J79-GE-15 turbojet engines.

Twenty-four RF-4Cs were fitted with AN/ALQ-125 TEREC (Tactical Electronic Reconnaissance) sensor for locating electronic emitters; 24 others employ the LOROP (LOng-Range Oblique Photography) suite, consisting of KS-127 optical camera with a 66-in (170-m) focal length. Other RF-4C equipment includes the AN/ARN-101 digital avionics navigation/reconnaissance system, recently supplemented by a new NWDS (navigation/weapons delivery system) and ring-laser gyro. The RF-4C's second crewman is a WSO who navigates, assists with communication and can operate the cameras.

The suitability of the big, sturdy Phantom airframe for the reconnaissance mission was apparent almost from the first flight of the **F4H-1** Phantom prototype on 27 May 1958. Early in the Phantom production run, two airframes which had begun life as Navy **F-4Bs** were modified to serve as USAF prototypes for the aircraft originally known as **RF-110A** and, on 16 July 1962, redesignated RF-4C. The first of these two service-test **YRF-4Cs** (62-12200/12201) flew on 8 August 1963.

The two YRF-4C aircraft tested the reconnaissance configuration and were subsequently used for other developmental duties. The first production-standard RF-4C (63-7740) flew on 18 May 1964.

Five hundred and three RF-4Cs were manufactured. A handful have gone from USAF inventory to South Korea and Spain. The type is no longer cost-effective to operate but the USAF has no ready substitute for its TEREC, LOROP and other capabilities.

During Operation Desert Storm, RF-4Cs operated with the 35th Tactical Fighter Wing (Provisional) from Sheikh Isa air base and with the 7440th Composite Wing at Incirlik AB, Turkey. Because the SR-71 reconnaissance aircraft had been retired and poor weather impeded KH-11 and other reconnaissance satellites, LOROP-equipped RF-4Cs were especially important in battlefield planning and played a secondary role in searching for Iraqi 'Scud' missile sites. LOROP-equipped RF-4C Phantoms flew several hundred day reconnaissance missions, including 'Scud' hunts, their cameras providing a slant range for useful photography up to 55 miles (88.51 km) on missions flown at 30,000 ft (9144 m).

MISSION PROFILE

Payload options: provision for various combinations of medium- to long-range and oblique reconnaissance cameras including one KS-72 or KS-87 forward oblique-framing camera plus one KA-56A low-altitude and one KA-55A high-altitude panoramic camera; or KS-127 LOROP (long-range oblique photography) camera; or AN/ALQ-125 TEREC (Tactical Electronic Reconnaissance) equipment package

Reconnaissance: on a reconnaissance mission, the RF-4C would refuel in flight but can cruise at medium to high altitude to a radius of about 740 miles (1191 km) unrefueled with centerline drop tank for medium to high-altitude LOROP day photography of a target region; on a hi-lo mission profile with run-in at medium to low altitude, the RF-4C would refuel in flight but can fly to a radius of about 600 miles (966 km) unrefueled with centerline drop-tank and two wing drop-tanks for photography of a point target or target region

USAF VARIANTS AND SERIALS

Original construction designations
RF-4C: The RF-4C was basically a standard F-4C with cameras installed in a modified nose. Five hundred and three were ordered between 1963 and 1972, with a small number of surplus aircraft supplied to Spain. 63-7740 to 63-7763; 64-0997 to 64-1085; 65-0818 to 65-0945; 66-0383 to 66-0478; 67-0428 to 67-0469; 68-0548 to 68-0611; 69-0349 to 69-0384; 71-0248 to 71-0259; 72-0145 to 72-0156

Conversion designations
GRF-4C: To date only one RF-4C has joined ATC to become a technical training airframe with the designation GRF-4C. 63-7751

NRF-4C: AFSC retains a pair of NRF-4C for photo-reconnaissance test work. 63-7744; 65-0850

SPECIFICATION

McDonnell Douglas RF-4C
Wing: span 38 ft 5 in (11.71); aspect ratio 2.82; area 530.0 sq ft (49.24 m²)
Fuselage and tail: length 62 ft 11 in (19.17 m); height 16 ft 6 in (5.03 m); tailplane span 17 ft 11.5 in (5.47 m); wheel base 24 ft 9 in (7.54 m)
Powerplant: two General Electric J79-GE-15 each rated at 10,900 lb (48.5 kN) dry and 17,000 lb (75.6 kN) afterburning thrust
Weights: basic empty 28,276 lb (12826 kg); maximum take-off 58,000 lb (26308 kg)
Fuel and load: internal fuel 1,771 US gal (6704 liters); external fuel up to one 600-US gal (2271-liter) and two 370-US gal (1401-liter) drop-tanks; maximum ordnance 16,00 lb (7257 kg), generally not carried
Speed: maximum level speed 'clean' at 40,000 ft (12190 m) 1,459 mph (2348 km/h) and at sea level 898 mph (1445 km/h)
Range: ferry range 1,750 miles (2816 km); combat radius 840 miles (1352 km)
Performance: maximum rate of climb at sea level 48,000 ft (14630 m) per minute; service ceiling 59,400 ft (18105 m)

USAF OPERATORS

Air Force Materiel Command (AFMC)				
6510th TW	6512th TS	'ED'	Edwards AFB, CA	NRF-4C

Air Training Command (ATC)				
3700th TTW	Sheppard TTC		Sheppard AFB, TX	GRF-4C

Air Combat Command (ACC)				
67th RW	12th RS	'BA'	Bergstrom AFB, TX	RF-4C

Air National Guard (ANG)				
117th RW	106th RS	'BH'	Birmingham MAP, AL	RF-4C
124th RG	189th RS		Boise Air Terminal, ID	RF-4C
	190th RS		Boise Air Terminal, ID	RF-4C
				converting to F-4G in 1992
152nd RG	192nd RS		Reno-Cannon IAP, NV	RF-4C
				converting to F-4G in 1992
155th RG	173rd RS		Lincoln MAP, NE	RF-4C
163rd RG	196th RS		March AFB, CA	RF-4C
186th RG	153rd RS		Key Fd, Meridian, MS	RF-4C

Below: The reconnaissance-dedicated RF-4C model of the Phantom II is now on the brink of being retired from front-line units but is expected to remain operational with second-line outfits of the Air National Guard for a few more years. Typical of the latter units is the 117th RW at Birmingham Municipal Airport, Alabama. One of their RF-4Cs is portrayed here at Alconbury during a European deployment accomplished under active-duty training (AcDuTra) obligations.

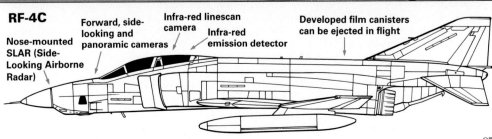

RF-4C

Nose-mounted SLAR (Side-Looking Airborne Radar)
Forward, side-looking and panoramic cameras
Infra-red linescan camera
Infra-red emission detector
Developed film canisters can be ejected in flight

McDonnell Douglas
F-15 Eagle

The **F-15 Eagle** is the air superiority fighter which succeeded in the Gulf War and which serves as flagship of the USAF's fighter force in the 1990s. Production of **F-15C/D** fighters for the USAF has ended and production of the F-15E is scheduled to end in 1993, but the Eagle will remain a first-line combat aircraft well into the new century. New versions were still being studied after the USAF's 1991 decision to eventually replace the F-15 with the Lockheed F-22 Rapier.

The F-15 pilot sits high atop the twin-engined fighter under a bubbled canopy. With its straightforward but very large wing of 608 sq ft (56 m^2), the Eagle is one of the few fast jets which has no need for a braking parachute as it lands smoothly and gently without one. The shoulder-mounted, swept wing has a fixed leading edge and plain unblown trailing-edge flaps.

The Eagle's pilot is equipped with ACES II zero-zero ejection seat and is intended to fight in the HOTAS (hands on throttle and stick) mode, the pilot getting key information from his HUD (head-up display) and cueing the aircraft with thumb and fingers. The F-15 Eagle's success in air-to-air combat owes much to its powerful Hughes APG-63 radar, its maneuverability and durability, and its heavy load of diverse weaponry. The APG-63 radar is being constantly improved, and on C and D model Eagles has become a lightweight X-band pulse-Doppler radar with a reprogrammable signal processor. In ideal circumstances, the F-15 can destroy enemy aircraft BVR (beyond visual range) using the radar-guided AIM-7M Sparrow or AIM-120 AMRAAM (Advanced Medium-Range Air-to-Air Missile). At closer quarters, where its high thrust-to-weight ratio and large wing make it fast and maneuverable, the F-15 can engage with AIM-9M Sidewinder infra-red missiles or with its 20-mm M61A1 Vulcan six-barrelled cannon.

In a European scenario, the F-15 Eagle would go aloft to attempt to achieve air superiority over the battlefield and would fly frequent missions of short duration in bad weather. In this setting, ease of maintenance for rapid turn-around is essential. In Operation Desert Storm, Eagles flew longer missions to escort strike aircraft. On these missions, F-15Cs took off, refueled in flight, cruised for two hours or more at medium altitude of around 28,000 ft (8534 m), typically at Mach 0.93 or 660 mph (1072 km/h), and engaged Iraqi aircraft 700 miles (1127 km) or more from their base. Quick turn-around was also a factor in the war against Iraq, and maintenance people reported that the F-15C met their expectations.

F-15C aircraft carry CFTs (conformal fuel tanks), which provide an additional 9,750 lb (4423 kg) of fuel. F-15C and D aircraft are powered by two 23,450-lb (104.3-kN) thrust Pratt & Whitney F100-PW-220 low-bypass turbofans. Plans to deliver F-15Es with the 20-per cent more powerful 29,000-lb (129.0-kN)

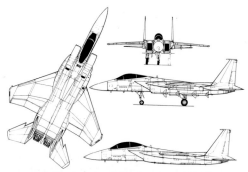

Above: Optimized to fulfil the air superiority role, the McDonnell Douglas F-15 Eagle racked up an impressive record in Desert Storm, when it single-handedly accounted for virtually all the Iraqi aircraft destroyed by coalition forces.

thrust F100-PW-229 engine beginning in August 1991 were delayed to later in the year.

The F-15 Eagle dates to 1965 when the USAF was looked for a superior long-range air superiority fighter. The resulting FX program led to the premier flight of the first **F-15A** (71-0280) on 27 July 1972. In 1973, plans were finalized to order 729 airplanes. The series began with the F-15A and the combat-capable two-seat model, originally the **TF-15A** and now designated **F-15B**. The first two-seater (71-0290) flew on 7 July 1973. A total of 355 F-15As and 57 F-15Bs was delivered to the USAF.

The operational career of the Eagle began with the first delivery of an F-15A (74-0083) to Tactical Air Command's (TAC's) 1st Tactical Fighter Wing at Langley AFB, Virginia, on 9 January 1976. The 36th TFW at Bitburg, Germany, received the Eagle in April 1977. Other operators have included the 21st TFW (Elmendorf AFB, Alaska – now 3rd Wing), 33rd TFW (Eglin AFB, Florida), 49th TFW (Holloman AFB, New Mexico), 57th Fighter Weapons Wing (Nellis AFB, Nevada) and 32nd TFG (Soesterberg, Netherlands). The 49th operated the F-15A model only before going out of the Eagle business and having its flag transferred to the USAF's F-117A wing on 1 January 1992. Other wings have acquired the F-15C.

In 1974-75, McDonnell fielded a modified F-15A (72-0119) in an attempt to capture world-class time-to-climb records for jet-powered aircraft. Under a 1 April 1974 contract, this **Streak Eagle** was modified for the record attempts by deleting non-mission critical systems including flap and speed brake actuators, armament, radar and fire control system. The Streak Eagle weighed some 1,800 lb (816 kg) less than comparable F-15A block 6 aircraft. The Streak Eagle made eight successful record attempts, the most dramatic being a climb to 98,425 ft (30000 m) in 207.80 seconds from brake release on a 1 February 1975 flight.

In the 1980s, the F-15A operated with TAC air defense squadrons in the interceptor role and was the carrier aircraft for the ASAT (anti-satellite) weapon; development of the latter was cancelled, but aircraft continue to be 'wired' for it. F-15A/B airplanes remaining in service will be assigned training and air superiority duties in ANG units, including those at Dobbins AFB, Georgia; New Orleans, Louisiana; Portland, Oregon; Otis, Massachusetts; St Louis, Missouri; and Hickam AFB, Hawaii.

Above: Sidewinder missiles are carried by this four-ship of F-15As from the Georgia ANG. While it makes for a stunning image, this formation is far from tactically sound.

Right: The first unit to acquire the improved F-15C version of the Eagle was the 18th Fighter Wing, which continues to operate the McDonnell Douglas fighter from Kadena, Okinawa, today.

Below: A brace of 57th FIS F-15C Eagles from Keflavik, Iceland, keeps a wary eye on a Soviet air force 'Bear-D' as it rumbles its way along on a mission to test USAF reaction times.

From June 1979, A and B models were succeeded in production by the F-15C and its two-seat equivalent, the F-15D. The 18th TFW (Kadena AB, Okinawa) operated the F-15C from the beginning and still has its original batch of C-model Eagles. Four hundred and 10 F-15Cs and 61 F-15Ds were delivered to the USAF. Foreign users of the Eagle are Israel (F-15A/B/C/D), Saudi Arabia (F-15C/D) and Japan (**F-15J/F-15DJ**).

The original Eagle two-seater (71-0290) was modified to become the SMTD (STOL/Maneuver Technology Demonstrator), equipped with Pratt & Whitney two-dimensional nozzles which can vector through 20° down and provide reverse thrust. The SMTD demonstrator flew on 7 September 1988. The SMTD used its vectored thrust, plus canard foreplanes, to improve low-speed performance. The result was an aircraft designed to operate on a much-shortened airfield – important in wartime, when fixed airfields are likely

to be cratered and under constant attack. After a three-year program, the SMTD Eagle made its 138th and final flight on 12 August 1991, making a short night landing under a simulated 200-ft (61-m) ceiling in total darkness.

When the US launched Operation Desert Shield on 6 August 1990, the 1st TFW at Langley AFB, Virginia, deployed F-15C/D Eagles of its 27th and 71st Tactical Fighter Squadrons on only hours' notice. Forty-eight Eagles made the longest fighter deployment in history, flying 14 to 17 hours from Langley to Dhahran with six to eight air refuelings *en route*. On 12 August 1990, F-15E Strike Eagles deployed from the 336th TFS, 4th TFW, at Seymour Johnson AFB, North Carolina. The early arrival of Eagles and Strike Eagles may have helped to deter Iraq from moving directly against Saudi oilfields.

In September 1990, the 33rd TFW from Eglin AFB, Florida, deployed its 58th TFS with F-15C Eagles to Tabuk, Saudi Arabia.

The 36th TFW at Bitburg, Germany, deployed F-15Cs to Tabuk and to Incirlik AB, Turkey. The 32nd TFS from Soesterberg, Netherlands, deployed to Incirlik as well. The F-15E Strike Eagle-equipped 335th TFS followed from Seymour Johnson.

On 17 January 1991, the US had five F-15C air-to-air and two F-15E strike squadrons fielded when the war against Iraq began. Most air-to-air engagements were fought by F-15Cs of the 58th TFS, part of the 33rd TFW, which scored 17 air-to-air victories.

No F-15C/D Eagle fighters were lost during Desert Shield/Storm. Two F-15E Strike Eagles were lost in combat. More than 2,200 missions totaling some 7,700 hours of combat time were logged. F-15Es joined other coalition aircraft in searching for and attacking 'Scud' ballistic missile launchers, on five- to six-hour sorties.

Most aerial victories were achieved against Iraqi aircraft caught by chance or attempting to flee to Iran, rather than in serious air-to-air

battles. F-15Cs scored 32 aerial kills (17 Eglin, 11 Bitburg, one Soesterberg, one Langley and two Saudi) of a total of 41 victories. Of these, all but eight were achieved with the Eagle's BVR weapon, the Sparrow missile. Seven kills were racked up by AIM-9 Sidewinders and one by out-maneuvering an opponent. The AIM-120A AMRAAM was not fired in anger, although more than 1,000 'captive carries' of the missile were racked up during combat missions in the final days of the war.

In the 1990s, F-15 Eagles will undergo staged improvements to radar and internal systems. Although committed to the F-22 ATF (advanced tactical fighter) as an F-15 replacement, the USAF is quietly studying a scaled-down, improved Eagle known as **F-15XX** in the event that budget realities cause cancellation of the F-22 program. Early F-15A/B Eagles will reach their projected 22-year service life in the 1990s and will require either a costly rebuild program or retirement.

Above: The sheer bulk of the F-15 Eagle is all too apparent in this near head-on study of one of these fighters taxiing for take-off.

Right: Four F-15A Eagles from the Georgia ANG unit at Dobbins AFB formate with a KC-135E from the Tennessee ANG before being called in to top up their stocks of fuel.

F-15 Eagle (continued)

MISSION PROFILE

Armament options: internal M61A1 Vulcan 20-mm cannon with maximum of 940 rounds; one fuselage and eight wing hardpoints for the carriage of drop-tanks, AN/ALQ-119(V) or AN/ALQ-131(V) ECM pods and missiles; F-15A/B/C/D do not normally carry air-to-ground ordnance but were designed with hardpoint provisions for carriage of most stores in US inventory, including conventional low-drag and retarded bombs, cluster-bomb units, gun and rocket pods; provision for up to four AIM-9J/L/M Sidewinder missiles and up to four AIM-7M Sparrow or AIM-120 AMRAAM missiles; two 600-US gal (2271-liter) drop-tanks are usually accommodated on mid-wing station; (F-15C) provision for two 750-US gal (2839-liter) CFTs (conformal fuel tanks)

HVA (high value asset) escort: escorting AWACS, J-STARS or other high-value aircraft in secure airspace carrying CFTs and two 600-US gal (2271-liter) drop-tanks, the F-15C would refuel in flight but can fly at medium- to high-altitude to a radius of about 1,000 miles (1610-km) unrefueled with 940 rounds of ammunition for the M61A1, four AIM-9M, four AIM-7M

Strike package escort: escorting strike aircraft to target carrying CFTs and two 600-US gal (2271-liter) drop-tanks, the F-15C would refuel in flight but can fly at medium- to high-altitude to a radius of about 1,000 miles (1610-km) unrefueled with 940 rounds of ammunition for the M61A1, four AIM-9M, four AIM-7M

Intercept: on an air defense/interceptor mission, the F-15A can fly at medium to high altitude to a radius of about 800 miles (1287 km) unrefueled with 940 rounds of ammunition for the M61A1, four AIM-9M, four AIM-7M, and two 600-US gal (2271-liter) drop-tanks on mid-wing hardpoints; the F-15C can fly at medium to high-altitude to a radius of about 1,100 miles (1770-km) unrefueled with 940 rounds of ammunition for the M61A1, four AIM-9M, four AIM-7M, two 600-US gal (2271-liter) drop-tanks on mid-wing hardpoints and two 730-US gal (2763-liter) CFTs

USAF VARIANTS AND SERIALS

YF-15A: The first 10 prototype/pre-production F-15As were given the Y prefix to indicate service test as all were initially employed by the manufacturer and the Air Force to evaluate the Eagle's capabilities.
71-0280 to 71-0289

YF-15B: The two prototype F-15Bs were allocated the designation YF-15B for the same reason as the YF-15A above.
71-0290 to 71-0291

F-15A: The initial production version with 355 ordered between 1972 and 1977 for TAC although most are operated in the air defense role. A limited number of surplus aircraft have been supplied to Israel.
72-0113 to 72-0120; 73-0085 to 73-0107; 74-0081 to 74-0136; 75-0018 to 75-0079; 76-0008 to 76-0120; 77-0061 to 77-0153

F-15B: Fifty-seven two-seat trainers were ordered between 1973 and 1977.
73-0108 to 73-0114; 74-0137 to 74-0142; 75-0080 to 75-0089; 76-0124 to 76-0142; 77-0154 to 77-0168

F-15C: Improved version of the F-15A, the F-15C featured external provision for conformal fuel tanks to increase range, with 420 ordered between 1978 and 1986.
78-0468 to 78-0550; 79-0015 to 79-0081; 80-0002 to 80-0053; 81-0020 to 81-0057; 82-0008 to 82-0038; 83-0010 to 83-0043; 84-0001 to 84-0031; 85-0093 to 85-0128; 86-0143 to 86-0180

F-15D: Tandem two-seat version of the F-15C with 61 built.
78-0561 to 78-0574; 79-0004 to 79-0014; 80-0054 to 80-0061; 81-0061 to 81-0065; 82-0044 to 82-0048; 83-0046 to 83-0050; 84-0042 to 84-0046; 85-0129 to 85-0134; 86-0181 to 86-0182

GYF-15A/GF-15A: Two pre-production aircraft and one F-15A were allocated the designation GYF-15A and GF-15A respectively, following their transfer to Air Training Command for the technical training role.
71-0284; 71-0286 (GY); 72-0115 (G)

SPECIFICATION

McDonnell Douglas F-15C
Wing: span 42 ft 9.75 in (13.05 m); area 608.0 sq ft (56.48 m²)
Fuselage and tail: length 63 ft 9 in) (19.43 m); height 18 ft 5.5 in (5.63 m); tailplane span 28 ft 3 in (8.61 m); wheel base 17 ft 9.5 in (5.42 m)
Powerplant: two Pratt & Whitney F100-P-220 each rated at 14,370 lb (63.9 kN) dry and 23,450 lb (104.3 kN) afterburning thrusts, or two F100-P-229 each rated at 18,000 lb (81.1 kN) intermediate and 29,000 lb (129.0 kN) afterburning thrusts
Weights: operating empty 28,600 lb (12793 kg); normal for interception mission 44,630 lb (20244 kg); maximum take-off with FAST packs 68,000 lb (30844 kg)
Fuel and load: internal fuel 13,455 lb (6103 kg); external fuel up to 9,750 lb (4423 kg) in two FAST packs and 11,895 lb (5395 kg) in three 600-US gal (2271-liter) drop-tanks; maximum ordnance 16,000 or 23,600 lb (7257 or 10705 kg) without or with FAST packs
Speed: maximum level speed 'clean' at 36,000 ft (10975 m) more than 1,650 mph (2655 km/h); cruising speed 570 mph (917 km/h)

Range: ferry range with drop-tanks more than 2,878 or 3,450 miles (4631 or 5560 km) without or with FAST packs; interception combat radius 1,222 miles (1967 km)
Performance: maximum rate of climb at sea level more than 50,000 ft (15240 m) per minute; service ceiling 60,000 ft (18290 m); absolute ceiling 100,000 ft (30480 m); take-off distance 900 ft (274 m) on an interception mission; landing distance 3,500 ft (1067 m) without a braking parachute

McDonnell Douglas F-15A
generally similar to the F-15C except in the following particulars:
Powerplant: two Pratt & Whitney F100-P-100 each rated at 14,670 lb (65.26 kN) dry and 23,830 lb (106.0 kN) afterburning thrusts
Weights: operating empty 28,600 lb (12973 kg); normal take-off for interception mission 41,500 lb (18884 kg); take-off with three 600-US gal (2271-liter) drop-tanks 54,400 lb (24675 kg); maximum take-off 56,000 lb (25401 kg)
Fuel and load: internal fuel 11,600 lb (5260 kg); external fuel up to 11,895 lb (5395 kg) in three 600-US gal (2271-liter) drop-tanks; maximum ordnance 16,000 lb (7257 kg)
Range: ferry range with drop-tanks more than 2,878 miles (4631 km)
Performance: landing distance 2,500 ft (762 m) with a braking parachute after an interception mission

McDonnell Douglas F-15D
generally similar to the F-15C except in the following particulars:
Weight: operating empty 29,400 lb (13336 kg)

USAF OPERATORS

Air Force Materiel Command (AFMC)

WR ALC		'RG'	Robins AFB, GA	F-15A
3246th TW	3247th TS	'ET'	Eglin AFB, FL	F-15A/B/C/D
6510th TW	6515th TS	'ED'	Edwards AFB, CA	F-15A/B/C/D

Air Training Command (ATC)

3400th TTW	Lowry TTC		Lowry AFB, CO	GF-15A
3700th TTW	Sheppard TTC		Sheppard AFB, TX	GYF-15A

Pacific Air Forces (PACAF)

18th Wg	12th FS	'ZZ'	Kadena AB, Okinawa	F-15C/D
	44th FS	'ZZ'	Kadena AB, Okinawa	F-15C/D
	67th FS	'ZZ'	Kadena AB, Okinawa	F-15C/D
3rd Wg	43rd FS	'AK'	Elmendorf AFB, AK	F-15C/D
	54th FS	'AK'	Elmendorf AFB, AK	F-15C/D

McDonnell Douglas F-15C MSIP Eagle

As the USAF's premier fighter for many years, the F-15 has received ongoing improvements, the latest fighter variant being the F-15C/D MSIP. In addition to new radar, the multi-stage improvement program enhances most aspects of the avionics suite, including the internal ECM system, computer capacity and processing speed. Most of the aircraft dispatched to the Gulf region were of this later variant.

Weapons
The F-15's primary weapon is the AIM-7M Sparrow radar-guided missile, which is being superseded by the smaller active-radar AIM-120 AMRAAM. Shorter range weapons include the AIM-9M Sidewinder and the internal 20-mm Vulcan cannon.

Radar
Based on the original APG-63, the MSIP's APG-70 provides outstanding long-range detection and tracking for the air-to-air role. The same radar is fitted to the F-15E, but used more for producing high resolution patch maps for targeting purposes

Markings
This machine is marked for Colonel Rick Parsons, commanding officer of the 33rd Tactical Fighter Wing during Desert Storm. The nose art alludes to the aircraft's normal basing at Eglin, on the shores of the Gulf of Mexico, but is especially apt given the unit's role against Iraq.

Kill marks
Colonel Parsons scored one victory against Iraqi warplanes, represented by the star under the cockpit. However, the aircraft itself was used to destroy three Iraqi aircraft, hence the three Iraqi flags.

Air Combat Command (ACC)

1st FW	27th FS	'FF'	Langley AFB, VA	F-15C/D
	71st FS	'FF'	Langley AFB, VA	F-15C/D
	94th FS	'FF'	Langley AFB, VA	F-15C/D
33rd FW	58th FS	'EG'	Eglin AFB, FL	F-15C/D
	59th FS	'EG'	Eglin AFB, FL	F-15C/D
	60th FS	'EG'	Eglin AFB, FL	F-15C/D
	One squadron to convert to OA-10A in 1992			

57th FW	422nd TES	'WA'	Nellis AFB, NV	F-15C/E
	F-15 FWS	'WA'	Nellis AFB, NV	F-15C/D
325th FW	1st FS	'TY'	Tyndall AFB, FL	F-15A/B
	2nd FS	'TY'	Tyndall AFB, FL	F-15A/B
	95th FS	'TY'	Tyndall AFB, FL	F-15A/B
AFI	57th FIS	'IS'	NAF Keflavik, Iceland	F-15C/D
ACW	4485th TS	'OT'	Eglin AFB, FL	F-15A/B/C

United States Air Forces in Europe (USAFE)

32nd FG	32nd FS	'CR'	Soesterberg AB, Netherlands	F-15C/D
36th FW	22nd FS	'BT'	Bitburg AB, Germany	F-15C/D
	53rd FS	'BT'	Bitburg AB, Germany	F-15C/D
	525th FS	'BT'	Bitburg AB, Germany	F-15C/D
	525th FS to inactivate in 1992			

Air National Guard (ANG)

102nd FW	101st FS		Otis ANGB, MA	F-15A/B
116th FW	128th FS		Dobbins AFB, GA	F-15A/B
131st FW	110th FS	'SL'	Lambert Fd, St Louis, MO	F-15A/B
142nd FG	123rd FS		Portland IAP, OR	F-15A/B
154th CG	199th FS		Hickam AFB, HI	F-15A/B
159th FG	122nd FS		NAS New Orleans, LA	F-15A/B

McDonnell Douglas
F–15E Strike Eagle

The **F-15E Strike Eagle** is a two-seat, dual-role aircraft assigned to the strike/interdiction mission while retaining a deadly capability for air-to-air combat.

Developed from the highly successful F-15 Eagle air superiority fighter, the Strike Eagle demonstrated its worth in Operation Desert Storm and is expected to form the backbone of US air power in Great Britain in the 1990s. Additional production, beyond airplanes purchased with FY 1992 funds, is unlikely, however, and manufacture of the F-15E Strike Eagle is expected to end in the early 1990s.

The pilot and WSO of the F-15E sit in tandem on ACES II zero-zero ejection seats. As a dual-role warplane, the F-15E has air-to-air capability and the pilot fights in the HOTAS (hands on throttle and stick) mode. Like its air-superiority predecessors, the F-15E has the capability to destroy enemy aircraft BVR (beyond visual range) using the radar-guided AIM-7M Sparrow or AIM-120 AMRAAM (Advanced Medium-Range Air-to-Air Missile). At closer range, the F-15E can engage with AIM-9M Sidewinder infra-red missiles or with its 20-mm M61A1 Vulcan six-barrelled cannon.

The F-15E Strike Eagle introduces redesigned controls, a wide field of vision HUD, and three CRTs which provide multi-purpose displays of navigation, weapons delivery and systems operations. The rear-cockpit WSO (weapon systems officer) employs four multi-purpose CRT terminals for radar, weapon selection and monitoring of enemy tracking systems. The WSO also operates AN/APG-70 synthetic aperture radar and Martin-Marietta LANTIRN (Low-Altitude Navigation and Targeting, Infra-Red, for Night) weapons and targeting pods, and has minimal flight controls.

The primary mission of the F-15E is the air-to-ground strike mission. The F-15E carries up to a maximum of 24,250 lb (11000 kg) of tactical ordnance, including Mk 20 Rockeye and CBU-87 cluster bombs, Mk 82 and Mk 84 250-lb (113-kg) and 1,000-lb (454-kg) bombs, AGM-65 Maverick missiles, and GBU-10, GBU-15 and GBU-28 guided weapons. The USAF has cancelled the SRAM-T (short-range air-to-ground missile, tactical) which was also slated for the Strike Eagle.

F-15E aircraft carry an additional 21,645 lb (9818 kg) of external fuel F-15Es, like the C and D models, are powered by two 23,450-lb (104.31-kN) thrust Pratt & Whitney F100-PW-220 low-bypass turbofans. Plans to deliver F-15Es with the 20 per cent more powerful 29,000-lb (129-kN) thrust F100-PW-229 engine beginning in August 1991, were delayed for a few months.

The F-15E has been a kind of second-generation Eagle, introducing a 'mud-moving' role for the first time. Following test work with the second two-seater built (71-0291), the first production F-15E (86-0183) flew on 11 December 1986.

In 1988, the 405th Tactical Training Wing at Luke AFB, Arizona, became the Tactical Air Command's RTU (replacement training unit) for the F-15E Strike Eagle aircraft. Soon thereafter, the first operational F-15Es were delivered to the 4th TFW, Seymour Johnson AFB, North Carolina, replacing the F-4E Phantom.

On 12 August 1990, as the US began Operation Desert Shield in response to the Iraqi invasion of Kuwait, F-15E Strike Eagles from the 336th TFS, 4th TFW, at Seymour Johnson AFB, North Carolina, deployed to Al Kharj air base, Saudi Arabia. F-15Es of the 4th Wing's 335th TFS followed. During Desert Storm, F-15Es were assigned strike missions against a variety of targets, including five- to six-hour sorties in search of 'Scud' missile launch sites. Two F-15E Strike Eagles were lost in combat.

In 1991, the Pentagon overruled USAF leaders who wanted to keep the F-15E Strike Eagle in production. The Air Force wanted to keep the line open in FY 1992, using $620 million in funds obtained from a sale of F-15Cs to Saudi Arabia directly from inventory. The USAF had wanted to order 12 additional F-15Es; the funds went to support equipment and spares for the existing fleet of F-15s.

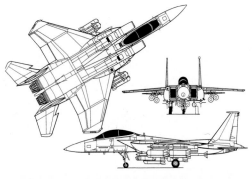

Above: Although it possesses air-to-air combat capability, the F-15E Strike Eagle specializes in the air-to-ground task and can carry a load exceeding 20,000 lb, which includes conventional and tactical nuclear weapons.

Left: 'Slick' bombs and Sidewinders constitute the armament carried by this F-15E Strike Eagle from the test center at Edwards AFB. LANTIRN navigation and targeting pods are also visible and the conformal fuel tanks introduced by the F-15C version are fitted as standard.

Below left: In ferry rig, with three fuel tanks and baggage pods, the first F-15E Strike Eagle to be delivered to the 48th Fighter Wing at RAF Lakenheath taxis towards a reception committee after completing a non-stop transatlantic ferry flight to its new home.

MISSION PROFILE

Armament options: internal M61A1 Vulcan 20-mm cannon with maximum of 450 rounds (512 rounds on early F-15Es); five fuselage and four wing hardpoints (plus four wing missile rails for AIM-9J/L/M Sidewinder or AIM-120A AMRAAM) for the carriage of most stores in US inventory, including nuclear gravity bombs, conventional low-drag and retarded bombs, and cluster-bomb units; centerline fuselage hardpoint (station 5) normally employed for drop-tank; four of the fuselage hardpoints (stations 3, 4, 6, 7) employed for AIM-7M Sparrow or AIM-120A AMRAAM missiles; fuselage-mounted LANTIRN (Low-Altitude Navigation and Targeting, Infra-Red, for Night) navigation (AN/AAQ-13) and targeting (AN/AAQ-14) pods; provision for AN/ALQ-119 or -131 ECM pod; provision for centerline (station 5) AN/AVQ-26 Pave Tack infra-red targeting designator/reader (not normally employed); provision for up to four AGM-88A HARM (high-speed anti-radiation missiles); provision for up to six AGM-65 Maverick missiles; future weapons are to include AGM-130 powered stand-off bomb and AGM-137 TSSAM

Nuclear strike: on a nuclear strike mission, the F-15E would refuel in flight but cruising at medium to high altitude can fly to a radius of about 1,000 miles (1610 km) unrefueled with two 610-US gal (2309-liter) drop-tanks (stations 1, 9), 450 rounds for the M61A1, four AIM-9M, and two Mk 51 or B61 nuclear stores on wing hardpoints (stations 2, 8)

SEAD (suppression of enemy air defenses): on a SEAD mission against air defense radars, the F-15E would refuel in flight but can cruise at medium to high altitude to a radius of about 1,000 miles (1610 km) unrefueled for attack from medium altitude with centerline drop-tank, two 610-US gal (2309-liter) drop-tanks (stations 1, 9), 450 rounds for the M61A1, four AIM-7M, and two AGM-88 HARM on wing hardpoints (stations 2, 8), or to a radius of about 730 miles (1174 km) with four AGM-88 HARM on wing hardpoints (stations 1, 2, 8, 9)

Close air support/battlefield area interdiction: on a CAS, BAI, or combined CAS/BAI mission the F-15E would refuel in flight but cruising at medium altitude with low-level time of 45 minutes and 30 minute loiter in target area can operate to a radius of about 660 miles (1062 km) unrefueled with two 610-US gal (2309-liter) drop-tanks (stations 1, 9), 450 rounds for the M61A1, four AIM-9M, four AIM-7M, and eight 12 Mk 82 500-lb (227-kg) bombs on MER-200 multiple ejector racks at mid-wing ordnance stations (stations 2 and 8); for an anti-armor mission the loadout would be eight 500-lb (227-kg) GBU-12 laser-guided bombs (stations 2 and 8)

HVA (high value asset) strike: on an HVA strike against a highly leveraged target, the F-15E would refuel in flight but can fly at medium- to high-altitude to a radius of about 900 miles (1448 km) unrefueled with two 610-US gal (2309-liter) drop-tanks (stations 1, 9), 450 rounds for the M61A1, four AIM-9M, AN/ANX-14 data-link pod on centerline (station 5), and two GBU-15 precision-guided glide bombs (stations 2, 8)

USAF VARIANTS AND SERIALS

F-15E: A two-seat, all-weather, deep-interdiction fighter with 163 ordered to 1990, with the final 37 to be acquired from FY 1991 budget.
86-0183 to 86-0190; 87-0169 to 87-0210; 88-1668 to 88-1708; 89-0471 to 89-0506; 90-0227 to 90-0262; plus other contracts

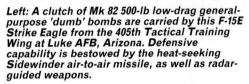

Left: A clutch of Mk 82 500-lb low-drag general-purpose 'dumb' bombs are carried by this F-15E Strike Eagle from the 405th Tactical Training Wing at Luke AFB, Arizona. Defensive capability is bestowed by the heat-seeking Sidewinder air-to-air missile, as well as radar-guided weapons.

Below: The first fully-operational Strike Eagle unit was the 4th Wing at Seymour Johnson AFB, North Carolina. One of their F-15Es is depicted here. Two squadrons from this organization were deployed to Saudi Arabia for the duration of the Gulf War.

McDonnell Douglas F-15E Strike Eagle

The F-15E is a highly versatile warplane that mirrors the USAF's goal of greater flexibility and efficiency in an era of reduced expenditure. While providing a superb all-weather attack platform capable of delivering PGMs, the F-15E retains the air-to-air fighting prowess of its fighter cousins. Strike Eagles are currently based with a rapid intervention wing in the US, and theater forces in Europe and Alaska. F-15Es will be included in future USAF composite wings.

Cockpit
The two-man cockpit is dominated by large multi-function CRT displays, three in the front and four in the back. These can display sensor imagery, terrain-following radar displays, threat information and a host of aircraft functions. The pilot can even see a FLIR image in the head-up display.

Weapons carriage
Twelve stub pylons are attached tangentially to the conformal fuel tanks, allowing the F-15E to carry a sizable load. The Eagle's standard wing pylons are also available. Here SUU-30H cluster-bomb dispensers are the load, in addition to a pair of self-defense AIM-9M Sidewinders on the wing pylon shoulder rails.

LANTIRN
Also fitted to late-model F-16s, the LANTIRN system consists of two pods attached under the F-15E's intakes. The navigation pod (starboard) and targeting pod (port) provide FLIR imagery, automatic terrain-following flight and laser designation.

Markings
All service F-15Es wear this overall dark gray camouflage, with low visibility national insignia. The two-color fin-flash and smart tail codes identify this aircraft as that assigned to the commander of the 48th Fighter Wing, based at Lakenheath in England.

SPECIFICATION

McDonnell Douglas F-15E
Wing: span 42 ft 9.75 in (13.05 m); area 608.0 sq ft (56.48 m²)
Fuselage and tail: length 63 ft 9 in (19.43 m); height 18 ft 5.5 in (5.63 m); tailplane span 28 ft 3 in (8.61 m); wheel base 17 ft 9.5 in (5.42 m)
Powerplant: two Pratt & Whitney F100-P-220 each rated at 14,370 lb (63.92 kN) dry and 20,450 lb (104.31 kN) afterburning thrusts
Weights: basic operating empty 31,700 lb (14379 kg); maximum take-off 81,000 lb (36741 kg)

Fuel and load: internal fuel 13,123 lb (5952 kg); external fuel 21,645 lb (9818 kg) in two FAST packs and up to three 610-US gal (2309-liter) drop-tanks; maximum ordnance 23,500 lb (10659 kg)
Speed: maximum level speed 'clean' at high altitude more than 1,650 mph (2655 km/h); cruising speed 570 mph (917 km/h)
Range: ferry range 3,570 miles (5745 km) with FAST packs and drop-tanks, and 2,878 miles (4631 km) with drop-tanks
Performance: maximum rate of climb at sea level more than 50,000 ft (15240 m) per minute; service ceiling 60,000 ft (18290 m); landing run 3,50 ft (1067 m) without braking parachute

USAF OPERATORS

Air Force Materiel Command (AFMC)

3246th TW	3247th TS	'ET'	Eglin AFB, FL	F-15E
6510th TW	6515th TS	'ED'	Edwards AFB, CA	F-15E

Pacific Air Forces (PACAF)

3rd Wg	90th FS	'AK'	Elmendorf AFB, AK	F-15E

Air Combat Command (ACC)

4th Wg	334th FS	'SJ'	Seymour Johnson AFB, NC	F-15E
	335th FS	'SJ'	Seymour Johnson AFB, NC	F-15E
	336th FS	'SJ'	Seymour Johnson AFB, NC	F-15E
57th FW	422nd TES	'WA'	Nellis AFB, NV	F-15E
	F-15 FWS	'WA'	Nellis AFB, NV	F-15E
58th FW	461st FS	'LF'	Luke AFB, AZ	F-15E
	550th FS	'LF'	Luke AFB, AZ	F-15E

General Dynamics
F-16 Fighting Falcon

The **F-16 Fighting Falcon**, also called the 'Viper', is the most numerous USAF aircraft. LANTIRN-equipped **F-16C** block 40/42 fighter-bombers equip the bulk of the active force's fighter wings while F-16C block 50/52s have begun delivery. A series of OCUs (operational capability upgrades) will continue enhancing the performance of Falcons already in service. **F-16A**s and some F-16Cs serve in Air National Guard units, the **F-16A ADF** (air defense fighter) version equipping ANG squadrons with an interceptor mission.

The F-16 is distinct in appearance, with its air intake or shock inlet located directly below the pilot. The fighter's configuration uses wing/body flare to enhance lift at high angles of attack. The wing itself is straight, albeit with leading-edge sweep, and has hinged leading and trailing flaps to increase maneuverability. The aircraft is often described as inherently unstable, relying upon a central computer and electronic fly-by-wire flight controls.

The F-16 pilot sits on a zero-zero ACES II (Advanced Concept Ejection Seat) canted to recline 30°. The cockpit has HUD and multi-function displays, a sidestick controller instead of a conventional control stick, and a one-piece canopy of blown polycarbonate which, in later versions, is lined with RAM (radar absorbent materials). Westinghouse APG-66/68 pulse-Doppler radar gives the F-16 'look down' capability and is being upgraded in the 1990s.

The F-16 is armed with an M61A1 Vulcan 20-mm cannon with 515 rounds, located on the port side of the fuselage at the blend between wing and fuselage. The F-16 carries up to a maximum of 29,450 lb (9276 kg) of ordnance, including Mk 20 Rockeye and CBU-87 cluster bombs, Mk 83 and Mk 84 500-lb (227-kg) and 1,000-lb (454-kg) bombs, AGM-65 Maverick missiles, and GBU-10 and GBU-15 guided weapons.

F-16C/D blocks 25, 30 and 40 aircraft are powered by 27,600-lb (122.77-kN) thrust General Electric F110-GE-100 engines or improved versions. F-16C blocks 32 and 42 Falcons have 23,840-lb (10814-kg) thrust P&W F100-PW-200s. Later F-16s use IPE (Improved Performance Engines) of the -220 and -229 subtypes.

After defeating the Northrop YF-17 in a 'fly-off' contest, the **YF-16** was chosen by the USAF on 13 January 1975. The USAF ordered eight full-scale development (FSD) F-16 airframes and the first (75-0745) flew at Fort Worth on 8 December 1976. The first two-seat FSD **F-16B** (75-0751) flew on 8 August 1977. The two-seat version retains wing and fuselage dimensions of the single-seater but sacrifices 1,500 lb (680 kg) of fuel.

In June 1975, four European countries (Belgium, Netherlands, Denmark and Norway) chose the **F-16A**. On both continents, an intricate MSIP (Multi-Stage Improvement Program) was launched to formalize cooperation in upgrading the aircraft on a planned, gradual basis. Numerous other foreign users have since

adopted the F-16 Fighting Falcon.

Delivery of operational airplanes began in January 1979 to the 388th TFW at Hill AFB, Utah. F-16s went next to the 56th TFW at MacDill AFB, Florida, one of the USAF's RTUs (replacement training units) for the type.

Despite a GAO (General Accounting Office) finding of engine malfunctions, structural cracks and other teething problems, the F-16 developed into a superb fighter-bomber. The F100-PW-100 engine was new and experienced problems including ground-start difficulties, compressor stalls, fuel-pump breakdowns and afterburner malfunctions. Much of this was corrected early and the engine, employed on all F-16A/B models, has proved successful.

The first YF-16 (72-1567) was rebuilt in December 1975, with twin canards added, to become the USAF Flight Dynamics Laboratory's Control-Configured Vehicle (CCV). Fly-by-wire flight controls and relaxed static stability made the YF-16 an ideal candidate to evaluate control of an aircraft beyond conventional means, with independent or 'decoupled' flight surfaces to permit maneuvering in one plane without movement in another – for example, turning without having to bank. The YF-16/CCV and the AFTI F-16 (below) could rise or fall using direct lift, move laterally by direct side force, or yaw, pitch or roll regardless of the direction of flight.

General Dynamics converted the fifth FSD F-16A (75-0750) into the Advanced Fighter Technology Integration aircraft, or **AFTI/**

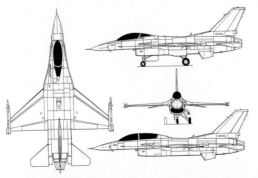

F-16A. The AFTI/F-16 has a triplex digital flight-control system, larger vertical canard surfaces at the air intake and a thick dorsal spine. From 1982, it underwent a two-year program of test flights.

In recent years, the AFTI/F-16 has become associated with close air support (CAS) studies, and is now known as the **AFTI/CAS F-16**. Upgraded with an F-16C block 25 wing and F-16C block 40 features including APG-68 radar and LANTIRN interface, the AFTI/F-16 has been through a five-phase CAS evaluation program over 1988-1991, applying an automatic target hand-off system, Pave Penny laser-designator pod, and digital systems to the low-level battlefield mission.

Versions of the F-16A were also tested with APG-65 radar, with J79 engine, and with YJ101 engine. A proposal for an F-16 with a much-changed wing shape was made in February 1980. Known as SCAMP (Supersonic Cruise And Maneuvering Prototype) and later as the **F-16XL**, this was a rebuild with a 'cranked delta' wing. The F-16XL's fuselage was lengthened to 54 ft 1.86 in (16.51 m) and grafted on a cranked-arrow wing incorporating carbon composite materials to save weight while increasing area and allowing up to 17 stores stations.

The first of two F-16XLs (75-0749) with single seat and F100 engine flew briefly in the mid-1970s. The second F-16XL (75-0747; originally a single-seat FSD F-16A), now a two-seater with F110 engine, flew in the 1980s and competed unsuccessfully with the F-15E Strike Eagle. Had it been chosen for production, the aircraft would have been designated **F-16F**.

F-16A/B airplanes were built in blocks 1, 5, 10 and 15, all powered by the Pratt & Whitney F100. F-16C/D models are in blocks 25, 30/32,

Left: Air-to-air and air-to-ground roles come within the compass of the General Dynamics F-16 Fighting Falcon, which is now the most numerous warplane in the USAF inventory. F-16C single- and F-16D two-seat versions are shown here.

Below: In addition to joining front-line units, the F-16C and its two-seat F-16D equivalent are now well established in service with Air Force Reserve and Air National Guard elements. One of the first second-line outfits to acquire F-16Cs was the Air Force Reserve's 944th TFG, which is stationed at Luke AFB, Arizona, and this example is specially marked to indicate assignment to the unit's commanding officer.

Top: The bulge at the base of this F-16A's tail surface identifies it as being one of the 270 Fighting Falcons that are undergoing conversion to the dedicated Air Defense Fighter standard for service with Air National Guard interceptor squadrons. This particular example is from the 114th FS at Kingsley Field, Oregon.

Above: Good handling qualities, extreme agility and plenty of power make the Fighting Falcon an almost ideal display mount, which is why it was selected for the 'Thunderbirds' display team in the 1980s when it replaced the T-38A Talon. The team's six single-seaters are portrayed here as they fly past the Statue of Liberty.

F-16 Fighting Falcon (continued)

40/42 and 50/52. C/D models in blocks 25, 30, 40 and 50 are powered by General Electric F110 engines, while otherwise identical ships in blocks 32, 42 and 52 have improved P&W F100s.

F-16A/B block 1s were early production ships (43 built), consisting of 21 F-16As and 22 F-16Bs distinguishable from later Fighting Falcons by their black radomes.

F-16A/B block 5s introduced the gray radome which is now standard. These 126 ships included 99 F-16As and 27 F-16Bs.

F-16A/B block 10 consists of 170 airplanes including 145 F-16As and 24 F-16Bs, in addition to earlier, now upgraded, machines.

F-16A/B block 15 (also known as MSIP I) introduced the first important changes to the F-16. Noteworthy is the extended horizontal stabilator, or 'big tail' now standard on these and all subsequent Fighting Falcons. Because of wing cracks and afterburner problems, the USAF is expected to retire pre-block 15 'small tail' ships by the mid-1990s, making these final F-16A/Bs the oldest F-16s to remain in service. Block 15 includes 457 American airplanes, including 410 F-16As and 47 F-16Bs.

Two hundred and seventy airframes in the F-16A/B block 15 series are being converted to ADF F-16A/B block 15 (air defense fighters). In October 1986, the USAF announced that these aircraft would take over the ANG fighter-interceptor mission, defending North America from bombers and cruise missiles. Principal additions are the AIM-7 Sparrow radar missile and a spotlight. The ADF F-16A/B block 15 interceptor also has provision for AIM-120 AMRAAM, advanced IFF (indentification, friend or foe), and HF radio for long-range communications. ANG interceptor pilots are trained by the 114th Fighter Squadron, Oregon ANG, at Kingsley Field in Klamath Falls. The cost of maintaining ADF units is likely to be reviewed in light of reduction of the Soviet threat.

The F-16C single-seat and F-16D two-seat fighters introduce progressive changes to enhance Fighting Falcon capability to operate at night. The first F-16C flew on 19 June 1984. All C and D models have an enlarged base or 'island' leading up to the vertical fin with a small blade antenna protruding up from it. The space was intended for the ASPJ (airborne self-protection jammer) but the USAF had abandoned this program. F-16C and D models also employ Hughes APG-68 multimode radar with increased range, sharper resolution and expanded operating modes. There is provision for the AGM-65D Maverick, and a variety of avionic advances. These models also give the pilot a bigger HUD, and a function keyboard control at the base of the HUD (located in a console to his left in earlier ships), called 'up front' controls. A data display with key items of information is located beside the HUD in front of the pilot at 'design eye' level for HOTAS flying.

F-16C/D block 25 airplanes (also known as MSIP II), production of which began in July 1984, are powered by the F100-PW-200 and number 319 aircraft: 289 F-16Cs and 30 F-16Ds.

The 27,600-lb (122.77-kN) thrust GE F110-GE-100 engine used in F-16 block 30s delivers about 5,000 lb (2268 kg) more thrust than P&W engines. This powerplant change brought a need to alter contours of the F-16 air intake to accommodate the larger amount of air ingested. Because the change was not made at first, early F-16C/D block 30s (MSIP III) are 'small inlet' airplanes, the 1-ft (0.3-m) larger air intake having become standard for GE power on 'big inlet' ships from 86-0262 onwards.

F-16C/D block 32 airplanes are identical to those in block 30 except that power is provided by a 23,770-lb (10782-kg) thrust F100-PW-220. Introduction of the 'dash 220' marks the maturation of the original F-16 engine. While the improved P&W engine is not as powerful as the GE powerplant, it is lighter and crew chiefs consider it 'smarter' and more dependable than Pratt & Whitney 200s.

F-16C/D block 30/32 aircraft have capability for AGM-45 Shrike I and AGM-88A HARM anti-radiation missiles, and AIM-120 AMRAAM. Avionics hardware changes are also introduced with block 30/32. A total of 501 of these airplanes was ordered during FY 1985-88, including 446 F-16Cs and 55 F-16Ds.

F-16C/D block 40/42 airplanes began to come off the Fort Worth production line beginning in December 1988. Among several F-16C/D blocks covered by MSIP III, this version introduces LANTIRN pods, GPS (Global Positioning System) receiver, HARM II, APG-68V radar, digital flight controls, auto

Searchlight
A night identification searchlight is fitted to the side of the ADF's nose.

General Dynamics F-16 ADF Fighting Falcon

Ordered in 1986, the F-16 ADF was chosen to equip fighter squadrons of the ANG engaged on air defense duties, replacing F-4 Phantoms and F-106 Delta Darts. The modification to ADF standard involves F-16A/B Block 15 aircraft only.

Markings
ADF aircraft retain the USAF's standard two-tone gray camouflage, but the Guard aircraft tend to feature more striking markings, and none more so than the griffon motif of the 144th Fighter Wing, California ANG.

Weapons
ADFs have been cleared to carry the AIM-7M Sparrow, AIM-9 Sidewinder and AIM-120 AMRAAM. This aircraft carries a typical load of four Sidewinders and two Sparrows. The ADF is the only operational F-16 model to carry the AIM-7.

Radar
Part of the ADF modification was an upgrade to the APG-66 radar to improve small target detection. Other ADF upgrades involved the fitment of HF/SSB long-range radio.

Service
Eleven ANG units operate the ADF variant, strategically placed around the outer states to cover all approaches to the United States. Training is handled by the Oregon unit.

matic terrain-following, and (as a logical consequence) increased take-off weight. With this block comes the configured (formerly 'common') engine bay, with options for the GE F110-GE-100 (block 40) or P&W F100-PW-220 (block 42).

Greater structural strength increases the F-16C/D **Night Falcon**'s 9-g capability from 26,900 lb (12201 kg) to 28,500 lb (12928 kg). The heavier all-up weight has resulted in larger landing gear to accommodate LANTIRN, bulged landing gear doors, and the move of landing lights to the nose gear door. Block 40/42 Night Falcons are slated for the USAF, Israel, Egypt, Turkey and Bahrain.

F-16C/D block 50/52 aircraft with IPE (Improved Performance Engine) are powered by the third major version of engines now in use – the GE F110-GE-129 and P&W F100-PW-229. These feature APG-68 (V5) radar and improved secure radios and radar warning receiver. Two hundred and forty-nine F-16 Fighting Falcons were deployed to Operation Desert Storm and flew almost 13,500 sorties, the highest sortie total for any aircraft in the war, while maintaining a 95.2-per cent mission capable rate, five per cent better than the F-16's peacetime rate. F-16s attacked ground elements in the Kuwaiti theater of operations, flew 'Scud' missions, and destroyed military production and chemical production facilities, and airfields.

In early 1991, USAF Tactical Air Command began quietly studying an MRF (Multi-Role Fighter) which would replace the F-16 in the 21st century. Most of the USAF's F-16s have relatively low airframe hours and will be among the last current aircraft to be replaced to phased out.

USAF Aircraft

F-16 Fighting Falcon (continued)

MISSION PROFILE

Armament options: internal M61A1 Vulcan 20-mm cannon with maximum of 500 rounds; three fuselage and six wing hardpoints for the carriage of most stores in US inventory, including nuclear and conventional low-drag and retarded bombs, and cluster-bomb units, plus two wingtip hardpoints for AIM-9M Sidewinder missiles; provision for AN/ALQ-119 or -131 ECM pod on either of two mid-wing ordnance stations or centerline; provision for up to six AGM-65 Maverick air-to-ground missiles, three each on two mid-wing ordnance stations; (F-16 block 15 ADF) provision for two AIM-7M Sparrow radar-guided missiles on mid-wing ordnance stations; (F-16C block 40/42 and block 50/52) LANTIRN (Low-Altitude Navigation and Targeting, Infra-Red, for Night) weapons and targeting pods; (F-16C block 50/52) LANTIRN weapons and targeting pods; provision for AGM-88B HARM (high-speed anti-radiation missile) and AGM-137 TSSAM (tri-service stand-off attack missile)

Close air support/battlefield area interdiction: on a CAS, BAI or combined CAS/BAI mission the F-16 would refuel in flight but can fly to a radius of about 500 miles (805 km) unrefueled to be on station for 45 minutes with 500 rounds of ammunition for the M61A1, two 600-US gal (2271-liter) wing drop-tanks on inboard ordnance stations, 12 Mk 82 500-lb (227-kg) bombs on MER (multiple ejector racks) at mid-wing ordnance stations, and two AIM-9M Sidewinder missiles on wingtips; for dedicated anti-armor work the load-out would be two wing-tanks, eight Mk 20 Rockeye CBUs on two mid-wing ordnance stations, and two Sidewinders; AN/ALQ-131(V) ECM pod on mid-wing ordnance station (not both) would be carried by one or two aircraft in a flight of four

Interdiction/strike: on an interdiction mission, the F-16 would refuel in flight but can fly at medium to high altitude to a combat radius of about 550 miles (885 km) unrefueled with 500 rounds of ammunition for the M61A1, two 600-US gal (2271-liter) wing drop-tanks on inboard ordnance stations, 12 Mk 82 500-lb (227-kg) general-purpose bombs on MER (multiple ejector racks) at mid-wing ordnance stations, and centerline AN/ALQ-131(V) ECM pod; in another typical interdiction configuration, the F-16 would refuel in flight but can fly at medium to high altitude to a combat radius of about 605 miles (973 km) unrefueled with 500 rounds of ammunition for the M61A1, two 600-US gal (2271-liter) wing drop-tanks on inboard ordnance stations, one 300-US gal (1136-liter) drop-tank on centerline, and six AGM-65 Maverick air-to-ground missiles on mid-wing ordnance stations

SEAD (suppression of enemy air defenses): on a SEAD mission against air defense radars, the F-16 would refuel in flight but can cruise at medium to high altitude to a radius of about 640 miles (1030 km) unrefueled for attack from medium altitude with 500 rounds for the M61A1 (not employed against SEAD targets), two 600-US gal (2271-liter) drop-tanks on inboard ordnance stations, and two AGM-88 HARM on mid-wing ordnance stations

Intercept: on an air defense/interceptor mission, the F-16A block 15 ADF (air defense fighter) can fly at high altitude to a radius of about 700 miles (1127 km) unrefueled with 500 rounds of ammunition for the M61A1, two AIM-9M on wingtip hardpoints, two AIM-7M on mid-wing hardpoints, centerline 300-US gal (1136-liter) drop-tank, and two 600-US gal (2271-liter) drop-tanks on mid-wing hardpoints

USAF VARIANTS AND SERIALS

YF-16A: Two prototype and six pre-production F-16As were given the Y prefix to indicate service test, as all were initially employed by the manufacturer and the Air Force to evaluate the capabilities of the type.
72-01567 and 72-01568; 75-0745 to 75-0750

YF-16B: The two pre-production F-16Bs have been allocated the designation YF-16B for the same reason as the YF-16A above.
75-0751 to 75-0752

Above: An F-16B Fighting Falcon assigned to the Edwards-based 6510th Test Wing is shown here as it takes part in trials with the AGM-45 Shrike anti-radiation air-to-surface missile (now replaced by the AGM-88 HARM).

Below: LANTIRN and ECM pods are carried by this F-16C from the 347th Fighter Wing at Moody AFB, Georgia, the 'Charlie' version of the General Dynamics warplane being the definitive model in USAF service.

F-16A: The initial production version with 743 ordered between 1978 and 1983, although most are operated by the Reserves or in the air defense role. These latter aircraft are known as F-16A (ADF) for Air Defense Fighter and are distinguishable by an avionics bulge at the base of the vertical stabiliser.
78-0001 to 78-0076; 79-0219 to 79-0409; 80-0474 to 80-0622; 81-0663 to 81-0811; 82-0900 to 82-1025; 83-1066 to 83-1117

F-16B: One hundred and twenty-one two-seat trainers were ordered between 1978 and 1983.
78-0077 to 78-0115; 79-0410 to 79-0432; 80-0623 to 80-0638; 81-0812 to 81-0822; 82-1026 to 82-1049; 83-1166 to 83-1173

F-16C: The F-16C has featured a host of improvements over the F-16A, including the option to fit either the General Electric F110-GE-129 or the Pratt & Whitney F100-PW-220 engine. Recent production has included the provision to fit the LANTIRN nav/attack system. Some 1,400 F-16Cs have been ordered or budgeted until 1993, when orders will terminate.
83-1118 to 83-1165; 84-1212 to 84-1318; 84-1374 to 84-1395; 85-1398 to 85-1505; 85-1544 to 85-1570; 86-0207 to 86-0371; 87-0217 to 87-0362; 88-0397 to 88-0550; 89-2000 to 89-2154; 90-0700 to 90-0776; 90-0801 to 90-0833; 91-0366 to 91-0461; 92-0100 to 92-0218; 93-0315 to 93-0464

F-16D: Tandem two-seat version of the F-16C with 237 built or budgeted until 1992.
83-1174 to 83-1185; 84-1319 to 84-1331; 84-1396 to 84-1397; 85-1506 to 85-1517; 85-1571 to 85-1573; 86-0039 to 86-0053; 87-0363 to 87-0396; 88-0150 to 88-0175; 89-2155 to 89-2179; 90-0777 to 90-0800; 90-0834 to 90-0849; 91-0462 to 91-0485; 92-0219 to 92-0249

GF-16A/GF-16C: Two F-16As and three F-16Cs were allocated the designations GF-16A and GF-16C respectively, following transfer to Air Training Command.
78-0013; 79-0408 (A); 83-1124; 83-1125; 83-1127 (C)

SPECIFICATION

General Dynamics F-16C
Wing: span over wingtip missile launchers 31 ft 0 in (9.45 m) and over wingtip missiles 32 ft 9.75 in (10.00 m); aspect ratio 3.0; area 300.0 sq ft (28.87 m²)
Fuselage and tail: length 49 ft 4 in (15.03 m); height 16 ft 8.5 in (5.09 m); tailplane span 18 ft 3.75 in (5.58 m); wheel base 13 ft 1.5 in (4.00 m)
Powerplant: one General Electric F110-GE-100 rated at 27,600 lb (122.77 kN) afterburning thrust or one Pratt & Whitney F100-P-220 rated at 23,450 lb (104.31 kN) afterburning thrust
Weights: empty 19,100 lb (8663 kg) with F110 turbofan or 18,335 lb (8316 kg) with F100 turbofan; typical combat take-off 21,585 lb (9790 kg); maximum take-off 25,971 lb (11372 kg) for an air-to-air mission without drop-tanks, or 42,300 lb (19187 kg) with maximum external load
Fuel and load: internal fuel 3162 kg (6,972 lb); external fuel up to 3066 kg (6,760 lb) in three 1136-, 1400-, 1703- and 2271-liter (300-, 370-, 450- and 600-US gal) drop-tanks; maximum ordnance 9276 kg (20,450 lb) for 5-g maneuver limit or 11,950 lb (5420 kg) for 9-g maneuver limit
Speed: maximum level speed 'clean' at 40,000 ft (12190 m) more than 1,320 mph (2124 km/h); maximum speed at sea level 915 mph (1472 km/h)
Range: ferry range more than 2,415 miles (3890 km); combat radius on a hi-lo-hi mission with six 1,000-lb (454-kg) bombs 340 miles (547 km)
Performance: maximum rate of climb at sea level more than 50,000 ft (15240 m) per minute; service ceiling more than 50,000 ft (15240 m); typical take-off distance 2,500 ft (762 m); typical landing distance 2,500 ft (762 m)

General Dynamics F-16A
generally similar to the F-16C except in the following particulars:
Fuselage and tail: height 16 ft 5.2 in (5.01 m);

*Left: Roughly half the F-16-equipped **ANG** units are employed on 'mud-moving' missions, weapons options including 'dumb' and 'smart' bombs plus the GPU-5/A 'Pave Claw' 30-mm cannon pod. This F-16A is assigned to the 174th FW, ANG.*

Air Combat Command (ACC)

31st FW	307th FS	'HS'	Homestead AFB, FL	F-16C/D
	308th FS	'HS'	Homestead AFB, FL	F-16C/D
	309th FS	'HS'	Homestead AFB, FL	F-16C/D
56th FW	61st FS	'MC'	MacDill AFB, FL	F-16C/D
	62nd FS	'MC'	MacDill AFB, FL	F-16C/D
	63rd FS	'MC'	MacDill AFB, FL	F-16C/D
	72nd FS	'MC'	MacDill AFB, FL	F-16C/D
57th FW	det 2	'WA'	Luke AFB, AZ	F-16C/D
	det 16	'WA'	Hill AFB, UT	F-16C/D
	422nd TES	'WA'	Nellis AFB, NV	F-16C
	F-16 FWS	'WA'	Nellis AFB, NV	F-16C/D
58th FW	310th FS	'LF'	Luke AFB, AZ	F-16C/D
	311th FS	'LF'	Luke AFB, AZ	F-16C/D
	314th FS	'LF'	Luke AFB, AZ	F-16C/D
347th FW	68th FS	'MY'	Moody AFB, GA	F-16C/D
	69th FS	'MY'	Moody AFB, GA	F-16C/D
	70th FS	'MY'	Moody AFB, GA	F-16C/D
363rd FW	17th FS	'SW'	Shaw AFB, SC	F-16C/D
	19th FS	'SW'	Shaw AFB, SC	F-16C/D
	33rd FS	'SW'	Shaw AFB, SC	F-16C/D
388th FW	4th FS	'HL'	Hill AFB, UT	F-16C/D
	34th FS	'HL'	Hill AFB, UT	F-16C/D
	421st FS	'HL'	Hill AFB, UT	F-16C/D
AWC	4485th TS	'OT'	Eglin AFB, FL	F-16A/B/C/D

United States Air Forces in Europe (USAFE)

52nd FW	23rd FS	'SP'	Spangdahlem AB, Germany	F-16C/D
	480th FS	'SP'	Spangdahlem AB, Germany	F-16C/D
86th FW	512th FS	'RS'	Ramstein AB, Germany	F-16C/D
	526th FS	'RS'	Ramstein AB, Germany	F-16C/D

Air National Guard (ANG)

113th FW	121st FS	'DC'	Andrews AFB, MD	F-16A/B
114th FG	175th FS	'SD'	Sioux Falls MAP, SD	F-16C/D
122nd FW	163rd FS	'FW'	Fort Wayne MAP, IN	F-16C/D
127th FW	107th FS		Selfridge ANGB, MI	F-16A/B
144th FW	194th FS		Frenso Air Terminal, CA	F-16A/B ADF
174th FW	138th FS	'NY'	Hancock Fd, Syracuse, NY	F-16A/B ADF
107th FG	136th FS		Niagara Falls IAP, NY	F-16A/B ADF
119th FG	178th FS		Hector Fd, Fargo, ND	F-16A/B ADF
120th FG	186th FS		Great Falls IAP, MT	F-16A/B ADF
125th FG	159th FS	'FL'	Jacksonville IAP, FL	F-16A/B ADF
132nd FW	124th FS	'IA'	Des Moines IAP, IA	F-16C/D
140th FW	120th FS	'CO'	Buckley ANFB, CO	F-16C/D
142nd FG	114th FS		Kingsley Fd, OR	F-16A/B ADF
147th FG	111th FS		Ellington AFB, TX	F-16A/B ADF
148th FG	179th FS		Duluth IAP, MN	F-16A/B ADF
149th FG	182nd FS	'SA'	Kelly AFB, TX	F-16A/B
158th FG	134th FS		Burlington IAP, VT	F-16A/B ADF
162nd FG	148th FS		Tucson IAP, AZ	F-16A/B
169th FG	157th FS		McEntire ANGB, SC	F-16A/B
177th FG	119th FS		Atlantic City IAP, NJ	F-16A/B ADF
181st FG	113th FS	'HF'	Hulman RAP, Terre Haute, IN	F-16C/D
183rd FG	170th FS	'SI'	Capital Apt, Springfield, IL	F-16A/B
184th FG	127th FS		McConnell AFB, KS	F-16C/D
185th FG	174th FS	'HA'	Sioux City, IA	F-16A/B
187th FG	160th FS	'AL'	Dannelly Fd, Montgomery, AL	F-16A/B
188th FG	184th FS	'FS'	Fort Smith MAP, AR	F-16A/B
191st FG	171st FS		Selfridge ANGB, MI	F-16A/B ADF

Air Force Reserve (AFRes)

301st FW	457th FS	'TF'	Carswell AFB, TX	F-16C/D
419th FW	466th FS	'HI'	Hill AFB, UT	F-16A/B
482nd FW	93rd FS	'FM'	Homestead AFB, FL	F-16A/B
507th FG	465th FS	'SH'	Tinker AFB, OK	F-16A/B
906th FG	89th FS	'DO'	Wright Patterson AFB, OH	F-16A/B
924th FG	704th FS	'TX'	Bergstrom AFB, TX	F-16A/B
944th FG	302nd FS	'LR'	Luke AFB, AZ	F-16C/D

Left: An unusual quad AIM-9 Sidewinder weapons load is carried by this Fighting Falcon as it receives a fresh load of fuel from a KC-135. In addition, it features auxiliary fuel tanks and an ECM pod and may well have been photographed during a transoceanic deployment, F-16s from first- and second-line units often being sent to overseas bases for training exercises.

Below left: This F-16A Fighting Falcon of the USAF Test Pilots School at Edwards AFB displays an unusual but not unattractive basically white-overall color scheme, which contrasts strongly with patches of high-visibility red on the tail and wings. A similarly marked aircraft is also flown by a small test unit managed by the Ogden Air Logistics Center.

Below: 'Hunter and killer'. In USAFE service, the F-16C has augmented F-4G 'Wild Weasels' of the Spangdahlem-based 52nd Fighter Wing in the defense suppression mission, whereby the high-value Phantoms locate hostile radar facilities which are then attacked by Fighting Falcons. In this task, the AGM-88 HARM is a key weapon but 'dumb' bombs and CBUs can also be used.

tailplane span 18 ft 0.34 in (5.495 m)
Powerplant: one Pratt & Whitney F100-P-100 rated at 14,670 lb (65.26 kN) dry and 23,830 lb (106.0 kN) afterburning thrusts
Weights: operational empty 14,567 lb (6607 kg); typical combat take-off 22,785 lb (10335 kg); maximum take-off 33,000 lb (14968 kg)
Fuel and load: internal fuel 6,972 lb (3162 kg); external fuel up to 6,760 lb (3066 kg) in three 300-, 370-, 450- and 600-US gal (1136-, 1400-, 1703- and 2271-liter) drop-tanks; maximum ordnance 15,200 lb (6894 kg)

General Dynamics F-16B
generally similar to the F-16A except in the following particulars:
Weights: operational weight empty 15,141 lb (6868 kg); typical combat take-off 22,160 lb (10051 kg)

General Dynamics F-16D
generally similar to the F-16C except in the following particulars:
Weights: normal take-off 24,502 lb (11114 kg); maximum take-off 37,500 lb (17010 kg)
Fuel and load: internal fuel 5,785 lb (2624 kg)

USAF OPERATORS

Air Force Materiel Command (AFMC)

Ogden ALC			Hill AFB, UT	F-16A
3246th TW	3247th TS	'ET'	Eglin AFB, FL	F-16A/B/C
6510th TW	6516th TS	'ED'	Edwards AFB, CA	F-16A/B/C

Air Training Command (ATC)

3400th TTW	Lowry TTC	Lowry AFB, CO	GF-16A/C
3700th TTW	Sheppard TTC	Sheppard AFB, TX	GF-16A

Pacific Air Forces (PACAF)

8th FW	35th FS	'WP'	Kunsan AB, RoK	F-16C/D
	80th FS	'WP'	Kunsan AB, RoK	F-16C/D
343rd Wg	18th FS	'AK'	Eielson AFB, AK	F-16C/D
432nd FW	13th FS	'MJ'	Misawa AB, Japan	F-16C/D
	14th FS	'MJ'	Misawa AB, Japan	F-16C/D
51st FW	36th FS	'OS'	Osan AB, RoK	F-16C/D

Lockheed/General Dynamics/Boeing

F-22 Rapier

The **F-22 Rapier** is the USAF's choice as its ATF (Advanced Tactical Fighter) and replacement for the F-15 Eagle. The F-22 meets a USAF requirement for long-range cruise at supersonic speeds without afterburning and makes use of low-observables (LO), or stealth, to defeat advanced radar defense systems.

The F-22 also uses thrust vectoring to maneuver at high angles of attack (AOA) in air-to-air combat. Two-dimensional engine nozzles can be vectored 20 per cent up or down at any power setting. Coupled with large leading-edge wing flaps and overall low wing loading, the nozzles permit maneuver at low speeds and high flight angles.

The short, angular F-22 has a comparatively large, diamond-shaped wing, splayed twin vertical tails, and large horizontal tails. The wing is, in fact, very nearly a delta, with 48° of sweep on the leading edge, a nearly straight trailing edge, and a very small tip chord. The wing blends into the fuselage to provide a lifting body area. Engine air intakes sit astride a short, tapered nose which houses the cockpit and most of the avionics. The inlet ducts curve inward and upward, shielding the front faces of the engine from direct illumination by radar. Radar-absorbent materials are employed in the forward fuselage and cockpit canopy.

The F-22 pilot sits upright on a zero-zero ACES II (Advanced Concept Ejection Seat) beneath an unbroken bubble-style canopy, and has a panel of liquid-crystal color displays and HUD (head-up display). Extensive use is made of VHSIC (Very High Speed Integrated Circuits), common modules and high-speed databuses. The avionics suite makes use of voice command/control, VHSIC 1750 computer, shared antennas, advanced data fusion/cockpit displays, INEWS (Integrated Electronic Warfare System), ICNIA (Integrated Communications, Navigation, Identification Avionics) and fiber optics data transmission.

The F-22 Rapier is intended to cruise at supersonic speed to a high-risk area and engage opposing aircraft BVR (beyond visual range) but, if necessary, to outmaneuver them at closer range. Details have not been released concerning the radar which will be crucial to the F-22 in BVR engagements, and in late 1991 a decision had not been made as to the type of cannon to be mounted internally in production F-22s for closer-in combat. The F-22's underside has a weapons bay with serrated edges, for AIM-120 AMRAAM missiles. The aircraft also has side-mounted weapons bays just aft of the engine inlets for AIM-9M Sidewinders.

Powerplant for the twin-engined F-22 is the Pratt & Whitney YF119, which is expected to have a thrust rating in the area of 30,000 lb (13607 kg).

The F-22 emerged from the free-spending Reagan years (1981-89) when the USAF saw an eventual need for an F-15 replacement to operate in the European theater. In 1984, the USAF formalized a requirement for a fighter capable of supersonic flight without afterburning, with a greater range than the F-15, and with vectoring and reversing engine nozzles for STOL performance.

An early decision was made to select the new ATF using a dem/val (demonstration/evaluation) process recommended by the 1986 Packard Commission: contractors would design and build candidate aircraft prototypes and would be told in general terms what was needed, then given wide latitude to devise solutions. Aircraft manufacturers would perform R&D (research and development) at their own expense. Engine manufacturers would compete similarly. There would not be a 'fly-off' competition: the ATF flight-test phase would be a wide-open, innovative setting which allowed builders to demonstrate what their aircraft could do.

Lockheed **YF-22A** and Northrop YF-23A candidates were developed for this ATF contest, initially in a 'black' program accessible only to those with compartmentalized security clearances. Boeing and General Dynamics were in partnership with Lockheed and the former's company-owned Boeing 757 was modified to become an avionics flying laboratory for the F-22 program.

The prototype YF-22A (87-3997/N22YF), powered by General Electric YF120 engines, made its first flight on 29 September 1990. The second YF-22A (87-3998/N22YX), powered by P&W YF119 engines, flew on 30 October 1990. The competing Northrop YF-23 also flew in both GE- and P&W-powered examples. Though the YF-23 flew earlier, the team headed by Lockheed decided to demonstrate its YF-22 prototypes more exhaustively than did Northrop. The two YF-22s flew 74 flights and 91.6 hours and made live firings of AIM-9 and AIM-120 missiles as well as single-engine landings, none of which were performed by the Northrop aircraft.

On 23 April 1991, the USAF announced its choice of the F-22 for the ATF production contract. The decision on the P&W engine came soon after. In September 1991, the USAF acknowledged that the F-22 will miss its weight goal by 10,000 lb (4536 kg) and will weigh 20 per cent more than the target weight of 50,000 lb (22680 kg). A Martin-Marietta infrared search-and-track system (IRST) for the F-22 was postponed due mainly to cost considerations.

Above: This artist's impression portrays the planned production configuration of the F-22A Rapier, some 650 examples of which are due to be delivered to the US Air Force. Production is expected to begin during the course of 1996, initially at a rate of 72 per year.

Below: The Rapier's distinctive planform is displayed to advantage in this study of one of the pair of YF-22A prototypes that were built to take part in the Advanced Tactical Fighter competition of 1990-91.

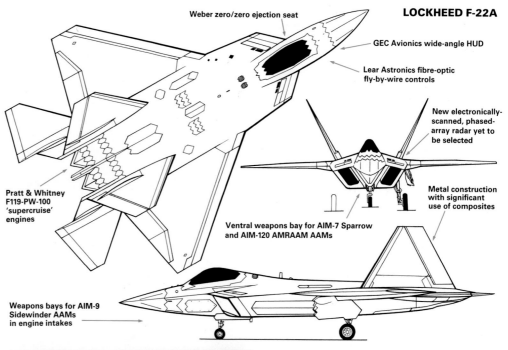

LOCKHEED F-22A

- Weber zero/zero ejection seat
- GEC Avionics wide-angle HUD
- Lear Astronics fibre-optic fly-by-wire controls
- New electronically-scanned, phased-array radar yet to be selected
- Metal construction with significant use of composites
- Ventral weapons bay for AIM-7 Sparrow and AIM-120 AMRAAM AAMs
- Pratt & Whitney F119-PW-100 'supercruise' engines
- Weapons bays for AIM-9 Sidewinder AAMs in engine intakes

Flight testing of the PW-powered YF-22 prototype resumed on 30 October 1991 at Edwards AFB, California. The prototype was were scheduled to fly extensively in 1991-92 to gather aerodynamic loads data, flight control aerodynamic effects data, vibration/acoustic noise data, and maximum coefficient of lift data. In April 1992 the aircraft suffered severe oscillations during a low pass and crashed on the runway. Lockheed pilot Tom Morgenfeld escaped, and the company had already acquired sufficient data to allow the completion of the design.

The USAF had planned originally to order 750 Advanced Tactical Fighters, with production beginning in 1994. Following the spring 1990 Major Aircraft Review (MAR), production was rescheduled to begin in 1996, saving $1.26 billion, for a total of 650 aircraft with maximum production rate of 72 planes per year in 1999 being changed to 48 per year in 2001.

MISSION PROFILE

Armament options: internal cannon (type not announced) scheduled for production aircraft; internal weapon bay for AIM-120 AMRAAM missiles and side-mounted weapon bay for AIM-9M Sidewinder missiles

Air-to-air combat: for various air-to-air scenarios, including point defense, HVA (high value asset) escort, and strike/interdiction escort, the F-22 would refuel in flight but can fly at supersonic cruise at high altitude to a radius of possibly 900 miles (1448 km) with an undisclosed number of AIM-120 AMRAAM and AIM-9M Sidewinder missiles

USAF VARIANTS AND SERIALS

YF-22A: The four evaluation aircraft for the Advanced Tactical Fighter program were allocated the designation YF-22A and YF-23A, with the former being selected as the next-generation air superiority fighter. 87-3997 and 87-3998 allocated N22YF and N22YX

SPECIFICATION

Lockheed/General Dynamics/Boeing YF-22A
Wing: span 43 ft 0 in (13.11 m); aspect ratio 2.2; area about 830.0 sq ft (77.1 m²)
Fuselage and tail: length 64 ft 2 in (19.56 m); height 17 ft 9 in (5.41 m)

Powerplant: two Pratt & Whitney F119-P-100 each rated at 35,000 lb (155.10 kN) afterburning thrust
Weights: empty more than 30,000 lb (13608 kg); maximum take-off 58,000 lb (26308 kg)
Speed: maximum level speed 'clean' Mach 1.58 in supercruise mode and at 30,000 ft (9145 m) Mach 1.7 in afterburning mode
Performance: service ceiling 50,000 ft (15240 m)

USAF OPERATORS

Air Force Materiel Command (AFMC)

6510th TW	6511th TS	'ED'	Edwards AFB, CA	YF-22A

Displaying civil identity letters, both of the YF-22A prototypes take time out from the test program to pose for the camera. Only the PW-powered aircraft was actively employed on test duties but this crashed beyond repair in April 1992 at Edwards.

USAF Aircraft

Schweizer

G-7

The **G-7** was specially designed to provide training in powered glider flying to cadets at the USAF Academy in Colorado Springs. The **TG-7A** is operated by the 94th Air Training Squadron at the Academy.

The Academy has long used 10 Schweizer 2-22 two-plane and five ASK-21 acrobatic sailplanes which do not have military designations and are not listed in USAF inventory. These required a powered aircraft to tow them aloft. The TG-7A, powered by a 112-hp Lycoming four-cylinder engine, is a conventional, low-wing glider with side-by-side seating. It requires no tow airplane and permits the cadet, under supervision of an Air Force pilot, to maneuver towards uncongested air space away from the Academy's airfield. Because it can stay aloft for extended periods, the longer flights provide cadets with more hands-on flying, increasing the opportunity to develop basic airmanship skills.

The first of these motorgliders was delivered to the Academy in 1984. Early in the TG-7A's service life, two were lost in crashes, attributed to a need to make minor changes to the flight surfaces of the aircraft. To check the TG-7A's tendency to stall and 'depart', locally-designed leading-edge fillets, or cuffs, were added following the second crash. Production of these aircraft seems to have totalled 11 airframes, which wear both their military serials and civil registration numbers.

Unlike the USAF Academy's training in Cessna T-41C, Boeing T-43A and de Havilland UV-18B aircraft – all part of the academic regimen – motorglider training in the TG-7A is voluntary and intended to be motivational. The TG-7A enables up to 1,200 Academy cadets each year to make their first solo flights.

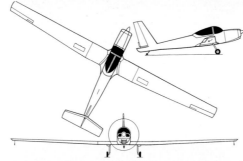

Above: Operated by the Air Force Academy from Colorado Springs, the Schweizer TG-7A motorized glider provides cadets with the opportunity to obtain initial flight experience. In the course of a typical year at the Academy, somewhere in the region of 1,200 students will fly solo for the first time on this type but use of the TG-7 is entirely voluntary, unlike other aspects of the academic program.

Left: Developed specifically to satisfy a USAF Academy requirement for a cheap and economical powered glider, the Schweizer TG-7A has been used in limited numbers since it first entered service during 1984.

MISSION PROFILE

Flight experience: used for initial flight experience and training flights for Air Force Academy students; motor-glider configuration allows the TG-7A to be launched under power and then revert to unpowered flight to extend flight duration

USAF VARIANTS AND SERIALS

TG-7A: Approximately a dozen TG-7A powered gliders were purchased, although only nine remain operational with the Air Force Academy.
81-0886 to 81-0887; 82-0039 to 82-0043; 87-0761 to 87-0764

SPECIFICATION

Schweizer TG-7A
Wing: span 59 ft 6 in (18.14 m); aspect ratio 18.1; area 195.71 sq ft (18.18 m²)
Fuselage and tail: length 27 ft 5 in (8.36 m); height 8 ft 0 in (2.44 m); wheelbase 18 ft 10 in (5.74 m)

Powerplant: one Avco Lycoming O-235-L2C rated at 112 hp (83 kW)
Weights: empty 1,300 lb (589 kg); maximum take-off 1,850 lb (839 kg)
Fuel and load: standard fuel capacity 15.5 US gal (59 liters); optional capacity 31 US gal (118 liters)
Speed: maximum level (unpowered) 150 mph (241 km/h); maximum cruising (powered) 111 mph (178 km/h)
Range: with standard fuel 300 miles (483 km); with optional fuel 598 miles (963 km)
Performance: rate of climb at sea level 1,075 ft (328 m) per minute; service ceiling above 24,000 ft (7315 m); take-off run 450 ft (137 m); landing run 412 ft (126 m); minimum sinking speed (unpowered) at 56 mph (90 km/h) 3.7 ft (1.13 m per second; best glide ratio (unpowered) at 60 mph (97 km/h) 22

USAF OPERATORS

Air Training Command (ATC)

94th ATS	Air Force Academy, Colorado Springs, CO	TG-7A

Sikorsky

H-53 Pave Low

The **H-53 Pave Low**, still widely known by its Vietnam-era nickname 'Super Jolly' is the USAF's largest and most powerful helicopter. The USAF operates the **TH-53A** for type training and **MH-53J** Enhanced Pave Low III version for special operations and combat rescue.

The H-53 is a conventional, long-range helicopter with twin turboshaft engines and self-lubricating, all-metal main and tail rotors. A large horizontal stabilizer is on the starboard side of the rotor pylon. The tricycle landing gear has twin wheels on each unit, and main units retracting into the rear of the sponsons on each side of the fuselage. The helicopter is equipped with inflight-refueling probe, two 315-US gal (1192-liter) self-sealing bladder-type fuel tanks, and two 450-US gal (1703-liter) external auxiliary fuel tanks. The helicopter ordinarily has a flight crew of two pilots and navigator, plus two pararescue technicians (PJs) for rescue and special operations work.

For conventional operations, the helicopter can transport 38 combat-equipped troops on side-facing troop seats or 22 litter patients and four medical attendants, or 18,500 lb (8391 kg) of freight.

Current missions assigned to the MH-53J reflect the increased emphasis on special operations in the 1990s: USAF Special Operations Command, formed in March 1990, employs the aircraft to penetrate enemy territory in support of Special Forces, Delta Force and SEAL teams operating in denied areas, or for combat rescue of friendly personnel. For these missions, the MH-53J is armed with 7.62-mm

(0.3-in) Miniguns operated by the PJ, whose duties have been expanded to include behind-the-lines work. MH-53Js are routinely made available for peacetime SAR (search and rescue) emergencies in both the military and civilian worlds.

The MH-53J has multi-mode radar for terrain following and terrain avoidance, FLIR, additional titanium armor plating, and increased fuel capacity.

The MH-53J is powered by two 4,380-shp General Electric T64-GE-415 turboshaft engines driving a five-bladed, 72-ft 3-in (22.02-m) main rotor.

The H-53 series began with the first flight of a US Marine Corps **YCH-53A** prototype on 14 October 1964, and with May 1966 deliveries of the **CH-53A** to the Marines. Four ex-Marine A models have since been transferred as TH-53A basic qualification trainers to the USAF's 542nd Crew Training Wing, Kirtland

SIKORSKY MH-53J

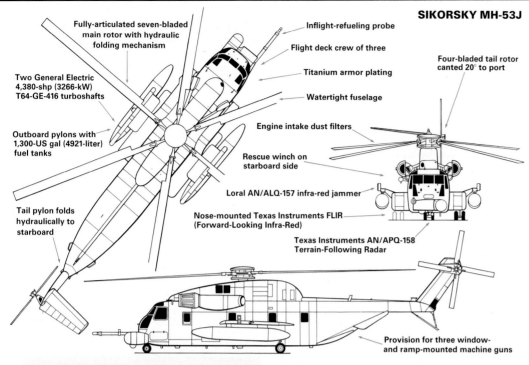

Fully-articulated seven-bladed main rotor with hydraulic folding mechanism

Inflight-refueling probe

Flight deck crew of three

Four-bladed tail rotor canted 20° to port

Two General Electric 4,380-shp (3266-kW) T64-GE-416 turboshafts

Titanium armor plating

Watertight fuselage

Outboard pylons with 1,300-US gal (4921-liter) fuel tanks

Engine intake dust filters

Rescue winch on starboard side

Loral AN/ALQ-157 infra-red jammer

Tail pylon folds hydraulically to starboard

Nose-mounted Texas Instruments FLIR (Forward-Looking Infra-Red)

Texas Instruments AN/APQ-158 Terrain-Following Radar

Provision for three window- and ramp-mounted machine guns

Above: Easily the most powerful and largest of the helicopter types in the USAF inventory, the Sikorsky H-53 has been subjected to extensive modification since entering service in 1967.

Left: Employed on a number of tasks which vary from combat search and rescue to covert 'black' operations, the MH-53J Enhanced Pave Low III is the latest manifestation of the 'Super Jolly' to see service with the US Air Force. It was in the thick of the special forces action during the Gulf War when it secretly infiltrated US and British personnel into Iraq.

Below: Although it is perhaps best known for a humanitarian role, the H-53 Pave Low routinely conducts training exercises with special forces personnel, and much of the peacetime flying task relates to covert operations. Here, one of the bulky Sikorsky helicopters hovers as a group of special forces troops is deposited in a remote forest clearing at the start of an exercise.

AFB, New Mexico, the RTU (replacement training unit) for the type. Versions of the helicopter are used by the US Marine Corps (CH-53A, **CH-53D, VH-53D, CH-53E**), US Navy (**RH-53A, MH-53A, RH-53D, MH-53D, YCH-53E, MH-53E**), Israel (**CH-53D**), and Germany (**CH-53G**). Other foreign variants include the **S-65C-2** (Austria) and **S-80M-1** (Japan).

Development of a USAF combat rescue model of the helicopter began on 28 November 1966 when the first of two Marine CH-53As was loaned to the Air Force. Eight USAF combat-rescue HH-53Bs (66-14428/ 14435) followed, first flying on 15 March 1967 and becoming operational by June 1967. The HH-53B replaced the HH-3E in Vietnam, acquiring its adaptation of the latter's nickname, 'Jolly Green Giant'. One HH-53B was tested in 1969 with a night/all-weather rescue system known as Pave Low I, which did not prove successful.

Twenty **CH-53C**s (68-10922/10933; 70-1625/1632) were delivered, these being transport versions lacking the air-refueling probe found on rescue helicopters. The CH-53C was initially employed for covert operations; later, eight CH-53Cs were used to provide battlefield mobility for the USAF Mobile Tactical Air Control System.

The 44 upgraded HH-53C combat-rescue helicopters (67-14993/14996; 68-8283/8286; 68-10354/10369; 69-5784/5797; 73-1647/1652) also served in Vietnam, from 1969 on. These aircraft participated in the attempt to rescue American prisoners of war in the celebrated Son Tay raid of November 1970. The HH-53C remained in service into the late 1980s. HH-53Cs supported Apollo space missions because their external cargo hook of 20,000-lb (9072-kg) capacity would have enabled them to retrieve the manned lunar capsule in the event of an abort just after launch.

The designation **VH-53F** was assigned to six aircraft ordered for the Air Force but with US Navy bureau numbers (159123/159128) for VIP transport by the 89th Military Airlift Wing. These were cancelled before deliveries could take place.

The sole **YHH-53H**, a former HH-53B (66-14433), tested a night/all-weather system dubbed Pave Low II, which served as a proof-of-concept vehicle for HH-53H and MH-53J Pave Low III variants to follow.

The HH-53H Pave Low III was a USAF rebuild of two CH-53Cs (68-10923; 70-1629) and eight HH-53B/Cs (69-5790/5791; 73-1647/ 1652) with night/all-weather search and rescue equipment including inertial navigation system, Doppler, projected map display, AN/ AAQ-10 infra-red and AN/APQ-158 terrain-following radar in a thimble fairing offset to port on the nose. The HH-53H modification was found to increase the maintenance demands of the type, a problem rectified in the subsequent J model. HH-53H aircraft were redesignated **MH-53H** in 1986 when upgraded for the special operations mission under the Constant Green program. The MH-53H was the first version to be fully cleared for nocturnal operations with the crew employing NVG (night vision goggles).

The decision to upgrade the USAF's H-53

H-53 Pave Low (continued)

fleet (including seven CH-53Cs) to MH-53J Enhanced Pave Low III standard was partly the result of poor performance by Navy RH-53D helicopters during the attempted rescue of American hostages in Iran in April 1980 and by less than full satisfaction with the HH-53H version. The MH-53J is intended to launch from a variety of environments, including ship decks, and includes folding rotors for storage aboard aircraft carriers and assault ships. The MH-53J introduces the –415 version of the T64 turboshaft engine, some 1,000 lb (454 kg) of additional titanium armor, and gross weight increased from 42,000 lb (19050 kg) to 50,000 lb (22680 kg). The first MH-53J was delivered on 17 July 1987. The J model entered service at Hurlburt Field, Florida, in 1988.

During Operation Just Cause in Panama, 20 December 1989, MH-53J Pave Low III, dropped US Navy SEAL commandos who assaulted Panama City's Patilla Airport to destroy a Lear Jet which might otherwise have been used by Panamanian leader Manuel Noriega to escape. In March 1990, MH-53Js were transferred to USAF Special Operations Command. During Operation Desert Storm, MH-53Js provided navigation and support for the US Army AH-64 Apaches which attacked Iraqi radar defense sites during the first hours of the war, 17 January 1991. During the war with Iraq, special operations MH-53Js inserted American and British commandos behind the lines including some who scouted Iraqi 'Scud' missile sites and rescued a down US Navy F-14 Tomcat pilot.

The USAF had hoped to replace its MH-53J fleet and several other types with some 55 Bell/Boeing CV-22 Osprey tilt-rotor special operations aircraft. The US Congress is endeavoring to overcome the Pentagon's cancellation of the Osprey, but the MH-53J fleet, which has no structural fatigue problems, is likely to remain in service through the end of the century.

MISSION PROFILE

Configuration options: the MH-53J Pave Low III helicopter was converted for special operations at night and in adverse weather; the helicopter has an aerial refueling probe and is equipped with inertial navigation system, stabilized FLIR, Doppler navigation equipment, a computer projected map display, and radar in an offset thimble fairing on the nose; the MH-53J can carry three 7.62-mm Miniguns operated from its door positions

Special operations/combat rescue: on a night insertion/extraction or combat rescue mission, the MH-53J when conducting one-third of the mission at altitude below 1,000 ft (305 m) cruises at 172 mph (277 km/h) and carries special operations personnel, rescue personnel, or equipment weighing up to 8,000 lb (3630 kg); the MH-53J can be refueled in flight or at designated ground waypoints, or can carry out such a mission to a radius of about 180 miles (90 km) unrefueled

USAF VARIANTS AND SERIALS

Original construction designations

CH-53A: Two surplus US Marine Corps CH-53As were transferred to the Air Force, adopting period serial allocations.
63-13693 to 63-13694

HH-53B: Long-range search and rescue version of the USMC CH-53A with an air refueling probe and external rescue hoist.
66-14428 to 66-14435

TH-53A: Five USMC CH-53As were redesignated to TH-53A standard for training duties with MAC.
66-14468 to 66-14472

CH-53C: Cargo/assault version of the HH-53C.
68-10922 to 68-10933; 70-1625 to 70-1632

HH-53C: Similar to the HH-53B but with an uprated engine and other minor improvements.
67-14993 to 67-14996; 68-8283 to 68-8286; 68-10354 to 68-10369; 69-5784 to 69-5797; 73-1647 to 73-1652

Conversion designations

NCH-53A: One of the CH-53As was assigned to permanent test duties connected with the launch and recovery of unmanned drones.
63-13694

MH-53H: A small number of CH/HH-53Cs were modified with nose-mounted FLIR, terrain-following radar and improved navigation equipment for special operations and combat rescue duties.
68-10923; 69-5791; 73-1647; 73-1648; 73-1649; 73-1650; 73-1651; plus others modified to MH-53J configuration

MH-53J: Advanced version of the MH-53H with terrain-following/avoidance radar, advanced avionics and ECM, secure communications, and global positioning system terminals.
66-14428; 66-14431; 66-14432; 66-14433; 67-14995; 68-8284; 68-8286; 68-10357; 68-10358; 68-10360; 68-10363; 68-10364; 68-10367; 68-10369; 69-5784; 69-5785; 69-5790; 69-5793; 69-5794; 69-5795; 69-5796; 69-5797; 70-1629; 70-1630; 73-1652; plus others

Below: The bulbous fairing on the port side of the nose of this MH-53J Pave Low III houses an AN/APQ-158 terrain-following radar, other items of kit including infra-red sensors and inertial navigation gear which bestow genuine night and all-weather capability. An inflight-refueling probe is also fitted as standard, while as many as three 7.62-mm Miniguns may be carried to lay down suppressive fire and for self-defense.

SPECIFICATION

Sikorsky HH-53C
Rotor system: main rotor diameter 22.02 m (72 ft 3 in); tail rotor diameter 4.88 m (16 ft 0 in); main rotor disc area 378.1 m^2 (4,070 sq ft); tail rotor disc area 18.68 m^2 (201.06 sq ft)
Fuselage and tail: length overall, rotors turning 26.90 m (88 ft 3 in) and fuselage 20.47 m (67 ft 2 in) excluding refueling probe; height overall 7.60 m (24 ft 11 in) and to top of rotor hub 5.22 m (17 ft 1.5 in); wheel base 8.23 m (27 ft 0 in)
Powerplant: two General Electric T64-GE-7 rated at 2927 kW (3,925 shp)
Weights: empty 10690 kg (23,569 lb); mission take-off 17344 kg (38,238 lb); maximum take-off 19050 kg (42,000 lb)
Fuel and load: internal fuel 2384 liters (630 US gal); external fuel up to two 1703 liter (450 US gal) auxiliary jettisonable tanks
Speed: maximum level speed 'clean' at sea level 315 km/h (196 mph); cruising speed 278 km/h (173 mph)
Range: maximum range 868 km (540 miles) with maximum auxiliary fuel
Performance: maximum rate of climb at sea level 631 m (2,070 ft) per minute; service ceiling 6220 m (20,400 ft); hovering ceiling 3565 m (11,700 ft) in ground effect, 1980 m (6,500 out of ground effect)

USAF OPERATORS

Air Force Special Operations Command (AFSOC)

1st SOW	20th SOS	Hurlburt Field, FL	MH-53J
39th SOW	21st SOS	RAF Woodbridge, UK	MH-53J
353rd SOW	31st SOS	Kadena AB, Okinawa	MH-53J

Air Force Materiel Command (AFMC)

6510th TW	6514th TS	Hill AFB, UT	NCH-53A

Air Mobility Command (AMC)

542nd CTW	1551st ATS	Kirtland AFB, NM	TH-53A, MH-53J

Sikorsky
H-60 Pave Hawk

The **H-60 Pave Hawk** is a versatile helicopter employed by the USAF as the **HH-60G** rescue platform and **MH-60G** special operations aircraft. Ten of the USAF's 92 H-60Gs are assigned to special operations forces, the remainder to combat rescue units of the active-duty, Reserve, and Air National Guard forces.

The H-60 is a conventional, medium-range helicopter with elastomeric (no lubrication) bearings carrying an advanced four-bladed titanium/glassfiber honeycomb rotor. The aircraft has a horizontal stabilizer, tail rotor, and electronic FBW (fly-by-wire) flight control system. The H-60 routinely has a crew of two pilots and one or more pararescue technicians (PJs) for rescue and special operations duties.

The H-60 series began with first flight of the US Army **YUH-60A** on 17 October 1974. Versions of the helicopter were planned for, or are used by, the US Army (**UH-60A, EH-60A, EH-60B, EH-60C, MH-60K, UH-60L, UH-60M, UH-60V**), US Coast Guard (**HH-60J**), and US Navy (**SH-60B, SH-60F, HH-60H**). Numerous foreign air forces also use versions of the Black Hawk.

SIKORSKY HH-60G

The USAF operated a single **HH-60A** (82-23718) first delivered to Hurlburt Field, Florida, in 1983, followed by 16 UH-60As (81-23643/23647; 88-26006/26016).

The USAF's variants, if early plans had reached fruition, would have included combat rescue full-system all-weather **HH-60D** machines and reduced-capability **HH-60E** models. At one time, 240 of these helicopters, called **Night Hawks**, were planned. Following first flight of its HH-60A on 4 February 1984, the USAF scaled down its interest in the D and E models. The eventual 'buy' of 91 machines have all been upgraded to H-60G standard. The H-60G Pave Hawk program stems from the cancellation of the Night Hawk and the upgrading of the 11 UH-60As originally procured by the USAF to train ground and air crews in Black Hawk operations.

The **HH-60G** is operated on combat rescue duties, lacking the FLIR of the MH-60G special operations aircraft. HH-60Gs have the option of mounting 7.62-mm Miniguns, while MH-60Gs are armed with 0.50-in guns.

Configuration options: the H/MH-60G is configured for rescue and special operations work; the helicopter incorporates an aerial refueling probe, additional internal auxiliary fuel tank of 117 US gal (443 liters), fuel management system, Doppler navigation equipment, an electronic map display, secure HF (high frequency) radio, FLIR (MH-60G only) and up to three .50-in machine guns (MH-60G) or 7.62-mm Minigun (HH-60G)

Air rescue: for an air rescue mission at medium altitude, the HH-60G can carry up to three rescue personnel, associated equipment, and three machine guns and fly (with two 230-US gal (871-liter) external fuel tanks) to a radius of about 400 miles (644 km); with addition of two 450-US gal (1703-liter) fuel tanks, radius becomes about 600 miles (966 km) with maximum endurance of 4 hr 51 min; the HH-60G can be refueled in flight

Special operations: on a day insertion/extraction or combat rescue mission, the MH-60G can be refueled in flight or, when conducting one-third of the mission at altitude below 1,000 ft (305 m), cruises at 167 mph (268 km/h) at 4,000 ft (1220 m) or 161 mph (258 km/h) at 1,000 ft (305 m), carrying special operations personnel, rescue personnel, or equipment weighing up to about 2,200 lb (997 kg) to a maximum radius of about 650 miles (1046 km)

Utility duties/conventional operations: although not normally so employed, the H/MH-60G can carry out various utility and conventional mission functions and can carry 11 combat troops or paratroopers, eight passengers, or four hospital litters and an 8,000-lb (3628-kg) load slung externally, operating to a maximum radius of about 650 miles (1046 km)

H/MH-60G: Air Force version of the Army UH-60A with an air refueling probe fitted along with defensive armor and provision for 0.50-in or 7.62-mm machine guns.
81-23643 to 81-23647; 82-23671; 82-23680; 82-23689; 82-23707; 82-23708; 88-26006 to 88-26016; 89-26112; 90-26229; 90-26236; 90-26238; plus other contracts

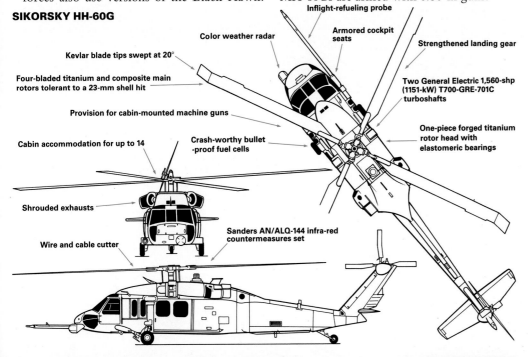

Inflight-refueling probe

Armored cockpit seats

Color weather radar

Strengthened landing gear

Kevlar blade tips swept at 20°

Four-bladed titanium and composite main rotors tolerant to a 23-mm shell hit

Two General Electric 1,560-shp (1151-kW) T700-GRE-701C turboshafts

Provision for cabin-mounted machine guns

One-piece forged titanium rotor head with elastomeric bearings

Cabin accommodation for up to 14

Crash-worthy bullet-proof fuel cells

Shrouded exhausts

Sanders AN/ALQ-144 infra-red countermeasures set

Wire and cable cutter

Above: Close to 100 examples of the H/MH-60G Pave Hawk have been obtained for service in special operations units and for combat SAR taskings.

Left: The inflight-refueling probe and rescue winch are clearly apparent in this view of an unarmed Sikorsky MH-60G Pave Hawk in standard camouflage battledress.

Below: The first variant of the versatile Black Hawk to be operated by the USAF was a solitary HH-60A.

SPECIFICATION

Sikorsky MH-60G
Rotor system: main rotor diameter 53 ft 8 in
(16.36 m); tail rotor diameter 11 ft 0 in (3.35 m). Main
rotor disc area 2.261.0 sq ft (210.05 m²); tail rotor disc
area 95.0 sq ft (8.83 m²)
Fuselage and tail: length overall, rotors turning 64 ft
10 in (19.76 m) and fuselage including retracted flight
refueling probe 57 ft 0.25 in (17.38 m); height overall,
rotors turning 16 ft 10 in (5.13 m) and to top of rotor hub
12 ft 4 in (3.76 m); tailplane span 14 ft 4.5 in (4.38 m);
wheel base 29 ft 0 in (8.84 m)
Powerplant: two General Electric T700-GE-700, each
rated at 1,560 shp (1163 kW)
Weight: maximum take-off 22,000 lb (9979 kg)
Fuel and load: internal fuel 360 US gal (1361 liters);
auxiliary internal fuel 117 US gal (443 liters); external fuel
two 450- or 230-US gal (1703- or 871-liter) drop-tanks;
maximum payload 8,000 lb (3629 kg)
Speed: maximum level speed 'clean' at sea level about
184 mph (296 km/h)
Range: endurance with maximum fuel 4 hours 51
minutes
Performance: maximum vertical rate of climb at sea
level more than 450 ft (137 m) per minute; service
ceiling 19,000 ft (5790 m)

USAF OPERATORS

Air Force Special Operations Command (AFSOC)

1st SOW	55th SOS	Hurlburt Field, FL	MH-60G

Air Mobility Command (AMC)

542nd CTW	1551st ATS	Kirtland AFB, NM	HH-60G

Air Rescue Service

	41st ARS	Patrick AFB, FL	HH-60G
	66th ARS	Nellis AFB, NV	HH-60G

Air National Guard (ANG)

106th RQG	102nd RGS	Suffolk County Apt, NY	HH-60G
129th RQG	129th RQS	NAS Moffett Field, CA	HH-60G
176th CG	210th RQS	Kulis ANGB, Anchorage, AK	HH-60G

*Door-mounted 0.50-in caliber machine guns are
part of the standard combat SAR configuration
of the MH-60G and were fitted to all helicopters
that participated in Desert Storm. The Pave
Hawk shown getting airborne here certainly has
them and must have been photographed during
the last stages of operations to liberate Kuwait.*

Bell

H-1 Iroquois

The **H-1 Iroquois**, better known as the
'Huey', still serves the USAF and its reserve
components in small numbers. The USAF in
recent years has had a handful of single-
engined **TH-1F**, **UH-1F**, **HH-1H** and
UH-1P, and twin-engined **UH-1N** aircraft.

The Huey is a conventional helicopter with
an all-metal fuselage structure, single main and
tail rotors, and a stabilizing bar above and at
right angles to the semi-rigid main rotor.
Small elevator surfaces are attached to the rear
fuselage. Tubular skid-type landing gear is
employed. The Huey is typically operated
with two pilots and a crew chief, with other
specialized personnel on board as required – for
example, a PJ (pararescue technician) for
rescue work. A typical configuration is for 10
passengers.

The single-engined UH-1F is powered by a
1,290-shp (1,290-shp) General Electric T58-
GE-3 turboshaft engine and has increased-
diameter rotors as compared with earlier
models. The twin-engined UH-1N is powered
by a Pratt & Whitney Canada T400-CP-400
Turbo 'Twin Pac', consisting of two PT6
turboshaft engines coupled to a combining
gearbox with a single output shaft, each flat-
rated to 1,290 shp (962 kW).

The Huey began life as the US Army's

XH-40, first flown 22 October 1956, and redesignated **HU-1A** in 1958. The series again received a new designation, **UH-1**, in 1962. Ver-

sions have served with the US Army (**UH-1A,
UH-1B, UH-1C, UH-1D, HH-1D, UH-1H,
EH-1H, UH-1M, UH-1V**), Navy (**HH-1K,
TH-1L, UH-1L, UH-1N**), and Marine Corps
(**UH-1E, UH-1N, VH-1N**).

The USAF began its Huey purchases with
the UH-1F (once briefly designated **XH-48A**)
first flown on 20 February 1964 and delivered
operationally on 23 September 1964. Some

BELL UH-1H

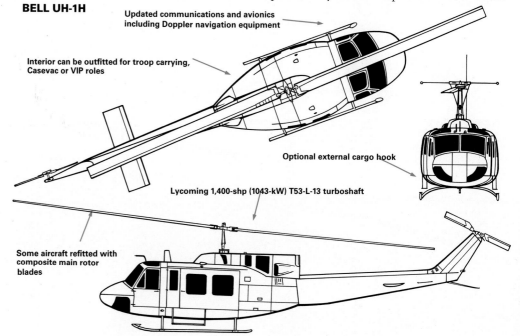

Updated communications and avionics
including Doppler navigation equipment

Interior can be outfitted for troop carrying,
Casevac or VIP roles

Optional external cargo hook

Lycoming 1,400-shp (1043-kW) T53-L-13 turboshaft

Some aircraft refitted with
composite main rotor
blades

UH-1Fs carried 'helevision' equipment to make TV recordings of the installation of missile and radar sites. Deliveries totalled 120 in standard form and 26 similar TH-1Fs configured as instrument trainers. The Huey was initially used to support Minuteman and Titan ICBM (intercontinental ballistic missile) sites.

On 4 November 1970, the USAF contracted for 30 HH-1H rescue ships for local base rescue to replace the aging HH-43 Huskie. Deliveries began in October 1971 and were completed in 1973. These helicopters are distinguished by their roof-mounted hoist capable of lifting a 600-lb (272-kg) load on a 250-ft (76.2-m) cable. The HH-1H was also equipped with all-weather instrumentation mounted in a radome on the aft fuselage belly.

The USAF ordered 70 examples of the UH-1N twin (also used by US Navy and Marine Corps), accepting the first on 2 October 1970. A follow-on order in 1970 added three more UH-1Ns as VIP transports used by the 89th Airlift Wing at Andrews AFB.

Twenty F models were diverted to UH-1P production and equipped with loudspeakers and leaflet-dropping apparatus for the psychological warfare mission.

Most of the UH-1Ns are still in inventory and some are used by the 542nd Crew Training Wing at Kirtland AFB, New Mexico, the RTU (replacement training unit) for the type.

Many of the UH-1Ns in USAF service are employed on staff transport tasks. This aircraft serves with the 58th Airlift Squadron, based at Ramstein for European theater support.

MISSION PROFILE

Configuration options: the H-1 Huey is employed for general-purpose duties by the USAF; aircraft are no longer configured for missions previously assigned, including ICBM (intercontinental ballistic missile) logistical support, rescue, and special operations

Utility/transport/training mission: the UH-1N cruises at 111 mph (178 km/h) to a maximum range of 374 miles (602 km/h) with an external load of 4,000 lb (1814 kg)

USAF VARIANTS AND SERIALS

Original construction designations
TH-1F: Twenty-six instrument/rescue training versions of the UH-1F were ordered in 1966.
66-1225 to 66-1250

UH-1F: Air Force version of the US Army UH-1B with 120 ordered between 1963 and 1966.
63-13141 to 63-13165; 64-15476 to 64-15501; 65-7911 to 65-7965; 66-1211 to 66-1224

HH-1H: Thirty HH-1H versions of the Army UH-1H were purchased in 1970 for base rescue and missile silo support.
70-2457 to 70-2486

UH-1N: Seventy-nine rescue models similar to the Army UH-1H but with a smaller engine. These were also employed to support the far-flung missile silos.
68-10772 to 68-10776; 69-6600 to 69-6670; 69-7536 to 69-7538

Conversion designations
GUH-1F: One GUH-1F remains assigned to Air Training Command for ground training.
65-7922

UH-1P: At least 14 UH-1Fs were converted to UH-1P standard for psychological warfare duties.
63-13146; 63-13149; 63-13156; 63-13160; 63-13161; 63-13162; 63-13165; 64-15476; 64-15486; 64-15493; 65-7925; 65-7926; 65-7929; 65-7948

SPECIFICATION

Bell UH-1F
Rotor system: main rotor diameter 44 ft 0 in (13.41 m); tail rotor diameter 8 ft 6 in (2.59 m); main rotor disc area 1,520.53 sq ft (141.26 m²); tail rotor disc area 56.8 sq ft (5.27 m²)
Fuselage and tail: length 41 ft 5 in (12.80 m); height 14 ft 4.5 in (4.39 m)

Powerplant: one General Electric T58-GE-3 rated at 1,290 shp (962 kW)
Weights: empty equipped 4,427 lb (2008 kg); maximum take-off 9,000 lb (4082 kg)
Fuel and load: internal fuel 410 US gal (1552 liters); maximum payload 4,000 lb (1814 kg)
Speed: maximum level speed at sea level 138 mph (222 km/h); cruising speed at sea level 130 mph (209 km/h)
Range: 380 miles (612 km)
Performance: maximum rate of climb at sea level 2,123 ft (647 m) per minute; service ceiling 6705 m (22,000 ft)

Bell HH-1H
generally similar to the UH-1F except in the following particulars:
Fuselage and tail: length overall, fuselage 41 ft 10.75 in (12.77 m); height 14 ft 6 in (4.42 m)
Powerplant: one Avco Lycoming T53-L-13 rated at 1,400 shp (1044 kW)
Weight: maximum take-off 9,500 lb (4309 kg)
Fuel and load: internal fuel 222 US gal (832 liters) increasable to 520 US gal (832 liters) with two overload tanks; maximum payload 3,880 lb (1759 kg)
Speed: cruising speed at sea level 138 mph (222 km/h)
Range: 327 miles (526 km)
Performance: maximum rate of climb at sea level 1,760 ft (535 m) per minute; service ceiling about 19,400 ft (5910 m)

Bell UH-1N
Rotor system: main rotor diameter 48 ft 2.25 in (14.69 m) with tracking tips; tail rotor diameter 8 ft 6 in (2.59 m); main rotor disc area 1,871.91 sq ft (173.90 m²) and tail rotor disc area 56.74 sq ft (5.27 m²)
Fuselage and tail: length overall, rotors turning 57 ft 3.25 in (17.46 m) and fuselage 42 ft 4.75 in (12.92 m); height overall 14 ft 10.25 in (4.53 m) and to top of rotor head 12 ft 10 in (3.91 m); tailplane span 9 ft 4.5 in (2.86 m)
Powerplant: one Pratt & Whitney Canada T400-CP-400 rated at 1,800 shp (1342 kW) but flat-rated to 1,290 shp (962 kW) for take-off and 1,130 shp (842 kW) for continuous running
Weights: empty 6,143 lb (2787 kg); maximum take-off 11,200 lb (5080 kg)
Fuel and load: internal fuel 215 US gal (814 liters); maximum payload 4,000 lb (1814 kg)
Speed: never exceed at sea level 161 mph (259 km/h); maximum cruising speed at sea level 142 mph (230 km/h)
Range: maximum standard at sea level 261 miles (420 km)
Performance: maximum rate of climb at sea level 1,320 ft (402 m) per minute; service ceiling 14,200 ft (4330 m); hovering ceiling 11,000 ft (3355 m) in ground effect.

Assigned to the 475th Air Base Wing at Yokota, Japan, this UH-1N wears an attractive VIP-type color scheme and is used as a staff transport by high-ranking officers of the Pacific Air Forces.

Below: White and red conspicuity colours are a feature of this UH-1N, which serves with the Air Force Flight Test Center at Edwards AFB. Rescue and range support are the primary tasks.

Cessna

T-37 Tweety Bird

The **T-37 Tweety Bird** is the USAF's primary jet trainer. The **T-37B**, employed since the late 1950s, has been the first airplane flown by tens of thousands of Air Force officers and pilots.

In addition to the mission of basic training carried out by some 550 T-37Bs of ATC (Air Training Command), a further 60-80 T-37Bs have been employed in low-cost pilot proficiency programs with the Tactical and Strategic Air Commands.

The T-37 dates to the mid-1950s when the USAF decided to conduct all pilot training from the *ab initio* phase onward in jet-powered aircraft. The aircraft is a conventional, all-metal, twin-jet monoplane with student pilot (at left) and instructor (at right) seated in side-by-side ejection seats beneath a single broad clamshell canopy. The aircraft is configured with two small engines in the wing roots with nozzles at the trailing edge. Tricycle landing gear is low and wide-tracked to ease landing and airfield performance. The horizontal tail of the aircraft is mounted above the fuselage about one-third of the way up the fin to assure that the airstream flowing past it is undisturbed by jet exhaust. The T-37 has manual controls with electric trim, hydraulic slotted flaps, and hydraulic landing gear.

The **XT-37** prototype (54-0716) made its first flight on 12 October 1954, followed by the first production **T-37A** (54-2729) on 27 Sep-

tember 1955. Five hundred and thirty-four T-37As were produced but were slow to take up the primary training mission, requiring considerable development work and at first being employed only to train students who had previously begun flying in the Beech T-34A.

In November 1959, the USAF introduced the T-37B with improved navigation and communications gear, and the more powerful 1,025-lb (4.56-kN) thrust Continental J69-T-25 turbojet engines. A **T-37C** version with wing hardpoints for ordnance and provision for armament has been exported but was not adopted by the USAF.

Two attempts were made in the 1950s to adopt the T-37 for an air-to-ground combat mission. The first came in 1958 when the US Army evaluated three T-37s at Ford Ord, California, one of several experiments which failed to overcome the statutory bar to the Army operating fixed-wing combat aircraft. The

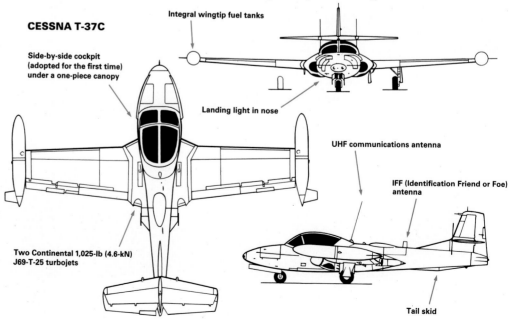

CESSNA T-37C

Integral wingtip fuel tanks

Side-by-side cockpit (adopted for the first time) under a one-piece canopy

Landing light in nose

Two Continental 1,025-lb (4.6-kN) J69-T-25 turbojets

UHF communications antenna

IFF (Identification Friend or Foe) antenna

Tail skid

Above: Introduced to service as long ago as the late 1950s, the Cessna T-37B continues in the basic training role at the present time and is unlikely to disappear from the inventory until early in the next century.

second attempt came with the USAF's **YAT-37D**, an armed version evaluated in the late 1950s.

Not until April 1961 did the USAF achieve its goal of all-jet pilot training, with students beginning in the Tweety Bird from the outset. The T-37B has been the USAF's primary trainer ever since.

During the Vietnam War, efforts to find a combat role for the basic T-37 resumed. The USAF on 2 May 1967 began to fly the **A-37A Dragonfly**, a converted T-37B, for close air support and special operations missions. Thirty-nine A-37As were built by converting T-37Bs on the production line. Some were assigned to the South Vietnamese Air Force.

The **A-37B** which followed was virtually a new aircraft, weighing nearly twice as much as a T-37 trainer and being powered by two 2,850-lb (12.68-kN) thrust General Electric J85-GE-17A turbojets. A total of 577 A-37Bs, some of which later became **OA-37B** forward air control (FAC) aircraft, served with USAF

and Air National Guard units well into the early 1990s. Numerous foreign air forces have operated T-37B, T-37C, and A-37B aircraft.

In 1986, the USAF abandoned long-standing plans to replace its T-37B Tweety Bird trainers with a new aircraft developed for the purpose, the Fairchild T-46. The latter aircraft was dropped not for any technical fault but because of program management problems. For a period thereafter, the USAF considered a proposal by Cessna's new owner, General Dynamics, for a new version of the T-37 with swept tail surfaces, designated **T-48**. No prototype T-48 was built. The USAF turned to service-life improvement as an alternative to new procurement.

In recent years, the USAF has conducted an EFS (enhanced flight screening) program under which certain intended future pilots are given their first flight experience in the propeller-driven Cessna T-41A. This is the only circumstance under which a few pilots begin their training curriculum in an aircraft other than the T-37B. The EFS program is intended to 'weed out' certain categories of personnel not likely to succeed as pilots and is not, in itself, considered to be training.

Looking towards prolonging the life of its

T-37B fleet, in August 1989 the USAF awarded a contract to Sabreliner Corp. for a T-37B SLEP (Service Life Extension Program). This effort has Sabreliner researching, designing and supplying kits which it submits to flight, static and structural tests before turning them over to the USAF for installation, replacing critical structural components of the service's fleet of T-37Bs (which numbered 632 in 1989). First flight of a 'SLEP Kit T-37B' took place in July 1991.

In the late 1980s, the USAF began planning again for a T-37B replacement, now dubbed PATS (Primary Aircraft Trainer System). In 1990, the US Navy joined the program which became JPATS, the first initial asserting the program's 'joint' service nature. At least nine aircraft types are in serious contention for a $3-billion contract to produce 888 trainers to replace the USAF T-37B beginning in 1997, and the US Navy Beech T-34C Turbo Mentor beginning in 2005. The services have specified that the JPATS aircraft, unlike the T-37B, must have tandem seating, but no decision had been reached in late 1991 as to whether the new trainer would be a jet or turboprop aircraft.

MISSION PROFILE

Configuration options: the T-37B is configured to carry two people to maximum weight of 250 lb (113 kg) each and has no stowage space; on cross-country flights, small items of baggage are stored behind the ejection seats

Training mission: for pilot training, typical *en route* (cruising) speed and airfield pattern speed is 200 kt; basic flight maneuver skills (stall recognition, spin recovery) are performed below 80 kt; aerobatics are performed between 200 and 270 kt; instrument work is performed at 100 to 200 kt; formation flying training is conducted at around 150 kt; typical training sorties are carried out in a 'box' 10 by 15 miles (16 by 24 km) in a 'block' of altitude from 8,000 to 10,000 ft (2438 to 3048 m) for low-altitude work, 18,000 to 25,000 ft (5486 to 7620 m) for high-altitude work; the syllabus-directed mission time for virtually all training flights is 1.3 hours in the T-37B; primary training of a student pilot takes 80 to 85 hours of flight time

Left: Although most Air Training Command T-37Bs are assigned to the basic pilot training role, a modest number undertake navigation tuition at Mather AFB, California, with the 323rd FTW. In order to extend the useful life of the 'Tweet', update work is presently in progress.

T-37 Tweety Bird (continued)

USAF VARIANTS AND SERIALS

XT-37: The three prototype aircraft were designated XT-37 to indicate the experimental nature of their evaluation for the basic training role.
54-0716 to 54-0718

T-37A: Five hundred and thirty-four production T-37As were ordered between 1954 and 1959, with the majority being upgraded to T-37B standard subsequently. Thirty-nine early production T-37As were converted to A-37A standard as proof of concept.
54-2729 to 54-2739; 55-2972; 55-4302 to 55-4321; 56-3464 to 56-3590; 57-2230 to 57-2352; 58-1861 to 58-1977; 59-0256 to 59-0390

T-37B: The T-37B was a development of the T-37A with more powerful engines and improved radio and navigation equipment. Four hundred and forty-nine were obtained between 1959 and 1968.
59-0241 to 59-0255; 60-0071 to 60-0200; 61-2494 to 61-2508; 61-2915 to 61-2919; 62-5952 to 62-5956; 64-13409 to 64-13470; 65-10823 to 65-10826; 66-7960 to 66-8006; 67-14730 to 67-14768; 67-22240 to 67-22262; 68-7981 to 68-8084

(**Note:** some aircraft were exported to Chile, Colombia, Greece, Jordan, Pakistan, Peru, South Vietnam, Thailand and Turkey.)

GT-37A: Four early production T-37As have been reassigned to the ground instruction role.
54-2733; 54-2734; 54-2736; 54-2738

SPECIFICATION

Cessna T-37B
Wing: span 33 ft 9.3 in (10.30 m); aspect ratio 6.2; area 183.9 sq ft (17.09 m²)
Fuselage and tail: length 29 ft 3 in (8.92 m); height 9 ft 2.3 in (2.80 m); tailplane span 13 ft 11.25 in (4.25 m); wheel base 7 ft 9 in (2.36 m)
Powerplant: two Continental J69-T-25 each rated at 1,025 lb (4.56 kN) dry thrust
Weights: empty 3,870 lb (1755 kg); maximum take-off 6,600 lb (2993 kg)
Fuel and load: internal fuel 309 US gal (1170 liters)
Speed: maximum level at 25,000 ft (7620 m) 426 mph (685 km/h); normal cruising speed at 25,000 ft (7620 m) 380 mph (612 km/h)
Range: maximum range at 25,000 ft (7620 m) 663 miles (1067 km); range at normal rated power at 25,00 ft (7620 m) 604 miles (972 km)
Performance: maximum rate of climb at sea level 3,020 ft (920 m) per minute; service ceiling 35,100 ft (10700 m); take-off distance 2,050 ft (625 m) to 50 ft (15 m); landing distance 2,700 ft (823 m) from 50 ft (15 m)

USAF OPERATORS

Air Training Command (ATC)

12th FTW	559th FTS	'RA'	Randolph AFB, TX	T-37B
14th FTW	37th FTS		Columbus AFB, MS	T-37B
47th FTW	85th FTS	'XL'	Laughlin AFB, TX	T-37B
64th FTW	35th FTS		Reese AFB, TX	T-37B
71st FTW	8th FTS		Vance AFB, OK	T-37B
80th FTW	88th FTS		Sheppard AFB, TX	T-37B
	89th FTS		Sheppard AFB, TX	T-37B
82nd FTW	96th FTS		Williams AFB, AZ	T-37B
323rd FTW	454th FTS		Mather AFB, CA	T-37B
3700th TTW			Sheppard AFB, TX	GT-37A

Northrop

T-38 Talon

The **T-38 Talon** is the USAF's standard advanced jet trainer. Seven-hundred Talons remain in service, most with ATC (Air Training Command) for high-performance pilot training. In the 1990s, the USAF plans to shift from a UPT (universal pilot training) scheme, in which all aviators progress through the T-38 before moving to their service aircraft, to SUPT (specialized undergraduate pilot training) in which T-38 training is provided only to those who will fly fighter, bomber or reconnaissance aircraft. This move will prolong the life of the aging T-38 fleet and keep the aircraft in service well into the next century.

The T-38 is a conventional twin-engined jet trainer, a cantilever low-wing monoplane with extremely small, sharp-edged wings, light-weight airframe, and a slender, area-ruled fuselage. The Talon is unique in being a trainer intended for routine flight at supersonic speed. The instructor is seated behind and 10 in (0.25 m) higher than the student pilot, both having rocket-assisted ejection seats. To assist the pilot, yaw and pitch flight-control channels incorporate stability augmenters, the aircraft having been consciously intended as one that

students could handle. The tandem cockpit is pressurized and air-conditioned.

A fully-powered rudder is fitted and the low-set tailplane is a one-piece, all-moving unit. The straight wing, with modest sweep on its forward leading edges, has no trim tabs, the ailerons being powered. The **T-38A** does not require a braking parachute, although it has two air brakes on the underside of the fuselage forward of the mainwheel wells. The T-38A has conventional tricycle landing gear with wide track and a steerable nosewheel, and is powered by two 3,850-lb (17.13-kN) thrust General Electric J85-GE-5A turbojets.

The student moves to the T-38A for advanced flying after first being trained in the Cessna T-37B. All USAF pilots followed this route from the early 1960s to the early 1990s. After the T-1A Jayhawk TTTS aircraft entered service, only those pilots on the RAFT (reconnaissance, attack, fighter) career track will progress from T-37B to T-38A, while those destined for transports and tankers will proceed from T-37B to T-1A.

In addition to the mission of advanced training carried out by some 700 T-38As of ATC (Air Training Command), a further 60-80 T-38As have been employed in low-cost pilot proficiency programs with the Tactical and Strategic Air Commands. The T-38A was viewed by the Strategic Air Command as an economical alternative to training co-pilots to

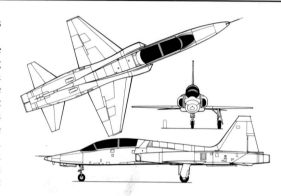

Above: The clean and elegant lines of the T-38A Talon are evident in this three-view drawing.

command standard and thus as a means of reducing wear on its aging B-52 bomber fleet. T-38As have been used by most SAC bomber wings and by the 9th Strategic Reconnaissance Wing (now 9th Wing), headquartered at Beale AFB, California. This ACE (Accelerated Co-pilot Enrichment) program usually involves some dozen or more T-38As.

Developed concurrently with the builder's F-5 fighter series, the first **YT-38** (58-1191) flew on 10 April 1959. Following tests with three YT-38s, the USAF placed the first in a series of T-38A production orders in late 1959. Production T-38As became operational on 17 March 1961, the first Talon unit being ATC's 3510th Flying Training Wing at Randolph AFB, Texas.

On 24 August 1961, Jacqueline Cochran became the first female to fly faster than sound in the course of establishing eight performance records in an early T-38A. In September and October 1961, Major Walter F. Daniel established four time-to-climb records in a T-38A (61-0849). Over 1978-84, the T-38A was flown by the USAF's Thunderbirds flight demonstration team.

In 1966, some 46 T-38As were acquired by the German government, to operate with US

Left: Although it is a two-seater, T-38As are regularly flown solo by pilot students as they move through the advanced phase of the training syllabus. This particular example of the Talon is a standard T-38A from Air Training Command's 82nd FTW at Williams AFB.

Above: A limited number of T-38A Talons are on the strength of the 49th (previously 37th) Fighter Wing, perhaps better known as being the unit with the F-117A Night Hawk 'Stealth Fighter'. Two attractively camouflaged 37th FW machines are seen here.

Above: In addition to more potent hardware, the USAF Test Pilots School also includes a handful of T-38A Talons in its fleet. Virtually all students will be familiar with Northrop's nippy trainer from their days with ATC.

markings to train German pilots in the American southwest. **T-38A(N)** variants are employed as astronaut 'hacks' by NASA. The T-38A(N) differs in having heated intake lips, VHF radio, and other minor changes. A small number of T-38As, **QT-38A** drones, and **DT-38A** drone controllers served with the US Navy.

An early T-38A (60-0576) was fitted with hardpoints for ordnance to test the concept of a 'lead-in fighter trainer' (LIFT) to provide a transition between pilot training and high-performance warplanes such as the F-15 Eagle. The program is also for experienced pilots making the transition from non-fighter to fighter aircraft.

Up to 132 airplanes were rebuilt as **T-38B LIFT** aircraft, often referred to by the designa-

Below: A four-ship formation of T-38As from the 12th Flying Training Wing at Randolph AFB passes low over the Texas countryside near their home base in a scene that is enacted almost daily at ATC facilities.

tion **AT-38B** (which does not have official status). In T-38B configuration, an ejector rack was attached to the centerline pylon beneath the second cockpit, stressed to accommodate the SUU-20/A rocket/practice bomb carrier, a practice bomb rack, or an SUU-11 0.3-in (7.62-mm) Minigun pod. LIFT training was conducted in both T-38As and T-38Bs by the 479th Tactical Training Wing at Holloman AFB, New Mexico, until 1991, when the wing was reduced to group status. The USAF has considered abandoning this program as a cost-saving measure but is expected, instead, to continue a LIFT program of greatly reduced size in the mid-1990s.

For three decades, every USAF pilot, even those assigned to relatively unglamorous types such as the C-130 Hercules or KC-135 Stratotanker, could boast of having flown at least one advanced, high-performance aircraft, the T-38A. As a result of UPT, every USAF pilot from 1961 to 1991 flew the T-38A. This system has been in dramatic contrast to the US Navy, which funnels its aviator trainees through 'pipelines' and uses fast jet fighters only for those destined for the tactical world.

The USAF now plans to change its system, with the primary purpose of prolonging the

service life of its T-38A fleet. Under SUPT, many student pilots who previously flew the T-38A will fly the T-1A Jayhawk. The T-38A is expected to need replacement between 2010 and 2015.

MISSION PROFILE

Configuration options: the T-38 trainer (T-38A) is configured to carry two people to maximum weight of 250 lb (113 kg) each plus up to 600 lb (272 kg) in a centerline external travel pod; the basic fighter training (BFT) aircraft (AT-38B) has an ejection rack in the centerline pylon stressed to take the SUU-20/A rocket/ practice bomb carrier, a practice bomb rack, or a Minigun pod

Training mission: for advanced pilot training (T-38A), typical en route (cruising) speed and airfield pattern speed is 300 kt; flying skills are taught through the full range of the aircraft's performance although only on an orientation basis beyond Mach 1.0

Basic fighter training (BFT): for basic fighter training (AT-38B), a typical mission of 1.5 hours is carried out at speeds averaging Mach 0.92 at altitudes from 20,000 to 35,000 ft (6096 to 10668 m) to rehearse fighter procedures, formations, and maneuvers; gunnery and rocket work is no longer part of the syllabus; BFT consists of 11 sorties per student

Northrop T-38A Talon

Still the world's only supersonic trainer, the T-38 has given Air Training Command many years' good service, and is set to do so until replaced by a new Bomber Fighter Training System aircraft in the next century. A shortfall in T-38 availability for advanced training has been redressed by diverting tanker/transport students to the T-1 Jayhawk now entering service, leaving the Talon solely for the bomber/fighter students.

Undercarriage
The T-38's landing gear is necessarily strong to handle the many landing cycles undertaken by training aircraft. In the event of systems failure, the landing gear extends and locks under gravity.

Powerplant
The two General Electric J85-GE-6 engines, each producing 3,850 lb (17.13 kN) thrust, provide advanced students with experience of both afterburning and twin-engine operation. One engine is sufficient to power the T-38 safely round a circuit.

Formation lights
Low intensity station-keeping light strips are incorporated in nose, wingtips and tail for students to practice night formation flight.

Markings
For many years the T-38s served in an all-white scheme, and indeed many still do. However, the fleet is slowly adopting this smart blue/white scheme for greater conspicuity in a variety of weather conditions.

USAF VARIANTS AND SERIALS

Original construction designations
YT-38: Three prototype Talons were allocated the designation YT-38 for service tests.
58-1191 to 58-1193

T-38A: More than 1,140 T-38As were purchased between 1958 and 1970 as the two-seat advanced jet trainer.
58-1194 to 58-1197; 59-1594 to 59-1606; 60-0547 to 60-0596; 61-0804 to 61-0947; 62-3609 to 62-3752; 63-8111 to 63-8247; 64-13166 to 64-13305; 65-10316 to 65-10475; 66-4320 to 66-4389; 66-8349 to 66-8404; 67-14825 to 67-14859; 67-14915 to 67-14958; 68-8095 to 68-8217; 69-7073 to 69-7088; 70-1549 to 70-1591; 70-1949 to 70-1956

Conversion designations
AT-38B: TAC acquired more than 100 aircraft fitted with a gunsight and practice bomb dispensers fitted to underwing hardpoints for the Lead-In Fighter Training (LIFT) role with designation T-38B being employed, although AT-38B is commonly used. More than 100 T-38As were modified, although most have been withdrawn.

GT-38A/GAT-38B: At least 15 T-38As and AT-38Bs have been assigned to ground instruction use.
60-0583; 60-0590; 60-0592; 60-0593; 61-0814; 61-0824; 61-0859; 61-0895; 61-0926; 61-0941 (GT) 61-0817; 61-0828; 61-0898; 61-0923; 61-0321 (GAT)

SPECIFICATION

Northrop T-38A
Wing: span 25 ft 3 in (7.70 m); area 170.0 sq ft (15.79 m²)
Fuselage and tail: length 46 ft 4.5 in (14.14 m); height 12 ft 10.5 in (3.92 m); tailplane span 14 ft 1.5 in (4.31 m); wheel base 16 ft 11.5 in (5.17 m)
Powerplant: two General Electric J85-GE-5 each rated at 2,680 lb (11.29 kN) dry and 3,850 lb (17.13 kN) afterburning thrusts
Weights: empty 7,174 lb (3254 kg); maximum take-off 12,050 lb (5465 kg)
Fuel and load: internal fuel 583 US gal (2206 liters)
Speed: maximum level speed at 36,000 ft (10975 m) 858 mph (1381 km/h); maximum cruising speed at 40,000 ft (12190 m) 578 mph (930 km/h)
Range: ferry range 1,093 miles (1759 km); typical range 860 miles (1384 km)
Performance: maximum rate of climb at sea level 33,600 ft (10241 m) per minute; service ceiling 53,600 ft (16335 m); take-off distance 2,500 ft (762 m) at maximum take-off weight; landing distance 3,000 ft (914 m) at maximum weight

USAF OPERATORS

Air Force Materiel Command (AFMC)

3246th TW	3247th TS	'ET'	Eglin AFB, FL	T-38A
6510th TW	6512th TS	'ED'	Edwards AFB, CA	T-38A

Air Training Command (ATC)

12th FTW	560th FTS	'RA'	Randolph AFB, TX	T-38A
14th FTW	50th FTS	'CM'	Columbus AFB, MS	T-38A
47th FTW	86th FTS	'XL'	Laughlin AFB, TX	T-38A
64th FTW	54th FTS	-	Reese AFB, TX	T-38A
71st FTW	25th FTS	'VN'	Vance AFB, OK	T-38A
80th FTW	90th FTS	'WF'	Sheppard AFB, TX	T-38A
82nd FTW	97th FTS	'WL'	Williams AFB, AZ	T-38A
3700th TTW			Sheppard AFB, TX	GT-38A, GAT-38B

Air Combat Command (ACC)

9th Wing	5th SRTS		Beale AFB, CA	T-38A
49th FW	433rd FS	'HO'	Holloman AFB, NM	AT-38B

Cessna
T-41 Mescalero

The **T-41** is a standard Cessna 172 light aircraft acquired 'off the shelf' by the USAF. It is a conventional, high-wing, propeller-driven aircraft with tricycle landing gear. Military T-41s are configured for side-by-side training with two persons on board and do not carry the second pair of rear seats found in the civilian counterpart.

The **T-41A** model (237 built; 98 in inventory) is used in generalized preliminary flight screening of pilot candidates. Although the similar **T-41B Mescalero** (255 built) is a US Army aircraft, two T-41Bs have been in USAF inventory in recent years. The more powerful **T-41C** (52 built; 50 in use) with fixed-pitch propellers, based on the Cessna R172E, is operated by the 557th Flying Training Squadron to provide cadet flight training at the USAF Academy in Colorado Springs. The **T-41D** designation applies to export versions (226 built) for other countries paid for with USAF funding under the Military Assistance Program (MAP).

The T-41A is powered by a 145-hp (108-kW) Continental O-300-C piston engine, while the T-41C has a 210-hp Continental O-360-E2D.

In 1955, Cessna developed its civilian Model 172 by modifying its successful Model 170B 'taildragger' with minor improvements and tricycle landing gear. Aircraft in the T-41 series

have the swept vertical tail introduced in 1960 with the Model 172A.

The T-41 owes its origins to USAF concern in the mid-1970s over the high cost of student failures in its all-jet training program, which uses the Cessna T-37 as a learning pilot's first aircraft. In search of a more cost-effective way of eliminating students unsuitable for pilot training, in July 1964 the USAF decided to introduce a light, piston-engined aircraft not so much to train pilots as to weed out those unsuitable for pilot duties in what has since become known as EFS (enhanced flight screening).

The Cessna 172 was selected and an order placed on 31 July 1964. The first T-41A flew in August 1964. The majority of T-41s are operated by civil flight schools under contract to the USAF, and the aircraft display both civil registration and military serial numbers, which are identical. In 1966, some T-41As were supplied to Peru through MAP. T-41A airplanes include 170 Cessna Model 172Fs, 26 Model 172Gs, 34 Model 172Hs, and seven Model 172Ks. The T-41A and subsequent models lack the cosmetic wheel 'pants' found on civilian airplanes.

The T-41B (US Army) and T-41C (USAF Academy) differ from the T-41A in having a more powerful engine and improved propeller

(as noted), openable right front cabin window, jettisonable doors, enlarged nose-wheel tire, no baggage door, fuselage/lift strut assist steps/cowl handle for fueling, and improved radios. The T-41C airframe and cowling were the same as the Army B Model, but with 14-volt electrical system (instead of 28) and standard R172E features. The aircraft finish is Alclad aluminum with flat black anti-glare panels. Again, both USAF serial and civil registration numbers were applied. Like the T-41A, the T-41C had only two front seats installed.

The USAF plans to replace its aging T-41A/C fleet in the 1990s with a new EFS (enhanced flight screener) aircraft to be chosen from off-the-shelf designs.

MISSION PROFILE

Configuration options: the T-41 is configured for pilot and student in side-by-side seating (rear seats are not installed) and to carry two people plus baggage/light cargo up to a combined total of about 980 lb (445 kg)

Flight screening/primary training: the T-41 cruises at 139 mph (224 km/h); a typical training/screening mission is carried out in a 'box' 10 by 15 miles (16 by 24 km) in a 'block' of altitude up to 10,000 ft (3048 m)

USAF VARIANTS AND SERIALS

T-41A: Air Force version of the Cessna 172F obtained between 1965 and 1969 for undergraduate pilot training with joint civilian/military identities.
65-5100 to 65-5269 (as N5100F to N5269F);
67-14959 to 67-14992 (as N4959R to N4992R);
69-7743 to 69-7749 (as N7743L to N7749L)

T-41C: The T-41C was similar to the US Army T-41B but with a fixed-pitch propeller.
68-7866 to 68-7910 (as N7866N to N7910N);
69-7750 to 69-7756 (as N7750L to N7756L)

Cessna 150: A single Cessna 150 was assigned to the 557th FTS, probably having been acquired from a civilian source.
84-0482

SPECIFICATION

Cessna T-41A
Wing: span 35 ft 7.5 in (10.86 m); area 174.0 sq ft (16.16 m²)
Fuselage and tail: length 26 ft 11 in (8.20 m); height 8 ft 9.5 in (2.68 m); tailplane span 11 ft 4 in (3.45 m); wheel base 5 ft 4 in (1.63 m)
Powerplant: one Continental O-300-C rated at 145 hp (108 kW)
Weights: operating empty 1,255 lb (565 kg); maximum take-off 2,300 lb (1043 kg)
Fuel and load: internal fuel 42 US gal (159 liters)
Speed: maximum level speed at sea level 139 mph (224 km/h); maximum cruising speed at 9,000 ft (2745 m) 131 mph (211 km/h)
Range: at economical cruising speed 640 miles (1030 km); at maximum cruising speed 615 miles (990 km)
Performance: maximum rate of climb at sea level 645 ft (196 m) per minute; service ceiling 13,100 ft (3995 m); take-off distance 865 ft (264 m) at maximum take-off weight; landing distance 520 ft (158 m) at maximum weight

CESSNA T-41C

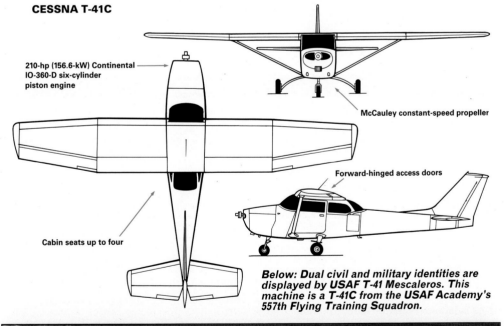

210-hp (156.6-kW) Continental IO-360-D six-cylinder piston engine

McCauley constant-speed propeller

Forward-hinged access doors

Cabin seats up to four

Below: Dual civil and military identities are displayed by USAF T-41 Mescaleros. This machine is a T-41C from the USAF Academy's 557th Flying Training Squadron.

USAF OPERATORS

Air Training Command (ATC)

Officer Training School	Orlando Apt, TX	T-41A
557th FTS	Air Force Academy, Colorado Springs, CO	T-41A/C

Boeing
CT-43

The **CT-43** trainer is derived from the commercial Boeing 737-200 airliner, and is operated by ATC (Air Training Command) to train USAF navigators. Of the 19 aircraft in inventory, 14 carry out this ATC mission, four perform general-purpose duties with the Air National Guard, and one is assigned as a VIP transport. The aircraft are being repainted in an all-white color scheme.

The 737 design is a conventional, low-wing, twin-jet aircraft with strong resemblance to earlier Boeing jet transports. The fuselage provides an internal cabin length of just over 62 ft (18.90 m). In ATC CT-43As, this space is densely packed for the navigator training function. In others, airline-style seating is provided.

Flight crew of the **CT-43A** consists of two pilots, with provision for an additional seat for crew chief or check-ride instructor. For its navigator training mission, the interior of the CT-43A is configured with stations for 12 student navigators, four advanced trainees, and three instructors. Training is carried out at all heights and under all weather conditions.

The CT-43A has a number of internal differences from its airliner counterpart. The fuselage mounts additional avionics aerials and has an 800-US gal (3028-liter) auxiliary fuel tank in the aft compartment. The CT-43A has only a single door and nine windows along each side of the cabin. The floor is strengthened to carry heavy avionics consoles and operating desks. The CT-43A is powered by two 14,500-lb (6577-kg) thrust Pratt & Whitney JT8D-9 turbofan engines.

The CT-43 traces its history to the Vietnam era when the USAF identified deficiencies in its navigator training program. To replace the Convair CT-29 used to train navigators, in May 1971 the USAF announced an order for 19 off-the-shelf Boeing 737-200s with an option (not taken up) for 10 more. The first CT-43A (71-1403) flew on 10 April 1973.

Beginning on 31 July 1973, the aircraft were delivered over one year's time. All initially served with the 323rd Flying Training Wing at Mather AFB, California. In more recent years, four airframes have gone to Detachment 1, Colorado Air National Guard, in Denver. These aircraft, designated **CT-43A** from late 1991, now provide training support to navigator-qualified cadets at the USAF Academy at Colorado Springs.

One aircraft (72-0286) was at one time assigned a civil registration identity (N99890 and, subsequently, N57JE). While listed as owned by Keyway Air Transport, Inc., this CT-43A based at Ramstein AB, Germany, apparently was used by the Central Intelligence Agency for general and VIP transport duties. There may have been other airframes with civil 737 or military CT-43A identities shuffled in and out of CIA duties at Ramstein. This airplane reportedly has reverted to military status with the 58th Air Lift Squadron at Ramstein, configured for VIP transport.

BOEING T-43A

Above: CT-43As were obtained for training, based on the Boeing 737 Series 200.

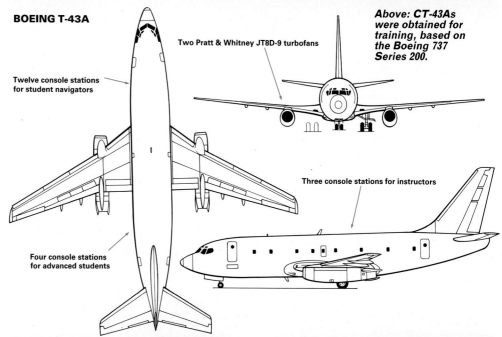

Twelve console stations for student navigators

Two Pratt & Whitney JT8D-9 turbofans

Three console stations for instructors

Four console stations for advanced students

MISSION PROFILE

Configuration options: the CT-43A is configured with strengthened flooring for avionics consoles, provision for overhead sextant viewing ports, and positions for up to 12 navigator trainees, four navigator proficiency students, and three instructors; the CT-43A is operated in conjunction with Honeywell T-45 electronic simulators to form the UNTS (Undergraduate Navigator Training System)

Navigator training: the CT-43A cruises typically at 505 mph (812 km/h) and carries out training missions at medium to high altitudes up to 38,000 ft (11582 m); employed in conjunction with UNTS, the CT-43A simulates a variety of operational missions, including low-level flights over land and water, night flights, airways navigation, and high-altitude operations up to 70,000 ft (21336 m); a training sortie typically lasts four hours

CT-43 aviation/navigation indoctrination program: the CT-43As assigned to the USAF Academy provide one indoctrination flight to each Academy cadet and standard USAF navigator training to a few hand-picked cadets who complete a summer training program

USAF VARIANTS AND SERIALS

CT-43A: Nineteen Boeing 737-253s were purchased between 1971 and 1973 for navigator training, with one located in Europe for VIP duties.
71-1403 to 71-1406; 72-0282 to 72-0288; 73-1149 to 73-1156

SPECIFICATION

Boeing CT-43A
Wing: span 93 ft 0 in (28.35 m); aspect ratio 8.8; area 980.0 sq ft (91.05 m²)
Fuselage and tail: length 100 ft 0 in (30.48 m); height 37 ft 0 in (11.28 m); tailplane span 36 ft 0 in (10.97 m); wheel base 37 ft 4 in (11.38 m)
Powerplant: two Pratt & Whitney JT8D-9 each rated at 14,500 lb (64.5 kN) dry thrust
Weights: operating empty 60,210 lb (27310 kg); maximum take-off 115,500 lb (52390 kg)
Fuel and load: internal fuel 5,151 US gal (19498 liters); maximum payload 34,790 lb (15780 kg)
Speed: never exceed at 20,000 ft (6095 m) 628 mph (1010 km/h); maximum level speed at 23,500 ft (7165 m) 586 mph (943 km/h); maximum cruising speed at 22,600 ft (6890 m) 576 mph (927 km/h)
Range: with maximum fuel 2,995 miles (4820 km); endurance 6 hours
Performance: maximum rate of climb at sea level 3,760 ft (1146 m) per minute; take-off distance 6,700 ft (2040 m) at 109,000 lb (49435 kg) to 35 ft (10.7 m); landing distance 4,300 ft (1310 m) at maximum landing weight from 50 ft (15 m)

USAF OPERATORS

Air Training Command (ATC)

323rd FTW	455th FTS	'NT'	Mather AFB, CA	CT-43A

US Air Forces in Europe (USAFE)

608th AG	58th AS		Ramstein AB, Germany	CT-43A

Air National Guard (ANG)

det 1	120th FS		Buckley ANGB, CO	CT-43A

Beech
T-1 Jayhawk

The **T-1 Jayhawk** is the USAF's TTTS (Tanker/Transport Trainer System) aircraft. Its mission is to provide advanced training to pilots in a SUPT (specialized undergraduate pilot training) program which makes it unnecessary for some pilots to train in the T-38 Talon. Under the SUPT scheme, student pilots destined for multi-engined aircraft types will proceed from the T-37B Tweet (and its replacement) to the T-1.

The **T-1A** is based on the civil Beechjet 400A, a version of the Mitsubishi MU-300 Diamond. The aircraft is conventional in design with low, swept wings and tail surfaces, T-tail, pressurized fuselage, and tricycle landing gear.

As configured for USAF's Air Training Command, the T-1A has cockpit seating for a student who will fly in the left seat, an instructor in the right seat, and a third crew seat for another student immediately behind. Rails are fitted to accommodate four extra seats in the rear cabin to carry passengers or additional students awaiting instruction. Structural enhancements, as compared to the civilian version, will provide for a large number of landings per flight hour, increased bird strike resistance, and an additional fuselage fuel tank. The T-1A also has single-point refueling and fewer cabin windows than its civilian equivalent. The T-1A Jayhawk is powered by two 2,700-lb (12.9-kN) thrust Pratt & Whitney JT15D-5B turbofan engines, mounted astride the rear fuselage.

The aircraft is, of course, part of an integrated system which includes simulators and a training syllabus. The USAF deems this aircraft type to be more cost-effective than any previous trainer in inventory.

Beech was awarded the TTTS contract in February 1990 after other aircraft designs from Cessna, Lear and British Aerospace were considered. Developmental and demonstration flying has been carried out by the company-owned 400T aircraft, which is similar to the production T-1A but does not have precisely the same fuselage configuration or internal configuration. The first production T-1A made its maiden flight at Beech Field, Wichita, Kansas, on 5 July 1991 and was formally delivered to the USAF in January 1992.

The USAF plans to acquire 180 T-1A Jayhawks, of which 77 are on firm order. The first production T-1A was delivered in July 1991. The first unit to receive the T-1A Jayhawk is the 64th Flying Training Wing at Reese AFB, Texas, which began instructor training in March 1992 and student training in September 1992.

Beech is scheduled eventually to produce three T-1A Jayhawks per month. The manufacturer was scheduled to deliver 27 aircraft in 1992, 30 in 1993, and 36 in 1994. Remaining Jayhawks would be built at a rate of 36 per year. Even long after T-1A deliveries began, the status of funding and Air Staff support for the TTTS program remained somewhat in doubt.

Obtained to satisfy the TTTS (Tanker/Transport Trainer System) requirement, plans anticipate a total of 180 Beech T-1A Jayhawks being bought for ATC during the 1990s.

The T-1A designation was used previously by the Lockheed T2V-1 SeaStar, a US Navy aircraft no longer in service. The Jayhawk nickname, selected in March 1990, has regional significance in Kansas (the T-1A is manufactured in Wichita) but is also assigned to the US Coast Guard's Connecticut-built Sikorsky HH-60J helicopter.

MISSION PROFILE

Configuration options: the T-1A has cockpit seating for a student pilot in the left seat, an instructor in the right seat, and a third crew seat for another student immediately behind; four more seats can be fitted in the rear cabin to carry passengers or additional students awaiting instruction

Multi-engined pilot training: the T-1A cruises typically at 447 mph (719 km/h) to a radius of about 800 miles (1287 km) with seven on board and 45-minute fuel reserve; a training syllabus was being developed as this volume went to print

USAF VARIANTS AND SERIALS

T-1A: 90-0400 plus other contracts

SPECIFICATION

Beech T-1A
Wing: span 43 ft 6 in (13.25 m); aspect ratio 7.5; area 241.4 sq ft (22.43 m²)
Fuselage and tail: length 48 ft 5 in (14.75 m); height 13 ft 9 in (4.19 m); tailplane span 16 ft 5 in (5.00 m); wheel base 19 ft 3 in (5.86 m)
Powerplant: two Pratt & Whitney Canada JT15D-5 each rated at 2,900 lb (12.9 kN) dry thrust
Weights: basic operating empty 10,115 lb (4588 kg); maximum take-off 15,780 lb (7157 kg)
Fuel and load: internal fuel 4,904 lb (2224 kg)
Speed: never exceed Mach 0.875; maximum level speed at 29,000 ft (8840 m) 531 mph (854 km/h); typical cruising speed at 39,000 ft (11890 m) 515 mph (828 km/h)
Range: with four passengers 2,222 miles (3575 km)
Performance: maximum operating altitude 41,000 ft (12500 m); take-off distance to 35 ft (10.7 m) 3,950 ft (1204 m) at maximum take-off weight; landing distance from 50 ft (15 m) 2,830 ft (862 m) at maximum weight

USAF OPERATORS

Air Training Command (ATC)

64th FTW	54th FTS	Reese AFB, TX	T-1A

BEECH T-1A

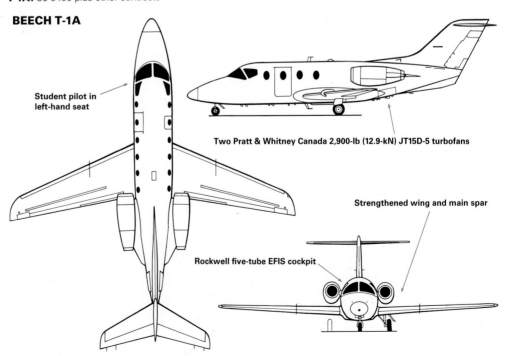

Student pilot in left-hand seat

Two Pratt & Whitney Canada 2,900-lb (12.9-kN) JT15D-5 turbofans

Strengthened wing and main spar

Rockwell five-tube EFIS cockpit

Lockheed
U-2R

Clarence L. 'Kelly' Johnson's famous **U-2** 'Dragon Lady' first flew on 4 August 1955 at the secret Groom Dry Lake facility in Nevada, and on 4 July the following year launched its first overflight of the Soviet Union. Four years later it became the most notorious aircraft of its era when one was shot down over Sverdlovsk and the pilot, Francis Gary Powers, was captured and imprisoned for espionage.

Early U-2 variants were initially powered by specially-prepared Pratt & Whitney J57 turbojets, and subsequently with the same manufacturer's J75. The new engine provided enough power, but the airframe limited the amount of sensors and fuel which could be carried. Long after the Powers shootdown, the U-2 was still regarded as a useful reconnaissance tool, and so Lockheed began a program to update the design.

The result was the **U-2R**, a much larger design sharing only the general layout and powerplant of its predecessor. First flying on 28 August 1967 from Edwards North Base, the U-2R offered a far greater payload capacity and much increased range. The notoriously tricky handling characteristics of the earlier aircraft were considerably improved. The first production batch amounted to 12 aircraft, six for the CIA and the remainder for the USAF. CIA aircraft were largely used for operations over China launched from Taiwan, and when these ended in 1974 the aircraft were handed over to the USAF, which had been flying its aircraft mostly in support of the war effort in Southeast Asia. In 1976, the Air Force rationalized its high-altitude strategic reconnaissance assets by moving the U-2Rs from their base at Davis-Monthan to Beale, where they shared ramp space with the SR-71.

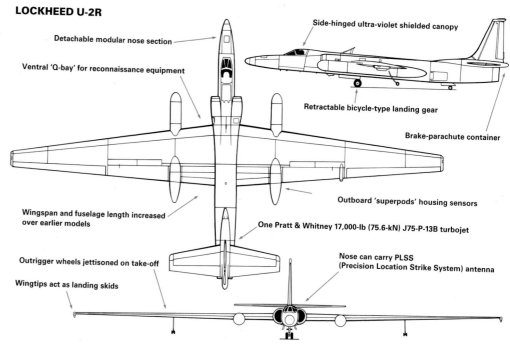

LOCKHEED U-2R

- Detachable modular nose section
- Ventral 'Q-bay' for reconnaissance equipment
- Side-hinged ultra-violet shielded canopy
- Retractable bicycle-type landing gear
- Brake-parachute container
- Wingspan and fuselage length increased over earlier models
- Outboard 'superpods' housing sensors
- One Pratt & Whitney 17,000-lb (75.6-kN) J75-P-13B turbojet
- Outrigger wheels jettisoned on take-off
- Wingtips act as landing skids
- Nose can carry PLSS (Precision Location Strike System) antenna

In November 1979 the production line was re-opened to produce 37 new aircraft. Of these, two were completed as **ER-2** aircraft for NASA's earth resources monitoring/exploitation program, two as two-seat **TR-1B** trainers, one as a similar **U-2RT** trainer and the remainder split between U-2Rs and **TR-1A**s. The latter differed only in minor detail, and was intended for a stand-off tactical reconnaissance mission, although in practice the missions and sensors of the U-2R and TR-1A were interchangeable. TR-1As were assigned mainly to training duties at Beale, and to the operational squadron based in England at RAF Alconbury (95th RS, 17th RW), from where they could patrol the Central European area. These were brought back under Beale's control with the disbandment of the 17th RW, but remain at Alconbury.

For sensor carriage, the U-2R is provided with six areas. Firstly, the nose cone is detachable and can be fitted with various radar systems or tracking cameras. Behind the cockpit is the Q-bay, which is useful for carrying bulky items such as large cameras. Further back on the fuselage is the smaller E-bay for electronic receivers, while the underside of the rear and central fuselage provides mounts for large 'farms' of electronic receiver antennas. Finally, various types of pods can be fitted to each wing for the carriage of radars, Elint equipment and other sensors.

Below: With a sunshade protecting the cockpit, a Lockheed U-2R of the 99th RS awaits a pilot at its home base at Beale, California. Despite being of 1960s vintage, the U-2 is still a very valuable reconnaissance tool.

Above: Caught moments before touchdown at Osan AB, South Korea, this U-2R is typical of those that now fly with the 6th SRS from this base. A total of four operational squadrons uses the U-2 at the present time.

Principal sensors identified for the U-2R are the ASARS-2 radar, Sigint suite, PLSS and optical cameras. The ASARS-2 was developed for the TR-1A and is housed in an extended nosecone. ASARS-2 is a synthetic aperture radar system that peers sideways into enemy territory and provides a picture of force dispositions. Allied to a comprehensive Sigint suite housed in various bays and pods and characterized by underfuselage antennas, the ASARS-2 forms part of the Tactical Reconnaissance System configuration, the most common among mission-configured aircraft.

Another style of extended nose identifies the PLSS-configured aircraft, which also has data-link equipment housed in the wing pods. This is used for the exact location of enemy radars, a ground station pinpointing the position by triangulation based on signals received from three PLSS-equipped aircraft. Cameras are still carried for some purposes, but use of these is restricted in the face of the capabilities of both modern defenses and the electronic sensors.

Information gathered by the onboard sensors is data-linked to a ground station via an antenna mounted under the rear fuselage. Alternatively, at least three aircraft have the dorsal mounting necessary for configuration with the 'Senior Span' satellite shunt. This large dorsal radome can uplink data to a satellite communications system, allowing it to be transmitted around the world. By using this equipment, planners in Washington can parti-

cipate in a U-2R mission in virtual real-time.

In operation, the U-2R retains some of the tricky handling qualities of its predecessors, especially during landing. For this reason a 'mobile' chase car is provided with an experienced U-2 pilot in radio contact with the landing aircraft to aid him through the approach and touchdown. Pilots wear David Clark S-1031 pressure suits to protect them in the case of ejection or depressurization at mission altitudes, which usually top 75,000 ft (22860 m). Mission profiles vary according to requirements, but often involve a duration of 9-10 hours, most of which is spent performing racetrack circuits.

Both U-2Rs and TR-1As were heavily involved in the war with Iraq, flying constant reconnaissance missions before, during and after the conflict to monitor ground movements and communications. Although a costly program, the high-flying 'Dragon Ladies' are still regarded as a crucial reconnaissance asset. An immediate prospect for the fleet is a re-engining program involving the replacement of the increasingly difficult to support J75 with the General Electric F118 (as developed for the Northrop B-2), which offers additional thrust, increased reliability and better fuel burn.

During December 1991 the Air Force decided to abandon the TR-1 designation. Therefore, the TR-1A became the U-2R, while the TR-1B changed to U-2RT. The three NASA ER-2s were unaffected by the change.

Above: One of the U-2Rs used on reconnaissance tasks during Desert Storm is dragged from its hangar at Taif in readiness for another mission along the border with Iraq.

Left: Pilot training for the U-2R is accomplished on a trio of specially-constructed two-seaters which feature a second cockpit in a raised position for use by an instructor.

Below: In common with other U-2s and TR-1s, the once glossy white TR-1B two-seaters adopted a standard matt black finish. Both of these machines have since been redesignated as U-2RTs, joining one aircraft built as such.

USAF VARIANTS AND SERIALS

U-2R: A dozen new-build U-2Rs were ordered in 1968 with seven additional aircraft included in the TR-1 batch.
68-10329 to 68-10340; 80-1066; 80-1070; 80-1071; 80-1076; 80-1095; 80-1096; 80-1098

U-2RT: One U-2RT was constructed as a two-seat trainer with the additional cockpit in a raised position.
80-1091

TR-1A: Twenty-five single-seat TR-1As were built, with one transferred to NASA as an ER-2.
80-1067 to 80-1068; 80-1072 to 80-1075; 80-1077 to 80-1090; 80-1092 to 80-1094; 80-1099 – survivors redesignated U-2R at end of 1991

TR-1B: Two TR-1Bs were ordered as two-seat trainers, also with the second cockpit in a raised position.
80-1064 to 80-1065 – both redesignated U-2RT at end of 1991

ER-2: NASA acquired a pair of TR-1As with the designation ER-2 applied. A third ER-2 was recently added when a 9th SRW (now 9th Wg) TR-1A was transferred.
80-1063; 80-1069; 80-1097

SPECIFICATION

Lockheed U-2R

Wing: span 103 ft 0 in (31.39 m); aspect radio 10.6; area about 1,000 sq ft (92.90 m²)
Fuselage and tail: length 62 ft 9 in (19.13 m); height 16 ft 0 in (4.88 m)
Powerplant: one Pratt & Whitney J75-P-13B rated at 17,000 lb (75.6 kN) dry thrust
Weights: basic empty, without powerplant and equipment pods, less than 10,000 lb (4536 kg); operating empty about 15,500 lb (7031 kg); maximum take-off 41,300 lb (18733 kg)
Fuel and load: internal fuel 7,649 lb (3469 kg); sensor weight 3,000 lb (1361 kg)
Speed: never exceed Mach 0.8; maximum cruising speed at 70,000 ft (21335 m) 430 mph (692 km/h)
Range: maximum range considerably more than 3,000 miles (4828 km); maximum endurance 12 hours
Performance: maximum rate of climb at sea level about 5,000 ft (1525 m) per minute; climb to 65,000 ft (19810 m) in 35 minutes 0 seconds; operational ceiling 90,000 ft (27430 m); take-off distance about 650 ft (198 m); landing distance about 12,500 ft (762 m)

U-2R (continued)

MISSION PROFILE

Signals intelligence gathering: mission loads often include sensors for the gathering of signals intelligence, from radar or communications sources, the Comint role being especially important as the U-2R can cruise for hours at a time at low speed, flying racetrack patterns to record long passages of communications; recorded data can be data-linked to ground stations in near real-time, or, on aircraft equipped with the Senior Span dorsal antenna, can be transmitted globally via the satellite communications network

Radar reconnaissance: from high altitude in friendly airspace, the U-2R provides an excellent platform for long-range stand-off radar reconnaissance; ASARS-2 radar is the main sensor, carried in an extended nose radome, the radar peering sideways and providing outstanding resolution imagery of force dispositions across the border; long border sweeps or racetrack patterns are flown to provide maximum area surveillance or long duration coverage

Photographic intelligence gathering: U-2Rs can carry a wide variety of camera systems for both vertical and oblique photography; the most important discipline is LOROP (LOng-Range Oblique Photography), very high-resolution cameras being used to provide imagery from long slant ranges, but this can be severely hampered by weather; vertical photography is little practiced due to the need to overfly the target

Emission location: PLSS (Precision Location Strike System) uses three aircraft flying orbits along a battlefront, all equipped with the PLSS sensor in an extended nosecone; each sensor records the direction of signals arriving from hostile radars and relays the data to a ground station, which uses the three recordings to compute the exact location of the emitter, and then passes on this information to attack systems

Earth resources survey: NASA's three ER-2 aircraft fly missions which can involve carrying various sensors to record earth and ocean data from great altitude, or sensors for monitoring the atmosphere, radiation or other subjects at high altitude

Training: three U-2RT aircraft are flown by the 9th Wing at Beale on training duties, a second stepped cockpit housing the instructor; the trainers are also detached to Alconbury to perform continuation training and check rides

USAF OPERATORS

Air Combat Command (ACC)

9th Wing			
	5th SRTS	Beale AFB, CA	U-2R/U-2RT
	5th SRS	RAF Akrotiri, Cyprus	U-2R
	6th SRS	Osan AB, RoK	U-2R
	95th SRS	RAF Alconbury, UK	U-2R
	99th SRS	Beale AFB, CA	U-2R

de Havilland Canada
V-18 Twin Otter

Below: Among the unusual collection of aircraft assigned to the Air Force Academy is a pair of de Havilland Canada UV-18B Twin Otters. These are used as platforms for parachute training of cadets and can carry up to 20 students.

The **de Havilland Canada V-18 Twin Otter** is employed by the USAF Academy, Colorado Springs, for parachute training for cadets.

The **UV-18B** is a military version of the DHC-6 Series 300 Twin Otter STOL (short take-off/landing) utility transport. The aircraft is a twin-turboprop, high-wing monoplane with fixed tricycle landing gear. In routine operations, the aircraft carries a flight crew of two pilots and up to 18 parachutists, including a jumpmaster.

The UV-18B is of conventional design, the wings incorporating double-slotted trailing-edge flaps and ailerons which can be drooped simultaneously with the use of the flaps to enhance STOL characteristics. The aircraft is powered by two 652-shp (486-kW) Pratt & Whitney Canada PT6A-27 turboprop engines.

De Havilland (now Boeing Canada) began design work on the civilian DHC-6 in January 1964. The Twin Otter made its first flight on 20 May 1965. The fourth principal variant, the Series 300 with PT6A-27 powerplants, was announced in 1969 and began with the 231st example of the type.

The **UV-18A** is a US Army aircraft, six of which are used by the Alaska National Guard's 207th Arctic Reconnaissance Group. This version was purchased beginning in 1976 as a STOL-capable administrative, logistical and personnel transport to operate through northern and western Alaska on a year-round basis.

The UV-18B was selected by the USAF Academy in 1977 and two aircraft were acquired 'off the shelf'. The two UV-18Bs are stationed at Peterson AFB, Colorado, a few miles from the Academy.

MISSION PROFILE

Configuration options: the UV-18B is configured for two pilots and 18 parachutists; the aircraft has STOL (short take-off/landing capability), anti-icing, de-icing system, and navigation/communications package for bad-weather capability

Airmanship/parachute training: to provide parachute training to cadets at the USAF Academy, the UV-18B cruises at 150 kt to a service ceiling of 25,000 ft (7620 m) and a range of 700 miles (1126 km) with a typical mission lasting 1.5 hours

USAF VARIANTS AND SERIALS

UV-18B: A pair of Twin Otter 300 utility transports was purchased in 1977 to conduct parachute duties with the Air Force Academy.
77-0464 and 77-0465 allocated N70464/N70465

SPECIFICATION

de Havilland Canada UV-18B
Wing: span 65 ft 0 in (19.81 m); aspect ratio 10.1; area 420,0 sq ft (39.02 m²)
Fuselage and tail: length 51 ft 9 in (15.77 m); height 18 ft 7 in (5.66 m); tailplane span 21 ft 0 in (6.40 m); wheel base 14 ft 9 in (4.5 m)
Powerplant: two Pratt & Whitney Canada PT6A-27 rated at 652 shp (486 kW)
Weights: operating empty 7,000 lb (3175 kg); maximum take-off 12,500 lb (5670 kg)
Fuel and load: internal fuel 2,583 lb (1171 kg);

maximum payload 5,100 lb (2313 kg) for 100-mile (161-km) range
Speed: maximum cruising speed at 10,00 ft (3050 m) 202 mph (324 km/h)
Range: with maximum fuel 945 miles (1521 km); range with 12 occupants 760 miles (1220 km)
Performance: maximum rate of climb at sea level 1,600 ft (488 m) per minute; service ceiling 26,700 ft (8140 m); take-off distance 1,010 ft (308 m) reducing to 820 ft (250 m) for STOL; landing distance 1,140 ft (348 m) reducing to 550 ft (171 m) for STOL

USAF OPERATORS

Air Training Command (ATC)

Air Force Academy	Colorado Springs, CO	UV-18B

DE HAVILLAND CANADA UV-18A

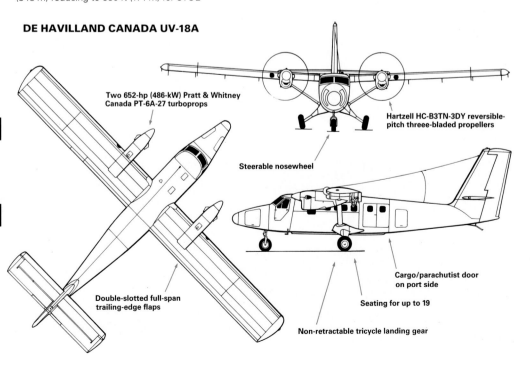

Two 652-hp (486-kW) Pratt & Whitney Canada PT-6A-27 turboprops

Hartzell HC-B3TN-3DY reversible-pitch threee-bladed propellers

Steerable nosewheel

Double-slotted full-span trailing-edge flaps

Cargo/parachutist door on port side

Seating for up to 19

Non-retractable tricycle landing gear

JPATS

JPATS (Joint Primary Aircraft Trainer System) is a program to develop a new primary flight trainer for the USAF and US Navy. About a dozen aircraft types are possible contenders for a long-term contract to produce 812 trainers to replace the USAF's Cessna T-37B Tweet beginning in 1997, and the US Navy Beech T-34C Turbo Mentor beginning in 2005. The contract is expected to be the largest single purchase of an American military aircraft type for the remainder of the century.

The program began as the USAF's PATS plan for a T-37B replacement and acquired its 'joint' status only after the Defense Department's Master Training Plan of 1989 called for both services to adopt the same primary trainer.

The aircraft types viewed as leading candidates for a JPATS production order all come from foreign manufacturers. The aircraft chosen would be assembled in the US by one of the American builders which has teamed up with the aircraft designer. Beech, Grumman, LTV, Learjet, Lockheed and Rockwell were, in 1992, the principal contenders.

On 1 May 1990, Beech announced a teaming arrangement with Pilatus of Switzerland to offer the Pilatus PC-9. Pilatus is supplying two PC-9 aircraft with design, test and certification data which Beech will use to develop two Beech-Pilatus demonstrators.

On 6 October 1988, Grumman signed with Italy's Agusta Group to submit the SIAI-Marchetti S.211A trainer as a candidate for what, at that time, was still the USAF's PATS program. The USAF evaluated the S.211A in San Antonio, Texas, as early as mid-1987, and a demonstrator aircraft has been based in Philadelphia as part of the sales effort.

In May 1990, LTV signed with Fabrica Militar de Aviones (FMA) of Argentina to offer the IA-63 Pampa 2000. A Pampa airframe made a tour of US training bases ending in November 1990.

Learjet was expected to market the EMBRAER EMB-312H, a Tucano variant, first flown in September 1991, in collaboration with Short Brothers, which produces a more powerful version for the RAF.

Rockwell teamed with Messerschmitt-Bölkow-Blohm to offer the Fan Ranger aircraft and to produce two demonstration aircraft expected to fly in 1992.

On 12 October 1989, Lockheed signed with

Above: Somewhere in the region of a dozen types are likely to do battle to secure the lucrative orders that will result from winning the Joint Primary Aircraft Trainer System contract. Among the highly promising candidates is Aermacchi's M.B.339, which is supported by Lockheed.

Right: Another contender for JPATS is the Swiss PC-9, which forms the cornerstone of a teaming agreement concluded between Pilatus and Beech. Two PC-9 aircraft are to be delivered to Beech for development and demonstration purposes as part of this bid.

Italy's Aermacchi SpA. to propose the M.B.339 jet tandem trainer. An Italian air force demonstrator aircraft leased to Aermacchi toured four US air bases in 1989, and a second round of demonstrations coincided with the 1991 Paris air show. The M.B.339 has significantly higher performance than other potential candidates.

Other aircraft builders with possible JPATS contenders include Bede, Cessna, Jaffe, and Teledyne Ryan.

When the JPATS requirement emerged from the US armed forces' Master Trainer Plan in 1989, the only requirement enunciated by the services was for a 'non-developmental, off-the-shelf' aircraft available at low cost with low maintenance, and a 20-year life cycle at 60 hours per month of operation to train 1,600 pilots per year. Recent studies show that the services will actually train half that number of pilots in the late 1990s, but an increase in the number of trainers needed by the Navy will keep the number of aircraft needed at around the 812 figure, revised from 888 in 1991. The JPATS seating configuration was decided by a brief JSON (Joint Statement of Operational Need) issued in November 1990 which specifies 'stepped tandem' seating and a pressurized cabin. This decision ruled out possible US team-ups with the manufacturers of Sweden's

Above: Fabrica Militar de Aviones of Argentina has joined forces with LTV in an attempt to win the JPATS contest, and the IA-63 Pampa has toured a number of key US Air Force and Navy training establishments in an attempt to 'win friends and influence people'.

Saab 2060 (an upgraded Sk.60), Switzerland's FFA AS-202, and Finland's Valmet L-90, all of which have side-by-side configuration.

Other JPATS requirements include zero-zero ejection seats, a canopy capable of withstanding the impact of a 4-lb (1.8-kg) bird at 250 kt, and stepped-down tandem seats to allow the instructor to see over the student. The JPATS schedule calls for source selection in fall 1993, contract award in early 1994, first USAF delivery in October 1996, and IOC in the summer of 1998.

MISSION PROFILE

Configuration options: the JPATS requirement calls for a non-developmental, off-the-shelf aircraft with 'stepped tandem' seating, a pressurized cabin, and a 20-year life cycle at 60 hours per month of operation to train 1,600 pilots per year; further configuration requirements and an aircraft type had not been decided upon in June 1992

Left: One of the first submissions to emerge in the battle for JPATS was SIAI-Marchetti's S.211, which is actually the subject of a proposal by Agusta and Grumman.

Teledyne Ryan
BQM-34 Firebee

The **BQM-34 Firebee** RPV (remotely piloted vehicle) is the USAF's current version of a drone which has evolved over decades and is employed for various missions including the testing and evaluation of air-to-air missiles.

This remotely piloted supersonic jet target vehicle is a cantilever shoulder-wing monoplane with 53° swept wing, conventional aluminium semi-monocoque fuselage, and numerous items of internal equipment including sensors for a missile scoring system.

The ground-launched **BQM-34A** Firebee is employed at Tyndall AFB, Florida, missile range. Some 18 more Firebee drones, designated **BQM-34L** and **BQM-34M**, were taken out of storage and employed by the 6514th Test Squadron at Hill AFB, Utah, for tests of the Over-The-Horizon Backscatter (OTH-B) and North Warning radar systems. The BQM-34A series has been re-engined with the 2,200-lb (9.79-kN) thrust General Electric J85-GE-17C engine and stressed for up to six *g*s of maneuver tolerance. The BQM-34M/L powerplant is the 1,920-lb (8.54-kN) thrust Continental J69-T-41A turbojet engine.

The Firebee aircraft (originally designated **Q-2A/B**) dates to 1951 and was employed initially in its present role as a flying target. Some impression of the type's age is illustrated by the fact that early, air-launched versions were carried aloft by a Douglas B-26 Invader. The Firebee I and II family of drones has been in production longer than any manned aircraft.

First flight of the current BQM-34A (originally **Q-2C**) took place on 19 December 1958 and the first production example flew on 25 January 1960. BQM-34A and **BQM-34D** versions (the latter no longer in service) have carried out a variety of duties, including simulating an unmanned jet fighter and releasing 500-lb (227-kg) bombs. The **MQM-34D** was a US Army version. US Navy versions included **BQM-34E** and **BQM-34T**.

Numerous air-launched Firebee I and II versions were employed for reconnaissance and intelligence-gathering programs as well as target and decoy duties. These included the **AQM-34G**, **AQM-34H**, **AQM-34J**, **AQM-34K**, **AQM-34L**, **AQM-34M**, **AQM-34N**, **AQM-34Q**, **AQM-34R**, **YAQM-34U**, **AQM-34V** and **XQM-103**. Other versions of the Firebee I employed in the air-to-ground tactical strike role include the **BGM-34A**, **BGM-34B** and **BGM-34C**. All of these numerous versions had been retired from service by the early 1990s.

The ground-launched BQM-34A Firebee has been the workhorse of the USAF's drone program for many years. It is used to simulate maneuvering subsonic targets.

SPECIFICATION

Teledyne Ryan BQM-34A
Wing: span 12 ft 10.8 in (3.93 m); area 36.0 sq ft (3.34 m²)
Fuselage and tail: length 22 ft 10.8 in (6.98 m); height 6 ft 8.4 in (2.04 m)
Powerplant: one JATO bottle rated at 11,300 lb (50.26 kN) thrust for ground launch, and one Teledyne CAE J69-T-9 rated at 1,700 lb (7.56 kN) dry thrust, later replaced by one General Electric J85-GE-17C rated at 2,200 lb (9.79 kN) dry thrust, for flight
Weights: basic empty 1,500 lb (680 kg); basic gross 2.060 lb (934 kg); maximum launching 2,500 lb (1134 kg)
Fuel and load: internal fuel 100 US gal (378 liters) and provision for one 25-US gal (94.5-liter) auxiliary fuel tank; external fuel up to two 100-US gal (378-liter) drop-tanks
Speed: never exceed at 50,000 ft (15240 m) 731 mph (1176 km/h); maximum level speed at 6,500 ft (1980 m) 690 mph (1112 km/h); maximum cruising speed at 50,000 ft (15240 m) 630 mph (1015 km/h)
Range: maximum range 796 miles (1282 km); endurance at 50,000 ft (15240 m) including a 160-glide after fuel exhaustion, 75 minutes 30 seconds
Performance: maximum rate of climb at sea level 16,000 ft (4875 m) per minute; operating height range between 50 and more than 60,000 ft (15 and more than 18300 m)

Beech
MQM-107 Streaker

The **MQM-107 Streaker** is a recoverable, variable-speed target drone or RPV (remotely piloted vehicle) used in the testing of air-to-air missiles.

The MQM-107 has a cylindrical fuselage with a prominent hook for recovery by helicopter winch. Its flat-airfoil, cantilever wing makes use of bonded honeycomb, with all-metal covering only on flight surfaces. Wing and tail surfaces are swept slightly at the leading edges.

All of this makes the MQM-107 a straightforward, low-cost pilotless aircraft. **MQM-107B** and **MQM-107D** versions are in USAF inventory and are assigned to Tyndall AFB, Florida. The vehicle is launched from the ground and can be employed to tow two TA-8 radar augmentation or infra-red augmentation targets which are deployed from beneath the wing and towed up to 8,000 ft (2438 m) behind the vehicle.

The MQM-107B/D guidance and control system permits either control by a ground operator or uncontrolled, pre-programmed flight. The flight control operator obtain relevant flight information by radio link from sensors located in the vehicle and can command both the maneuver and the recovery of the RPV.

The MQM-107B is powered by an 831-lb (3.7-kN) thrust Microturbo TRI 60-2 Model 074 turbojet engine slung in a pod beneath the fuselage. The MQM-107D model is powered by a similarly-mounted 960-lb (4.27-kN) thrust Teledyne CAE 373-8 turbojet engine.

This RPV traces its lineage to the VSTT (Variable-Speed Training Target) program which produced the **MQM-107A** drone for the US Army following exhaustive flight trials in 1974-75. Operational deliveries of the Army variant began in 1976.

The USAF acquired the type as a lower-cost alternative to RPV targets in the BQM-34 Firebee series. The recoverable MQM-107B/D was viewed as preferable to an expendable target drone system.

SPECIFICATION

Beech MQM-107B
Wing: span 9 ft 10 in (3.00 m); area 27.16 sq ft (2.52 m²)
Fuselage and tail: length 18 ft 1 in (5.51 m); height 4 ft 10 in (1.47 m)
Powerplant: one JATO bottle for ground launch, and one Microturbo TRI 60-2 Model 074 rated at 831 lb (3.7 kN) dry thrust for flight
Weights: maximum launch including booster 1,090 lb (494 kg)
Fuel and load: internal fuel 438 lb (199 kg)
Speed: operating speed range between 317 and 610 mph (510 and 982 km/h)
Range: endurance more than 3 hours 0 minutes
Performance: operating height range between sea level and 40,000 ft (12190 m)

The Streaker is available in two service versions, this being the MQM-107D with pod-mounted Teledyne turbojet. The Streaker is usually used to tow targets behind it for live air-to-air missile tests and is employed by the 475th Weapons Evaluation Group.

Sperry/Tracor North American
QF-100 Super Sabre

The **F-100 Super Sabre** has enjoyed a prolonged extension of its service career in the form of the **QF-100D/F** full-scale pilotless aerial target drone. Converted to pilotless drone configuration by Tracor Flight Systems (Sperry, prior to 1984), QF-100D/F Super Sabres are employed as full-scale aerial targets for air-to-air and surface-to-air missile work at Eglin Gulf Test Range, Florida, and White Sands Missile Range, New Mexico.

A typical mission employs the QF-100D/F as a target for an air-to-air test of an infra-red missile and is flown 'nullo' (with no pilot aboard). The QF-100 is controlled by ground operators, although practice missions in the QF-100D/F are flown with a pilot aboard when a ground controller is being trained. A self-destruct mechanism takes over within six minutes if contact with the ground controller is lost. Otherwise, the QF-100 target drone is expected to engage an air-to-air missile, serve as a target, and survive to be used again. The wing pylons of the QF-100 have been modified with a chaff-and-flare dispenser to enable the drone to imitate enemy aircraft.

QF-100D/F aircraft have been equipped with wingtip propane burner pods intended to serve as an infra-red target for heat-seeking missiles. During the engagement portion of a mission, the aircraft engine (a Pratt & Whitney 16,950-lb/75.4-kN J57-P-21A turbojet) is put to idle and the burner pods at the wingtips are ignited. The drone can then be engaged by a heat-seeking missile (with inert warhead) with a high prospect that a 'hit' or near-miss will not destroy the drone. The intention is to have each QF-100D/F aircraft accomplish up to seven flights involving engagements before being lost.

The F-100 Super Sabre dates to the early 1950s when it became the USAF's first fighter in the 'century series' (those with designations in the 100s) and its first fighter capable of sustained supersonic speed in level flight. The first service-test **YF-100** (52-5754) flew on 24 April 1953, the first production **F-100A** (52-5756) on 29 October 1953. Additional designations of aircraft in the series were **F-100B** (a test prototype of the 1950s later redesignated **F-107**),

F-100C, **F-100D**, **F-100E** (a proposed version not built), and **F-100F** (the two-seat version).

F-100s served as fighter-bombers in Vietnam and equipped Air National Guard squadrons well into the late 1970s. When Super Sabres were replaced by newer fighter types, the decision was made in 1979 to modify F-100D (single-seat) and a few F-100F (two-seat) aircraft to serve as piloted or pilotless drones.

The first 100 QF-100D drones were modified over 1980-85 by Sperry Flight Systems at Litchfield Park, Arizona. An additional 240 aircraft (about 210 QF-100D and about 30 QF-100F) were converted over 1986-90 by Tracor Flight Systems at Mojave, California. As of late 1991, of the total 340 drone Super Sabres, 319 had flown, one was yet to make its first flight, and 20 had been rejected by the USAF for technical reasons. Operation of the drones at Tyndall AFB, Florida, and Holloman AFB, New Mexico, is carried out under contract by General Electric. The 82nd Tacti-

cal Aerial Targets Squadron at Tyndall AFB, Florida, operates the Eglin Range QF-100D/Fs. More than two-thirds of the 319 have been lost in air-to-air drone engagements.

Production of QF-100D/F drones is now complete. The USAF is well advanced in plans to replace the Super Sabre drones with QF-106A Delta Darts.

SPECIFICATION

Sperry/North American QF-100

Wing: span 38 ft 9.5 in (11.82 m); area 385.9 sq ft (35.77 m²)

Fuselage and tail: length excluding probe 47 ft 1.25 in (14.357 m); height 16 ft 2.67 in (4.945 m)

Powerplant: one Pratt & Whitney J57-P-21A rated at 11,700 lb (52.04 kN) dry and 16,950 lb (75.4 kN) afterburning thrusts

Weight: normal take-off 29,762 lb (13500 kg); mission take-off 31,000 lb (14062 kg)

Fuel and load: internal fuel 770 US gal (2915 liters)

Speed: maximum level speed 'clean' at 36,00 ft (10975 m) 864 mph (1390 km/h) and at sea level 770 mph (1239 km/h)

Range: typical range 600 miles (966 km); guidance radar-limited range 222 km (138 miles); endurance 40-55 minutes

Performance: maximum rate of climb at sea level 16,550 ft (5045 m) per minute; service ceiling 46,000 ft (14020 m); operating height range between 200 and 50,000 ft (60 and 15240 m)

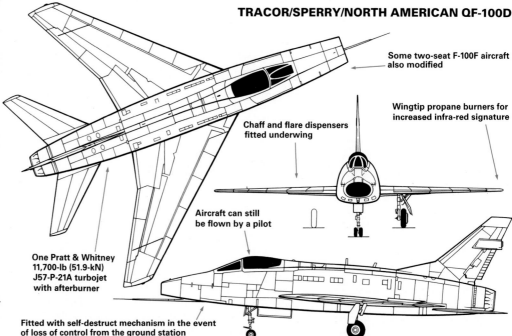

TRACOR/SPERRY/NORTH AMERICAN QF-100D

Some two-seat F-100F aircraft also modified

Wingtip propane burners for increased infra-red signature

Chaff and flare dispensers fitted underwing

Aircraft can still be flown by a pilot

One Pratt & Whitney 11,700-lb (51.9-kN) J57-P-21A turbojet with afterburner

Fitted with self-destruct mechanism in the event of loss of control from the ground station

Left: Following a long and distinguished career with first- and second-line elements, the Super Sabre was selected in 1979 to serve as a target drone. More than 300 QF-100Ds and QF-100Fs had been accepted by 1992.

Below: Tracor Flight Systems at Mojave has had sole responsibility for the Super Sabre drone conversion program since 1986. One of the last QF-100Fs to be modified is seen here.

Honeywell/Convair

QF-106 Delta Dart

The **F-106 Delta Dart** now serves in the USAF solely as a full-scale aerial target/pilotless drone under the designation **QF-106A**.

In late 1991, the QF-106A began to replace the QF-100D/F Super Sabre as the USAF's FSAT (full-scale aerial target), first at the White Sands Missile Range, New Mexico, and thereafter at the Eglin Gulf Test Range, Florida. The QF-106A is deemed better able to simulate an enemy aircraft for air-to-air missile engagements because of its higher speed and greater maneuverability. The aircraft is powered by a 24,500-lb (108.98-kN) thrust afterburning Pratt & Whitney J75-P-17 turbojet engine.

As with earlier FSATs, a typical mission employs the QF-106A as a target for an air-to-air test of an infra-red missile and is flown 'nullo' (with no pilot aboard), although it can be flown with a pilot aboard for training purposes. The QF-106 is controlled by ground operators. The intent is for the QF-106A target drone to survive repeated engagements with air-to-air missiles.

The delta wing of the QF-106 makes it impossible for the aircraft to employ wingtip propane burners used on earlier drones to create an infra-red source for heat-seeking missiles. The burners have been placed beneath wing pylons which are located below the wing and rather far forward. This has proven less than fully satisfactory, in part because most test-range missile engagements occur with the missile being fired down at the target.

The Convair F-106 Delta Dart (originally designated **F-102B**) first flew in the form of a **YF-106A** service-test aircraft (56-0451) on 26 December 1956, and is generally considered to be the last of the 'century series' (USAF fighters with designations in the 100s). Two hundred and seventy-seven single-seat **F-106A** interceptors and 63 **F-106B** two-seat, combat-capable trainers, had been delivered when production of the total of 340 ended in 1961. Delta Darts served with fighter-interceptor squadrons in the US, and on brief deployments to Europe and Korea, and with the Air National Guard until mid-1989. Two two-seaters were transferred to NASA for test work using the designation **NF-106B**. One aircraft in the series is understood to have evaluated different radar and fire-control systems using the designation **YF-106C**.

In the late 1980s, the USAF chose the F-106A Delta Dart as its future target drone to replace the PQM-102A Delta Dagger (no longer in service) and eventually the QF-100D/F Super Sabre.

Conversion of F-106As to target drones is accomplished by Honeywell. Following the completion of an initial batch of 10 QF-106As in 1990, responsibility for major portions of the work has been shifted to the USAF itself. This work is performed before the aircraft are removed from storage at AMARC (Aerospace Maintenance And Regeneration Center); further work is performed in East St Louis, Illinois. Start-up of conversion of the 11th and subsequent aircraft was delayed from May 1991 to September 1991 and the program is now underway with some four QF-106As being produced per month towards an eventual goal of 194.

As with previous fighters converted into pilotless drone targets, operation of Delta Darts at Holloman AFB, New Mexico, and Tyndall AFB, Florida, is managed under contract by General Electric. The 82nd Tactical Aerial Targets Squadron at Tyndall AFB, Florida, operates Eglin Range QF-106As.

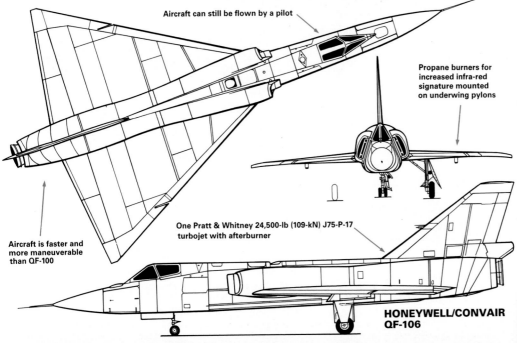

Aircraft can still be flown by a pilot

Propane burners for increased infra-red signature mounted on underwing pylons

One Pratt & Whitney 24,500-lb (109-kN) J75-P-17 turbojet with afterburner

Aircraft is faster and more maneuverable than QF-100

HONEYWELL/CONVAIR QF-106

SPECIFICATION

Honeywell/Convair QF-106
Wing: span 38 ft 3.5 in (11.67 m); area 697.8 sq ft (64.83 m²)
Fuselage and tail: length including probe 70 ft 8.75 in (21.55 m); height 20 ft 3.33 in (6.18 m)
Powerplant: one Pratt & Whitney J75-P-17 rated at 17,200 lb (76.51 kN) dry and 24,500 lb (108.98 kN) afterburning thrusts
Weight: normal take-off 35,500 lb (16012 kg)
Fuel and load: internal fuel 1,514 US gal (5731 liters)
Speed: maximum level speed 'clean' at 40,000 ft (12190 m) 1,487 mph (2393 km/h)
Range: typical radius 575 miles (925 km)
Performance: maximum rate of climb at sea level 30,000 ft (9145 m) per minute; service ceiling 58,000 ft (17680 m)

Above: The third and last member of the 'century series' fighters to be reconfigured as a target drone will be the Delta Dart, current planning anticipating the conversion of just under 200 aircraft to either QF-106A or QF-106B standard. One of the first QF-106Bs is depicted here.

Left: In service, the QF-106 Delta Darts are flown by the 82nd TATS of the 475th Weapons Evaluation Group. The aircraft are still capable of piloted flight.

USAF
ORDNANCE

This article simplifies weapon designations as much as possible. Most of the prefixes and suffixes which identify them have been omitted. For instance, the prefix 'AF/' indicates an item used only by the Air Force, while 'AN/' means one used by both the Air Force and Navy. Using the current weapon designation system, a '/B' suffix indicates the device is released from the aircraft to do whatever it is designed to do, while an '/A' indicates that it remains attached to the aircraft. While the original design has just a numerical designation, subsequent models are indicated by a letter following the number (e.g., GBU-12/B, -12A/B, etc). This article uses only sufficient designation to visually distinguish between versions. For example, while a new explosive filler may result in a new bomb version, since the bomb's external appearance is unchanged, it is ignored in the designation.

Weapon development is an ongoing process, with some interesting programs currently underway. Have

Dash II is working on air-to-air missiles with reduced radar cross-section and increased maneuverability. Other programs are testing 'not-so-dumb' bombs with either inertial or global positioning systems (GPS) guidance to help them hit where they're aimed instead of where the wind tries to blow them. The Joint Direct Attack System (formerly the Adverse Weather PGM – AWPGM program) incorporates 'pattern recognition' terminal guidance seekers to find preprogrammed targets based on intelligence from imaging infra-red systems or synthetic-aperture, millimeter-wave or laser radar. In theory, this will allow aircraft like the B-52 to drop multiple PGMs per pass. It will also give single-seat aircraft a low-workload PGM capability. (The interesting part will be programming the weapons – the mind boggles at the thought of programming over 150 bombs for a three-ship cell of B-52s!) Finally, the search to replace the M61 Vulcan cannon continues – as it has for the last 20 years or so.

GENERAL-PURPOSE BOMBS

General-purpose (**GP**) bombs are the most commonly used weapons of aerial warfare. They are inexpensive, easy to produce, and have numerous applications, including providing the warhead for most PGMs. The USAF inventory includes the 500-lb (227-kg)

Mk 82, 750-lb (340-kg) **M117** and 2,000-lb (907-kg) **Mk 84**. All have suspension lugs spaced 14 in (36 cm) apart, except for the Mk 84s, which are spaced at 30 in (76 cm). Except as noted, GP bombs are carried by the A-7, A-10, B-52, F-111, F-4, F-15E and F-16.

GENERAL PURPOSE BOMBS

BOMB	WARHEAD	CLASS	FIN KIT	REMARKS
Mk 82 LDGP	Mk 82	500 lb	Mk 82	conical fin
Mk 82 SE	Mk 82	500 lb	Mk 15	Snakeye retard fin
Mk 82 AIR	Mk 82	500 lb	BSU-49	Air Inflatable Retard
M117	M117	750 lb	MAU-103	original conical fin; B-52 only
M117	M117	750 lb	MAU-103A	conical fin w/strakes; B-52 only
M117R	M117	750 lb	MAU-91	retard fin; B-52 only
M117 AIR	M117	750 lb	BSU-93	Air Inflatable Retard; B-52 only
UK 1,000-lb	Mk 10	1,000 lb	No 107	conical fin; B-52 only
UK 1,000-lb	Mk 18	1,000 lb	No 114	conical fin; B-52 only
UK 1,000-lb	Mk 20	1,000 lb	No 117	retard fin; B-52 only
Mk 84 LDGP	Mk 84	2,000 lb	Mk 84	conical fin
Mk 84 AIR	Mk 84	2,000 lb	BSU-50	Air Inflatable Retard

Left: The USAF's most versatile weapons platform, the F-15E, is seen surrounded by most of the weapons in the inventory. Of note are the Durandal cratering munitions at far left, a wide range of bombs and precision-guided munitions (PGMs), and a B61 tactical nuclear weapon in the foreground.

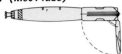

Mk 82 LDGP (M904 fuze)

Mk 82 SE (M904 fuze)

Mk 82 AIR (nose plug)

Mk 84 LDGP (M904 fuze)

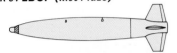

Mk 84 AIR (FMU-113 fuze)

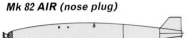

M117 (MAU-103 fin)

M117 (MAU-103A fin)

M117R (MAU-91 fin)

UK 1,000-lb (No. 114 fin)

UK 1,000-lb (No. 117 fin)

500-lb Mk 82 AIRs are seen carried in a 'flat-four' by an F-111D.

The Mk 84 LDGP is a 2,000-lb bomb.

The larger tail identifies the Mk 84 Air Inflatable Retard.

B-52Gs primarily use the M117 750-lb class weapon.

A number of different fins can be fitted to Mk 80-series GP bombs. The most common is the low-drag, general-purpose (**LDGP**) conical fin. High-drag fins include both the new air inflatable retard (**AIR**) series as well as the Vietnam War-era **Snakeye** (**SE**). (The 'eye' suffix identifies a weapon developed by the Naval Weapons Center at China Lake, California.) While the Snakeye can only be used with the Mk 82 (and forces many aircraft to slow down to deliver them), AIRs exist for both the Mk 82 and Mk 84 and can be released at much higher airspeeds. AIRs are often referred to by their canister designations, munition stabilizing and retarding unit: (**BSU**) **-49** and **-50** for the Mk 82 and Mk 84, respectively. The explosive content of LDGP bombs is roughly 50 per cent.

The **M117** (not Mk 117) was widely used in Vietnam, but is now only employed by the B-52. The low-drag version is fitted with the miscellaneous munitions unit (**MAU**) -103 conical fin while the high-drag **M117R** uses the MAU-91 Snakeye-type fin. The new **M117 AIR** uses the BSU-93 fin, a modification of the Navy 1,000-lb (454-kg) Mk 83's BSU-85. The Korean War-vintage M117 has a US Army Air Force designation, while the Vietnam War-era Mk 80 series bombs have US Navy designations. The explosive content is about 65 per cent.

During the Gulf War with Iraq, B-52Gs employed the **British 1,000-lb (454-kg) bomb**. There are several versions of this bomb and although the table matches warheads to fin-types, it is believed that all warhead/fin combinations are compatible. Explosive content is about 50 per cent.

Often overlooked, the different fuzes used with GP bombs are absolutely crucial to inflicting the desired damage to a given target. While nose fuzes are usually identifiable visually, most tail fuzes are hidden by the fin assembly – except for the M905, which uses the ATU-35 anemometer for spin arming. The fuzes used by USAF GP bombs are summarized in the following table.

GENERAL-PURPOSE BOMB FUZE OPTIONS

FUZE	LOCATION	TYPE	REMARKS
M904	nose	instantaneous/short delay	
M905/ATU-35	tail	instantaneous/short delay	
Mk 43	nose	proximity	high-drag bombs only
FMU-26	nose or tail	instantaneous/short delay	
FMU-54	tail	instantaneous	high-drag bombs only
FMU-72	nose or tail	long delay	
FMU-113	nose	proximity	modern 'daisy-cutter'
FMU-139	nose or tail	instantaneous/short delay	

PENETRATION BOMBS

The USAF adopted the French Durandal for use by F-111s as the **BLU-107** runway denial weapon. Its delivery requires a non-maneuvering, level flight path at low altitude across the target: a highly defended runway. Durandals were used during the Gulf War. A television report showing bomb disposal teams at a Kuwaiti airfield a year after the end of the war clearly showed one being prepared for destruction. The probability is that they were dropped by French Jaguar As on the first day of the war. No USAF source has admitted their use. The 450-lb (204-kg) Durandal penetrator consists of a warhead, rocket motor and parachute. Designed for carriage on bomb release unit (**BRU**) **-3**, an aerodynamic fairing is installed over the nose of the weapons carried on the front stations, while the blunt penetrator nose is exposed on the aft weapons. When released, a braking chute extracts the main chute and then drops away. The main chute slows the weapon and points it at the ground. When the proper downwards angle is achieved, the main chute is released and the rocket motor fires the warhead through up to 16 in (41 cm) of unreinforced concrete. After it has penetrated beneath the runway, the 15-kg (33-lb) warhead detonates, heaving the runway surface upwards, thus making it unusable.

The success of the Israeli air force in destroying the Arab air forces on the ground during the opening minutes of the 1967 Six-Day War prompted the major tactical air forces on both sides of the Iron Curtain to spend billions of dollars on hardened aircraft shelters (**HAS**s). These shelters are impervious to most GP bombs. Naturally, the need arose for a bomb capable of penetrating HASs and other hardened facilities. The answer to this requirement is commonly referred to as the improved 2,000-lb (907-kg) bomb, or I-2,000, although its actual designation is bomb live unit (**BLU**) -109. To prevent it from breaking up before it penetrates the hardened exterior of its target, the BLU-109 has an explosive content of only 25 per cent. The rear of the bomb is flared slightly so as to be compatible with any Mk 84 fin group. Since all of its targets require precise aiming, BLU-109s are only used as part of a PGM.

The ultimate (to date) penetration warhead, the **BLU-113**, was developed, produced, deployed and used in combat in only 17 days! Used for the 4,700-lb (2132-kg) GBU-28 'Deep Throat' bombs, they were machined from spare 20-cm (8-in) howitzer barrels to resemble very long BLU-109s, but with an explosive content of only 15 per cent. Published reports indicate the bomb was dropped from relatively high altitude at supersonic speed, maximizing both its kinetic energy and impact angle, thus enabling it to penetrate over 100 ft (31 m) of earth or 20 ft (6 m) of concrete.

Fuzing for penetration bombs is an ongoing challenge. The goal is to survive the initial impact, penetrate the target's hard 'shell'and destroy whatever is inside without passing through the target and into the ground. While the Durandal has a built-in fuze, the BLU-109 and -113 penetration bombs use the FMU-143 tail fuze. Suspension lug spacing on BLU-107 is 14 in (36 cm), while the BLU-109 and -113 use 30 in (76 cm).

BLU-107 Durandal

PAVEWAY LASER-GUIDED BOMBS

The precision avionics vectoring equipment (**PAVE**) effort began during the Vietnam War and resulted in a number of programs, the most successful of which was the Paveway laser guidance kit for 'dumb' bombs. The formal designation for this class of weapon is guided-bomb unit (**GBU**). **Paveway I** LGBs used during Vietnam had fixed wings (the front fins are called canards, while the rear ones are wings). The so-called 'Long Wing' versions of these bombs are still used occasionally for training. Of all the Paveway I LGBs, only the Mk 82-based **GBU-12** and Mk 84-based **GBU-10** were retained and improved. **Paveway II** bombs are externally distinguishable from Paveway Is by their 'pop-out' wings, which make handling and carriage easier. Both bombs have 'bang-bang' computer control and guidance

(CCG) sections which use full control deflection to alter the bombs' paths, thus shortening their range. **Paveway III** CCGs use proportional guidance, which increases bomb range and accuracy. They are also known as low-level, laser-guided bombs (**LLLGBs**). LLLGB kits were developed for both 500-lb (227-kg) **GBU-22** and 2,000-lb (907-kg) **GBU-24** bombs but, at four times the price of Paveway IIs, only the latter generated a performance increase warranting production

The **GBU-27** Paveway III bombs used with the F-117 have shorter canards and Paveway II wings to enable them to fit within that aircraft's weapons bay. Also, the adapter collar between the CCG and the warhead has been shortened from the GBU-24's 9 in (23 cm) to 6 in (15 cm). The **GBU-28** used by the F-111F and F-15E has the GBU-27's airfoil group, but the GBU-24's 9-in (23-cm) adapter collar.

The table below identifies the various members of the USAF Paveway LGB family still used operationally. When several models have the same external configuration, with the differences being internal to the CCG, they are all shown on the same line.

Delivery of LGBs requires laser designation of the target. While ground-based designation is an option, it is an extremely problematical one requiring extensive coordination to ensure the proper laser codes are used, and that the target is illuminated at the right time and direction. The preferred method is aerial designation from the delivery aircraft, if at all possible. There are four systems used by USAF aircraft for laser designation: Pave Spike, Pave Tack, LANTIRN and the F-117A's F/DLIR system.

A small number of the rapidly disappearing Block 36 through 45 Air National Guard F-4Es flown by the 108th TFW (NJ), and 122nd TFW and 181st TFG (IN) are equipped with the airborne, visual, special-type (**AVQ**)-23A Pave Spike pod. This system is only capable of daytime designation and is carried in the left forward missile

GBU-10A Paveway I

GBU-10C/D/E/F Paveway II (Mk 84)

GBU-10G/H/J Paveway II (BLU-109)

GBU-12A Paveway I (Mk 82)

GBU-12B/C/D Paveway II (Mk 82)

GBU-24 Paveway III (Mk 84)

GBU-24A Paveway III (BLU-109)

well. F-4Es drop Paveway I and Paveway II LGBs.

An even smaller number of RF-4Cs and F-4Es, but all F-111Fs, are equipped with the **AVQ-26 Pave Tack** pod, capable of day or night designation. F-4s carry Pave Tack on their centerline station, in place of a 600-US gal (2271-liter) fuel tank (aircrew refer to it as 'Pave Drag'). F-111Fs carry it on a rotating cradle in the weapons bay. F-111s drop all LGBs except GBU-27s.

All F-15Es and Block 42 F-16C/Ds are equipped with the low-altitude navigation and targeting, infra-red, for night (**LANTIRN**) system, comprising the airborne, infra-red, special type (**AAQ**)-13 navigation pod and

GBU-12 Paveway IIs carried under the wing pylons of an F-111F, which is also armed with an AIM-9P.

The GBU-12 500-lb LGB was used by F-111Fs during Desert Storm for anti-armor missions known as 'tank-plinking'.

The GBU-24A features the BLU-109 hardened-case penetration warhead. The Paveway III nose is distinctive.

AAQ-14 targeting pod. (F-15Es carry the AAQ-13 on the right side and the AAQ-14 on the left, while the F-16s reverse this arrangement.) LANTIRN gives these aircraft capabilities similar to AVQ-26-equipped F-111Fs, with the AAQ-14 responsible for laser designation. F-15Es drop the GBU-10A Paveway I, as well as all Paveway IIs and IIIs, except for GBU-27s. F-16s can carry LGBs, but do not designate targets.

The F-117A uses its internal infra-red attack and designation system (**IRADS**) to provide its designation capability. It can drop Paveway II LGBs and GBU-27s.

Two other related systems deserve mention here: Pave Penny and LANA. Both of these items are used in target acquisition, but they are sometimes mistakenly credited with a laser designation capability.

The airborne, infra-red, detecting and/or range and bearing search (**AAS**)-35 Pave Penny target identification set, laser (**TISL**) is used by the A-10 and has been tested with the F-16. A-10s carry this small pod on its own pylon on the front right portion of the fuselage. It senses targets designated with lasers by ground troops and projects a symbol on the head-up display (HUD) to help the pilot locate the targets more quickly. A-10s do not drop LGBs, although they are authorized to carry them.

The airborne infra-red, receiving/ passive detecting (**AAR**)-45 low-altitude night attack (**LANA**) pod was developed for US Navy A-7Es and adopted by the Air National Guard for use on its A-7Ds flown by the 150th TFG (NM), 132nd TFG (IA) and 138th

The AAQ-14 targeting pod of the LANTIRN system is carried to the starboard by the F-16C.

The port pod on the F-16/LANTIRN is the AAQ-13 navigation pod, with TFR and FLIR.

Tailored to fit the bays of the F-117 is the GBU-27 (foreground), with cropped tail fins.

GBU-27 Paveway III (Mk 84)

GBU-27A Paveway III (BLU-109)

GBU-28 Paveway III (BLU-113)

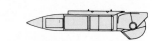
AVQ-26 Pave Tack pod

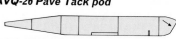
AAR-45 LANA pod (for A-7D)

TFG (OK). The pod is only carried on the right inboard pylon. Strictly a navigation system, it displays a FLIR image on the HUD so the pilot can see to fly at night. It has no laser capability. As the A-7D is retired, use of LANA with both the A-10 and F-16 is being explored. A-7s do not normally drop LGBs.

PAVEWAY BOMBS

BOMB	WARHEAD	CLASS	FIN KIT	REMARKS
GBU-10	Mk 84	2,000 lb	MXU-600	Paveway I short wing
GBU-10A	Mk 84	2,000 lb	MXU-600A	Paveway I long wing
GBU-10C-D-E-F	Mk 84	2,000 lb	MXU-651	Paveway II
GBU-10G-H-J	BLU-109	2,000 lb	MXU-651	Paveway II 'GBU-10I'
GBU-12	Mk 82	500 lb	MXU-602	Paveway I short wing
GBU-12A	Mk 82	500 lb	MXU-602A	Paveway I long wing
GBU-12B-C-D	Mk 82	500 lb	MXU-650	Paveway II
GBU-24	Mk 84	2,000 lb	BSU-84	Paveway III
GBU-24A	BLU-109	2,000 lb	BSU-84	Paveway III
GBU-27	Mk 84	2,000 lb	unknown	Paveway III for F-117
GBU-27A	BLU-109	2,000 lb	unknown	Paveway III for F-117
GBU-28	BLU-113	4,700 lb	WGU-25/36	Paveway III 'Deep Throat'

Fuzing for LGBs depends on which Paveway version and warhead is being used:

PAVEWAY FUZE OPTIONS

FUZE	LOCATION	TYPE	REMARKS
M905/ATU-35	tail	short delay	Paveway I
FMU-26	nose or tail	short delay	Paveway I
FMU-81	nose or tail	short delay	Paveway II/III
FMU-139	nose or tail	instantaneous/short delay	Paveway II/III
FMU-143	tail	instantaneous/short delay	penetration warheads

Providing the F-111F with autonomous precision attack capability is the AVQ-26 pod.

GBU-15

The modular guided weapon system (**MGWS**) bomb family was developed from the homing bombs (**HOBO**s) used in Vietnam. Basically, a **GBU-15** is the seeker head from a Maverick missile mated to a Mk 84 warhead fitted with large wings so it can be launched from beyond the range of enemy defenses. It is also fitted with a data-link capability, making it possible to guide the bomb from a second aircraft well away from the combat zone, allowing the launching aircraft to escape. Data-link control is exercised through the airborne television, special-type (**AXQ**) -14 pod.

Costing approximately $150,000 each, GBU-15s are used sparingly against well-defended, high-value targets. With the deactivation of the 3rd TFS F-4Es, this workload-intensive weapon is presently employed only by the 493rd FS's F-111Fs, which launched 70 GBU-15(V)-2s during the war with Iraq. GBU-15 is scheduled to become operational with F-15Es soon.

Both electro-optical (**EO**) and imaging infra-red (**IIR**) seeker heads are used. There are also two types of fin groups, the original 'long-chord' wing and the newer 'short-chord'. Both wings give the same guide performance and are compatible with both warheads. However, to minimize costs, a decision was made to use long-chord wings with only the Mk 84 and short-chord wings with only the BLU-109, popularly known as the **GBU-15I**. GBU-15s utilize the FMU-124 instantaneous or short-delay impact fuze.

GBU-15 SUMMARY

VERSION	SEEKER	WARHEAD	FIN GROUP	WEIGHT	REMARKS
GBU-15(V)-1	DSU-27	Mk 84	MXU-724	2,510 lb	long-chord EO
GBU-15(V)-2	WGU-10	Mk 84	MXU-724	2,560 lb	long-chord IIR
GBU-15(V)-31	DSU-27	BLU-109	MXU-787		'GBU-15I' EO
GBU-15(V)-32	WGU-10	BLU-109	MXU-787		'GBU-15I' IIR

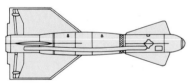

GBU-15(V)-1/2 (Mk 84)

GBU-15(V)-1 with EO guidance mounted on an F-111F.

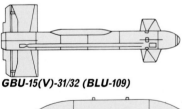

GBU-15(V)-31/32 (BLU-109)

AXQ-14 Data Link pod

The AXQ-14 data link is carried under the F-111F's rear fuselage.

BLAST BOMB

Used in Vietnam to clear helicopter landing zones and in Iraq to detonate minefields, the 15,000-lb (6804-kg) class **BLU-82** blast bomb is the largest bomb in the Air Force arsenal. It is currently delivered only by MC-130Es, being released via the cargo door strapped to a cargo pallet. The bomb's descent is slowed and stabilized by parachutes, and detonated by an M904 fuze attached to the end of a 4-ft (1.2-m) length of pipe. This fuzing arrangement, called a 'daisy cutter', was developed and used with many bombs in Vietnam to ensure above-ground detonation, thus maximizing blast and fragmentation effects. The explosive content of the BLU-82 is about 80 per cent.

BLU-82 (M904 fuze)

When dropped from an MC-130E, the BLU-82 has the pallet attached.

CLUSTER BOMBS

While structures and other 'hard' targets are best dealt with by classical bombs, area targets such as troop and armor concentrations, truck parks and artillery batteries are more susceptible to cluster munitions. Many early cluster munitions were dispersed from containers retained by the aircraft. This had two major drawbacks: first, it increased aircraft drag, thus decreasing range; and second, the dispersion pattern of the bomblets was very dependent on speed and altitude, forcing the aircraft to maintain a predictable flight path during delivery – never a wise move in combat. For these reasons, only dispensers released from the delivery aircraft are used today. All cluster bomb dispensers have 14-in (36-cm) suspension lug spacing.

Modern cluster bombs, like general-purpose bombs, are employed by all tactical fighters as well as B-52s, and all work basically the same way. Once released from the aircraft, the dispenser shell breaks apart, scattering the bomblets. Once again, fuzing is of critical importance. Two types can be used: time delay and proximity. A time delay fuze is set on the ground, and requires bomb release at a specific altitude and airspeed to produce optimum bomblet dispersion. Proximity fuzing uses a radar in the fuze to sense height above the ground, providing much greater latitude in delivery parameters. Proximity fuzes are, of course, more expensive.

The **Mk 20 Rockeye II** was developed by the Navy, adopted by the Air Force and used extensively in both Vietnam and Iraq. Its shaped charge bomblets look very much like throwing darts.

The suspension underwing unit (**SUU**) -30H dispenser family also dates from the Vietnam War. All utilize spherical bomblets with sharp-edged ridges, called 'flutes', on their exteriors. These flutes cause the bomblets to spin-arm as they disperse. The cluster bomb unit (**CBU**) -52 contains grapefruit-sized bomblets which explode on impact. The **CBU-58** has a larger number of orange-sized bomblets, but functions the same way. The **CBU-58A** adds an incendiary capability to the CBU-58. The **CBU-71** is identical to the CBU-58A except that its bomblets explode at random times, serving as mines. The **CBU-71A** bomblets function like those in the CBU-71, but have a different fuze.

The one dispenser with an added twist is the **SUU-65** version of the tactical munitions dispenser (**TMD**). After release, its fins unfold and cant to spin the dispenser to a preselected rate before it opens. This permits ideal

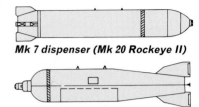

Mk 7 dispenser (Mk 20 Rockeye II)

SUU-30H (M907 fuze/CBU-58A)

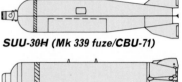

SUU-30H (FMU-56 fuze/CBU-52B)

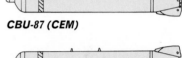

SUU-30H (Mk 339 fuze/CBU-71)

CBU-87 (CEM)

CBU-89 (Gator)

bomblet dispersion, even when released from very low altitudes. The SUU-65 can be distinguished from the very similar **SUU-64** by the large crossbar at the back of the fin assembly. At present, this is only used with the **CBU-87** combined effects munition (**CEM**). CEM bomblets, similar in size and shape to a beer can, are stabilized by a tail-mounted ballute, have an anti-material shaped charge in the nose, and a body that explodes into anti-personnel and incendiary fragments.

The **CBU-89 'Gator'** contains both anti-tank and anti-personnel mines. The former senses magnetic disturbances as a tank passes nearby and fires a self-forging warhead at it. The latter deploys tripwires and detonates when the wires are disturbed. Both mines eventually self destruct.

The **CBU-97** sensor fuzed weapon (**SFW**), as of early 1992, was poised to enter low-rate initial production. Each of its 10 BLU-108 orientation/stabilization devices (OSDs) contain four 'skeets', explosively forged penetrator anti-armor submunitions. Each OSD descends by parachute until it is properly aligned above the target area and the skeets have extended from its body. Then the parachute is released and a rocket fires to spin the OSD and stop its descent. This also flings the skeets away from the OSD along a

CLUSTER BOMB DISPENSER FUZES

FUZE	LOCATION	TYPE	REMARKS
M907	nose	time delay	SUU-30
Mk 339	nose	time delay	SUU-30 and Mk 20
FMU-26	nose	time delay	SUU-30
FMU-56	nose	proximity	SUU-30
FMU-110	nose	proximity	SUU-30
FZU-39	nose	proximity	SUU-64 and -65

horizontal trajectory. As they deploy from the OSD, each skeet actively searches for targets with an infra-red sensor. When positioned over a target the skeet explodes, transforming a flat 5.25-in (13.3-cm) diameter copper plate into a 6,000-ft (18239-m) per second kinetic energy projectile directed at the target. The projectile penetrates reactive and/or main battle tank armor to destroy the interior of the tank and kill its crew. In tests against armored formations, kill rates of over 2.5 tanks

per CBU-97 dropped have been demonstrated. This ability to kill multiple targets per pass will become crucial as the size of the fighter force shrinks.

The Air Force now plans to acquire some Joint Stand-off Weapons (formerly known as the Navy's advanced interdiction weapons systems – AIWS) to give it the ability to deliver BLU-108s at stand-off ranges of more than 20 nm (23 miles/37 km).

Above: The CBU-87 Combined Effects Munition carried by an F-111E.

Top left: CBU-71 is based on the SUU-30H dispenser with frag/incendiary mines.

Left: A Mk 7 dispenser is moved towards a waiting A-10A.

CLUSTER BOMB SUMMARY

BOMB	DISPENSER	SUBMUNITIONS	TYPE	WEIGHT
Mk 20	Mk 7	247 Mk 118	anti-tank	490 lb
CBU-52	SUU-30H	217 BLU-61	fragmentation	790 lb
CBU-58	SUU-30H	650 BLU-63	fragmentation	810 lb
CBU-58A	SUU-30H	650 BLU-63A	fragmentation/incendiary	820 lb
CBU-71	SUU-30H	650 BLU-86	fragmentation/incendiary	810 lb
CBU-71A	SUU-30H	650 BLU-68	fragmentation/incendiary	820 lb
CBU-87	SUU-65	202 BLU-97	combined effects	960 lb
CBU-89	SUU-64	72 BLU-91	anti-personnel	
		22 BLU-92	anti-tank	700 lb
CBU-97	SUU-64	10 BLU-108	anti-armor	920 lb

UNDERWATER MINES

During the early 1980s, two B-52G units were modified to undertake maritime operations. As part of this program they were authorized to employ several naval underwater mines, including the **Mk 36 and 40 Destructors**, **Mk 55** bottom mine, **Mk 56** moored mine and **Mk 60 Captor** (for enCAPsulated TORpedo).

While most aircraft are capable of carrying the Destructors, it is believed that B-52s with a maritime mission are the only ones that actually train to employ them. (The USAF's only use for the Navy's 1,000-lb (454-kg) **Mk 83** warhead is as part of the Mk 40.)

Basically, these are standard GP bombs with Mk 75 long-delay arming kits, intended primarily for use as underwater mines. Although technically cleared for use with standard conical fins, given GP bombs' propensity for exploding when they hit the water at high speeds it is doubtful that they would ever be used with anything but Snakeye-type fins.

The **Quickstrike** family are influence-fuzed bottom mines, the name coming from the short amount of time needed to assemble these weapons. They are useful down to about 300 ft (91 m).

UNDERWATER MINES

MINE	WARHEAD	WEIGHT	FIN KIT	REMARKS
Mk 36	Mk 82	560 lb	Mk 15	time-delay
Mk 40	Mk 83	1,060 lb	MAU-91	time-delay
Mk 41	Mk 84	2,000 lb	unknown	time-delay
Mk 55 Mod 2		2,160 lb	n/a	magnetic, 600 ft
Mod 3		2,180 lb	n/a	pressure/magnetic, 150 ft
Mod 5		2,180 lb	n/a	acoustic/magnetic, 150 ft
Mod 6		2,190 lb	n/a	pressure/acoustic/magnetic, 150 ft
Mod 7		2,190 lb	n/a	dual-channel magnetic, 600 ft
Mk 56 OA 05		2,150 lb	n/a	dual-channel magnetic, 1,200 ft
OA 06		2,215 lb	n/a	faired nose
Mk 60	Mk 46	2,360 lb	n/a	Captor anti-submarine torpedo
Mk 62	Mk 82	580 lb	Mk 15	Quickstrike
Mk 63 Mod 0	Mk 83	1,020 lb	EX 9	Quickstrike
Mod 1	Mk 83	1,080 lb	EX 126/9	Quickstrike
Mk 64 OA 1/2	Mk 84	2,130 lb	EX 127/9	Quickstrike
OA 3	Mk 84	2,145 lb	EX 128/9	Quickstrike
Mk 65		2,360 lb	EX 7	Quickstrike

2.75-in UNGUIDED ROCKETS

Widely used during the Vietnam War, unguided rockets are seldom used by today's US Air Force. While RF-4Cs have been seen on rare occasions with rocket pods, the usual rocket users are the forward air control (FAC) aircraft such as the OA-10 and the aircraft it is replacing, the rapidly disappearing OV-10 and OA-37.

There are five types of 2.75-in (70-mm) rocket motors, seven warheads and five rocket pods in use. The rockets include the older Mk 4 and Mk 40 folding fin aircraft rockets (**FFAR**s), Mk 66 wrap-around-fin aircraft rockets (**WAFAR**s), and the very similar Canadian rocket vehicle (**CRV**) -7 C14 and C15 rockets. The Mk 66 and C14/15 have about 40 per cent more range than the earlier Mk 4/40.

Warheads include the Mk 1 high-explosive (HE), Mk 5 high-explosive, anti-tank (HEAT), Mk 61 training warhead unit (WTU) -1 for target practice, M151 pearlite malleable iron (PMI), M156 white phosphorous (WP) and the warhead unit (WDU) -4 flechette. The HEAT warhead has a shaped charge, PMI is for fragmentation, WP is used for target marking and the flechette warhead contains 2,200 anti-personnel darts.

While most combat warheads are olive drab with yellow nose bands, WP are green with red letters; TP heads are blue with white lettering. All warheads use impact fuzes, with the exception of the WDU-4, which senses deceleration before firing its flechettes. Rocket pods are made of treated paper with a thin aluminum outer skin. They also have paper front fairings which shatter upon rocket impact.

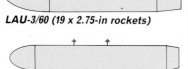

LAU-5003 (19 x 2.75-in rockets)

LAU-3/60 (19 x 2.75-in rockets)

LAU-68/131 (7 x 2.75-in rockets)

The following chart matches warheads with motors and gives 'all-up' lengths and weights.

2.75-in WARHEAD/ROCKET MOTORS COMBINATIONS/LENGTHS

WARHEAD	TYPE	FFARs		WAFARs		CRV-7s	
		length	weight	length	weight	length	weight
Mk 1	HE	48 in	18 lb	50 in	20 lb	53 in	21 lb
Mk 5	HEAT	48 in	18 lb	50 in	20 lb	53 in	21 lb
Mk 61	TP (Mk 1)	48 in	18 lb	50 in	20 lb	53 in	21 lb
M151	PMI	53 in	22 lb	55 in	24 lb	58 in	24 lb
M156	WP	53 in	22 lb	55 in	24 lb	58 in	24 lb
WTU-1	TP (M151)					58 in	24 lb
WDU-4	flechette	52 in	22 lb				

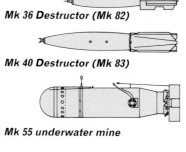

Mk 36 Destructor (Mk 82)

Mk 40 Destructor (Mk 83)

Mk 55 underwater mine

Mk 56 OA 05 moored mine

Mk 56 OA 06 moored mine

Mk 60 Captor mine (Mk 46 torpedo)

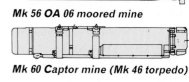

Mk 63 Mod 1 Quickstrike mine

Mk 65 Quickstrike mine

The B-52G is the main USAF launch platform for mines. This example is seen releasing a Mk 56 OA 05 moored mine.

NUCLEAR BOMBS

All US nuclear bombs are thermonuclear (i.e., hydrogen bombs). Delivery options are dependent on the bomb/aircraft combination and the type of target destruction required. All bombs incorporate parachutes which can be used to assist in level weapon delivery (and aircraft escape!). With the relatively recent retirement of the older B28 strategic and B43 tactical weapons, the table below presents the currently active, aircraft-delivered gravity weapons. While there may be several variants of a given weapon, only the basic designations are presented here. (The term 'Mk' is sometimes seen instead of 'B'.)

The **B53** is based on the warhead used by the Titan II missile. It was recalled into the inventory for use against deeply-buried Soviet command centers and submarine pens. While it has free-fall and parachute-retarded airburst options, it would normally use

a laydown (delayed surface burst) or immediate contact (surface) burst.

The **B57** was designed as a nuclear depth charge, but was later adopted for use as a low-yield tactical nuclear weapon. Nicknamed the 'Dr Pepper' bomb (after the American soft drink), its delivery options include laydown, and toss (sometimes called loft) with either air or surface burst.

The **B61**, in addition to its strategic use, is the weapon most commonly used by tactical fighters. It is nicknamed the 'Silver Bullet', because of its shape and color. Delivery options include free-fall or retarded airburst, laydown, and toss (with either air or surface burst).

The **B83** is designed for attacking hardened strategic targets such as command bunkers, and nuclear weapon storage sites. It has free-fall or retarded airburst as well as surface burst and laydown delivery options.

B53 strategic nuclear bomb

B57 tactical/maritime nuclear bomb

B61 tactical/strategic nuclear bomb

Several tactical aircraft are cleared to carry the B61, including the F-15E.

B83 strategic nuclear bomb

USAF NUCLEAR BOMBS

BOMB	WEIGHT	YIELD	INVENTORY	SHAPE	USE
B53	8,850 lb	9 mt	small	BDU-13	strategic, B-52 only
B57	500 lb	5-20 kt	about 1,000	BDU-12	tactical and maritime
B61	700 lb	10-500 kt	over 3,000	BDU-38	tactical and strategic
B83	2,400 lb	1-2 mt	over 1,000	BDU-46	strategic

GUNS

The **M2A1 Bofors** is a recoil-operated, clip-fed, air-cooled 40-mm cannon originally designed as an AAA weapon. It weighs 1,050 lb (476 kg) and fires at a rate of 120 rounds per minute (rpm). Two are used by the AC-130A, one by the AC-130H.

The **M3** 0.50-caliber machine gun is a modification of the earlier M2 dating from 1933. The M3 uses a disintegrating link feed system and is recoil-operated. It fires 1,200 rpm with a muzzle velocity of 2,840 ft per second (fps) (866 m per second; m/s) and an effective range of 3,000 ft (914 m). Four of the 70-lb (32-kg) M3s are used in the tail turret of the B-52G, each with 600 rounds of ammunition.

The **M60** 0.3-in machine gun uses a disintegrating link feed system and is gas operated. It fires 600 rpm with a muzzle velocity of 2,800 fps (853 m/s) and a maximum range of 3,500 ft

(1067 m). Four of the 25-lb (11-kg) M60s are used in the OV-10. The H-3 also uses this gun.

The **M61 Vulcan** 20-mm six-barrelled Gatling gun was developed in the 1950s. It uses a linkless feed system and is externally powered from the aircraft's hydraulic or electrical system. It fires up to 6,000 rpm with a muzzle velocity of 3,400 fps (1036 m/s). At its maximum rate of fire, prolonged bursts can generate nearly 4,000 lb (1814 kg) of reverse thrust! Active Air Force aircraft equipped with the 265-lb (120-kg) M61 include the A-7D, B-52H, AC-130A/H, F-4E, F-15 and F-16. In all probability, the F-22 will also be equipped with it. F-111s can carry the M61 in their weapons bay, but haven't since the 1970s.

The aircraft gun unit (**GAU**) -2 0.3-in six-barrelled Gatling gun is a scaled-down version of the M61. It can

SUU-11 pod (GAU-2)

GPU-5 Pave Claw (GAU-13)

Armorers load the GAU-8 Avenger cannon of an A-10A.

The GPU-5 pod is deployed with close air support F-16As.

use either linkless or belted feed systems and is externally powered from the aircraft's electrical system. It fires up to 6,000 rpm with a muzzle velocity of 2,850 fps (869 m/s). Active Air Force aircraft equipped with the 67-lb (30-kg) GAU-2 include the A-37 and MH-53. The AC-130A uses the GAU-2 as part of its MXU-470 gun module. The GAU-2 also forms the basis for the 325-lb (147-kg) **SUU-11** gun pod used by the A-37, OV-10 and AT-38B.

The **GAU-8 Avenger** 30-mm seven-barrelled Gatling gun is the anti-tank cannon around which the A-10 was designed. It uses a linkless feed system and is externally powered from the aircraft's hydraulic and electrical systems. It fires at either 2,100 or 4,200 rpm with a muzzle velocity of 3,500 fps (1067 m/s). When loaded with 1,350 rounds of ammunition, the total gun system weighs 3,800 lb (1724 kg). Only the A-10 uses the GAU-8.

The **GAU-13** 30-mm four-barrelled Gatling gun is the basis of the gun pod unit (**GPU**) -5 anti-tank cannon pod. It uses a closed loop feed and storage system and is pneumatically driven. It fires at 2,400 rpm with a muzzle velocity of 3,200 fps (975 m/s). When loaded with 353 rounds of ammunition, the gun pod weighs 1,865 lb (846 kg). Several aircraft have been evaluated with the GPU-5, but only the F-16As of the 174th TFW (NY ANG) are known to operate it.

TRAINING WEAPONS AND OTHER STORES

Dropping and firing live weapons is something done infrequently during training, and most of the time training ordnance is used. For missiles this means rounds with working seekers, but no rocket motors, warheads or guidance sections. Where a live missile would display black (guidance), yellow (warhead), or brown (rocket motor) bands, training rounds display either blue bands or paint the entire section blue. The designation of air-to-ground training missiles is **ATM** rather than AGM. Air-to-air missiles are normally referred to as 'captive', e.g., AIM-9P-**CAP**.

Full-scale training bombs are normally referred to as 'inert Mk 82' rather than the formal title of bomb, dummy unit (**BDU**) -50. There are also **inert Mk 84s** (but without a BDU designation). These bombs are usually painted overall blue and are filled with concrete instead of explosives.

The most commonly carried training bombs are referred to as 'blue bombs' and 'beer cans'. Both of these bombs were developed by the Navy and adopted by the Air Force. The 'blue bombs' are a streamlined 25-lb (11-kg) bomb called **Mk 76** by the Navy and **BDU-33** by the Air Force. It simulates the ballistics of a Mk 82 SE. 'Beer cans' are painted Dayglo orange, weigh 10 lb (4.5 kg), and are shaped like a beer can with fins. Called by their naval designation of **Mk 106** for years, the Air Force has only recently given a slightly altered version the designation of

SUU-20 (four rocket/six bomblets)

SUU-21 (six bomblets)

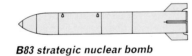

MXU-648 baggage pod

Mk 76 'blue bombs' with dummy Mk 7 CBUs and Mk 82 iron bombs seen prior to loading on an A-10.

BDU-48. Its ballistics most closely resemble a retarded nuclear weapon. Both of these bombs can be mounted on specially-modified multiple or triple ejector racks (MERs or TERs) or in SUU-20 or SUU-21 dispensers.

The **SUU-20** dispenser holds six practice bombs and four 2.75-in (70-mm) rockets (the latter option is rarely used).

The explosively ejected bombs are exposed on the bottom of the dispenser and a mix of Mk 106s and BDU-33s is common. The **SUU-21** was developed because aircraft based in Europe overfly populated areas more frequently than those based elsewhere. The SUU-21 bombs are contained within enclosed bomb bays and ejected by springs. No rocket capability exists with the SUU-21.

The miscellaneous unit (**MXU**) **-648** is a baggage pod converted from old BLU-1/27 firebomb shells. While a few have removable tailcones, most have a small door on the left side of the pod. Virtually all fighter and attack aircraft carry these on flights away from their home base, except for non-Pave Tack F-111s, which use their large weapons bay instead.

The aircraft instrumentation system (**AIS**) pods are used as part of the air combat maneuvering instrumentation (**ACMI**) system. These systems allow real-time and post-mission evaluation of exercises. This system allows the battle to be viewed from any angle, even from the 'cockpits' of opposing aircraft. It also evaluates surface-to-air and air-to-air engagements and, recently, has begun to include bombing accuracy. AIS pods resemble unfinned Sidewinder missiles with pitot tubes and are mounted to AIM-9 launchers. There are several versions, including the airborne, special type (**ASQ**) **T-11**, **-13**, **-17**, **-20**, **-21** and **-25**, as well as the airborne, telemetering, special type (**AKQ**) **-T1**. Except for the T-11, which has a ram air scoop on its side, all pod differences are internal.

363rd Fighter Wing F-16Cs with the SUU-20 training pod. Four rockets can be carried outboard, with six 'blue bombs' underneath.

ELECTRONIC COUNTERMEASURES (ECM) PODS

ECM pods were introduced during the Vietnam War to counter SAMs. Over the years they have been refined and updated to cope with newer SAMs. Although some new pods look very similar to earlier ones, many have completely new electronics. These pods use deception techniques to make radars think an aircraft is in a slightly different location than where it actually is, causing radar-guided SAMs to detonate just far enough away from their target to allow the aircraft to escape. Current ECM pods include the airborne, countermeasures, special purpose (**ALQ**) **-119**, **-131** and **-184**, as well as the quick reaction capability (**QRC**) **80-01**. All pods use 30-in (70-cm) suspension lug spacing.

OPERATIONAL ECM PODS

POD	WEIGHT	LENGTH	HEIGHT	COVERAGE	REMARKS
ALQ-119(V)-15	575 lb	143 in	21 in	low/med/hi	US-based aircraft
QRC 80-01(V)-3	575 lb	143 in	21 in	low/med/hi	US-based aircraft
ALQ-119(V)-17	400 lb	115 in	21 in	med/hi	US-based aircraft
QRC 80-01(V)-4	400 lb	115 in	21 in	med/hi	US-based aircraft
ALQ-131 DEEP	680 lb	111 in	24.5 in	bands 3/4/5	Europe-based aircraft
ALQ-131 SHALLOW	585 lb	111 in	20 in	bands 4/5	Europe-based aircraft
ALQ-184(V)-1	680 lb	156 in	20 in	bands 4/5	US-based aircraft
ALQ-184(V)-2	510 lb	116 in	20 in	bands 4/5	US-based aircraft

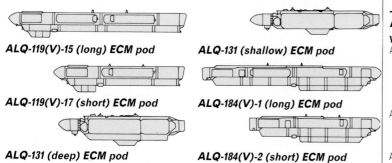

ALQ-119(V)-15 (long) ECM pod

ALQ-131 (shallow) ECM pod

ALQ-119(V)-17 (short) ECM pod

ALQ-184(V)-1 (long) ECM pod

ALQ-131 (deep) ECM pod

ALQ-184(V)-2 (short) ECM pod

AIM-7 SPARROW

The 500-lb (227-kg) class, medium-range, air intercept missile (**AIM**) **-7** Sparrow began as Project 'Hot Shot' in May 1946. It didn't actually intercept a target until December 1953, even though production began in 1951. Early versions were developed to shoot down non-maneuvering targets. When the Vietnam War came, experience proved the **AIM-7E** to be virtually useless against maneuvering, fighter-sized targets, especially at low level. The **AIM-7E-2** 'dogfight' modification, identifiable by the 'L' markings on its wings, was introduced in 1969 to answer these shortcomings. This missile served as the jumping-off point for both the British SkyFlash and Italian Aspide missiles. Further refinements resulted in the **AIM-7E-3** and **-4**, limited numbers of which still exist. Up to this point, the configuration of AIM-7s had been guidance and control section, wing, warhead and rocket motor. With the advent of the **AIM-7F**, avionics improvements enabled the high-explosive, blast-fragmentation warhead to be moved in front of the wing, allowing the rocket motor to be enlarged, thereby improving range. This virtually new

AIM-7F/M Sparrow MRAAM

The AIM-7M Sparrow/F-15C Eagle combination was responsible for most of the kills in the Gulf War.

missile introduced a Doppler seeker and improved virtually all other components to make it more capable against maneuvering, low-altitude targets. The current front-line version is the **AIM-7M**, which has a monopulse seeker and numerous other evolutionary improvements to increase reliability and decrease cost.

AIM-9 SIDEWINDER

Development of the 200-lb (91-kg) class Sidewinder missile family began in 1951. Forty years and nearly 30 versions later, it is by far the most successful and deadly air-to-air missile in USAF inventory. The **AIM-9** has evolved from a missile which could only be launched at close range from directly behind a non-maneuvering target to an all-aspect weapon with up to five times the range of the original. It has served as the basis for the MIM-72 Chapparal, AGM-122 Sidearm, and AA-2 'Atoll' missiles. Beginning as a Navy missile adopted by the Air Force, requirements soon drove the two services along separate development paths. This persisted throughout the Vietnam War, until costs forced common

development of the AIM-9L and subsequent versions.

The AIM-9L/M is standard armament on all tactical fighters except F-111s, which use only the AIM-9P-3 on their outboard shoulder stations because of wing clearance problems. However, AIM-9L/Ms can be carried on the inboard F-111 pylons, if desired.

AIM-9J/P versions are launched from the **Aero 3B** launcher rail. Modification of those launchers to accept the AIM-9L/M/R missiles resulted in the **LAU-105**, while the newest launcher for Sidewinders is the **LAU-114**.

The following list defines just the currently active versions of the AIM-9 family.

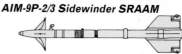

AIM-9P-2/3 Sidewinder SRAAM

AIM-9L/M/R Sidewinder SRAAM

NWC 'Boa-M' test version (AIM-9X)

Raytheon AIM-9X test version

AIM-9 SIDEWINDER VARIANTS

VERSION	REMARKS
AIM-9J	About 13,000 built, both AIM-9B/E/J modifications and new builds
	30.5-in long guidance and control section (**GCS**) with modified servo, electronic and 130211 double-delta fins
	3-in long Mk 303/304 target detector device (**TDD**) or Mk 303 Mod 4 with combined functions
	75-in long Mk 17 motor
AIM-9J-1	Modified AIM-9J with 25.5-in long GCS which incorporates rate bias and solid state electronics
	3-in long target detecting device unit (**DSU**) -21/B active optical target detector (**AOTD**) which utilizes gallium-arsenide (**GaAs**) lasers
AIM-9J-2	AIM-9J with 75-in long SR116 rocket motor
AIM-9J-3	AIM-9J-1 with SR116 rocket motor

AIM-9P	Redesignation of AIM-J-1
AIM-9P-1	AIM-9P with DSU-21/B TDD
AIM-9P-2	AIM-9P with SR116 rocket motor
AIM-9P-3	AIM-9P-1 with SR116 rocket motor
AIM-9P-4	AIM-9J GCS modified to be all-aspect capable, DSU-21/B TDD, Mk 8 warhead and an improved SR116 rocket motor; foreign military sales (**FMS**) only
AIM-9L	About 16,000 built for USN and USAF, 3,500 for Europe; Swedish designation Rb 74 25.5-in long AN/DSQ-29 GCS has an indium-antimony (InSb) seeker which gives it an all-aspect capability; BSU-32/B 22-in span 'pointy' fins USAF versions are argon (A) cooled from a bottle contained in the missile while USN versions are nitrogen (N₂) cooled from a launcher rail bottle 6.5-in DSU-15/B AOTD 11.5-in long WDU-17 annular blast-fragmentation (**ABF**) warhead 71-in long Mk 36 rocket motor with Mk 1 wings
AIM-9M	Originally AIM-9L product improvement program (**PIP**); over 7,000 built Modified with closed cycle cooling, infra-red countermeasures (**IRCM**) and background discrimination Reduced-smoke version of Mk 36 rocket motor
AIM-9R	AIM-9M with imaging infra-red (**IIR**) GCS which doesn't require refrigeration system
AIM-9X	Program to develop an internal-carriage Sidewinder for use with F-22 Two versions currently in test: Raytheon-developed version of AIM-9M which replaces old wings/canards with 11-in span tail controls; NWC-developed 'Boa-M' program with 16-in span wings and AIM-9D canards controlled by a digital autopilot

The AIM-9M is the current standard Sidewinder version, seen here on an F-15C together with AIM-7M Sparrows.

LGM-30 MINUTEMAN

The Minuteman silo-launched, surface attack, guided missile (**LGM**) -30 has been operational for over 20 years. A solid-fuel, three-stage missile named for the quickness of its response as much as for the volunteer soldiers of the American Revolution, 10 Minutemen are controlled from each two-man command site. The 73,000-lb (33113-kg) **LGM-30F Minuteman II** had a 6,000-nm (6,905-mile; 11112-km) range and carried a single, 1.2-megaton

warhead. Operational since 1965, these 450 missiles were stood-down from alert during September 1991 as part of a US initiative to reduce nuclear tensions. The 78,000-lb (35381-kg) **LGM-30G Minuteman III** has a 7,000-nm (8,056-mile; 12964-km) range and carries three 335-kiloton warheads. First launched in 1968, 50 of the original force of 550 have been replaced by the LGM-118. The remainder are still operational but, during his January 1992 State of the Union address, President Bush announced plans to remove from each missile two of its three warheads.

LGM-30G Minuteman III protective nosecone and the three multiple independent re-entry vehicle warheads.

The Minuteman III is the last version operational and accounts for the majority of US silo-launched ICBMs.

AGM-45 SHRIKE

The 400-lb (181-kg) air-to-ground missile (**AGM**) -45 was developed by the Navy during the Vietnam War as the first anti-radiation missile (**ARM**). The original **AGM-45A** had a single burn motor and became operational in 1965. The **AGM-45B** introduced a dual burn motor, with the initial acceleration thrust followed by a second, sustaining thrust. Altogether, 12 guidance, eight warhead, three control and seven motor sections were developed by the time production of over 13,000 Shrikes ceased in 1978. All versions maintained the same external configuration, and six guidance sections remain operational. The AGM-45 can be launched from either the **LAU-34** or the newer **LAU-118** (also used to launch the AGM-88). The Shrike in USAF service is carried by 'Wild Weasel' F-4Gs and F-16Cs.

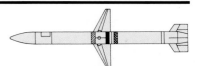

AGM-45 Shrike ARM

This Shrike is seen carried by an F-16C, which is used by the 52nd Fighter Wing for defense suppression duties.

AGM-65 MAVERICK

Developed during the Vietnam War as a subsonic, launch-and-leave replacement for the AGM-12 Bullpup, Maverick has evolved over the years and remains in production. While all the same size, AGM-65s utilize a variety of guidance and warhead sections. The original 125-lb (57-kg) high-explosive, shaped-charge warheads have been replaced in later AGM-65s by 300-lb (136-kg) blast-penetration warheads. All versions use the same rocket motor, with maximum launch range depending on target size and seeker performance. While maximum aerodynamic range is about 12.5 nm (14 miles; 23 km), a more realistic range is nearer 8 nm (9 miles; 14 km). Mavericks are used by A-7Ds, F-4Es, F-4Gs, F-15Es and F-16s; however, during the Gulf War over 90 per cent of the AGM-65s fired were from A-10s. Maverick is a very workload-intensive weapon which pilots of faster aircraft, such as the F-16, found very difficult to employ in combat.

AGM-65A has an electro-optical (television) seeker which the pilot uses to acquire the target. After designating the target and ensuring the missile is locked on, the pilot fires the missile and can either select another target or commence escape maneuvers. The **AGM-65B** has the advantage of 'scene-magnification', which enables it to be locked on to the same target as an AGM-65A from twice the range. Both missiles are white, with clear seeker domes. The AGM-65B has 'SCENE MAG' stenciled on its side.

AGM-65C was a semi-active laser (**SAL**) version developed in the late

AGM-65 Maverick

Maverick, the main USAF anti-armor weapon, is used by F-16s.

1970s. However, in 1979 both the USAF and USN decided to forego this seeker in favor of imaging infra-red (IIR). The USMC became the only user of SAL guidance, in the form of the **AGM-65E**, which features the larger warhead. SAL permits ground troops to designate targets for their close air support. During the Gulf War, this capability was used fewer than 10 times. AGM-65Es are gray.

AGM-65D was the first IIR version produced, becoming operational during 1986 with 81st TFW A-10s. The advantage of IIR over EO guidance is its ability to be used at night and in conditions of smoke and haze. For the **AGM-65F**, the Navy modified the IIR seeker's tracking function for anti-ship attacks and incorporated the larger warhead. The **AGM-65G** combines the guidance features of both the 'D' and 'F' with the latter's warhead.

AGM-65 MAVERICK VARIANTS

VERSION	GUIDANCE	WEIGHT	WARHEAD	REMARKS
AGM-65A	EO	465 lb	125 lb	
AGM-65B	EO (Scene Mag)	465 lb	125 lb	
AGM-65C	SAL	465 lb	125 lb	not produced
AGM-65D	IIR	485 lb	125 lb	USAF only
AGM-65E	SAL	645 lb	300 lb	USMC only
AGM-65F	IIR (anti-ship)	675 lb	300 lb	USN only
AGM-65G	IIR	675 lb	300 lb	USAF/USN

AGM-69 SHORT-RANGE ATTACK MISSILE (SRAM)

Deployed since 1972 on strategic bombers, the 2,200-lb (998-kg) class SRAMs were removed from alert on B-52s and B-1Bs and placed in storage during 1990 after doubts about their safety were raised. Equipped with a 170-kiloton nuclear warhead, the supersonic AGM-69s have a range of about 100 nm (115 miles; 185 km). Inertially guided, the SRAM's main function is the elimination of terminal area defenses. When FB-111As were converted to F-111Gs and transferred to Tactical Air Command, their SRAM capability was eliminated.

The SRAM was mounted on a rotary launcher in B-52 bomb bays.

AGM-84 HARPOON

Harpoon is a 1,200-lb (544-kg) class anti-ship missile which has been operational with the US Navy since the mid-1970s. It can be launched from ships (RGM-84) and submarines (UGM-84), as well as aircraft (AGM-84). The AGM-84A through D are externally identical. All versions of this subsonic missile are turbojet powered, with the inlet located on the bottom of the missile between the wings. Used successfully by the US Navy against Libyan patrol boats in 1986, no anti-ship Harpoons were used during the Gulf War.

The **AGM-84A** uses a radar altimeter to fly at sea-skimming heights. Its inertial guidance section is programmed prior to launch to direct it to the target area, where an active radar seeker controls terminal guidance. As it attacks its target, the AGM-84A performs a pop-up maneuver to enhance warhead penetration. The **AGM-84B** has a

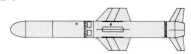

AGM-84 Harpoon anti-ship missile

guidance program which dispenses with the terminal pop-up maneuver. The **AGM-84C** has a refined pop-up maneuver. The **AGM-84D** features an increase in range from 57 to 75 nm (66 to 86 miles; 106 to 139 km), and the ability to navigate to several turnpoints *en route* to the target area and then execute one of several terminal attack maneuvers.

Two squadrons of B-52Gs (at Anderson AFB, Guam, and Loring AFB, Maine), were equipped with Harpoons beginning in 1983. However, with the closure of the former and the announced closure of the latter, it is unclear whether this capability will be retained.

AGM-86 AIR-LAUNCHED CRUISE MISSILE (ALCM)

The ALCM was initially envisioned as a replacement for the ADM-20 Quail decoy missile and called subsonic cruise armed decoy (**SCAD**). It was finally developed as the **AGM-86A** to be a long-range complement to the AGM-69 SRAM, with which it had launcher compatibility. The length of the AGM-86A was defined by the length of the B-1A's weapons bay. After cancellation of the B-1A, the AGM-86 was redesigned prior to competing against the AGM-109H Tomahawk to see which missile would arm the B-52G. Called **AGM-86B**, the new missile had a longer fuselage, since it

would only be used with the B-52. Equipped with a 200-kiloton warhead, the 3,200-lb (1452-kg) AGM-86B is a subsonic, turbojet-powered missile with a range in excess of 1,500 nm (1,762 miles; 2778 km). As B-52Gs are withdrawn from service, B-52Hs are becoming ALCM carriers.

It was revealed a year after the Gulf War that seven B-52Gs fired 35 conventionally-armed **AGM-86C**s

B-52Gs carry 12 AGM-86B ALCMs on the wing pylons.

against eight targets in northern Iraq. These missions had launch points about 50 nm (58 miles/93 km) south of the Saudi-Iraq border and were conducted prior to the start of missions from Turkey. The attack, with the previously secret ALCM variants, was mounted from Barksdale AFB, LA, resulting in mission lengths in excess of 34 hours. The full extent of modifications from the AGM-86B is unknown, but some fuel capacity was sacrificed for the 1,000-lb (454-kg) blast-fragmentation warhead size. GPS is used to supplement the TERCOM guidance system.

The most interesting aspect of cruise missiles is their guidance system. Although the altitude flown is controlled by a radar altimeter, the clearance level commanded varies during the mission, depending on terrain, so the missile flies just high enough to avoid hitting terrain rising faster than the radar altimeter and flight controls can compensate for.

AGM-88 HIGH-SPEED ANTI-RADIATION MISSILE (HARM)

Based on lessons learned in Vietnam, the 800-lb (363-kg) class AGM-88 is fast enough to give SAM operators minimum opportunity to shut down their radar before the HARM does it for them. HARM has three modes of employment: (**1**) In the **long-range stand-off** mode the missile is preprogrammed on the ground for up to three specific sites. Upon detecting those sites, the missile is launched on a ballistic trajectory. (Although HARM can be launched in the direction of a target, it guides in azimuth only, not range, thus relying on the target to emit and identify itself.) (**2**) The **self-protection** mode launches the missile against threats detected by the launching aircraft's radar warning receiver. (**3**) The **target of opportunity** mode uses the HARM's seeker to help determine when to launch against a previously unknown threat. One interesting technique used during the opening stages of the Gulf War was to use multiple-launchers, drone missile (BQM) -74C targets as decoys, thus enticing the SAM sites into turning on their radars for the incoming barrage of HARMs.

There are three versions of the AGM-88, differing mainly in the features of the guidance section electronics. The **AGM-88A** requires the seeker to be sent back to a depot in the US to be reprogrammed. The **AGM-88B** allows the seeker to be reprogrammed on the flight line. This version, with Block-3 software, was the primary one used during the Gulf War. The **AGM-88C** will incorporate further seeker improvements and replace the steel cubes in the warhead with considerably more lethal tungsten alloy

AGM-88 HARM

The USAF's principal HARM platform is the F-4G 'Wild Weasel'.

ones. HARMs are launched from the **LAU-118** launch rail, which can also accommodate the older AGM-45.

Although many aircraft can launch HARMs, the Air Force only employs them from F-4Gs and F-16C 'Wild Weasels'. The F-4G is by far the HARM's most effective launch platform, because the airborne radar receiving, passive detecting (APR) -47 system allows it to detect, identify and precisely locate threat radars and then attack them or direct other aircraft to attack them. No other aircraft has this capability, and the Air Force faces a dilemma in replacing it as it nears retirement. The main focus of current efforts is to improve the F-16C to be something more than the 'extra set of pylons for the F-4G' that it is right now. Consideration has also been given to arming EF-111As with HARM.

LGM-118 PEACEKEEPER

Commonly known as the MX, the 195,000-lb (88452-kg) LGM-118 was originally conceived as a mobile system to decrease its vulnerability to attack. The Peacekeeper is a four-stage missile which can deliver 10 500-kiloton warheads at intercontinental ranges.

A controversial system, development of the hardware proceeded faster than

Fifty LGM-118s ICBMs are deployed, each equipped with 10 warheads. They use existing Minuteman silos.

the political debate surrounding its basing. While several concepts were considered, a railroad-based system was eventually settled upon. As an interim solution, 50 of the 100 authorized missiles were deployed beginning in 1986 in former Minuteman III silos.

The other missiles have been stored, and plans to develop the rail-based system were cancelled in September 1991, in response to the dramatic changes in the world situation. President Bush announced cancellation of further production during his State of the Union address in January 1992, and proposed scrapping the existing missiles if the CIS (former USSR) would scrap their large multiple-warhead ICBMs.

AIM-120 ADVANCED, MEDIUM-RANGE AIR-TO-AIR MISSILE (AMRAAM)

The AIM-120 is the replacement for the AIM-7 Sparrow. An extremely controversial weapon, it has had a long and difficult gestation, emerging as a missile far more lethal than the one it replaces.

AMRAAM's most important improvement is the incorporation of an active radar seeker. Although incorporated previously into the AIM-54 Phoenix, putting this feature into a Sparrow-sized airframe is a significant achievement. It allows the launching aircraft to simultaneously engage several targets and maneuver 'out of the fight' before the missiles hit their targets. The Sparrow, by comparison, requires the launching aircraft to maintain radar contact with a single target until the missile hits it. The disadvantage of this was dramatically demonstrated during the famous Aimval/Aceval tests during the mid-1970s. In one engagement, which became known as 'The Towering Inferno', four F-15s engaged four F-5s with simulated AIM-7s. Before they were all 'shot down' by the Sparrows, the F-5s were able to launch simulated AIM-9s which 'destroyed' all the F-15s. AMRAAM would have allowed a single F-15 to target all four F-5s before withdrawing beyond the range of their AIM-9s.

The other main area of emphasis with AMRAAM has been reliability and maintainability. Sparrow was infamous during the Vietnam War for its unreliability. Getting this feature right has been one of the main reasons it has taken so long to get the AIM-120 into production. Virtually all other areas of performance have been improved over

AIM-120 AMRAAM

AIM-120 mounted on the wingtip rail of an F-16C. A Mk 84 AIR is underwing.

the AIM-7, such as reducing motor smoke, increasing speed and range, improving warhead fuzing and lethality, and providing better ECCM.

Because it only weighs 350 lb (160 kg), the missile can be rail-launched from stations previously associated only with AIM-9 Sidewinders. This was done during the Gulf War, when the F-15Cs of the 33rd TFW were the first unit to take AMRAAM into combat. Unfortunately, by the time the aircraft software was set up to allow carriage of AIM-7s, -9s and -120s, the aircraft of the Iraqi air force were hiding in their shelters or fleeing to Iran, and there was no opportunity to actually use the new missile in combat.

AIM-120 will eventually replace AIM-7 on all F-15s and F-16s, as well as the new F-22.

AGM-129 ADVANCED CRUISE MISSILE

Intended as a stealthy replacement for the AGM-86B, deliveries of production AGM-129As began in June 1990. The 2,750-lb (1247-kg) class ACM has a range of more than 1,800 nm (2,071 miles; 3340 km) and features improved accuracy and targeting flexibility. With about 640 missiles completed through FY91, plans for a total of 1,461 to arm

B-52Hs were abandoned when President Bush announced cancellation of further production during his State of the Union address in January 1992. Operational training launches began during 1991.

The B-52H force is receiving the AGM-129A. The ACM is more stealthy than the AGM-86B.

AGM-130

The AGM-130 is a GBU-15 equipped with a rocket motor to increase its stand-off range even further.

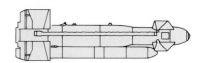

AGM-130 (Mk 84 warhead)

AGM-130 VARIANTS

VERSION	SEEKER	WARHEAD	FIN GROUP	WEIGHT	REMARKS
AGM-130A	DSU-27	Mk 84	MXU-787	2980 lb	rocket-boosted EO
AGM-130B	WGU-10	Mk 84	MXU-787	3026 lb	rocket-boosted IIR

AGM-131 SRAM II/T

In line with a change of US policy announced in September 1991, development of the AGM-131A SRAM II strategic replacement for the AGM-69, and the AGM-131B SRAM-T tactical derivative, was cancelled.

MGM-134 SMALL INTER-CONTINENTAL BALLISTIC MISSILE

The SICBM was originally developed as a mobile strategic missile which would be less vulnerable than existing missiles based in fixed locations. Popularly known as 'Midgetman', this 37,000-lb (16783-kg), three-stage missile would have been armed with a single 500-kiloton warhead, and have a range of about 6,800 nm (7,826 miles; 12594 km). In compliance with the September 1991 change in US policy, plans to develop the MGM-134 as a mobile missile were cancelled. Plans to develop it for basing in existing Minuteman III silos were abandoned when President Bush announced cancellation of the program during his State of the Union address in January 1992.

AGM-137 TRI-SERVICE STAND-OFF ATTACK MISSILE (TSSAM)

TSSAM, a stealthy missile under development, will have a range of up to 300 nm (345 miles; 556 km) and employ brilliant anti-tank (BAT) autonomously-guided submunitions. They are hit-to-kill weapons employing conventional shaped-charge warheads.

AGM-142 POPEYE

Popeye is a 3,300-lb (1497-kg) conventional stand-off missile armed with a 1,975-lb (896-kg) high-explosive warhead. It was developed by Israel's Rafael Armament Development Authority and procured by the US Air Force under the 'Have Nap' program. Co-produced by Martin Marietta, it features inertial guidance coupled with EO terminal homing. Tested on several aircraft, the 50-nm (58-mile; 93-km)

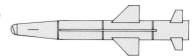

AGM-142 Popeye ('Have Nap')

range missile has entered service with conventionally dedicated B-52Gs. Popeye was not used during the Gulf War, reportedly because of concerns about the effects using an Israeli-developed weapon would have had on the coalition.

AIRCRAFT ORDNANCE CONFIGURATIONS

A-10A (Fairchild Thunderbolt II)

On one outboard wing station, two AIM-9L/Ms are carried on LAU-105s mounted to a dual rail adapter (DRA). On the other is an ECM pod, either ALQ-119(V)-15 (US-based aircraft), or ALQ-131 (shallow) (overseas-based aircraft). The ALQ-184(V)-1 and ALQ-131 (deep) are also authorized.

AGM-65 Mavericks (only carried on stations 3/9) are normally half EO and half IIR versions. They are primarily carried on single-rail LAU-117s and, if carried on triple-rail LAU-88s, are slant loaded.

Triple ejector racks (TERs) are carried on stations 4/8. The racks can carry three bombs, although normally have only two. Loading is sometimes slant (weapons on the bottom and outboard stations), but normally flat (weapons on shoulder stations).

Primary bombs are Mk 82 LDGP, Mk 20 Rockeye II and SUU-30H, one type per mission. Other authorized weapons include Mk 82 SE and Mk 82 AIR. The A-10, of course, is built around the GAU-8 Avenger cannon.

The centerline pylon (station 6) is not loaded for combat operations, and pylons 2/10 and 5/7 are sometimes removed in high-threat situations to improve maneuverability.

B-52G/H (Boeing Stratofortress)

Conventional:
Unlike B-52D/Fs used in Vietnam, B-52G/Hs never received the 'Big Belly' modification which allowed the internal carriage of clips holding up to 108 bombs. They carry two four-bomb, or up to three nine-bomb, clips internally. Loads include: 27 each of SUU-30, SUU-64, SUU-65, Mk 82 LDGP, Mk 82 SE, Mk 82 AIR, Mk 36 Destructor, M117, M117R, M117 AIR or M129 leaflet bombs; 18 British 1,000-lb (454-kg) bombs; eight each of Mk 84 LDGP, Mk 84 AIR, Mk 55 mine, Mk 56 mine, or Mk 60 mine.

Two types of external pylons are used. The longer pylon was originally used for carriage of the AGM-28 'Hound Dog' nuclear cruise missile; the shorter pylon was designed for conventional weapons carriage and is known as the 'Stub' wing pylon, and is only compatible with aircraft not modified for carriage of ALCMs. There are two types of mounting hardware attached to the pylons for carriage of conventional weapons: (**A**) The most common is the 'I-beam' rack adapter to which two multiple ejector racks (MERs) are attached. This arrangement allows the carriage of 12 weapons on each wing and it can be used with either pylon. I-beam equipped aircraft can carry 24 each of SUU-30, SUU-64, SUU-65; Mk 82 LDGP, Mk 82 SE, Mk 82 AIR, Mk 36 Destructor, M117, M117R, M117 AIR or M129. (**B**) For stores too long and/or heavy to be attached to MERs, the heavy stores adapter beam (HSAB) is used. This permits carriage of up to nine weapons from each pylon, depending on the weapons' size and weight, and it can only be used with the Stub pylon. HSAB-equipped aircraft can carry 10 each of Mk 84 LDGP, Mk 84 AIR, or Mk 60 mine; 12 each of Mk 55 mine, Mk 56 mine, or AGM-84 Harpoon; 18 each of any bomb carried by the I-beam; 18 each of Mk 40 Destructor, British 1,000-lb (454-kg) bomb, CBU-87 CEM, or CBU-89 Gator; four each of AGM-142 Popeye.

In addition, the B-52G has four tail-mounted .50-caliber M3 machine guns, and the B-52H a tail-mounted M61 Vulcan cannon.

Above: An A-10 with standard CAS load including 'slant two' Mavericks, CBUs and self-defense Sidewinders.

Below: The bomb bay of the B-52G is able to accommodate a wide variety of stores.

Nuclear:
Internally, nuclear-armed B-52s are probably capable of carrying the following carriage device/weapon combinations: forward – MHU-29 carrying a single B53 or a MHU-14 clip with four B61/83s; aft – SRAM Rotary Launcher with eight AGM-69As or another MHU-14 clip of B61/83s, or a single Common Strategic Rotary Launcher (CSRL) with a total of eight of B61, B83, AGM-86, or AGM-129.

Externally, nuclear-armed B-52s can use either two SRAM pylons with a total of 12 AGM-69s or two ALCM pylons with a total of 12 AGM-86Bs or AGM-129s.

F-111 (General Dynamics)

There are three types of interchangeable F-111 bomb bay doors in use. The original doors are used with an internal luggage rack, 'Tokyo' fuel tank, or for nuclear weapons. The M61 gun installation has not contained a gun since about 1980. The gun port has been faired over and the fixed right-hand side of the installation is used as a luggage rack. The F-111F usually carries a Pave Tack pod on a rotating cradle in its bay. Both the gun and Pave Tack installations can mount ECM pods (currently shallow ALQ-131 for UK-based aircraft and QRC 80-01(V)-4 for those at Cannon AFB, NM), although this is usually done only when AXQ-14 data-link pods are carried on the aft ECM station of F-111Fs.

Although F-111s were constructed with provisions for four pylons fixed for carriage at 26° of wingsweep, this was only done to carry fuel tanks on the FB-111A. Only the four movable inboard pylons are considered here.

Since AIM-9 Sidewinder missiles are usable primarily during daylight and

Left: F-111Fs can carry up to four 2,000-lb PGMs each. The middle aircraft of this group has GBU-10 LGBs; the outer aircraft carry GBU-15 EOGBs.

Right: Eagles on patrol show the typical load of four AIM-9Ms and four AIM-7Ms. AIM-7 is being replaced by the AIM-120 AMRAAM, which can also be carried on wing racks.

Above: F-4G 'Wild Weasel' aircraft carrying AGM-88 and AGM-65 (near) and AGM-45 (far). Both have AIM-7 Sparrows for self-defense.

F-111s prefer to work at night whenever possible, the missiles are optional equipment. Clearance problems with the aircraft wings mean that short-winged missiles are carried on stations 3A and 6A, mounted halfway up the outside of the outboard pylons. The 'go to war' missile used for this purpose is the AIM-9P-3. AIM-9L/M missiles can be carried on launchers mounted on the bottom of the pylons. With the exception of GBU-12s, PGMs preclude use of stations 3A and 6A for AIM-9 carriage.

The mission of F-111s is to attack targets deep (for a tactical scenario) in enemy territory, so maximum range is usually a mission requirement. For this reason up to four of the following low-drag, pylon-mounted stores are often carried: Mk 84 LDGP, Mk 84 AIR, SUU-64, SUU-65, GBU-10, GBU-12, GBU-24. These loads are not normally mixed, although both Mk 84 LDGPs and GBU-10s have been used on inboard pylons with GBU-24s on outboard pylons. Paveway I versions of the GBU-10/12 are still occasionally used for training missions, although Paveway IIs are used in combat. Both Mk 84 and BLU-109 warhead versions of GBU-10/24s are used. Two GBU-15s are carried, always on the outboard pylons. Only F-111Fs carrying the AXQ-14 pod can guide these weapons. As noted above, when this happens the ECM pod is carried on the forward station (preventing use of the Pave Tack pod).

Two F-111Fs have employed the GBU-28 in combat and, of these, only the 495th TFS commander's aircraft, 70-2391, was successful. These aircraft mounted a single GBU-28 on the left outboard pylon and a Mk 84 LDGP (for ballast) on the right outboard pylon.

When bombs are carried on BRU-3s,

Right: The F-117 carries its weapons (mostly 2,000-lb LGBs) in an internal bay with extending pylons for easy fitment.

it is almost always on the outboard pylons, with the inboard pylons left empty. While each BRU-3 can carry six bombs, it is not unusual for four to be carried. When the BRU's bottom stations are empty, the load is called a 'flat four'; when the inboard stations are empty, it is a 'slant four'. Weapons normally carried on BRUs include: SUU-30H, Mk 20, Mk 82 (any version, but AIRs normally preferred), and BLU-107.

Only F-111Es and Fs carry 600-US gal (2270-liter) external fuel tanks, and only on the outboard pylons. As training aircraft, F-111Gs no longer carry these tanks. Operationally, fuel tanks would probably only be used in conjunction with B57 or B61 nuclear weapons on the inboard pylons.

EF-111As carry no operational stores.

F-117A (Lockheed Night Hawk)

Operationally, F-117As have been used primarily to delivery Paveway II GBU-10 and Paveway III GBU-27 LGBs with both Mk 84 and BLU-109 warheads. Although they can carry Paveway II GBU-12s, it is not clear that this was actually done during Operation Desert Storm. Carriage of the B61 and B83 may also be possible.

A-7D (Vought Corsair II)

For the Air Force, the A-7 has been primarily a close air support asset. The aircraft have three pylons on each wing, as well as two fuselage pylons for carriage of AIM-9s. All USAF Sidewinders have been carried, including the current AIM-9L/M. A-7Ds are equipped with a nose-mounted M61 Vulcan cannon.

The right outboard pylon appears to be the primary ECM pod location. The

Above: The F-15E usually carries its weapons on stub pylons attached to the strap-on conformal fuel tanks.

Below: The F-16 ADF version in service with the ANG interceptor fleet can fire the AIM-7 Sparrow.

current pod is the ALQ-119(V)-17. The left outboard pylon is usually left empty, but can also be used for ECM or MXU-648 baggage pod carriage. The inboard pylons are normally used for the 300-US gal (1136-liter) external fuel tanks. However, the AAR-45 LANA pod can be mounted on the right inboard pylon of aircraft equipped to use it. The middle pylons are normally equipped with TERs carrying a mix of Mk 82 (all versions), Mk 20, SUU-30, SUU-64 or SUU-65.

Multiple ejector racks (MERs) were used during Vietnam and can still be carried. However, they would not often be found in a modern combat scenario where their use would seriously degrade the maneuverability of the aircraft.

There are Vietnam War-vintage photos of A-7Ds carrying Mk 84 LDGPs on the four inboard pylons, but it is doubtful this capability has been exploited to carry LGBs. Unlike Navy A-7s, Air Force aircraft do not employ Shrikes, HARMs, Walleyes or other PGMs.

F-4G (McDonnell Douglas Phantom II)

ALQ-184(V)-1 (37th TFW) or deep ALQ-131 (52nd TFW) ECM pods are carried in the front-left missile well. If needed, AIM-7Fs can be carried in the aft missile wells. F-4Gs seldom, if ever, carry AIM-9 Sidewinders. All F-4Gs now use only the F-15's 600-US gal (2271-liter) centerline fuel tank. Fuel tanks of 370-US gal (1400-liter) capacity are usually carried on the outboard pylons.

Primary ordnance carriage on F-4Gs is on the inboard pylons. Weapons include: AGM-88 HARMs mounted on LAU-118 launcher (while the normal load is two, up to four have been carried using all four wing pylons); AGM-45 Shrikes mounted on either the LAU-34 or LAU-118 (this is not the preferred weapon and would probably be used only if stocks of AGM-88s ran low); or AGM-65 Mavericks mounted on either triple-rail LAU-88s or single-rail LAU-117s. The old AGM-78 Standard ARM has been retired.

F-15A/B/C/D (McDonnell Douglas Eagle)

All F-15s are equipped with an internally-mounted M61 Vulcan cannon. Three 600-US gal (2271-liter) fuel tanks are carried on the fuselage centerline and wing pylons. Although Eagles were originally designed with two additional wing pylons for carriage of ALQ-119(V)-12 (long) ECM pods, they were never used because of their adverse effect on aircraft handling. F-15A/B/Ds have rarely, if ever, been known to carry centerline-mounted ECM pods, and F-15Cs are equipped with the internal ALQ-135 ECM system.

Four AIM-9 Sidewinders are mounted to the sides of the wing pylons on LAU-114 launchers. Although the AIM-9J/P versions can be carried, the normal complement is the later AIM-9L/M series.

Four AIM-7F/M Sparrows are mounted to the 'corner' fuselage stations. Eagles never carried the older AIM-7Es. AIM-120A AMRAAMs will eventually replace the Sparrow. However, since it is lighter than the older missile, the AIM-120 can also be rail-mounted on LAU-114 launchers. In fact, this was how the missile was first carried into combat on 33rd TFW F-15Cs during the Gulf War.

During the early 1980s, F-15C/Ds assigned to the 1st TFW at Langley AFB, Virginia, were given a Rapid Deployment Force mission which resulted in them being equipped with conformal fuel tanks (CFTs) and MER-200 bomb racks for a secondary air-to-ground mission. They were probably trained to employ Mk 82 and Mk 84 LDGP bombs, as well as Mk 20 and SUU-30 cluster bombs. In any event, this tasking was eventually removed and it is believed the CFTs and MER-200s were sold to Saudi Arabia.

F-15E (McDonnell Douglas Strike Eagle)

F-15Es retain all the air-to-air capabilities of older Eagles but, with a range capability falling between the F-111 and F-16, are mainly intended for interdiction missions. During the Gulf War they were used almost exclusively at night.

Although the wing and centerline pylons are cleared for weapon carriage, they are primarily used to mount three 600-US gal (2271-liter) fuel tanks. AIM-9L/Ms mounted to the wing pylons on LAU-114s are standard, as are LANTIRN pods. The AAQ-13 navigation pod is mounted on the right inlet station, while the optional AAQ-14 targeting pod is mounted on the left.

CFTs are a standard configuration item for F-15Es. Although the Strike Eagle demonstrator aircraft was equipped with MER-200 bomb racks, these were deleted on production aircraft in favor of pylons mounted on the CFTs. Up to 12 bombs can be carried in this way, with the following configurations noted during the Gulf

War: 12 each of Mk 82 LDGP, Mk 20, SUU-30H, SUU-64 or SUU-65; eight each of GBU-12 Paveway II LGBs on front and back, top and bottom stations; four each of GBU-10 Paveway II LGBs, with Mk 84 warheads, on front and back, bottom stations. Some F-15Es were also seen armed with AIM-7F/Ms or a mixed load of two Sparrows on the left side of the fuselage and six Mk 20s on the right. These loads were probably used in an attempt to shoot down 'Scud' missiles soon after launch. Other stores authorized for carriage, but not noted during the Gulf War, include: 12 each of Mk 82 SE or Mk 82 AIR; six each of AGM-65A/B/D Mavericks mounted on LAU-88s carried on wing pylons; four each of Mk 84 LDGP or Mk 84 AIR on front and back, bottom stations; three each of GBU-24 Paveway III LGBs or B61 nuclear bombs mounted on wing and centerline pylons; two each of GBU-15(V)-1/2 on wing pylons with AXQ-14 on centerline.

Stores which will undoubtedly become a standard part of the F-15E's arsenal in the near future include AGM-65Gs from LAU-117s, BLU-109 versions of already authorized PGMs, the GBU-28 and the AGM-130.

F-16A/B/C/D (General Dynamics Fighting Falcon)

The standard F-16 combat configuration noted during the Gulf War was the internal M61 Vulcan cannon, two wingtip-mounted AIM-9L/Ms, two 370-US gal (1400-liter) fuel tanks mounted on the inboard wing pylons, and either an ALQ-119(V)-15 (US-based units) or deep ALQ-131 (Europe-based units) ECM pods. Early in the war, two additional AIM-9L/Ms were sometimes carried on the outboard wing pylons. This left the center wing pylons available for bombs, including: pylon-mounted Mk 84 LDGP, Mk 84 AIR, SUU-64, AGM-65A/B/D on LAU-117s, AGM-45 or AGM-88 on LAU-118s ('Wild Weasels' only); six TER-mounted Mk 82 LDGPs or Mk 20s, or four slant-two SUU-30H, SUU-64 or SUU-65. On some missions it was possible to remove the fuel tanks and carry four Mk 84s.

F-16As from the 174th FW are a trial F-16 close air support unit. As such, they are the only F-16s equipped with the GPU-5 30-mm gun pod. The GPU-5 is carried on the centerline, with the ALQ-119 moved to one wing pylon and an LAU-117-mounted AGM-65D on the other.

Block 42 F-16Cs are capable of mounting LANTIRN pods. The AAQ-13 is mounted on the left chin station with the AAQ-14 mounted on the right, the reverse of the F-15E installation.

Other authorized stores include Mk 82 AIR, Mk 82 SE, AGM-65G, GBU-10/12/24 LGBs and B61 nuclear bombs. While LAU-88s are authorized for AGM-65A/B/Ds, they reduce aircraft range so much that their use in combat is very unlikely.

USAF Air Bases

Below is an alphabetical review of the USAF's bases, both at home and overseas. Included are the smaller Air National Guard and Air Force Reserve facilities attached to civilian airfields, and the major non-aircraft operating facilities. Several of these bases are due for imminent closure as part of the general force reduction, and all are subject to change as the USAF completes its radical reorganization.

Since 1944 Andersen AFB on Guam has been associated with heavy bombers, starting life as a B-29 base for the campaign against Japan, and later being the primary B-52 base during the Vietnam conflict. Although the B-52 unit there was deactivated in 1990, the base still hosts detachments from bomber units such as the 96th Wing, which sent this B-1B.

RAF Alconbury, UK

Command: USAFE
Major unit: 10th SW to 628th SW (see text)
Tenant unit: 9th Wing U-2R (ACC)
Location and origin of name: three miles northwest of Huntingdon, and named for nearby village

Base opened in 1938 with US forces in residence from September 1942. The base was administered by 7560th ABG, with the 86th BS operating the B-45 from 1955 as a satellite of the 47th BW at RAF Sculthorpe, Norfolk, until the end of the year. In August 1959 the 10th TRW moved here from Spangdahlem AB. Although wing headquarters was located at Alconbury, the 19th TRS was stationed at RAF Bruntingthorpe with the 42 TRS at RAF Chelveston. However, following the closure of the other two bases, the 10th consolidated its squadrons at Alconbury. The wing operated the RB-66 until May 1965 when it began conversion to the RF-4C. The wing gradually reduced complement to just one squadron of Phantoms before adding an aggressor role with the formation of the 527th TFTAS in April 1976. Most USAFE squadrons deployed to Alconbury for aggressor training until July 1988 when the 527th relocated to RAF Bentwaters. The wing became the 10th TFW in August 1987 with two squadrons of A-10As relocating from the 81st TFW. However, the rundown of USAFE units resulted in the A-10s being withdrawn in late 1991/early 1992 with the 10th becoming a Support Wing prior to changing designation to 628th SW later in 1992. Europe-based Special Operations forces began moving to Alconbury from RAF Woodbridge and Rhein Main AB during 1992. SAC began operations from Alconbury in October 1982 when the 17th RW was formed to operate the TR-1A. However, a realignment of reconnaissance assets resulted in the wing inactivating during 1991 with assets reassigned to the 9th SRW (later 9th Wing).

Altus AFB, Oklahoma

Command: AMC
Major unit: 443rd AW C-5B, C-141B
Tenant units: 340th Wg KC-135R (AMC), ACE det 71st FTW T-37B (ATC)
Location and origin of name: adjacent to the northeast suburbs of the city of the same name

Formerly known as Altus Army Airfield until closed May 1945. Reopened March 1953 under TAC control with the 63rd Troop Carrier Wing in residence. 96th BW assigned in November 1953 and transferred to SAC in June 1954. Various other SAC units stationed until July 1968 when the base came under MAC control. 443rd MAW took up residence in May 1969 followed by 340th ARG in July 1977. Facility conducts C-5 and C-141 aircrew training as well as conventional airlift duties.

Andersen AFB, Guam

Command: PACAF
Major unit: HQ 13th AF/633rd ABW – no aircraft assigned
Tenant unit: 605th MASS no aircraft assigned (AMC)
Location and origin of name: two miles north of Yigo, and named after General James Roy Andersen, Chief of Staff, HQ Army Air Forces Pacific Ocean, lost at sea between Kwajalein and Hawaii on 26 February 1946

Base opened late 1944 and was later a major SAC base supporting B-52 and KC-135 operations during the Vietnam War. Base operated by the 3960th Strategic Wing until April 1970 when replaced by the 43rd Strategic Wing. B-52Ds assigned to 60th BS until upgraded to B-52G, with the wing deactivated in April 1990. Facility now supports Joint Typhoon Warning Center. HQ 13th Air Force moved to Andersen AFB from Clark AB during 1991.

Andrews AFB, Maryland

Command: AMC
Major unit: 89th AW C-12F, C-20B/C, C-21A, VC-25A, C-135B, C-137B/C, UH-1N
Tenant units: det 1 4950th TW C-21A, C-135C (AFMC); 113th FW F-16A/B (ANG); det 1 113th FW C-22B/C (ANG); 459th AW C-141B (AFRes); plus US Navy and Marine Corps squadrons
Location and origin of name: 11 miles southeast of Washington DC, and named for Lieutenant General Frank M. Andrews, World War II Commander of European theater, killed in a B-24 accident in Iceland on 3 May 1943

Previously titled Camp Springs Air Base when opened in September 1942 and later an Army Air Field before changing to Andrews Field in February 1945. Administered by MATS in November 1948, Bolling Field Command in April 1949, MATS again in August 1952 and Bolling Field Command for the second time in October 1957 (redesignated Headquarters Command in March 1958). Finally transferred to MAC in July 1976. Housed VIP units for most of its career including 1401st Flight Operations Group from August 1952, 1254th Air Transport Wing in July 1961 and 89th MAW January 1966. HQ MATS in residence from December 1958 until moved to Scott AFB in January 1958. HQ Air Research and Development Command (later HQ AFSC) assigned in January 1958.

Ankara AS, Turkey

Joint Turkish/USAFE facility located near the city of Ankara and operated by 7217th ABG to support transit US military aircraft. The base has HQ TUSLOG, Turkey/US Logistics Group, in residence as headquarters for US activities in Turkey.

Arnold AFB, Tennessee

AFMC facility located seven miles southeast of Manchester housing the Arnold Engineering Development Center with a large complex of wind tunnels and rocket/jet engine test cells. Named after General Hap Arnold, wartime chief of the AAF.

Atlantic City IAP, New Jersey

Located 10 miles west of Atlantic City with the 177th FG operating the Air Defense Fighter version of the F-16A/B by the New Jersey ANG.

Aviano AB, Italy

Command: USAFE
Major unit: 40th SW – no aircraft assigned
Tenant unit: US Army helicopter unit
Location and origin of name: south of town of the same name

Originally an Italian flying school when opened in 1939. US forces stationed at Aviano since 1955 when the 7207th ABS was formed to administer the base which was used by USAFE squadrons on temporary assignment. The 40th Tactical Group was formed in April 1966. A US Army CH-47D unit is in residence but no USAF aircraft are assigned, although the facility is a strategically important transit base for USAFE aircraft staging from Germany and the UK to central and eastern Mediterranean bases. The 401st TFW regularly deployed squadrons to Aviano until the wing ceased flying during the latter half of 1991. However, the wing is believed to have moved from Torrejon to Aviano in name only pending a final decision being made as to its future. Aviano provided facilities for numerous aircraft deploying to and from the USA for Desert Shield/Desert Storm.

Avon Park AFS, Florida

Small Air Force Station operated by ACC and located at the bombing range of the same name in central Florida.

Bangor ANGB, Maine

Bangor IAP is four miles northwest of the city with the KC-135E assigned to the 101st ARW Maine ANG. The 158th FG Vermont ANG maintains an alert detachment here, while the Army National Guard has a small presence.

Barksdale AFB, Louisiana

Command: ACC
Major unit: HQ 8th Air Force, 2nd Wg B-52G, KC-10A, KC-135A/Q
Tenant units: det 3 1401st AS C-21A (AMC); ACE det 14th FTW T-38A (ATC); 917th FW A-10A (AFRes); 98th ARG (Associate) KC-10A (AFRes)
Location and origin of name: located in the suburbs of Bosier City and named after Lieutenant Eugene H. Barksdale, World War I airman killed in a Douglas O-2 observation aircraft accident near Wright Field in August 1926

Established in November 1930 with various pursuit units assigned until World War II, when the base conducted training of replacement aircrew of entire groups destined for overseas service. After the war the base was operated by Air Training Command with the Pilot Instructor School among the units in residence. The 47th BW was stationed at Barksdale briefly from November 1948, with the base becoming a SAC installation in November 1949. Other SAC units at Barksdale included the 91st SRW for two years from October 1949, 301st BW from November 1949 until April 1958, and 376th BW from October 1951. Between them these units operated the B-29 and later the B-47 plus the KC-97 tanker. In addition, a variety of reconnaissance types was located, ensuring the huge flight line was packed with SAC aircraft. The 2nd BW was assigned from April 1963, while Continental Air Command's 917th TCG was in residence from December 1962, although CONAC squadrons were stationed from February 1959. Headquarters 8th Air Force was relocated from Andersen AFB, Guam, in January 1975.

Barnes MAP, Westfield, Massachusetts

Barnes MAP is three miles north of Westfield with the 104th FG flying the A-10A of the Massachusetts ANG.

Beale AFB, California

Command: ACC
Major unit: 9th Wg KC-135Q, T-38A, U-2R/RT; HQ 2nd Air Force (ACC)
Tenant unit: nil
Location and origin of name: 13 miles east of Marysville, and named in honor of Brigadier General Edward F. Beale, Californian pioneer and founder of the US Army Camel Corps

Constructed as Camp Beale and opened in October 1942. Transferred to the Air Force in November 1948 initially for Air Training Command until April 1951 when reassigned to Continental Air Command. In July 1956 SAC took over the base, which was left dormant until 1958 when the runway was constructed. The first aircraft arrived in July 1959 when KC-135As were assigned to 4126th Strategic Wing. B-52s were added later, with the 456th SAW replacing the 4126th from February 1963. The wing flew the B-52G and KC-135A until September 1975 when the unit was replaced by the 17th BW. The 4200th Strategic Wing was stationed from January 1965 to prepare for the arrival of the first operational SR-71s one year later. The 9th SRW replaced the 4200th SW in June 1966 and added the U-2R in 1976, followed by the TR-1A. Huge PAVE PAWS surface-launched ballistic missile detection system became operational in July 1979. Headquarters 2nd Air Force activated in September 1991 to control all SAC reconnaissance assets.

RAF Bentwaters, UK

Command: USAFE
Major unit: 81st TFW A-10A
Tenant unit: nil
Location and origin of name: six miles northeast of Woodbridge, and named for a local landmark

Base operated by the RAF from 1944 and made available for US forces in 1951. The 81st FIW moved to Bentwaters in September 1951, although the 116th FIS (a mobilized ANG squadron attached to the 81st) equipped with the F-86A preceded the parent wing by one month and was stationed at RAF Shepherd's Grove, Suffolk, while the 92nd FIS was located at RAF Manston. The 116th FIS returned to state control in November 1952 and was replaced by the 78th FIS. The latter unit moved to Woodbridge when Shepherd's Grove closed in 1957 and the 92nd transferred to Bentwaters. Subsequently, the wing HQ remained at Bentwaters while exercising control over the twin bases. The F-86A was replaced by the F-84F, F-101A/C, F-4C/D and most recently the A-10A. The 81st TFW began retiring the A-10 during 1992, with the first aircraft returning to the USA in January for a six-week Air Warrior exercise, prior to the aircraft re-equipping other units. The re-equipment program was due to be completed by March 1993, enabling the wing to inactivate and the base to close.

Bergstrom AFB, Texas

Command: ACC
Major unit: HQ 12th Air Force; 67th RW RF-4C
Tenant units: HQ 10th Air Force (AFRes); 924th TFG

Beale has been associated with strategic reconnaissance since the mid-1960s, and is now headquarters for the USAF's U-2R fleet. The barns in the background used to house SR-71s.

F-16C/D (AFRes)
Location and origin of name: seven miles southeast of Austin, and named after Captain John A. Bergstrom, an administrative officer killed 8 December 1941 during Japanese attack on Clark Field, becoming the first serviceman from Austin to die in World War II

Established as Del Valle Airfield in September 1942 but renamed Bergstrom Army Air Field six months later. Originally intended to teach photographic and observation training, the base was, however, primarily involved in troop carrier operations. Administered by TAC from March 1946, but transferred to Continental Air Command and SAC before reverting to TAC usage in July 1966. The 27th FW (later 27th Fighter Escort Wing) was stationed in 1949/1950 and again from 1951 until 1959 operating the F-51, F-84 and later the F-101A/C, plus the KB-29P tanker. SAC's 4130th Strategic Wing based from October 1958 until replaced by the 340th BW in September 1963 when TAC activated the 75th TRW as the RF-4C replacement training unit, and the Tactical Control Group without aircraft assignment initially. The latter subsequently became a flying unit with the O-2 assigned. The 75th inactivated in July 1971 when replaced by the 67th TRW (later 67th RW). The reduction in requirement of tactical reconnaissance operations has seen the wing shrink from four squadrons to just one, with the 67th RW due to inactivate in September 1992 with the base closing one year later.

Birmingham MAP, Alabama

Located in the northeast suburbs of Birmingham with the 117th RW flying the RF-4C of the Alabama ANG. In addition there is an Army National Guard unit, while nearby is the Pemco Aeroplex facility which conducts maintenance of C-130s and C-135s.

Bitburg AB, Germany

Command: USAFE
Major unit: 36th FW F-15C/D
Tenant unit: nil
Location and origin of name: adjacent to town of same name

Base activated in 1952 when 36th Fighter-Bomber Wing moved from Fürstenfeldbrück AB with the F-84E. F-86F operated from 1953 until 1956 when the wing converted to the F-100C, reforming the 'Skyblazers' aerobatic team for six seasons. The wing was responsible for operations at nearby Spangdahlem between 1969 and 1971. Base deployed the majority of its aircraft and personnel to Turkey and Saudi Arabia for Desert Shield/Desert Storm, gaining 17 aerial victories.

Boise Air Terminal (Gowen Field), Idaho

The Air Terminal is six miles west of Boise with the 124th RG Idaho ANG in residence flying the RF-4C in the replacement training role, but is currently transitioning to the F-4G. An Army National Guard unit is a tenant operating a sizeable number of helicopters.

Bolling AFB, District of Columbia

Command: AMC
Major unit: 1100th ABG – no aircraft assigned
Tenant unit: nil
Location and origin of name: southeast of Washington DC, south of the confluence of the Potomac and Anacostia Rivers. Named for Colonel Raynal C. Bolling, assistant chief of the Air Service killed near Amiens, France, on 26 March 1918 in exchange of fire on the ground with German soldiers

One of the oldest flying establishments in the USA, the base was constructed beginning in May 1918, becoming Bolling Field two months later. Accommodated flying proficiency operations for the Washington area, extending throughout the 1920s and 1930s. Upgraded shortly before World War II as a protective base for the vicinity of Washington, as well as training aircrews destined for combat operations overseas. Additionally, the base was the main facility for air transportation of senior military and political figures until 1945, when this function moved to the larger base at Andrews. Flight operations markedly reduced after World War II when mission changed from flying to administration and support. VIP helicopter operations continued until September 1968 when the last flying squadron relocated to Andrews AFB.

Bradley ANGB/Bradley IAP, Connecticut

Bradley ANGB is adjacent to the International Airport which is 15 miles north of Hartford at East Granby. The A-10As of the 103rd FG Maryland ANG are in residence along with an Army National Guard battalion.

Brooks AFB, Texas

Command: AFMC
Major unit: 6570th ABG, Human Systems Division and School of Aerospace Medicine (AFMC) – no aircraft assigned
Tenant unit: nil
Location and origin of name: southeast of San Antonio, named for Cadet Sidney Brooks who was killed at Kelly Field on 13 November 1917 when his Curtiss JN-4 nosed down on landing. He was posthumously awarded his wings and commission

Established February 1918 as a satellite of Kelly Field, and named Brooks Field housing a balloon and airship school, and a primary flying school. School of Aerospace Medicine moved here from New York in 1926. Conducted observation training and the Air Corps Advanced Flying School during the early 1940s. Limited flight operations continued after World War II, including pilot training and troop carrier, until June 1960 when all flying activities ceased. Subsequently the base has concentrated on aviation medicine and all manner of health matters for the Air Force.

Buckley ANGB, Colorado

Located eight miles east of Denver with the 140th FW Colorado ANG, currently converting from

the A-7D/K to the F-16C/D. Detachment 1 has four CT-43As to train ANG navigators and provide transportation duties. An Army National Guard unit is also stationed at Buckley along with non-flying Naval Reserve and Marine Corps Reserve squadrons. Buckley is close to the popular Colorado ski resorts and attracts a large number of visiting aircraft at weekends.

Burlington IAP, Vermont

Located three miles east of Burlington with the 158th FG operating Air Defense Fighter version of the F-16A/B by the Vermont ANG.

Byrd IAP, Richmond, Virginia

Byrd IAP is four miles southeast of Richmond and has the 192nd FG in residence, which recently completed conversion from the A-7D/K to the F-16C/D with the Virginia ANG. The facility is named in honor of polar explorer Admiral Richard E. Byrd.

Cannon AFB, New Mexico

Command: ACC
Major unit: 27th FW F-111D/G
Tenant unit: nil
Location and origin of name: seven miles west of Clovis, and named for General John K. Cannon who was air commander for the invasion of southern Europe in August 1944, and Commander-in-Chief, Allied Air Force in the Mediterranean Theater. Subsequently CinC USAFE and TAC until retired in 1954

Opened in late 1942 as a heavy bombardment training base during World War II and subsequently a processing center for personnel separating from service in 1945 and 1946. Base under ATC control from April 1950 until July 1951, when transferred to TAC. Housed ANG unit in 1951 and 1952 before tactical units took up residence, including the 37th Fighter-Bomber Wing briefly followed by 388th FBW, 312th FBW and 474th FBW, before the 27th TFW was assigned in February 1959. Wing converted from the F-100 to F-111D in 1969 and commenced upgrading to the F-111E/F and EF-111A during early 1992. Cannon AFB will be sole operational F-111 base by the middle of the decade.

Cape Canaveral AFS, Florida

Air Force Space Command site at the NASA facility primarily to support the launch of rockets and space shuttles containing US Air Force satellites. Operated as launch center by Eastern Space and Missile Center with headquarters at Patrick AFB.

Cape Cod AFS, Massachusetts

Facility jointly used as ballistic missile early warning system (BMEWS) and for the tracking of satellites. Operated by Air Force Space Command.

Capital Airport, Springfield, Illinois

Located two miles northwest of Springfield with the 183rd FG Illinois ANG flying the F-16A/B.

Carswell AFB, Texas

Command: ACC
Major unit: 7th Wing B-52H, KC-135A
Tenant unit: 301st FW F-16C/D (AFRes); ACE det 12th FTW T-37B (ATC)

Location and origin of name: two miles northwest of Fort Worth and named in honor of Major Horace S. Carswell, killed in a B-24 crash in the South China Sea near Tungchen, China, on 26 October 1944

Occupied from August 1942 for medium and heavy bomber training until 1945. Assigned to Continental Air Force in April 1945 (redesignated to SAC on 21 March 1946) with the 7th BW activated in November 1947 and currently still in residence. Other SAC units stationed at Carswell AFB have included the 11th BW between 1951 and 1960, 4123rd Strategic Wing from 1957 to 1959, and 403rd BW during 1960 and 1961. The 43rd BW was assigned between 1960 and 1964 as the combat crew training unit for the B-58 Hustler before the unit moved to Little Rock AFB. The unit was stationed at Carswell primarily because the huge Convair production line was located across the runway from Carswell AFB and the close location of the first unit would ease the transition to the revolutionary new bomber. The 340th BG was formed at Carswell in July 1968 to conduct a similar role for the FB-111A. The 7th BW operated the B-29 and B-36 before converting to the B-52F in 1957, and subsequently the B-52D and B-52H. The wing is scheduled to transfer its B-52s to the 2nd Wing by December 1992, with the unit inactivating early in 1993 and the base closing by September 1993.

Castle AFB, California

Command: ACC
Major unit: 93rd Wg B-52G, KC-135A/R
Tenant unit: ACE det 323rd FTW T-37B (ATC)
Location and origin of name: six miles northwest of Merced and named after Brigadier General Frederick W. Castle, killed on 25 December 1944 when shot down in a B-17 near Liège, Belgium

Constructed in 1941 as Air Corps Basic Flying School, Merced and later Merced Army Airfield before gaining its current name in January 1948. The primary duties were that of basic flying training and the Women's Air Service Pilot (WASP) advanced training during World War II. The 93rd BG was formed in June 1946, with the 93rd BW activating in August of the following year. Initially operated the B-29 and B-50 plus the KB-29P tanker before switching to the KC-97 in 1953 and B-47 in 1954. Converted to the B-52B in 1955 and commenced Stratofortress and KC-135 tanker aircrew training in 1956. Maintained an air defense commitment between 1955 and 1968 with the 456th FIS operating the F-106A, followed by the 84th FIS from September 1973 also flying the F-106A. Castle AFB is scheduled to close by September 1995 with the 93rd Wing inactivating after having transferred the bomber and tanker training commitment to the 92nd Wing.

Cavalier AFS, North Dakota

Operated by Air Force Space Command as an early warning site with the ballistic missile early warning system (BMEWS).

Channel Island ANGB, California

Channel Island ANGB is located in one corner of Naval Air Station Point Mugu which is eight miles from Camarillo. The facility is comparatively new as the C-130Es of the 146th AW California ANG only moved to the site from their former base at Van Nuys Airport in February 1989.

The F-111 fleet is concentrated at Cannon with the 27th Fighter Wing. This wing currently operates F-111Ds (illustrated) and Gs, but is receiving Es and Fs from UK bases.

Chanute AFB, Illinois

Command: ATC
Major unit: 3330th TTW (see text)
Tenant unit: nil
Location and origin of name: adjacent to southern Rantoul, and named after Octave Chanute, the pioneer aeronautical engineer and designer

Opened in 1917 and named Rantoul Aviation Field, before being renamed Chanute Field. Facility initially conducted pilot training during World War I before switching to that of a storage depot. Technical training introduced in February 1921 when the Air Service Mechanics School transferred from Kelly Field. Continued to conduct technical training during and after World War II with maintenance training for Thor, Bomarc and Hound Dog missiles added between 1958 and 1960. Employed numerous static airframes. However, the base was earmarked for closure with the duties of Chanute Technical Training Center dispersed to other ATC locations during 1991, with the base due to cease operating in October 1993.

Charleston AFB, South Carolina

Command: AMC
Major unit: 437th AW C-141B
Tenant units: 315th AW (Associate) C-141B (AFRes); det 1 107th FG F-16A/B ADF (NY ANG)
Location and origin of name: located in the northwest section of North Charleston and named after the adjacent city

Formerly Charleston MAP and occupied by the Army in 1942 as a training base for B-17 and B-24 aircrew and ground personnel. Subsequently conducted C-54 aircrew training. Assigned to Air Transport Command (ATC) after World War II as a terminus for C-54 flights to Europe and the Near East. Assigned to TAC from 1952 to 1955 when transferred to Military Air Transport Service (MATS). The 1608th Air Transport Wing was the primary unit at Charleston from March 1955 until January 1966, when MATS became MAC and most four-digit units were redesignated; the 1608th ATW became the 437th MAW. The C-141A was delivered in 1966 and the C-5A in 1970, although the latter type was transferred to 436th MAW in 1973. The base is currently preparing to become the first operational C-17A facility with deliveries scheduled to commence late in 1992.

Charlotte/Douglas IAP, North Carolina

Douglas IAP is to the west of Charlotte with the C-130Bs of the 145th AG North Carolina ANG. Apart from conventional airlift duties, the aircraft perform fire fighting duties and are marked with Dayglo orange areas during the summer and autumn 'dry season'.

Cheyenne MAP, Wyoming

Cheyenne MAP is located in the northern suburbs of the city with the 153rd AG Wyoming ANG in residence operating the C-130B. The unit performs a similar role to that of the C-130s based at Charlotte.

Cheyenne Mountain AFB, Colorado

Command: AFSPACECOM
Major unit: 3rd Space Support Wing – no aircraft assigned
Tenant unit: nil
Location and origin of name: six miles south of Colorado Springs and named after the mountain range in which the site is located

The facility was opened in 1966 as the nerve center of the North American Aerospace Defense Command (NORAD) command center and is now operated by US Space Command. The site is buried deep inside the Cheyenne Mountains and is manned by more than 1,400 personnel from the Army, Navy and Air Force, plus Canadian Forces and civilian technicians. US Space Command has no aircraft assigned and there are no facilities at Cheyenne Mountain AFB, as Peterson AFB is located nearby.

RAF Chicksands, UK

Facility operated by 7274th ABG of USAFE with an Electronic Security Wing and Group as part of AF Intelligence Command.

Unit markings carried by USAF aircraft often reflect their basing, this 93rd Wing KC-135R carrying a castle on the fin. Castle is currently a major training base, handling type conversion for both the KC-135 and B-52. The base is due for deactivation, with the training commitment passing to Fairchild.

Clark AB, Republic of the Philippines

Command: PACAF
Major unit: 3rd TFW (see text)
Tenant units: 353rd SOW (AFSOC); det 1 1403rd AS (AMC); HQ 13th Air Force (PACAF) (see text)
Location and origin of name: 65 miles north of Manila and named after Major Harold M. Clark, an early aviator raised in the Philippines who was killed in a seaplane accident at Miraflores Locks, Panama Canal Zone

The base was activated as Fort Stotsenberg in 1903 and was transferred from the Army to the Air Force in 1948. 405th FW activated at Clark AB in April 1959 to replace the 6200th ABW operating the F-100D and F-102A. During the Vietnam War the base was heavily involved providing support, as it was the closest permanent US installation to Vietnam. The 405th was assigned until September 1974 when it was replaced by the 3rd TFW. As part of an agreement between the US and Philippine governments the base at Clark was to be vacated by September 1992, although the explosion of Mount Pinatubo combined with the arrival of tropical storm Typhoon Yunya early on the morning of 15 June 1991 effectively ended operations. A thick deposit of ash rendered the base useless, and the AFSOC Hercules and helicopters, together with the based C-12F, were flown to NAS Cubi Point next day as a temporary measure. By coincidence, the last of the resident F-4E/Gs had been flown back to the USA just one week earlier. Subsequent evaluation of the damage revealed it to be very extensive and far beyond economical repair, so the base was vacated by the US earlier than planned. The facility was officially returned to the Philippine government on 26 November 1991, ending almost 90 years of US occupancy.

Columbus AFB, Mississippi

Command: ATC
Major unit: 14th FTW T-37B, T-38A
Tenant unit: nil
Location and origin of name: 10 miles northwest of town of same name

Established in 1941 as Air Corps Advanced Flying School Columbus and retitled several times to reflect the base's role before being named Columbus AFB in June 1948. Like numerous other bases located in the southern states, Columbus was a training facility conducting primary and basic flying education until 1955, when transferred to SAC with the 4228th Strategic Wing forming in July 1958 flying the B-52F and KC-135A. Unit redesignated 454th BW in February 1963 but inactivated in July 1969. Base transferred back to ATC in July 1969 although the 3650th Pilot Training Wing had formed five months earlier. Fighter pilot training commenced in 1969 with the 3650th PTW redesignated 14th FTW in June 1972.

NAS Dallas, Texas

NAS Dallas is to the southwest of Dallas between the city and Fort Worth, and is also known as Hensley Field. The 136th AW Texas ANG operates the C-130H from the base along with Naval and Marine Corps Reserve fighter squadrons and an Army National Guard unit. The NAS is adjacent to the huge LTV Corporation facility which housed the production lines for the F-8 Crusader and A-7 Corsair II.

Dannelly Field, Montgomery, Alabama

Dannelly Field is seven miles southwest of Montgomery with the 187th FG operating the F-16A/B of the Alabama ANG. The Alabama ARNG has a helicopter unit based at the same location. Field named for Ensign Clarence Dannelly, a Navy pilot killed in an accident at Pensacola, Florida, in World War II.

Davis-Monthan AFB, Arizona

Command: ACC
Major unit: 355th FW A-10A
Tenant units: 41st ECS EC-130E (ACC); 71st SOS CH-3E (AFRes); det 1 120th FG F-16A ADF (MT ANG); Aerospace Maintenance & Regeneration Center (AFLC)
Location and origin of name: located in the southwest suburbs of Tucson, and named in honor of Second Lieutenants Samuel H. Davis and Oscar Monthan. The former was killed in the crash of a Curtiss JN-6 on 28 December 1921 at Carlstrom Field, Arcadia, Florida, while the latter died on 27 March 1924 at Luke Field, Oahu, Hawaii, in the crash of a Martin NS-1 bomber. Both had attended high school in Tucson

Formerly Tucson and renamed Davis-Monthan landing field in November 1925 with a small Army presence to handle and service the frequent visiting military aircraft. Upgraded during the early 1940s to enable bomber aircrew training to be conducted, initially with the B-24 and later the B-29. Immediately after World War II the base was one of many southern locations which were employed to store surplus aircraft, with Davis-Monthan housing the largest concentration of B-29s and C-47s. The arid weather conditions prevailing were found to be ideal for long-term storage, with the base expanding to accommodate and dispose of retired US military aircraft. Base operated by Air Technical Service Command from November 1945 until transferred to SAC in March 1946. Housed several bomber units including 43rd and 303rd BWs flying B-29s and B-50s, and later the B-47 and KC-97 until 1960 and 1964, respectively; 390th SMW equipped with Titan II missiles in January 1962; followed by 4080th SRW operating the U-2 in June 1963. 4453rd CCTW activated in July 1964 to train TAC F-4C aircrew. Military Aircraft Storage and Disposition Center (MASDC) formed in February 1965 to process surplus aircraft, helicopters and missiles from all branches of the Department of Defense. More recently renamed Aerospace Maintenance & Regeneration Center (AM&RC). 4080th SRW replaced by 100th SRW in June 1966. Drone operations conducted by both SAC and TAC, but consolidated under the 432nd TDG in July 1976. 355th TFW replaced the 4453rd CCTW in July 1971 to conduct A-7 aircrew training until 1976, when the unit switched to A-10A training. EC-130H squadron assigned in July 1980 and 602nd TACW (later 602nd ACW) for forward air controller operations added in September 1982. Base consolidated operations under 355th FW by the spring of 1992, with the 602nd ACW inactivating.

Decimomannu AB, Sardinia

USAFE operation located at the large Italian Air Base on Sardinia which conducts air combat maneuvering and dissimilar air combat training for NATO forces. Administered by det 4 of the 40th SW.

Des Moines MAP, Iowa

Des Moines MAP is adjacent to the city of the same name and houses the 132nd FW Iowa ANG flying the A-7D/K.

Dobbins AFB, Georgia

Dobbins AFB is two miles south of Marietta and is an AFRes base with the 94th AW operating the C-130H. In addition, the 116th FW Georgia ANG flies the F-15A/B, while co-located are US Army Reserve and Naval Reserve units. Located on the same site is the huge Lockheed Aeronautical Systems Company with the C-130 Hercules production line, which is known by the Air Force as Plant 6. The base was named after Captain Charles Dobbins, who was killed near Sicily during World War II.

Dover AFB, Delaware

Command: AMC
Major unit: 436th AW C-5A/B
Tenant unit: 512th AW (Associate) C-5A/B (AFRes)
Location and origin of name: three miles southeast of town of the same name

Occupied since 1941 and initially known as Municipal Airport, Dover Airdrome before being renamed Dover AFB January 1948. Conducted anti-submarine warfare operations in 1942/1943 and trained P-47 aircrew from 1943. Assigned to TAC April 1946 but without a flying commitment and transferred to Continental Air Command December 1948. Intercept duties began in August 1950 with the base under ADC control between January 1951 and April 1952, when transferred to MATS. Upgraded with air freight terminal for transatlantic operations. 1607th ATW formed January 1954 with the C-54 and later the C-124C and C-133A. Replaced by 436th MAW January 1966 with C-141A assigned followed by the C-5A in 1971, although the StarLifters were relocated elsewhere in 1973. The C-5A was joined by the C-5B in 1986.

Duluth IAP, Minnesota

The International Airport is five miles northwest of Duluth and houses the 148th FG Minnesota ANG with the F-16A/B ADF.

Duke Field, Florida

Duke Field is one of several facilities located within the Eglin complex and is near Valparaiso. The field, which is also known as Eglin Air Force Auxiliary number 3, is an AFRes facility with AC-130As of the 919th SOG.

Dyess AFB, Texas

Command: ACC
Major unit: 96th Wg B-1B, KC-135A
Tenant units: 463rd AW C-130H (MAC); ACE det 12th FTW T-38A (ATC)
Location and origin of name: three miles southwest of Abilene, and named after Lieutenant Colonel William E. Dyess who was caught by the Japanese on Bataan in April 1942 and escaped one year later. After fighting with guerrilla forces in Mindanao he was repatriated to the USA and commenced flight retraining. On 23 December 1943 his P-38 caught fire over Burbank, California, and he was killed when he guided the stricken aircraft away from a populated area

Established as Abilene Army Air Base in December 1942 as a fighter pilot training facility during World War II until closed in 1945. Assigned to SAC from October 1953 and prepared for bomber and tanker operations with the 341st BW taking up residence in September 1955 flying the B-47E and KC-97G. The 96th BW moved to Dyess from Altus AFB in September 1957 and became the major SAC unit when the 341st moved to Malm-

strom AFB in June 1961. 96th BW upgraded to B-52 in 1963. Cargo operations began in February 1961 with the assignment of the 64th TCW, which was replaced by the 516th TCW in January 1963. Became first operational B-1B base when 96th BW commenced deliveries in June 1985.

Eaker AFB, Arkansas

Command: ACC
Major unit: 97th Wg B-52G, KC-135A
Tenant unit: ACE det 14th FTW T-37B (ATC)
Location and origin of name: two miles northwest of Blytheville, and named after General Ira C. Eaker, aviation pioneer and commander of the 8th Air Force in World War II

Established as Blytheville Army Airfield June 1942 and later Blytheville AFB until taking up its current name in 1988. Conducted flying training duties including advanced and instrument training. Later changed to women transport pilots and troop-carrier combat crew training before base closed at the end of World War II. Reactivated under TAC control June 1953 but transferred briefly to Air Material Command from October 1953 until July 1954 when TAC gained the base again. B-57s operated by 461st BW from 1955 until 1958, when reassigned to SAC in April 1958, with the 97th BW moving from Biggs AFB, TX, in July 1959 with the B-52G. The KC-135A was added in 1961. The 97th BW is scheduled to inactivate during 1992 with the B-52s being retired and its KC-135s redistributed prior to the base closing in September 1993.

Edwards AFB, California

Command: AFMC
Major unit: Air Force Flight Test Center and 6510th TW with a wide variety of types (see unit listing)
Tenant units: USAF Astronautics Laboratory (AFMC); US Army Engineering Flight Activity with various test helicopters and fixed-wing types; NASA Ames Dryden Flight Research Facility also with a mix of aircraft and helicopters
Location and origin of name: 20 miles east of Rosamond, and named in honor of test pilot Captain General G. W. Edwards, killed 5 June 1948 in crash of Northrop YB-49 flying wing near Muroc

Established as Muroc Lake Bombing and Gunnery Range in September 1933 as a range for aircrew stationed at March Field, and retitled several times retaining the Muroc lineage until December 1949, when the name Edwards AFB was applied. The range continued to host locally-based bomber and fighter units during World War II, although the remoteness and settled weather conditions attracted the Army Air Force to begin flight testing in 1946. The Air Force Flight Test Center (AFFTC) was formally established in June 1951 with the Experimental Flight Test Pilots School (later AF Test Pilots School) added in January 1953. Numerous test and evaluation squadrons, groups and wings have been formed to enable the AFFTC to expand and contract its operations according to the needs of the Air Force. The 6510th TW is the current flight organization and was formed in March 1978, although it had previously existed in Group and ABW status since June 1951.

Eglin AFB, Florida

Command: AFMC
Major unit: Air Force Development Test Center and 3246th TW with a wide variety of types (see unit listing)
Tenant units: 33rd FW F-15C/D (ACC); Air Warfare Center/4485th TS RF-4C, F-15A/B/C, F-16A/B/C/D (ACC); 1st SOW HC-130N/P, MH-60G (AFSOC); det 4 1402nd AS C-21A (AMC)

Location and origin of name: two miles southwest of the twin towns of Niceville and Valparaiso, and named after Lieutenant Colonel Frederick I. Eglin, killed on 1 January 1937 in the crash of a Northrop A-17 pursuit aircraft while assigned to the General Headquarters, Army Air Force

Established in 1935 as Valparaiso Bombing and Gunnery Base and changed to Eglin Field in 1944 to encompass the entire Proving Ground area including 10 auxiliary fields and hundreds of thousands of acres of ranges. Assigned to AAF Proving Ground Command April 1942, becoming the second-largest AAF installation after Wendover Bombing Range, Utah. Air Proving Ground Command formed July 1948 as forerunner of today's AF Armament Division. Climatic Laboratory opened May 1947. Air Material Armament Test Center established December 1949. Overwater Eglin Gulf Test Range covering 15,000 square miles opened January 1961 followed by the Special Air Warfare Center the following year. Air Rescue operations began in January 1955 initially with the 48th ARS and eventually the Aerospace Rescue and Recovery Center, which has an indirect connection to the AFSOC units currently in residence. The Tactical Air Warfare Center (TAWC – later AWC) was established November 1963 as liaison between the test phase of weapons evaluation and their operational employment. The 4485th TS was formed as the Center's flying unit in April 1971. The 33rd TFW moved from Otis AFB, MA, in April 1965. SAC operations at Eglin were restricted to the 4135th Strategic Wing equipped with the B-52G but without tankers and stationed between December 1958 and February 1963, when replaced by the 39th BW until inactivated in February 1965.

Eielson AFB, Alaska

Command: PACAF
Major unit: 343rd Wg OA-10A, F-16C/D
Tenant units: 6th Wg RC-135S/X, TC-135S (ACC); 168th ARG KC-135D/E (ANG)
Location and origin of name: 26 miles southeast of Fairbanks, and named after Colonel Carl B. Eielson, an Alaskan pioneer who was killed 9 November 1929 in crash of a Hamilton airplane while attempting a rescue of crewman on a schooner off the Siberian North Cape

Opened in 1943 as Mile 26 Satellite Field due to its location from Fairbanks and renamed Eielson AFB January 1948. Assigned to AAF Transport Command and initially a satellite to Ladd Field, but closed in June 1945. Reopened under Alaskan Air Command control September 1946 and became independent the following year as a winter training facility for units in temporary residence. Upgraded in the mid-1950s to provide facilities for SAC bombers and tankers staging through on global missions. Major SAC presence began July 1960 when 4157th Combat Support Group, later Strategic Wing, was formed. Unit replaced by 6th Strategic Wing March 1967 with the primary role of strategic reconnaissance, employing a variety of RC-135s including RC-135S Cobra Ball and RC-135X Cobra Eye. Tactical operations commenced in 1971 and were expanded with the activation of the 343rd Composite Wing in October 1981. 6th Wing to deactivate in 1992 with aircraft reassigned to 55th Wing control.

Eldorado AFS, Texas

Operated by Air Force Space Command ballistic missile early warning system (BMEWS).

The prototype B-2 wheels over the vast USAF and NASA test base at Edwards, which has extensive runways marked out on Rogers Dry Lake.

Ellington ANGB, Texas

Ellington ANGB is 17 miles southeast of Houston and adjacent to City of Houston Airport. The facility was formerly an Air Force Base. The 147th FG Texas ANG operates the F-16A/B ADF, while also resident are an Army National Guard facility and a US Coast Guard station. In addition, NASA operates the Lyndon B. Johnson Space Center nearby with a large number of aircraft stationed at Ellington. Base named for Lieutenant Eric L. Ellington, a pioneer pilot killed in November 1913.

Ellsworth AFB, South Dakota

Command: ACC
Major unit: 28th Wg B-1B, KC-135R, EC-135A/C/G/H/L
Tenant units: 44th SMW LGM-30F (ACC); 99th Wg – no aircraft assigned (ACC); ACE det 64th FTW T-38A (ATC)
Location and origin of name: two miles northwest of Box Elder, and named after Brigadier General Richard E. Ellsworth, CO of 28th SRW, killed 18 March 1953 in crash of an RB-36 near Nut Cove, Newfoundland

Initially known as Rapid City Army Air Base when established in 1942 as a bomber base and has retained the mission ever since. Large numbers of bomber units assigned for short periods during World War II, with the current unit, the 28th Wg, established in August 1947. The base operated the B-29 and converted to the B-36 in 1949, but switched to reconnaissance the following year. An air defense commitment was added in 1952 with the 54th FIS based until 1960. Reconnaissance operations were retained until 1956 when the 28th BW converted to the B-52D. The KC-135A began deliveries in 1959. Strategic missile operations commenced early in 1962 with the 44th SMW operating the Titan I and the Minuteman I from 1963. The Strategic Warfare Center, together with its operating unit the 99th Strategic Warfare Wing, began operations at Ellsworth AFB in 1989. The Center provides ACC aircrew with regular courses designed to develop tactics and improve routine operations, specializing in the delivery of conventional and nuclear weapons under simulated combat conditions.

Elmendorf AFB, Alaska

Command: PACAF
Major unit: HQ 11th Air Force; 3rd Wg F-15C/D/E
Tenant units: 962nd ACS E-3B/C (PACAF); 616th AG C-12F, C-130H (PACAF)
Location and origin of name: positioned adjacent to Anchorage, and named after Captain Hugh M. Elmendorf, killed 13 January 1933 flight testing a P-25 aircraft near Patterson Field, Ohio

Housed a mixed complement during World War II, including interceptors, bombers, rescue and transport aircraft to support and defend the Alaskan landmass. All of these duties with the exception of bombardment continued during the 1950s. Major SAC presence returned July 1960 when 4157th Combat Support Group, later Strategic Wing, was formed, until June 1966 when the unit inactivated. The 21st Composite Wing formed in July 1966 operating the F-102A and C-130D with the 5041st Tactical Operations Squadron assigned in October 1971 operating the B-57E, C-118A, C-124C and T-33A. The strategic position of the base ensured it provided facilities to aircraft deploying to and from Southeast Asia during the Vietnam War. The F-4E was assigned in 1970 followed by the F-15A in 1982, and the F-15C from May 1987. The F-15E joined the unit at the end of 1991 with the 3rd Wg forming to replace the 21st FW in December 1991.

England AFB, Louisiana

Command: ACC
Major unit: 23rd FW A-10A
Tenant unit: nil
Location and origin of name: five miles west of Alexandria, and named after Lieutenant John B. England, a World War II and Korean War veteran who was killed 17 November 1954 in the crash of an F-86 near Toul, France

Known as Alexandria Army Air Base from 1942 until 1955 when it was renamed to its current title. Conducted B-17 combat crew training during World War II until flight operations ceased in 1945. Assigned to TAC from 1950 in readiness to commence fighter operations, initially housing a mobilized Air National Guard Group, but with the 366th Fighter-Bomber Wing assigned in January 1953. Joined by 401st Fighter-Bomber Wing in September 1957. Both wings subse-

quently relocated to Europe, the former to France in 1962 and the latter to Spain in 1966. Base hosted air warfare operations in 1966 with the assignment of the 1st ACW until 1969 when the unit moved to Hurlburt Field. England conducted special operations crew training from 1969 until the early 1970s with several squadrons which were gradually inactivated or transferred elsewhere. Tactical fighter duties began in September 1970 operating F-100-equipped squadrons transitioning between service in Southeast Asia and their parent wings in the USA. The 23rd TFW arrived from McConnell AFB in July 1972 and is current at the base. Wing is in the process of retiring their A-10As, with the 23rd FW due to be inactivated by September 1992 and the base closing 12 months later. However, the 23rd will be reborn in Composite Wing form at Pope AFB.

Fairchild AFB, Washington

Command: ACC
Major unit: 92nd Wg B-52H, KC-135R
Tenant units: 141st ARW KC-135E (ANG); det 24 37th ARS UH-1N (AMC); ACE det 323rd FTW T-37B (ATC)
Location and origin of name: 12 miles southwest of Spokane, and named for General Muir S. Fairchild, a World War I pilot who subsequently became Air Force Vice Chief of Staff and who died on 17 March 1950

Popularly known as Galena Field and later Spokane Air Depot, along with other role suffixes before gaining its present title in November 1950. During the whole of World War II the base served as a supply and maintenance depot for the Pacific Northwest and Alaska overhauling aircraft engines. Postwar the base was upgraded to operate B-29 bombers with assignment to SAC in September 1947 shortly before the 92nd BW was formed. During the Korean War a number of mobilized Strategic Reconnaissance units were stationed at Fairchild. Air Force Cold Weather Survival School established in March 1966. The bomber and tanker aircrew training role will transfer from Castle AFB to Fairchild by the middle of the decade.

RAF Fairford, UK

USAFE standby facility which is periodically returned to active service to support SAC B-52 bombers during NATO exercises. Formerly a SAC KC-135 base as part of the European Tanker Task Force and administered by the 11th SG until June 1990 when the last operational sortie was flown. Latter unit inactivated two months later when 7020th ABS took over, with responsibility to the 20th TFW (now 20th FW).

Falcon AFB, Colorado

Satellite operations unit and remote tracking station which is part of Air Force Space Command and administered by the 2nd Space Wing.

Forbes Field, Kansas

Forbes Field is two miles south of Topeka with the 190th ARG Kansas ANG operating the KC-135E. The field was formerly known as Forbes AFB housing SAC and TAC units until the 1970s.

Fort Smith MAP, Arkansas

The Municipal Airport is within the southern suburbs of Fort Smith and has the 188th FG Arkansas ANG flying the F-16A/B in residence.

Fort Wayne MAP, Indiana

Fort Wayne MAP is five miles southwest of the city and houses the 122nd FW Indiana ANG which recently converted from the F-4E to the F-16C/D.

Francis E. Warren AFB, Wyoming

Command: ACC
Major unit: 90th SMW LGM-30G, LGM-118A
Tenant unit: 37th ARS UH-1N (AMC)
Location and origin of name: adjacent to west side of Cheyenne, and named for Wyoming's first Senator, Francis E. Warren, who served in the Civil War during 1863 and died in 1929

Installation has a long record of military use as it first served as a camp to guard construction workers, becoming Fort David A. Russell in 1867 (honoring a Union General), and Fort Francis E. Warren in 1930. Transferred to the Air Force in June 1947 under control of ATC. Converted from an aviation engineering school to a Technical School in May 1948. Commenced conversion to accommodate intercontinental ballistic missiles (ICBMs) in 1957 with 706th SMW assigned in February 1958 equipped with the Atlas. Unit replaced by 389th SMW in April 1961 until March 1965 when the wing inactivated. The 90th SMW was formed at Francis E. Warren AFB in July 1963. The base is the only facility to deploy the LGM-118A Peacekeeper missile with 50 silos beginning in June 1986. The wing was due to convert fully to 100 Peacekeepers, although a budget cap restricted the number at 50, resulting in a mixed complement.

Fresno Air Terminal, California

The Air Terminal is five miles northeast of Fresno with the 144th FW California ANG operating the F-16A/B ADF. The base also has an Army National Guard repair facility which performs overhaul of helicopters from many of the western states.

Galena Airport, Alaska

PACAF facility with an alert shelter complex enabling Elmendorf-based F-15s to be dispersed from home base.

George AFB, California

Command: ACC
Major unit: 35th FW F-4E/G
Tenant unit: det 1 144th FW F-16A ADF (ANG)
Location and origin of name: six miles northwest of Victorville, and named after Brigadier General Harold H. George, a World War I fighter ace who died in an aircraft accident near Darwin, Australia, on 29 April 1942

Initially known as Air Corps Advanced Flying School and later Victorville Army Air Field/Air Force Base, the facility was given its present name in June 1950. Established as an advanced flying training site until the end of World War II when it was converted to a storage depot for B-29 bombers and several types of trainers until the end of 1948, when these had been disposed of. The base passed from Air Material Command to Continental Air Command briefly before joining Air Defense Command (ADC) in January 1951 and SAC six months later, with the assignment of the mobilized 452nd BW prior to the unit being sent to the Far East. Despite an ADC presence for many years TAC took over responsibility of the base in November 1951 and has maintained control ever since. The 479th Fighter-Bomber Wing was established as the first major TAC unit at George AFB conducting operational training for the F-51 and F-86 before converting to the F-100. The unit received the F-104A beginning in October 1954 and deployed to numerous worldwide trouble spots as well as training Starfighter pilots from overseas countries. The wing was the only TAC unit to be fully equipped with the Starfighter. Began converting to the F-4 in 1965 for an association with the Phantom which was to last for more than 27 years! During the tenure of the 479th, several other units were resident for short periods including the 21st Fighter-Bomber Wing (1953/1954), 31st TFW (1959/1962), 355th TFW (1962/1964), 8th FBW (1964/1965). The 479th inactivated in October 1971 when the 35th TFW took over as the major unit at George AFB, assuming control of the F-4s and adding the F-105G two years later. Training of German Phantom pilots was also undertaken from 1973, initially with eight F-4Fs but later by 10 Luftwaffe-ordered F-4Es. The requirement for specialist F-4G operations and training resulted in the 37th TFW being assigned at George in March 1981. However the gradual rundown of Phantom operations and corresponding reduction in aircrew requirement resulted in all George-based F-4s being assigned to the 35th TFW in October 1989. The Phantom withdrawal, which commenced in earnest in 1990, continued throughout 1991 with operations due to cease in 1992, with the 35th TFW (now 35th FW) inactivating and the base closing.

Gila Bend AFAF, Arizona

ACC range located over the vast empty wasteland in southwest Arizona, and run by the 832nd Combat Support Squadron. Employed by various units, but primarily used for training sorties launched from Luke AFB.

Goodfellow AFB, Texas

Command: ATC
Major unit: 3480th TTW
Tenant unit: 8th Missile Warning Squadron (AFSPACECOM)
Location and origin of name: two miles southeast of San Angelo, and named for Second Lieutenant John J. Goodfellow Jr, killed in aerial engagement with Fokkers near Thiaucourt, France, 14 September 1918

Established in 1940 as a pilot training school during World War II, and served in the primary training role postwar. Base gradually increased a non-flying role with the assignment of cryptographic training, with flying activities finally ceasing in March 1975. Currently undertakes technical training for personnel entering an intelligence career, including civilians as well as a host of other non-flying specialists.

Grand Forks AFB, North Dakota

Command: ACC
Major unit: 319th Wg B-1B, KC-135R
Tenant units: 321st SMW LGM-30G (ACC); det 3 37th ARS HH-1H (AMC); ACE det 64th FTW T-38A (ATC)
Location and origin of name: 16 miles west of Grand Forks and named after the city of the same name

Base completed early in 1957 under the control of Air Defense Command as a fighter interceptor facility with the 18th FIS flying the F-101B. SAC element added in September 1958 when 4133rd Strategic Wing was assigned, although the KC-135A did not arrive until February 1960 and the B-52H until 23 months later. The Strategic Wing was replaced by the 319th BW in February 1963, with the base transferred to SAC five months later. 321st SMW assigned November 1964 with major development to house ICBMs beginning two months later.

The 120th FG's F-16s operate from the civil airport at Great Falls, in Montana's 'Big Sky Country'. The unit has an air defense tasking with the ADF variant.

Great Falls IAP, Montana

The International Airport is five miles southwest of Great Falls housing the F-16A/B ADF of the 120th FG Montana ANG.

Greater Wilmington-New Castle County Airport, Delaware

The airport is five miles south of Wilmington and is home for the C-130Hs of the 166th AG Delaware ANG. In addition a small Army National Guard unit is tenant, while Boeing Helicopters have a flight test facility at the Airport.

RAF Greenham Common, UK

USAFE base with Tomahawk ground-launched cruise missiles assigned to the 501st TMW which formed in October 1982. Missiles removed and returned to the USA beginning in 1990 as part of the INF treaty, with the 501st inactivating in June 1991. Base transferred back to the 7273rd ABG.

Griffiss AFB, New York

Command: ACC
Major unit: 416th Wg B-52G, KC-135R
Tenant units: Rome Air Development Center – no aircraft assigned (AFMC); ACE det 71st FTW T-37B (ATC); plus US Army aviation brigade
Location and origin of name: one mile northeast of Rome and named after Lieutenant Colonel Townsend E. Griffiss, killed 15 February 1942 when mistakenly shot down near Plymouth, England

Formerly known as Rome Air Depot when opened in 1942 and subsequently identified by several other suffix identities before gaining its current name in January 1948. Assigned to Material Command and conducted aircraft engine maintenance as well as training air depot groups in engine repair. Limited aviation operations postwar, but electronic research activities commenced in 1949 with the Watson Laboratory transferred

from Red Bank, NJ, in 1950. The Rome Air Development Center was established in June 1951 followed by a new intelligence and reconnaissance laboratory opened in 1952 to evaluate radar and ECM systems. SAC presence established in August 1958 with the formation of the 4039th Strategic Wing, with the KC-135A operated from April 1959 and B-52G from January 1960. Strategic Wing replaced by 416th BW in February 1963.

Grissom AFB, Indiana

Command: AMC
Major unit: 305th Wg KC-135R, EC-135G/L
Tenant units: 930th FG A-10A (AFRes); 434th ARW KC-135E (AFRes); ACE det 71st FTW T-37B (ATC)
Location and origin of name: seven miles south of Peru, and named for astronaut Lieutenant Colonel Virgil I. Grissom, killed in fire aboard Apollo spacecraft under test at Kennedy Space Center on 27 January 1967

Established as a US Naval facility in 1942 and transferred to the Air Force as a Storage Branch in November 1951. Renamed Bunker Hill AFB in June 1954 and given its current identity in May 1968. Assigned to TAC with the 323rd Fighter-Bomber Wing established in August 1955 operating the F-86 and later the F-100. Transferred to SAC in September with the assignment of KC-97 tanker operations, followed by the establishment of the 305th BW in June 1959 equipped with the B-47E. The Stratojet was replaced by the B-58A beginning in 1961. A post-attack command control system equipped with the EC-135 assigned mid-1966. Unit changed to an Air Refueling Wing with withdrawal of B-58s in January 1970.

Gulfport-Biloxi Regional Airport, Mississippi

Gulfport-Biloxi Airport is within the city limits of Gulfport and has no aircraft assigned, although Reserve units are frequently in temporary residence to use air-to-ground gunnery range located 70 miles to the north.

Gunter AFB, Alabama

Facility housing Air Force Communications Command's Computer Systems Division, and Air Force Logistics Command's Logistics Management Center. In addition, the Air University has a Senior NCO Academy and an Extension Course Institute at Gunter AFB.

Hahn AB, Germany

Former home of the 50th TFW flying the F-16C/D until 1991 when the unit was returned to the USA. The base is now a non-flying station administered by an Air Base Group.

Hancock Field, Syracuse, New York

Hancock Field is five miles northeast of Syracuse and has the 174th FW New York ANG flying the F-16A/B in residence.

Hanscom AFB, Massachusetts

Command: AFMC
Major unit: Electronic Systems Division and 3245th ABW – no aircraft assigned
Tenant units: nil

Location and origin of name: 17 miles northwest of Boston, and named after Massachusetts aviation pioneer Laurence G. Hanscom, killed in the crash of his Fleet biplane on 9 February 1941

Established as Laurence G. Hanscom Field, Boston Auxiliary Airport in June 1941 and gained its present title in January 1977. Employed as a P-47 operating base in 1943 and a test facility for radar and radio research by Harvard University and the Massachusetts Institute of Technology during late 1944. In addition, the base hosted research into developing technologies including electronic, nuclear, geophysics and chemistry. Base became part of the Air Force Cambridge Research Center in 1952, with the AFCRC moving to Hanscom in 1955. By 1960 the base had become the principal Air Force site for electronics research, with the Electronic Systems Division established in April 1961. Various airframes were operated during the development of electronic tests, with some aircraft directly assigned while others were borrowed as required. The base was administered by Air Material Command and Air Defense Command until August 1951 when Air Research and Development Command (the forerunner of AFSC) took over. The 3rd BW was stationed at Hanscom from December 1946 until June 1949, when Continental Air Command squadrons were in residence. Flying activities were gradually transferred elsewhere and eventually ceased in September 1973, although the base is still capable of full-scale aircraft operations as evidenced by the large static display at periodic air shows.

Harrisburg IAP, Middletown, Pennsylvania

The International Airport is 10 miles east of Harrisburg with the EC-130Es of the 193rd SOG Pennsylvania ANG in residence. The base is also known as Olmstead Field.

Hector Field, Fargo, North Dakota

Hector Field is three miles north of Fargo and has the 119th FG North Dakota ANG operating the F-16A/B ADF.

Hickam AFB, Hawaii

Command: PACAF
Major unit: HQ PACAF/15th ABW EC-135J
Tenant units: det 1 89th AW C-135C (AMC); 154th CG F-15A (ANG)
Location and origin of name: on Oahu Island nine miles west of Honolulu, and named for Lieutenant Colonel Horace M. Hickam, a pioneer aviator killed in A-12 accident on 5 November 1934 at Fort Crockett, TX

George AFB was the last major home for the USAF's active-duty Phantom fleet.

Originally named Hickam Field when opened in 1935, and gained its present title in March 1948. Construction of facilities enabled many flying activities from Fort Shafter and Luke Field to move to Hickam by 1940. The Japanese attack on Pearl Harbor in December 1941 killed 121 personnel and wounded others, while 64 aircraft were destroyed. Facilities were rebuilt subsequently, with numerous units based at various times during World War II. Postwar, several air transport units were resident, along with air rescue and communications squadrons. Base operated by Pacific Air Command from 1946 for three years until transferred to MATS, but reverted to Far East Air Forces (the forerunner of PACAF) in 1955. The 1502nd Air Transport Wing formed July 1955 as the major unit at Hickam, operating the C-124. The 6594th Recovery Control Group (later Test Group) was formed with C-119Js in November 1959 to recover re-entering satellites. The C-119 proved unsatisfactory for the task and was replaced by the JC-130B and JC-130H. The 6486th ACCS operated the EC-135P from April 1965 until October 1969, when the unit was redesignated 9th ACCS. The 1502nd ATW was replaced by the 61st MAW in January 1966 but was later changed to the support role before deactivating. The 15th ABW formed in November 1971 as the primary unit at Hickam.

RAF High Wycombe, UK

USAFE command facility operating alongside its RAF equivalent.

Hill AFB, Utah

Command: AFMC
Major unit: HQ Ogden Air Logistics Center
Tenant units: 388th FW F-16C (ACC); 419th TFW F-16A (AFRes); 6545th TG C-130B, DC-130A, HC/NC-130H, NCH-53A (AFMC)
Location and origin of name: five miles south of Ogden, and named for Major Ployer P. Hill, a military test pilot killed 30 October 1935 in crash of Boeing 299 at Wright Field, OH

Known as Ogden Air Depot initially until renamed Hill Field in 1939. Facilities completed for an aircraft repair shop in March 1942, gaining command status in 1943 as the Ogden Air Depot Control Area Command. Under Air Technical Services Command the base was a postwar storage site for the B-29, C-45 and C-82 until 1953. Became center for Air Force munitions in the 1950s, with the Minuteman missile engineering test facility opened in 1966. B-26-equipped 461st BW was resident from 1953 until relocating to Blytheville AFB in April 1956. 4677th Radar Electronic Evaluation ECM Flight established in November 1954 with surplus bombers such as the B-29 employed to conduct various test programs. Unit changed designation and upgraded to become 4677th Defense Systems Evaluation Squadron with the EB-57 before moving to Malmstrom AFB in 1972. 945th TCG formed by Continental Air Command in 1962 with the C-119 and later the C-124. Absorbed by the AFRes when CONAC was renamed in August 1968, with group's 733rd MAS replaced by 466th TFS operating the F-105B in January 1973. Group replaced by 419th TFW in October 1982. 1550th Aircrew Training and Test Wing formed April 1971 to train aircrew for fixed- and rotary-wing rescue types. Drone operations conducted by 6514th TS and consolidated at Hill AFB January 1979 with formation of 6545th TG. 388th TFW re-formed with the F-4D in December 1975.

Holloman AFB, New Mexico

Command: ACC
Major unit: 49th FW F-117A
Tenant units: 6585th Test Group QF-86H, QF-100D/F, QF-106A (AFMC)
Location and origin of name: eight miles southeast of Alamogordo, and named after Colonel George V. Holloman, inventor and guided missile pioneer killed in B-17 crash on Formosa 19 March 1946

Known as Alamogordo Bombing and Gunnery Range when opened in 1942 and renamed Holloman AFB in January 1948. Employed as training site for bomber crews during World War II. In 1947 Air Material Command took over the base from SAC and moved the AAF guided missile program from Wendover and established the New Mexico Joint Guided Missile Range. Snark missile launching facility opened in 1950. White Sands and Holloman Proving Grounds merged in 1952 with the Holloman Air Development Center established shortly afterwards. 3225th Drone Squadron assigned from 1953 until 1963 with a number of drone launch aircraft including the GB-26 and later the GC-130A. A 35,000-ft test track for missile guidance system testing completed in 1959. Base administered by Air Research and Development Command (later AFSC) until 1971 when transferred to TAC. 366th TFW moved from France in July 1963 with the F-84F, but converted to the F-4C before transferring to Phan Rang AB, South Vietnam. 49th TFW relocated to Holloman AFB from Spangdahlem AB, Germany, in July 1968. Numerous test units established over the years for various periods of duty, with the 6585th Test Group formed August 1970 and currently in residence operating unmanned drone aircraft such as the QF-86H, QF-100 and QF-106 as targets for Army and Air Force missile tests. Lead-in fighter training (LIFT) role established August 1973 with T-38As of 465th TFTS. Role expanded greatly from January 1977 with formation of 479th TTW and three additional squadrons of Talons fitted with a gunsight and practice bomb dispensers as AT-38Bs. However, the reduction in requirement forced a major cutback to just one squadron during 1990/1991. 49th FW commenced re-equipping with the F-117A beginning April 1992 when aircraft transferred from 37th FW at Tonopah TR.

Homestead AFB, Florida

Command: ACC
Major unit: 31st FW F-16C/D
Tenant units: 482nd FW F-16A (AFRes); 301st ARS HC-130H/N, HH-3E to HH-60G (AFRes); det 1 125th FG F-16A (ANG); Inter-American Air Force Academy GOA-37B, GC-47D, GC-130A/B, GF-5B, GT-33A (ACC)
Location and origin of name: five miles northeast of Homestead, and named after the nearby city

Established as Homestead Army Field in 1941 as a staging base for Air Transport Command aircraft being ferried abroad, and for the training of ferry pilots. Base badly damaged by hurricane in September 1945 and closed three months later. Assigned to SAC and rebuilt during the mid-1950s, with the 19th BW moving from Pinecastle AFB, FL, in June 1956 equipped with the B-47 and KC-97, and upgraded to B-52H and KC-135A in 1962. The 19th BW was resident until July 1968 when the base was transferred to TAC. Continental Air Command presence established in 1960 with 435th TCW and 76th TCS operating the C-119, plus 301st ARS with the SA-16B (later HU-16B). 31st TFW moved from George AFB in May 1962 with the F-100 until December 1966 when the unit relocated to Huy Hoa AB, South Vietnam. However, prior to the wing moving to the Far East the 4531st TFW was established to

administer the base for the next four years, with a variety of flying squadrons assigned. The 31st TFW returned to Homestead AFB in October 1970. AFRes operated the EC-121T in the airborne early warning role by the 79th AEW&CS until October 1978 when replaced by the 93rd TFS operating the F-4C. The 482nd TFW was re-formed as the AFRes unit in command in April 1981. The Inter-American Air Force Academy moved from Albrook AFS, Canal Zone, by January 1990.

Hondo MAP, Texas

Civilian Airport with the Officer Training School in residence flying several dozen T-41s under ATC control.

Howard AFB/Albrook AFS, Canal Zone

Command: TAC – assignment after June 1992 unknown
Major unit: Air Forces Panama
Tenant unit: 61st MAG C-21A, C-22A, C-27A, C-130H, CASA 212 (AMC)
Location and origin of name: located close to Panama City, and named after Major Charles H. Howard

Originally established as Bruja Point Military Reservation in 1928. Air Forces Panama is the USAF representative for operations throughout Latin America. Unit was part of TAC and reports to 12th Air Force. Hosts Coronet Cove deployments of ANG fighter and attack aircraft for two-week deployments from the USA, and Volant Oak reserve C-130 rotations for airlift duties in the region.

Hulman Regional Airport, Terre Haute, Indiana

Hulman Airport is five miles east of Terre Haute with the 181st FG Indiana ANG, which recently converted from the F-4E to the F-16C/D.

Hurlburt Field, Florida

Command: AMC
Major unit: HQ AFSOC, 1st SOW MC-130E/H, AC-130H, MH-53J (AFSOC)
Tenant unit: AF Special Operations School (AFSOC)
Location and origin of name: five miles west of Fort Walton Beach, and named after First Lieutenant Donald W. Hurlburt, killed in crash of an AT-18 near Eglin Field 1 October 1943

Established in 1943 as Eglin-Hurlburt Airdrome and given its present name in January 1948. Frequently referred to as Eglin Air Force Auxiliary Field #9. Base served as headquarters of Electronics Section of Air Proving Ground Command and as a radar countermeasures training facility during World War II. Base inactive until 1955 when 17th BW moved from Miho AB, Japan, operating the B-26 and B-57, but converted to the B-66B the following year. Wing inactivated June 1958 when B-66s relocated to Europe. 4751st Air Defense Missile Wing formed January 1958 with the Bomarc missile until July 1962 when the system was phased out. Base switched to Air Commando role in April 1962 with the activation of the 1st ACW operating a variety of elderly types including the A-1, RB-26, C-46, C-47, C-123, AT-28 and U-10. The wing moved to England AFB in January 1966 having been replaced by 4410th CCTW. The 1st SOW returned to Hurlburt Field in July 1969 and has subsequently been the major operator at the base, apart from the period between July 1974 and July 1975 when replaced by the 834th Tactical Composite Wing.

Incirlik AB, Turkey

Command: USAFE
Major unit: 39th TG – no aircraft assigned
Tenant unit: nil
Location and origin of name: 10 miles east of Adana, the name Incirlik is Turkish for 'fig orchard'

Base activated in May 1954 with 39th Tactical Group commencing operations in March 1966. Base supports rotational training deployments of USAFE fighter aircraft to conduct weapons delivery on the nearby ranges. 7440th Provisional Wing formed late 1990 for Operation Proven Force to operate the mixed fleet of USAFE fighters along with SAC KC-135As and MAC C-130s during combat operations against Iraq.

Indian Springs AFAF, Nevada

ACC range complex which is run by the 57th FW from Nellis AFB and houses the UH-1Ns of 4440th HS.

Iraklion AB, Crete

Command: USAFE
Major unit: 7276th ABG – no aircraft assigned
Tenant unit: nil
Location and origin of name: 10 miles east of Iraklion, and named after the nearby city which is the capital of Crete

A joint Greek/US base for many years supporting USAFE aircraft operating in the eastern Mediterranean. Houses an Electronic Security and a Communications Squadron.

Izmir AS, Turkey

USAFE facility located at Cigli Air Base and administered by 7241st ABG. Izmir is the headquarters of the 6th Allied Tactical Air Force.

Jacksonville IAP, Florida

The International Airport is 15 miles northwest of the city with the 125th FG Florida ANG operating the F-16A/B ADF.

Joe Foss Field, Sioux Falls, South Dakota

Joe Foss Field is located on the northside of Sioux Falls and houses the 114th FG South Dakota ANG which is currently converting from the A-7D/K to the F-16C/D. The field is named after Brigadier General Joseph J. Foss, former governor of the state and founder of the South Dakota ANG.

Kadena AB, Okinawa

Command: PACAF
Major unit: 18th Wg F-15C/D, KC-135R, E-3B/C
Tenant units: 33rd ARS HH-3E (AMC); 353rd SOW MC-130E, HC-130N/P, MH-53J (AFSOC); 13th MAS C-12F (AMC)
Location and origin of name: 15 miles north of Naha, and named after nearby city

A US installation for more than four decades, with the 18th Fighter-Bomber Wing assigned since November 1954 operating the F-86, F-100, F-105, F-4 and currently the F-15C. SAC presence during Vietnam War included the 4252nd Strategic Wing from January 1965 until April 1970 when replaced by the 376th Strategic Wing. Initially the resident KC-135As were composed of aircraft rotating from the USA, with the B-52

added later to conduct long-range bombing missions of targets in North and South Vietnam. The 376th SW continued to operate tanker aircraft from the US and added a number of KC-135A and Q models which were directly assigned to the 909th ARefS. The unit supported SR-71As located at Kadena and rotational RC-135s of the 55th SRW from Offutt AFB. An E-3 squadron was formed during 1979. Following the explosion of Mount Pinatubo in the Philippines in June 1991, Special Operations forces stationed at Clark AB were moved here to join the rescue Hercules squadron already in residence. 18th Wing became the single manager for PACAF F-15C/D squadrons, together with KC-135R and E-3 Sentry units, at the end of 1991.

Keesler AFB, Mississippi

Command: ATC
Major unit: 3300th TTW – no aircraft assigned
Tenant units: 7th ACCS EC-130E (ACC); 403rd AW C-130E/H, WC-130E/H (AFRes)
Location and origin of name: located adjacent to Biloxi, and named after Second Lieutenant Samuel R. Keesler Jr, shot down in a Camel near Lamourie, France, on 8 October 1918 and died next day

Opened as Biloxi Air Corps Technical School in June 1941 to train aircraft mechanics. A radar school relocated from Boca Raton AAFd late 1947, making Keesler one of the two largest technical schools in the AAF. Various training roles added including aircraft weapons training facility in 1969. Several C-130 units were assigned to Keesler in 1973 including the 1st Aerial Cartographic & Geodetic Squadron (1st ACGS) with RC-130As, 53rd WRS with the WC-130E/H, and 815th TAS operating the C-130B and later the WC-130H. The former two units were subsequently inactivated. The EC-130Es of 7th ACCS were reassigned from Southeast Asia during August 1975. The 3300th TTW was operational during 1977 and 1978 before briefly inactivating, only to be re-formed in October 1979.

Keflavik Naval Station, Iceland

Command: US Navy
Major unit: Air Forces Iceland (ACC); 57th FS F-15C/D (ACC), 960th ACS E-3B/C (ACC)
Tenant units: 56th ARS HH-3E to HH-60G (AMC)
Location and origin of name: located near Reykjavik

Base housed an Air Defense Command presence for more than 40 years with the 57th FIS assigned since November 1954, operating the F-89C and later the F-102A, F-4E and currently the F-15C/D. Responsibility for the squadron and its parent organization Air Forces Iceland changed from ADC to TAC in October 1979 when the latter assumed the few remaining flying units of the former. ADC also EC-121s operated from the

base, although the reduction in status of the Command resulted in AFRes EC-121Ts of 79th AEW&CS rotating to the base until the type was retired in 1978. E-3 Sentry airborne early warning operations took over from October 1978, initially by det 2 552nd AW&CW, but from September 1979 by the 960th AW&CSS (Airborne Warning & Control Support Squadron). The squadron changed its designation in December 1980 with the deletion of the word 'Support' from its title.

A quartet of 31st Fighter Wing F-16s overflies their base at Homestead. The base also houses a Reserve F-16 unit, a Reserve combat rescue unit and a ground school.

William K. Kellogg Airport, Battle Creek, Michigan

Kellogg Airport is on the northern outskirts of Battle Creek, with the 110th FG Michigan ANG currently converting from the OA-37B to the OA-10A.

Kelly AFB, Texas

Command: AFMC
Major unit: San Antonio Air Logistics Center
Tenant units: 433rd AW C-5A (AFRes); 149th FG F-16A/B (ANG)
Location and origin of name: five miles southwest of San Antonio, and named after Second Lieutenant George M. Kelly, killed in crash of Curtis Type IV near an infantry encampment close to the present site of Fort Sam Houston, Texas, on 10 May 1911. Second Lieutenant Kelly was the first US Army pilot casualty

Originally known as the Aviation Camp at Fort Sam Houston when opened in 1917 but renamed Camp Kelly soon afterwards. Initially a Signals Corps supply office and a repair and training facility. Pursuit and bomber training base from 1921 and observation school established in 1922. Kelly bombing range acquired in 1931, but later disposed of to become Lackland AFB. HQ Air Corps Advanced Flying School established in 1931. Gunnery School formed July 1941 and Air Corps Replacement Training Center formed as part of Advanced Flying Training School. San Antonio Air Service Command established in 1943 as major air logistics center. 518th Air Transport Group formed June 1948 as forerunner of 1700th Air Transport Group. HQ MATS Continental Division located August 1948. Various Air Transport Squadrons/Groups located during the 1950s, including 1700th Test Squadron, which evaluated turboprop powerplants fitted to piston-engined types such as the C-97 and C-121. CONAC 433rd TCW formed November 1960, operating the C-119 and later the C-124. Air Logistics Center operated examples of the F-5, F-106 and T-38, but at present has no aircraft.

RAF Kemble, UK

Former RAF maintenance unit, now a USAFE overhaul, storage and distribution center run by AFMC. The base conducts maintenance of Europe-based USAF aircraft including A-10As, C-130s and F-15s and has a small number of retired F-5Es in storage awaiting export sale.

Key Field, Meridian, Mississippi

Key Field is six miles southwest of Meridian and operates the 186th RG Mississippi ANG with the RF-4C, although the base is scheduled to become a KC-135 facility. The Mississippi ARNG has a helicopter unit located nearby.

King Salmon Airport, Alaska

PACAF facility with an alert shelter complex enabling Elmendorf-based F-15s to be dispersed from home base.

Kingsley Field, Klamath Falls, Oregon

Kingsley Field is five miles southeast of Klamath Falls and has the 114th FS Oregon ANG operating the F-16A/B ADF to train ANG Fighting Falcon pilots. Base houses an alert detachment of F-15As of the 142nd FG from Portland. Named for Second Lieutenant David R. Kingsley, who was shot down over Ploesti, Romania, on 23 June 1944.

Kirtland AFB, New Mexico

Command: AFMC
Tenant units: AF Weapons Laboratory – no aircraft assigned (AFMC)
Major unit: 542nd Crew Training Wing HC-130N/P, HH-3E, TH-53A, MH-53J, MH-60G (AMC); 150th FG A-7D/K to F-16C/D (ANG)
Location and origin of name: southeast outskirts of Albuquerque, and named after Colonel Roy C. Kirtland who died at Moffet Field, California, 2 May 1941 aged 65, as the oldest military pilot in the Air Corps at the time

Established as Albuquerque Army Air Base in 1941 and renamed to its present title in January 1948. Initially a four-engined aircraft training station and bombardier school in 1942. Base changed to support of Manhattan Project, and Sandia Atomic base in 1946. 428th Army Air Force Base Unit formed February 1946 as forerunner of the 4901st Special Weapons Wing and Air Force Special Weapons Center. Base administered by Air Material Command until December 1949 when it was reassigned to Air Research and Development Command. 3170th Special Weapons Group assigned from August 1948 until 1961, having changed to 4925th Special Weapons Group/Test Group in the meantime. Special Weapons School added in 1966 and laser laboratory constructed in 1968. Sandia Base incorporated July 1971 (also known as Kirtland East) increasing base area from 2,800 to 54,000 acres. Electromagnetic research facility opened in 1975 incorporating a huge framework large enough to accommodate a C-130 Hercules. Air Rescue training center and 1550th ATTW moved from Hill AFB in February 1976 with the base becoming a MAC facility in July 1977. 1550th ATTW and 1606th ABW merged to form 542nd CTW in October 1991.

K. I. Sawyer AFB, Michigan

Command: ACC
Major unit: 410th Wg B-52H, KC-135A
Tenant unit: nil
Location and origin of name: seven miles northeast of Gwinn, and named for Mr Kenneth I. Sawyer, a county road commissioner who formed the plan for the county airport that later became K. I. Sawyer AFB

Facility changed from a civilian airport to military use in April 1956. Initially assigned to Air Defense Command housing an interceptor unit. 4042nd Strategic Wing formed August 1958 and replaced by 410th BW in February 1963 with base transferring to SAC in January 1964. 56th FW operated the F-101B at the base between 1961 and 1964. 62nd FIS assigned from August 1959 until replaced by 87th FIS in May 1971. Latter squadron flew the F-106A/B until inactivated during 1985.

Kulis ANGB, Anchorage, Alaska

The Air National Guard Base is located at Anchorage IAP with two Alaska ANG squadrons assigned to the 176th CG, operating the C-130H, and more recently the HC-130H(N) and HH-60G. Base named for Lieutenant Albert Kulis, who was killed in a training flight in 1954.

Kunsan AB, Republic of Korea

Command: PACAF
Major unit: 8th FW F-16C/D
Tenant unit: nil
Location and origin of name: eight miles southwest of Kunsan City, and named for nearby city

Base built by Japanese in 1938 and occupied by the US at the end of World War II. 354th TFW arrived from Myrtle Beach AFB in July 1968 and remained until June 1970 when it returned to its stateside base. During its stay in South Korea the wing was composed of mobilized Air National Guard squadrons flying the F-100. The 354th was replaced by the 54th TFW activated in June 1970 for four months, operating two squadrons of F-4Es deployed from stateside units. 8th TFW assigned in September 1974 operating the F-4D until September 1981, when the unit converted to the F-16A as the first active overseas Fighting Falcon wing.

Lackland AFB, Texas

Command: ATC
Major unit: 3250th TTW – no aircraft assigned
Tenant unit: nil
Location and origin of name: eight miles southwest of San Antonio, and named for Brigadier General Frank D. Lackland, who was Commandant of the Advanced Flying School at Kelly Field and died in April 1943

Facility separated from Kelly Field June 1942 and known as San Antonio Aviation Cadet Center, although frequently referred to as 'The Hill', making it the largest such installation in the USA at the time. Renamed several times before becoming Lackland AFB in January 1948. Lackland has no runway and therefore no aircraft operations, although a number of displayed airframes sited throughout the complex are believed to be employed for instructional purposes. The AAF Basic Military School formed February 1946 to conduct basic military training for active-duty, ANG and Reserve airmen. In addition the facility conducts technical training for security police, training instructors, the Officer Training School, plus many other courses. 3250th TTW formed November 1979.

Lajes Field, Azores

Command: MAC – operator unknown after June 1992
Major unit: 1605th ASW – no aircraft assigned
Tenant unit: nil
Location and origin of name: on Terceira Island, Azores, 900 miles west of Portugal, and named for locality

Portuguese facility which has supported US operations since 1946. No US aircraft assigned, although the base has a very important role providing support for flights across the Atlantic for all branches of the Department of Defense. During Desert Shield/Desert Storm Lajes had a number of KC-10As in residence to refuel cells of fighter aircraft deploying non-stop from the USA to the Middle East.

RAF Lakenheath, UK

Command: USAFE
Major unit: 48th FW F-111F changing to F-15E
Tenant unit: nil
Location and origin of name: three miles southwest of Brandon, and named after village adjacent to the base

Base activated in 1941, becoming a SAC rotational base for heavy bombers in the late 1940s with B-29s from the 2nd BG arriving in August 1948 and were followed by other units. B-36s began deploying to Lakenheath from stateside bases in January 1951 when the 7th BW deployed six aircraft from Carswell AFB. B-47 squadrons also regularly deployed to Lakenheath as part of SAC's policy of basing a sizeable portion of its fleet in Europe and North Africa. However, towards the end of the 1950s SAC vacated the East Anglian facilities as it concentrated operations at the four bases in the Cotswolds, Berkshire and Oxfordshire. Lakenheath was prepared for fighter operations with the 48th TFW moving from Chaumont AB, France, in January 1960. The wing was equipped with the F-100D but changed to the F-4D prior to converting to the F-111F in 1977. The unit began transferring its aircraft back to the USA early in 1992 in preparation to convert to the F-15E. The first Eagle was delivered to the 48th FW on 21 February 1992, with the unit expected to be fully equipped by 1993.

Lambert Field/St Louis IAP, Missouri

Lambert Field is 12 miles northwest of St Louis and houses the 131st FW Missouri ANG flying the F-15A/B. Apart from the International Airport and the ANG facility, McDonnell Douglas has a huge production complex where the F/A-15 Eagle and F-18 Hornet are constructed.

Langley AFB, Virginia

Command: ACC
Major unit: HQ 1st Air Force; 1st FW F-15C/D, EC-135P, UH-1N
Tenant units: det 1 1402nd MAS C-21A (AMC); det 2 158th FG F-16 ADF (VA ANG); NASA Langley Research Center – various aircraft assigned
Location and origin of name: to the north of Hampton, and named in honor of Professor Samuel P. Langley, pioneer aeronautical scientist and Secretary of the Smithsonian Institute, who died in February 1906

Established December 1916 as Aviation Experimental Station and Proving Ground, and renamed Langley Field in August 1917. The base is one of the oldest continuously active air bases in the USA. Aircraft and airship facilities constructed in 1917, with three nearby ranges acquired in 1917 and 1919. Various early test facilities and training schools established during the 1920s and 1930s. General HQ, Air Force established March 1935. Upgraded for heavy bomber operations in 1941. Extensive wartime National Advisory Committee for Aeronautics (NACA – the forerunner of NASA) usage. Several troop carrier units based for short periods postwar, with HQ TAC in residence May 1946. TAC units assigned included the 363rd TRW located from 1947 until 1951, 4th FW 1949 to 1950, and 20th FBW during 1951/1952. 463rd TCW with the C-130B based from July 1963 to November 1965 when replaced by 316th TCW, until inactivated October 1975. 48th FIS located at Langley from January 1953. Inactivated in 1991, becoming the last front-line air defense squadron. 8th ACCS equipped with EC-135Ks assigned between 1969 and 1971, and 6th ACCS operating the EC-135P from October 1972. 1st TFW moved from Mac-Dill AFB in June 1975.

Laughlin AFB, Texas

Command: ATC
Major unit: 47th FTW T-37B, T-38A
Tenant unit: nil
Location and origin of name: six miles east of Del Rio, and named for First Lieutenant Jack T. Laughlin, the first resident of Del Rio to be killed in World War II; his B-17 was brought down by ground fire on 29 January 1942 over Java

Base opened late 1942 as Laughlin AAF to conduct bombardier training and closed at the end of World War II. Upgraded and reopened for F-84 training in 1952, with T-33A training added in 1954 under the 3645th PTW. Transferred from ATC to SAC in April 1957 with 4025th and 4080th SRWs in residence to conduct RB-57 and U-2 operations. Former inactivated June 1960 and latter moved to Davis-Monthan AFB in July 1963. Base returned to ATC April 1962 with 3646th PTW activated six months earlier. 47th FTW replaced 3646th in September 1972.

Lincoln MAP, Nebraska

The airport is one mile northwest of Lincoln with the 155th RG Nebraska ANG operating the RF-4C, plus an Army National Guard unit.

Lindsey AB, Germany

USAFE base situated at Wiesbaden with the 7100th CSW in residence. The wing is responsible for a large Medical Center plus 25 operating bases and five munitions support sites in and around the Frankfurt area.

Little Rock AFB, Arkansas

Command: AMC
Major unit: 314th AW C-130E
Tenant unit: 189th AG C-130E (ANG)
Location and origin of name: 17 miles northeast of Little Rock, and named for nearby city

Base established in February 1955 for SAC with 70th SRW formed at same time operating the RB-47 and KC-97. Joined by 384th BW six months later. 70th inactivated June 1962 after arrival of the 308th SMW in April 1962 with Titan II missiles. 384th BW moved to McConnell AFB prior to 43rd BW relocating to Little Rock from Carswell AFB with the B-58A in September 1964. SAC operations ceased early in 1970 when the base was transferred to TAC April 1970 with the C-130E-equipped 64th TAW assigned. 314th TAW replaced 64th in May 1971, with both the base and the airlift role transferring to MAC in December 1974. Wing conducts Hercules aircrew training for US and overseas nations.

Loring AFB, Maine

Command: ACC
Major unit: 42nd Wg B-52G, KC-135R
Tenant unit: nil
Location and origin of name: four miles west of Limestone, and named for Major Charles J. Loring, killed 22 November 1952 when he flew his crippled F-80 into enemy gun emplacement at Sniper Ridge, Korea

Established as Limestone AFB in June 1950 although the Air Force began operations 18 months earlier. Renamed to its present title October 1954. SAC base housing 42nd BW from February 1953 operating the B-36 until converting to the B-52 late 1956 and KC-135 from 1957. Both types currently operated by the wing. 27th FIS resident from 1959 until 1971 flying the F-106A. Most northeasterly USAF base in the USA and frequently used for SAC aircraft deploying to Europe. The wing is scheduled to inactivate and the base to close by 1994.

Los Angeles AFB, California

An AFMC base housing the Space Systems Division and operated by the 6592nd ABG.

Lowry AFB, Colorado

Command: ATC
Major unit: Lowry TTC/3400th TTW with several instructional airframes – see unit listing
Tenant unit: nil
Location and origin of name: between Denver and Aurora, and named for First Lieutenant Francis B. Lowry, killed 26 September 1918 when his Salmon 2A2 aircraft was shot down near Crepion, France

Base activated late 1937 as Denver Branch, Air Corps Technical School, and renamed Lowry Field March 1938. Initially conducted technical school courses during World War II, but changed to B-29 crew training in 1945/1946. 322nd TCW assigned June 1947 to June 1949. Postwar, returned to technical training role. Site of Air Force Academy 1954 to 1958 pending construction of facilities at Colorado Springs. Lowry TTC established January 1959. 451st SMW equipped with the Titan I in residence between April 1961 until June 1965. Flight operations ceased July 1966. 3400th TTW formed November 1979. The base is scheduled for closure by 1994 with duties being transferred to other ATC facilities.

Luke AFB, Arizona

Command: ACC
Major unit: 58th FW F-15E, F-16C/D
Tenant unit: 944th FG F-16C/D (AFRes)
Location and origin of name: 20 miles northwest of Phoenix, and named after Second Lieutenant Frank Luke Jr, who crashed his Spad near Petain, France, on 29 September 1918 and was killed in ground fire exchange

Established as Litchfield Park Air Base February 1941 but renamed Luke Field four months later. The title Litchfield Park was subsequently allocated to Naval storage facility near Phoenix in the 1950s and 1960s. Flying training base during World War II, becoming the largest single-engined and advanced flying training facility by the end of the war. Postwar, Luke was placed on limited operational status and used as fighter storage depot. Under Air Training Command control until late 1946 when a satellite of Williams AFB. Regained flying training role in 1951 under ATC and upgraded for F-84 operations in 1954. Transferred to TAC in July 1958 with F-86 training transferred from Williams AFB mid-1960, adding some F-100 training for USAF and over-

seas air arms. 3600th FTW assigned November 1952 and replaced by 4510th CCTW before inactivating October 1969. F-86 program transferred to Nellis AFB late 1962 in exchange for major F-100 training role. German training program in residence since the early 1960s, switching from the F-84F to F-104G June 1964. 58th TFTW formed October 1969 as primary flying unit and joined by 405th TTW August 1979. F-100 training ceased in 1971 in favor of the F-4C and F-5A/B. Began F-15 training in November 1974 and F-16 in 1979. 405th TTW transferred its F-15A/B/C/D models to Tyndall AFB, while F-15E absorbed into 58th FW, commencing late 1991.

Luke offers excellent flying weather throughout the year, and vast ranges nearby for tactical instruction. Conversion to the F-16 and F-15E is undertaken here.

MacDill AFB, Florida

Command: ACC
Major unit: 56th FW F-16C/D
Tenant unit: HQ US Central Command
Location and origin of name: adjacent to southwest Tampa city limits, and named for Colonel Leslie MacDill, killed in the crash of a North American BC-1 at Anacostia, DC, on 8 November 1938

Established as Southeast Air Base, Tampa, in May 1939 and renamed MacDill Field in December 1939. Base conducted B-17 and B-18 flight operations from February 1941. Postwar, the base performed B-50 aircrew training for SAC with 306th BW assigned September 1950 and the 305th BW four months later. Upgraded to accommodate B-47s and KC-97s late in 1951. SAC operations ceased by July 1962 when the base transferred to TAC. 12th TFW operated the F-84F from April 1962 and converted to the F-4C in 1964. Joined by 15th TFW in July 1962 and replaced by 1st TFW October 1970. 1st TFW moved to Langley AFB in June 1975 when the 56th TFW returned to USA from Nakhon Phanom RTAFB, Thailand.

Malmstrom AFB, Montana

Command: AMC
Major unit: 301st Wg KC-135R (AMC); ACE det 12th FTW T-38A (ATC)
Tenant unit: 341st SMW LGM-30F to G (ACC)
Location and origin of name: two miles east of Great Falls, and named for Colonel Einar A. Malmstrom, killed in crash of a T-33A near Great Falls AFB on 21 August 1954

Established as Great Falls Army Air Base in 1942 and renamed to its current title in October 1955. Hosted bomber aircraft crew training during 1942/1943 before changing to that of preparing lend-lease aircraft for shipment to the USSR in 1944/1945. Base served as aerial port for personnel and cargo destined for Alaska between 1946 and 1953 under MATS control until February 1954 when transferred to SAC. 517th Air Transport Wing formed June 1948 and changed to 1701st

ATW until inactivated May 1953. 407th Strategic Fighter Wing assigned between December 1953 and July 1957 operating the F-84. 4061st ARefW operated the KC-97 between July 1957 and July 1961. Site of SAC's first Minuteman unit when the 341st SMW formed in July 1961. EB-57Es of 4677th DSES moved from Hill AFB in August 1972 and changed to 17th DSES July 1974 before inactivating in July 1979. 301st ARW re-formed with the KC-135R in January 1988.

Mansfield Lahm Airport, Ohio

Lahm Airport is three miles north of Mansfield and houses the 179th AG Ohio ANG flying the C-130H. Facility is named after nearby city and for aviation pioneer Brigadier General Frank P. Lahm.

March AFB, California

Command: AMC
Major unit: HQ 15th Air Force, 22nd Wg KC-10A
Tenant units: 452nd ARW KC-135E (AFRes), 943rd AG C-130B (AFRes); 163rd RG RF-4C (ANG); ACE det 82nd FTW T-38A (ATC)
Location and origin of name: nine miles southeast of Riverside, and named for Second Lieutenant Payton C. March, killed 12 February 1918 in crash of a Curtiss JN-4 at Fort Worth, Texas

Established as Alesandro Aviation Field in March 1918, and renamed March Field the same month. Performed pilot training between 1917 and upgraded for heavy bomber crew training in World War II. Postwar, the base was assigned to SAC with the 22nd BW activated May 1949. Expanded prior to the introduction of the B-47 and KC-97 in 1952/1953 and the B-52B in 1963. Various other bomb wings were assigned for short periods including the 330th BW in 1949/1951, 44th BW in 1951, and 320th BW 1952/1960. The 452nd TCW (later MAW and ARefW) formed at March in November 1960 and has been assigned ever since apart from the period between 1972 and 1976 when it relocated to Hamilton AFB, California.

Glenn L. Martin State Airport, Baltimore, Maryland

Glenn L. Martin Airport is located eight miles east of Baltimore with two Maryland Air National Guard units in residence, consisting of the 175th FG flying the A-10A and the 135th AG operating the C-130E.

Mather AFB, California

Command: ATC
Major unit: 323rd FTW T-37B, CT-43A
Tenant unit: 940th ARG KC-135E (AFRes)
Location and origin of name: 12 miles southeast of Sacramento, and named for Second Lieutenant Carl S. Mather, killed in mid-air collision with JN-4D near Ellington Field, Texas, on 30 January 1918

Opened as Mather Field in February 1918 as a training base, but used for aerial forestry patrols and inactivated June 1922. Reopened briefly between 1930 and 1932, and served as an outpost for Hamilton Field in 1935 and Stockton Field in February 1941 until established as a separate facility in May 1941. B-25 training base in 1943 and port of embarkation for the Far East in 1944/1945. Bombardment and Flight Engineer School opened March 1946. 3535th Bomber Training Wing formed August 1948 and subsequently

changed title to Observer Training Wing before becoming Navigator Training Wing. The 3535th NTW was replaced by the 323rd FTW in April 1973. SAC had 4134th Strategic Wing assigned in May 1958 with the B-52, and replaced by 320th BW February 1963 until inactivated in October 1989.

May ANGB/Reno-Cannon IAP, Nevada

The International Airport is five miles southeast of Reno and has the 152nd RG Nevada ANG flying the RF-4C. ANG area is named after Major General James A. May, former Nevada Adjutant General.

Maxwell AFB, Alabama

Command: Air University
Major unit: HQ Air University/3800th ABW – no aircraft assigned
Tenant unit: 908th AG C-130H (AFRes)
Location and origin of name: one mile northwest of Montgomery, and named for Second Lieutenant William C. Maxwell, killed in crash of a DH-4 in the Philippines on 12 August 1920

Entitled Engine and Repair Depot when opened in April 1918, and changed to Maxwell Field in November 1922. Served as Air Repair Depot during World War I and continued in use postwar as a landing field for air mail operations. Base expanded during late 1920s/early 1930s. Air Corps Tactical School arrived in 1931, and base conducted pilot training during World War II. AAF School moved from Orlando, Florida, in December 1945 and changed to Air University three months later. 3800th Air University Wing formed July 1948 and subsequently changed to ABW status. AFRes unit activated in April 1969.

McChord AFB, Washington

Command: AMC
Major unit: 62nd AW C-141B
Tenant unit: 446th AW (Associate) C-141B (AFRes)
Location and origin of name: eight miles south of Tacoma, and named for Colonel William C. McChord, killed in crash of an A-17 near Maidens, Virginia, on 18 August 1937

Known as Pierce County Airport and Tacoma Airport in 1934 before being renamed McChord Field in December 1937. Became largest bomber training base, principally with the B-25 between 1940 and 1944. Later served as a P-39 modification center until the end of the war, when the base was assigned airlift and air defense functions. 62nd TCW activated in August 1947 and moved to Larson AFB, Washington, April 1952 when the 1705th Air Transport Group formed. However, the 62nd TCW returned to McChord in June 1960. Several interceptor units assigned during the 1950s and 1960s, although the 318th FIS activated in August 1955 was the longest in residence as it did not deactivate until December 1989.

McClellan AFB, California

Command: AFMC
Major unit: Sacramento Air Logistic Center F-111A/D/E/F, EF-111A, T-38A
Tenant units: HQ Air Rescue Service (AMC); 431st T&ES F-111A/D/E/F/G (ACC); 55th WRS WC-135B (AMC); also US Coast Guard facility
Location and origin of name: nine miles northeast of Sacramento, and named for Major Hezekiah McClellan, killed in crash of a Consolidated PB-2A near Centerville, Ohio, on 25 May 1936

Established as Sacramento Air Depot in 1935, and retitled McClellan Field in December 1939. Performed repair and overhaul of fighter aircraft, with P-38 and P-39 assembly lines supplemented by the P-40 in 1940. 4127th AAF Base Unit formed in April 1944, subsequently becoming the Sacramento Air Material Area/Air Logistics Center. Became a B-29 storage area postwar, with F-80s and F-86s stored during the early 1950s. 55th Weather Reconnaissance Squadron activated in February 1951 and has remained at the base ever since, apart from a six-month period of inactivity in 1961. 552nd AW&CW formed July 1955 with the EC-121 until April 1976, when the unit moved to Tinker AFB prior to receiving the E-3 Sentry.

McConnell AFB, Kansas

Command: ACC
Major unit: 384th Wg B-1B, KC-135R
Tenant units: 184th FG F-16C/D (ANG); ACE det 12th FTW T-38A (ATC)
Location and origin of name: five miles southeast of Wichita, and named for Second Lieutenant Thomas L. McConnell and Captain Fred McConnell who were both assigned to 307th BG. Tom McConnell was killed in crash of B-17 into a mountainside on Bougainville Island on 10 July 1943, while Fred McConnell was killed in crash of a private biplane in Kansas on 25 October 1945

Base known as Wichita Municipal Airport when established in March 1942, and changed to McConnell AFB in April 1954. Assigned to Air Material Command which received aircraft from the adjacent Boeing facility between 1942 and 1946. Returned to civilian control between 1946 and 1951, when it became Wichita AFB with the 3520th CCTW to train B-47 aircrew under ATC. Unit transferred to SAC as 4347th CCTW until inactivated in June 1963. Base administered by SAC from July 1958 until transferred to TAC in July 1963. 381st SMW formed in March 1962 with the Titan II missile. Major TAC presence began in October 1962 with 388th TFW assigned until relocated to Korat RTAFB, Thailand, in February 1964. The 355th TFW was based for just 16 months from July 1964 when it moved to Takhli RTAFB, Thailand. 23rd TFW re-formed in February 1964 with the F-105 until relocated to England AFB in July 1972. Base reverted to SAC control in July 1972 with 384th ARW re-formed five months later.

McEntire ANGB, Columbia, South Carolina

McEntire ANGB is 12 miles east of Columbia with the 169th FG South Carolina ANG F-16A/B assigned, along with an Army National Guard helicopter unit. Base is named for Brigadier General B. B. McEntire Jr, who was killed in the crash of an F-104A in 1961.

McGhee Tyson Airport, Knoxville, Tennessee

McGhee Tyson Airport is 10 miles southwest of Knoxville and has the 134th ARG Tennessee ANG in residence flying the KC-135E.

McGuire AFB, New Jersey

Command: AMC
Major unit: HQ 21st AF; 438th AW C-141B
Tenant units: 170th ARG KC-135E (ANG); 108th FW F-4E to KC-135E (ANG); 514th AW (Associate)

C-141B (AFRes)
Location and origin of name: 18 miles southeast of Trenton, and named for Major Thomas B. McGuire, killed on 7 January 1945 in crash of a P-38 on Los Negros Island in South Pacific

Formerly known as Fort Dix Airport when established in 1942 and renamed to its present title in January 1948. Training and staging area for units relocating to Europe in 1942 and 1943. Performed overhaul, servicing and preparation of aircraft being sent overseas during 1944, before conducting processing and inactivating of units postwar. Base administered by various commands during the latter half of the 1940s including Air Transport Command, SAC, CONAC, and ADC before transfer to MATS in July 1954. SAC's 91st SRW was based for 10 months in 1948, followed by ADC's 52nd FW between October 1949 and February 1952. The 1611th Air Transport Wing was activated in May 1954 and was assigned until January 1966 when it was replaced by the 438th MAW. MATS Atlantic Division was established in June 1955, later becoming MATS Eastern Transport AF before changing to the 21st Air Force in 1966 when MATS became MAC. Naval Air Transport Wing Atlantic (NATWA) was formed in May 1958 to administer the East Coast Naval squadrons which operated Air Force transport aircraft on a pool basis. The squadrons, including VR-3 based at McGuire AFB, flew various types including the C-118 and C-121 initially, and the C-130E later, before the arrangement was terminated in 1967 and the aircraft returned to the Air Force. The 305th ARefS operated the KC-97G at McGuire AFB between January 1960 and March 1965 as a detached unit of the 4050th ARefW/499th ARefW with HQ at Westover AFB.

Memphis IAP, Tennessee

The International Airport is within the city limits of Memphis with the 164th AG Tennessee ANG, which is currently converting from the C-130A to the C-141B.

RAF Mildenhall, UK

Command: USAFE
Major unit: HQ 3rd Air Force; 100th ARW (USAFE) (see text)
Tenant units: 306th Wg rotational KC-135s, RC-135s (ACC); 313th TAG rotational C-130E/Hs (AMC); Naval Air Facility
Location and origin of name: one mile northwest of and named for Mildenhall

Base opened in 1934 by the RAF, with the USAF commencing operations in July 1950 with assignment to SAC as a bomber and maintenance base. The bomber presence was limited as Mildenhall housed the supporting KC-97 tankers from the Bombardment Wings. However, as the SAC presence in East Anglia declined, Mildenhall was transferred to USAFE control in July 1959, becoming a cargo facility for MATS aircraft delivering supplies and personnel to England. The 7120th ACCS moved to Mildenhall from Chateauroux AB, France, in 1965 initially with the C-118A for airborne command post duties, but upgraded to the EC-135A upon arrival in the UK. These were subsequently converted to EC-135H standard, with the unit being replaced by the 10th ACCS in January 1970. The 513th TCW moved to Mildenhall from Evreux AB, France, in July 1966, bringing with it the rotational C-130 operation consisting of 32 aircraft. However, this number was halved prior to MAC assigning the 313th TAG to coordinate C-130 operations in January 1976. The 513th changed to an Airborne Command and Control Wing in June 1987. SAC operations resumed with the transfer of det 1 of the 98th SW from Upper Heyford in October 1976 to operate the rotational KC-135s and RC-135s. The 306th SW was activated at Ramstein in August 1976 with control of the Mildenhall det, although the wing moved to Mildenhall in July 1978 when the 7th Air Division was activated at Ramstein. SAC increased its presence with the activation of detachment 4 of the 9th SRW in March 1979 to operate the U-2R initially, and later the SR-71A. However, the SR-71 was withdrawn from service in January 1990 with the det inactivated later in the year. The reorganization of USAF operations has resulted in the SAC and MAC assets in Europe being transferred to USAFE during 1992. In preparation for this the 100th ARW was formed in January 1992 to replace the 513th ACCW, which was inactivated. The 100th will assume responsibility for KC-135 tankers directly assigned to USAFE, replacing 306th Wing.

Minot AFB, North Dakota

Command: ACC
Major unit: 5th Wg B-52H, KC-135A; 91st SMW LGM-30G
Tenant units: det 7 37th ARS HH-1H (AMC); ACE det 64th FTW T-38A (ATC)
Location and origin of name: 13 miles north of Minot, and named for the nearby city

Established in 1957 as an Air Defense Command

base with interceptor squadrons located there. 4136th Strategic Wing formed in September 1958 until replaced by 450th BW in February 1963. Base transferred to SAC in July 1962 with 455th SMW formed at same time with the Minuteman I ICBM. Latter wing replaced by 91st SMW, while 450th BW inactivated when 5th BW moved from Travis AFB in June 1968. 91st SMW upgraded to Minuteman III in 1971.

Misawa AB, Japan

Command: PACAF
Major unit: 432nd FW F-16C/D
Tenant unit: US Naval Facility
Location and origin of name: adjacent to Misawa, and named after the town

Base occupied by US forces in September 1945, with 49th FW assigned between August 1948 and December 1950. The unit returned to Misawa in April 1953 following combat duty during the Korean War. Wing relocated to France in December 1957 and was replaced by 21st TFW from July 1958 to June 1960. The 45th TRS was stationed at Misawa during the early 1960s operating the RF-101C until the squadron moved to Tan Son Nhut AB, South Vietnam. The 475th TFW was reactivated at Misawa operating the F-4C and later the F-4D, plus the RF-4C until March 1971, when inactivated. Base administered by the AF Security Service until October 1978 when returned to PACAF control with the 6112th ABW activated. 432nd TFW was reactivated in July 1984 to operate the F-16A for air defense of the area to the north of Japan.

Minneapolis St Paul IAP, Minnesota

The International Airport is in Minneapolis near the confluence of the Mississippi and Minnesota Rivers, with an AFRes section operated by the 934th AG and the 133rd AW of the Minnesota ANG, both flying the C-130E.

General Mitchell IAP, Milwaukee, Wisconsin

The International Airport is three miles south of Milwaukee and is named after the legendary aviation pioneer Billy Mitchell. The military area is run by the AFRes and has the 440th AW operating the C-130H, while the Wisconsin ANG operates the KC-135R assigned to the 128th ARG.

Moffett Field, California

The Naval Air Station is two miles north of Mountain View and is the main P-3 Orion base on the West Coast of the USA. The California ANG has the 129th RQG in residence flying the HC-130N/P and HH-60G. The station is earmarked for closure by the middle of the decade, which will require the ANG unit to move elsewhere.

Overshadowed by the San Bernadino Mountains, March AFB proclaims itself as 'Tanker Town, USA'. 15th Air Force, which controls all active-duty tanker assets, is headquartered here, and the base supports the activities of a KC-10 wing and a Reserve KC-135 squadron. Other flying units are a Reserve Hercules squadron and one flying ANG RF-4Cs. Like many other bases, March also maintains a well-kept museum, numbering among its exhibits a U-2 and an SR-71.

Moody AFB, Georgia

Command: ACC
Major unit: 347th FW F-16C/D
Tenant unit: nil
Location and origin of name: 10 miles northeast of Valdosta, and named for Major George P. Moody, killed on 5 May 1941 in crash while flight testing an AT-10 trainer at Wichita, Kansas

Established as Valdosta Airfield in June 1941 and renamed to its present title in January 1948. Conducted aircrew training during World War II, and transferred postwar variously between Air Training Command, SAC and TAC before assigned to ATC in September 1951 with the 3350th FTW in residence. Unit redesignated 38th FTW in December 1973 but inactivated two years later. The 347th TFW was re-formed in September 1975 with the F-4E assigned, but upgraded to the F-16A. The wing was scheduled to transfer their aircraft to other units during 1992/1993 prior to Moody AFB closing, although the base has been given a reprieve and will now house a composite wing instead.

Mountain Home AFB, Idaho

Command: ACC
Major unit: 366th FW F-111A, EF-111A
Tenant units: det 2 57th FW (ACC); det 3 AWC (ACC) – aircraft borrowed as required
Location and origin of name: 10 miles southwest of Mountain Home, and named after nearby city

Established as Army Air Base Mountain Home in November 1942 and retitled to its present name in January 1948. Operated training for heavy bomber crews during World War II but closed in 1945. Reopened in 1949 when 5th SRW was assigned for four months. Briefly operated by MATS until May 1953 when transferred to SAC with the 9th BW assigned flying the B-29 and later the B-47. Operated the Stratojet until 1966 and was one of the last SAC units to operate the type. Wing relocated to Beale AFB in 1966 when Mountain Home was transferred to TAC with the 67th TRW in residence until July 1971. The 347th TFW was based for a short time from May 1971 until October 1972 when replaced by the 366th TFW, which returned to USA from Takhli RTAFB, Thailand. Mountain Home housed the F-111F from June 1971 until 1977 when the type was delivered to Europe and replaced by the F-111A. The EF-111A was added in November 1981. Most of the Raven personnel were deployed to the Middle East for Desert Shield/Desert Storm. Mountain Home AFB has been identified as the facility to house the Air Force's first major composite wing, with fighters, bombers and support aircraft all operated by a single manager. The first F-15Es were delivered in 1992.

Muniz ANGB/San Juan IAP, Puerto Rico

The ANG Base is to the east of San Juan with the 156th FG Puerto Rico ANG operating the A-7D.

Myrtle Beach AFB, South Carolina

Command: ACC
Major unit: 354th FW A-10A
Tenant unit: nil
Location and origin of name: adjacent to Myrtle Beach, and named after nearby city

Opened in 1940 and known as Myrtle Beach MAP, before changing to Myrtle Beach General Bombing and Gunnery Range in 1942. Returned to MAP status for a short time in 1947 before becoming an AFB in January 1948. As the title suggests the facility conducted gunnery and bombardment training during World War II. Base inactive between November 1947 and June 1954 when prepared for flight operations with assignment to TAC. 342nd Fighter-Day Wing based for a few months in 1956 followed by the 354th FDW from November 1956 until July 1968, when the unit moved to South Korea. Base administered by 4554th CCTW until June 1970 when the 354th TFW returned from duty overseas. Equipped with the A-7D and later the A-10A. Two squadrons of A-10As and most of the personnel from the base were deployed to Saudi Arabia for Desert Shield/Desert Storm. Wing is in the process retiring the A-10 prior to inactivating later in 1992, with the base closing 12 months later.

Nashville Metropolitan Airport, Tennessee

The Metropolitan Airport is six miles southeast of Nashville and houses the 118th AW Tennessee ANG operating the C-130H.

Nellis AFB, Nevada

Command: ACC
Major unit: HQ Air Warfare Center; 57th FW A-10A, F-15C/D/E, F-16C/D, 'Thunderbirds' Air Demonstration Unit F-16C/D
Tenant units: 4440th TFTG/Red Flag (ACC); 4443rd TTG/Air Warrior (ACC); det 3 1400th MAS C-12F (AMC)
Location and origin of name: eight miles northeast of Las Vegas, and named for First Lieutenant William H. Nellis, killed on his 70th mission on 27 December 1944 when his P-47 was shot down near Bastogne, Belgium

Opened in 1941 as Las Vegas Air Field with various other titles until renamed Nellis AFB in April 1950. Trained AAF gunners during World War II and expanded postwar with additional facilities for the USAF Aircraft Gunnery School in May 1949 (later Fighter Weapons School). Base administered by Air Corps Flying Training Command and later ATC before switching to TAC in July 1958. 3595th Air Demonstration Flight, alias 'The Thunderbirds', moved from Luke AFB in June 1956 and changed designation to 4520th Air Demonstration Flight and Squadron before becoming the USAF Air Demonstration Squadron in February 1967. Nellis base and range complex expanded to more than three million acres by 1962, making it the largest USAF installation. 4525th Fighter Weapons Wing formed in September 1966 as the flying unit of the Tactical Fighter Weapons Center (TFWC). 4525th FWW replaced by 57th FWW in October 1969. 4480th TFW activated in July 1967 but replaced by 474th TFW six months later. Red Flag realistic tactical exercises began late 1975 with 4440th TFTG assigned in March 1976 to coordinate activities. The 57th FWW organized aggressor training with the 64th and 65th FWSs, becoming TFTASs and operating the F-5E around the same time.

New Boston AFS, New Hampshire

Air Force Space Command Satellite remote tracking station.

NAS New Orleans, Louisiana

The Naval Air Station is 15 miles south of New Orleans with the 159th FG Louisiana ANG flying the F-15A/B, while the AFRes unit is the 926th FG operating the A-10A. The base is Headquarters of the US Naval Reserve and is home for USN and Marine Corps Reserve squadrons.

Newark AFB, Ohio

AFMC facility near Newark which has the Aerospace Guidance and Metrology Center in residence to overhaul and repair inertial guidance and navigation systems for aircraft and missiles.

Niagara Falls IAP, New York

The International Airport is six miles east of Niagara Falls with a complex administered by the AFRes. Resident unit is the 914th AG flying the C-130E, while the New York ANG has the 107th FG flying the F-16A/B ADF. The New York ARNG has an Aviation Company flying a mixed helicopter force.

Norton AFB, California

Command: AMC
Major unit: 63rd AW C-141B
Tenant units: 1400th AS C-12F, C-21A (AMC); 445th AW (Associate) C-141B (AFRes)
Location and origin of name: within San Bernardino city limits, and named for Captain Leland Norton, killed when his A-20 was shot down near Amiens, France, on 27 May 1944

Established as MAP San Bernardino in 1942 but under AAF control with an air depot in residence which was known as the San Bernardino Air Material Area (AMA) from February 1943. Changed title twice before inactivating in June 1947. Base assigned to AAF Material and Services, and later AAF Technical Service Command which was the forerunner of AF Logistics Command. San Bernardino AMA re-formed in December 1949 to perform jet aircraft overhauls. Base served as Atlas and Titan missile logistics and storage facility between 1962 and 1964. AMA inactivated in July 1966 with overhaul duties redistributed to other centers. Base transferred to MAC at the same time with 63rd MAW transferring from Hunter AFB, GA, in April 1967. However, the wing is scheduled to inactivate prior to the base closing by 1994.

Offutt AFB, Nebraska

Command: ACC
Major unit: 55th Wg C-135A, NKC-135A, EC-135C, KC-135E, RC-135S/U/V/W/X, TC-135S/W, E-4B
Tenant unit: det 1 1401st AS C-21A (AMC)
Location and origin of name: eight miles south of Omaha, and named for First Lieutenant Jarvis J. Offutt, the first native of Omaha to be killed in World War I, when his SE.5 crashed near Valheureux, France, on 13 August 1918

Known as Fort George Cook from March 1891, and established as Offutt Field for flying duties in 1924. However, this was predated by the presence of the 61st Balloon Company late 1918 for combat reconnaissance training. Field accommodated interim reserve flying training and Post Office airmail flights during 1920s and 1930s. Limited military presence until 1940, with the Glenn L. Martin Company leasing all flying facilities in 1941 to erect a bomber plant. Bomber production and modification carried out during World War II. Base administered by AAF Material Command. Postwar, hosted a separation center for personnel leaving the service. 438th TCW in residence between June 1949 and March 1951. Transferred to SAC in October 1948 with Headquarters of the Command moving from Andrews AFB the following month. New SAC HQ building and command control center opened late 1956, with a KC-135A squadron activated in October 1958. The latter unit, designated 34th ARefS, operated the first airborne command posts from 1961 onwards. These ACPs performed a continuous airborne relay from February 1961 for almost 25 years, with one aircraft performing an eight-hour sortie before being relieved by another. 4321st Strategic Wing in residence from October 1959 to January 1963 when replaced by 385th SAW. The 385th inactivated in December 1964 with the 34th ARefS believed unattached until June 1966, when the squadron moved to Pease AFB. The ACP KC-135s were again autonomous for two months until the 55th SRW moved to Offutt from Ramey AFB, PR, in August 1966. The 2nd ACCS was activated in April 1970 to operate the EC-135Cs and was joined by the 1st ACCS with the E-4B seven years later. The 55th Wg will assume the operations of the 6th Wg in 1992.

O'Hare Air Reserve Forces Facility, Chicago, Illinois

The Facility is run by the AFRes and is in one area of O'Hare Airport, which is 22 miles northwest of Chicago. Resident is the 928th AG operating the C-130H, and the 126th ARW Illinois ANG flying the KC-135E.

Onizuka AFB, California

Satellite operations unit near San Francisco operated by the 2nd Satellite Tracking Group for AF Space Command.

Osan AB, Republic of Korea

Command: PACAF
Major unit: HQ 7th Air Force, 51st FG OA-10A, F-16C/D
Tenant unit: det 3 1403rd AS C-12F (AMC)
Location and origin of name: 38 miles south of Seoul, and named for nearby town which was the scene of the first fighting between US and North Korean forces in July 1950

The base was originally known as K-55 when the runway was opened in December 1952, and was retitled to its present name in 1956. 58th FBW assigned between March 1955 and July 1958 operating the F-86 until inactivated. Base administered by 6314th Support Wing until November 1971 when replaced by the 51st ABW flying a variety of transport aircraft and helicopters in support of the 314th Air Division. Unit changed to 51st CW with a tactical role, operating the F-4E and OV-10A.

Otis ANGB, Falmouth, Massachusetts

The base is seven miles northeast of Falmouth, with the 102nd FW Massachusetts ANG flying the F-15A/B. Adjacent are Cape Cod AFS, Cape Cod US Coast Guard Station, and Camp Edwards Army National Guard Training Site. Facility was formerly an Air Force Base and was named for First Lieutenant Frank J. Otis, pilot and flight surgeon killed in an air crash in 1937.

Patrick AFB, Florida

Command: AFSPACECOM
Major unit: Eastern Space and Missile Center – no aircraft assigned; 9th Space Division
Tenant units: det 15 41st ARS HH-3E (AMC); 71st ARS HC-130N/P (AMC)
Location and origin of name: two miles south of Cocoa Beach, and named for Major General Mason M. Patrick, Chief of AEF's Air Service in World War I, and subsequently the architect of legislation to create the Air Corps from the Air Service

Established by the Navy as NAS Banana River and transferred to the USAF as Joint Long Range Proving Ground and Long Range Proving Ground AFB before gaining its current title in 1950. Primarily involved in missile tracking duties, with the 550th Guided Missile Wing assigned briefly during December 1950, followed by the 4800th GMW and 6555th GMW. Latter unit and 6550th Test Group assigned in various forms for many years. Base operated by ARDC and later AFSC until early 1980s when transferred to Space Command. TAC assets assigned in 1975 with the 549th TASTG operating the O-2 and OV-10A until inactivated by mid-1988. Base supports rocket launches from nearby Cape Canaveral with NASA aircraft frequently in residence. The 9th SRW maintained detachment 5 operating a single U-2R for operations over the Caribbean until inactivated in February 1991. The only permanently assigned unit at present is the 41st ARS det flying the HH-3E for local rescue duties, and the 71st ARS which formed in October 1991 flying the HC-130.

Another base in the Los Angeles area, Norton houses a StarLifter transport wing. It is on the current list for base closures, its 63rd Airlift Wing scheduled to deactivate in 1993.

Pease ANGB, New Hampshire

The base is one mile east of Portsmouth and houses the 157th ARG New Hampshire ANG flying the KC-135E. Formerly an Air Force Base until 1991 when operational units were withdrawn and the site was transferred to the ANG. Named for Captain Harl Pease, who was killed when his B-17 was shot down while attacking Rabaul, New Britain, on 7 August 1942.

Greater Peoria Airport, Illinois

The Airport is seven miles southwest of Peoria with the 182nd FG Illinois ANG in residence, flying the OA-37B and the C-26A.

Peterson AFB, Colorado

Command: AFSPACECOM
Major unit: HQ Air Force Space Command; 1st Space Wing – no aircraft assigned
Tenant unit: 302nd AW C-130B (AFRes)
Location and origin of name: at eastern edge of Colorado Springs, and named for First Lieutenant Edward J. Peterson, killed on 8 August 1942 when his reconnaissance P-51 (F-4) crashed on take-off at the field which bears his name

Known as Air Support Command Base when opened in 1942 and later Peterson Field. Con-

ducted photo-reconnaissance training until mid-1943, when it switched to heavy bomber training. Later undertook fighter pilot training in 1944 with an instructors' school formed in 1945. Postwar, the base was closed to flying duties and assigned to Air Defense Command to support nearby Ent AFB. Regular flying duties resumed in 1967 with the 3253rd PTS in residence until July 1974. The 4600th ABW flew the T-33A in support of HQ ADC from November 1971 until March 1975 when the unit changed to the 46th ADW. Base transferred to SAC in October 1979 but reassigned to Space Command by the mid-1980s. HQ AFSPACECOM formed in September 1982.

Phelps Collins ANGB, Michigan

The ANG base is seven miles west of Alpena and has no resident flying squadron or aircraft assigned. Primarily an ANG and AFRes facility used for annual field training and by Army National Guard and Marine Corps Reserve for special training. Base named for Captain W. H. Phelps Collins, who was killed in France in March 1918.

Greater Pittsburgh IAP, Pennsylvania

The International Airport is 15 miles northwest of Pittsburgh and has a military area administered by the AFRes. Resident unit is the 911th AG flying the C-130H, while the Pennsylvania ANG has the 171st ARW flying the KC-135E and the 112th FG operating the A-7D/K.

Plattsburgh AFB, New York

Command: AMC
Major unit: 380th Wg KC-135A/Q
Tenant unit: ACE det 71st FTW T-37B (ATC)
Location and origin of name: adjacent to and named after town of Plattsburgh

Established in February 1955 as Plattsburgh AFB under SAC control with the 380th BW activated in July 1955 to operate the B-47E and KC-97G, plus the EB-47. Base was one of a handful selected to service test the Super Wing concept operating 70 B-47s and 40 KC-97s between July 1959 and June 1960. These were assigned to the 380th BW and the 308th BW which was in residence between July 1959 and June 1961. 4108th ARefW flying the KC-97G was stationed here between January 1961 and January 1963, before being replaced by the 497th ARW which inactivated in September 1964. Plattsburgh was one of two SAC bases which housed operational FB-111As until July 1991 when the final examples were retired.

Pope AFB, North Carolina

Command: ACC
Major unit: 23rd Wg (ACC); 317th AW C-130E (AMC); USAF Airlift Center
Tenant unit: nil
Location and origin of name: 12 miles northwest of Fayetteville, and named for First Lieutenant Harley H. Pope, killed on 7 January 1919 when his JN-4 crashed near Fayetteville, North Carolina

Base established as Camp Bragg Flying Field in 1919 and renamed Pope Field later in the year. Conducted observation and balloon training between 1919 and 1927 followed by bomber training. Became the first US installation used for joint air/ground operations in 1929 due to the close proximity of the huge Fort Bragg Army complex. Base adapted for major troop carrier training duties during World War II and postwar operating chiefly the C-82. Base assigned to TAC in April 1946 and CONAC from December 1948, before reverting to TAC two years later. 464th TCW assigned in September 1954 until August 1971 when replaced by 317th TAW. USAF Tactical Airlift Center in residence from September 1966 to June 1971, and re-formed during the late 1970s. Base upgraded in 1969/1970 to conduct C-5 and C-141 operations in connection with 82nd Airborne based at Fort Bragg. Transferred from TAC to MAC in December 1974. Pope AFB is the only MAC base scheduled to be transferred to Air Combat Command as it is due to house the composite 23rd Wg with C-130s and A-10s.

Portland IAP, Oregon

The International Airport is five miles north of Portland, with the 142nd FG Oregon ANG flying the F-15A/B. In addition, the AFRes 939th ARW is stationed, operating the HC-130H, HH-1H and HH-3E.

Quonset Point State Airport, Providence, Rhode Island

The State Airport is 20 miles south of Providence and is home base for the 143rd AG Rhode Island ANG flying the C-130E. The Rhode Island ARNG has a large helicopter Aviation Company at the airport.

Ramstein AB, Germany

Command: USAFE
Major unit: HQ USAFE, 86th FW F-16C/D
Tenant units: 7th Air Division (ACC); 608th MAG C-12F, C-20A, C-21A, C-135B, UH-1N, CT-43A (AMC)
Location and origin of name: 10 miles west of Kaiserslautern, and named after nearby town

Base opened in 1952 as Landstuhl AB, and re-named Ramstein-Landstuhl AB before gaining its present title. The 86th FBW moved to the base from Neubiberg AB, Germany, in August 1952, but was upgraded to Air Division status in November 1960 with responsibility for four F-102A interceptor squadrons at Ramstein and three other bases (Bitburg, Hahn and Soesterberg). However, the unit returned to wing level exactly eight years later, and moved to Zweibrücken in November 1969. In the meantime the 26th TRW, had moved to Ramstein from Toul-Rosières AB, France, in October 1966. The 26th TRW remained until January 1973 when it was transferred to Zweibrücken in exchange for the 86th TFW, which returned to Ramstein. The 306th SW was activated by SAC in August 1976 although no aircraft were stationed at Ramstein as the unit was formed to control detachments at Mildenhall and Zaragoza AB, Spain. However, the need for an effective liaison between SAC HQ and HQ USAFE resulted in the 7th Air Division being formed at Ramstein. The 608th MAG was formed to operate the mixed fleet of VIP types flown in support of HQ USAFE and HQ 17th Air Force.

Randolph AFB, Texas

Command: ATC
Major unit: HQ ATC; 12th FTW T-37B, T-38A
Tenant unit: nil
Location and origin of name: 17 miles northeast of San Antonio, and named for Army Captain William M. Randolph, killed in the crash of an AT-4 on 17 February 1928

Base known as Aviation Field, San Antonio when opened in 1928, but renamed Randolph Field shortly afterwards. Performed primary and basic pilot training from 1931 and upgraded during the latter part of World War II for B-29 operations. Postwar, the base continued primary pilot training until 1951 with the base concentrating on conversion training of B-29 aircrew, plus the C-119 and T-33 between 1954 and 1956, B-57 in 1954/1955, and KC-97 between 1956 and 1958. The 3510th Basic Pilot Training Wing was formed in August 1948 and remained as the major flying unit until May 1972 when replaced by the 12th FTW. HQ ATC was transferred from Scott AFB in August 1957. Randolph housed a limited SAC presence with the 4397th ARefW assigned between July 1958 and June 1962, and is believed to have been responsible for KC-97 aircrew training with the 4397th CCTS. The facility is rather unusual as all of its buildings, flightline areas and operation complexes are laid out neatly between the two main runways.

Reese AFB, Texas

Command: ATC
Major unit: 64th FTW T-37B, T-38A
Tenant unit: nil
Location and origin of name: adjacent to Lubbock, and named after First Lieutenant Augustus F. Reese, killed on 14 May 1943 when his P-38 was shot down near Cagliari, Sardinia

Established as Air Corps Advanced Flying School, Lubbock in 1941 and renamed Reese AFB in November 1949. Hosted Air Corps Advanced Flying School in 1941 and upgraded postwar to conduct all-jet training by mid-1951. However, continued to provide TB-25N training between 1955 and 1959 before switching completely to the T-33A. The T-38A was added in 1963 and the T-41 two years later. Major flying unit was the 3500th PTW from October 1949 until October 1972, when replaced by the 64th FTW.

Rhein Main AB, Germany

Command: USAFE
Major unit: 435th AW C-9A, C-130E
Tenant unit: nil
Location and origin of name: five miles south of Frankfurt, and named after the confluence of the Rhein and Main rivers to the west of Frankfurt

Base opened in July 1936, with US forces stationed since March 1945. The base was one of three which were heavily involved in Operation Vittles, the resupply by air of the besieged city of Berlin in 1948 and 1949 with hundreds of daily flights by C-54s and C-47s. The 61st TCW was established at the base in July 1948, but inactivated in June 1951 when the 60th TCW moved from nearby Wiesbaden AB. The unit operated the C-119 until October 1955 when it moved to Dreux AB, France. The 433rd TCW was stationed at Rhein Main between August 1951 and July 1952 during its period of mobilization before returning to the USA and Reserve status. The 317th TCW was also in residence during 1952 and 1953 before being transferred to Neubiberg AB. The 7407th CSW was activated at Rhein Main in the mid-1950s to operate a mixed fleet of RB-57Ds and specialist C-130As from Rhein Main, plus a squadron of intelligence-gathering C-97Gs flying from Wiesbaden. The wing eventually inactivated, with their Hercules absorbed into the 435th TAW. The 7310th TAW operated the base for many years until the 322nd TAW was re-formed from Air Division status in January 1970. The 322nd became an Air Division again in June 1975 with the 435th TASW changing to a TAW as the primary unit at Rhein Main. The base operates the largest combined cargo and passenger terminal in the Air Force and shares the runway with one of the busiest commercial airports on the continent. The base was one of the primary support facilities for MAC airlifters flying to and from the Middle East during Desert Shield/Desert Storm.

Richards-Gebaur AFB, Missouri

Although an AFRes installation, Richards-Gebaur is still an Air Force Base and is located 17 miles south of Kansas City. The base houses the 442nd FW flying the A-10A, along with Navy and Army Reserve units. Base named for First Lieutenant John F. Richards II and Lieutenant Colonel Arthur W. Gebaur Jr. The former was killed when his Nieuport was shot down during the Argonne Offensive on 26 September 1918, while the latter was killed when his F-84 was brought down over North Korea on 29 August 1952. The wing is due to move to Whiteman AFB in mid-1994 before Richards-Gebaur AFB closes at the end of that year.

Rickenbacker ANGB, Ohio

The base is 13 miles southwest of Columbus and has been administered by the ANG since April 1980, when transferred from SAC. Ohio ANG residents include the 121st FW operating the A-7D/K, and the 160th ARG flying the KC-135E (ANG), while the AFRes has the 907th AG with the C-130E. Formerly known as Lockbourne AFB but renamed for Captain Edward V. Rickenbacker, legendary World War I ace who died on 23 July 1973. All resident Reserve units to move to Wright-Patterson AFB during 1993 with Rickenbacker closing in 1994.

Robins AFB, Georgia

Command: AFMC
Major unit: Warner Robins ALC
Tenant units: HQ AFRes; 19th Wg KC-135R, EC-135Y, EC-137E (AMC); ACE det 71st FTW T-37B (ATC)
Location and origin of name: 15 miles southeast of Macon, and named after Brigadier General Augustine Warner Robins who died on 16 June 1940 at Randolph Field while commandant of the Air Corps Training Center

Established as Robins Field in 1941 primarily as a logistics depot but also trained 50,000 personnel for overseas duty in World War II. Warner Robins Depot Area Command formed in February 1944 as forerunner of today's Air Logistics Center. Reduced to limited flying duties between 1945 and 1949. Upgraded for SAC operations with two ARefSs located in 1954 and 1956, which appear to have operated without wing assignment, both inactivated when the 4137th Strategic Wing was formed in February 1959. Latter wing replaced by 465th BW in February 1963, which itself was inactivated in July 1968 when the 19th BW moved from Homestead AFB. HQ Continental Air Command located between April 1961 and August 1968 when the service was renamed Air Force Reserve, with HQ at Robins AFB.

Rosecrans Memorial Airport, St Joseph, Missouri

Rosecrans Airport is four miles west of St Joseph and has the 139th AG Missouri ANG in residence flying the C-130H.

Salt Lake City IAP, Utah

The International Airport is three miles west of

Salt Lake City and houses KC-135Es of the 151st ARG Utah ANG flying the KC-135E. The Utah ARNG has a small helicopter detachment located at the airport.

San Vito del Normanni AB, Italy

Facility near Brindisi has an Electronic Security Group as part of AF Intelligence Command and is run by the 7275th ABG of USAFE.

Savannah IAP, Georgia

The International Airport is four miles northwest of Savannah with the 165th AG Georgia ANG flying the C-130H. The airport has a Gulfstream production and overhaul facility located.

Schenectady County Airport, New York

The County Airport is two miles north of Schenectady and has the 109th AG New York ANG operating a mixture of C-130Hs and ski-equipped LC-130H models.

Scott AFB, Illinois

Command: ACC
Major unit: HQ AMC, 375th AW C-9A, C-12F, C-21A
Tenant units: HQ AF Communications Command, HQ Air Weather Service (AMC); 932nd AG (Associate) C-9A (AFRes)
Location and origin of name: six miles northeast of Belleville, and named for Corporal Frank S. Scott, the first enlisted airman to lose his life in an aircraft accident. He was killed at College Park, Maryland, on 28 September 1912 in the crash of a Wright Type B biplane for which he was a chief mechanic.

Base established as Scott Field in 1917 for lighter than air training with airship facilities between 1919 and 1938. World War I vintage facilities replaced by permanent structures with the training of radio operators and a mechanics' school during World War II. Postwar, the training level was reduced, but increased during the Korean War with the base serving as stateside terminus for MATS. HQ ATC located until October 1957 when base transferred to MATS control, with HQ of the service moving from Andrews AFB at the same time. HQ AF Communications Service became independent of MATS in July 1961, with HQ Air Rescue and Recovery Service moving from Orlando AFB, Florida, in June 1968. SAC presence between June 1947 and June 1949 with the 96th BW. 1405th ABW (later Aeromedical Transport Wing) operated aeromedical duties from August 1948 until January 1966 when the unit was replaced by the 375th AAW (later 375th AW).

Seymour Johnson was chosen as the first base for a composite wing, the 4th Wing combining the F-15Es of the former 4th TFW with the KC-10 Extenders of the 68th ARW.

Selfridge ANGB, Michigan

Selfridge ANGB is three miles northeast of Mount Clemens and was formerly a major Air Force Base. Several Reserve units are in residence, including the 127th FW and 191st FG (both Michigan ANG) operating the F-16A/B and F-16A/B ADF, respectively. Air Force Reserve units include the 927th AG flying the C-130E and the 305th RQS operating the HC-130H/N and HH-3E. In addition, the base houses Navy, Marine Corps and Army Reserve units, as well as an Army National Guard squadron. US Coast Guard Detroit has a number of helicopters operating from Selfridge.

Sembach AB, Germany

Command: USAFE
Major unit: HQ 17th Air Force – no aircraft assigned
Tenant unit: nil
Location and origin of name: nine miles northeast of Kaiserslautern, and named after nearby farming community

Base activated in 1930, with US presence since July 1953 when the 66th TRW moved from Shaw AFB. Wing relocated to Laon AB, France, in July 1958 prior to the base being readied for the assignment of tactical missiles. The 38th Tactical Missile Wing relocated from Hahn AB in August 1959 with the Matador and later the Mace missiles. Unit inactivated in September 1966. The 601st Tactical Control Wing (later Tactical Air Control Wing) was assigned to Sembach during the late 1970s operating the CH-53C and OV-10A. Base was one of four Forward Operating Locations for the UK-based A-10As until 1991 when the detachment was withdrawn. 66th ECW assigned from March 1987 until mid-1991 operating the EC-130H. Currently has no aircraft in residence.

Seymour Johnson AFB, North Carolina

Command: ACC
Major unit: 4th Wg KC-10A, F-15E
Tenant units: 916th ARG (Associate) KC-10A (AFRes); OL AD 191st FG F-16A/B (MI ANG); ACE det 12th FTW T-38A (ATC)
Location and origin of name: within city limits of Goldsboro, and named for Navy Lieutenant Seymour A. Johnson, killed while flight testing a Grumman monoplane near Norbeck, Maryland, on 5 March 1941

Established as Technical School, AAFTTC Goldsboro in 1942 and renamed Seymour John-

son Field soon afterwards. Field accommodated Aviation Cadet Pre-Technical School Training program during World War II, before becoming an AAF Separation Center postwar. Inactive from 1947 until April 1956 when under TAC control. 83rd FDW in residence in 1956 and 1957 operating the F-86 and F-100 when replaced by the 4th FDW which returned to the USA from the Far East. 4241st Strategic Wing formed by SAC in October 1958 and replaced by 68th BW in April 1963. Latter unit changed to an ARefG in September 1982 and later an ARefW with the KC-10A assigned. Wing merged with the 4th TFW to become the 4th Wing under TAC as the first composite wing to evaluate the principal before the creation of more complex units.

Shaw AFB, South Carolina

Command: ACC
Major unit: HQ 9th Air Force; 363rd FW F-16C/D
Tenant unit: 507th ACW OA-10A (ACC)
Location and origin of name: 10 miles northwest of Sumter, and named for Second Lieutenant Erwin D. Shaw, killed when his Bristol Fighter was shot down over enemy lines on 9 July 1918

Base known as Shaw Field when opened in 1941 as a primary flying school. Postwar, the base accommodated P-61 night fighter operations. Facility operated by Continental Air Command until transferred to TAC in December 1950. 20th FW in residence from August 1947 until November 1951, and 437th TCW briefly at the end of 1950. 363rd TRW moved from Langley AFB in April 1951 and is current as a Fighter Wing (since October 1982 as a TFW). Unit conducted reconnaissance operations and training for more than 30 years with numerous squadrons assigned. 507th Tactical Control Group formed in July 1954.

Shemya AFB, Alaska

Command: PACAF
Major unit: 5073rd ABG – no aircraft assigned
Tenant unit: nil
Location and origin of name: located at western end of the Aleutian Islands chain, midway between Anchorage, Alaska, and Tokyo, Japan, and named after the island on which the base is situated

Established as Shemya Army Air Base in 1943 and served as a bomber base during World War II. Operated by Alaskan Air Command until August 1990 when PACAF absorbed all AAC assets. Housed a cryptological unit for the Security Service from 1956 until 1975, and ADC's Cobra Dane radar from the spring of 1976. Det 1 6th Wing (formerly 6th SRW) established to operate the Eielson-based RC-135s which frequently terminate missions at Shemya. Base known as 'The Rock' as it is only 11 square miles in area. The Aleutian chain has the international date line bent around it so that the date is the same as the remainder of the USA.

Shepherd Field, Martinsburg, West Virginia

Shepherd Field is four miles south of Martinsburg and is home for the C-130Es of the 167th AG West Virginia ANG.

Sheppard AFB, Texas

Command: ATC
Major unit: Sheppard TTC; 80th FTW T-37B, T-38A, 3700th TTW – various aircraft types (see unit listing)
Tenant unit: nil

Location and origin of name: four miles north of Wichita Falls, and named in honor of Morris E. Sheppard, a Texas senator and chairman of the Senate Military Affairs Committee who died on 9 April 1941

Base known as Technical School at Wichita Falls when opened in 1941 and renamed Sheppard Field soon afterwards. Constructed as a Technical School, and expanded to accommodate basic training in 1943/1944. Postwar served as Separation Center before being declared surplus. Reactivated for basic training role in 1948, and for aircraft maintenance instruction. Various other training specialties transferred to Sheppard including Atlas and Titan missile training. Base upgraded to accommodate SAC presence with 4245th Strategic Wing formed in January 1959, and renumbered 494th BW in February 1963. Wing inactivated in April 1966. Base commenced German Air Force pilot training program in March 1967 with the T-37B and T-38A. 3630th FTW formed in December 1965 and replaced by 80th FTW in January 1973.

Sioux Gateway Airport, Sioux City, Iowa

Gateway Airport is seven miles south of Sioux City with the 185th FG Iowa ANG, currently exchanging their A-7D/Ks for the F-16C/D.

Sky Harbor IAP, Phoenix, Arizona

The International Airport is to the east of central Phoenix and has the 161st ARG Arizona ANG operating the KC-135E.

Soesterberg AB, the Netherlands

Command: USAFE
Major unit: 32nd FG F-15C/D
Tenant unit: nil
Location and origin of name: three miles from Zeist, and named for locality

Base originally activated in 1913, although it was not until 1954 that US forces were in residence. The 32nd Fighter Day Squadron was assigned from October 1956 operating the F-86F. The squadron was allocated to the 36th FDW with HQ at Bitburg until April 1960, when parented to the 86th FIW with HQ at Ramstein. In November 1968 the squadron was assigned the status of reporting directly to the HQ 17th Air Force, as it was assigned the joint role of integrated air defense of the Netherlands along with its prescribed commitment to USAFE. The squadron continued in this autonomous format until November 1989, when the 32nd TFG was activated as the controlling element.

Sondestrom AB, Greenland

Air Force Space Command operates a radar support complex.

Spangdahlem AB, Germany

Command: USAFE
Major unit: 52nd FW F-4G, F-16C/D
Tenant unit: nil
Location and origin of name: eight miles east of Bitburg, and named for nearby village

Base opened in 1953 as a USAFE facility with the 10th TRW taking up residence from Toul-Rosières AB, France, in May 1953. The unit relocated to RAF Alconbury in August 1959 when the 49th TFW moved to Spangdahlem AB from Etain-Rouvres AB, France. Wing returned home in July 1968 as the USAF's first 'dual-based' NATO-committed fighter unit prepared to return to Europe if and when necessary. The unit returned to Germany annually as part of this commitment under Operation Crested Cap, although other units were substituted when the 49th TFW sent aircraft and personnel to Thailand in 1972. The 39th TEWS formed in April 1969 operating the EB-66C/E but was assigned to the 36th TFW with HQ at Bitburg AB as Spangdahlem did not have a resident flying wing. The base was attached to the 36th TFW later in the month, with the 23rd TFS transferred from Bitburg to Spangdahlem. The 52nd TFW was formed at Spangdahlem in December 1971 to operate the two squadrons independently of the 36th TFW. The 39th TEWS inactivated in January 1973 and was replaced by the 81st TFS, before finally becoming a three-squadron wing when joined by the 480th TFS in November 1976. The base will add the A-10A by early 1993 to become the first USAFE composite wing.

Springfield-Beckley MAP, Ohio

The Municipal Airport is five miles south of Springfield, with the 178th FG Illinois ANG flying the F-16A/B.

Standiford Field, Louisville, Kentucky

Standiford Field is four miles south of Louisville, with the 123rd AW Kentucky ANG flying the C-130B.

Stewart ANGB/Stewart IAP, New York

Stewart Air National Guard Base is four miles west of Newburgh and was formerly Stewart Air Force Base. The base houses the 105th AG New York ANG operating the C-5A, together with an Army Reserve unit and a Marine Corps air refueling squadron.

Stuttgart/Echterdingen Airport, Germany

The 608th AG has three C-21As assigned to the European Command (EUCOM) Flight Section and flown by the 7005th ABS, along with a small number of US Army C-12s and UH-1s for VIP duties.

Suffolk County Airport, Westhampton Beach, New York

Suffolk County Airport is adjacent to Westhampton, with the 106th RQG New York ANG flying the HC-130N/P and HH-60G.

Tempelhof Central Airport AS, Germany

USAFE terminal at Tempelhof Airport located in the suburbs of Berlin and operated by the 7350th ABG since July 1948. Base also houses an Electronic Security Wing as part of AF Intelligence Command.

Allen C. Thompson Field, Jackson, Mississippi

Thompson Field is seven miles east of Jackson, flying the C-141B with the 172nd AG Mississippi ANG.

Thule AB, Greenland

Command: AFSPACECOM
Major unit: 1012th ABG; 12th Missile Warning Group
Tenant unit: nil
Location and origin of name: on the northwest coast of Greenland, 700 miles north of the Arctic Circle and 900 miles south of the North Pole, and named for nearby locality

Base activated in 1952 but has no aircraft assigned as it is primarily concerned with early warning duties. Presently assigned to Air Force Space Command housing missile warning and satellite tracking equipment. Only a couple of hundred US military and civilian personnel are stationed at Thule, along with approximately 1,000 Danish contractors.

Tinker AFB, Oklahoma

Command: AFMC
Major unit: Oklahoma City ALC
Tenant units: 28th AD C-135E, EC-135K (ACC); 552nd ACW E-3B/C (ACC); 507th FG F-16A/B (AFRes)
Location and origin of name: eight miles southeast of Oklahoma City, and named for Major General Clarence L. Tinker, commander of the 7th Air Force whose LB-30 disappeared over the Pacific while leading a raid against Wake Island on 7 June 1942

Base known as Midwest Air Depot when opened in 1941, becoming the Oklahoma City Air Depot and later still Tinker Field. Base produced A-26s, C-47s and C-54s at the Douglas plant, while conducting repairs to B-17s, B-24s and B-29s during World War II. The Oklahoma City Air Depot Control Area Command was activated in February 1943 as the forerunner of today's Air Logistics Center. Postwar, the base carried out overhaul and modification of aircraft, engines and associated equipment. 323rd BW activated as a Reserve unit and assigned between June 1949 and March 1951. The 506th Strategic Fighter Wing was based between March 1955 and April 1959. 1707th Air Transport Wing was located in June 1959 to conduct aircrew training for MATS, until January 1966 when replaced by the 443rd MAW. The latter relocated to Altus AFB in May 1969. The 4552nd AW&CS was formed in October 1974 to make preparations for the arrival in TAC service of the E-3 Sentry. The 4552nd was inactivated in July 1976 when the 552nd AW&CW relocated from McClellan AFB.

Toledo Express Airport, Ohio

Express Airport is 14 miles west of Toledo, with the 180th FG Ohio ANG flying the A-7D/K.

Tonopah Test Range Airfield, Nevada

Some 30 miles southeast of the town of Tonopah, situated within the Nellis range complex. Purpose-built to house F-117 operations in secrecy. Home of the F-117-equipped 37th Fighter Wing but has reverted to range support facility after F-117s moved to Holloman AFB.

Torrejon AB, Spain

Former home of the 401st TFW flying the F-16C/D until early 1992, the base no longer has US military forces in residence, and was returned to wholly Spanish operations from May 1992. HQ 16th Air Force was also located at Torrejon although its present assigned base is unknown.

Travis AFB, California

Command: AMC
Major unit: HQ 22nd Air Force; 60th AW C-5A/B, C-141B
Tenant unit: 349th AW (Associate) C-5A/B, C-141B (AFRes)
Location and origin of name: 50 miles northeast of San Francisco, and named for Brigadier General Robert F. Travis, killed in the crash of a B-29 at Fairfield-Suisun AFB on 5 August 1950

Base opened as Fairfield-Suisun Army Air Base and renamed Travis AFB in October 1950. Operated by Air Transport Command to provide ferrying of aircraft overseas and airlifting supplies and troops to the Far East during World War II. Postwar, the base became the West Coast's aerial embarkation and disembarkation point for the Pacific theater with the 530th Air Transport Wing (and later the 1501st ATW) before the base was transferred to SAC in May 1949. The 9th SRW was formed in May 1949 followed by the 5th SRW six months later. The former moved to Mountain Home AFB in May 1953 while the latter relocated to Minot AFB in July 1968. Several Air Transport Squadrons were assigned during 1953 followed by the 1501st ATW in July 1955. Base transferred to MATS in July 1958 with the 1501st replaced by the 60th MAW in January 1966. The 916th ARefS was operated from September 1959 initially under control of the 5th BW but from July 1968 as an autonomous unit. The unit inactivated during the 1980s.

Truax Field/Dane County Regional Airport, Madison, Wisconsin

Field is two miles north of Madison and houses the 128th FW Wisconsin ANG operating the A-10A, plus an Army National Guard unit.

Tucson IAP, Arizona

Tucson Airport is seven miles south of Tucson, with the 162nd FG Arizona ANG operating the F-16A/B. The group conducts ANG Fighting Falcon pilot training for the Air National Guard and for the Royal Netherlands Air Force. Tucson is a mecca for lovers of elderly aircraft as many former military types are in store or flown by civilian operators. The Learjet Corporation has a production and overhaul facility for the C-21A located there.

Tulsa IAP, Oklahoma

The International Airport is four miles northeast of Tulsa, with the 138th FG Oklahoma ANG operating the A-7D/K. The Oklahoma ARNG has a helicopter unit in residence, while the McDonnell Douglas Corporation has a facility at the airport.

Tyndall AFB, Florida

Command: ACC
Major unit: HQ Air Defense Weapons Center; 325th FW F-15A/B
Tenant unit: 475th Weapons Evaluation Group QF-100D/F, QF-106A/B, E-9A (ACC)
Location and origin of name: 12 miles east of Panama City and named for First Lieutenant Frank B. Tyndall, killed in the crash of a P-1 near Moresville, North Carolina, on 15 July 1930

Base established as Tyndall Field in 1941 under AAF Training Command to conduct flexible gunnery training during World War II. Postwar, the base accommodated all-weather jet interceptor training and aircraft controllers, with assignment to the 3625th Training Wing (later FTW and CCTW). Base transferred to Air Defense Command in July 1957 with the 4756th ADW as the primary flying unit. Tyndall became the primary weapons center evaluating the effectiveness of ADC units involving the use of unmanned drones. Conducted F-101, F-102 and F-106 aircrew transition training from July 1962. Air Defense Weapons Center formed in November 1967 with flying squadrons assigned directly following the inactivation of the 4756th ADW in January 1968. Separate runway for drone operations completed in July 1978. Air Combat Maneuvering Instrumentation (ACMI) system opened in 1978. Interceptor Weapons School established in October 1979. Base transferred to TAC in October 1979 when ADC was absorbed into the former Command. 325th Fighter Weapons Wing formed at Tyndall AFB in July 1981 as the flying component of the Air Defense Weapons Center. Redesignated to Tactical Training Wing status 1983. Conducts all F-15A and C aircrew training following transfer of additional aircraft from Luke AFB during 1992. 475th Weapons Evaluation Group formed in October 1983 to operate the drones.

RAF Upper Heyford, UK

Command: USAFE
Major unit: 20th FW F-111E, EF-111A
Tenant unit: nil
Location and origin of name: 13 miles north of Oxford, and named after nearby village

The base was originally opened during World War I, but not transferred to USAF control until the early 1950s. Initially a SAC base housing rotational stateside-based B-47 units, commencing with the 22nd BW from March AFB in December 1953. Other units rotated to Upper Heyford until 1958 when the Reflex Action system was introduced, with wings deploying small quantities of aircraft for three-week periods instead of whole wings for three months at a time. The retirement of the B-47 from service resulted in Reflex Action being terminated in March 1965 at Upper Heyford (and Brize Norton). Brize Norton was subsequently returned to the RAF, but Upper Heyford continued to support SAC activities with small numbers of KC-135As rotating from the USA along with RB-47Hs of the 55th SRW (and later the RC-135). While stationed at Upper Heyford these aircraft were operated by det 1 of the 98th SW with headquarters at Torrejon AB, Spain. The SAC unit later transferred to Mildenhall with the base transferred to USAFE. The 66th TRW moved to Upper Heyford from Laon AB, France, in September 1966 with the RF-101C, but commenced conversion to the RF-4C in 1969. The wing inactivated in April 1970 when the 20th TFW relocated to Upper Heyford from RAF Wethersfield. The wing began transferring its aircraft back to the USA in 1992 prior to inactivating and the base closing.

Tyndall is the premier air defense training base, handling all F-15A/C conversion with the 325th Fighter Wing, and providing range facilities with ACMI system and target drones.

US Air Force Academy

Command: Direct Reporting Unit
Major unit: Air Force Academy
Tenant units: 557th FTS T-41A/C (ATC); 94th ATS TG-7A (ATC)
Location: north of Colorado Springs

Established in April 1954 but remained at Lowry AFB until facilities completed in August 1958. AFA has a staff of 2,500 and approximately 4,400 cadets and 220 preparatory school students. The Academy has a small airfield housing a T-41 squadron to provide primary flight training to cadets, a TG-7A motor glider squadron, and a Cessna 150 for the cadet flying team.

Vance AFB, Oklahoma

Command: ATC
Major unit: 71st FTW T-37B, T-38A
Tenant unit: nil
Location and origin of name: three miles southeast of Enid, and named for Lieutenant Colonel Leon R. Vance, wounded when his B-24 ditched into the English Channel on 5 June 1944, but disappeared without trace on 26 July 1944 when his aircraft went missing between Iceland and Newfoundland

Base known as Air Corps Basic Flying School, Enid when opened in 1941 and renamed Enid AFB before gaining its present title in July 1949. Base provided undergraduate and advanced pilot training during World War II, before inactivating briefly postwar. Reopened when the 3575th PTW was activated in August 1948. 3575th replaced by the 71st FTW in November 1972.

Vandenberg AFB, California

Command: AFSPACECOM
Major unit: Western Space and Missile Center
Tenant unit: 11th Training & Test Wing (ACC)
Location and origin of name: eight miles northwest of Lompoc, and named in honor of General Hoyt S. Vandenberg, director of the CIA in 1946 and 1947 and Chief of Staff of the Air Force between 1948 and 1953. General Vandenberg died on 2 April 1954

Established as Camp Cooke in April 1957 when transferred from the Army, and renamed Vandenberg AFB in October 1958. Initially under Air Research & Development Command, but transferred to SAC seven months later. Established to launch polar orbiting satellites and to train ICBM launch crews. AFSC responsible for actual launches under AF Western Test Range between 1964 and 1970, Space and Missile Test Center from 1970 until 1979, and Western Space and Missile Center after 1979. 4392nd Aerospace Support Wing formed in July 1961 and was joined by 6595th Space Test Group in May 1970 (subsequently retitled Satellite Test Group and Aerospace Test Group). Base transferred to AF Space Command after September 1982. The 11th Training and Test Wing was established by SAC during 1991 to control the 4315th CCTS as the ICBM unit at Vandenberg.

Volk Field, Madison, Wisconsin

Located 90 miles northwest of Madison, the field is operated by the Air National Guard as a training site with an air-to-ground and air-to-air range. No aircraft are assigned, although squadrons rotate on a regular basis from their home stations.

Westover AFB, Massachusetts

Westover is five miles northeast of Chicopee and was formerly a major SAC base until becoming an AFRes site in 1974. The 439th AW operates the C-5A from the base, along with Army, Navy and Marine Corps Reserve units and an Army National Guard helicopter squadron. The base was named for Major General Oscar Westover, Chief of the Air Corps, who was killed in the crash of a Northrop A-17AS near Burbank, California, on 21 September 1938.

Wheeler AFB, Hawaii

Command: PACAF
Major unit: 15th ABS – no aircraft assigned
Tenant unit: US Army flying units
Location and origin of name: adjacent to US Army Schofield Barracks in the center of the island of Oahu, and named for Major Sheldon H. Wheeler, the commanding officer of Luke Field, Hawaii, killed in the crash of a biplane on 13 July 1921

Base opened in February 1922 with a variety of AAF units assigned before, during and after World War II. Base became a satellite of Hickam in 1971 and assigned to 15th ABW with HQ at Hickam AFB. The 22nd TASS was assigned at Wheeler operating the O-2A by November 1971 and later the OV-10A until inactivated in September 1988. The squadron was the last Air Force flying unit to be stationed at Wheeler.

Whiteman AFB, Missouri

Command: ACC
Major unit: 351st SMW LGMN-30F
Tenant unit: nil
Location and origin of name: two miles south of Knob Noster, and named for Second Lieutenant George A. Whiteman, killed on 7 December 1941 when his P-40 was shot down while taking off from Wheeler Field, during the attack on Pearl Harbor

Base originally known as Sedalia Glider Base when opened in 1942 and was renamed seven more times before becoming Whiteman AFB in October 1955. As the title suggests the base performed glider operations initially, but switched to providing training for aircrew transitioning to transport aircraft, with more than 60 squadrons being temporarily based. Base operated by Air Transport Command and later TAC but inactive between September 1946 until reopened in July 1951 with assignment to SAC the following month. The 340th BW was in residence from October 1952 operating the B-47 and KC-97 combination until September 1963, when the wing moved to Bergstrom AFB. The facility was selected to accommodate the Minuteman I missile with the 351st SMW forming in February 1963. More recently Whiteman AFB has been chosen as

the first, and most likely the only, B-2A 'Stealth Bomber' base, with det 509 being formed at the end of 1990 to begin preparations for the new aircraft. The 509th Wing is believed to be the unit due to operate the type at Whiteman AFB when the B-2A becomes operational in the mid-1990s.

Will Rogers World Airport, Oklahoma City, Oklahoma

Will Rogers Airport is seven miles southwest of Oklahoma City with the 137th AW Oklahoma ANG flying the C-130H. The airport houses a large FAA facility, which operates a number of former military aircraft.

Williams AFB, Arizona

Command: ATC
Major unit: 82nd FTW T-37B, T-38A
Tenant unit: nil
Location and origin of name: 10 miles east of Chandler, and named for First Lieutenant Charles L. Williams, killed on 6 July 1927 in the crash of a Boeing PW-9A near Fort DeRussy, Hawaii

Base known as Mesa Military Airport when established in 1941 and later titled Williams Field. Administered by Air Corps Flying Training Command which subsequently became ATC. Base performed aircrew training initially for twin-engined and later single-engined aircraft types during World War II. 3525th PTW formed in August 1948 and assigned until February 1973 when replaced by the 82nd FTW. Fighter gunnery school added in 1953 and 1954 as the AF Advanced Flying School (Fighter). Base became an undergraduate pilot training base exclusively in 1961, although the 4441st CCTS was activated by TAC in December 1963 to conduct F-5 pilot training for USAF and numerous overseas air arms. The squadron changed to 425th TFTS in October 1969 and was inactivated in September 1989. The 82nd FTW is scheduled to inactivate in September 1992 with the base due to close 12 months later.

Willow Grove Air Reserve Forces Facility, Pennsylvania

Willow Grove facility is 14 miles north of Philadelphia and is also known as a Naval Air Station. The Pennsylvania ANG has the 111th FG operating the OA-10A, while the AFRes operates the C-130E with the 913th AG. The base also has Army, Navy and Marine Corps Reserve units in residence.

RAF Woodbridge, UK

Command: USAFE
Major unit: 81st TFW A-10A
Tenant unit: 39th SOW HC-130N/P, MH-53J (AFSOC)
Location and origin of name: seven miles east of and named after town of Woodbridge

Base operated by the RAF from 1943 and made available for US forces in 1952. A single squadron from the 81st FIW, the 78th FIS, was stationed at Woodbridge initially, and was joined by the 79th TFS operating the F-100D which was assigned to the 20th TFW at RAF Wethersfield. The latter subsequently moved to Upper Heyford along with the parent in April 1970. The 67th ARRS was assigned in March 1970 operating the HC-130H/N together with the HH-3E. The squadron was subsequently redesignated to special operations and joined by the 21st SOS with

the MH-53J, and later still by the 39th SOW. These units were transferred from MAC to AFSOC when the latter organization was established in May 1990. However, all AFSOC units in Europe will relocate to Alconbury during 1992.

Woomera AS, Australia

Operated by Air Force Space Command with a ballistic missile early warning system (BMEWS).

Wright-Patterson AFB, Ohio

Command: AFMC
Major unit: HQ AFMC
Tenant units: HQ Aeronautics Systems Division/ASD (AFMC); 4950th TW C-18A, EC-18B/D, NKC-135A, EC-135E, NC-141A, CT/NT-39A, T-39B (AFMC); 906th FG F-16A/B (AFRes)
Location and origin of name: 10 miles northeast of Dayton, and named in honor of aviation pioneers Orville and Wilbur Wright, and First Lieutenant Frank S. Patterson. The former pair were the first to pilot a powered, heavier-than-air flying machine, at Kitty Hawk, North Carolina, on 17 December 1903. Lieutenant Patterson was killed on 19 June 1918 near Fairfield Aviation General Supply Depot while testing machine gun synchronization through the propeller of a DH-4

The facility currently called Wright-Patterson AFB is an amalgamation of Wilbur Wright Field and Fairfield Aviation General Supply Depot. The latter subsequently became Patterson Field housing aviation supplies and equipment, and became a repair site. During World War II the site was chiefly in support of Fairfield Air Depot. Air Corps Maintenance Command formed in 1941. Wright Field absorbed the aeronautical engineering role from McCook Field in 1927 and concentrated on this activity during World War II. The two bases were merged in January 1948 when Wright-Patterson AFB was created. Air Research and Development Command (ARDC) was located between November 1950 and May 1951 when it moved to Baltimore, Maryland. The Wright Air Development Center was established in April 1951, and changed to Divisional status in 1959 for two years before becoming the Aeronautical Systems Division (ASD). Base upgraded in 1958/1959 to accommodate SAC bombers, with the 4043rd Strategic Wing formed in April 1959. Unit inactivated in February 1963 having been replaced by the 17th BW which re-formed three months earlier. Latter wing moved to Beale AFB in September 1975, ending SAC operations at the base. Aeronautical Museum established in December 1960 as the primary location for preserved USAF aircraft and associated systems. The 4950th Test Wing activated in March 1971 as the flying unit of the test aircraft flown by ASD. All AFSC aircraft are to be concentrated at Edwards AFB in due course, with Wright-Patterson acquiring the ANG and AFRes aircraft currently stationed at Rickenbacker ANGB by the middle of the decade.

Wurtsmith AFB, Michigan

Command: ACC
Major unit: 379th Wg B-52G, KC-135A
Tenant unit: ACE det 71st FTW T-37B (ATC)
Location and origin of name: three miles northwest of Oscoda, and named for Major General Paul B. Wurtsmith, killed on 13 September 1946 in crash of a B-25 on Cold Mountain near Asheville, North Carolina

Base established as Camp Skeel in 1931 and was renamed Oscoda AFB before gaining its present title in February 1953. Employed for winter maneuvers and aerial gunnery practice prewar and during World War II, until closed at the end of 1945. Reopened early in 1947 but with limited operations until 1951 when assigned to ADC as an interceptor base. The 4026th Strategic Wing was formed in August 1958 with the base transferred to SAC in April 1960. 4026th replaced by the 379th BW in January 1961. The wing is due to inactivate in 1993 prior to the base closing during September of that year.

Yeager Airport, Charleston, West Virginia

Yeager Airport is four miles northeast of Charleston, with the 130th AG West Virginia ANG flying the C-130H. Airport named for Brigadier General Charles 'Chuck' Yeager, who was born and raised in West Virginia.

Yokota AB, Japan

Command: PACAF
Major unit: HQ 5th Air Force; 475th ABW UH-1N
Tenant unit: 374th AW C-9A, C-21A, C-130E/H (AMC)
Location and origin of name: 28 miles west of Tokyo and named for the nearby town

The base was occupied by US forces after World War II and was heavily involved in the Korean War. The 3rd Bomb Group was one of the first USAF units in residence operating the B-26 during 1948/1949. The 35th FIW was in residence for a short time from April 1950, and returned to Yokota from Johnson AB, Japan, in October 1954. Wing inactivated in October 1957 having been replaced by the 67th TRW three months earlier. The wing inactivated in December 1960 and returned to the USA. The 6000th Operations Wing was assigned during the 1950s and 1960s with two operations squadrons flying the C-119G and a pair of reconnaissance squadrons equipped with the RB-57A and RB-50E/G. Latter type was withdrawn in July 1961 when replaced by the C-130B-II. Elements of the 8th TFW were in short-term residence at Yokota in 1964 with the F-105, although the wing was stationed at George AFB. The 421st ARS was stationed at Yokota from 1953 until 1965 to provide air refueling with the KB-29 and later the KB-50J. The 6441st TFW was formed in April 1965 and was assigned until November 1966. The 347th TFW activated in January 1968 operating the F-4 as well the remainder of the RB-57 and C-130B reconnaissance types of the 556th RS until May 1971, when the wing returned home. The reduction in activities at Yokota resulted in the base being administered by the 475th ABW from November 1971 with the UH-1N and CT-39A to support HQ 5th Air Force. The 374th TAW formed at Clark AB November 1973 as the primary MAC unit in the Far East, with one squadron of C-130s located at Yokota from late 1974. The 316th TAG was formed to control the squadron, but was inactivated in September 1989 when the parent wing moved to Yokota.

Youngstown MAP, Ohio

The Municipal Airport, 16 miles north of Youngstown, is an AFRes site, with the 910th AG operating the C-130H.

Zaragoza AB, Spain

Formerly a support base operated by the 406th TFTW with central region USAFE fighter squadrons in residence for weapons training at the nearby Bardenas bombing range. Base also had a SAC presence with the 34th SS assigned operating tankers on periods of temporary duty with KC-10As from the USA and KC-135s detached from RAF Mildenhall. Base ceased US operations at the end of 1991 with the rotational pair of KC-10s deploying to RAF Mildenhall.

Right: The Naval Air Station at New Orleans houses a mixed bag of units from three services. In addition to US Navy and Marine Corps Reserve units, there is an AFRes A-10 unit and the F-15As of the Louisiana Air National Guard's 159th Fighter Group.

Above: Vandenberg AFB on the Californian coast is Space Command's major space launch and missile test facility. Here a pair of Minuteman III ICBMs is launched simultaneously on a test flight. The re-entry area is mainly in the Marshall Islands.

Below: Nellis AFB, on the outskirts of Las Vegas, is the USAF's main tactical exercise center, a vast range complex in the Nevada desert being attached to the base. Here an RAF Hercules lands in front of a packed apron at the end of a multi-national Red Flag exercise.

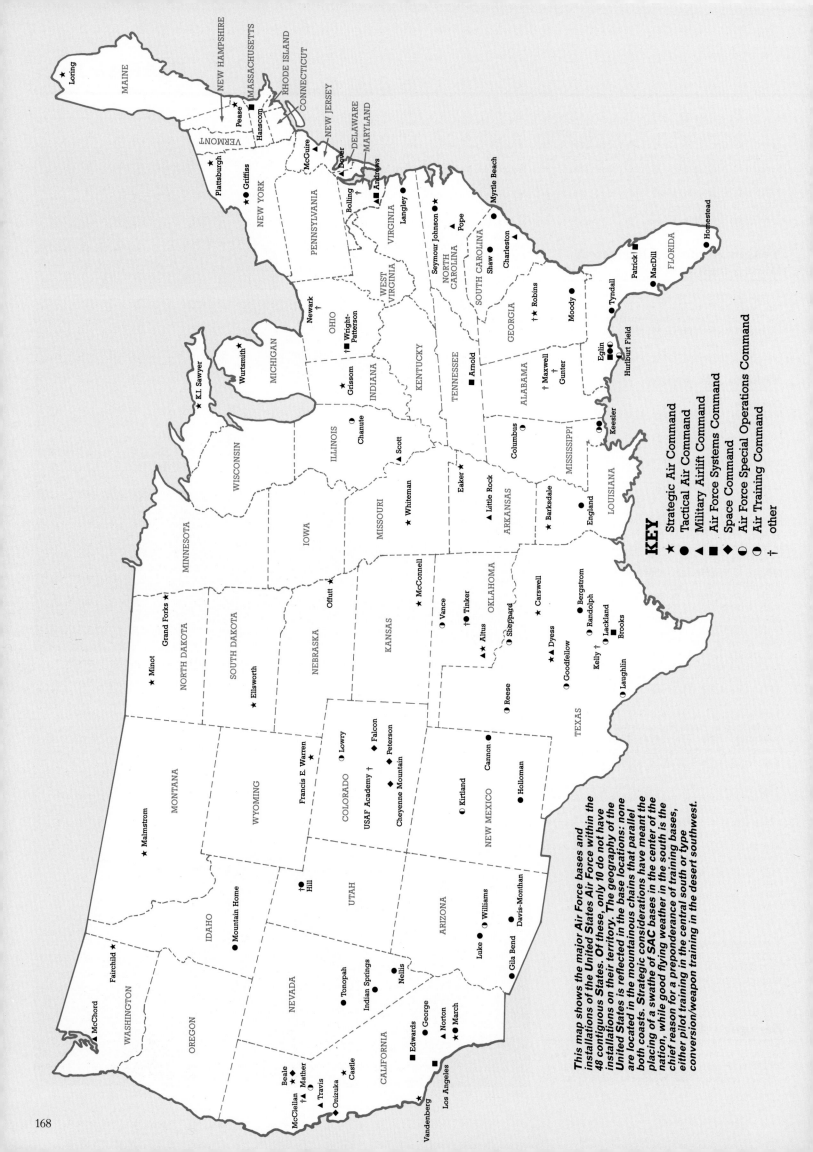

KEY

★ Strategic Air Command
● Tactical Air Command
▲ Military Airlift Command
■ Air Force Systems Command
◆ Space Command
◖ Air Force Special Operations Command
◔ Air Training Command
† other

This map shows the major Air Force bases and installations of the United States Air Force within the 48 contiguous States. Of these, only 10 do not have installations on their territory. The geography of the United States is reflected in the base locations: none are located in the mountainous chains that parallel both coasts. Strategic considerations have meant the placing of a swathe of SAC bases in the center of the nation, while good flying weather in the south is the chief reason for a preponderance of training bases, either pilot training in the central south or type conversion/weapon training in the desert southwest.

WASHINGTON
McChord ■
Fairchild ★ †

OREGON

IDAHO
Mountain Home ●
† Hill ●

NEVADA
Tonopah ●
Indian Springs ●
Nellis ●

CALIFORNIA
Beale ★ ◆
† ▲ Mather
Travis ▲
McClellan ▲ †
Onizuka ◆
Castle ★
Edwards ■
George ●
Norton ▲
March ★ ●
Los Angeles ■
Vandenberg ★

MONTANA
Malmstrom ★

WYOMING
Francis E. Warren ★

UTAH

ARIZONA
Luke ●
Williams ●
Gila Bend ●
Davis-Monthan ●

COLORADO
Lowry ◔
USAF Academy †
Cheyenne Mountain ◆
Falcon ◆
Peterson ◆

NEW MEXICO
Cannon ●
Kirtland ◔
Holloman ●

NORTH DAKOTA
Minot ★
Grand Forks ★ ★

SOUTH DAKOTA
Ellsworth ★

NEBRASKA
Offutt ★

KANSAS
McConnell ★

OKLAHOMA
Vance ◔
Tinker ●
† Altus ▲
Sheppard ◔

TEXAS
Carswell ★
Bergstrom ●
Randolph ◔
Lackland ■
Brooks †
Dyess ▲ ●
Goodfellow ★ ◔
Kelly †
Laughlin ◔
Reese ◔
Dyess ▲ ▲

MINNESOTA

IOWA

MISSOURI
Whiteman ★

ARKANSAS
Little Rock ▲
Eaker ★

LOUISIANA
Barksdale ★
England ●

WISCONSIN

ILLINOIS
Chanute ◔
Scott ▲

MICHIGAN
K.I. Sawyer ★
Wurtsmith ★

INDIANA
Grissom ★

KENTUCKY

TENNESSEE
Arnold ■

MISSISSIPPI
Columbus ◔
Keesler ◔

ALABAMA
† Maxwell ★
† Gunter

OHIO
Newark †
Wright-Patterson † ■

WEST VIRGINIA

VIRGINIA
Langley ●
Bolling †

GEORGIA
† Robins ★
Moody ●

FLORIDA
Eglin ■ ◔
Hurlburt Field ◖
Patrick ■
MacDill ■
Homestead ●

NORTH CAROLINA
Seymour Johnson ●
Pope ▲

SOUTH CAROLINA
Shaw ●
Charleston ▲
Myrtle Beach ●

MAINE
Loring ★

NEW HAMPSHIRE
Pease ★

MASSACHUSETTS
Hanscom ■

VERMONT

NEW YORK
Plattsburgh ★
Griffiss ● ★

PENNSYLVANIA

NEW JERSEY
McGuire ▲

DELAWARE
Dover ▲

MARYLAND
Andrews ▲ ■

168

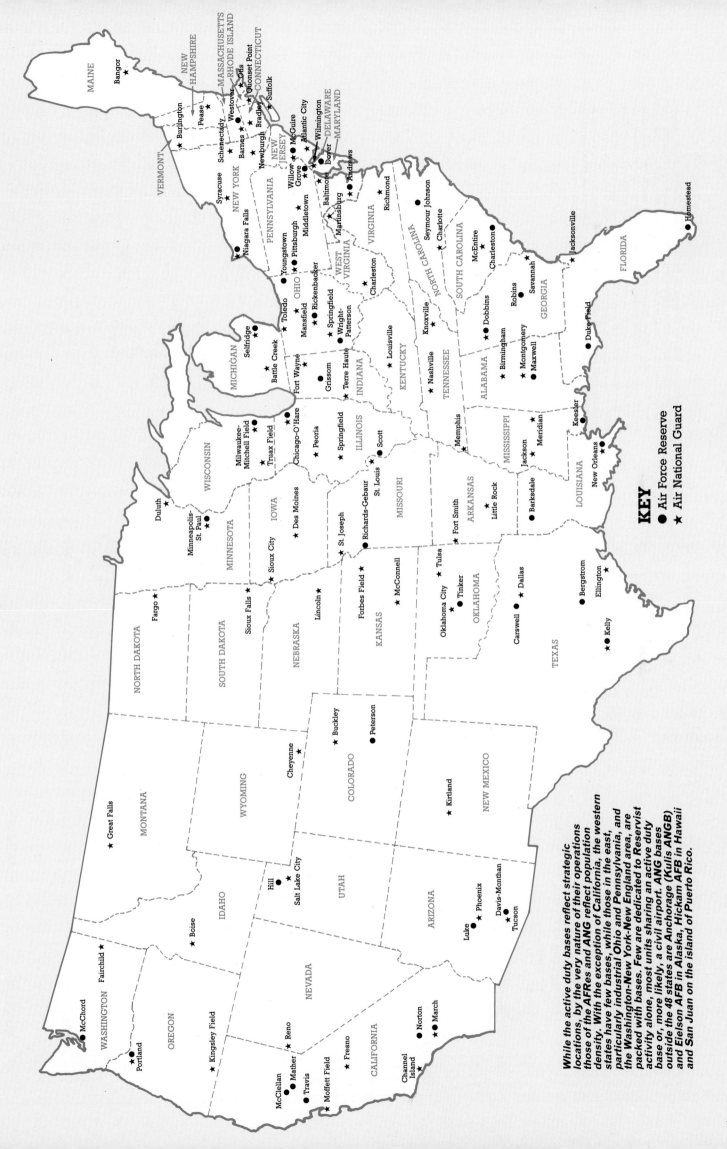

KEY

● Air Force Reserve

★ Air National Guard

MAINE

Bangor ★

NEW HAMPSHIRE

MASSACHUSETTS

RHODE ISLAND

CONNECTICUT

Otis ★

Quonset Point ★

Burlington ★

Pease ★

Westover ★★

Barnes ★

Bradley ★

Suffolk ★

VERMONT

Schenectady ★

Syracuse ★

NEW YORK

Newburgh ★

NEW JERSEY

McGuire ●

Atlantic City ★

Willow Grove ★

Wilmington ★

DELAWARE

Dover ●

MARYLAND

Niagara Falls ★

PENNSYLVANIA

Youngstown ●

Pittsburgh ●

Middletown ★

Baltimore ★

Martinsburg ★

Andrews ●★

Richmond ●

OHIO

Toledo ★

Mansfield ★

Rickenbacker ★

WEST VIRGINIA

Charleston ★

VIRGINIA

Seymour Johnson ●

Charlotte ★

NORTH CAROLINA

MICHIGAN

Selfridge ●

Battle Creek ★

Fort Wayne ★

Grissom ●

Terre Haute ★

INDIANA

Springfield ★

Wright-Patterson ●

Louisville ★

KENTUCKY

Knoxville ★

Nashville ★

TENNESSEE

McEntire ★

SOUTH CAROLINA

Charleston ●

Dobbins ●

Birmingham ★

ALABAMA

Montgomery ★

Maxwell ●

Robins ●

Savannah ★

GEORGIA

Jacksonville ★

FLORIDA

Homestead ●

Duke Field ●

Milwaukee-Mitchell Field ●

Truax Field ★

WISCONSIN

Chicago-O'Hare ●

Peoria ★

Springfield ★

ILLINOIS

Scott ●

Duluth ★

Minneapolis-St. Paul ●★

MINNESOTA

Des Moines ★

IOWA

Sioux City ★

Sioux Falls ★

SOUTH DAKOTA

Fargo ★

NORTH DAKOTA

St. Joseph ★

Richards-Gebaur ●

St. Louis ●

MISSOURI

Forbes Field ★

Lincoln ★

NEBRASKA

McConnell ★

KANSAS

Memphis ★

Jackson ★

MISSISSIPPI

Meridian ★

Keesler ●

New Orleans ●★

LOUISIANA

Barksdale ●

Little Rock ●

Fort Smith ★

ARKANSAS

Tulsa ★

Oklahoma City ●

Tinker ●

OKLAHOMA

Dallas ★

Carswell ●

Bergstrom ★

Ellington ★

TEXAS

Kelly ●

Great Falls ★

MONTANA

WYOMING

Cheyenne ★

Buckley ★

Peterson ●

COLORADO

Kirtland ★

NEW MEXICO

Hill ●

Salt Lake City ★

UTAH

Boise ★

IDAHO

NEVADA

Reno ★

Phoenix ★

Luke ★

Davis-Monthan ●

Tucson ★

ARIZONA

Fairchild ★

McChord ●

Portland ●

WASHINGTON

Kingsley Field ★

OREGON

McClellan ●

Mather ★

Travis ●

Moffett Field ★

Fresno ★

Channel Island ★

Norton ●

March ●

CALIFORNIA

*While the active duty bases reflect strategic
locations, by the very nature of their operations
those of the AFRes and ANG reflect population
density. With the exception of California, the western
states have few bases, while those in the east,
particularly industrial Ohio and Pennsylvania, and
the Washington-New York-New England area, are
packed with bases. Few are dedicated to Reservist
activity alone, most units sharing an active duty
base or, more likely, a civil airport. ANG bases
outside the 48 states are Anchorage (Kulis ANGB)
and Eielson AFB in Alaska, Hickam AFB in Hawaii
and San Juan on the island of Puerto Rico.*

169

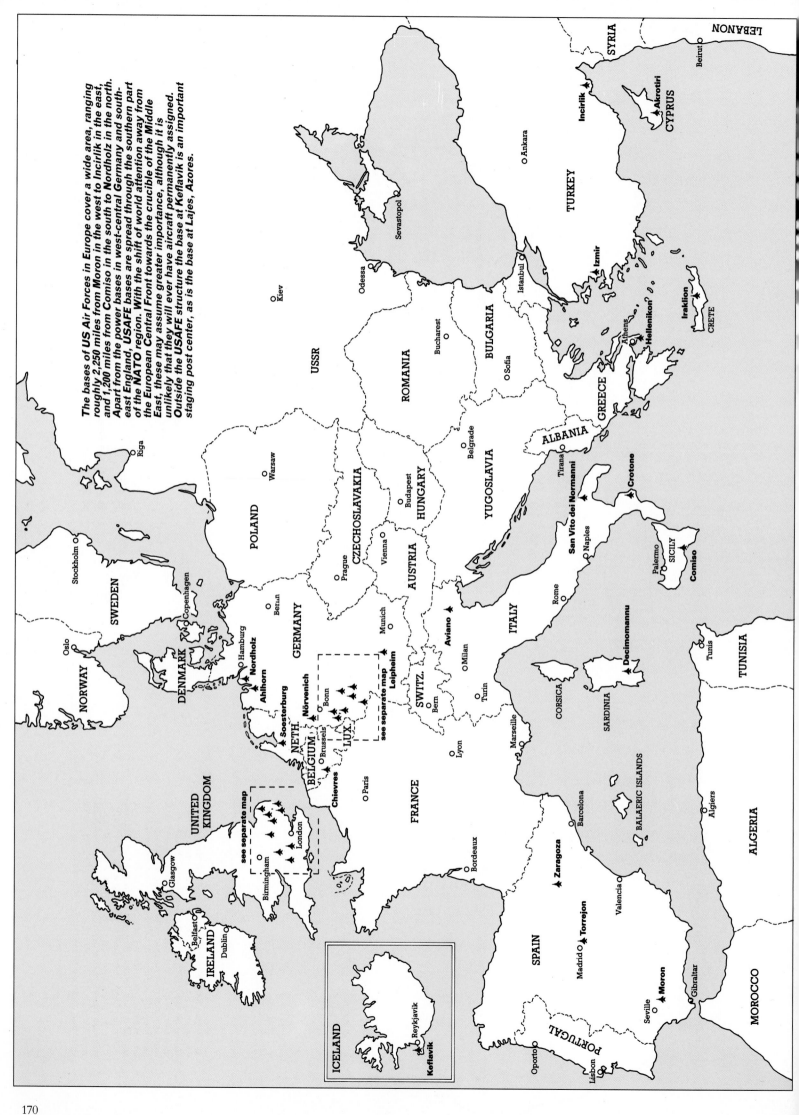

The bases of US Air Forces in Europe cover a wide area, ranging roughly 2,250 miles from Moron in the west to Incirlik in the east, and 1,200 miles from Comiso in the south to Nordholz in the north. Apart from the power bases in west-central Germany and south-east England, USAFE bases are spread through the southern part of the NATO region. With the shift of world attention away from the European Central Front towards the crucible of the Middle East, these may assume greater importance, although it is unlikely that they will ever have aircraft permanently assigned. Outside the USAFE structure the base at Keflavik is an important staging post center, as is the base at Lajes, Azores.

LEBANON

SYRIA

Beirut

Akrotiri
CYPRUS

Incirlik

Iraklion
CRETE

Izmir

Hellenikon?

Ankara

TURKEY

Istanbul

Athens

GREECE

Sevastopol

Odessa

Kiev

Bucharest

ROMANIA

BULGARIA

Sofia

USSR

ALBANIA

Tirana

Crotone

San Vito dei Normanni

YUGOSLAVIA

Belgrade

Budapest

HUNGARY

Warsaw

POLAND

CZECHOSLAVAKIA

Prague

Vienna

AUSTRIA

Naples

Palermo

SICILY

Comiso

Rome

ITALY

Decimomannu

Stockholm

SWEDEN

Copenhagen

Berlin

GERMANY

Munich

Aviano

Milan

Turin

SWITZ.

Bern

CORSICA

SARDINIA

Oslo

NORWAY

DENMARK

Hamburg

Nordholz

Ahlhorn

Soesterburg

NETH.

Nörvenich

Bonn

Leipheim

see separate map

BELGIUM

Brussels

LUX.

Chievres

Paris

FRANCE

Lyon

Marseille

BALAERIC ISLANDS

Barcelona

Algiers

ALGERIA

Riga

UNITED
KINGDOM

see separate map

Glasgow

Belfast

Dublin

IRELAND

Birmingham

London

Bordeaux

Zaragoza

SPAIN

Madrid Torrejon

Valencia

Seville

Moron

Gibraltar

PORTUGAL

Oporto

Lisbon

MOROCCO

TUNIS

TUNISIA

Tunis

ICELAND

Reykjavik

Keflavik

Tripoli

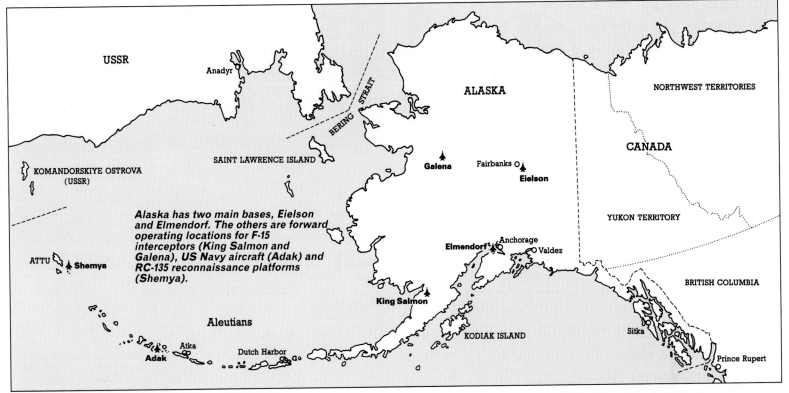

USSR
Anadyr
ALASKA
NORTHWEST TERRITORIES
KOMANDORSKIYE OSTROVA
(USSR)
SAINT LAWRENCE ISLAND
Galena
Fairbanks O
Eielson
CANADA

Alaska has two main bases, Eielson and Elmendorf. The others are forward operating locations for F-15 interceptors (King Salmon and Galena), US Navy aircraft (Adak) and RC-135 reconnaissance platforms (Shemya).

YUKON TERRITORY
ATTU
Shemya
Elmendorf
Anchorage
Valdez
BRITISH COLUMBIA
King Salmon
Aleutians
KODIAK ISLAND
Sitka
Atka
Dutch Harbor
Adak
Prince Rupert
BERING STRAIT

The map at left covers the USAFE area, while below are insets showing the location of bases in the UK and Germany, several of which are due for imminent closure. Above and right are the areas covered by the PACAF brief, recently expanded to include Alaska, which was previously a separate command.

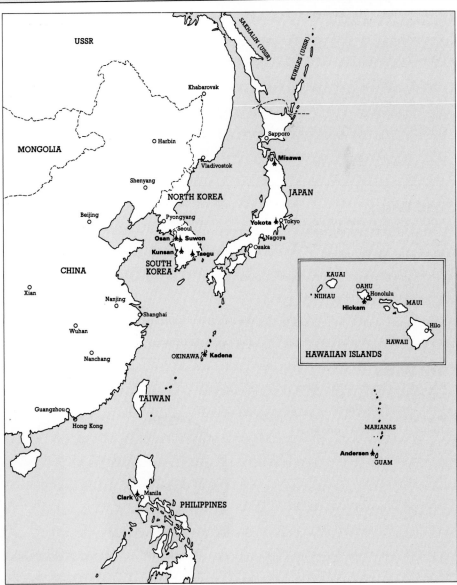

USSR
SAKHALIN (USSR)
KURILES (USSR)
Khabarovsk
Sapporo
MONGOLIA
Misawa
Harbin O
Vladivostok
JAPAN
Shenyang
Yokota
Tokyo
NORTH KOREA
Beijing
Pyongyang
Nagoya
Seoul
Osaka
Osan
Suwon
CHINA
Kunsan
Taegu
SOUTH KOREA
Xian
Nanjing
Shanghai
Wuhan
Nanchang
OKINAWA
Kadena
TAIWAN
Guangzhou
Hong Kong
Clark
Manila
PHILIPPINES

KAUAI
OAHU
NIIHAU
Honolulu
Hickam
MAUI
Hilo
HAWAII
HAWAIIAN ISLANDS

MARIANAS
Andersen
GUAM

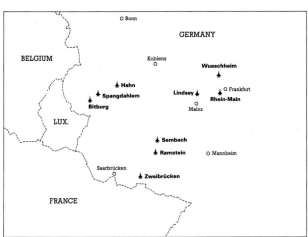

BELGIUM
Bonn O
GERMANY
Koblenz O
Wueschheim
Hahn
Spangdahlem
Lindsey
Frankfurt O
Bitburg
Rhein-Main
Mainz O
LUX.
Sembach
Saarbrücken O
Ramstein
Mannheim O
Zweibrücken
FRANCE

Sculthorpe
Norwich O
Alconbury
Lakenheath
Mildenhall
Chicksands
Cambridge
Bentwaters
Upper Heyford
Ipswich O
Woodbridge
Oxford O
Luton O
Wethersfield
Fairford
Swindon
Reading O
Greenham Common
London
ENGLAND
Southampton
Brighton

Units of the USAF

1st Fighter Wing

ACC Langley AFB, VA: F-15C/D, EC-135P, VH-1N ('FF')
27th/71st/94th Fighter Squadrons
6th Airborne Command and Control Squadron
4401st Helicopter Squadron

Established in July 1947 as the 1st Fighter Wing at March Field, CA, with P-80s, the wing changed designation several times before becoming a Tactical Fighter Wing in October 1970 with the F-4 at MacDill AFB, FL. The wing moved to Langley AFB in June 1975 and converted to the F-15A. The 6th ACCS with EC-135Ps was added in August 1976. The wing subsequently upgraded to the F-15C/D. The 71st and 27th TFSs were the first two USAF fighter units to deploy to Saudi Arabia for Operation Desert Shield, on 7 and 8 August 1990, respectively. The wing was credited with an Iraqi Mirage F1 kill on 17 January 1991. The designation was changed from Tactical Fighter Wing to the current Fighter Wing in October 1991. The 6th ACCS is due to deactivate during 1992, with the EC-135s being retired or transferred to the 55th Wing.

Above: Badges of the 1st FW's three F-15 squadrons. The wing also has EC-135s and VH-1Ns.

The 'FF' tailcode stands for 'First Fighter', and in keeping with this tradition the wing was the first to respond to the call following the Iraqi invasion of Kuwait.

1st Special Operations Wing

AFSOC Hurlburt Field, FL: AC-130H, C-130E, MC-130E/H, MH-53J
Eglin AFB, FL: HC-130N/P, MH-60G
8th/9th/20th/55th Special Operations Squadrons

The wing was initially created as 1st Air Commando Group in August 1944 in Hailakandi, India, and inactivated in November 1945. It was reactivated in April 1962 to replace the 4400th CCTG as the primary unit for air commando operations and training at Hurlburt Field, then upgraded to Wing status in June 1963 and redesignated 1st Special Operations Wing in July 1968. The 834th Tactical Composite Wing temporarily replaced the 1st SOW at Hurlburt between July 1974 and July 1975.

The 1st SOW transferred from TAC to AF Special Operations Command on 22 May 1990, and in that same year was awarded the Mackay Trophy for 'the most meritorious flight of the year' for an AC-130H combat sortie against Panamanian Defense Forces during Operation Just Cause. The unit has operated a variety of air commando, psychological warfare and special operations types including A-37, B-26, AC/EC-47, AC-119, AC/MC-130, UH-1, O-2, AT-28, QU-22, and OV-10. The MC-130H 'Combat

Talon II' is currently being introduced to replace the MC-130E, and the wing will receive the AC-130U in place of the AC-130H by 1994.

The 1st SOW operates a mix of helicopters and Hercules 'specials' in its Special Operations role. Below left is an AC-130H gunship; below are Sikorsky MH-53J Pave Low IIIs.

2nd Wing

ACC/AMC Barksdale AFB, LA: B-52H, KC-135A/Q, KC-10A
62nd/596th Bomb Squadrons
32nd/71st Air Refueling Squadrons

The 2nd Bombardment Wing (Very Heavy) was activated in October 1947 operating the B-29 at Davis-Monthan AFB and has subsequently operated the B-50, B-47 and B-52, together with KB-29, KC-97 and KC-135 tankers. The unit moved to Hunter AFB, GA, in 1950 before relocating to its present home at Barksdale AFB in April

1963, replacing the 4238th Strategic Wing. The 2nd Wing won the Fairchild Trophy as the top bomber team at SAC's Proud Shield bombing and navigation competition in 1963. Currently, it operates two squadrons of B-52Gs together with a KC-135A and KC-10A squadron, although the B-52H is due to be assigned during 1992 when the B-52G models retire. The unit was redesignated 2nd Wing in October 1991.

During the Gulf War, the B-52Gs of the 2nd Wing launched cruise missiles and, as here, carried conventional bombs.

3rd Wing

PACAF Elmendorf ABF, AK: F-15C/D/E ('AK'), E-3C
43rd/54th/90th Fighter Squadrons
962nd Air Control Squadron

Originally established as the 3rd Bombardment Wing (Light) in August 1948 at Yokota AB, Japan, the wing became a Bombardment Wing (Tactical) and later Tactical Fighter Wing. The wing has been located in the Far East for virtually all of its operational career and moved to Clark AB in September 1974, replacing the 405th FW. Aircraft types operated include the F-4 Phantom from 1971 onwards, with the F-4E and G models assigned in recent years. The unit was due to deactivate by September 1992 as part of an agreement to vacate the Philippines, although the eruption of Mount Pinatubo pre-empted the rundown of Clark AB. Instead, the unit relocated to Elmendorf

AFB in December 1991, replacing the 21st FW, adopting two of the 21st's F-15C squadrons and activating one of F-15Es. Two E-3s were added in 1992.

The 43rd FS is one of the 3rd Wing's two F-15C squadrons.

Still bearing 21st FW legends, this quartet of F-15s represents the commander's aircraft and examples from the three squadrons.

4th Wing
ACC Seymour Johnson AFB, NC: KC-10A, F-15E ('SJ')
334th/335th/336th Fighter Squadrons
344th/911th Air Refueling Squadrons

Created as the 4th Fighter Wing in July 1947 at Andrews AFB as a SAC unit flying the P-80, the unit changed to Fighter Interceptor Wing status and transferred to TAC in January 1950. It relocated to the Far East between 1950 and 1957 before moving to Seymour Johnson AFB in December 1957, and becoming a Tactical Fighter Wing the following year. The unit won the F-4 category in the 1976 William Tell competition at Tyndall AFB with the F-4E, and has operated a variety of fighter aircraft including the F-86, F-100, F-105 and F-4, before becoming the first operational F-15E wing in 1990. Two squadrons of F-15Es deployed to Al Kharj, Saudi Arabia, for

The 4th Wing badge is carried on the F-15E's intake.

Operation Desert Storm as part of the 4th TFW (Provisional). Upon return to the US in spring 1991, the unit was redesignated 4th Wing and, as the first composite wing, gained two KC-10A squadrons from SAC.

Chosen as the operational CONUS-based F-15E unit, the 4th Wing also has two squadrons of KC-10s so that the fighters can rapidly deploy to any point on the globe.

5th Wing
ACC/AMC Minot AFB, ND: B-52H, KC-135A
23rd Bomb Squadron
906th Air Refueling Squadron

Formed as the 5th Strategic Reconnaissance Wing at Mountain Home AFB in July 1949, the unit relocated to Fairfield-Suisun AFB (later Travis AFB) five months later. It operated the RB-29 and RB-36 before switching roles to become a Bombardment Wing in October 1955 with the B-36 assigned. After upgrading to the B-52 and KC-135 in 1959, the unit moved to Minot AFB in July 1968 and absorbed the resources of the 450th BW. The wing won the Fairchild Trophy as the top bomber team with the B-52H at SAC's Proud Shield bombing and navigation competition in 1988, and was redesignated 5th Wing in October 1991.

Left: A winged skull motif adorns the tails of both the B-52s and KC-135s of the 5th Wing.

Above: A 5th Wing B-52H lives up to the unit's motto: 'Guardians of the Upper Realm'.

6th Wing
ACC Eielson AFB, AK: RC-135S/X, TC-135S
24th Strategic Reconnaissance Squadron

This wing was established at Walker AFB, NM, as the 6th Bombardment Wing in January 1951 flying the B-29 and later the B-36 and B-52. In March 1967 it was redesignated 6th Strategic Wing and moved to Eielson AFB, replacing the 4157th SW and operating various RC-135s (some directly assigned), including RC-135S Cobra Ball and

RC-135X Cobra Eye. In addition, KC-135s from SAC units in the 'lower 48' regularly rotate to Eielson for the Alaskan Tanker Task Force. The unit, which has specialized in conducting reconnaissance operations to gather atmospheric particles for analysis in connection with Soviet nuclear tests, was redesignated 6th Strategic Reconnaissance Wing before changing to 6th Wing in October 1991. The wing deactivated in 1992, control of its aircraft passing to the 55th Wg.

Two RC-135S Cobra Ball aircraft fly with the 6th Wing.

7th Wing
ACC/AMC Carswell AFB, TX: B-52H, KC-135A
9th/20th Bomb Squadrons
7th Air Refueling Squadron

Another early SAC unit, the 7th Bombardment Wing was formed in November 1947 at Fort Worth AAF (later Carswell AFB) but was not activated until August 1948. As with many other SAC units, the 7th BW has operated a variety of types, including the B-29 and B-36, before receiving the B-52 in 1957. The KC-135A

tanker was assigned to the wing in 1958. The unit is due to deactivate in 1993 with B-52Hs transferred to the 2nd Wing.

7th Wing aircraft proclaim their geographical basing by carrying a fin stripe with the words 'Fort Worth, Texas' and the stylized head of a longhorn. The unit still operates the 'stovepipe' KC-135A tanker, which it will keep until deactivation in 1993.

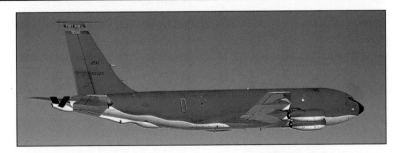

8th Fighter Wing
PACAF Kunsan AB, RoK: F-16C/D ('WP')
35th/80th Fighter Squadrons

The unit has spent the majority of its operational career stationed in the Far East at bases in Japan, South Korea and Thailand since being activated in August 1948, apart from 17 months located in the US. The wing has a distinguished lineage with successful operations during the Korean and Vietnam Wars where the unit became known as the 'MiG Killers'. The wing moved to Kunsan AB at end of the Vietnam War, flying the F-4D

until re-equipping with the F-16A in September 1981 and the F-16C subsequently. The unit was redesignated 8th FW at the end of 1991.

Right: Patch of the 8th FW.

Below: One of two 'Viper' units in Korea, the 8th Fighter Wing flies the F-16C variant.

9th Wing

ACC Beale AFB, CA: KC-135Q, T-38A, U-2R, U-2RT
5th/6th/99th Strategic Reconnaissance Squadrons
95th Reconnaissance Squadron
5th Strategic Reconnaissance Training Squadron
349th/350th Air Refueling Squadrons

The 9th Strategic Reconnaissance Wing was established at Beale AFB in June 1966 after 16 years of mixed bomber and reconnaissance operations. The SR-71 was operated initially, with the U-2 being added in September 1976 with the transfer of

'Dragon Lady' operations from the 100th SRW at Davis-Monthan AFB. The two KC-135Q squadrons joined the wing in 1983. The TR-1 was assigned in 1981. SR-71 operations ceased during early 1990 when the type was prematurely retired from service, permitting the overseas U-2 detachments to be reorganized into numbered squadrons. The unit changed its designation to 9th Wing in October 1991. The 349th ARS was due to deactivate in mid-1992, with the KC-135Qs being re-engined and transferred elsewhere.

Since the SR-71's retirement in 1990, the 9th Wing's main operational type has been the Lockheed U-2R, although it maintains tankers.

10th Support Wing

USAFE RAF Alconbury, UK: A-10A ('AR')
509th/511th Tactical Fighter Squadrons

Established at Pope AFB in December 1947 as the 10th Reconnaissance Wing, the unit added the 'Tactical' prefix to its designation before transferring from TAC to USAFE in July 1952 with a relocation to Toul-Rosières AB, France, flying the RB-26 and RF-80. The unit moved to Spangdahlem AB, Germany, in May 1953 and RAF Alconbury in August

1959. Among the reconnaissance types operated in Germany and the UK were the RF-84F, RB-45, RB-57, WB/RB-66 and the RF-4C from 1965, before switching to the tactical fighter role in August 1987 with two squadrons of A-10As being transferred from RAF Bentwaters. The A-10s began returning to the USA in October 1991 as part of the

Conventional Forces in Europe (CFE) Treaty. The unit became the 10th Support Wing in January 1992 and was scheduled to be renumbered 628th SW during the first half of 1992.

12th Flying Training Wing

ATC Randolph AFB, TX: T-37B, T-38A ('RA')

Although now assigned to Air Training Command, the unit was originally part of SAC, having formed in November 1950 at Turner AFB, GA, as the 12th Fighter Escort Wing. The unit modified its role designation several times before deactivating in January 1958. Reactivated as a Tactical Fighter Wing in April 1962 at MacDill AFB, the wing transferred to Cam Ranh Bay AB, South Vietnam, flying the F-4, and remained there until deactivating in November 1971. The designation was changed to Flying Training Wing in March 1972 and the wing reactivated six weeks later, replacing the 3510th FTW with the T-37 and T-38.

Above: Patch of the 12th FTW.

Right: This 12th FTW T-37B wears the wing's 'RA' tailcode.

14th Flying Training Wing

ATC Columbus AFB, MS: T-37B, T-38A ('CM')
559th/560th Flying Training Squadrons

The unit was established in July 1947 as the 14th Fighter Wing at Dow AFB, ME, operating the P-47 and P-84 (later F-47 and F-84). Inactivating in October 1949, the wing remained dormant until redesignated as an Air Commando Wing with PACAF in February 1966 at Nha Trang AB, South

Vietnam. The wing was redesignated the 14th SOW in August 1968 and moved to Phan Rang AB 14 months later, operating various special forces types including the A-1, AC-47, AC-119, C-123, O-2 and U-10. Inactivated in September 1971, the unit was reorganized as a Flying Training Wing with ATC and reactivated in June 1972, replacing the 3650th PTW.

'CM' tailcodes adorn only the T-38s of the 14th FTW. Some of the aircraft are finished in the dark blue/white scheme, while others remain in all-white.

15th Air Base Wing

PACAF Hickam AFB, HI: EC-135J
9th Airborne Command and Control Squadron

Created as the 15th Tactical Fighter Wing in April 1962 at MacDill AFB, the unit operated the F-84F for two years and the F-4C from 1964 onwards. The wing also flew the B-57G, training aircrew for night interdiction duties. Following inactivation in October

1970 the unit was redesignated 15th ABW and moved to Hickam AFB, where it was activated again in November 1971 to administer the Hawaiian base. The T-33A and O-2 were employed alongside four EC-135Ps, although the former two types

have since been retired. The four EC-135Ps were subsequently replaced by the EC-135J, although these are due to be relocated to Offutt AFB by late 1992 when airborne command post duties are centralized with the 55th Wing.

18th Wing

PACAF Kadena AB, Okinawa: F-15C/D, KC-135R, E-3B/C ('ZZ')
12th/44th/67th Fighter Squadrons
909th Air Refueling Squadron
961st Air Control Squadron

The 18th Fighter Wing was formed at Clark AB in August 1948 and operated various liaison, reconnaissance and fighter types. The unit was redesignated 18th Fighter-Bomber Wing in January 1950 and 18th Tactical Fighter Wing in July 1958. Despite the Fighter-Bomber designation, the unit employed the F-86 and F-100, with the F-105, RF-101 and RF-4C subsequently operated. The F-4 was assigned for many years until the end of the 1970s, when the

unit converted to the F-15C. 18th TFW squadrons have won the Hughes Achievement Trophy for excellence in air defense five times since 1981. In addition, the unit won the F-15C category at the 1982 and 1988 William Tell competitions at

Tyndall AFB. At the end of 1991, the wing became the 18th Wing with a squadron of KC-135s and another operating the E-3B/C directly assigned. The wing was the first overseas unit to assume a composite wing format.

Above: Patch of the 18th TFW (now Wing).

Left: 18th Wing Eagles now wear PACAF's darker scheme.

19th Wing
AMC Robins AFB, GA: KC-135R, EC-135Y
99th/912th Air Refueling Squadrons

The 19th Bombardment Wing was activated in August 1948, operating the B-29, B-47 and B-52 until 1984, when the unit changed to an Air Refueling Wing with two squadrons of KC-135As. The wing was awarded the Mackay Trophy in 1982 for 'the most meritorious flight of the year' when a B-52 crew successfully landed their aircraft after losing its rudder and elevator hydraulic system; this feat had not previously been accomplished without significant damage or total loss of the aircraft. The wing upgraded to the KC-135R beginning in 1987 and assumed responsibility for the two EC-135Ys operated on behalf of the CinC US Central Command. The unit changed to 19th Wing in October 1991.

The 19th Wing's role is principally air refueling, for which it has the KC-135R.

20th Fighter Wing
USAFE RAF Upper Heyford, UK: F-111E, EF-111A ('UH')
55th/77th/79th Fighter Squadrons
42nd Electronic Combat Squadron

Formed at Shaw AFB as the 20th Fighter Wing in August 1947, the unit was redesignated 20th Fighter-Bomber Wing in January 1950. The wing moved to Langley AFB in November 1951 for six months before transferring from TAC to USAFE for assignment at RAF Wethersfield with the F-84. Equipment was upgraded to the F-100D in 1957 and the designation was changed to 20th Tactical Fighter Wing in July 1958. The unit moved to RAF Upper Heyford in April 1970, where it converted to the F-111E with the EF-111A added later. F-111Es and EF-111As supported Operation Desert Storm while operating from Incirlik AB, Turkey, with the 7440th Provisional Wing. The 20th FW was due to be deactivated following transfer of the F-111Es and EF-111As back to the US beginning in 1992.

The F-111Es of Upper Heyford are returning to the US, where 25 will enter service with the 27th Fighter Wing at Cannon.

22nd Wing
AMC March AFB, CA: KC-10A
6th/9th Air Refueling Squadrons

Activated in August 1948 as the 22nd Bombardment Wing at Smokey Hill AFB, KS, the unit moved to March AFB nine months later and has remained at the base ever since. The B-47 and B-52 were employed for more than three decades, with the KC-135A assigned from 1963 and the KC-10A subsequently. The unit retired the last of their B-52Ds in 1983, becoming an Air Refueling Wing at the same time. The KC-135s were transferred to other SAC Wings in 1989, with the final example departing during December 1989. The unit was redesignated 22nd Wing in October 1991.

Previously operating KC-135s as well as the KC-10, the 22nd Wing has now settled on the latter.

23rd Fighter Wing
ACC England AFB, LA: A-10A ('EL')
74th/76th Fighter Squadrons

Established as the 23rd Fighter Wing in August 1948 at Northwest Guam AFB, Guam, with the F-47, the unit moved to Howard AFB, Canal Zone, in mid-1949 for a brief period, followed by 13 months at Presque Isle AFB, Maine, before inactivating. The unit was redesignated 23rd Tactical Fighter Wing and reactivated at McConnell AFB in February 1964 with the F-105D, before moving to England AFB to replace the 4403rd TFW in July 1972 and converting to the A-7D. The A-10A began to replace the A-7 in 1980. Two squadrons from the 23rd TFW deployed to King Fahd, Damman, Saudi Arabia, for Desert Storm. The wing is scheduled to inactivate by 1993, although the unit is to re-form at a later date as a composite unit at Pope AFB, with a mix of A-10s, C-130s and F-16s.

A-10s will remain with the 23rd Fighter Wing after it becomes a rapid-reaction 'super wing'.

24th Composite Wing
ACC Howard AFB, Canal Zone: OA-37B ('HW')

Formed as the 24th Composite Wing (Special) in November 1942, the unit spent various periods of duty in Iceland and Puerto Rico before inactivating in July 1948. The unit reactivated at Albrook AFB, Canal Zone, in November 1967 and changed to Air Commando Wing status five months later, with a further change to 24th Special Operations Wing during the summer of 1968. The wing moved to Howard AFB in January 1968 and downgraded to Group status in June 1972. The designation was changed to 24th Composite Group in November 1973 and upgraded to Wing standard in January 1976, when control passed from Southern Command to TAC. The 24th employed a variety of aircraft types, including the OA-37B, while hosting numerous AFRes and ANG fighter units on temporary duty.

27th Fighter Wing
ACC Cannon AFB, NM: F-111D/G ('CC')
428th/522nd/523rd/524th Fighter Squadrons

Established as the 27th Fighter Wing in July 1947 and activated 13 months later at Kearney AFB, NE, with the P-51, the wing moved to Bergstrom AFB in March 1949 and was redesignated 27th Fighter Escort Wing in February 1950 with the F-84. The unit subsequently changed to Strategic Fighter Wing and Fighter-Bomber Wing before finally becoming a Tactical Fighter Wing in July 1958. The F-101 was flown before switching to the F-100 in 1959, when the wing moved to Cannon AFB. Despite commencing F-111D deliveries in October 1969 the wing continued to operate the F-100F until mid-1972. The F-111G began to be received from SAC during 1990, although only one squadron was assigned, rather than two as originally planned. The unit changed to Fighter Wing status in 1991, and is to receive the F-111E and F models, along with the EF-111A, from USAFE commencing 1992.

Above: The 27th FW has four F-111 squadrons assigned.

Left: F-111Gs are unique to the 27th FW, and will be retired in 1992.

28th Air Division
ACC Tinker AFB, OK: EC-130E/H, C-135E, EC-135K
7th Airborne Command and Control Squadron
8th Tactical Deployment and Control Squadron
41st Electronic Combat Squadron

The 28th Air Division was formed in April 1985 with three specialist electronic squadrons of C-130s and C-135s directly assigned, and with responsibility for the E-3 Sentry Wing at Tinker AFB. The Air Division took control of the 7th ACCS operating the EC-130E Airborne Battlefield Command, Control and Communications (ABCCC), and the 41st ECS flying the EC-130H 'Compass Call' in April 1985, while the 8th TDCS, employing a C-135E and two EC-135K command platforms, was transferred from the 552nd AW&CW to the 28th AD in March 1986. The 552nd AW&CW (now 552nd ACW) became subordinate to the 28th Air Division in April 1985, providing liaison between HQ TAC and the operational wing.

Among the 28th AD assets are the Lockheed EC-130E (ABCCC) aircraft of the 7th ACCS.

28th Wing
ACC/AMC Ellsworth AFB, SD: B-1B, KC-135R, EC-135A/C/G/H/L
37th/77th Bomber Squadrons
4th Airborne Command and Control Squadron
28th Air Refueling Squadron

The unit formed as the 28th Bombardment Wing (Very Heavy) in July 1947 at Rapid City AFB (later Ellsworth AFB), SD, with a variety of strategic bombers, such as the B-29, B-36 and B-52, plus strategic reconnaissance aircraft including the RB-29 and RB-36. Designation was changed to Strategic Reconnaissance Wing between April 1950 and October 1955, when it reverted to Bombardment Wing. The unit added the EC-135 in 1965 and converted from the B-52H to the B-1B during 1987, and won the 1989 Fairchild Trophy as the first B-1B competition winner at SAC's Proud Shield bombing and navigation meet. Designation was changed to 28th Wing in October 1991.

Above: The 37th BS operates the B-1B.

Left: 28th Wing aircraft carry the Mt Rushmore faces on the fin, with the inscription 'Ellsworth'.

31st Fighter Wing
ACC Homestead AFB, FL: F-16C/D ('HS')
307th/308th/309th Fighter Squadrons

Created as the 31st Fighter Wing in November 1947 at Turner AFB, GA, with the P-51, the unit was redesignated a Fighter-Bomber Wing, followed by Fighter-Escort Wing and Strategic Fighter Wing, before becoming a Tactical Fighter Wing in July 1958 with the F-100. The wing moved to George AFB in March 1959 and Homestead AFB in May 1962, finally relocating to Tuy Hoa AB, South Vietnam, in December 1966. In October 1970 the unit returned to Homestead AFB to replace the 4531st TFW, assuming that unit's F-4s. The wing became the 31st Tactical Training Wing in March 1981, and in 1985 converted to the F-16A and reverted to TFW status. After upgrading to the F-16C in 1990, this unit changed designation yet again in late 1991 to its original Fighter Wing.

The 31st Fighter Wing is currently flying the F-16C/D model, although this is one of their earlier F-16As. The 'HS' tailcode stands for Homestead.

32nd Fighter Group
USAFE Soesterberg AB, Netherlands: F-15C/D ('CR')
32nd Fighter Squadron

The 32nd Fighter Interceptor Squadron initially operated the F-100, before switching to the F-102A and joining the 86th Fighter Interceptor Wing in April 1960. The latter unit upgraded to Air Division status in November 1960 but reverted to FIW standard in November 1968. The squadron transferred from 86th FIW to HQ 17th Air Force control in 1968, and converted to the F-4E commencing July 1969, when it became a Tactical Fighter Squadron. It remained assigned to the 17th AF until November 1989, when the 32nd TFG was activated. The 32nd TFS converted to the F-15A beginning September 1978 and to the F-15C in June 1980. The unit was awarded the Hughes Achievement Trophy for excellence in air defense in 1979 and 1980, and won the F-15 Top Gun award at the 1984 William Tell competition at Tyndall

Patch of the 32nd (Tactical) Fighter Group.

AFB. The squadron transferred several Eagles to the Royal Saudi Air Force in September 1990 before the remainder were deployed to Incirlik AB, where they gained a single air-to-air kill against a Mirage F1EQ on 19 January 1991. The squadron was redesignated 32nd Fighter Group in November 1991, by which time the first Multi-Stage Improvement Program (MSIP) Eagles had commenced delivery.

The 32nd FG aircraft come under operational control of the Royal Netherlands Air Force, but remain part of USAFE.

33rd Fighter Wing
ACC Eglin AFB, FL: F-15C/D ('EG')
58th/59th/60th Fighter Squadrons

The 33rd Fighter Wing was formed at Roswell AFB (later Walker AFB), NM, in November 1947 with the F-51 and redesignated Fighter Interceptor Wing in January 1950. The wing moved to Otis AFB, MA, in November 1948 and was inactivated in February 1952. The unit was redesignated 33rd Fighter Wing (Air Defense) and activated in October 1956 at Otis AFB with the F-89 and F-94, although it inactivated in August 1957. The wing was reactivated April 1965 as a Tactical Fighter Wing at Eglin AFB with the F-4, which was operated until 1979 when conversion to the F-15A commenced. The F-15C began replacing the F-15A in October 1984. The unit won the F-15 category in the 1984, 1986 and 1988 William

Patch of the 33rd (Tactical) Fighter Wing.

Tell competitions at Tyndall AFB. The 58th TFS deployed to Tabuk, Saudi Arabia, for Desert Storm, with 16 air-to-air kills credited to them. The unit changed designation to Fighter Wing late in 1991, and was scheduled to exchange one squadron of Eagles for the A/OA-10A in late 1992.

Gulf victors: Eagles of the Eglin-based 33rd FW scored the bulk of air-to-air kills in Desert Storm with F-15C MSIP aircraft.

35th Tactical Fighter Wing
ACC George AFB, CA: F-4E ('GA'), F-4E/G ('WW')
20th/561st/562nd Fighter Squadrons

The unit was established as the 35th Fighter Wing at Johnson AB, Japan, in August 1948, operating the F-51. The wing was redesignated 35th Fighter Interceptor Wing in January 1950 and relocated to various bases in Japan and Korea operating the F-80, F-94 and F-86 before inactivating in October 1957. The unit was reactivated at Da Nang AB, South Vietnam, as a Tactical Fighter Wing with the F-4, replacing the 7252nd TFW in April 1966. The wing was inactivated in July 1971 and moved to

George AFB three months later to replace the 479th TFW. They operated the F-105G 'Wild Weasel' alongside the F-4 from July 1973 until July 1980. The unit was redesignated Tactical Training Wing to concentrate on F-4E/G aircrew training in July 1984 until October 1989, when it reverted to a TFW and the 35th assumed the squadrons of the co-located 37th TFW. The wing has conducted German Air Force Phantom aircrew training since 1972 with eight F-4F and later 10 F-4E aircraft specially assigned for the purpose. The wing is gradually reducing in size as the Phantom is retired from service, with inactivation due during 1992.

The F-4Gs of the 35th FW are due for reassignment to the Air National Guard.

36th Fighter Wing
USAFE Bitburg AB, Germany: F-15C/D ('BT')
22nd/53rd/525th Fighter Squadrons

The wing was activated with the F-80 as the 36th Fighter Wing in June 1948 at Howard AFB, Canal Zone, and moved to Fürstenfeldbruck AB, Germany, in August of that year. The unit was redesignated 36th Fighter-Bomber Wing and Fighter Day Wing before changing to Tactical Fighter Wing in July 1958. They relocated to Bitburg AB in December 1952, and flew the F-84 and F-86 before switching to the F-100D in 1956. The unit formed the 'Skyblazers' demonstration team between 1949 and 1952, and again from October 1956 to January 1962. The F-105D was operated between 1961 and 1966 before the wing converted to the F-4D. The wing controlled the EB-66C/F and F-4 squadrons at nearby Spangdahlem between September 1969 and December 1971, when the 52nd TFW was established. The F-15A was operated between 1977 and 1980, when the wing converted to the F-15C. The

22nd TFS won the Hughes Achievement Trophy for excellence in air defense in 1988. During Desert Storm one squadron was assigned to Al Kharj, Saudi Arabia, while a second operated from Incirlik AB, Turkey, with the 7440th Provisional Wing, being

credited with 14 air-to-air kills during the war and three more in late March. The unit changed to Fighter Wing in October 1991. The 525th FS is due to inactivate during 1992.

Below are the three squadron badges comprising the 22nd FS (bee), 53rd FS (tiger) and 525th FS (bulldog).

37th Fighter Wing

ACC Tonopah TR, NV: F-117A, T-38A ('TR')
415th/416th/417th Fighter Squadrons

The wing was created as the 37th Fighter-Bomber Wing in April 1953 at Clovis AFB, NM, although it was not operational and inactivated two months later. The unit was reactivated in March 1967 as a Tactical Fighter Wing at Phu Cat AB, South Vietnam, with the F-100 and later the F-4. They conducted forward air control operations with the F-100F between 1967 and 1969, and were inactivated in March 1970. The unit reactivated at Tonopah Test Range with the F-117A in October 1989. Two squadrons operated from Khamis Mushait, Saudi Arabia, during Desert Storm with the 37th TFW (Provisional). The unit changed to Fighter Wing in October 1991, with the wing due to transfer their aircraft to the 49th FW when it moves to Holloman AFB in 1992.

Above: The night hawk badge of the 37th (Tactical) Fighter Wing.

Right: A 37th FW F-117 approaches a tanker for refueling. When the F-117s transferred to Holloman in mid-1992, they joined the 49th Fighter Wing, with the 7th, 8th and 9th Fighter Squadrons.

39th Special Operations Wing

AFSOC RAF Woodbridge, UK: HC-130N/P, MH-53J
Rhein Main AB, Germany: MC-130E
7th/21st/67th Special Operations Squadrons

The unit was designated 39th Air Rescue and Recovery Wing and stationed at Eglin AFB, FL, during the 1960s and 1970s, with several squadrons and a host of detachments assigned. These were located across the US and at numerous overseas outposts including Greenland, Spain, the Canal Zone and the UK. The designation changed to Aerospace Rescue and Recovery Wing status during the 1970s and was reorganized in July 1988 to become the 39th Special Operations Wing. The unit moved to Rhein Main AB, Germany, the following year to assume control of three special operations squadrons in Germany and the UK prior to the creation of Air Force Special Operations Command in May 1990. Most of the aircraft and helicopters flown by the wing were actively engaged in Desert Storm while operating from Turkey. The wing relocated to Alconbury in January 1992 prior to its three squadrons joining the parent unit.

The 39th SOW operates all USAFE Special Operations assets, including the 7th SOS MC-130Es (below) and 21st SOS MH-53Js (below left).

39th Tactical Group

USAFE Incirlik AB, Turkey

The 39th Tactical Group was created to control tactical range support activities at the base involving visiting USAFE fighter aircraft. During the 1970s the primary unit at Incirlik was detachment 10 TUSLOG (Turkey/US Logistics), but changed in 1983 to the 39th Tactical Air Control Group and to its present title in 1984.

40th Tactical Support Wing

USAFE Aviano AB, Italy

The 40th Tactical Group has administered Aviano AB for many years, hosting visiting fighter aircraft from USAFE units. The unit was upgraded to wing standard when it became the 40th Tactical Support Wing in 1990. Following the withdrawal of the F-16Cs from the 401st TFW at Torrejon AB, Spain, the wing was believed to have relocated to Aviano pending its future being finalized.

42nd Wing

ACC/AMC Loring AFB, ME: B-52G, KC-135R
69th Bomb Squadron
42nd/407th Air Refueling Squadrons

The unit was established as the 42nd Bombardment Wing (Heavy) in February 1953 at Limestone AFB (later Loring AFB), ME, with the B-36 and KC-97, which were respectively replaced by the B-52 in 1956 and the KC-135A a year later. The unit was awarded the Mackay Trophy in 1983 for 'the most meritorious flight of the year' when a KC-135A crew successfully refueled an F-4E 2,000 ft (610 m) above the ocean, towing the aircraft 160 miles (257 km) while continuing to refuel until the fighter pilot could regain sufficient thrust to maintain flight on his own. The wing deployed most of its B-52Gs during Desert Shield/Storm, with operations mainly conducted at Diego Garcia. The unit became the 42nd Wing in October 1991, and is due to inactivate prior to the base closing in September 1994, with its B-52Gs relocating to the 410th BW while the KC-135s are redistributed.

Based close to the North Atlantic coast, the 42nd Wing has a secondary maritime commitment which originally involved the use of Harpoon anti-ship missiles. These are no longer carried, but the B-52Gs can still sow naval mines in addition to their conventional bombing tasks.

44th Strategic Missile Wing

ACC Ellsworth AFB, SD: LGM-30F
60th/61st/62nd Strategic Missile Squadrons

The unit was formed with the B-29 and TB-29 as the 44th Bombardment Wing (Medium) in January 1951 at March AFB. The wing moved to Lake Charles AFB (later Chennault AFB), LA, in August 1951 before converting to the B-47 and KC-97 and deactivating in June 1960. The unit was redesignated 44th Strategic Missile Wing and reactivated in January 1962 with the Titan I missile, followed a year later by the Minuteman I. The unit upgraded to the LGM-30F Minuteman II in 1972. The wing was scheduled to inactivate in late 1991 with their 150 missiles retired.

47th Flying Training Wing

ATC Laughlin AFB, TX: T-37B, T-38A ('XL')
85th/86th Flying Training Squadrons

The unit was established with the A-26 as the 47th Bombardment Wing (Light) at Biggs AFB, TX, in July 1947. The unit moved to Barksdale AFB in November 1948 and inactivated in October 1949 before reactivating at Langley AFB in March 1951. They moved to RAF Sculthorpe, UK, with USAFE in June 1952 and were redesignated 47th BW (Tactical) in October 1955. The B-45, RB-45 and B-66 were operated, plus the KB-50J tanker, before the wing deactivated in June 1962. The wing was redesignated 47th Flying Training Wing with ATC and activated in September 1972, replacing the 3646th PTW at Laughlin AFB.

Like most ATC units, the 47th FTW has two squadrons, the 85th flying the Cessna T-37B and the 86th operating the Northrop T-38A Talon. This example of the latter carries the 'XL' tailcode and an inscription for the local Texas town.

48th Fighter Wing
USAFE RAF Lakenheath, UK:
F-111F, F-15E ('LN')
492nd/494th Fighter Squadrons

Formed by USAFE at Chaumont AB, France, in June 1952 as the 48th Fighter-Bomber Wing with the F-84 and F-86, the unit converted to the F-100 before being redesignated 48th Tactical Fighter Wing in July 1958. They moved to RAF Lakenheath in January 1960 and converted to the F-4D in 1972, subsequently exchanging the Phantom for the F-111F in 1977. Three squadrons deployed to Taif, Saudi Arabia, for Desert Storm, becoming the largest unit located in the Gulf, with assignment to the

48th TFW (Provisional). The unit was redesignated 48th Fighter Wing in October 1991, and began converting to the F-15E in 1992. The first F-15E was delivered on 21 February 1992, with conversion due for completion by 1993.

1992 is a year of transition for the 48th FW, which changes from F-111F (above left) to F-15E. Both of these aircraft are marked for the unit's commander.

49th Fighter Wing
ACC Holloman AFB, NM:
F-15A/B, AT-38B ('HO')
7th/8th/9th Fighter Squadrons
433rd Fighter Squadron

Created as the 49th Fighter Wing in August 1948 at Misawa AB, operating the P-51, the unit was redesignated 49th Fighter-Bomber Wing in February 1950 and relocated to several bases in Japan and South Korea before transferring from PACAF to USAFE in December 1957 and converting to the F-100 at the same time. The unit was based at Etain/Rouvres AB, France, until August 1959, when it moved to Spangdahlem AB, Germany, having become a Tactical Fighter Wing in July 1958. The wing converted to the F-105D in 1961 and the F-4D in 1967. They relocated to Holloman AFB as the USAF's first 'dual-based' NATO-committed wing, stationed in the US but organized to return to Europe immediately if necessary (a forerunner of the rapid deployment force). The unit received the Mackay Trophy in 1969 for 'the most meritorious flight of the year' when the wing relocated 72 F-4Ds non-stop from Germany to Holloman AFB without a single abort, completing 504 air refuelings. Equipment was upgraded to F-15A

The wing commander's F-15A also carries an inscription for the local city of Alamogordo.

beginning October 1977. The unit won the F-15 category and the individual 'Top Gun' award at the 1988 William Tell competition at Tyndall AFB. The single squadron of AT-38Bs was absorbed when the 479th TTW was relegated to Group status. The unit changed designation to 49th Fighter Wing in October 1991, with preparations initiated for the unit to receive the F-117A at Holloman AFB commencing 1992.

Above are the patches of the 49th's three main fighter squadrons. Left is a tactically camouflaged AT-38B flown by the wing for the fighter lead-in role.

51st Fighter Wing
PACAF Osan AB, RoK: OA-10A,
F-16C/D ('OS')
19th/36th Fighter Squadrons

The unit was established at Naha AB, Okinawa, in August 1948 as the 51st Fighter Wing operating the F-61. They were redesignated 51st Fighter Interceptor Wing in February 1950 and moved to several bases in Japan, Okinawa and South Korea before inactivating in May 1971. The wing was reactivated as the 51st Air Base Wing in November 1971 at Osan AB, replacing the 6314th Support Wing, and changed to 51st Composite Wing (Tactical) in September 1974 with the F-4E and the OV-10A. The unit was redesignated the 51st TFW in January 1982 with squadrons located at Suwon,

Taegu, as well as wing headquarters. The wing was subsequently downgraded to Group status with the F-16C assigned during 1989, and the A-10A one year later.

Two units fly the F-16C in Korea, the other being the 8th Fighter Wing. In addition to the Fighting Falcons, the 51st operates the OA-10A in the forward air control role.

52nd Fighter Wing
USAFE Spangdahlem AB,
Germany: F-4G, F-16C/D ('SP')
23rd/81st/480th Fighter
Squadrons

The 52nd Fighter Wing (All Weather) was activated at Mitchel Field, NY, in June 1948, operating the P-61. They were redesignated Fighter All-Weather Wing and Fighter Interceptor Wing before inactivating in February 1952, having moved to McGuire AFB. Designation changed to 52nd Fighter Wing (Air Defense) and the unit was

activated at Suffolk County AFB, NY, in July 1963, with the F-101B, later inactivating in September 1968. The unit became the 52nd Tactical Fighter Wing and was reactivated at Spangdahlem AB in December 1971, assuming responsibility for the squadrons formerly under 36th TFW control. They operated in the 'Wild Weasel' 'hunter-killer' role with the F-4C and D models before converting to the F-4E and F-4G. The F-16C replaced the F-4E in 1987. F-4Gs from the wing operated from Sheikh Isa, Bahrain, during Desert Storm while other F-4Gs and F-16Cs were stationed at Incirlik AB, Turkey.

The unit changed designation to Fighter Wing in October 1991, and is due to become a Composite Wing with the assignment of the A-10A by early 1993.

F-16Cs are used by the 52nd FW for defense suppression missions on behalf of USAFE.

55th Wing
ACC Offutt AFB, NE: C-135A, EC-135C, KC-135E, NKC-135A, RC-135S/U/V/W/X, TC-135S/W, E-4B
1st/2nd Airborne Command and Control Squadrons
24th/38th/343rd Strategic Reconnaissance Squadrons

The 55th Strategic Reconnaissance Wing was formed in June 1948 at Topeka AFB (later Forbes AFB), KS, with a variety of reconnaissance platforms assigned, including the RB-29, RB-47 and, more recently, the RC-135. The unit moved to Ramey AFB, PR, in November 1950 and Offutt AFB in August 1966 and assumed responsibility for 'Looking Glass' airborne command post relay. The unit gained the E-4 National Emergency Airborne Command Post (NEACP) when the 1st ACCS moved from Andrews AFB in November 1975. The wing gained a number of VIP C-135A/B aircraft, with examples of the EC-135H, J and P due from USAFE, PACAF and TAC during 1991/1992 to centralize airborne command post operations under a single manager. The unit changed designation to 55th Wing in October 1991.

Two of the 55th Wing's important roles are depicted here. Below left is an E-4B of the 1st ACCS, while below is an RC-135W from the electronic reconnaissance fleet.

56th Fighter Wing
ACC MacDill AFB, FL: F-16C/D ('MC')
61st/62nd/63rd/72nd Fighter Squadrons

The unit was established as the 56th Fighter Wing at Selfridge AFB in August 1947 with the P-80 and was changed to Fighter Interceptor Wing status in January 1950, before inactivating in February 1952. Redesignated 56th Fighter Wing (Air Defense) at K. I. Sawyer AFB, the unit was activated in February 1961 with the F-101B and then inactivated in January 1964. The wing changed to 56th Air Commando Wing and activated at Nakhon Phanom RTAFB, Thailand, in April 1967 with a variety of special operations types including the A-1, C-123, T-28 and U-10, before becoming the 56th SOW in August 1968. Designation was changed to Tactical Fighter Wing and the unit moved to MacDill AFB in June 1975, operating the F-4E. Re-equipped with the F-16A commencing 1979, the unit became a Tactical Training Wing in July 1982. The F-16C was assigned in 1989 with the unit redesignated a TFW, and then changed to Fighter Wing at the end of 1991. The unit is due to transfer its aircraft to Luke AFB, AZ, in 1994 prior to a realignment of activities at MacDill AFB.

MacDill's F-16 wing is assigned the type conversion role, and consequently has a high number of F-16D two-seaters. It is due to move to Luke.

58th Fighter Wing
ACC Luke AFB, AZ: F-15E, F-16C/D ('LF')
310th/311th/314th/461st/550th Fighter Squadrons

Established with the F-84 as the 58th Fighter-Bomber Wing at Itazuke AB, Japan, in July 1952, the unit operated at several bases in the Far East until inactivated in July 1958. The wing was redesignated 58th Tactical Fighter Training Wing and activated at Luke AFB in October 1969, replacing the 4510th CCTW training F-100 and later F-4 aircrew. A squadron of A-7Ds was assigned between 1969 and 1971, and the F-5 training unit was located at Williams AFB from 1969 until transferred to the 405th TTW in August 1979. The unit began converting to the F-15A in 1974 and changed designation to 58th Tactical Training Wing in April 1977. F-15 training was transferred to the 405th TTW in August 1979 with the 58th TTW concentrating on the F-4C until 1983, when the F-16A commenced delivery. The wing began receiving the F-16C in 1984, and was redesignated 58th Fighter Wing in October 1991 with F-15Es transferred from the 405th TTW to consolidate training duties at Luke.

Luke offers excellent weather for tactical training, and the resident 58th FW provides type training for both the F-16C and F-15E. The latter has recently adopted the 'LF' tailcode of its new 'owner', having transferred from the 405th TTW.

60th Airlift Wing
AMC Travis AFB, CA: C-5A/B, C-141B
7th/22nd/75th/86th Airlift Squadrons

The 60th MAW replaced the 1501st Air Transport Wing at Travis AFB in January 1966 operating the C-124C, C-130E, C-133A/B and C-141A. The former two types were transferred to other commands when the wing completed transition to the C-141, while the C-133 was retired when replaced by the C-5A beginning in 1971. The unit changed designation to 60th Airlift Wing in September 1991.

In addition to four active-duty squadrons, the 60th AW aircraft are also manned by Reservists.

61st Airlift Group
AMC Howard AFB, Canal Zone: C-21A, C-22A, C-27A, C-130H, CASA 212
310th Airlift Squadron

The group was activated in 1985 to coordinate MAC activities within the Canal Zone and Central America, consisting of reserve airlift units on temporary duty at Howard AFB. The unit was assigned a single C-22A and a pair of former US Coast Guard HC-130Hs which had been reconfigured from the rescue role to basic airlifters. These were later joined by a C-21A and a CASA 212, although five C-27As were ordered as the most suitable airlifter for duties in the region, with deliveries commencing at the end of 1991.

62nd Airlift Wing
AMC McChord AFB, WA: C-141B
4th/8th/36th Airlift Squadrons

The 62nd MAW was redesignated from Air Transport Wing status in January 1966, having originally formed in July 1947 as a Troop Carrier Wing. The wing equipped with the C-124C and C-141A, although the latter type had replaced the faithful Globemaster by 1969. One squadron of C-130Es was assigned from July 1975 until 1989 when that unit converted to the C-141B. In keeping with other MAC units the change to 62nd Airlift Wing took place in September 1991.

Most of the 62nd AW's C-141 missions are concerned with the Far East.

63rd Airlift Wing
AMC Norton AFB, CA: C-141B
14th/15th/53rd Airlift Squadrons

The 63rd Troop Carrier Wing was created as a reserve unit in June 1949 at NAS Floyd Bennett, NY, with the C-47. The unit was ordered to active service in May 1951 and inactivated after only eight days. They were reactivated at Altus AFB in January 1953 and moved to Donaldson AFB, SC, 10 months later to convert to the C-124. One squadron of Globemasters was maintained at Rhein Main AB, Germany, between August 1956 and January 1967. The wing relocated to Hunter AFB, GA, in April 1963 before moving to Norton AFB in April 1967 and converting to the C-141A. Designation was changed to 63rd MAW in January 1966 and to 63rd Airlift Wing in September 1991. The unit, which won the 1990 Airlift Rodeo competition, was due to deactivate commencing 1992, with their C-141Bs transferring to the Reserves.

The 63rd AW is a wing chosen for deactivation, the C-141Bs being redistributed.

64th Flying Training Wing
ATC Reese AFB, TX: T-37B, T-38A
35th/54th Flying Training Squadrons

The unit was formed as the 64th Troop Carrier Wing with TAC at Donaldson AFB, SC, in July 1952 operating the C-82, and inactivated two years later. They were reactivated at Dyess AFB in February 1961 with the C-130A/D, but inactivated in January 1963 when replaced by the 516th TCW. The wing was reactivated at Sewart AFB, TN, in July 1966 with the C-130E and redesignated 64th Tactical Airlift Wing in May 1967 before moving to Little Rock AFB in March 1970. After being inactivated in May 1971, the unit transferred to ATC and was redesignated 64th Flying Training Wing with activation at Reese AFB in October 1972, replacing the 3500th PTW. It is the first recipient of the T-1A Jayhawk.

The 54th FTS have used part of this T-38's serial to highlight the squadron. T-1A Jayhawks are joining the unit.

67th Reconnaissance Wing
ACC Bergstrom AFB, TX: RF-4C ('BA')
12th Reconnaissance Squadron

The wing was established as the 67th Reconnaissance Wing at March AFB in November 1947 (although only its subordinate unit, the 67th Recon Group, was operational) with assignment to the 1st Fighter Wing. The 67th RW changed designation to Tactical Reconnaissance Wing and was activated in August 1948 with the RB-26 and RF-80, but was inactivated in March 1949. The unit transferred to FEAF and was reactivated in February 1951 at Komaki AB, Japan, with several assignments in the Far East operating RB-50, RB-66, RF-84, RF-86 and RF-101 before inactivating in December 1960. They transferred to TAC and reformed at Mountain Home AFB in January 1966 with the RF-4C assigned, but moved to Bergstrom AFB in July 1971. A small number of RF-4Cs from Bergstrom flew strike recon sorties during Desert Storm from Sheikh Isa, Bahrain. The unit changed to the 67th Reconnaissance Wing in October 1991. General rundown of tactical reconnaissance assets has resulted in three of the unit's four squadrons deactivating in recent years, with just the 12th RS remaining. The wing was due to inactivate in September 1992 prior to the base closing.

In the fall of 1992 the 67th RW will deactivate, spelling the end of the RF-4C as an active-duty type, although it will continue in ANG service. Only one squadron remains, despite having put up a good showing in Desert Storm.

71st Flying Training Wing
ATC Vance AFB, OK: T-37B, T-38A ('VN')
8th/25th Flying Training Squadrons

Activated at Kadena AB in August 1948 as the 71st Tactical Reconnaissance Wing with the RB-17 and RB-29 formed into a single squadron, the wing inactivated after just two months of operations. It was redesignated 71st Strategic Reconnaissance Wing and re-formed at Larson AFB, WA, in January 1955 to evaluate the GRF-84 and GRB-36 parasite/mothership concept for SAC, but also conducted conventional recon duties with the RF-84F until inactivated in July 1957. The unit was re-formed as the 71st Surveillance Wing (Ballistic Missile Early Warning System) at Ent AFB, CO, in January 1962 and changed to 71st Missile Warning Wing five years later. They were responsible for radar sites in Alaska, Greenland and the UK. The wing moved to McGuire AFB in July 1969 but inactivated in April 1971. The unit was transferred to ATC and was redesignated 71st Flying Training Wing with activation at Vance AFB in November 1972, replacing the 3575th PTW.

'VN' tailcodes adorn this strikingly marked T-38 of the 25th FTS. At left is the 71st FTW's patch.

80th Flying Training Wing

ATC Sheppard AFB, TX: T-37B, T-38A ('WF')
88th/89th/90th Flying Training Squadrons

The wing was activated as the 80th Flying Training Wing at Sheppard AFB in January 1973 to replace the 3630th FTW. The unit conducted undergraduate pilot training for US, German and South Vietnamese air forces, and later added several allied nations including Iran, El Salvador, Kuwait and Saudi Arabia.

The 80th FTW trains European pilots, hence the NATO star on the fin.

81st Tactical Fighter Wing

USAFE RAF Bentwaters, UK: A-10A ('WR')
RAF Woodbridge, UK: A-10A ('WR')
78th/91st/92nd/510th Tactical Fighter Squadrons

Formed as the 81st Fighter Wing with the P-47 at Wheeler AFB, Hawaii, in May 1948, the unit moved to Camp Stoneman, CA, in May 1949 for a few days before relocating to Kirtland AFB. It was redesignated 81st Fighter Interceptor Wing in January 1950 and moved to Moses Lake AFB (later Larson AFB), WA, in May 1950. The unit moved to RAF Bentwaters, UK, in September 1951

and transferred from ADC to USAFE. Redesignated 81st Tactical Fighter Wing in July 1958, the unit converted from the F-84F to the F-101A/C. Equipment was changed to the F-4C in 1965 and subsequently to the F-4D, before the unit converted to the A-10A beginning in 1978. An aggressor squadron of F-16Cs was assigned from June 1988 until inactivated in early 1990. Reduced from six squadrons to four in 1988 when 38 A-10As were transferred to the 10th TFW at Alconbury, the wing is due to retire its A-10s between April 1992 and March 1993 before inactivating.

Once the largest wing in the USAF, with six squadrons of A-10s, the 81st is running down its operations prior to deactivation.

82nd Flying Training Wing

ATC Williams AFB, AZ: T-37B, T-38A ('WL')
96th/97th Flying Training Squadrons

The unit was formed with the P-51 as the 82nd Fighter Wing at Grenier AFB, NH, in August 1947 and attached to the 307th BW SAC, but was inactivated in October 1949. The wing transferred to ATC and was redesignated 82nd Flying Training Wing at Williams AFB in February 1973, replacing the 3525th PTW. The unit was due to inactivate by September 1992, with the base closing 12 months later.

The 82nd FTW is the casualty as far as ATC wing deactivations go. This T-38 is marked 'Willie One' for the wing commander.

86th Fighter Wing

USAFE Ramstein AB, Germany: F-16C/D ('RS')
512th/526th Fighter Squadrons

The unit was established as the 86th Fighter Wing at Neubiberg AB, Germany, in July 1948 and redesignated the 86th Fighter-Bomber Wing in January 1950 when they converted to the F-84. The wing moved to Landstuhl AB (later Ramstein AB) in August 1952 and changed to Fighter Interceptor Wing in August 1954. The unit upgraded to 86th Air Division in November 1960 with responsibility for F-102A-equipped air defense squadrons located at three West German and one Dutch bases. Designation reverted to 86th Fighter Interceptor Wing in

November 1968 and changed to Tactical Fighter Wing in October 1969. The wing moved to Zweibrücken AB, Germany, in November 1969 with the RF-4C and F-4C, and returned to Ramstein in January 1973, acquiring a squadron of F-4Es with a second added in 1977. The unit won the F-4 category in the 1978 William Tell competition at Tyndall AFB, and converted to the F-16C beginning September 1985. The unit changed to 86th Fighter Wing during the spring of 1991.

Despite force cutbacks, the 86th FW remains in Germany with two squadrons of F-16Cs.

89th Airlift Wing

AMC Andrews AFB, MD: C-9C, C-12A, C-20B/C, VC-25A, C-135B/C, C-137C, UH-1N
1st Airlift Squadron
1st Helicopter Squadron

The wing was formed on 8 January 1966 to replace the 1254th Air Transport Wing at Andrews AFB as the primary unit performing special missions duties to transport Presidential, governmental, VIP and senior

military passengers. Despite being downgraded to Group status for a brief period in 1977, the unit has retained its mission unchanged. A detachment at Hickam AFB operates a pair of C-135s for VIP duties within the Pacific region on behalf of the CinC PACAF. 89th MAW aircraft were active in the Gulf during Desert Shield/Storm, transporting statesmen between the Middle East and European capitals. The unit was redesignated 89th Airlift Wing on 12 July 1991 when the former 89th MAW was amalgamated with the 1776th ABW.

The 89th AW's best-known aircraft are the pair of 'Air Force One' VC-25A Presidential transports.

90th Strategic Missile Wing

ACC F. E. Warren AFB, WY: LGM-30G, LGM-118A

The unit was created as the 90th Bombardment Wing in January 1951 at Fairchild AFB with the B-29, RB-29 and TB-29 as a replacement training unit for Superfortress crews destined for FEAF. The wing moved to Forbes AFB, KS, in March 1951 and was redesignated 90th Strategic Reconnaissance Wing in June 1956, with the RB-29 and later the RB-47 assigned. It was inactivated in June 1960, but was redesignated 90th Strategic Missile Wing at Francis E. Warren AFB and re-formed in July 1963 with the Minuteman I and later the Minuteman III. The LGM-118A Peacekeeper was added in June 1986.

91st Strategic Missile Wing

ACC Minot AFB, ND: LGM-30G 319th/320th/321st/400th Strategic Missile Squadrons

The unit was established as the 91st Strategic Reconnaissance Wing at McGuire AFB in November 1948, operating the B-17, RB-17, TB-17, RB-29 and RC-54. It moved to Barksdale AFB in October 1949 and Lockbourne AFB, OH, in September 1951, with the RB-45, RB-47 and RB-50 added. The wing was inactivated in November 1957, redesignated 91st Bombardment Wing at Glasgow AFB, MT, and activated in February 1963 with the B-52 and KC-135. The unit moved to Minot AFB when it was redesignated 91st Strategic Missile Wing in June 1968, equipped with the Minuteman I and Minuteman III, although only the latter ICBM is currently assigned.

92nd Wing

ACC/AMC Fairchild AFB, WA B-52H, KC-135R 325th Bomb Squadron 43rd/92nd Air Refueling Squadrons

Formed as the 92nd Bombardment Wing with the B-29 at Spokane AFB (later Fairchild AFB), WA, in November 1947, the unit has remained at the base ever since. The unit was redesignated 92nd Strategic Aerospace Wing in February 1962 but reverted to Bombardment Wing status in March 1972.

They operated the B-36 between 1951 and 1957 and the B-52 from 1957 onwards, and won the Fairchild Trophy as the top bomber team at SAC's Proud Shield bombing and navigation competition in 1953 and 1986. The unit changed to 92nd Wing in October 1991, and is scheduled to gradually increase its complement before assuming the aircrew training role from the 93rd Wing by 1995.

92nd Wing B-52s and KC-135Rs (illustrated) carry the 'Seattle Seahawk' badge on the fin.

93rd Wing

ACC/AMC Castle AFB, CA: B-52G, KC-135A/R 328th Bomb Squadron 329th Combat Crew Training Squadron 93rd/924th Air Refueling Squadrons

The unit was activated as the 93rd Bombardment Wing at Castle AFB in August 1947, with the B-29 and later the B-50 assigned. The wing operated the KB-29 and KC-97 plus the B-47 before becoming the first SAC unit to convert to the B-52 in 1955. The wing was also the first KC-135A unit. They conducted aircrew training for the B-52 and KC-135 from 1956 to date, apart from the periods September 1959 to September 1963 and April 1974 to March 1977 when this function was assigned to other SAC units. The wing won the Fairchild Trophy as the top bomber team at SAC's Proud Shield bombing and navigation competition in 1952 (jointly with 97th BW) and 1970. The unit changed designation to 93rd Wing in October 1991. The wing is scheduled to run down operations, with some B-52Gs being transferred to the 410th Wing and KC-135s to other units, before inactivating in 1994. The aircrew training task will go to the 92nd Wing.

At present the main B-52 and KC-135 training unit, the 93rd is to pass this duty to the 92nd upon deactivation in 1994. Here a castle-marked KC-135A provides a refueling platform for tests with the two YF-22 prototypes.

94th Airlift Wing

AFRes Dobbins AFB, GA: C-130H 700th Airlift Squadron

The unit was formed as the 94th Bombardment Wing at Marietta AFB (later Dobbins AFB), GA, in June 1949 as a light bombardment wing in the Reserve, with the B-26 and a variety of trainers. The wing was ordered to active service in March 1951 but inactivated in April 1951. The unit was redesignated 94th Tactical Reconnaissance Wing and activated in June 1952 in the Reserves. Designation changed to 94th Bombardment Wing in May 1955 when it moved to Scott AFB, becoming the 94th Troop Carrier Wing in July 1957 and relocating to L. G. Hanscom Field in November 1957. The wing moved back to Dobbins AFB in July 1972. The unit was ordered to active service in October/November 1962 and changed designation to the 94th Military Airlift Wing in October 1966 and to Tactical Airlift Wing in July 1972. They won Volant Rodeo (the forerunner of Airlift Rodeo) at Pope AFB in 1985, and have operated a variety of transport aircraft since 1957, including the C-47, C-119, C-124, C-7 and C-130H from 1985.

A C-130 of the 700th AS overflies Dobbins, bearing the legend 'City of Marietta' on the nose.

96th Wing

ACC/AMC Dyess AFB, TX: B-1B, KC-135A 337th/338th Bomb Squadrons 917th Air Refueling Squadron

The unit was established as the 96th Bombardment Wing at Altus AFB in November 1953 with the KC-97 assigned, followed two years later by the B-47. Designation was changed to Strategic Aerospace Wing in April 1962 but reverted to Bombardment Wing in March 1972. They were equipped with the B-52 from 1963 until 1985, when the unit converted to the B-1B. The wing received the Mackay Trophy in 1989 for 'the most meritorious flight of the year' when a crew successfully landed its aircraft with the nosewheel retracted. The KC-135A has been operated from 1965 to date. The unit changed to 96th Wing in October 1991.

Two squadrons of the 96th Wing fly the B-1B bomber.

97th Wing

ACC/AMC Eaker AFB, AR: B-52G, KC-135A 340th Bomb Squadron 97th Air Refueling Squadron

The 97th Bombardment Wing was formed with the B-29 at Mile 26 Air Field (later Eielson AFB), AK, in December 1947 and moved to Smokey Hill AFB, KS, in March 1948 and Biggs AFB two months later. The wing relocated to Blytheville AFB, AR, in July 1959, with the facility renamed Eaker AFB in 1988. The unit operated the B-47 from 1955 until it converted to the B-52 in 1960, and received the KC-135A in 1962. The wing won the Fairchild Trophy as the top bomber team at SAC's Proud Shield bombing and navigation competition in 1951, 1952 (jointly with 93rd BW) and 1985. The unit changed to 97th Wing in October 1991 and was due to inactivate in 1992, prior to the base closing.

97th Wing B-52Gs have a conventional bombing commitment.

98th Air Refueling Group (Associate)

AFRes Barksdale AFB, LA: KC-10A
78th Air Refueling Squadron (Associate)

The unit was formed in 1987 as an Associate Group with the AFRes to crew active-duty KC-10As in place of full-time aircrew.

99th Wing

ACC Ellsworth AFB, SD

The 99th Strategic Reconnaissance Wing was activated at Fairchild AFB in January 1953 with the RB-29 and RB-36. The unit was redesignated 99th Bombardment Wing in October 1955 and moved to Westover AFB in September 1956. The B-52 was operated from 1956 and the KC-135A from 1966 until 1972, with the unit inactivating in March 1974. The 99th Strategic Weapons Wing activated in 1989 as an operational component of SAC's Strategic Warfare Center to develop and teach tactics to bomber and tanker aircrew.

100th Air Refueling Wing

USAFE RAF Mildenhall, UK: KC-135R

Formed as 100th Bombardment Wing at Portsmouth AFB (later Pease AFB), New Hampshire, in January 1956 operating the B-47E and KC-97G under SAC control. Redesignated 100th Strategic Reconnaissance Wing in June 1966 and moved to Davis-Monthan AFB, Arizona, to replace the 4080th Strategic Wing operating a mixed fleet of U-2s, together with a small number of DC-130E drone launch aircraft

and BQM-34 drones. Unit maintained detachments in South Vietnam during the late 1960s and early 1970s. Wing began phasing down operations at Davis-Monthan with drone operations transferring to TAC in mid-1976, and U-2s reassigned to the 9th SRW at Beale AFB, California. Redesignated 100th ARW in September 1976 and moved to Beale AFB to operate two squadrons of KC-135Qs until 1982, when tanker operations were absorbed into the 9th SRW and the 100th was inactivated. Reformed at RAF Mildenhall in January 1992 under USAFE to replace the 513th ACCW as the primary unit at the base. The unit was established to operate the KC-135Rs due for assignment with USAFE by mid-1992.

101st Air Refueling Wing

ANG Bangor IAP, ME: KC-15E
132nd Air Refueling Squadron

The 132nd ARS is the wing's flying unit, operating the KC-135E since 1984. It was formed as 132nd Fighter Squadron in February 1947 with P-47Ds, and flew the F-80C in 1948 and the F-51D in 1950. The

unit mobilized between February 1951 and October 1952, followed by conversion to F-51H as the 132nd FIS. The F-94A was assigned prior to F-89D in 1957 and F-89J from December 1959. The 101st FIG was

assigned in December 1960. The F-102A was flown for just four months in 1969 before conversion to the F-101B. The unit changed to ARefS in 1976 with the KC-135A and the group upgraded to Wing status.

102nd Fighter Wing

ANG Otis ANGB, MA: F-15A/B, C-12J
101st Fighter Squadron

The 101st FS is directly assigned at Otis, operating the F-15A/B and a C-12J support. Squadron lineage dates from 1918 although it was not activated with the Massachusetts National Guard until November 1921. The unit was mobilized in November 1940 and flew observation and reconnaissance sorties until July 1946, when it inactivated. The unit reformed one month later as the 101st

Fighter Squadron at Boston's Logan Airport, initially with the P-47 and later with the F-84B. Equipment reverted to the P-51H for stateside service during the Korean War, with a change to FIS status in July 1954 with F-94A/B. The F-86H was delivered in 1958, with the unit becoming a TFS. The unit mobilized during the Berlin crisis and was

stationed at Phalsbourg AB, France, between October 1961 and August 1962. The 102nd TFG was formed in October 1962 as the controlling element of the squadron. F-84Fs were assigned in March 1964 followed by F-100Ds from June 1971. The unit moved to Otis AFB in August 1968 and reverted to a FIS in June 1972 with the

F-106A, and was assigned to the 102nd FIW in July 1976. Conversion to the F-15A took place from September 1987.

The 101st Fighter Squadron is the East Coast ANG F-15 interceptor unit.

103rd Fighter Group

ANG Bradley ANGB, CT: A-10A, C-12F ('CT')
118th Fighter Squadron

The 118th FS is the group's flying unit, operating the A-10A since May 1979 with a C-12F support. The squadron was organized in November 1923 and called to active duty February 1941, until November 1945 when it transferred back to the National Guard. The unit was federalized in August 1946 as the 118th Fighter Squadron at Bradley Field with T-6s and a C-47, before acquiring the P-47N. Mobilized between February 1951 and October 1952 as 118th FIS and assigned to 103rd FIG, they converted to the F-51H in December 1952 and the F-84D the following year. The F-94B was assigned in 1956 and the F-86H two years later. The FIS designation was retained, with F-100As operated from October 1959 and F-102As from December 1965. The unit became a TFS with the F-100D in April 1971, and was the first ANG unit to convert to the A-10A in 1979. The 118th will re-equip with F-16C/D in mid-1993.

Several ANG units fly the A-10, including the Connecticut unit. This squadron is one earmarked for conversion to the F-16.

104th Fighter Group

ANG Barnes MAP, Westfield, MA: A-10A ('MA')
131st Fighter Squadron

The 131st FS is the group's operational unit, flying the A-10A since July 1979. The unit formed in February 1947 as the 131st Fighter Squadron at Barnes Field with the P-47N, and took on the F-51H in November 1951.

The unit converted to the F-94A/B and was designated 131st FIS in July 1954, changing to a TFS in 1958 when it received the F-86H. The unit was mobilized for active duty in October 1961, with assignment to

Phalsbourg AB, France, until August 1962. It joined the 104th TFG in October 1962 and converted to the F-84F in March 1964 and the F-100D in June 1971. The 131st is to gain six OA-10As late in 1992.

105th Airlift Group
ANG Stewart ANGB, NY: C-5A
137th Airlift Squadron

The 137th AS is the flying unit of the group, with the C-5A operated since 1984. The unit was established as the 105th Fighter Squadron in June 1948 at White Plains, operating the P-47D before changing to an FIS with the F-51H in September 1952. The squadron flew the F-94A/B from June 1953 until May 1958, when the newly-designated TFS adopted the F-86H. The 105th TFG was organized at the same time. The unit was redesignated as Aeromedical Transport Squadron with the C-97A, before changing to Air Transport Squadron and Military Airlift Squadron in 1966 with the C-97G. It later changed to Tactical Air Support Squadron in March 1970 with the U-3A assigned, re-equipping with the O-2A in April 1971. The squadron reverted to a MAS when the C-5A entered service, thereby converting from one of the smallest aircraft in ANG service to the largest. Relocation to Stewart ANGB occurred when the squadron received the C-5A.

This New York ANG unit had an amazing change when it handed in its Cessna O-2s for C-5 Galaxies!

106th Rescue Group
ANG Suffolk County Apt, NY:
HC-130N/P, HH-60G
102nd Rescue Squadron

The group is responsible for the 102nd RQS which operates the HC-130N and P versions of the Hercules and the HH-60G Pave Hawk. Another unit with a history dating from World War I, it had various observation types assigned. The unit was mobilized in October 1940 for reconnaissance duties until being disbanded in April 1944. It was federalized in November 1947 with the B-26, initially based at Mitchel Field and White Plains before moving to NAS Floyd Bennett in 1948. Activated for the Korean War with B-29, the unit reverted to the B-26 when it was returned to state control. The F-94B was assigned in 1957, the unit briefly becoming the 102nd FIS before converting to the MC-119J as the 101st Aeromedical Transport Squadron in September 1958. In January 1963 the unit changed to Air Transport Squadron with the C-97A and G models. A change of role to air refueling took place mid-1969, with the KC-97L. The move to Suffolk County Airport was completed in June 1970 before the unit changed to an FIS, with the F-102A operated from December 1972. Diversity of role continued with the delivery of the HC-130P and HH-3E in 1975, with designation to the 102nd Aerospace Rescue and Recovery Squadron and, more recently, the Air Rescue Squadron. The HH-3E was replaced by the MH-60G during 1990, with the HC-130N added.

The 106th RQG operates a mix of HC-130s and HH-60Gs for the rescue role in the east.

107th Fighter Group
ANG Niagara Falls IAP, NY:
F-16A/B (ADF)
136th Fighter Squadron

The 136th FS is the group's flying unit, with the F-16A (ADF) assigned since October 1990. The unit formed as the 136th Fighter Squadron in December 1948 with the P-47D at NAS Niagara Falls, but moved to nearby Municipal Airport two years later and was placed on active duty between March 1951 and October 1952. The unit became an FIS and converted to F-51H at the end of 1952, then to the F-94B in January 1954. Designation was changed to a TFS in October 1957 with the F-86H, and the F-100C was assigned from August 1960. The unit was called to active duty between October 1961 and August 1962 for the Berlin crisis, and again in January 1968 for the *Pueblo* crisis with a period of duty at Tuy Hoa AB, South Vietnam. Returned to state control in June 1969, the unit was redesignated an FIS in April 1971. The F-101B and F-4C were received from 1982, the F-4D joining the unit in mid-1986.

108th Fighter Wing
ANG McGuire AFB, NJ: F-4E,
C-26A ('NJ')
141st Fighter Squadron

The 141st FS is the wing's flying unit, operating the F-4E and supporting C-26A but currently converting to the KC-135E to become the 141st ARefS. The unit was established as the 141st Fighter Squadron in May 1949 at Mercer Airport, Trenton, with the F-47D. Called to active duty between March 1951 and December 1952, the unit was redesignated a Fighter-Bomber Squadron with the F-51H and moved to McGuire AFB. During 1955, it switched to the F-86E and became an FIS. The TFS designation was applied in 1958 when the unit received the F-84F. A second call-up occurred between October 1961 and August 1962 with deployment to Chaumont AB, France, the unit leaving their aircraft in France when they returned to state control and converted to the F-86H. The 108th TFG was assigned in October 1962 and upgraded to wing standard in December 1974. F-105Bs assigned April 1964 were flown for 17 years until replaced by the F-4D, followed by re-equipment with the F-4E July 1985.

The 141st FS was the last ANG unit to operate the F-4E in a fighter role, but now flies KC-135 tankers. Phantoms will remain with the Guard in RF-4C and F-4G versions.

109th Airlift Group
ANG Schenectady County Apt,
NY: LC-130H, C-130H, C-12J
139th Airlift Squadron

The 139th AS is the group's flying unit, with C-130H and LC-130H assigned from late 1984 along with a C-12J for support. The unit was established as the 139th Fighter Squadron in November 1948 with the P-47D, but converted to the F-51H in 1951. The squadron was redesignated to FIS status in 1952, with the F-94B assigned in 1954. The 109th FIG was formed in 1956, followed a year later by the F-86H and a change to a TFS. The unit received the C-97A in January 1960 to become an Air Transport Squadron before upgrading to the C-97G and changing to an MAS in 1966. The unit was ordered to active service between October 1961 and August 1962, and became a TAS in March 1971 with the C-130A. Equipment changed to the ski/wheel C-130D mid-1975 for resupply of the Distant Early Warning (DEW) radar sites above the Arctic circle.

A speciality of the 109th AG is

USAF Units

110th Fighter Group

ANG W. K. Kellogg Apt, MI:
A-10A/OA-10A ('BC')
172nd Fighter Squadron

The 172nd FS is the group's flying unit, and re-equipped with the A-10A and OA-10A in mid-1991. Formed with F-51Ds as the 172nd Fighter Squadron in September 1947, the squadron was called to active service in February 1951 and redesignated 172nd FIS three months later. The unit returned to state control with the F-51H assigned until 1954, when it converted to the F-86E. The 172nd received F-89Cs in April 1955 before changing to a TRS in April 1958. The unit converted to O-2As and was redesignated 172nd TASS in June 1971 before re-equipping with the OA-37B in 1981. Designation was changed to 172nd TFS.

111th Fighter Group

ANG NAS Willow Grove, PA:
OA-10A, C-26A ('PA')
103rd Fighter Squadron

The 103rd FS started life in June 1924 with trainer and observation types until mobilized in February 1941 for wartime duty. The unit returned to the Pennsylvania National Guard after the war, with federalization in December 1948 and the operation of the B-26 at Southwest Philadelphia Airport. The 103rd mobilized for the Korean War with RB-29s as a Strategic Reconnaissance Squadron, and returned to state duty in December 1952 as a Fighter-Bomber Squadron with the P-51D and later the F-84F. The F-94A/B was operated from 1955 as the 103rd FIS, followed by the F-89H/J in 1959. The unit became an Air Transport Squadron in April 1962 with the C-97G, with a move to NAS Willow Grove the following year. A Tactical Air Support role began in May 1969 with the U-3A/B, followed by the O-2A and OA-37B March 1981. The OA-10A began replacing the Dragonfly in mid-1990.

The 111th Tactical Air Support Group became a Fighter Group on 15 March 1992, but it retained a FAC role with its OA-10As.

112th Fighter Group

ANG Gtr Pittsburgh IAP, PA:
KC-135E
146th Fighter Squadron

The 146th FS is the operational unit of the wing, with the A-7D assigned since April 1975. Formed as the 146th Fighter Squadron in June 1948 with the F-47N, the unit converted to F-51H in June 1951 as an FIS, with the F-84F assigned in 1954. The F-86D was operated from 1957, progressively being replaced by the F-86L. The F-102A was flown from 1960 until transition to the A-7D in 1975. The squadron won the F-102A category at the 1963 William Tell competition. The unit commenced a transition to the KC-135E in late 1991, changing to the 146th ARS with assignment to the 171st ARW.

A change of role has seen the 112th Fighter Group replace its A-7Ds (illustrated) with KC-135E tankers.

113th Fighter Wing

ANG Andrews AFB, MD:
F-16A/B, C-21A, C-22B ('DC')
121st Fighter Squadron

The 121st FS is the flying component of the wing, operating the F-16A since January 1990. The only ANG unit which resides in a state other than its base, the 121st TFS is operated by the District of Columbia. The unit was activated in April 1941 and mobilized five months later before disbanding in November 1945. It was given federal recognition as the 121st Fighter Squadron in October 1946 with the P-47D. The F-84C was delivered in 1949, the unit becoming the 121st FIS in July 1951. Re-equipped with the F-94B and mobilization preceded a return to state control in October 1952 with the F-51H assigned. The F-86A was operated from March 1954, with the F-86E received in 1955 and the F-86H in 1957. The unit became a TFS in November 1958 when it converted to the F-100A. A second period of active duty began in October 1961 until demobilization in August 1962. The 113th TFG was organized in October 1962. The F-100C was assigned from January 1968 until 1969, the F-105D joining the squadron in 1971 until it was replaced by the F-4D in June 1981. The 113th TFG changed to Wing status in 1975. Detachment 1 of the 121st FS is organized to operate four C-22Bs and a C-21A on behalf of Headquarters Air National Guard East.

The 113th Fighter Wing is better known as an operator of 'DC' coded F-16As, but it also maintains the C-22B transports of the NGB.

114th Fighter Group

ANG Joe Foss Fd, Sioux Falls, SD: F-16C/D, C-12F ('SD')
175th Fighter Squadron

The 175th FS is the group's operational unit, activated as the 175th Fighter Squadron in September 1946 with P-51Ds, mobilized from March 1951 to November 1952 and redesignated 175th FIS. The unit converted to the F-94A in mid-1954 and to the F-94C in 1956, with the F-89D operated from 1958 until 1960 when the F-102A entered service. The squadron joined the 114th FIG, and became the 175th TFS when it converted to the F-100D in May 1970. They flew the A-7D from 1977 until mid-1991, when the squadron began to convert to the F-16C/D.

Patch of the 175th (Tactical) Fighter Squadron.

116th Fighter Wing
ANG Dobbins AFB, GA F-15A/B:
128th Fighter Squadron

The 128th FS is the wing's flying unit, operating the F-15A since spring 1986. The squadron was organized in May 1941 at Chandler Field, Atlanta, and called to active duty between September 1941 and September 1945. The 128th Fighter Squadron received federal recognition in August 1946 with the P-47N. The unit received the F-84D in 1950 and moved to Marietta AFB (later Dobbins AFB) before being recalled to active duty from October 1950 to July 1952 and equipping with F-51H. The F-84D was assigned again in late 1952 before conversion to the F-84F in 1955. The unit changed to an FIS in 1960 with the F-86L, although the role was shortlived as the C-97F was assigned in April 1961, the unit then becoming an Air Transport Squadron. The C-97G replaced the F model before the C-124C was assigned and unit was redesignated 128th MAS in January

F-15A/Bs are flown by the 128th FS, which has a battlefield air superiority role rather than a US air defense tasking.

1966. In April 1973 unit again changed to a TFS with the F-100D assigned. The 116th TFG was replaced by the 116th TFW in December 1974. The F-105G was assigned mid-1979 until 1983, when the unit converted to the F-4D.

117th Reconnaissance Wing
ANG Birmingham MAP, AL:
RF-4C ('BH')
106th Reconnaissance Squadron

The 106th RS is the wing's flying component, operating RF-4Cs since February 1971. The unit was created as the 106th Observation Squadron in January 1924 and was called to active duty in November 1940 at Birmingham Airport. They returned to state control in November 1946 with the A-26, and became the 106th TRS in February 1951. The squadron was mobilized for the Korean War with the RB-26 in April 1951 and

released from active duty in December 1952. The RF-84F was assigned early in 1957 with a further period of active duty for the Berlin crisis, the squadron locating at Dreux AB, France, between November 1961 and August 1962. The 117th TRG was activated in October 1962 and upgraded to Wing status in December 1974.

The Alabama ANG was not reticent about celebrating its 20th year of operating the Phantom. Its RF-4Cs were heavily involved in Desert Storm, flying tactical reconnaissance missions.

118th Airlift Wing
ANG Nashville Metro Apt, TN:
C-130H
105th Airlift Squadron

The 105th AS is the wing's flying unit, with the C-130H assigned since February 1990. The unit formed in World War I and operated as the 136th Squadron from 1921 until combined with the 105th Observation Squadron in 1936. They were mobilized at Nashville Airport in September 1940 until

disbanded in August 1943. The unit was federalized in February 1947 as the 105th Fighter Squadron with the P-47, with active duty between March 1951 and December 1952. They became the 105th TRS with the RF-51D, followed by RF-80A in September 1954. The transport role began in April 1961

when the 105th Air Transport Squadron received the C-97G, followed by the C-124C in April 1967, the unit having changed to an MAS in January 1966. They became a TAS March 1971, switching to the C-130A, with the 118th TAG elevated to Wing status in February 1975.

119th Fighter Group
ANG Hector Fd, Fargo, ND:
F-16A/B (ADF), C-130B
178th Fighter Squadron

The 178th FS is the group's flying unit, with the F-16A (ADF) assigned since September 1990. The unit was formed as the 178th Fighter Squadron in January 1947 with P-51Ds and mobilized between April 1951 and December 1952. They were redesignated the 178th Fighter-Bomber Squadron in June 1951, and the 178th FIS when returned to state control. The unit converted to the F-94A/B in June 1954 and later the F-94C, with the 119th FIG assigned in April 1956. The squadron has retained the air defense role, subsequently re-equipping with the F-89D in June 1958, the F-89J in November 1959, the F-102A in July 1966, the F-101B in November 1969 and the F-4D in 1977, before receiving the F-16A. The unit won the F-101B category at the 1970 and 1972 William Tell competitions, and the F-4D section in 1986, and was awarded the Hughes Achievement Trophy as the top air defense unit for 1974.

The 'Happy Hooligans' of North Dakota are responsible for US air defense to the north, flying the Air Defense Fighter model of the F-16A.

120th Fighter Group
ANG Great Falls IAP, MT:
F-16A/B (ADF), C-130B
186th Fighter Squadron

The 186th FS is the group's operational unit, with the F-16A (ADF) assigned since June 1987. The unit was formed as the 186th Fighter Squadron in June 1947 with P-51Ds. They were mobilized between April 1951 and December 1952, and redesignated 186th FIS with the F-86A in November 1953. The squadron converted to the F-89C in April 1956 with the 120th FIG assigned. The

F-89H was operated from April 1958 and the F-89J from March 1960, before switching to the F-102A in July 1966. The F-106A was assigned in April 1972 until conversion to the F-16A. The unit won the F-106A category at the 1974 and 1976 William Tell competitions, and was awarded the Hughes Achievement Trophy as the top air defense unit for 1985.

Another northern air defense outfit is the 120th FG at Great Falls. Here is the two-seat F-16B assigned to the unit.

121st Fighter Wing
ANG Rickenbacker ANGB, OH:
A-7D/K, C-26A ('OH')
166th Fighter Squadron

The 166th FS is the wing's flying unit, operating the A-7D. The unit was established as the 166th Fighter Squadron at Lockbourne AFB in January 1947 with F-51Ds and later F-51Hs. The squadron re-equipped with F-84Cs in April 1950 and was mobilized between February 1951 and October 1952. They reverted to the F-51H but converted to the F-80C in March 1954. The unit became a TFS with the F-84E assigned in January 1955 and the F-84F in late 1957. The squadron was called to active duty in October 1961 with deployment to Etain AB, France, as part of the 7121st TFW. They were demobilized in August 1962 and returned to state control, although the unit's aircraft remained in Europe. The squadron converted to the F-100C and joined the 121st TFG in October 1962. They were activated again from January 1968 to July 1969 with assignment to Kunsan AB, South Korea. The unit upgraded to the F-100D in November 1971 and the A-7D in December 1974. They are due to change to the 166th ARS/121st ARW with KC-135Rs and move to Wright-Patterson AFB by 1994.

122nd Fighter Wing
ANG Fort Wayne MAP, IN:
F-16C/D, C-26A ('FW')
163rd Fighter Squadron

The 163rd FS is the wing's flying unit, operating the F-16C since 1991. The unit was formed as the 163rd Fighter Squadron in October 1947 with P-51Ds. They were redesignated the 163rd Fighter-Bomber Squadron and mobilized between February 1951 and October 1952, before changing designation to the 163rd FIS in September 1954 with F-80Cs. The unit converted to the F-86A in March 1956 and the F-84F in January 1958, becoming a TFS. The squadron was called to active duty again in February 1961 with deployment to Chambley AB, France, as part of the 7122nd TFW. They were demobilized in August 1962 and returned to state control, although the unit's aircraft remained in Europe. The squadron joined the 122nd TFG and was assigned RF-84Fs from October 1962 to April 1964, despite retaining the TFS designation. The

Unlike previous ANG units, the 122nd Fighter Wing received C/D models when it transferred to the F-16. The 'FW' tailcode stands for Fort Wayne, the unit's base.

unit re-equipped with the F-84F in May 1964 and the F-100D in June 1971. The squadron has reported directly to the 122nd TFW since December 1974, having converted to the F-4C in April 1979 and the F-4E in mid-1986.

123rd Airlift Wing
ANG Standiford Fd, Louisville, KY: C-130B, C-12F
165th Airlift Squadron

The 165th AS is the wing's flying component, operating the C-130B. The 165th Fighter Squadron was formed in February 1947 with P-51Ds and was called to active service between October 1950 and July 1952. The unit converted to the F-84E and deployed to RAF Manston, UK, in November 1951 before returning to state control and taking up the F-51H and, soon after, the F-51D. They re-equipped with the F-86A in late 1956 before being redesignated the 165th TRS in 1958 with the RB-57A. The 123rd TRG formed in October 1962. The RF-101G/H was assigned in July 1965 and the unit was called to active duty from January 1968 to July 1969 with deployments to Itazuke AB, Japan, as well as Alaska and Panama. The squadron switched to the RF-101C and to the RF-4C in 1976, with the 123rd TRG upgraded to Wing status. The unit became the 165th TAS with the C-130B assigned in January 1989, and is to upgrade with the C-130H during 1992.

124th Reconnaissance Group
ANG Boise Air Terminal, ID:
RF-4C, C-26A
189th/190th Reconnaissance Squadrons

The 189th RS and 190th RS are the group's flying components, with the RF-4C currently assigned. The 190th Fighter Squadron was formed in October 1946 with P-51Ds. The unit was called to active service in April 1951 as the 190th Fighter-Bomber Squadron until returned to state control in December 1952. They were redesignated the 190th FIS with F-86As in November 1953, with F-94Bs assigned in September 1955. The unit joined the 124th FIG in April 1956 and converted to the F-89B, before re-equipping with the F-86L in July 1959 and the F-102A in October 1964. The unit won the F-102A category at the 1974 William Tell competition. They became the 190th TRS in October 1975 with conversion to the RF-4C. The unit is due to be redesignated the 190th FS with the F-4G, and is currently in the process of conversion. The 189th TRTS re-formed as a replacement training unit (RTU) for ANG reconnaissance aircrew during the early 1980s.

High over the barren landscape of its home state, an Idaho ANG RF-4C formates on a tanker. The RF-4C fleet is concentrated in the ANG, and it is the Idaho unit's task to train aircrews on this type.

125th Fighter Group
ANG Jacksonville IAP, FL:
F-16A/B (ADF), C-130H ('FL')
159th Fighter Squadron

The 159th FS is the group's flying component, operating the F-16A (ADF) since September 1986 with a C-130H support. They were formed as the 159th Fighter Squadron in February 1947 with F-51Ds at Thomas Cole MAP, Jacksonville. The squadron was the first ANG unit to receive jet aircraft, with P-80s assigned in August 1948. They were called to active service in October 1950 and converted to the F-84E with a deployment to Misawa AB, Japan, before returning to state control in July 1952. They became the 159th FIS in 1952 and reverted to F-51s. The unit received F-86As in 1954 but changed to the P-80C, with the 125th FIG assigned in July 1956. They upgraded to the F-86D in August 1956, the F-86L in June 1959 and the F-102A one year later. The unit won the F-86D category at the 1956 William Tell competition. The Delta Dagger gave way to the Dart in late 1974. The squadron is unique, conducting the air defense role but with tail code applied.

The southeast tip of the United States is defended from aerial attack by the F-16s of the 125th Fighter Group.

126th Air Refueling Wing
ANG Chicago-O'Hare IAP, IL:
KC-135E
108th Air Refueling Squadron

The 108th ARS is the flying component of the 126th ARW, with KC-135Es since 1983. The unit was activated in July 1927 and called up from February 1941 to November 1943. They were federalized in January 1947 with the A-26 as the 108th Bombardment Squadron at Chicago Municipal Airport, and

mobilized again in April 1951 during the Korean War. The squadron returned to state control and was redesignated the 108th Fighter-Bomber Squadron with the F-51D, and moved to O'Hare Airport in April 1954. The unit converted to the F-84F in July 1955 with a change to FIS status. The squadron

became the first ANG ARefS in July 1961 with the KC-97F, subsequently upgrading to the KC-97L before converting to the KC-135A in December 1976.

127th Fighter Wing
ANG Selfridge ANGB, MI:
F-16A/B, C-130B
107th Fighter Squadron

The wing has the 107th FS as its flying unit, operating the F-16A since April 1990 with a C-130B support. The 107th was established in 1918 for duty in France and was mobilized in October 1940. The unit returned to federal control in September 1946 as the 107th Bombardment Squadron with the A-26 at Detroit-Wayne Major Airport. They changed to the F-84B in 1950, becoming a Fighter

Squadron before being called to active duty in February 1951 for 21 months. The unit became an FIS at the end of 1952 with the F-51H, followed by F-86Es and F-89Cs. In April 1958, the squadron became a TRS with the RF-84F. The 127th TRG was activated in

October 1962 and upgraded to Wing standard in December 1974. Conversion to the RF-101A/C took place in January 1971, followed in June 1972 by a change to TFS status with assignment of F-100Ds. The A-7D was received in September 1978.

Two Michigan Guard units are equipped with the F-16, this being the multi-role fighter-bomber unit. The other unit is assigned an air defense mission.

Above: Unofficial badge of the 107th FS.

128th Air Refueling Group
ANG Gen Mitchell IAP, Milwaukee, WI: KC-135R
126th Air Refueling Squadron

The 126th ARS is the group's operational unit, flying the KC-135E from 1982. The 126th Observation Squadron was activated in November 1940 and ordered to active duty seven months later, until November 1945. Federal recognition came in June 1947 at General Mitchell Field for the 126th Fighter Squadron, with the P-51D. Conversion to F-80As began in September 1949 with recall to active duty in February

1951, operating the F-86A until November 1952 when the squadron was returned to state control and took on the F-51D. In August 1953 they received the F-86A again and became an FIS. The unit operated the F-89B, C, D and J models of the Scorpion between October 1954 and January 1960. The squadron changed role in August 1961 when the first KC-97F was delivered to the 126th ARefS. The KC-97F was replaced by the KC-97G model and later upgraded to KC-97L standard; conversion to the KC-135A took place during December 1977.

The 128th ARG is gaining KC-135Rs in place of the KC-135E (illustrated).

128th Fighter Wing
ANG Dane County RAP, Truax, WI: A-10A, C-130B ('WI')
176th Fighter Squadron

The 176th FS is the wing's flying component, operating the A-10A since June 1981. Established as the 176th Fighter Squadron in October 1948 with P-51Ds, the unit mobilized in February 1951, with the F-89A partially assigned in April 1952. They returned to state control equipped with the F-51H, becoming the 176th Fighter-Bomber Squadron. The unit converted to the F-86A in December 1953 when it became the 176th FIS, and received the F-89B/C in 1954 with the 115th FIG attached in April 1956. Equipment was upgraded to the F-89D in July 1957, the F-89H in 1959 and the F-89J in January 1960. The unit flew the F-102A from April 1966 until October 1974, when it was redesignated the 176th TASS, with the O-2A. The 115th TASG was exchanged for the 128th TASW early in 1975, with O-2s replaced by OA-37Bs late in 1979. The unit became the 176th TFS in June 1981 when the A-10A was assigned. The squadron is due to convert to the F-16C/D early in 1993.

Below: Wisconsin's A-10 squadron is known informally as the 'Raggidie Ass Militia'.

129th Rescue Group
ANG NAS Moffett Field, CA:
HC-130N/P, MH-60G
129th Rescue Squadron

The 129th RSQ is the operational unit of the group, flying the HC-130N/P and MH-60G since May 1975 and 1990, respectively. The squadron was established in April 1955 as the 129th Air Resupply Squadron at Hayward MAP, with the C-46D initially and the SA-16A soon afterwards. The unit joined the 129th Troop Carrier Group in January 1962, with the U-10 added in 1963 followed by the C-119C. Designation was changed to 129th Air Commando Squadron in 1963 and to Special Operations Squadron in 1968. The unit converted to C-119Gs and later C-119Ls until May 1975, when the HC-130P and HH-3E were assigned and they became the 129th Aerospace Rescue and Recovery Squadron. The unit moved to NAS Moffett Field in 1980 and became an ARS before exchanging the HH-3E for the HH-60G and adding the HC-130N.

Air Rescue, California-style. An HH-60G Pave Hawk practices refueling from an HC-130 over San Francisco's Bay Bridge. Below is the 129th ARRS (RQS) badge.

130th Airlift Group
ANG Yeager Apt, Charleston, WV: C-130H
130th Airlift Squadron

The 130th AS is the group's flying unit, operating the C-130H since early 1987. The unit was organized as the 130th Troop Carrier Squadron with the C-46D at Kanawha County Airport in October 1955, and added the SA-16A/B soon after. The squadron joined the 130th Troop Carrier Group in January 1962, with U-10s added in 1963 followed by C-119Cs. Designation was changed to 130th Air Commando Squadron

in 1963 and to Special Operations Squadron in 1968. The unit converted to the C-119G and later the C-119L until October 1975, when the unit became a TAS with the C-130E. The 130th served with the 1630th TAW (Provisional) at Al Ain, UAE, for Desert Storm.

The C-130 Hercules of the West Virginia Air National Guard are no strangers to overseas deployments. This aircraft is seen in the UK while on a 'summer camp', while the unit took part in Desert Storm.

131st Fighter Wing
ANG Lambert Fd, St Louis, MO: F-15A/B, C-12F ('SL')
110th Fighter Squadron

The 110th FS is the flying component of the 131st FW, operating the F-15A since 1991 with a C-12F support. Activated in June 1923, the squadron was mobilized from December 1940 until February 1946. The squadron returned to federal control in September 1946 as the 110th Fighter Squadron and flew the P-51D when recalled to active duty in March 1951. The unit was returned to state control again in December 1952 and re-equipped with the B-26B, becoming the 110th Bombardment

Squadron. They changed to FIS in 1957 with the F-80C, followed by the F-84F, before switching to TFS in January 1960. During the Berlin crisis the squadron was activated and relocated to Toul-Rosières AB, France, from the end of 1961 until August 1962. Upon return to Lambert Field the squadron converted to the F-100C and later the F-100D, before upgrading to the F-4C in 1979. The unit operated the F-4E from February 1985 until 1991, when the F-15A was introduced.

The latest ANG F-15 user is the 131st FW, based across the runway from the McDonnell Douglas plant which produces the Eagle.

132nd Fighter Wing
ANG Des Moines MAP, IA: A-7D/K, C-12J ('IA')
124th Fighter Squadron

The 124th FS is the wing's flying unit, operating the A-7D since January 1977 and a supporting C-12J. The unit was formed in February 1941 at Des Moines and called to active service seven months later, until May 1944. Equipped with the P-51D, the 124th Fighter Squadron was federalized in August 1946, with recall to active Air Force duty from April 1951 to December 1952. The unit became the 124th FIS in January 1953 with F-80Cs, and F-84Es in September 1956. The F-86L was assigned in April 1958, followed by the F-89J in April 1962. The squadron

changed to TFS in August 1969 with F-84Fs, and F-100Ds from April 1971. The unit is scheduled to convert to the F-16C/D by mid-1993.

The A-7 Corsair II operational fleet is concentrated in the Guard units, although time is running out for the popular 'SLUF'. This is a two-seat A-7K, assigned to Iowa's 124th Fighter Squadron at Des Moines.

Patch of the 124th FS.

133rd Airlift Wing
ANG Minneapolis St Paul IAP, MN: C-130E
109th Airlift Squadron

The 109th AS is the wing's flying unit, operating the C-130E since 1981. The 109th Aero Squadron was organized in August 1917 and ordered to active duty from February 1941 to May 1945. The unit returned to federal service in September 1946 as the 109th Fighter Squadron with P-51Ds at Holman Field, St Paul. The

squadron was recalled to active duty as an FIS, with duty for the Korean War from March 1951 to December 1952, when it returned to peacetime levels. The unit moved to Minneapolis St Paul Airport and was assigned the T-28A for a year until mid-1957, when F-94A/Bs were delivered, although F-89Hs were received at year's

end. These were operated until January 1960 when the C-97A was delivered, with the unit becoming an Air Transport Squadron. The unit upgraded to the C-97G and was redesignated an MAS in January 1966. C-130As were delivered in March 1971, resulting in a change of designation to TAS.

134th Air Refueling Group
ANG McGhee Tyson Apt, Knoxville, TN: KC-135E
151st Air Refueling Squadron

The 151st ARS is the group's operational unit, flying the KC-135E since 1982. The squadron was federally recognized in December 1957 as the 151st FIS, attached to the 134th FIG with F-86Ds and later F-86Ls. The unit converted to F-104A/Bs in July 1960 and was activated between November 1961 and August 1962 for deployment to Ramstein AB, Germany. The squadron transferred to the F-102A from March 1963 until April 1964, when it re-equipped with the KC-97G as the 151st ARefS. Equipment was upgraded to the KC-135A in July 1976.

A Tennesse ANG KC-135E refuels Guard Eagles from Georgia. Above is the unit's badge, carried on the 'Milky Way' fuselage sash.

135th Airlift Group
ANG Glenn L. Martin State Apt, Baltimore, MD: C-130E
135th Airlift Squadron

The 135th AS is the group's flying component, operating the C-130E since 1990. The unit was activated in September 1955 as the 135th Air Resupply Squadron at Harbor Field, Baltimore, with C-46Ds and SA-16Bs. Redesignated the 135th Troop Carrier Squadron in October 1958, the squadron moved to Glenn L. Martin Airport in April 1960 and joined the 135th TCG in January 1962. Shortly afterwards the unit

became an Air Commando Squadron with the U-10 assigned in August 1963, although the Helio Couriers were transferred to Southeast Asia in August 1965 and replaced by U-6As. Special Operations Squadron status applied in 1968. The U-10s returned in August 1967, operating alongside HU-16Bs until 1971 when the unit became a TASS with the O-2A. TAS designation was assigned in April 1977 with the arrival of the C-7B Caribou, which was replaced by the C-130B in October 1980.

Beginning Hercules operations with C-130Bs, the 135th AG now flies the E model.

136th Airlift Wing
ANG NAS Dallas, TX: C-130H
181st Airlift Squadron

The 181st AS is the wing's operational flying unit, with the C-130H assigned since August 1986. Created as the 181st Fighter Squadron in February 1947 with P-51Ds, the unit re-equipped with F-84Bs in 1950 with F-51Hs assigned the following year. The F-80C was operated in January 1955, the unit becoming the 181st FIS and converting to the F-86D in August 1957 and the F-86L in June 1959. The squadron became the 181st ARefS early in 1965 when the KC-97G was assigned and then upgraded in 1966 to the KC-97L. The 136th ARefG upgraded to Wing standard in December 1974. The unit switched to the 181st TAS in February 1978 when it re-equipped with C-130Bs and subsequently C-130Hs. They won Volant Rodeo, the

forerunner of Airlift Rodeo, at Pope AFB in 1986. The squadron was stationed at Al Ain, UAE, with the 1630th TAW (Provisional) for Desert Storm.

Badge of the 181st (Tactical) Airlift Squadron.

In its career, the 181st Squadron has been a fighter and tanker unit, but now flies the airlift mission with the C-130H. These aircraft were deployed during Desert Storm.

137th Airlift Wing
ANG Will Rogers World Apt, Oklahoma City, OK: C-130H
185th Airlift Squadron

The 185th AS is the wing's operational unit, flying the C-130H. The unit was formed as the 185th Night Pursuit Squadron in 1918 with the Sopwith Camel and called to active duty during World War II. They were federalized as the 185th Fighter Squadron in February 1947 at Westheimer Field, Norman, OK, with P-51Ds. The squadron

moved to Will Rogers Airport in September 1949, becoming the 185th TRS in February 1951 with RF-51Ds. The unit was mobilized in May 1951, with RF-80As operated until a return to state control with reversion to

F-51Ds, and a redesignation to 185th Fighter-Bomber Squadron at the same time. The unit converted to the F-80B/C in April 1953 and changed to the 185th FIS with F-86Ls operated from May 1958. The squadron

became the 185th Air Transport Squadron in April 1961, with the C-97F initially and the C-97G later. The unit was redesignated the 185th TAS in December 1974 with C-130As, upgrading to C-130Hs mid-1979.

The 185th is another squadron which has switched from a fighter to an airlift role.

138th Fighter Group
ANG Tulsa IAP, OK: A-7D/K ('OK')
125th Fighter Squadron

The 125th FS is the operational component of the group, flying A-7Ds since July 1978. The unit was formed as the 125th Observation Squadron in November 1940 and placed under active Air Force control two months later, and inactivated in December 1945. Federal recognition took place in February 1947 as the unit became the 125th Fighter Squadron, operating

P-51Ds until June 1950 when the F-84B was delivered, followed by a corresponding change to Fighter-Bomber Squadron status. The squadron was recalled from October 1950 until July 1952, when it acquired the F-51D. Conversion to the F-80C began in 1954, followed in 1957 by the F-86D and a change to FIS status, plus activation of the 138th FIG. The C-97F was assigned in January 1960, the unit becoming the 125th Air Transport Squadron. A short period of active duty began in October 1961 for the Berlin crisis, with the C-97G assigned. The unit was redesignated the 125th MAS in

January 1966, with the C-124C replacing the C-97 in February 1968. The squadron became a TFS in January 1973 with the F-100D, and is due to re-equip with the F-16C/D by mid-1993.

The 125th (Tactical) Fighter Squadron currently flies the A-7D with the Oklahoma ANG. In 1993 the A-7 will be retired in favor of F-16C/Ds.

139th Airlift Group
ANG Rosecrans MAP, St Joseph, MO: C-130H
180th Airlift Squadron

The 180th AS is the group's operational unit, with the C-130H assigned since February 1987. The unit was created as the 180th Bombardment Squadron in August 1946 with A-26B/Cs and activated in April 1951, with a deployment to Bordeaux-Mérignac

AB and Laon AB, France. The squadron was returned to state control in January 1953 and redesignated the 180th FIS in January 1957 with the F-94C. The unit re-equipped with RF-84Fs as the 180th TRS in April 1958, and changed to the 180th Air Transport Squadron in March 1962 when assigned the C-97F. The C-97G model was subsequently operated, with a change to the 180th MAS in January 1966. The unit became the 180th ARefS with the KC-97L assigned from

September 1969 until October 1976, when the C-130A was delivered to the 180th TAS. The squadron was assigned to the 1630th TAW (Provisional) at Al Ain, UAE, during Desert Storm.

Badge of the 180th Airlift Squadron, a C-130H operator which flew Desert Storm missions.

USAF Units

140th Fighter Wing
ANG Buckley ANGB, CO:
F-16C/D, CT-43A ('CO')
120th Fighter Squadron

The 120th FS is the flying unit of the wing, with the A-7D assigned in April 1974. Another unit organized during World War I, the 120th was called to active duty from January 1941 until November 1943. In June 1946 the 120th Fighter Squadron became the first National Guard flying unit to receive federal recognition in a postwar reorganization. The unit was based at Denver Airport with the P-51D. The squadron was mobilized for two months during mid-1951, although most personnel had already volunteered for service in Korea. The unit became the 120th FIS and equipped with the F-80C in 1953, forming the Minutemen aerial display team. Conversion to the F-86E began in 1958 and to the F-86L two years later. In January 1961 the unit became a TFS when it re-equipped with the F-100C. A second period of activation took

place between October 1961 and August 1962 for the Berlin crisis. The 140th TFG was activated in October 1962. The unit was mobilised for the third time in January 1968 and, following relocation to three active bases in the US, deployed in May to Phan Rang AB, South Vietnam. The squadron flew more than 5,000 combat sorties before being returned to state control in April 1969. F-100Cs were exchanged for F-100Ds in 1971. The 140th TFG was changed to Wing level December 1974. The squadron won the Top Gun award at the 1981 Gunsmoke Competition held at Nellis AFB. Detachment 1 of the 120th TFS was organized to operate four CT-43A navigation trainers on behalf of Headquarters Air National Guard West. The squadron began conversion to the F-16C at the end of 1991.

In addition to its F-16 fighters, the Colorado ANG at Buckley flies the CT-43A on behalf of the HQ ANG West.

141st Air Refueling Wing
ANG Fairchild AFB, WA:
KC-135E, C-12J
116th Air Refueling Squadron

The 116th ARS in the operational unit of the wing, flying KC-135Es since 1984 with a support C-12J. The unit began life in August 1924 and was one of the first National Guard units to be mobilized in September 1940, remaining on active duty until the end of 1943. The squadron was reorganized as the 116th Fighter Squadron at Felts Field in February 1947 with the P-51D, and moved to Geiger Field in 1948 to re-equip with the F-84B in April 1950. The squadron was called to active duty in February 1951 and converted to the F-86A before moving to

RAF Bentwaters, UK. The unit was returned to state control in November 1952 and equipped with the F-51D, until receiving the F-86A again in 1954 and being redesignated the 116th FIS. The squadron converted to the F-94B in August 1955, the F-89D in December 1957 and the F-89J in July 1960 before switching to the F-102A in March 1966. The 141st FIG was organized in July 1960. F-101Bs were assigned from November 1969 until July 1976, when the unit re-equipped with the KC-135A for the 116th ARefS and moved to Fairchild AFB. The Stratotankers were subsequently re-engined to become KC-135Es.

The 141st Air Refueling Wing operates the KC-135E. Here one refuels an F-16 of the nearby Montana ANG.

142nd Fighter Group
ANG Kingsley Fd, OR: F-16A/B
Portland IAP, OR: F-15A/B,
C-26A
114th/123rd Fighter Squadrons

The group has two flying units assigned, consisting of the 114th FS with F-16As and the 123rd FS operating F-15As. The former squadron was organized in June 1947 as the 114th Bombardment Squadron at Floyd Bennett Field, New York, with the B-26B. The unit was ordered to active duty between March 1951 and November 1952 with the B-29A, but reverted to the B-26 when returned to state control. The squadron was redesignated the 114th FIS in June 1957 with F-94Bs, until inactivated in September 1958. Reactivated as the 114th TFTS at Kingsley Field, Oregon, with the F-4C in 1984, the unit switched to the F-16A/B early in 1989 to train ANG interceptor aircrew.

The 123rd Observation Squadron was established in April 1941 and ordered to active service five months later for three years. The 123rd Fighter Squadron was given federal recognisation in August 1946 with the P-51D and recalled to active duty in March 1951. The squadron was returned to state control in December 1952 before becoming an FIS with F-86As in mid-1953. The 123rd subsequently operated the F-94B from October 1955 and F-89D from June 1957, followed by the F-89H and J models. The F-102A arrived in January 1966, with the F-101B entering service in March 1971. The unit won the F-101B category at the 1976 William Tell competition and the F-4C section in 1984. Conversion to the F-4C began in 1982, followed by the F-15A in June 1989.

The 142nd Fighter Group has two component squadrons: the 114th at Klamath Falls, which trains ANG F-16 ADF pilots, and the 123rd at Portland, which flies the F-15 on operational air defense duties. Both units apply flamboyant fin markings.

143rd Airlift Group
ANG Quonset Point State Apt,
Providence, RI: C-130E
143rd Airlift Squadron

The 143rd AS is the group's operational unit, with the C-130E employed since 1990. The unit was formed in November 1955 as the 143rd Air Resupply Squadron at Theodore F. Green Airport with C-46Ds and SA-16As. The squadron was redesignated the 143rd Troop

Carrier Squadron in October 1958 when the C-46 was retired, with the 143rd TCG formed in January 1962. Air Command Squadron status was achieved in July 1963, followed in August 1968 by change to Special Operations Squadron. U-10Ds were

assigned in 1963 and C-119G/Ls in September 1971. Conversion to the C-130A took place during October 1975 with a corresponding change to a TAS, with the unit moving to Quonset Point Airport in July 1980.

144th Fighter Wing
ANG Fresno Air Terminal, CA:
F-16A/B, C-26A
194th Fighter Squadron

The 194th FS is the wing's operational unit, assigned the F-16A (ADF) since October 1989. The unit was established as the 194th Fighter Squadron in March 1949 at Hayward MAP with F-51Ds. Redesignated 194th FIS with the F-86A assigned in October 1954, the squadron moved to Fresno Air Terminal. The 144th FIG formed in April 1956. The unit converted to the F-86L mid-1958, F-102A late 1964, and F-106A mid-1974. The squadron won the F-106A category at the 1980 William Tell competition. The 144th FIG upgraded to Wing standard in July 1976, re-equipping with F-4Ds before switching to F-16As.

Another link in the defensive chain around the United States is provided by the 144th Fighter Wing, which guards the southwest. Its strikingly-marked equipment is the F-16 ADF, based at Fresno Air Terminal.

145th Airlift Group
ANG Charlotte/Douglas IAP, NC:
C-130B
156th Airlift Squadron

The 156th AS is the group's flying unit, equipped with C-130Bs since May 1971. The 156th Fighter Squadron formed in May 1946 with the P-47D at Morris Field, Charlotte, but was not granted federal recognition until March 1948. The squadron converted to the F-51D in December 1949 and was called to active duty in October 1951. They became the 156th Fighter-Bomber Squadron and received F-84Es for deployment to RAF Manston, UK, until July 1952, when the unit was returned to state control. The squadron reverted to the F-51D and converted to the F-86A in January 1954. Designation changed to 156th FIS in July 1955, with the unit receiving the F-86E in October 1957 and the F-86L in March 1959. The squadron changed to 156th Aeromedical Airlift Squadron in January 1961 with the C-119C, followed by the C-121C in 1962. The unit was redesignated the 156th Air Transport Squadron in January 1964 and 156th MAS in January 1966, with the C-124C operated from April 1967 to May 1971.

146th Airlift Wing
ANG NAS Point Mugu, CA:
C-130E
115th Airlift Squadron

The 115th AS is the flying component of the 146th AW, operating the C-130E since 1975. The unit was activated in June 1924 and stationed in California throughout the World War II until reorganized at Van Nuys Airport as the 115th Bombardment Squadron in October 1946, with the A-26. The squadron moved to Lockheed Air Terminal, Burbank, and saw active duty between April 1951 and December 1952. They relocated at Van Nuys as the 115th Fighter-Bomber Squadron, equipped with F-51Hs, before converting to F-86As in January 1955 and becoming a TFS. In January 1960 C-97A/Cs were assigned to the 115th Air Transport Squadron, with mobilization between October 1961 and August 1962 during the Berlin crisis. The C-97G was subsequently operated. The squadron became the 115th TAS in April 1970 when the C-130A was assigned. The

The California state bear forms the basis of the 115th Airlift Squadron's badge. The unit flies the C-130E from Point Mugu.

unit operated a mix of C-130A and B models until 1975 when the C-130E was received. The 146th TAG upgraded to Wing standard in February 1975. The unit moved to Channel Island ANGB, located in a corner of NAS Point Mugu, at the end of 1989.

147th Fighter Group
ANG Ellington ANGB, TX:
F-16A/B (ADF), C-26A
111th Fighter Squadron

The 111th FS is the group's flying unit, employing the F-16A (ADF) since December 1989 with a C-26A in support. The squadron was organized in June 1923 and called to active duty in November 1940. The unit was given federal recognition in February 1947 as the 111th Fighter Squadron, operating P-51Ds at Ellington Field. The squadron was mobilized again in October 1950 and converted to the F-84E before reverting to state control in July 1952 with the F-51H. The unit was redesignated the 111th Fighter-Bomber Squadron from January 1953 until early 1955, when it changed back to an FIS with the arrival of the F-80C. F-86Ds were delivered in August 1957 with the ANG jet

instrumentation school operating the T-33A. The 147th FIG was activated in May 1958 before the F-86L was assigned the following year. The F-102A was delivered in the summer of 1960 with the Delta Dagger operated until 1975, despite the delivery of the first F-101Bs to the 111th FIS in May 1971. The unit won the F-101B category at the 1978 and 1980 William Tell competitions. The squadron was responsible for training air defense aircrew for the ANG from January 1970 until April 1976, hence the assignment of both aircraft types. F-4Cs were operated from 1981 until replaced by F-4Ds.

This is one of the original F-16As used by the 147th FG, since upgraded to ADF standard for the interceptor mission.

148th Fighter Group
ANG Duluth IAP, MN: F-16A/B (ADF)
179th Fighter Squadron

The 179th FS operates as the group's flying unit, with the F-16A (ADF) assigned since July 1990. The unit was formed as the 179th Fighter Squadron in September 1948 with F-51Ds and called to active service between March 1951 and November 1952. The squadron was redesignated 179th FIS and re-equipped with the F-94A/B in July 1954, followed by the F-94C mid-1957. The squadron converted to F-89Js in July 1959,

joined the 148th FIG in July 1960, and converted to the F-102A late in 1966, before accepting delivery of F-101Bs in April 1972. The unit won the F-102A category at the 1970 William Tell competition. The squadron changed to 179th TRS with the assignment of RF-4Cs in January 1976, but reverted to the air defense role in 1984 with delivery of the F-4D.

Minnesota ANG F-16 ADFs feature the North Star and Little Dipper motif on the fin to reflect the north-facing defense role.

149th Fighter Group
ANG Kelly AFB, TX: F-16A/B ('SA')
182nd Fighter Squadron

The 182nd FS is the group's flying component, with the F-16A operated since May 1986. The squadron was established as the 182nd Fighter Squadron in October 1947 at Brooks AFB, with P-51Ds, and redesignated the 182nd Fighter-Bomber Squadron in October 1950 when mobilized with F-84Es prior to deployment to the Far East. The unit was returned to state control in July 1952 with operating F-51H. The 182nd moved to Kelly AFB in August 1956, re-equipping with F-84Fs and being redesignated the 182nd FIS in January 1957. The squadron converted to the F-86D at the end of 1957, and subsequently the F-86L in July 1960 and joining the 149th FIG. The unit changed to the 182nd TFS with F-84Fs assigned from September 1969 until April 1971, when the F-100D was delivered. F-4Cs were operated from early 1979.

150th Fighter Group
ANG Kirtland AFB, NM: A-7D, C-130B
188th Fighter Squadron

The 188th FS is the group's operational unit, with the A-7D assigned since late 1973. The unit was created as the 188th Fighter Squadron in July 1947 with the P-51D and was mobilized between February 1951 and October 1952. Redesignated the 188th FIS, the squadron converted to the F-80C in August 1953, before re-equipping with the F-100A in April 1958. The 150th FIG was added in July 1960. The unit upgraded to the F-100C as the 188th TFS in 1964, and was called to active duty in January 1968, including a period of deployment to Tuy Hoa AB, South Vietnam. The 188th was returned to state control in June 1969 and converted to the F-100D in 1972. The squadron is due to convert to the F-16C/D in 1993.

A New Mexico ANG A-7 fires its internal Vulcan cannon during strafing practice.

151st Air Refueling Group
ANG Salt Lake City IAP, UT: KC-135E
191st Air Refueling Squadron

The 191st ARS is the group's flying unit, operating the KC-135E. Formed as the 191st Fighter Squadron in November 1946 with P-51Ds, the unit was called to active duty between April 1951 and December 1952. They were redesignated the 191st Fighter-Bomber Squadron in early 1952, remaining so until 1955 when the unit became 191st FIS with the F-86A. The 151st FIG was formed in August 1957. The F-86L was assigned from 1958 until April 1961, when the unit became the 191st Air Transport Squadron with C-97Cs and later C-97Gs. The squadron was redesignated 191st MAS in January 1966 and switched to C-124Cs in February 1969. They converted to the KC-97L in October 1972 as the 191st ARefS, before upgrading to KC-135As in April 1978, and re-engined KC-135Es in 1982.

Most of the Guard tanker fleet has adopted the charcoal gray color scheme, including this Utah ANG example.

152nd Reconnaissance Group
ANG Reno-Cannon IAP, NV: RF-4C, C-12J
192nd Reconnaissance Squadron

The 192nd RS is the group's operational unit, flying the RF-4C since July 1975. Established as the 192nd Fighter Squadron in April 1948 with the F-51D assigned, the unit was called to active duty in March 1951. They were redesignated the 192nd Fighter-Bomber Squadron and returned to state control in December 1952. The unit became the 192nd FIS in June 1955 and converted to the F-86A. The 152nd FIG was formed in April 1958, with F-86Ls assigned four months later. The squadron re-equipped with RB-57Bs and changed to the 192nd TRS in March 1961. RF-101G/Hs were operated from October 1965, and subsequently the RF-101C until conversion to the RF-4C. The squadron was mobilized between January 1968 and June 1969 with a period of deployment to Itazuke AB, Japan. The unit won the 1986 and 1990 Reconnaissance Air Meet competition held at Bergstrom AFB. The squadron is due to convert to F-4Gs as the 192nd FS/152nd FG in mid-1992, with first examples received in August 1991.

The Nevada ANG are known as the 'High Rollers', an allusion to the state's lucrative gambling industry. The RF-4Cs are based at one of the main centers: Reno.

153rd Airlift Group
ANG Cheyenne MAP, WY: C-130B
187th Airlift Squadron

The 187th AS is the group's operational unit, with the C-130B assigned since April 1972. The unit was established as the 187th Fighter Squadron in August 1946 with the P-51D, and mobilized in April 1951, becoming the 187th Fighter-Bomber Squadron. The squadron was returned to state control in December 1952 and converted to F-80Cs in August 1953. Redesignated 187th FIS in February 1955, the unit converted to F-86Ls three years later. The 153rd FIG was assigned in February 1958. The squadron became the 187th Aeromedical Transport Squadron with MC-119Js in February 1961. C-121Gs were assigned in June 1963 with a change to Air Transport Squadron status, until redesignated the 187th MAS in January 1966. The unit became the 187th TAS in April 1972 with conversion to C-130Bs.

This Wyoming ANG C-130B was painted to commemorate the state's centenary in 1990.

154th Composite Group
ANG Hickam AFB, HI: F-15A/B, C-130H
199th Fighter Squadron

The 199th FS is the group's operational unit, flying the F-15A since March 1987. The unit was created as the 199th Fighter Squadron in November 1946 at Bellows Field with T-6s and a mixed bag of non-combat types, until July 1947 when the P-47N was delivered. The squadron moved to Hickam Field in late 1947 and was redesignated the 199th Fighter-Bomber Squadron in July 1952 and the 199th FIS four months later. They equipped with T-33As in November 1953 and F-86Es in February 1954. The squadron upgraded to the F-86L early in 1958, with the 165th FIG allocated in December 1960. The unit converted to F-102As in January 1961 until June 1976, when they re-equipped with the F-4C and became the 199th TFS. The designation changed to Composite Group in November 1978. The squadron is due to add four KC-135Rs early in 1993 as the first ANG composite unit.

F-15s from the Hawaii ANG handle the air defense of the island group and are to be augmented by KC-135R tankers.

155th Reconnaissance Group
ANG Lincoln MAP, NE: RF-4C, C-12F
173rd Reconnaissance Squadron

The 173rd RS is the group's flying unit, with the RF-4C assigned since February 1972. The unit was formed as the 173rd Fighter Squadron in July 1946 with P-51Ds, until August 1948 when they converted to the F-80C. The unit was redesignated the 173rd Fighter-Bomber Squadron with F-51s and mobilized from April 1951 until December 1952. Designation changed to 173rd FIS in September 1953, with F-80Cs followed by F-86Ds in January 1957 and F-86Ls late in 1959. The unit joined the 155th FIG in July 1960, and was redesignated the 173rd TRS in May 1964 with conversion to RF-84Fs.

Few aircraft have a more distinctive back end than the 'Double Ugly' Phantom. The Nebraska ANG flies the RF-4C model on tactical reconnaissance duties.

156th Fighter Group
ANG Muniz ANGB/Puerto Rico IAP, San Juan, PR: A-7D, C-26A ('PR')
198th Fighter Squadron

The 198th FS is the group's flying unit, operating the A-7D since July 1975. The unit was formed as the 198th Fighter Squadron in November 1947 at Isla Grande Airport with P-47Ns. They were redesignated the 198th FIS in November 1952 prior to converting to the F-86E, which involved a partial move to San Juan Airport. The 156th FIG was formed in May 1956 when the move was completed to the latter facility, the unit re-equipping with F-86Ds. F-86Hs were assigned in 1960 and the unit, now the 198th TFS, converted to F-104C/Ds from mid-1967 until 1975. The 198th is due to convert to the F-16A/B late in 1992.

157th Air Refueling Group
ANG Pease AFB, NH: KC-135E
133rd Air Refueling Squadron

The 133rd ARS is the group's flying unit, operating the KC-135E since 1984. The unit was formed as the 133rd Fighter Squadron at Grenier Field, Manchester, NH, in April 1947 with the P-47D and was on active duty between February 1951 and October 1952. They were redesignated an FIS and equipped with F-51Hs from 1952 until June 1954, when the F-94A/B entered service. The squadron operated F-86Ls from April 1958 until September 1960 when they became an Air Transport Squadron with C-97As and later C-97Gs. The unit was assigned to the 157th ATG and called to active duty in October 1961 for 11 months. The 133rd moved to Pease AFB in 1966 and changed to MAS in January, with C-124Cs operated from 1968. The squadron became a TAS in April 1971 with the C-130A, and an ARefS in 1975 with the KC-135A.

New Hampshire KC-135Es feature a stylized treatment around the nose and cockpit, with the state name carried on the fin.

158th Fighter Group
ANG Burlington IAP, VT: F-16A/B (ADF), C-12F
134th Fighter Squadron

The 134th FS is the group's operational unit, flying F-16As since July 1986 with a C-12F support. The 134th Fighter Squadron formed in August 1946 with P-47Ds, and F-51s from July 1950, with active duty performed between February 1951 and October 1952. The squadron changed to FIS and converted to the F-94A/B in April 1954, followed by the F-89D in 1958. The 158th FIG was allocated in July 1960 with conversion to the F-102A in August 1965. In June 1974 the unit changed to a Defense Systems Evaluation Squadron, flying the EB-57B. F-4Ds were assigned in October 1981 with redesignation to a TFS, before reverting to FIS status with the F-16A.

The 134th FS until recently had a tactical role, but with the assignment of the F-16 the tasking has changed to air defense.

159th Fighter Group

ANG NAS New Orleans, LA:
F-15A/B, C-130H
122nd Fighter Squadron

The 122nd FS is the flying unit of the group, operating the F-15A since June 1985 with a C-130H in support. Activated as the 122nd Observation Squadron at New Orleans in March 1941, the unit operated a selection of antiquated types. They were mobilized from October 1941 until October 1945, when allocated back to the National Guard. The unit was federalized as the 122nd Bombardment Squadron in December 1946 at New Orleans Airport with the A-26, until mobilized again between April 1951 and December 1952. The squadron changed to an FIS in June 1957 with F-80Cs and was incorporated into the 159th FG. The unit was assigned F-86Ds later in the year and moved to NAS New Orleans. Conversion to the

The 'Coonass Militia' of the Louisiana ANG organize the 122nd FS in four flights, with different-colored fin bands.

F-102A was implemented in July 1960, followed exactly 10 years later by the F-100D and a change to TFS. F-4Cs were operated from April 1979 before upgrading to the F-15A.

160th Air Refueling Group

ANG Rickenbacker ANGB, OH:
KC-135R
145th Air Refueling Squadron

The 145th ARS is the group's flying unit, with the KC-135E assigned since late 1983. The unit was formed in March 1956 as the 145th Air Transport Squadron at Akron-Canton Airport with C-46Ds. The unit was redesignated to Aeromedical Transport Squadron standard in February 1957 with the MC-119J. The 145th moved to Clinton County AFB and became an ARefS in July 1961, although the first KC-97F did not arrive until February 1962. The 160th ARG was organized in July 1961. Aircraft were replaced by the KC-97L in March 1965 and the KC-135A 10 years later. The unit moved to Lockbourne AFB (renamed Rickenbacker AFB/ANGB) in September 1971. The unit

Patch of the 145th Air Refueling Squadron, Ohio ANG.

The 145th differs from other units by having 'Ohio Air Guard' along the fuselage. R-model tankers are now flown.

commenced conversion to KC-135Rs late in 1991 with a transfer from the 160th ARG to the 121st ARW, and should have moved to Wright-Patterson AFB by 1994.

161st Air Refueling Group

ANG Sky Harbor IAP, Phoenix, AZ: KC-135E
197th Air Refueling Squadron

The 197th ARS is the group's operational unit, flying the KC-135E since 1982. The unit was formed as the 197th Fighter Squadron in December 1946 at Luke AAF with P-51Ds, before moving to Sky Harbor Airport two years later. The 197th converted to the F-84B in November 1950 prior to mobilization in February 1951 as the 197th Pilot Training Squadron. The squadron was returned to state control in October 1952 as the 197th FIS with F-51Ds. They re-equipped with F-86As in 1953 with the 161st FIG assigned in October 1957. Aircraft were upgraded to the F-86L in November 1957 before conversion to the F-104A/B in April 1960. The unit performed active duty between November 1961 and August 1962 with deployment to Ramstein AB, Germany.

Nicknamed the 'Copperheads', the Arizona Air Guard's 197th ARS operates the KC-135A from Sky Harbor Airport, Phoenix.

Redesignated the 197th Air Transport Squadron in October 1962 with C-97Gs, the unit became the 197th MAS in January 1966. The squadron changed to 197th ARefS in August 1972 with KC-97Ls assigned until October 1977, when the unit re-equipped with the KC-135A.

162nd Fighter Group

ANG Tucson IAP, AZ: A-7D/K, F-16A/B, C-130B
148th/162nd/195th Fighter Squadrons

The group has three squadrons assigned, consisting of the 148th FS, 152nd FS and 195th FS all operating the F-16A/B. The 152nd FIS was formed in May 1956 with F-86As and converted to F-86Fs as a TFS in 1957. A year later the first F-100As were delivered, with the 162nd FIG assigned. The unit exchanged the F-100 for the F-102A in February 1966 until September 1969, when they reverted to F-100D/Fs supplemented by F-100Cs. The squadron became a TFTS and was allocated a role as the replacement training unit (RTU) for ANG F-100 aircrew. The squadron continued as an RTU until 1977 when the F-100 was replaced by the A-7D, with a number of two-seat A-7Ks assigned subsequently. The unit was

redesignated 152nd TFS in July 1979 and began converting to F-16As during late 1991. The other two squadrons were reformed by the Arizona ANG from inactivated units acquired from other states. The 148th TFTS was activated with F-16A/Bs early in 1986 and the 195th TFTS received A-7Ds in 1983. The last A-7 was retired in the third quarter of 1991, additional F-16s being assigned. The change to a single type may well result in one of the squadrons being disbanded. The Royal Netherlands Air Force has a dozen F-16A/Bs detached to Arizona ANG for aircrew training.

The state flag adorns the tails of Arizona's F-16s. The unit utilizes its exceptional flying weather to train crews, including those destined for the Dutch air force.

163rd Reconnaissance Group
ANG March AFB, CA: RF-4C
196th Reconnaissance Squadron

The 196th RS is the group's flying unit, operating the RF-4C since early 1990. The unit was established as the 196th Fighter Squadron in November 1946 at Norton AFB with P-51Ds, before converting to the F-80C June 1948. The 196th was mobilized in October 1950 and re-equipped with F-84Es as a Fighter-Bomber Squadron before undertaking a period of duty in Japan. They joined the 116th FBG in October 1950. The squadron was back under state control in July 1952 with relocation to Ontario IAP, flying the F-51H. The unit was redesignated the 196th FIS in March 1954 with the F-86A, switching to the 163rd FIG in May 1958. Equipment was upgraded to F-86Ds and F-86Ls before converting to F-102As in 1965. The unit changed to the 196th TASS with the O-2A in March 1975 before moving to March AFB and reverting to jets, with the F-4C operated from 1983. The squadron upgraded to the F-4E before becoming a TRS with the RF-4C.

The 196th RS has only recently adopted the RF-4C, having previously flown the F-4E on tactical duties.

164th Airlift Group
ANG Memphis IAP, TN: C-141B
155th Airlift Squadron

The 155th AS is the group's operational unit, previously flying the C-130A and currently converting to the C-141B. The 155th Fighter Squadron was formed December 1946 with P-51Ds and mobilized in April 1951 as the 155th TRS, flying RF-51Ds. The 155th was demobilized in January 1953 with the RB-26C and converted to the RF-84F April 1956. The unit changed to 155th Air Transport Squadron with C-97Gs in April 1961 and was joined by the 164th ATG. The unit was redesignated 155th MAS in January 1966 and switched to the C-124C in May 1967. They became the 155th TAS in August 1974 with C-130As and was the last US unit to operate the type. The squadron commenced conversion to C-141Bs early in 1992.

The 164th Airlift Group was remarkable as the last operator of the C-130A model. It is now converting to the C-141 StarLifter, the second Guard unit to convert to the jet airlifter, following Mississippi.

165th Airlift Group
ANG Savannah IAP, GA: C-130H
158th Airlift Squadron

The 158th AS is the group's flying unit, operating the C-130H since September 1981. The 158th Fighter Squadron was established in October 1946 with the P-47N at Chatham Field, Savannah. The 158th converted to F-80s in August 1948 and was called to active duty in October 1950. The unit converted to F-84Ds with a temporary assignment to Misawa AB, Japan, before returning to state control in July 1952. The squadron was redesignated 158th FIS with F-51Hs and re-equipped with F-84Fs in March 1957. The 165th FIG was formed in July 1958. The unit received C-97F/Gs in April 1962 with a redesignation to 158th Air Transport Squadron. The squadron became the 158th MAS in January 1966 with C-124Cs assigned in 1967. The 158th was the last operational C-124C unit, with the final pair retired in September 1974 when the unit became the 158th TAS with C-130Es.

In addition to an F-15A squadron, the Georgia Air National Guard is responsible for the 158th Airlift Squadron, which flies the C-130H from Savannah.

166th Airlift Group
ANG Gtr Wilmington Apt, DE: C-130H
142nd Airlift Squadron

The 142nd AS is the group's flying unit, operating the C-130H since November 1985. The unit was organized as the 142nd Fighter Squadron in September 1946 with the P-47N, and the F-84C from February 1950. Active duty was performed between February 1951 and October 1952, with F-94Bs assigned. The squadron was redesignated 142nd Fighter-Bomber Squadron upon return to state control with the F-51H, before converting to F-86As in March 1954 and becoming an FIS. The F-86E gradually replaced the A model of the Sabre, with F-86Hs operated from November 1958 and a corresponding change to a TFS. The unit became an Air Transport Squadron in 1962 with the C-97F and later the G model, with the 166th ATG assigned. In May 1971 the 142nd converted to C-130As and became a TAS. The unit served with the 1630th TAW (Provisional) at Al Ain, UAE, during Desert Storm.

Delaware was one of the states which was used to provide airlift support during Desert Storm. The C-130Hs joined other Guard units at Al Ain in the United Arab Emirates.

167th Airlift Group
ANG Shepherd Fd, Martinsburg, WV: C-130E
167th Airlift Squadron

The 167th AS is the group's flying unit, operating the C-130E since 1990. The unit was established as the 167th Fighter Squadron in March 1947 at Kanawha County Airport, with P-47Ds. The 167th was mobilized in October 1950 and converted to F-84Bs one year later, before deploying to RAF Manston, UK. The squadron was returned to state control in July 1952, and converted to the F-51D as the 167th FIS. The 167th was the final ANG unit to fly the F-51D, converting from Mustangs during early 1957. T-28As were flown until September 1957, when the unit converted to F-86Hs with a redesignation to TFS status. They became the 167th Aeromedical Transport Squadron with C-119Cs in 1961 and C-121Cs in 1963. The squadron joined the 167th ATG in January 1964, and was redesignated 167th MAS in January 1966 and 167th AAS in August 1968. The unit converted to the C-130A in June 1972 as 167th TAS, upgrading to C-130Bs in 1978 and moving to Shepherd Field in 1981.

Patch of the 167th Airlift Squadron, which flies the C-130E.

168th Air Refueling Group

ANG Eielson AFB, AK:
KC-135D/E
168th Air Refueling Squadron

The 168th ARS is the group's flying unit, operating the KC-135D/E since it was formed October 1986. Initially under 176th Composite Group, the unit was assigned in July 1990 to the 168th ARG.

A newly-formed Guard squadron is the 168th ARS, which flies the tanker mission in Alaska, using a mix of KC-135Es (illustrated) and the rare KC-135D model.

169th Fighter Group

ANG McEntire ANGB, SC:
F-16A/B, C-130H
157th Fighter Squadron

The 157th FS is the group's flying unit, operating the F-16A since July 1983 with a C-130H support. The unit was formed as the 157th Fighter Squadron in December 1946, with the P-51D. The squadron was called to active duty in October 1950 and redesignated 157th TRS with RF-51Ds. The 157th converted to RF-80As in 1951 and deployed to Moron AB, Spain, until returned to state control in July 1952. The unit was redesignated 157th FIS with F-51Hs and added a mix of F-86As until January 1955, when they re-equipped with F-80Cs. The

169th FIG was formed in September 1957. Aircraft changed to the F-86L mid-1958 and the F-104A in February 1960. The unit was mobilized from November 1961 to August 1962 and deployed to Ramstein AB, Germany. F-102As were assigned from early 1963 until April 1975, when the squadron converted to A-7Ds and became the 157th TFS. The 157th became the first ANG F-16A squadron when it converted from A-7Ds in 1983. The unit was called to active duty in December 1990 and deployed to Al Kharj, Saudi Arabia, for Desert Storm.

An AGM-65 anti-armor missile is carried by this SC ANG F-16. The aircraft wears the 'Swamp Fox' badge on the fuselage.

170th Air Refueling Group

ANG McGuire AFB, NJ: KC-135E
150th Air Refueling Squadron

The 150th ARS is the group's flying component, with the KC-135E assigned since 1983. The unit was established in February 1956 as the 150th Aeromedical Transport Squadron at Newark, NJ, with C-46Ds and then the MC-119J in 1958. The 150th re-equipped with C-121Cs in 1961 as an Air Transport Squadron, with the 170th ATG activated in January 1964. The unit moved to McGuire AFB in July 1965 and was redesignated 150th Aeromedical Airlift Squadron with C-121C/Gs. The 150th changed to a TAS in June 1973 with the C-7A/B, before switching to an ARefS with the KC-135A in April 1977.

KC-135Es equip the 150th ARS, part of New Jersey's ANG. Other state units are an F-16 air defense squadron and an F-4 unit.

171st Air Refueling Wing

ANG Gtr Pittsburgh IAP, PA:
KC-135E
147th Air Refueling Squadron

The 147th ARS is the wing's operational unit, flying the KC-135E since 1983. The unit was formed as the 147th Fighter Squadron in April 1949 with F-47Ns, then was redesignated 147th FIS and re-equipped with F-51Hs in June 1951. Equipment was upgraded to the F-84F in late 1954 and F-86D/Ls early in 1958. The squadron converted to the C-119J in May 1961 as the 147th Aeromedical Transport Squadron before receiving C-121Gs in 1963. The 171st ATG was formed in February 1964. The 147th was redesignated a MAS and was mobilized between May 1968 and December 1969. The unit switched to KC-97Ls in October 1972 as the 147th ARefS, and upgraded to KC-135As in July 1977.

The KC-135E-equipped 147th ARS incorporates the ANG's Minuteman motif into its badge.

172nd Airlift Group

ANG Allen C. Thompson Fd, Jackson, MS: C-141B
183rd Airlift Squadron

The 183rd AS is the group's flying unit, with the C-141B operated since mid-1986. The 183rd TRS was formed at Hawkins Field, Jackson, in July 1953, with RB-26Cs. The unit was redesignated 183rd Aeromedical Transport Squadron in November 1957 with

C-119Fs, which were replaced by C-121Cs in mid-1961. The 183rd became an Air Transport Squadron and moved to Thompson Field in January 1963, with the 172nd ATG assigned in 1964. Designation changed to 183rd MAS in January 1966, with

C-124Cs assigned in February 1967. The unit converted to C-130Es in May 1972 as the 183rd TAS, upgrading to C-130Hs in 1980. The 183rd reverted to an MAS when it re-equipped with the C-141B.

174th Fighter Wing
ANG Hancock Fd, Syracuse, NY: F-16A/B ('NY')
138th Fighter Squadron

The 138th FS is the wing's operational unit, flying the F-16A. The unit was created in October 1947 as the 138th Fighter Squadron, with P-47Ds assigned soon afterwards. F-84Bs were operated briefly for nine months from January 1950, until the F-51H was received. The unit was redesignated 138th FIS in 1953 with the F-94B assigned, and became a TFS with F-86Hs in December 1957. The 174th TFG had been formed by late 1958. The unit was called to active duty in 1961 and deployed to Phalsbourg AB, France, until returned to state control in August 1962. A second period of active duty

came between May and December 1968 for the *Pueblo* crisis, involving a relocation at Cannon AFB to operate a FAC and crew training school. A-37Bs were assigned from late 1970 until mid-1979, when A-10As were received and the group was elevated to Wing standard. The squadron converted to F-16As commencing in November 1988 with the role of close air support, and was called to active duty in December 1990 and deployed to Al Kharj, Saudi Arabia, for Desert Storm.

During Desert Storm the F-16As of the 174th Fighter Wing undertook close support missions, this pair seen carrying cluster bombs. The squadron also uses the Pave Claw gun pod.

175th Fighter Group
ANG Glenn L. Martin State Apt, Baltimore, MD: A-10A ('MD')
104th Fighter Squadron

The group was activated in June 1921 with 104th Squadron as its flying unit, the first National Guard squadron to be equipped with Curtiss Jennies as its own aircraft. The unit was called to active duty between February 1941 and September 1943. The 104th was reorganized as a Fighter Squadron at Harbor Field with P-47Ds and later P-51Ds, with federal recognition in August 1946. In July 1954 the unit received T-33As which, along with F-86Es, were operated from Friendship Airport, Baltimore, while F-51s continued to fly from Harbor

Field. The transition to jets was finally completed when the unit received F-86Hs and moved to Glenn L. Martin State Airport in November 1958, becoming a TFS. The 175th TFG was activated in October 1962. The unit was mobilized between May and December 1968 during the *Pueblo* crisis, before receiving the A-37B in April 1970. Conversion to the A-10A began in October 1980. The unit is due to add six OA-10As in late 1992.

Maryland's 104th Fighter Squadron has operated the A-10 since 1980, and is now in the process of adding OA-10A FAC platforms.

176th Composite Group
ANG Kulis ANGB, Anchorage, AK: C-130H, HC-130H(N), HH-60G
144th Airlift Squadron
210th Rescue Squadron

The 144th AS and 210th RQS are the two operational units of the group. The 144th Fighter-Bomber Squadron was formed in July 1953 at Elmendorf AFB with the F-80C assigned the following year. The squadron moved to Anchorage IAP in 1955. F-84Es were assigned in July 1955 along with a change to an FIS, until July 1957 when the unit converted to C-47s and became the

144th Air Transport Squadron. Ski-equipped C-123Js were assigned in July 1960, with a change to TAS in April 1969. The 176th TAG was formed at the same time. The Provider was replaced by the C-130E early in 1976, followed by the C-130H late in 1983. The 210th RQS is the Guard's newest squadron, being activated during 1990 with HC-130H(N) and HH-60G delivered shortly after formation.

One of the 176th CG's two squadrons is used for airlift tasks, flying the C-130H (illustrated). The other unit provides rescue cover for the 49th state, both squadrons flying from Anchorage.

177th Fighter Group
ANG Atlantic City IAP, NJ: F-16A/B (ADF)
119th Fighter Squadron

The 119th FS operates as the flying unit of the 177th FG, with the F-16A (ADF) assigned since July 1988. The unit was activated in January 1930 and called to active service in September 1940, until disbanded in May 1944. The 119th Fighter Squadron was organized under state control at Newark, NJ, in January 1947 with P-47Ds. The unit was not mobilized during the Korean War and flew P-51Hs and later P-51Ds from its home base. Redesignated 119th FIS, the squadron converted to F-86Es in May 1955. The unit changed to F-84Fs in 1958 and moved to Atlantic City IAP, becoming a TFS in 1960. The 119th served on active duty between October 1961 and August 1962, with the 177th FIG forming in October 1962 before converting to F-86Hs later that year. F-100Cs

were assigned mid-1963, with an additional period of active service between January 1968 and June 1969 following the *Pueblo* seizure. The squadron re-equipped with the F-105B from June 1970 until January 1973, when F-106As were assigned and the 119th became an FIS for the second time. The unit won the final F-106A category at the 1984 William Tell competition.

178th Fighter Group
ANG Springfield-Beckley MAP, OH: A-7D/K ('OH')
162nd Fighter Squadron

The 162nd FS is the group's flying unit, with the A-7D assigned. The 162nd Fighter Squadron was established in November 1947 with P-51Ds at Cox MAP, Dayton. The squadron converted to F-51Hs in May 1950 and F-84Es in August 1955, becoming the

162nd FIS and moving to Springfield MAP two months later. The 162nd changed to TFS status when it upgraded to F-84Fs in November 1957, and was mobilized between October 1961 and August 1962. The 178th TFG was added in October 1962. The unit re-equipped with F-100Ds in April 1970 and A-7Ds in April 1978, and is to re-equip with F-16C/Ds early in 1993.

The 162nd FS is one of three Ohio ANG A-7 units, identified by the red fin band.

179th Airlift Group
ANG Mansfield-Lahm APT, OH:
C-130H
164th Airlift Squadron

The 164th AS is the group's operational component, with the C-130H assigned since 1991. The unit was formed as the 164th Fighter Squadron in June 1948 with P-51Ds and switched to F-51Hs in July 1949. The 164th was redesignated a Fighter-Bomber Squadron in November 1952 with F-80Cs and F-84Es from October 1954. The unit converted to F-84Fs in September 1957, becoming a TFS in November 1958. The 164th was mobilized between October 1961 and August 1962, with the 179th TFG assigned in October 1962. The unit re-equipped with the F-100D in February 1972 and changed to a TAS with the C-130B in January 1976.

In 1976 the 164th Squadron of the Ohio ANG became a Hercules operator, with the B model. It has now upgraded to the latest C-130H, operating from Mansfield.

180th Fighter Group
ANG Toledo Express Apt, OH:
A-7D/K ('OH')
112th Fighter Squadron

The 112th FS currently operates as the group's flying unit, operating A-7Ds since mid-1979. Another unit born during World War I, the squadron was mobilized in November 1940 for war service until August 1945. The unit was federally recognized in December 1946 as the 112th Bombardment Squadron with A-26Bs at Cleveland Hopkins Airport. The 112th was called back to active duty from October 1950 until March 1952, becoming the 112th Fighter-Bomber Squadron with F-51Hs at Berea Airport.

Shortly afterwards the unit moved to Akron-Canton Airport and changed to a Fighter Interceptor Squadron. They moved temporarily to Toledo Municipal Airport with a mix of T-28As, T-33As and a few F-84Es, before finally relocating to Toledo Express Airport in January 1959 and completing transition to F-84Fs as a TFS. The unit was activated between October 1961 and August 1962 but remained at its home base. The 112th TFS converted to F-100Ds in October 1970, and is due to receive the F-16C/D in mid-1992.

The 112th FS occasionally deploys to Howard AFB as part of Coronet Cove.

181st Fighter Group
ANG Hulman Fd, Terre Haute, IN:
F-16C/D ('HF')
113th Fighter Squadron

The 113th FS is the group's flying unit, and began converting to the F-16C in 1991. The unit was organized in August 1917 and mobilized from January 1941 until November 1943. The squadron received federal recognition as the 113th Fighter Squadron in April 1947 with P-51Ds at Stout Field, and was called to active duty in February 1951. The 113th was returned to state control in November 1952 and moved to Hulman Field in 1954. Transition to F-80Cs coincided with a change to FIS status in 1955. One year later the F-86A was assigned, before the F-84F arrived in April 1958, designation changing to a TFS. While retaining the TFS designation the 113th operated the RF-84F, until May 1964, when the unit reverted to F-84Fs. The 181st TFG was activated in October 1962. F-100Ds were delivered in

August 1971, the 113th being the last ANG unit to operate the Super Sabre before converting to F-4Cs in July 1979. F-4Cs were replaced by F-4Es mid-1987.

182nd Fighter Group
ANG Gtr Peoria Apt, IL: OA-37B,
C-26A ('IL')
169th Fighter Squadron

The 169th FS is the group's operational squadron, with the OA-37B assigned since mid-1980. The 169th Fighter Squadron was formed in June 1947 with P-51Ds, until October 1952 when the F-51H was delivered. The 169th was redesignated a Fighter-Bomber Squadron with just the T-28A, until becoming the 169th FIS in March 1956 with the F-84F. The unit changed to a TFS and was mobilized between October 1961 and August 1962, with the 182nd TFG assigned in October 1962. The 169th changed to a TASS in May 1969 with the U-3A, until 1971 when it converted to the O-2A.

F-16C of the 113th FS wear 'HF' (for Hulman Field) codes.

183rd Fighter Group
ANG Capital Apt, Springfield, IL:
F-16A/B ('SI')
170th Fighter Squadron

The 170th FS is the operational unit, flying the F-16A since October 1989. The unit was established as the 170th Fighter Squadron in September 1948 with F-51Ds and ordered to active service in March 1951. The 170th was redesignated a Fighter-Bomber Squadron in April 1951 and returned to state control in November 1952. The squadron converted to F-86Es in late 1953 and F-84Fs at the end of 1954. Designation changed to 170th FIS in July 1955 and 170th TFS in November 1958. The unit was mobilized from October 1961 until August 1962, with the 183rd TFG assigned in October 1962. The F-4C was

The 170th FS has among the most colorful markings applied to the F-16, which it flies on general fighter-bomber duties.

operated from January 1972 and the F-4D from July 1984, until the F-16A arrived.

184th Fighter Group
ANG McConnell AFB, KS:
F-16C/D, C-12J
127th/161st Fighter Squadrons

The 127th FS is one of the group's two operational flying units, with F-16Cs assigned since 1991 and a C-12J support. The unit was formed in August 1941 at Wichita Municipal Airport and mobilized two months later, until November 1945. The 127th Fighter Squadron returned to state control in September 1946 with P-51Ds. The 127th re-equipped with F-84Cs in 1950 and was redesignated a Fighter-Bomber

Squadron shortly afterwards. Active duty began in October 1950, involving assignment to Chaumont AB, France, before returning to reserve status and the F-51D in July 1952. The unit moved to McConnell AFB and converted to the F-80C in June 1954, changing designation to an FIS. F-86Ls were assigned from January 1958 until April 1961, when they converted to F-100Cs as a TFS. The 184th TFG was activated in

October 1962, while another recall to active duty took place between January 1968 and June 1969 involving a short period at Kunsan AB, South Korea. The 127th re-equipped with the F-105D in March 1971 and became a TFTS as Replacement Training Unit (RTU) for active and reserve Thunderchief aircrew. The squadron retained the RTU role with F-4Ds commencing 1979, before switching to the F-16A in September 1987 and the

F-16C in 1991. The 161st TFTS was established in March 1987 with F-16As but upgraded to F-16C/Ds early in 1991, while the 177th TFTS was assigned F-4Ds until 1987, when it disbanded.

The Kansas Jayhawks of the 184th Fighter Group undertake training for other Guard units on the F-16. Shown is an F-16B, but the group has now upgraded to the C/D.

185th Fighter Group
ANG Sioux Gateway Apt, Sioux City, IA: A-7D/K ('HA')
174th Fighter Squadron

The 174th FS is the group's operational unit, flying the A-7D since July 1977. The unit was established as the 174th Fighter Squadron in December 1946 with P-51Ds. The 174th converted to the F-84B in May 1950 and was mobilized from April 1951 until January 1953. They reverted to F-51Ds in 1953 and re-equipped with F-80Cs in July 1953 and F-84Es in August 1956. The 174th became a TRS in April 1958 with RF-84Fs

assigned until redesignating to a TFS with the F-100C in May 1961. The squadron joined the 185th TFG in October 1962 and mobilized between January 1968 and May 1969, involving a lengthy period of combat operations from Phu Cat AB, South Vietnam. The unit upgraded to F-100Ds in 1974 and is scheduled to receive F-16C/Ds mid-1992.

In the process of converting to the F-16, the 174th Fighter Squadron was one of two Iowa units flying the A-7D/K, carrying the 'HA' tailcode instead of the 'IA' applied to the other unit.

186th Reconnaissance Group
ANG Key Fd, Meridian, MS: RF-4C, C-26A
153rd Reconnaissance Squadron

The 153rd RS is the operational unit of the group, flying the RF-4C since September 1978. The unit was formed as the 153rd Observation Squadron in September 1939 and called to active duty from October 1940 until December 1945. The 153rd was federalized with P-47Ns as a Fighter Squadron in September 1946 and recalled to active duty from March 1951 until November 1952. The unit converted to RF-51Ds as the

153rd TRS in December 1952, and then to RF-80As in June 1955. The squadron was temporarily based at Gulfport Airport from October 1956 to March 1958 and re-equipped with RF-84Fs. The 153rd was called to active service from October 1961 to August 1962, then 186th TRG was assigned. The unit received RF-101Cs in November 1970 and was the last US operational unit with the reconnaissance Voodoo when the

final example was retired in January 1979. The 153rd is due to convert to KC-135Es as the 153rd ARS during 1992.

187th Fighter Group
ANG Dannelly Fd, Montgomery, AL: F-16A/B, C-130H ('AL')
160th Fighter Squadron

The 160th FS is the group's flying unit, with F-16As operated since October 1988 with C-130H support. The 160th Fighter Squadron was formed in October 1947 with P-51Ds. The unit was redesignated the 160th TRS in September 1950 when called to active duty, converting to the RF-80A in May 1951. The 160th deployed to Europe in January 1952, operating from bases in Germany and France before returning to state control in July 1952 and re-equipping with the RF-51D. The squadron received RF-80s again in June 1955, with RF-84Fs assigned one year later. The unit was mobilized for a second time between October 1961 and August 1962,

Alabama's F-16s wear a distinctive variation to the camouflage theme.

before joining the 187th TRG two months later. The squadron converted to RF-4Cs in 1971 and changed to F-4Ds in July 1983, becoming the 160th TFS.

188th Fighter Group
ANG Fort Smith MAP, AR: F-16A/B, C-12F ('FS')
184th Fighter Squadron

The 184th FS is the group's flying component, with the F-16A assigned since June 1988. The unit was formed as the 184th TRS in October 1953 with RB-26Cs, until replaced by RF-80As in June 1956. The squadron converted to RF-84Fs early in 1957 and was called to active duty between November 1961 and August 1962. The 184th joined the 188th TRG in October 1962. RF-101Cs were operated from December 1970 until June 1972, when the F-100D was delivered and the unit became the 184th TFS. The 184th re-equipped with F-4Cs mid-1979, and flew F-4Ds until 1988, when the F-16A was assigned.

Known as the 'Flying Razorbacks' in honor of the hog variety associated with the state, the 184th Fighter Squadron of the Arkansas ANG is an F-16A operator employed on battlefield duties. This pair of aircraft carries practice bomb/rocket dispensers for an exercise.

189th Airlift Group
ANG Little Rock AFB, AR: C-130E
154th Airlift Squadron

The 154th AS is the group's operational unit, flying the C-130E since mid-1987. The unit was established at Adams Field, Little Rock, during December 1917 as the 154th Aero Squadron and was demobilized from February 1919 until October 1925. Reformed as the 154th Observation Squadron, the unit was mobilized from September 1940 until December 1945. The 154th was redesignated a Fighter Squadron in August

1946 with P-51Ds and was called to active service again in October 1950, with temporary duty at Langley AFB and later in South Korea and Japan, flying F-84Es. The unit was returned to state control in July 1952 as the 154th TRS, flying RF-51Ds. The squadron re-equipped with the RF-80A in December 1954, the RF-84F in April 1957, the RB-57A/B in March 1958, and the RF-101H mid-1965. The 154th relocated to

Little Rock AFB in 1962 and joined the 189th TRG. The unit was recalled to active duty from January to December 1968, with a period of duty at Itazuke AB, Japan. The squadron converted to KC-135As in January 1976 as the 154th ARefS and upgraded to KC-135Es in 1983. The 154th changed to a TATS when the C-130E was assigned mid-1987.

190th Air Refueling Group

ANG Forbes Field, Topeka, KS: KC-135E
117th Air Refueling Squadron

The 117th FIS was formed at NAS Hutchinson in February 1957 from a defunct unit deactivated by the Pennsylvania ANG. Operating F-80Cs initially, the unit re-equipped with the RB-57A in April 1958, becoming a TRS, with the 190th TRG activated in October 1962. The unit relocated to Forbes AFB in August 1967 and changed to Tactical Bombing Squadron with the B-57G, before acquiring the EB-57B as the 117th Defense Systems Evaluation Squadron. After 20 years of operating B-57s, the unit changed to KC-135As and became an Air Refueling Squadron. The Stratotankers were redesignated KC-135E in 1984 following re-engining.

The 'Kansas Coyotes' of the 117th ARS fly the Boeing KC-135E Stratotanker. The badge features a cartoon canine in a grainfield.

191st Fighter Group

ANG Selfridge ANGB, MI: F-16A/B
171st Fighter Squadron

The 171st FS is the group's flying unit, with the F-16A(ADF) assigned since August 1990. The unit was established as the 171st Fighter Squadron in April 1948 at Wayne Major Airport, Detroit, with F-51Ds. The squadron converted to F-84Bs in 1950 and was mobilized February 1951. The 171st was assigned to the 127th Pilot Training Group along with its sister unit the 107th Fighter Squadron. The squadron was returned to state control in October 1952, becoming an FIS with the F-51H in November 1952 and the F-86E in November 1953. The 171st

converted to the F-89C in June 1955 and was redesignated 171st TRS in February 1958 with RF-84Fs. The 191st TRG was activated in October 1962. The unit moved to Selfridge AFB and converted to the

RF-101A/C in January 1971, followed by a change to the F-106A in June 1972, becoming the 171st FIS. The 171st switched to F-4Cs in 1978 and upgraded to F-4Ds before receiving the F-16A.

These F-16As were among the first 'Vipers' assigned to the 191st FG. The ADF version is now used for the air defense mission.

Unofficial badge of the 'Michigan Wolves' – the 191st FG.

192nd Fighter Group

ANG Byrd IAP, Richmond, VA: F-16C/D, C-26A ('VA')
149th Fighter Squadron

The 149th FS is the group's flying unit, having converted from the A-7D to the F-16C during July 1991. The unit was established as the 149th Fighter Squadron in June 1947 with P-47Ds. The 149th was activated from March 1951 until December 1952, when it was redesignated a Fighter-Bomber

Squadron. The squadron changed to Bombardment Squadron in November 1953 with B-26s. The unit was redesignated 149th FIS in June 1957 and 149th TRS in April 1958, before reverting to FIS status two months later, despite operating the B-26 throughout plus a handful of F-84Fs, F-86Es

and an RB-57B. The F-84F finally entered service in November 1958 under the 149th TFS. The 149th was mobilized between October 1961 and August 1962, with the 192nd TFG assigned in October 1962. The unit flew F-105Ds from January 1971 until converting to the A-7D in June 1981.

193rd Special Operations Group

ANG Harrisburg IAP, Middletown, PA: EC-130E
193rd Special Operations Squadron

The 193rd SOS is the group's operational squadron, flying the EC-130E since 1977. The unit was formed in September 1967 at Olmstead AFB (now Harrisburg IAP) as the 193rd Tactical Electronic Warfare Squadron with the EC-121S and C-121C. The 193rd was redesignated an SOS from April 1977 until December 1977, when it reverted to TEWS status. The squadron began conversion to

EC-130Es in 1977. The unit changed designation to 193rd Electronic Composite Squadron in October 1980 but changed to 193rd SOS again mid-1984.

Two special Hercules versions are flown by the 193rd SOS, this being the EC-130E Rivet Rider which performs battlefield broadcasting. The more shadowy EC-130E Comfy Levi is believed to have an Elint function.

301st Fighter Wing

AFRes Carswell AFB, TX: F-16C/D ('TF')
457th Fighter Squadron

The unit was established as the 301st Fighter Wing with P-47s at Seymour Johnson Field in October 1944, as a B-29 escort unit for western Pacific operations. The 301st was based at several locations in Okinawa with P-61s and P-80s before inactivating in January 1949. The unit was

reactivated as the 301st TFW at Carswell AFB in July 1972, operating the F-105D (including the Thunderstick II version) until 1981 when the unit re-equipped with the F-4D. The wing upgraded to the F-4E in August 1987 before exchanging the Phantom for the F-16C December 1990.

301st FW F-16Cs wear the 'TF' tailcode for 'Texas Falcon'. Phantoms were previously used.

301st Wing
AMC Malmstrom AFB, MT:
KC-135R
91st Air Refueling Squadron

The unit was established in October 1947 as a Bombardment Wing at Smokey Hill AFB, KS, with B-29s and moved to Barksdale AFB, LA, in November 1949. The wing operated KB-29s and KC-97s plus B-47Es, EB-47Es and RB-47s before relocating to Lockbourne AFB (renamed Rickenbacker AFB), OH, in April 1958. The 301st converted to the KC-135A in 1963, becoming an ARW in June 1964. The unit was deactivated in September 1979 with the base transferred from SAC to ANG in April 1980. The wing was re-formed at Malmstrom AFB with KC-135Rs during January 1988, and changed to 301st Wing in October 1991.

A steer's skull adorns the fin of the Montana-based 301st Wing, which flies the KC-135R.

302nd Airlift Wing
AFRes Peterson AFB, CO:
C-130B
731st Airlift Squadron

The unit was created as the 302nd Troop Carrier Wing at McChord AFB in June 1949, with the C-54 and C-82. The 302nd was mobilized in June 1951 and inactivated immediately. The wing reformed at Clinton County AFB, OH, in June 1952 with C-46s initially and later C-119s. The 302nd was redesignated a TAW in July 1967 and a SOW in July 1970 with the A-37B and U-3A. Designation changed back to 302nd TAW in August 1971 when the unit moved to Lockbourne AFB (later Rickenbacker AFB), OH, with the UC/C-123K. The wing relocated to Peterson AFB with the C-130B assigned in October 1982. The unit is also responsible for a C-130B-equipped group stationed at March AFB.

C-130B Hercules are now becoming rare in the USAF structure, having largely been replaced by C-130Es and Hs. One remaining user is the Air Force Reserve's 731st AS at Peterson AFB.

305th Wing
AMC Grissom AFB, IN: KC-135R, EC-135G/L
70th/305th Air Refueling Squadrons

The unit was formed as the 305th Bombardment Wing at MacDill AFB in January 1951 with the B-29A and KC-97E, to conduct training for SAC crews destined for the Korean War. The B-47 was received late in 1952. The wing moved to Bunker Hill AFB (renamed Grissom AFB), IN, in June 1959 and converted to the KC-135A. The 305th became the second B-58A Hustler wing in May 1961 until January 1970, when the type was retired and the unit was redesignated the 301st ARW. The EC-135 post attack command control system was assigned in 1966 and was operated by the 3rd ACCS from April 1970 to December 1975, when it was absorbed into the 70th ARefS. The 305th upgraded to the KC-135R during the latter half of 1988. Redesignated 305th Wing in October 1991, the unit is scheduled to inactivate by 1994, permitting Grissom to cease Air Force operations.

Among the 305th Wing C-135 oddities is this KC-135R(RT), which incorporates an air refueling receptacle above the cockpit.

306th Wing
ACC RAF Mildenhall, UK

The unit, as the 306th Bombardment Wing, has operated B-29 and B-50 bombers and KC-97E tankers at MacDill AFB since activated in September 1950, subsequently converting to the B-47E in 1951. The wing won SAC's Proud Shield bombing and navigation competition in 1958. The 306th moved to McCoy AFB, FL, in April 1963 and re-equipped with B-52Cs and KC-135As. The unit was deactivated in July 1974. The 306th was redesignated a Strategic Wing and activated at Ramstein AB, Germany, in August 1976, assuming the support task of the 98th SW, whose HQ was at Torrejon AB, Spain, prior to the latter unit phasing down operations by that year's end. The unit operated as liaison between SAC and USAFE until replaced by the 7th Air Division at Ramstein, with the wing relocating to RAF Mildenhall in July 1978. Designation changed to 306th Wing in October 1991. The wing is due to be inactivated in late 1992, having been replaced by the 100th ARefW.

313th Airlift Group
USAFE RAF Mildenhall, UK

The group was formed in January 1976 as the controlling element for C-130 Hercules rotations at Mildenhall, and was subordinate to the Ramstein-based 322nd Airlift Division until the latter was disbanded in 1991. Under a proposed reorganization of MAC assets, the 313th will probably be assigned aircraft directly, rather than operate rotations from the USA.

314th Airlift Wing
AMC Little Rock AFB, AR:
C-130E
50th/61st/62nd Airlift Squadrons
16th Airlift Training Squadron

The 314th was established as a Troop Carrier Wing at Smyrna AFB (later Sewart AFB), TN, in November 1948, specializing in airborne assault and operating C-47s and C-82s alongside two versions of towed gliders. The wing converted to C-119s in 1949 and added a mixed fleet of C-46s plus various light helicopters and liaison types. The unit re-equipped with the C-123B and C-130A in 1956, then upgraded to the C-130B in 1961. The 314th relocated to Kung Kuan AB (later Ching Chuan Kang AB), Taiwan, in January 1966 and re-equipped with the C-130E. Designation changed to 314th TAW in August 1967. The unit relocated to Little Rock AFB in May 1971, replacing the 64th TAW and the 4442nd CCTW, assuming the operational commitment of the former and the training role of the latter. The C-130H was assigned in 1974, although these aircraft were reassigned elsewhere during the 1980s. The wing won Volant Rodeo, the predecessor of Airlift Rodeo, at Pope AFB in 1981 and 1983. The unit changed designation to 314th Airlift Wing at the end of 1991.

In addition to normal airlift operations, the 314th AW is assigned the C-130 conversion role for the active-duty fleet.

315th Airlift Wing (Associate)

AFRes Charleston AFB, SC: C-141B
300th/701st/707th Airlift Squadrons (Associate)

The unit was organized as the 315th Troop Carrier Wing under PACAF control at Brady AB, Japan, in June 1952, with a variety of transport aircraft including the C-46. The wing was inactivated in January 1955, but was redesignated 315th Air Commando Wing in February 1966 and activated at Tan Son Nhut AB, South Vietnam, with the UC/C-123B and C-130E-I Combat Talon I. The

315th moved to Phan Rang AB, South Vietnam, in June 1967 and changed to a SOW in August 1968. In January 1970 the unit became the 315th TAW, operating A-37Bs and AC-47Ds alongside C-123Ks. The wing was inactivated in March 1972, but redesignated by AFRes as 349th MAW (Associate) in July 1973 to provide Reservist personnel to operate front-line C-5A and

C-141A aircraft at Charleston AFB. The C-5As were transferred to Dover AFB mid-1973 with the unit upgrading to C-141Bs in 1980/1981.

317th Airlift Wing

AMC Pope AFB, NC: C-130E
39th/40th/41st Airlift Squadrons

The 317th spent 10 years stationed in Europe before relocating from Evreux-Fauville AB, France, to Lockbourne AFB, Ohio, in June 1964. The unit received their first C-130As in 1957 and has operated the Hercules ever since. It moved to its current location in August 1971 and re-equipped with the C-130E at the same time. Two

squadrons of C-130Es were stationed at Masirah, Oman, with the 1640th TAW (Provisional) throughout Desert Shield/Storm to conduct theater tactical airlift. The unit may be reorganized as a Composite Wing and assigned to Air Combat Command. The unit changed designation to 317th Airlift Wing at the end of 1991.

The 317th AW is one of the units which regularly deploys C-130s to Mildenhall's 'Bravo' Squadron.

319th Wing

ACC/AMC Grand Forks AFB, ND: B-1B, KC-135R
46th Bomb Squadron
905th Air Refueling Squadron

The 319th was established in June 1949 as a BW at Reading MAP, PA, as a Reserve unit operating the B-26 alongside a variety of training aircraft. The unit moved to Birmingham MAP, AL, in October 1949 before inactivating in March 1951. The wing was re-formed as the 319th Fighter-Bomber Wing in May 1955 at Memphis MAP, TN, with F-84s and T-33As but was inactivated in November 1957. The unit was transferred to SAC as the 319th BW at Grand Forks AFB and activated in February 1963, replacing the 4133rd Strategic Wing with B-52Hs and KC-135As. The wing won SAC's Proud Shield bombing and navigation competition in 1969. The 319th converted to B-52Gs in 1983 and B-1Bs in 1988, exchanged its KC-135As for KC-135Rs in 1987, and changed to 319th Wing in October 1991.

The 319th is one of four wings with Rockwell B-1Bs assigned, these flying with the 46th Bomb Squadron. A second squadron within the wing flies the KC-135R tanker, both types featuring the wing's blue and orange fin-stripe. Most of the B-1Bs have nose art applied.

321st Strategic Missile Wing

ACC Grand Forks AFB, ND: LGM-30G
446th/447th/448th Strategic Missile Squadrons

The unit began life as the 321st Bombardment Wing in March 1953, operating B-47Bs and KC-97s at Pinecastle AFB (later McCoy AFB), FL, until inactivated in October 1961. The wing won SAC's Proud Shield bombing and navigation competition in 1957. The 321st was redesignated an SMW, replacing the 4047th Strategic Wing in November 1964 and re-forming at Grand Forks AFB with the LGM-30F Minuteman II, upgrading to LGM-30G Minuteman III in 1972.

323rd Flying Training Wing

ATC Mather AFB, CA: T-37B, CT-43A ('NT')
454th/455th Flying Training Squadrons

The 323rd Bombardment Wing was formed in May 1949 as a Reserve unit at Tinker AFB with B-26s and a mixed fleet of trainer types. The unit was called to active duty in March 1951 with personnel reassigned to numerous units worldwide before the wing was inactivated. The 323rd was reassigned to TAC as the 323rd Fighter-Bomber Wing in August 1955 and was activated at Bunker Hill AFB, IN, operating F-86s and F-100s until being inactivated in September 1957. The unit was transferred to ATC as the 323rd FTW, replacing the 3535th Navigator Training Wing, and activated in April 1973 operating the T-29B/C and T-43A, with T-37Bs added in 1974. The wing conducted navigator training for the USAF, ANG and AFRes, plus many allied nations, before

extending operations to encompass Navy and Marine Corps flight officers in July 1976. The 323rd was scheduled to relocate to Beale AFB, although the plans were changed and the unit will now move to Randolph AFB instead.

Navigation training is undertaken by the 323rd FTW, hence the 'NT' tail code. The principal type employed is the CT-43A (illustrated).

325th Fighter Wing

ACC Tyndall AFB, FL: F-15A/B ('TY')
1st/2nd/95th Fighter Squadrons

The 325th Fighter Wing was established at Hamilton AFB, CA, in June 1948, operating the F-61 and F-82. The unit was relocated to Moses Lake AFB, WA, and McChord AFB before disbanding in February 1952. The 325th was reactivated as a Fighter Wing (Air Defense) in October 1956 at McChord AFB, operating F-102As until 1968 when the unit switched to F-106As. The wing maintained a large detachment at Osan AB, RoK, from February 1968 until it was inactivated in July 1968. The unit was redesignated the 325th Fighter Weapons Wing at Tyndall AFB in July 1981 as the flying component of the Air Defense Weapons Center. The 325th was

redesignated to Tactical Training Wing status in 1983. The unit converted to the F-15A/B in April 1982, and was redesignated the 325th Fighter Wing in August 1991.

Based at Tyndall, the 325th Fighter Wing (previously TTW) undertakes training on the F-15C/D models.

340th Wing
**AMC Altus AFB, OK: KC-135R
11th/306th Air Refueling
Squadrons**

Established as the 340th Bombardment Wing in October 1952 at Sedalia AFB (later Whiteman AFB), MO, the wing was confined to supervision of base construction until May 1964, when YRB-47Bs and KC-97s were delivered. The unit relocated to Bergstrom AFB in September 1963 with B-52Ds and KC-135As, until inactivated in October 1966. The 340th was downgraded to Group status and re-formed at Carswell AFB as an FB-111A training unit in July 1968, although the first aircraft was not delivered to the 4007th CCTS until October 1969. The unit was inactivated in December 1971 when the training role was transferred to the 380th BW. The wing was redesignated 340th ARG in July 1977 and activated at Altus AFB with KC-135As, subsequently upgrading to Wing standard in 1984. The unit converted to the KC-135R mid-1987 and changed to 340th Wing in October 1991.

Flying KC-135R tankers only, the 340th Wing decorates the tails of its aircraft with a silhouette of Oklahoma state, over which is superimposed a covered wagon.

341st Strategic Missile Wing
**ACC Malmstrom AFB, MT:
LGM-30F to G
10th/12th/490th/564th Strategic
Missile Squadrons**

The 341st was formed as a Bombardment Wing in September 1955 at Abilene AFB (later Dyess AFB), TX, with the B-47 and KC-97 until redesignated 341st SMW in July 1961. The wing was relocated to Malmstrom AFB with the LGM-30B Minuteman I assigned from July 1962 until 1969, when it was replaced by the LGM-30F Minuteman II. In 1975 the LGM-30G Minuteman III was added. The wing is due to complete conversion to the LGM-30G imminently.

343rd Wing
**PACAF Eielson AFB, AK:
OA-10A, F-16C/D ('AK')
11th Tactical Air Support
Squadron
18th Fighter Squadron**

The unit was established as the 343rd Composite Wing in October 1981, operating the A-10A and O-2A with 18th TFS and 23rd TASS, respectively. Designation changed to TFW by 1985, with the OV-10A replacing the O-2 during 1986. The Broncos were withdrawn in 1990, with the 23rd TASS being disbanded and partially replaced by a small number of OA-10As assigned to the 18th TFS. The unit has been identified as a future Composite Wing and began to receive the F-16C/D at the end of 1991.

Partnering the OA-10s are newly-delivered F-16Cs with LANTIRN equipment. They fly with the 18th Fighter Squadron.

Below: The 11th TASS operates the OA-10A in the FAC role.

347th Fighter Wing
**ACC Moody AFB, GA: F-16C/D
('MY')
68th/69th/70th Fighter
Squadrons**

The unit was created as the 347th Fighter Wing at Itazuke AB, Japan, in August 1948, operating F-51s and F-61s. The 347th was redesignated a Fighter All-Weather Wing in January 1950, prior to inactivating six months later. Now an FW, the unit activated at Yokota AB, Japan, in January 1968 with the F-4C, F-105D, EB-57E and C-130B-II. The wing returned to the USA, assigned to Mountain Home AFB from May 1971 until October 1972. The 347th was inactive until July 1973 when the wing reformed at Takhli RTAFB, Thailand, replacing the 474th TFW with the F-111A. The unit moved to Korat RTAFB, Thailand, from July 1974 until June 1975, when it was inactivated. The 347th was relocated to Moody AFB in September 1975, operating the F-4E until January 1988 when the unit re-equipped with the F-16A. The wing won the F-4 catagory at the William Tell competition in 1980 at Tyndall AFB. Conversion to the F-16C began during 1990, with one squadron deployed to Al Minhad, UAE, for assignment to the 388th TFW (Provisional) for Desert Storm.

Moody F-16Cs were committed to action during the Gulf War, flying from Al Minhad. LANTIRN pods are available.

349th Airlift Wing (Associate)
**AFRes Travis AFB, CA: C-5A/B,
C-141B
301st/312th/708th/710th Airlift
Squadrons (Associate)**

The 349th was established as a Troop Carrier Wing at Hamilton AFB, CA, in June 1949, operating the C-46 and a number of trainer types. The unit was redesignated the 349th Fighter-Bomber Wing in May 1952 shortly after mobilization, but returned to reserve service one month later. The wing operated T-33As along with F-51s, F-80s and F-84s before reverting to 349th TCW in September 1957. C-119s were operated from 1958 and C-124As arrived in 1965, the unit becoming the 349th MAW in January 1966. The 349th moved to Travis AFB in July 1969 as the first Associate Wing, providing Reservist personnel to operate front-line MAC aircraft at McChord AFB, Norton AFB and Travis AFB until June 1973, when the former two bases were assigned their own associated wings.

351st Strategic Missile Wing
**ACC Whiteman AFB, MO:
LGM-30F
508th/509th/510th Strategic
Missile Squadrons**

The unit was formed as the 351st SMW in February 1963 at Whiteman AFB, with the LGM-30B Minuteman I assigned from January 1964 until May 1966 when it was replaced by the LGM-30F Minuteman II. The wing is scheduled to inactivate during 1992 with the withdrawal of the Minuteman II.

353rd Special Operations Wing
**AFSOC Kadena AB, Okinawa:
MC-130E, MH-53J, HC-130N/P
1st/17th/31st Special Operations
Squadrons**

The wing was established in 1990 as the air component for special operations in the western Pacific region, operating the MC-130E, MH-53J and HC-130N/P. The 353rd was stationed at Clark AB with a squadron based at Kadena AB, although the eruption of Mount Pinatubo in 1991 forced the USAF to vacate Clark and move to NAS Cubi Point initially, then to Kadena.

The PACAF Special Operations wing includes HC-130s in its inventory.

354th Fighter Wing
ACC Myrtle Beach AFB, SC:
A-10A ('MB')
353rd/355th/356th Fighter
Squadrons

The unit was established as the 354th Fighter-Day Wing in November 1956 at Myrtle Beach AFB with the RF-80, replacing the 342nd FDW. Shooting Stars were replaced by F-100s in 1957, with the unit redesignated the 354th TFW in July 1958. The 354th moved to Kunsan AB, RoK, in July 1968 and was composed of squadrons rotated from the USA, including two ANG F-100C units, four with the F-4D and two with the F-4E. The wing's assets passed to the 54th TFW when the 354th returned to Myrtle Beach AFB in June 1970, where it replaced the 4554th TFW and converted to

A-7Ds, with a number of T-33As operated for combat crew training duties. The wing split into Advanced and Rear echelons in October 1972, many of the unit's aircraft deploying to Korat RTAFB, Thailand. A-7 aircraft drawn from the deployed Myrtle Beach squadrons were formed into the 3rd TFS and assigned to the 388th TFW in March 1973. Dual operations continued until May 1974. The unit re-equipped with the A-10A in 1976. Two squadrons of A-10As deployed to King Fahd Airport, Damman, Saudi Arabia, in August 1990 to form the 354th TFW (Provisional) for Desert Storm. The A-10A is scheduled to be retired and the wing to be inactivated during 1992.

This 354th Fighter Wing A-10 wears a kill tally from its service in the Gulf.

355th Fighter Wing
ACC Davis-Monthan AFB, AZ:
A-10A ('DM'), OA-10A ('NF')
333rd/354th/357th/358th Fighter
Squadrons

The unit was activated as the 355th TFW in July 1962 at George AFB with the F-105D, but relocated to McConnell AFB in July 1964. The wing moved to Takhli RTAFB, Thailand, in November 1965 and added the EB-66B/C/E. The wing was inactivated in December 1970, but reformed at Davis-Monthan AFB in July 1971, replacing the 4453rd CCTW and initially operating F-4Cs. The unit began converting to A-7Ds as a Corsair II replacement training unit (RTU) in July 1971, gaining the additional role of tactical drone launch and recovery with the DC-130A. A second drone squadron was

added in July 1976, although all operational drone activities ceased in April 1979. The unit commenced conversion to the A-10A in March 1976, and changed to the 355th Tactical Training Wing in September 1979. Designation was changed to 355th Fighter Wing in late 1991. The 355th assumed responsibility for front-line flying operation of aircraft based at Davis-Monthan AFB from April 1992.

Based at Davis-Monthan, the 355th has a training role for the A-10, and is now also responsible for the operation of the OA-10A forward air control aircraft previously assigned to the 602nd Air Control Wing.

363rd Fighter Wing
ACC Shaw AFB, SC: F-16C/D
('SW')
17th/19th/33rd Fighter
Squadrons

The unit was established as the 363rd Reconnaissance Wing in July 1947 at Langley Field with FP-80s and FA-26s (later RF-80s and RB-26s). The wing was redesignated the 363rd TRW in August 1948 before inactivating from April 1949 until September 1950, when it re-formed at Langley AFB, moving to Shaw AFB in April 1951. The unit operated a variety of tactical reconnaissance types including the RB-45C, RB-57A, B-57E, EB-66B/C/E, RF-84F,

RF-101A/C, RT-33A and RF-4C, before being redesignated to Tactical Fighter Wing status in October 1981. The 363rd converted to the F-16A in April 1982, with one squadron of RF-4Cs retained until September 1989. Equipment was upgraded to the F-16C in March 1985. Two squadrons of F-16Cs deployed to Al Dafra AB, Sharjah, UAE, for Desert Storm. Designation changed to 363rd FW by October 1991.

The 17th FS is known as the 'Hooters', and wear the name on the fin-stripe. Other 363rd squadrons are the 19th 'Gamecocks' and 33rd 'Falcons'.

366th Fighter Wing
ACC Mountain Home AFB, ID:
EF/F-111A ('MO')
389th/391st Fighter Squadrons
390th Electronic Combat
Squadron

The unit was activated as the 366th Fighter-Bomber Wing at Alexandria AFB (later England AFB), LA, in January 1953 with the F-51D initially, but immediately began conversion to F-86s. The wing added F-84Fs in 1954 and an air-refueling capability with the KB-29P, which was later replaced by the KB-50J in 1957. Equipment was upgraded to the F-100D in 1957 and designation changed to 366th TFW in July 1958. The wing was inactivated in April 1959, but reorganized at Chaumont AB, France, in May 1962, acquiring the Air National Guard F-84Fs which remained in Europe when the mobilized squadrons were returned to state

control. The wing returned to the USA for assignment to Holloman AFB in July 1963 and operated the F-84F for a further two years, alongside the F-100. The 366th commenced conversion to the F-4C in 1965 and moved to Phan Rang AB, South Vietnam, in March 1966. The unit transferred north to Da Nang AB in exchange for the 35th TFW which moved to Phan Rang AB. The wing was relocated to Takhli RTAFB, Thailand, in June 1972 for four months prior to assignment to Mountain Home AFB, replacing the 347th TFW and equipping with the F-111F. The 366th received F-111As in July 1977 and EF-111As in November 1981. The EF-111As were deployed to Taif, Saudi Arabia, and assigned to the 48th TFW (Provisional) for Desert Storm.

The EF-111As of the 366th Fighter Wing are shortly to move to Cannon to join the 27th FW.

374th Airlift Wing
PACAF Yokota AB, Japan: C-9A,
C-130E/H
20th Aeromedical Airlift
Squadron
345th Tactical Airlift Squadron
1403rd Military Airlift Squadron

The unit was formed as the 374th Troop Carrier Wing in August 1948 at Harmon AFB, Guam, with C-54s. The 374th moved to Tachikawa AB, Japan, in March 1949, acquiring the C-46, C-47, C-119 and C-124 until inactivated in July 1957. The wing was reactivated at Naha AB, Okinawa, in August

1966 with the C-130A and upgraded to the C-130E when the wing moved to Ching Chuan Kang AB, Taiwan, in May 1971. The unit was relocated to Clark AB, Philippines, in November 1973 and to Yokota AB, Japan, in September 1989. Some of the 374th's aircraft were deployed to Thumrait, Oman, for Desert Storm. The wing changed designation to 374th Airlift Wing at the end of 1991.

The 374th AW provides airlift duties in the PACAF region. Among its duties is flying an air ambulance service using the C-9A.

375th Airlift Wing
AMC Scott AFB, IL: C-9A, C-12F, C-21A
11th Aeromedical Airlift Squadron
1375th/1400th/1401st/1402nd Military Airlift Squadrons

The unit was established as the 375th Troop Carrier Wing in June 1949 at Greater Pittsburgh Apt, PA, as a Reserve unit operating C-46s and C-82s alongside a mix of trainer types. The wing was called to active duty in October 1950 and stationed at Greenville AFB (later Donaldson AFB), SC, until July 1952, when it returned to Reserve status. The unit converted to C-119s before inactivating in November 1957. The 375th was reactivated as an Aeromedical Airlift Wing at Scott AFB in January 1966, replacing the 1405th Aeromedical Transport Wing. The unit operated C-118As and C-131As from 1966, plus the C-121G in 1968 when the Pennsylvania ANG was mobilized. The former two types were replaced by the

C-9A in 1968. In April 1975 the wing gained responsibility for numerous VIP squadrons and detachments located across the USA. These dets and squadrons were formerly assigned to the major commands to provide transportation for senior officers and were equipped with the CT-39A but converted to C-12F and C-21A in 1984 and 1985.

Above right: Large numbers of C-21As serve with the 375th Airlift Wing, detached to various USAF bases to provide staff transport for major headquarters.

Right: The 11th AAS is the main CONUS aeromedical unit, operating the C-9A. The interior is equipped to handle all but the most serious medical cases.

379th Wing
ACC/AMC Wurtsmith AFB, MI: B-52G, KC-135A
524th Bomb Squadron
920th Air Refueling Squadron

The unit was formed as the 379th Bombardment Wing at Homestead AFB in November 1955, operating the B-47E and KC-97G. The wing moved to Wurtsmith AFB in January 1961 and converted to the KC-135A and B-52H, becoming the first SAC

unit to receive the final version of the Stratofortress. The 379th switched to B-52Gs by 1980. The wing won SAC's Proud Shield bombing and navigation competition in 1987. Designation changed to the 379th Wing in October 1991. The wing is due to inactivate in 1993 with the B-52s retired and KC-135s transferred elsewhere.

Seen on a Desert Storm mission, this B-52G displays the 379th's 'Triangle K' insignia.

380th Wing
AMC Plattsburgh AFB, NY: KC-135A/Q
310th/380th Air Refueling Squadrons

The unit was established as the 380th Bombardment Wing at Plattsburgh AFB in July 1955 with the B-47E and KC-97G. EB-47s were added in July 1962. The wing re-equipped with KC-135As in 1964 and B-52Gs in 1966. A mix of the KC-135A and Q models was assigned. B-52s were operated until July 1971 when the wing converted to

the FB-111A, the training role being transferred from Carswell AFB in December 1971. The wing won SAC's Proud Shield bombing and navigation competition an unprecedented five times in 1974, 1976, 1977, 1978 and 1984. The FB-111A was retired from service in July 1991 when the unit was redesignated the 380th ARW, although this title was changed to 380th Wing three months later.

The 380th Wing operates the KC-135Q aircraft, formerly dedicated to support of the SR-71.

384th Wing
ACC/AMC McConnell AFB, KS: B-1B, KC-135R
28th Bomb Squadron
384th Air Refueling Squadron

The unit was formed as the 384th Bombardment Wing at Little Rock AFB in August 1955 with the B-47E. KC-97Gs were added in 1961 and replaced by KC-135As in 1964, before the unit was inactivated in September 1964. The 384th was redesignated an ARW and activated at McConnell AFB in December 1972 equipped with the KC-135A. The wing upgraded to the KC-135R during the latter half of 1985 as the first unit to receive the modified tanker.

Badge of the 384th (Bomb) Wing.

Designation reverted to Bombardment Wing status in July 1987, with the B-1B assigned in 1988, and changed to 384th Wing in October 1991.

A single squadron operates the B-1B within the 384th Wing. All wing aircraft carry the 'Keepers of the Plains' fin logo.

388th Fighter Wing
ACC Hill AFB, UT: F-16C/D ('HL')
4th/34th/421st Fighter Squadrons

The unit was created as the 388th Fighter-Day Wing at Clovis AFB, NM, in November 1953 with F-86s, before relocating to Etain/Rouvres AB, France, in December 1954. The wing converted to F-100s but was inactivated in December 1957 when it was replaced by the 49th FBW. The unit was re-formed as the 388th TFW at McConnell AFB in October 1962 with the F-100 assigned initially, and the F-105D operated from 1963. The wing was inactivated in February 1964 when replaced by the 23rd TFW. The 388th was reactivated at Korat RTAFB, Thailand, in April 1966 with a mix of combat types including the F-105D. The wing converted to the F-4E in 1969 and added EB-66C/Es in

1970, F-105Gs in 1971, EC-130Es in 1972, A-7Ds in 1973, and AC-130Hs and F-4Ds in 1974. EC-121Rs were assigned briefly from the end of 1970 and into 1971. The wing ceased operations in November 1975 and moved to Hill AFB one month later, operating the F-4D. The 388th converted to the F-16A in January 1979, upgrading to the F-16C in May 1989. The wing was the winner of the Gunsmoke competition at Nellis AFB in 1983. Two squadrons were deployed to Al Minhad AB, UAE, for service with 388th TFW (Provisional) during Desert Storm. Designation changed to the 388th FW by October 1991.

Hill's 388th FW was the first front-line unit anywhere to adopt the F-16, and it is still flying the aircraft 13 years later, albeit in upgraded F-16C/D form.

403rd Airlift Wing
AFRes Keesler AFB, MS: C-130H, WC-130E/H
815th Airlift Squadron

The unit was established as the 403rd Troop Carrier Wing at Portland IAP, OR, in June 1949, operating a mix of C-46s and trainers. The 403rd was mobilized in April 1951 and moved to Ashiya AB, Japan, one year later operating the VC-47, C-54 and C-119. The wing was returned to Reserve service in January 1953 and moved to Selfridge AFB in November 1957. Designation changed to 403rd TAW in July 1967, then to 403rd Composite Wing in December 1969 with the

A-37B, O-2A and U-3A assigned, before re-equipping with the C-130A and reverting to 403rd TAW in July 1971. The 403rd became an Aerospace Rescue & Recovery Wing in March 1976 with the HC-130H/N, HH-1N and CH/HH-3C/E, the WC-130B being added when the unit became the 403rd Rescue & Weather Reconnaissance Wing in January 1977. The unit moved to Keesler AFB in 1984 and changed to 403rd TAW in 1987 with the assignment of the C-130E alongside the WC-130E/H. The wing is responsible for a C-130E group located at Minneapolis St Paul IAP, MN.

The USAF's small WC-130 weather reconnaissance fleet is entrusted to the 403rd AW.

410th Wing
ACC/AMC K. I. Sawyer AFB, MI: B-52H, KC-135A
46th/307th Air Refueling Squadrons
644th Bomb Squadron

The unit was established as the 410th Bombardment Wing at K. I. Sawyer AFB in February 1963 with the B-52H and KC-135A assigned, and has operated the two types subsequently. The 410th BW replaced the 4042nd Strategic Wing. Designation

changed to 410th Wing in October 1991. The wing is due to exchange their B-52Hs for the B-52G late in 1993, with a further influx of G models in 1995 consolidating all conventionally-armed Stratofortresses on one base.

410th Wing aircraft carry a rainbow on the fin, although this has been toned down on dark gray-painted B-52s and KC-135s. Far right is the patch of the 644th BS, which flies the B-52H.

416th Wing
ACC/AMC Griffiss AFB, NY: B-52G, KC-135R
41st Air Refueling Squadron
668th Bomb Squadron

The unit was formed as the 416th Bombardment Wing at Griffiss AFB in February 1963, operating the B-52G and KC-135A and replacing the 4039th Strategic Wing. The G version of the Stratofortress has been operated ever since, while the KC-135R replaced the A version during 1990. Designation changed to 416th Wing in October 1991.

Badge of the 668th BS.

One of the more striking tail markings carried by B-52s is the 416th's Statue of Liberty, applied for the wing's home state.

419th Fighter Wing
AFRes Hill AFB, UT: F-16A/B ('HI')
466th Fighter Squadron

The unit was established as the 419th Troop Carrier Wing at Scott AFB in June 1949 with C-46s and a variety of trainer types, until May 1951 when it was inactivated. The wing was re-formed as the 419th TFW at Hill AFB in October 1982, with the F-105D/F operated until January 1984 when the 419th

converted to F-16A/Bs as the first Fighting Falcon unit in the AFRes. The wing won the Gunsmoke competition at Nellis AFB in 1987. The 419th is responsible for AFRes F-16 squadrons at Luke and Tinker AFBs.

Hill is in many ways 'F-16 Town', hosting an active-duty wing, the main maintenance center for the type and the 466th FS, which flies F-16As for 10th Air Force.

432nd Fighter Wing
PACAF Misawa AB, Japan: F-16C/D ('MJ')
13th/14th Fighter Squadrons

The unit was formed as the 432nd TRW at Shaw AFB in February 1958, operating the RF-84F and RF-101A/C, but was inactivated in June 1959. The 432nd was reactivated at Udorn RTAFB, Thailand, in September 1966 with the F-4C and RF-4C. Several stateside F-4E and one F-4D squadrons were temporarily assigned during 1972. The unit was redesignated the 432nd TFW in November 1974 with the F-4E, until December 1975 when the unit was inactivated. The 432nd was redesignated a Tactical Drone Group at Davis-Monthan AFB in July 1976 with drone assets from the 355th TFW (TAC) and 100th SRW (SAC), including DC-130A/E and AQM-34 drones.

The group was inactivated in April 1979, but was redesignated 432nd TFW and re-formed at Misawa AB in July 1984, with the F-16A assigned in April 1985. The wing upgraded to the F-16C/D in July 1986 and became the 432nd Fighter Wing mid-1991.

Based in northern Japan, the F-16C/Ds of the 432nd Fighter Wing are close to a large concentration of CIS airfields. The wing has two squadrons, the 13th FS 'Panthers' with black/white checkerboard fin stripe, and the 14th FS (illustrated) with black/yellow fins.

433rd Airlift Wing
AFRes Kelly AFB, TX: C-5A
68th Airlift Squadron

The unit was established as the 433rd Troop Carrier Wing at Cleveland MAP, OH, in June 1949, with the C-46 and a mix of trainers. The wing saw active service in October 1950 at Greenville AFB (later Donaldson AFB), SC, and Rhein-Main AB, Germany, with the C-119, until July 1952 when it was returned

to Reserve duty and inactivated. The 433rd was re-formed at Brooks AFB, TX, in May 1955 with C-46s, converting to C-119s in 1957 and the C-124C in 1963, until 1972. The wing moved to Kelly AFB in November 1960 and was redesignated the 433rd TAW in July 1967 before changing to 433rd MAW in

July 1969. C-130Bs were delivered in June 1971 when the unit became the 433rd TAW. The 433rd converted to C-5As in mid-1985 when it again became an MAW. The wing is responsible for just one squadron at present and was mobilized for Desert Shield/Desert Storm in late 1990/early 1991.

434th Air Refueling Wing

AFRes Grissom AFB, IN: KC-135E
72nd Air Refueling Squadron
78th Air Refueling Squadron (Associate)
79th Air Refueling Group (Associate)

The unit was created as the 434rd Troop Carrier Wing at Atterbury AFB, IN, in July 1949, with the C-46 and C-47 plus a number of trainers. The 434th was mobilized in May 1951 and moved to Lawson AFB, GA, in January 1952, until returned to Reserve service in February 1953. The wing returned to Atterbury AFB (later Bakalar AFB) in

February 1953 and re-equipped with C-119s in 1957 and U-3As in 1969. The unit was redesignated the 434th TAW in July 1967 and was inactivated in December 1969. The 434th was re-formed as an SOW at Grissom AFB in January 1971 with the O-2A and A-37B, plus, briefly, responsibility for a C-124C unit in 1972. The unit changed to 434th TFW in October 1973 with the A-10A assigned in June 1981. The wing was redesignated the 434th ARefW in 1987 with the KC-135E and responsibility for two KC-10A Associate Groups at Barksdale and Seymour Johnson AFBs.

Identified by its blue fin stripe, the 72nd ARS is one of three AFRes KC-135E units.

435th Airlift Wing

USAFE Rhein Main AB, Germany: C-9A, C-130E
37th Airlift Squadron
55th Aeromedical Airlift Squadron

The 435th Troop Carrier Wing was formed at Miami IAP, FL, in June 1949 as a Reserve unit with the C-46, until mobilized from March 1951 until December 1952. The 435th returned to Reserve status and re-equipped with C-119. The unit moved to Homestead AFB in July 1960 and converted to the C-124. The wing was mobilized again from October 1961 until August 1962, then inactivated in December 1965. The 435th was redesignated a Military Airlift Support Wing at RAF High Wycombe, UK, in December 1968 without aircraft assigned. The unit moved to Rhein Main AB, Germany, in July 1969 and upgraded to the

435th TAW in July 1975 to control an airlift and an aeromedical evacuation squadron located at Rhein Main. The 37th TAS deployed 15 C-130Es to Al Ain, Abu Dhabi, in August 1990 for Desert Shield/Storm. Under a proposed reorganization of MAC assets overseas, the unit will probably become part of USAFE. The wing changed designation to 435th Airlift Wing at the end of 1991.

Like its counterpart in PACAF, USAFE's main airlift unit not only flies the C-130 Hercules on general transport missions (above), but also has a C-9-equipped Aeromedical Airlift Squadron.

436th Airlift Wing

AMC Dover AFB, DE: C-5A/B
3rd/9th Airlift Squadrons

The unit was established as a Reserve unit as the 436th Troop Carrier Wing at Godman AFB, KY, in June 1949, with C-45s and C-47s. The 436th moved to Standiford MAP, KY, in October 1950 and was mobilized in April 1951, then inactivated immediately. The wing was re-formed in May 1955 with the C-45 and C-46 at NAS New York, NY, until inactivated again in May 1958. The 436th MAW was activated in January 1966 to replace the 1607th Air Transport Wing at Dover AFB when MATS changed to MAC.

The C-124C and C-133A were operated until the C-141A StarLifter commenced delivery in 1966, followed by the C-5A Galaxy in 1971. By mid-1973 the wing was equipped solely with the C-5, as their C-141s had been transferred elsewhere. The wing has won or has been joint winner of the Mackay Trophy for 'the most meritorious flight of the year' no fewer than three times, in 1977 (along with the 512th MAW (Associate)), 1978 and 1988. The unit changed to the 436th Airlift Wing in September 1991.

Seen in the now-rare white and gray scheme, this is a C-5A of the East Coast-based 436th AW, a regular visitor to European bases.

437th Airlift Wing

AMC Charleston AFB, SC: C-141B
17th/20th/41st/76th Airlift Squadrons

The 437th Troop Carrier Wing was formed at Chicago-Orchard Apt (later Chicago-O'Hare IAP), IL, in June 1949 with C-46s. The 437th was ordered to active service in August 1950 at Shaw AFB until returned to Reserve service in June 1952 at Chicago. While mobilized, the 437th was stationed in Japan. The wing operated C-119s until inactivated in June 1952. The 437th was redesignated an MAW and replaced the 1608th ATW in January 1966, equipped with the C-124C and C-130E, although the arrival of the C-141A in

1966 resulted in the other two types being relocated to other units. Three squadrons were operated initially and were joined by the 20th MAS in 1973. The unit was redesignated 437th AW in September 1991, and has been selected as the first operational wing to receive the C-17A, with the 17th AS scheduled to commence delivery by the end of FY 1992 with initial operating capability due in 1994.

Also on the East Coast, and again heavily involved in transatlantic transport missions, the 437th AW is equipped with the C-141B StarLifter.

438th Airlift Wing

AMC McGuire AFB, NJ: C-141B
6th/18th/30th Airlift Squadrons

The unit was established as a Reserve unit as the 438th Troop Carrier Wing at Offutt AFB in May 1949 with the C-46, until mobilized in March 1951. The wing was redesignated the 438th Fighter-Bomber Wing in May 1952 but returned to Reserve service, operating the C-46 and F-51

followed by the F-80 and F-86. The wing moved to General Mitchell Field, WI, in June 1952 and Milwaukee Apt, WI, in January 1953, until inactivated in November 1957. The 438th was established as an MAW in January 1966 to replace the 1611th ATW, operating the C-130E and C-135A/B. C-141Bs entered service in 1967, the C-135As being reassigned to TAC and the C-135s allocated to various Commands for VIP and test duties.

439th Airlift Wing

AFRes Westover AFB, MA: C-5A
337th Airlift Squadron

The unit was formed as the 439th Troop Carrier Wing in May 1949 at Selfridge AFB, MI, with trainers including the TC-46. The wing was mobilized in April 1951 and redesignated the 439th Fighter-Bomber Wing in May 1952 with the C-46 and T-28, and later the F-51, T-33, F-80, F-84 and F-86. The 439th returned to Reserve service in

June 1952 and was inactivated in November 1957. The wing was re-formed as 439th TAW at Westover AFB, MA, in March 1974, operating the C-123K and C-130B. C-130Bs were replaced by C-130Es in 1982. In 1987 the 439th was redesignated an MAW with the assignment of the C-5A. The unit was mobilized for Desert Shield/Desert Storm operations in late 1990/early 1991. The wing is responsible for two groups located at Greater Pittsburgh IAP, PA, with C-130Hs and Niagara Falls IAP, NY, with C-130Es.

Operating from McGuire AFB in New Jersey, the 438th Airlift Wing has flown the C-141 since 1967. Three active-duty squadrons are assigned, and are augmented by the Reserve's 514th AW Associate unit.

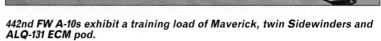

440th Airlift Wing
AFRes Gen Mitchell Fd, WI: C-130H
95th Airlift Squadron

The unit was established as the 440th Troop Carrier Wing at Wold-Chamberlain MAP (later Minneapolis-St Paul IAP), MN, in June 1949 with C-46s and various trainers. The 440th was activated for operational duty in May 1951 and redesignated a Fighter-Bomber Wing in June 1952, moving to Fort Snelling, MN. The unit returned to Reserves with the F-51, T-33A and F-80 assigned. Designation reverted to 440th TCW in September 1957 with the C-119, and the wing moved to General Mitchell Field, WI, two months later. The 440th converted to C-130As in January 1971 and upgraded to C-130Hs in 1989. The wing is responsible for a C-130E group at Selfridge ANGB and a C-130H group at Chicago-O'Hare IAP.

This 95th AS C-130H carries the legend 'Spirit of Wisconsin' on the nose.

442nd FW A-10s exhibit a training load of Maverick, twin Sidewinders and ALQ-131 ECM pod.

442nd Fighter Wing
AFRes Richards Gebaur AFB, MO: A-10A ('KC')
303rd Fighter Squadron

The unit was formed as the 442nd Troop Carrier Wing in June 1949 at Fairfax Field, KS, with the C-46 and various trainers. The 442nd was relocated to NAS Olathe, KS, in May 1950 until mobilized in March 1951, and was inactivated immediately. The wing returned to Reserve service when it re-formed in June 1952 with C-46s. The unit moved to Grandview AFB (later Richards Gebaur AFB), MO, and was called to active duty again in October 1961 with the C-124 assigned. The wing returned to Reserve duty and was redesignated 442nd Air Transport Wing in December 1965, before changing to 442nd MAW one month later. The 442nd changed designation to a TAW in June 1971 when the C-130A was assigned. Equipment was upgraded to the C-130E mid-1975 and converted to the A-10A mid-1982, with the unit changing to 442nd TFW. The wing has the responsibility for an A-10A group at Grissom AFB.

443rd Airlift Wing
AMC Altus AFB, OK: C-5B, C-141B
56th/57th Airlift Squadrons

The unit was established as the 443rd Troop Carrier Wing in May 1949 at Hensley Field, TX, as a Reserve unit, with C-46s and a mix of trainers. The 443rd was mobilized in May 1951 and moved to Donaldson AFB, SC, between August 1951 and January 1953, when it was inactivated. The wing was assigned to MAC and redesignated the 443rd MAW at Tinker AFB in January 1966, replacing the 1707th ATW and conducting aircrew training with C-124C until 1968, and the C-141A. The wing moved to Altus AFB in May 1969 and added the C-5A later in the year. Equipment was upgraded to the C-141B in 1980 and the C-5B in January 1986. The wing won Volant Rodeo, the forerunner of Airlift Rodeo, at Pope AFB in 1979. Designation changed to 443rd Airlift Wing in September 1991.

The Altus airlift wing has both C-141s and C-5Bs (illustrated) on charge.

445th Airlift Wing (Associate)
AFRes Norton AFB, CA: C-141B
728th/729th/730th Airlift Squadrons (Associate)

The unit was formed as the 445th Fighter-Bomber Wing at Buffalo, NY, in July 1952, with the F-51 and T-6. The 445th converted to the F-80 and F-84 and moved to Niagara Falls MAP, NY, in June 1955, before being redesignated 445th TCW in September 1957. The wing moved to Dobbins AFB, GA, in November 1957, with the C-45 and TC-47. The 445th operated a variety of types including the C-47, C-117, VC-117 and U-3. The unit was redesignated 445th Air Transport Wing in December 1965 before changing to 445th MAW one month later. The wing flew the VC-47, VT-29 and HU-16 before being inactivated in June 1971. The 445th was redesignated an MAW (Associate) at Norton AFB in July 1973 with three Associate squadrons operating front-line C-141Bs of the 63rd MAW (now 63rd AW) in place of front-line crews.

446th Airlift Wing (Associate)
AFRes McChord AFB, WA: C-141B
97th/313th Airlift Squadrons (Associate)

The unit was established as the 446th Troop Carrier Wing at Ellington AFB, TX, in May 1955, with C-45s and C-46s. The 446th converted to the C-119 before being redesignated 446th TAW in July 1967, and re-equipping with the C-130A March 1968. A pair of RC-130Ss was assigned between 1970 and 1972, with the C-124C operated from 1971. The wing was inactivated in July 1972, but was redesignated 446th MAW (Associate) and reactivated at McChord AFB in July 1973, with two Associate squadrons performing duties similar to the 445th MAW (A).

452nd Air Refueling Wing
AFRes March AFB, CA: KC-10A, KC-135E
336th Air Refueling Squadron
79th Air Refueling Squadron (Associate)

The unit was formed as the 452nd Bombardment Wing at Long Beach MAP, CA, in June 1949, with the B-26. The 452nd was mobilized in August 1950 and relocated to George AFB before serving in the Far East until May 1952, when it was returned to Reserve service. The wing was redesignated 452nd TRW in June 1952 with B-26s and F-80s, before reverting to 452nd BW in May 1955. The unit converted to the C-46 and C-119 as the 452nd Troop Carrier Wing, moving to March AFB in October 1960. The 452nd re-equipped with C-124s in 1965 as the 452nd ATW/MAW and moved to Hamilton AFB, CA, in January 1972. The unit became the 452nd TAW in April 1972 when the C-130B was assigned. The wing moved to March AFB in January 1976 when it was redesignated 452nd ARefW, with the KC-135A assigned. Equipment was upgraded to the KC-135E during 1985. The wing was initially responsible for three KC-135 squadrons, but a reorganization of assets in 1987 resulted in one squadron transferring to the 434th ARefW and being replaced by a KC-10A (Associate) unit.

Based at March AFB, the 452nd ARW not only has a directly-assigned KC-135E squadron (with orange fin-stripe), but also an Associate KC-10 squadron flying active-duty aircraft of the 22nd Wing.

459th Airlift Wing
AFRes Andrews AFB, MD: C-141B
756th Airlift Squadron

The unit was formed as the 459th Troop Carrier Wing at Andrews AFB in January 1955, with the C-45 and C-46. The 459th changed to the C-119 in 1957 and the C-124C when the unit became an MAW in July 1966. The wing converted to the C-130A and became the 459th TAW in June 1971. Equipment was upgraded to C-130Bs briefly in 1974 and the C-130E in 1975. The 459th re-equipped with the C-141B late in 1986, as the first and, so far, only AFRes StarLifter unit, changing to 459th MAW again. The wing is responsible for two C-130E groups located at NAS Willow Grove, PA, and Rickenbacker ANGB, OH.

463rd Airlift Wing
AMC Dyess AFB, TX: C-130H
772nd/773rd Airlift Squadrons

The unit was established as the 463rd Troop Carrier Wing at Memphis MAP, TN, in January 1953, with the C-46 and C-119. The 463rd moved to Ardmore AFB, OK, eight months later and re-equipped with the C-130A in December 1956 as the first operational Hercules unit. The wing moved to Sewart AFB, TN, in January 1959 and upgraded to the C-130B in early 1961. The 463rd relocated to Langley AFB in July 1963 before moving to Mactan Isle Afd, Philippines, in November 1965. The unit was

redesignated 463rd TAW in July 1967 and transferred to Clark AB, Philippines, in July 1968. The 463rd returned to the USA in June 1972 for assignment to Dyess AFB with the C-7A and C-130E. Caribous were operated for one year only and the C-130E was exchanged for the C-130H during 1975. Many of the wing's aircraft were deployed to the Middle East for Desert Storm. The wing changed designation to 463rd Airlift Wing at the end of 1991.

The 463rd Airlift Wing shares its Dyess base with the B-1Bs and KC-135s of the 96th Wing. It is equipped with the C-130H.

475th Air Base Wing
PACAF Yokota AB, Japan: UH-1N

The unit was formed as the 475th Fighter Wing at Itazuke AB, Japan, in August 1948 with the F-51, until inactivated in April 1949. The wing was redesignated 475th TFW at Misawa AB, Japan, and activated in January 1968 with F-4Cs and F-4Ds, with the RF-4C added in 1970. The wing's assets were transferred to the 3rd TFW in March 1971 when the 475th was inactivated. The unit was re-formed as the 475th Air Base Wing,

replacing the 6100th Air Base Wing, with the C-130B-II of the 347th TFW operated briefly before that version of the Hercules was transferred to USAFE. The wing assumed the VIP and support roles for HQ 5th Air Force, operating a variety of types including the C-54, VC-118A, T-29, T-33A, CT-39A and UH-1P before upgrading to the UH-1N.

Since formation in the early 1970s, the 475th ABW has operated a variety of types in the VIP/staff transport role.

475th Weapons Evaluation Group
ACC Tyndall AFB, FL: E-9A, QF-106A/B
82nd Tactical Aerial Targets Squadron

The Weapons Evaluation Group was formed in October 1983 as the primary operator of the variety of target drones employed by the Air Defense Weapons Center. Three squadrons were assigned to the group, with the 82nd Tactical Aerial Targets Squadron operating the QF-100D/F and, more recently,

the QF-106A/B, alongside BQM-34A Firebee and MQM-107B/D Streaker target drones. The drones are employed as practice targets for pilots transitioning to the intercept role and for qualified pilots attending exercises at Tyndall. The intention is for pilots to score a

near miss, enabling the drone to be recovered and reused. In addition, the 81st Range Control Squadron and 83rd Fighter Weapons Squadron are assigned to the group. The two de Havilland Canada E-9A Dash 8M aircraft are operated by the 475th WEG.

In addition to specialized drones, the 475th operates the QF-106.

Badge of the 475th WEG, alluding to the drone mission.

482nd Fighter Wing
AFRes Homestead AFB, FL: F-16A/B ('FM')
93rd Fighter Squadron

The unit was established as the 482nd Troop Carrier Wing at Miami IAP, FL, in June 1952, with C-46s, for just six months before being inactivated. The wing was re-formed as the 482nd Fighter-Bomber Wing at Dobbins AFB, GA, in May 1955, operating the F-84 and T-33, before converting to the

F-86 until the wing was inactivated in November 1957. The 482nd was redesignated a TFW in April 1981 at Homestead AFB with the F-4C, replacing the 915th TFG. Equipment was upgraded to the F-4D in September 1983 and changed to the F-16A in July 1989. The wing is also

responsible for an F-16A group at Wright Patterson AFB.

507th Air Control Wing
ACC Shaw AFB, SC: OA-10A ('SF')
21st Fighter Squadron

The unit was created as the 507th Tactical Control Group at Shaw AFB in March 1954, but with no aircraft assigned. The wing was redesignated 507th Communications Control Group and later Tactical Air Control Group in June 1974, replacing the 68th Tactical Air

Support Group. CH-3Es, O-2As and OV-10As were operated. Designation changed to the 507th Tactical Air Control Wing. O-2As were replaced by OT-37Bs in March 1986, then OV-10As in April 1988. The unit changed to the 507th Air Control Wing in September 1991 and began re-equipping with the OA-10A one month later.

Previously flying OV-10 Broncos, the Shaw FAC wing is now equipped with the Fairchild OA-10A.

507th Fighter Group
AFRes Tinker AFB, OK: F-16A/B ('SH')
465th Fighter Squadron

The group was established at Tinker AFB in May 1972 as the controlling element of the 465th TFS, with the F-105D assigned. The 507th was inactive between March 1973

and October 1975. The group re-equipped with the F-4D in October 1980 and the F-16A exactly eight years later.

The 'SH' tailcode of the 507th TFG is said to stand for the fighter pilot's favorite saying: 'Shit Hot!'

512th Airlift Wing (Associate)

AFRes Dover AFB, DE: C-5A/B
326th/709th Airlift Squadrons (Associate)

The unit was formed as the 512th Troop Carrier Wing at Reading MAP, PA, in September 1949, with the C-46 and some trainer types. The wing moved to New Castle County Apt, DE, in April 1951 until it was mobilized in March 1951. The 512th returned to Reserve control in November 1952, converted to the C-119 in 1957 and relocated to NAS Willow Grove, PA, in July 1958. The wing transferred to Carswell AFB and was redesignated 512th Air Transport Wing in January 1965, with the C-124 assigned. The 512th became an MAW in January 1966 and was inactivated June 1971.

The unit was re-formed as the 512th MAW (Associate) at Dover AFB in July 1973, providing Reservist personnel to operate front-line C-5A/Bs on a regular basis. The wing was a joint winner, with 436th MAW, of the Mackay Trophy for 'the most meritorious flight of the year' for 1977.

513th Airborne Command and Control Wing

USAFE RAF Mildenhall, UK: EC-135H, WC-135B
10th Airborne Command and Control Squadron

The unit was created as the 513th Troop Carrier Group at Rhein Main AB, Germany, in November 1948, with C-47s and C-54s for duty during the Berlin Airlift. The 513th was inactivated shortly after the airlift ended, to be re-formed in November 1955 as the 513th Troop Carrier Group at Sewart AFB, TN, operating the C-123B. The unit was upgraded to Wing level in September 1957 until being inactivated in December 1958.

The wing was re-formed at Evreux-Fauville AB, France, in April 1966 to conduct the relocation of rotational C-130 operations from France to RAF Mildenhall, taking up residence at the latter in July 1966. Designation was changed to 513th TAW in July 1967. The wing operated the C-130A, B, E and H models on temporary duty from the USA until 1976, when the 313th TAG assumed this duty. EC-135Hs were assigned from 1966 as European Command airborne command post until mid-1991, when the type commenced retirement. Mobilized AFRes C-124C units were assigned from July 1968 until May 1969 under the 1648th MAS (Provisional). The wing was redesignated the 513th Airborne Command and Control Wing in June 1987. The 513th was inactivated in January 1992, when the 100th ARefW was formed.

514th Airlift Wing (Associate)

AFRes McGuire AFB, NJ: C-141B
335th/702nd/732nd Airlift Squadrons (Associate)

The unit was formed as the 514th Troop Carrier Wing at Birmingham MAP, AL, in June 1949, with the C-46 and a mixture of trainer types. The 514th moved to Mitchel AFB, NY, in October 1949 and was mobilized in May 1951. The wing converted to C-119s in 1952 and was inactivated briefly between February and April 1953, when it then returned to Reserve control, re-forming at Mitchel AFB. The 514th relocated to McGuire AFB in March 1961 and re-equipped with C-124Cs in 1966. The unit was redesignated 514th TAW in July 1967 before becoming the 514th MAW (Associate) in September 1968 as the first associate unit. The wing initially provided Reservist personnel for the C-9A, C-141A and C-5A at MAC bases within the 21st Air Force region, although additional associate units at Dover, Charleston and Scott AFBs enabled the 514th to concentrate on StarLifter operations at McGuire.

Badge of the 514th AW(A).

542nd Crew Training Wing

AMC Kirtland AFB, NM: HC-130N/P, HH-3E, TH-53A, MH-53J, MH-60G
1550th/1551st Flying Training Squadrons

The 542nd Crew Training Wing formed in October 1991 to replace the 1550th ATTW and 1606th ABW. The wing is responsible for training aircrew for rescue and special operations duties.

Training for the Special Operations and air rescue squadrons is undertaken by the 542nd CTW. Among the types on charge is the Sikorsky HH-60G Pave Hawk.

552nd Air Control Wing

ACC Tinker AFB, OK: E-3B/C
8th Tactical Deployment and Control Squadron
960th/963rd/964th/965th Airborne Warning and Control Squadrons
966th Airborne Warning and Control Training Squadron

The unit was created as the 552nd Airborne Early Warning and Control Wing at McClellan AFB in March 1955, with a variety of EC- and RC-121s operated until 1976. The unit was redesignated to Group status in July 1974 until it was inactivated in April 1976. The 552nd was reformed as an AW&CW at Tinker AFB in July 1976 in readiness for the assignment of the E-3 Sentry. EC-130Es were operated from October 1976. The unit upgraded to Division standard in October 1983 until the formation of the 28th Air Division in April 1985, when it reverted to 552nd AW&CW.

The 552nd Air Control Wing operated all of the USAF's E-3 Sentries, although some are now detached to PACAF and, in the future, USAFE. The wing undertakes its own training, and comes under control of the 28th Air Division.

602nd Air Control Wing

ACC Davis-Monthan AFB, AZ: OA-10A ('NF')
333rd/354th Fighter Squadrons

The unit was created as the 602nd Tactical Control Group at Bergstrom AFB in April 1966, but with no aircraft assigned. The 602nd was redesignated a Tactical Air Control Group in June 1974, replacing the 71st Tactical Air Support Group. CH-53Cs and O-2As were operated. Designation changed to 602nd Tactical Air Control Wing in October 1976. The wing relocated to Davis-Monthan AFB in September 1982. The O-2As were retired in July 1980. One squadron of OV-10As was located at George AFB from May 1984 until June 1990, while a second squadron operated the Bronco from October 1988 until December 1990. OA-37Bs were assigned from May 1981 until March 1988, when the wing re-equipped with the OA-10A. The unit changed to 602nd Air Control Wing in September 1991. The 602nd was inactivated in April 1992, when the 355th FW assumed control of the front-line flying operations at Davis-Monthan AFB.

The OA-10s of the 602nd ACW have now amalgamated with the 355th Fighter Wing.

603rd Air Support Group
AMC Kadena AB, Okinawa: C-12F
13th Airlift Squadron

The group was formed to provide facilities for MAC aircraft delivering cargo and personnel to Okinawa. A MAC squadron is stationed at Kadena, operating the C-12F since 1984.

608th Airlift Group
USAFE Ramstein AB, Germany: C-12F, C-20A, C-21A, C-135B, UH-1N, CT-43A
58th Airlift Squadron

The group was organized during the early 1980s to replace the 435th TAW as the controlling unit for the 58th MAS. The unit was tasked with conducting VIP and communications duties within USAFE, employing a variety of aircraft types. A 58th MAS C-20A was assigned to General Norman Schwarzkopf for operations within the Middle East during Desert Storm.

A mix of types is flown by the 58th AS for transport duties. Here is a C-20A.

611th Air Support Group
AMC Osan AB, RoK: C-12F
1403rd Airlift Squadron Det 3

The group was established to provide facilities for MAC aircraft delivering personnel and cargo to South Korea. A detachment is stationed at Osan, operating the C-12F since 1984.

616th Airlift Group
PACAF Elmendorf AFB, AK: C-12F, C-130H
517th Airlift Squadron

The group took charge of the 17th TAS operating C-130Es in April 1975, replacing the 21st TFW. The group upgraded to C-130Hs at the end of 1986, and added the C-12F assigned to detachment 1 during the mid-1980s. It is subordinate to the 3rd Wg.

624th Air Support Group
AMC Clark AB, Philippines: C-12F
1403rd Airlift Squadron Det 1

The group was formed to provide facilities for MAC aircraft delivering cargo and personnel to the Philippines. A detachment was stationed at Clark, operating the C-12F since 1984. However, US forces vacated Clark during mid-1991. The C-12F supported PACAF's HQ 13th Air Force, which has subsequently moved from Clark to Andersen AFB, Guam, and it is probable the detachment has moved eastwards also.

906th Fighter Group
AFRes Wright-Patterson AFB, OH: F-16A/B ('DO')
89th Fighter Squadron

The 906th TCG was assigned to the 302nd TCW in February 1963 with the C-119 and changed to the C-123K in 1971, until September 1975. The group re-formed at Wright-Patterson AFB in July 1982 with the 89th TFS flying the F-4D until October 1989, when the unit changed to the F-16A.

'DO' (for Dayton, Ohio) adorns the fins of the 906th FG's F-16As. The unit comes under control of the 482nd FW at Homestead.

907th Airlift Group
AFRes Rickenbacker ANGB, OH: C-130E
356th Airlift Squadron

The 907th TCG was assigned to the 302nd TCW in February 1963 with the C-119 until 1967, when designation changed to 907th TAW. The unit re-equipped with the C-123K in 1971, until September 1975. The group is responsible for the 356th TAS, which was transferred to the 302nd TAW until the early 1980s, when it was reassigned to the 94th TAW. The unit subsequently joined the 459th TAW operating the C-130A, and currently flies the C-130E.

A 459th AW subsidiary, the 907th AG flies C-130Es under 14th Air Force control.

908th Airlift Group
AFRes Maxwell AFB, AL: C-130H
357th Airlift Squadron

The group was assigned as the 908th TAG in April 1969 at Maxwell AFB and became the 908th TASG operating the O-2A until December 1971, when it reverted to TAG status with the C-7A. The group is responsible for the 357th TAS and was assigned to the 94th TAW in July 1972. The 908th converted to the C-130E in 1983 and upgraded to the C-130H in 1986.

Badge of the 908th AG.

910th Airlift Group
AFRes Youngstown MAP, OH: C-130H
757th Airlift Squadron

The group operated U-3As with the 757th TASS until it was redesignated 757th SOS/910th SOG in April 1971, operating the A-37B. Designation changed to 757th TFS in October 1973. The group was subordinate to the 434th TFW until April 1981, when it converted to C-130Bs and joined the 459th TAW. The 910th upgraded to C-130Es in 1989 and C-130Hs in 1991.

911th Airlift Group
AFRes Gtr Pittsburgh IAP, PA: C-130H
758th Airlift Squadron

The group operated the C-124C until it was redesignated 758th TAS/911th TAG in February 1972, with the C-123K assigned. The group was attached to the 302nd TAW until reassigned to the 439th MAW in 1980, re-equipping with the C-130A. The group upgraded to C-130Hs in 1987.

913th Airlift Group
AFRes NAS Willow Grove, PA: C-130E
327th Airlift Squadron

The group operated the C-119 until September 1970, when its 327th TAS converted to C-130As. The group was assigned to the 403rd TAW from April 1971 until January 1976, when it transferred to the 459th TAW. The 913th converted to the C-130E in January 1976. The group deployed to Thumrait, Oman, for Desert Storm and was assigned to the 1660th TAW (Provisional).

914th Airlift Group
AFRes Niagara Falls IAP, NY: C-130E
328th Airlift Squadron

The group operated C-119s until December 1970, when its 328th TAS converted to C-130As. The group was assigned to the 403rd TAW from April 1971 until January 1976, when it transferred to the 439th TAW. The group converted to the C-130E by mid-1976. The 914th deployed to Sharjah, UAE, for Desert Storm and was assigned to the 1650th TAW (Provisional).

916th Air Refueling Group (Associate)
AFRes Seymour Johnson AFB, NC: KC-10A
77th Air Refueling Squadron (Associate)

The group was re-formed as Associate status in 1987 to provide personnel to operate front-line KC-10As of the 68th ARW and, more recently, the 4th Wing at Seymour Johnson AFB. The group has the 77th ARS assigned, which is believed to be a unit new to AFRes.

USAF Units

917th Fighter Wing
AFRes Barksdale AFB, LA: A-10A ('BD')
46th Fighter Training Squadron
47th Fighter Squadron

The 917th SOG was assigned to the 434th SOW from February 1972 with the A-37B assigned until October 1973, when it changed to 917th TFG. The group converted to A-10As in October 1980 with the 47th TFS assigned. The 47th was joined by the 46th TFTS as an AFRes A-10 training unit in September 1983, with the 917th being upgraded to Wing standard in July 1987, replacing the 434th TFW.

The 917th FW has two squadrons of A-10s, acting as the type conversion unit for reserve forces.

919th Special Operations Group
AFRes Duke Field, FL: AC-130A
711th Special Operations Squadron

The 919th TAG/711th TAS was activated in July 1971 and assigned to the 459th TAW until December 1974, initially with the C-130A but upgraded to the C-130B in July 1973. The group converted to the AC-130A as the 919th SOG early in 1975 and operated without wing control until it was assigned to the 939th Air Rescue Wing in 1990.

The angel of death is fitting for the AC-130A-equipped 919th SOG, shortly to receive the AC-130H.

924th Fighter Group
AFRes Bergstrom AFB, TX: F-16A/B ('TX')
704th Fighter Squadron

The 924th TCG operated C-119s at Ellington AFB under control of the 446th TCW since January 1963. The group was redesignated 924th TAG in July 1967 and converted to C-130As in March 1968. The 704th and 705th TASs were both assigned to the group. The group transferred to the 433rd TAW in July 1972 and moved to Bergstrom AFB in 1976 when it upgraded to the C-130B. The training role was assigned to the 705th TATS in July 1972 until it was inactivated mid-1976. The group switched to the tactical fighter role in July 1981 with the 924th TFG assigned to the 482nd TFW, operating the F-4D. The unit upgraded to F-4Es in January 1989 and re-equipped with the F-16A/B in 1991.

The 'Outlaws' of the 924th FG proudly proclaim their Texan associations on their aircraft with the 'Lone Star' state flag and 'TX' tailcode.

926th Fighter Group
AFRes NAS New Orleans, LA: A-10A ('NO')
706th Fighter Squadron

The 926th TCG operated C-119s at NAS New Orleans under control of the 446th TCW since January 1963. The unit was redesignated 926th TAG in July 1967 and converted to C-130As in December 1969. The 926th was transferred to the 442nd TAW in July 1972 and converted to C-130Bs in November 1973, before converting to the A-37B in April 1978 as the 926th TFG. The 706th TFS was assigned to the 434th TFW. Equipment changed to the A-10A in January 1982.

The 926th FG deployed A-10s during Desert Storm, and one aircraft scored a cannon kill over an Iraqi helicopter.

927th Airlift Group
AFRes Selfridge ANGB, MI: C-130E
63rd Airlift Squadron

The 927th TCG has operated C-119s at Selfridge AFB under control of the 403rd TCW since February 1963. The unit was redesignated 927th TAG in July 1967 and converted to U-3As as the 927th TASG in 1969s. The group changed to 927th TAG in June 1971 when it re-equipped with C-130As. The group transferred to the 459th TAW in March 1976 until early 1985, when it moved to the 440th TAW and converted to C-130Es shortly afterwards. The 927th deployed to Sharjah, UAE, for Desert Storm and was assigned to 1650th TAW (Provisional).

The patch of the 927th AG highlights the paradrop role.

928th Airlift Group
AFRes Chicago-O'Hare IAP, IL: C-130H
64th Airlift Squadron

The group operated C-119s under the 403rd TCW from January 1963 until it was redesignated 928th TAG in July 1967. The group converted to C-130As in September 1970. The 928th transferred to the 440th TAW at the same time. Equipment changed to C-130Hs in 1988.

'City of Chicago' is proclaimed on the nose of this 928th AG C-130H, seen in flight over its home town. The unit has flown the Hercules since 1970.

930th Fighter Group
AFRes Grissom AFB, IN: A-10A ('IN')
45th Fighter Squadron

The unit was designated 930th SOG with the A-37B in July 1970 under 403rd Composite Wing, until January 1971 when it was transferred to the 434th SOW. The group was redesignated 930th TFG in September 1973 and converted to the A-10A in June 1981.

Patch of the 932nd AAG(A).

932nd Aeromedical Airlift Group (Associate)
**AFRes Scott AFB, IL: C-9A
73rd Aeromedical Airlift Squadron (Associate)**

The group operated the C-119 as the 932nd TCG between February 1963 and October 1966. The 932nd was re-formed in Associate status in 1973 to provide aircrew and medical staff to replace active Air Force personnel manning 375th AW C-9As.

934th Airlift Group
**AFRes Minneapolis St Paul IAP, MN: C-130E
96th Airlift Squadron**

The 934th TCG operated C-119s at Minneapolis St Paul under control of the 440th TCW since February 1963. The unit was redesignated 934th TAG in July 1967 and converted to the C-130A in December 1969. The 934th was transferred to the 442nd TAW in 1977 and the 433rd TAW in 1982. The group converted to C-130Es and transferred to the 403rd TAW.

The 934th AG is subordinate to the 403rd AW, which has its headquarters at Keesler AFB, Missouri.

939th Rescue Wing
**AFRes Davis-Monthan AFB, AZ: CH-3E
Portland IAP, OR: HC-130H/P, HH-3E
Homestead AFB, FL: HC-130H/N/P, HH-3E
Selfridge ANGB, MI: HC-130H/N/P, HH-3E**

**Duke Field, FL: AC-130A
71st Special Operations Squadron
301st/304th/305th Rescue Squadrons**

The wing was formed in 1991 as the controlling element for the three autonomous rescue units and the two Special Operations units.

This HC-130H is from the Selfridge-based 305th Rescue Squadron.

940th Air Refueling Group
**AFRes Mather AFB, CA: KC-135E
314th Air Refueling Squadron**

The group was assigned to the 452nd MAW at McClellan AFB with C-124Cs from January 1968 until April 1972, when it converted to C-130As, becoming the 940th TAG. Seven months later the group

upgraded to C-130Bs and switched to the air-refueling role with KC-135As, moving in October 1976 to Mather AFB. Equipment was upgraded to the KC-135E in 1985.

Reserve tanker units are equipped with the KC-135E and come under the control of the 10th Air Force. The 314th Air Refueling Squadron has a red fin-stripe.

943rd Airlift Group
**AFRes March AFB, CA: C-130B
303rd Airlift Squadron**

The group operated under the 452nd TCW from January 1963 to April 1969 with C-119s. The 943rd was re-formed as a TAG at March AFB under the 302nd TAW mid-1985 with C-130Bs.

The 943rd AG has a secondary firefighting role using the MAFFS equipment.

944th Fighter Group
**AFRes Luke AFB, AZ: F-16C/D ('LR')
302nd Fighter Squadron**

The group was re-formed in July 1987 as the controlling element of the 302nd TFS when the squadron converted from the CH-3E to the F-16C. The unit won the 1989 Gunsmoke competition at Nellis AFB.

First Reserve unit to receive the F-16C/D, the 302nd FS is known as the 'Sun Devils'.

3245th Air Base Group
AFMC Hanscom AFB, MA: no aircraft assigned

The 3245th Air Base Wing was formed in April 1960 to administer facilities at the base, with the Cambridge Research Laboratory established at the same time and the Electronics Systems Division activated 12 months later. No aircraft are assigned at present, although CRL and ESD have aircraft on loan from manufacturers and other AFSC departments when required. The 3245th changed to Group status in July 1964. ESD is currently involved in the evaluation of the E-8 Joint STARS program.

3246th Test Wing
**AFMC Eglin AFB, FL: F-4D/E, F-15A/B/C/D/E, F-16A/B/C, F-111E, F-117A, UH-1N, T-38A ('ET')
3247th Test Squadron**

The 3246th Test Wing was formed in July 1970 as the flying component of the Air Proving Ground Command (APGC) which was organized in July 1948. APGC subsequently changed title to Air Proving Ground Center (APGC), Armament Development & Test Center (ADTC),

Headquarters Armament Division and, more recently, the Air Force Development Test Center and Munitions Systems Division. The Center is responsible for evaluating new and developing existing aerospace weapons systems prior to their implementation to combat units.

A mixed fleet flies with the 3246th TW on weapons development and clearance work.

3300th Technical Training Wing

ATC Keesler AFB, MS: no aircraft assigned

The 3300th Technical Training Wing was activated in November 1979 as the administrative unit for ATC activities at Keesler AFB. No aircraft are assigned to the unit, which conducts courses on such diverse subjects as avionics, command and control systems, communications, computers, electronics and radar systems.

3400th Technical Training Wing

ATC Lowry AFB, CO: GA-7D, GA-10A, GB-1A, GB-52F, GF-4E, GF-15A, GF-16A/C, GF-111A

The 3400th Technical Training Unit formed in November 1979 as the operational unit for the Lowry TTC, responsible for training subjects including avionics, logistics, munitions and space operations. A small number of airframes are employed, varying in size from an A-7 Corsair II up to a B-52.

3700th Technical Training Wing

ATC Sheppard AFB, TX: GYA-10A, GA-10A, GB-52D/F/G, GC-130A/B/D, GNKC-135A, GF-4C/D/E, GRF-4C, GYF-15A, GF-16C, GF-101B, GF-111A, GUH-1F, GCH-3C, GT-37A, GT-38A, GAT-38B

The 3700th Technical Training Wing, activated in November 1979, is the operational component of the Sheppard TTC, which is the main aircraft maintenance training center with several dozen aircraft used as training aids. The base has been involved in technical training since 1942 and has enlisted hundreds of surplus aircraft types during its 50 years of operations. These include types which are no longer in operational service, such as the B-52D/F and F-101B. The G prefix of the aircraft is applied to indicate ground instruction duties.

4950th Test Wing

AFMC Wright-Patterson AFB, OH: C-18A, EC-18B/D, NKC-135A, EC-135E, NC-141A, CT-39A, NT-39A, T-39B
4951st/4952nd/4953rd Test Squadrons

The 4950th Test Wing was established in March 1971 as the flying unit of the Wright Air Development Center, which was created in June 1951. Wright ADC changed to Division status in December 1959 until it was replaced by Aeronautical Systems Division (ASD) in April 1961. The 4951st, 4952nd and 4953rd Test Squadrons were activated in July 1975. ASD is responsible for the design, development and acquisition of aeronautical systems including transports, tankers and utility aircraft, rescue helicopters, long- and short-range air-to-surface missiles, aircraft engines and simulators, plus reconnaissance and electronic warfare systems. In addition, the wing supports programs conducted by other AFMC departments. The majority of AFMC's large transport aircraft are assigned to the 4950th TW and are loaned to other agencies as required. The 4950th TW/ASD has operated a host of test C-135s, many of which have featured major modifications.

An important task of the 4950th Test Wing is range instrumentation using the Boeing EC-18B ARIA platform.

Assigned to the 4950th TW is an original short-body NC-141A StarLifter used for trials.

6510th Test Wing

AFMC Edwards AFB, CA: YA-7D, A-7K, OA-37B, NOA-37B, B-1B, B-2A, B-52G/H, C-17A, C-23A, MC-130H, AC-130U, NF-4C, NF-4E, YF-4E, F-15A, F-15E, F-16A/B/C, F-117A, UH-1N, T-38A ('ED')
6510th/6511th/6512th/6515th/6516th/6517th/6518th/6519th

Test Squadrons
Hill AFB, UT C-130B, DC-130A, HC-130H, NC-130H, NCH-53A
6514th Test Squadron

The 6510th Test Wing was reformed in March 1978 as the flying component of the Air Force Flight Test Center (AFFTC), which was organized in June 1951. The 6510th had existed since June 1951, initially as an Air Base Wing until November 1954, when it changed to Air Base Group status. The 6510th Test Group was assigned, together with the 6512th Test Squadron, from July 1959 until October 1963 and July 1962, respectively. The latter unit was active again between October 1969 and January 1973. Several other Test and Support Squadrons have been formed for varying periods since 1951 to conduct evaluation programs. The major flying squadron at Edwards AFB is currently the 6512th TS, while the 6514th TS is located at Hill AFB for drone development work. Virtually every operational aircraft type and numerous proof-of-concept prototypes have been assigned to the AFFTC. As the title suggests, AFFTC performs flight evaluation and development of manned aircraft prior to the operational testing and service phase of a type's career. The Center also operates the Test Pilot School where experienced pilots and engineers are trained for flight test and aerospace research work. The giant Utah Test and Training Range is administered by the AFFTC to evaluate and develop RPVs and cruise missiles.

Virtually every USAF aircraft is represented in the 6510th TW, including the F-15E.

Vought A-7Ds are used for general chase duties and for training test pilots.

6545th Test Group

AFMC Hill AFB, UT: C-130B, DC-130A, HC-130H, NC-130H, NCH-53A
6514th Test Squadron

The Test Group was activated in January 1979, although its subordinate unit – the 6514th Test Squadron – was formed in September 1973 reporting directly to the Air Force Flight Test Center at Edwards AFB until the 6545th was created. The group conducts tests of drone and RPV assets and has day-to-day control of the Utah Test and Training Range where evaluation and development of remotely piloted vehicles and cruise missiles are undertaken.

6585th Test Group

AFMC Holloman AFB, NM: QF-100D, QF-106A

Holloman AFB has conducted drone operations in conjunction with missile tests for more than two decades, with the 6585th Test Group activated in August 1970, replacing the Holloman Air Development Center (and later the Air Force Missile Development Test Center). The group is assigned a mixture of manned and unmanned drones flown as targets for Air Force and Army missile tests. PQM-102As were expended in large numbers during the 1970s, followed by the QF-100 and latterly the QF-106. The Army has utilized a number of QF-86Fs obtained from Canada. Many of the drones operated by the 6585th TG have survived operations at Tyndall AFB prior to their reassignment to Holloman. However, their fate is assured at Holloman AFB as the Air Force and Army are in the business of evaluating the accuracy of ground-to-air and air-to-air weapons rather than providing practice for aircrew.

Air Forces Iceland

ACC NAS Keflavik, Iceland:
F-15C/D ('IS')
57th Fighter Interceptor
Squadron

Air Forces Iceland (AFI) was formed by TAC in October 1979 when the Command absorbed the duties of Aerospace Defense Command. Prior to this the duties were coordinated by ADC and Atlantic Command. AFI has the 57th FIS as its flying squadron, which has been located at Keflavik since November 1954. AFI is responsible for the defense of the huge area surrounding Iceland and works closely with Norwegian and United Kingdom forces to maintain

surveillance of Soviet long-range bombers and reconnaissance aircraft while in the respective air defense zones. E-3 Sentries of the 552nd AW&CW (now 552nd ACW) detach to Iceland and are placed under control of AFI during their stay. However, the 552nd E-3s were committed to the Gulf War and have been replaced at Keflavik by NATO Sentries since August 1990.

The 'Black Knights' of the 57th FIS are no strangers to Russian aircraft. Most of the intercepts are Tupolev 'Bears' patrolling the North Atlantic.

Air Weather Service

AMC McClellan AFB, CA:
WC-135B
55th Weather Reconnaissance
Squadron

With its headquarters at McClellan, the Air Weather Service reports directly to MAC (AMC from June 1992). It supplies global weather information for all USAF activities, and has a small fleet of Boeing WC-135Bs.

The 55th WRS operates the WC-135B meteorological reconnaissance aircraft from McClellan.

HQ Air Warfare Center

ACC Eglin AFB, FL: A-10A, F-4G, RF-4C, F-15B/C, F-16A/B/C/D ('OT')
4485th Test Squadron

Known as the Tactical Air Warfare Center (TAWC) since established in November 1963, until late 1991 when the prefix 'Tactical' was removed. The Air Warfare Center (AWC) has had the 4485th Test Squadron as its flying unit since it was formed in April 1971, although other

squadrons have been assigned for various periods. In addition, the 4485th Test Wing was active for 15 months during 1964 and 1965. The Center acts as the link between the Air Force Development Test Center, which conducts evaluation of new and existing weapons systems, and operational units. AWC operates a small mixed fleet of fighter, attack and reconnaissance airframes, with detachment 5 of the 4485th TS based at George AFB with a pair of F-4Gs, although the det will inactivate in 1992.

Among the 4485th TS fleet assigned to the AWC is this F-15, used for missile tests.

HQ Fighter Weapons Center

ACC Nellis AFB, NV: A-10A, F-15C/D/E, F-16C/D, F-111A/D/E/ F/G, UH-1N ('WA')
57th Fighter Wing
  A-10 Fighter Squadron
  F-15 Fighter Squadron
  F-16 Fighter Squadron
  422nd Test and Evaluation
    Squadron
  541st Test and Evaluation
    Squadron
  4440th Helicopter Squadron
  4477th Test and Evaluation
    Squadron
  USAF Air Demonstration
    Squadron 'Thunderbirds'

Below: F-16s figure prominently in the FWC's activities, used for operational and tactical tests.

The Tactical Fighter Weapons Center (TFWC) was formed in September 1966, with the 4525th Fighter Weapons Wing and four squadrons activated as its flying organization. The primary duty of the Center was to teach fighter pilots various tactics and techniques to enable them to be effective and proficient. The Center

operated the F-100 and F-105 initially, with the A-7, F-4 and F-111A added later. The 4525th FWW was replaced by the 57th Fighter Interceptor Wing (later Fighter Weapons Wing) in October 1969. The two 'century-series' types were replaced by additional F-4s, before examples of the A-10, F-15 and F-16 were assigned. TFWC

established small detachments at other bases to assist with the introduction into service of new aircraft types, including Hill AFB for the F-16A/B, Luke AFB with the A-7D, F-15A/B and F-16C, and McClellan AFB for various F-111 types. The prefix 'Tactical' was removed in late 1991, the unit becoming Fighter Weapons Center.

Above: The 57th Fighter (Weapons) Wing is the main FWC operating unit.

Above: An A-10 fighter squadron is still in existence to evaluate new tactics with the 'Warthog'.

Above: As the latest tactical aircraft to enter USAF service, the 57th FW has several F-15Es.

The FWC is also responsible for the Air Demonstration Squadron, better known as the 'Thunderbirds'. The team flies the F-16A.

USAF Tail Codes

The US Air Force has employed the use of two-letter tail codes, or Distinctive Unit Aircraft Identification Markings to give them their official title, for more than 25 years. The first usage was in Southeast Asia at the end of 1966 and spread rapidly during the following year as more units were assigned to the war effort. These were assigned to tactical units whose aircraft, by that time, had received a brown and green camouflage pattern which eliminated markings and unit identification. With the massive influx of additional squadrons into PACAF there was a need to quickly identify aircraft by units. The position, size and colour of tail codes, which were initially white, were prescribed in a Technical Order to ensure uniformity. As each aircraft/helicopter type had a different size tail there were variations in the height of the tail code, ranging from 10 in (25 cm) for UH-1 Iroquois to 36 in (91 cm) on C-7 Caribou and C-130 Hercules. The majority of fighter types had a tail code either 18 or 24 in (46 or 61 cm) tall. In all cases the tail code was positioned above the aircraft serial number.

The first three units to display tail codes were the 8th TFW at Ubon RTAFB, Thailand, the 12th TFW at Cam Ranh Bay, South Vietnam, and the 366th TFW at Da Nang AB, South Vietnam. The former two wings adopted a system with the first letter identifying the wing, followed by a second letter for the individual squadron. The 8th TFW chose the letter 'F' for the wing, with FG, FP and FY as the three flying squadrons; the 8th TFW had wing letter 'X' with XC, XD, XN and XT as its assigned squadrons. The 366th TFW selected a unique system which involved each of the wing's F-4Cs being assigned an individual code within the range AA to AZ, BA to BZ and CA to CZ. The first letter was assigned to the squadron, with the second letter to the aircraft itself. This system was retained for almost two years until it was realigned in 1969 into the recognized format.

Within PACAF, tail codes were allocated on the basis of the letter combination not having been assigned to another unit, with almost 100 being consigned by 1968. Tail codes were extended to stateside tactical squadrons commencing in 1968, although with a little more uniformity as many units chose the first letter to correspond with the base name or mission, and with the second letter assigned in sequence. For example the F-111As of the 474th TFW at Nellis AFB were coded NA, NB, NC and ND, while codes BA, BB and BC were assigned to the RF-4Cs of the 67th TRW at Bergstrom AFB. The ANG adopted tail codes beginning in 1968, while the AFRes did not begin to use the system until 1972.

Tail code allocation was altered in 1972 when aircraft maintenance was transferred from squadron to wing level and the aircraft themselves were removed from squadron assignment. The change resulted in the majority of units adopting a wing code irrespective of the number of squadrons assigned. As stated earlier, PACAF, TAC, AAC and USAFE used the system widely, while ANG and AFRES units (with TAC as their gaining command in the event of mobilization) also displayed tail codes. MAC and SAC did not choose this form of unit identification. Air Force Logistics Command has operated only a handful of aircraft types, with just the Warner Robins ALC coding their F-15A until 1991, when the Sacramento ALC began applying codes to their F-111s. The two major Air Force Systems Command units at Eglin AFB and Edwards AFB began applying tail codes to their aircraft in 1982 and 1983, including those which are painted in the attractive gloss white scheme with large red areas. Finally, Air Training Command became the latest user of tail codes commencing in 1985. At that time ATC began experimenting with a dark blue color scheme to the underside and tail section of their T-37Bs and T-38As, with tail codes applied to the small number of repainted aircraft.

SAC bombers and tankers have not been included in the system, although some of their aircraft have had codes applied while operated by other Commands. The Air Force Flight Test Center at Edwards AFB has applied tail code 'ED' to B-52s on loan from SAC. During 1991 two Seymour Johnson AFB-based KC-10A squadrons were transferred from SAC to TAC as the first composite unit, with tail code 'SJ' applied. MAC, SAC and TAC were replaced by ACC and ALC in June 1992, which is certain to result in a number of tail code changes. Additional ACC bombers are due to be formed into composite units along with AMC tankers and C-130s and ACC fighters, resulting in the adoption of tail codes. This has already become reality at Kadena AB, Okinawa, where the F-15s of the 18th Wing have been joined by KC-135Rs of 909th ARefS and E-3s of 961st ACS, all displaying tail code 'ZZ'.

USAF TAIL CODES

Tail Code	Fin Color	Sqn	Group/ Wing	Base	Type/ Command
'AK'	r	11th TASS	343rd Wg	Eielson AFB, AK	OA-10A [PACAF]
	bl	18th FS	343rd Wg	Eielson AFB, AK	F-16C/D [PACAF]
'AK'	bl	43rd FS	3rd Wg	Elmendorf AFB, AK	F-15C/D [PACAF]
	y	54th FS	3rd Wg	Elmendorf AFB, AK	F-15C/D [PACAF]
	r	90th FS	3rd Wg	Elmendorf AFB, AK	F-15E [PACAF]
'AL'	r/wt	160th FS	187th FG	Dannelly Fd, AL	F-16A/B [ANG]
'AZ'	y/r/bl	152nd FS	162nd FG	Tucson IAP, AZ	A-7D/K [ANG]
'AZ'	y/r/bl	195th FS	162nd FG	Tucson IAP, AZ	A-7D/K [ANG]

Note: A-7s should have been withdrawn by early 1992 with the tail code ceasing to be current, as the AZ ANG F-16s do not display this form of identification.

Tail Code	Fin Color	Sqn	Group/ Wing	Base	Type/ Command
'BA'	or	12th RS	67th RW	Bergstrom AFB, TX	RF-4C [ACC]
'BC'	nil	172nd FS	110th FG	Battle Creek ANGB, MI	OA-10A [ANG]
'BD'	bl	46th FTS	917th FG	Barksdale AFB, LA	A-10A [AFRes]
	gn	47th FS	917th FG	Barksdale AFB, LA	A-10A [AFRes]
'BH'	nil	106th RS	117th RW	Birmingham MAP, AL	RF-4C [ANG]
'BT'	r	22nd FS	36th FW	Bitburg AB, Germany	F-15C/D [USAFE]
	y	53rd FS	36th FW	Bitburg AB, Germany	F-15C/D [USAFE]
	bl	525th FS	36th FW	Bitburg AB, Germany	F-15C/D [USAFE]
'CC'	bl/bk	428th FS	27th FW	Cannon AFB, NM	F-111G [ACC]
	r	522nd FS	27th FW	Cannon AFB, NM	F-111D [ACC]
	bl	523rd FS	27th FW	Cannon AFB, NM	F-111D [ACC]
	y	524th FS	27th FW	Cannon AFB, NM	F-111D [ACC]
'CM'	nil	50th FTS	14th FTW	Columbus AFB, MS	T-38A [ATC]
'CO'	bl/wt	120th FS	140th FW	Buckley ANGB, CO	F-16C/D [ANG]
'CR'	or/gn	32nd FS	32nd FG	Soesterberg AB, Netherlands	F-15C/D [USAFE]
'CT'	nil	118th FS	103rd FG	Bradley ANGB, CT	A-10A [ANG]
'DC'	gy/wt	121st FS	113th FW	Andrews AFB, MD	F-16A/B [ANG]
'DM'	y/bk	357th FS	355th FW	Davis-Monthan AFB, AZ	A-10A [ACC]
	bk/wt	358th FS	355th FW	Davis-Monthan AFB, AZ	A-10A [ACC]
'DO'	or/bk	89th FS	906th FG	Wright-Patterson AFB, OH	F-16A/B [AFRes]
'ED'	bl/wt	6510th TS	6510th TW	Edwards AFB, CA	B-2A [AFMC]
	bl/wt	6511th TS	6510th TW	Edwards AFB, CA	YF-22A [AMSC]
	bl/wt	6512th TS	6510th TW	Edwards AFB, CA	YA-7D, A-7K, OA-37B, NOA-37B, B1-B, C-23A, NF-4C, NF-4E, YF-4E, F-117A, UH-1N, T-38A [AFMC]
	bl/wt	6515th TS	6510th TW	Edwards AFB, CA	F-15A, F-15E [AFMC]
	bl/wt	6516th TS	6510th TW	Edwards AFB, CA	F-16A/B/C [AFMC]
	bl/wt	6517th TS	6510th TW	Edwards AFB, CA	C-17A [AFMC]
	bl/wt	6518th TS	6510th TW	Edwards AFB, CA	MC-130H, AC-130U [AFMC]
	bl/wt	6519th TS	6510th TW	Edwards AFB, CA	B-52G/H [AFMC]
'EG'	bl	58th FS	33rd FW	Eglin AFB, FL	F-15C/D [ACC]
	y	59th FS	33rd FW	Eglin AFB, FL	F-15C/D [ACC]
	r	60th FS	33rd FW	Eglin AFB, FL	F-15C/D [ACC]
'EL'	bl/wt	74th FS	23rd FW	England AFB, LA	A-10A [ACC]
	r/wt	76th FS	23rd FW	England AFB, LA	A-10A [ACC]
'ET'	wt/r	3247th TS	3246th TW	Eglin AFB, FL	F-4D/E, F-15A/B/C/D/E, F-16A/B/C, F-111E, F-117A, UH-1N, T-38A [AFMC]
'FF'	nil	6th ACCS	1st FW	Langley AFB, VA	EC-135P [ACC]
	y	27th FS	1st FW	Langley AFB, VA	F-15C/D [ACC]
	r	71st FS	1st FW	Langley AFB, VA	F-15C/D [ACC]
	bl	94th FS	1st FW	Langley AFB, VA	F-15C/D [ACC]
	nil	4401st HS	1st FW	Langley AFB, VA	UH-1N [ACC]
'FL'	nil	159th FS	125th FG	Jacksonville IAP, FL	F-16A/B [ANG]
'FM'	gy	93rd FS	482nd FW	Homestead AFB, FL	F-16A/B [AFRes]
'FS'	r/wt	184th FS	188th FG	Fort Smith MAP, AR	F-16A/B [ANG]
'FT'	?	75th FS	23rd Wg	Pope AFB, NC	A-10A [ACC]
'FW'	bl/gld	163rd FS	122nd FW	Fort Wayne MAP, IN	F-16C/D [ANG]
'GA'	sil/bk	20th FS	35th FW	George AFB, CA	F-4E [ACC]
'HA'	bk/wt	174th FS	185th FG	Sioux City MAP, IA	F-16C/D [ANG]
'HF'	?	113th FS	181st FG	Hulman Fd, Terre Haute, IN	F-16C/D [ANG]
'HI'	y/bk	466th FS	419th FW	Hill AFB, UH	F-16A/B [AFRes]
'HL'	y/bk	4th FS	388th FW	Hill AFB, UH	F-16C/D [ACC]
	r/wt	34th FS	388th FW	Hill AFB, UH	F-16C/D [ACC]
	bk/r	421st FS	388th FW	Hill AFB, UH	F-16C/D [ACC]
'HO'	y	8th FS	49th FW	Holloman AFB, NM	F-117 [ACC]
	r	9th FS	49th FW	Holloman AFB, NM	F-117 [ACC]
	gn	433rd FS	49th FW	Holloman AFB, NM	AT-38B [ACC]
'HS'	r/wt	307th FS	31st FW	Homestead AFB, FL	F-16C/D [ACC]
	gn/wt	308th FS	31st FW	Homestead AFB, FL	F-16C/D [ACC]
	bl/wt	309th FS	31st FW	Homestead AFB, FL	F-16C/D [ACC]
'IA'	r/y	124th FS	132nd FW	Des Moines MAP, IA	A-7D/K [ANG] to convert to F-16C/D in 1993

Some aircraft assigned to squadron or wing commanders feature the tail code in stylized form, usually dropped shadows. This is an F-111G of the 27th FW.

The 'TR' tail code (standing for 'Tonopah Range') of the 37th Fighter Wing is shortly to disappear when the T-38s and F-117s transfer to Holloman.

Some units have changed their codes, the 3246th Test Wing changing from 'AD' (Armaments Division) to the more explicit 'ET' (Eglin Test).

The code worn by more aircraft types than any other is the 'ED' of the 6510th Test Wing, which flies virtually every type in the inventory, including this F-4E.

Code	Color	Squadron	Wing	Base	Aircraft
'IL'	r/wt/bl	169th FS	182nd FG	Gtr Peoria Apt, IL	OA-37B [ANG]
					to convert to F-16A/B in 1992
'IN'	bl	45th FS	930th FG	Grissom AFB, IN	A-10A [AFRes]
'IS'	bk/wt	57th FIS	AFI	NAF Keflavik, Iceland	F-15C/D [ACC]
'KC'	bk/y	303rd FS	442nd FW	Richards Gebaur AFB, MO	A-10A [AFRes]
'LF'	gn/y	310th FS	58th FW	Luke AFB, AZ	F-16C/D [ACC]
	bl/wt	311th FS	58th FW	Luke AFB, AZ	F-16C/D [ACC]
	y/bk	314th FS	58th FW	Luke AFB, AZ	F-16C/D [ACC]
	bk/y	461st FS	58th FW	Luke AFB, AZ	F-15E [ACC]
	sil/bk	550th FS	58th FW	Luke AFB, AZ	F-15E [ACC]
'LN'	bl	492nd FS	48th FW	RAF Lakenheath, UK	F-111F [USAFE]
	y	493rd FS	48th FW	RAF Lakenheath, UK	F-111F [USAFE]
	r	494th FS	48th FW	RAF Lakenheath, UK	F-111F [USAFE]
					converting to F-15E in 1992
'LR'	y/r	302nd FS	944th FG	Luke AFB, AZ	F-16C/D [AFRes]
'MA'	r/wt	131st FS	104th FG	Barnes MAP, MA	A-10A [ANG]
					to convert to F-16A/B in 1992
'MB'	r/bk	353rd FS	354th FW	Myrtle Beach AFB, SC	A-10A [ACC]
	bl/wt	355th FS	354th FW	Myrtle Beach AFB, SC	A-10A [ACC]
	gn/wt	356th FS	354th FW	Myrtle Beach AFB, SC	A-10A [ACC]
'MC'	y/wt	61st FS	56th FW	MacDill AFB, FL	F-16C/D [ACC]
	bl/wt	62nd FS	56th FW	MacDill AFB, FL	F-16C/D [ACC]
	r/wt	63rd FS	56th FW	MacDill AFB, FL	F-16C/D [ACC]
	bk/wt	72nd FS	56th FW	MacDill AFB, FL	F-16C/D [ACC]
'MD'	bk/wt	104th FS	175th FG	Martin Apt, Baltimore, MD	A-10A [ANG]
'MJ'	r	13th FS	432nd FW	Misawa AB, Japan	F-16C/D [PACAF]
	y	14th FS	432nd FW	Misawa AB, Japan	F-16C/D [PACAF]
'MO'	y	389th FS	366th FW	Mountain Home AFB, ID	F-111A [ACC]
	nil	390th ECS	366th FW	Mountain Home AFB, ID	EF-111A [ACC]
	bl	391st FS	366th FW	Mountain Home AFB, ID	F-111A [ACC]
'MY'	r	68th FS	347th FW	Moody AFB, GA	F-16C/D [ACC]
	sil	69th FS	347th FW	Moody AFB, GA	F-16C/D [ACC]
	bl/wt	70th FS	347th FW	Moody AFB, GA	F-16C/D [ACC]
'NJ'	r	141st FS	108th FW	McGuire AFB, NJ	F-4E, C-26A [ANG]
'NO'	r	706th FS	926th FG	NAS New Orleans, LA	A-10A [AFRes]
					to convert to F-16C/D
'NT'	nil	454th FTS	323rd FTW	Mather AFB, CA	CT-43A [ATC]
'NY'	bl/wt	138th FS	174th FW	Hancock Field, NY	F-16A/B [ANG]
'OH'	gn/wt	112th FS	180th FG	Toledo Express Apt, OH	A-7D/K [ANG]
					to convert to F-16C/D
	r/y	162nd FS	178th FG	Springfield MAP, OH	A-7D/K [ANG]
					to convert to F-16C/D
	bl/wt	166th FS	121st FW	Rickenbacker ANGB, OH	A-7D/K [ANG]
'OK'	bk	125th FS	138th FG	Tulsa IAP, OK	A-7D/K [ANG]
					to convert to F-16C/D
'OS'	bk/y	19th FS	51st FW	Osan AB, RoK	OA-10A [PACAF]
	bk/r	36th FS	51st FW	Osan AB, RoK	F-16C/D [PACAF]
'OT'	bk/wt	4485th TS	AWC	Eglin AFB, FL	A-10A, RF-4C, F-15B/C, F-16A/B/C/D [ACC]
	bk/gy	4485th TS	det 5	George AFB, CA	F-4G [ACC]
'PA'	bl/r/y	103rd FS	111th FG	NAS Willow Grove, PA	OA-10A [ANG]
'PR'	bl/r/y	198th FS	156th FG	Muniz ANGB, PR	A-7D/K [ANG]
					to convert to F-16C/D
'RA'	nil	559th FTS	12th FTW	Randolph AFB, TX	T-37B [ATC]
	nil	560th FTS	12th FTW	Randolph AFB, TX	T-38A [ATC]
'RG'	nil	nil	WR ALC	Robins AFB, GA	F-15A [AFMC]
'RS'	gn/bk	512th FS	86th FW	Ramstein AB, Germany	F-16C/D [USAFE]
	r/bk	526th FS	86th FW	Ramstein AB, Germany	F-16C/D [USAFE]

Code	Color	Squadron	Wing	Base	Aircraft
'SA'	r/wt	182nd FS	149th FG	Kelly AFB, TX	F-16A/B [ANG]
'SD'	bk/wt	175th FS	114th FG	Joe Foss Fd, SD	F-16C/D [ANG]
'SF'	bl/wt	21st FS	507th ACW	Shaw AFB, SC	OA-10A [ACC]
'SH'	bl	465th FS	507th FG	Tinker AFB, OK	F-16A/B [AFRes]
'SI'	or/wt/bl	170th FS	183rd FG	Capitol MAP, IL	F-16A/B [ANG]
'SJ'	bl/wt	334th FS	4th Wg	Seymour Johnson AFB, NC	F-15E [ACC]
	gn/wt	335th FS	4th Wg	Seymour Johnson AFB, NC	F-15E [ACC]
	y/wt	336th FS	4th Wg	Seymour Johnson AFB, NC	F-15E [ACC]
	bk/wt	344th ARS	4th Wg	Seymour Johnson AFB, NC	KC-10A [AMC]
	r/wt	911th ARS	4th Wg	Seymour Johnson AFB, NC	KC-10A [AMC]
'SL'	r/wt/bk	110th FS	131st FW	Lambert-St Louis MAP, MO	F-15A/B [ANG]
'SM'	r	2874th TS	SM ALC	McClellan AFB, CA	F-111A/D/E [AFMC]
'SP'	bl/wt	23rd FS	52nd FW	Spangdahlem AB, Germany	F-16C/D [USAFE]
	y/bk	81st FS	52nd FW	Spangdahlem AB, Germany	F-4G [USAFE]
	r/wt	480th FS	52nd FW	Spangdahlem AB, Germany	F-16C/D [USAFE]
'SW'	wt/bk	17th FS	363rd FW	Shaw AFB, SC	F-16C/D [ACC]
	y/bk	19th FS	363rd FW	Shaw AFB, SC	F-16C/D [ACC]
	bl/y	33rd FS	363rd FW	Shaw AFB, SC	F-16C/D [ACC]
'TF'	bl/r	457th FS	301st FW	Carswell AFB, TX	F-16C/D [AFRes]
'TH'	r/wt/bk	113th FS	181st FG	Hulman Fd, IN	F-16C/D [ANG]
'TR'	nil	415th FS	37th FW	Tonopah TR, NV	F-117A [ACC]
	nil	416th FS	37th FW	Tonopah TF, NV	F-117A [ACC]
	nil	417th FS	37th FW	Tonopahn TF, NV	F-117A, T-38A [ACC]
'TX'	bl/r	704th FS	924th FG	Bergstrom AFB, TX	F-16A/B [AFRes]
'TY'	r	1st FS	325th FW	Tyndall AFB, FL	F-15A/B [ACC]
	y	2nd FS	325th FW	Tyndall AFB, FL	F-15A/B [ACC]
	bl	95th FS	325th FW	Tyndall AFB, FL	F-15A/B [ACC]
'UH'	nil	42nd ECS	20th FW	RAF Upper Heyford, UK	EF-111A [USAFE]
	bl/wt	55th FS	20th FW	RAF Upper Heyford, UK	F-111E [USAFE]
	r	77th FS	20th FW	RAF Upper Heyford, UK	F-111E [USAFE]
	y/bk	79th FS	20th FW	RAF Upper Heyford, UK	F-111E [USAFE]
'VA'	r/wt/bl	149th FS	192nd FG	Richard E. Byrd Fd, VA	F-16C/D [ANG]
'VN'	nil	25th FTS	71st FTW	Vance AFB, OK	T-38A [ATC]
'WA'	y/bk	A-10 FWS	57th FW	Nellis AFB, NV	A-10A [ACC]
	y/bk	F-15 FWS	57th FW	Nellis AFB, NV	F-15C/D [ACC]
	y/bk	F-16 FWS	57th FW	Nellis AFB, NV	F-16A/B/C/D [ACC]
	y/bk	422nd TES	57th FWW	Nellis AFB, NV	A-10A, F-15C/D, F-16A/B/C/D [ACC]
	y/bk	431st TES	57th FWW	McClellan AFB, CA	F-111D/F [ACC]
	gy	4477th TES	57th FWW	Nellis AFB, NV	T-38A [ACC]
'WF'	nil	90th FTS	80th FTW	Sheppard AFB, TX	T-38A [ATC]
'WI'	nil	176th FS	128th FW	Truax ANGB, WI	A-10A [ANG]
					to convert to F-16C/D in 1993
'WL'	nil	97th FTS	82nd FTW	Williams AFB, AZ	T-38A [ATC]
'WP'	bl	35th FS	8th FW	Kunsan AB, RoK	F-16C/D [PACAF]
	y	80th FS	8th FW	Kunsan AB, RoK	F-16C/D [PACAF]
'WR'	r/wt	78th TFS	81st TFW	RAF Woodbridge, UK	A-10A [USAFE]
	bl/wt	91st TFS	81st TFW	RAF Woodbridge, UK	A-10A [USAFE]
	y/wt	92nd TFS	81st TFW	RAF Bentwaters, UK	A-10A [USAFE]
	pr/wt	510th TFS	81st TFW	RAF Bentwaters, UK	A-10A [USAFE]
'WW'	y/wt	561st FS	35th FW	George AFB, CA	F-4E/G [ACC]
	bl/wt	562nd FS	35th FW	George AFB, CA	F-4E/G [ACC]
'XL'	nil	85th FTS	47th FTW	Laughlin AFB, TX	T-37B [ATC]
	nil	96th FTS	47th FTW	Laughlin AFB, TX	T-38A [ATC]
'ZZ'	y	12th FS	18th Wg	Kadena AB, Okinawa	F-15C/D [PACAF]
	bl	44th FS	18th Wg	Kadena AB, Okinawa	F-15C/D [PACAF]
	r	67th FS	18th Wg	Kadena AB, Okinawa	F-15C/D [PACAF]
	bl/r	909th ARS	18th Wg	Kadena AB, Okinawa	KC-135R [PACAF]
	nil	961st ACS	18th Wg	Kadena AB, Okinawa	E-3B/C [PACAF]

Color code: bl = blue, bk = black, gld = gold, gn = green, gy = gray, or = orange, pr = purple, r = red, sil = silver, wt = white, y = yellow

USAF ORDER OF BATTLE

On 1 June 1992, the US Air Force underwent its most radical reorganization since its inception in 1947. The major combat forces of Strategic and Tactical Air Commands were amalgamated into Air Combat Command, while US-based support aircraft such as tankers and transports were grouped under Air Mobility Command. The two theater commands have had their taskings widened to incorporate some former TAC, SAC and MAC assets, while AFLC and AFSC have combined into a single command (AFMC). What follows is the reshuffle, although the far-reaching structural changes to the order of battle will result in further alterations as more composite wings are formed.

AIR COMBAT COMMAND (ACC)

Headquarters Air Combat Command (ACC) Langley AFB, Virginia

Air Combat Command (ACC) was formed on 1 June 1992 to manage the US Air Force's war-fighting assets located on American soil. The creation of ACC confirmed the predominant role of the fighter pilot in Air Force leadership of the 1990s and marked the end, for most purposes, of doctrine split between 'tactical' and 'strategic' forces. In what amounted to a 'hostile takeover', Tactical Air Command (TAC) with its fighters, fighter-interceptors, strike and electronic warfare aircraft absorbed the bomber and missile forces until then operated by the Strategic Air Command (SAC).

Under US warfighting plans, air operations are controlled by theater commanders such as General Norman Schwarzkopf, who headed Central Command during the Gulf War, or by unified/specified commanders like the head of today's US Strategic Command (Stratcom) who, in wartime, takes charge of nuclear bombers, missiles and submarine-launched missiles. Until it was disestablished SAC was one of the unified/specified commands with a direct warfighting role, while TAC, in its lesser status as an Air Force major command, was not. An early bid by ACC's first commander, General John M. (Mike) Loh, to have ACC upgraded to become part of the national unified command structure drew little interest in Congress and ACC remains (like its predecessor, TAC) a service component.

ACC's spearhead is the composite wing, an integrated package of aircraft and capabilities able to serve as an expeditionary force for rapid overseas deployment. These serve under ACC's 9th and 12th Air Forces which would, themselves, deploy overseas for conflict and have new battle staff in the form of Air Operations Groups, which also came into existence on 1 June 1992. The 23rd Wing at Pope AFB, North Carolina, carrying on in the tradition of the World War II 'Flying Tigers', is equipped with A-10, OA-10, F-16 and C-130, is located adjacent to the US Army's rapid-deployment 82nd Airborne Division, and is described by an Air Force general as "the nation's premier forcible-entry capability for the future." Still in its early days, ACC may eventually have half a dozen expeditionary wings, and will also have an increased number of combat wings designated for the close air support role. By the turn of the century, ACC wants its expeditionary force upgraded with F-22, A-XX and MRF (multi-role fighter) aircraft.

ACC is also responsible for the bomber force and ICBM force. 15th and 20th Air Forces will not have battle staff Air Operations Groups since they normally do not deploy overseas. The manned bomber will remain vital to US warfighting plans. The B-2 will be a 'silver bullet' for quick-reaction strikes against high-value targets. The B-1B will remain the fleet workhorse and principal nuclear penetrator, with the B-52H retained for stand-off nuclear attack and conventional fighting and the B-52G for the conventional mission only.

1st Air Force
HQ Tyndall AFB, FL

325th FW	1st FS	'TY'	Tyndall AFB, FL	F-15A/B
	2nd FS	'TY'	Tyndall AFB, FL	F-15A/B
	95th FS	'TY'	Tyndall AFB, FL	F-15A/B
475th WEG	82nd TATS		Tyndall AFB, FL	E-9A, QF-100, QF-106A/B
AFI	57th FIS	'IS'	NAS Keflavik, Iceland	F-15C/D
Northeast ADS			Griffiss AFB, NY	no aircraft assigned
Northwest ADS			McChord AFB, WA	no aircraft assigned
Southeast ADS			Tyndall AFB, FL	no aircraft assigned
Southwest ADS			March AFB, CA	no aircraft assigned

ADS = Air Defense Sector

2nd Air Force
HQ Beale AFB, CA (all reconnaissance assets)

9th Wg	5th SRTS	Beale AFB, CA	U-2R/RT, T-38A
	5th SRS	RAF Akrotiri, Cyprus	U-2R
	6th SRS	Osan AB, RoK	U-2R
	95th RS	RAF Alconbury, UK	U-2R
	99th SRS	Beale AFB, CA	U-2R
	349th ARS	Beale AFB, CA	KC-135Q
	350th ARS	Beale AFB, CA	KC-135Q
55th Wg	1st ACCS	Offutt AFB, NE	E-4B
	2nd ACCS	Offutt AFB, NE	EC-135C
	24th SRS	Eielson AFB, AK	RC-135S/X, TC-135S
	38th SRS	Offutt AFB, NE	C-135A, NKC-135A
	343rd SRS	Offutt AFB, NE	KC-135E, RC-135U/ V/W, TC-135W

8th Air Force
HQ Barksdale AFB, LA (all manned bombers)

2nd Wg	62nd BS	Barksdale AFB, LA	B-52H
	596th BS	Barksdale AFB, LA	B-52H
5th Wg	23rd BS	Minot AFB, ND	B-52H
7th Wg	9th BS	Carswell AFB, TX	B-52H
	20th BS	Carswell AFB, TX	B-52H
28th Wg	4th ACCS	Ellsworth AFB, SD	EC-135A/B/ C/G/H/L
	37th BS	Ellsworth AFB, SD	B-1B
	77th BS	Ellsworth AFB, SD	B-1B
42nd Wg	69th BS	Loring AFB, ME	B-52G
92nd Wg	325th BS	Fairchild AFB, WA	B-52H
93rd Wg	328th BS	Castle AFB, CA	B-52G
	329th CCTS	Castle AFB, CA	B-52G
96th Wg	337th BS	Dyess AFB, TX	B-1B
	338th BS	Dyess AFB, TX	B-1B
97th Wg	340th BS	Eaker AFB, AR	B-52G
319th Wg	46th BS	Grand Forks AFB, ND	B-1B
379th Wg	524th BS	Wurtsmith AFB, MI	B-52G
384th Wg	28th BS	McConnell AFB, KS	B-1B
410th Wg	644th BS	K. I. Sawyer AFB, MI	B-52H
416th Wg	668th BS	Griffiss AFB, NY	B-52G
			to convert to B-52H in 1992

9th Air Force
HQ Shaw AFB, SC

1st FW	6th ACCS	'FF'	Langley AFB, VA	EC-135P
	27th FS	'FF'	Langley AFB, VA	F-15C/D
	71st FS	'FF'	Langley AFB, VA	F-15C/D
	94th FS	'FF'	Langley AFB, VA	F-15C/D
	4401st HS	'FF'	Langley AFB, VA	UH-1N
4th Wg	334th FS	'SJ'	Seymour Johnson AFB, NC	F-15E
	335th FS	'SJ'	Seymour Johnson AFB, NC	F-15E
	336th FS	'SJ'	Seymour Johnson AFB, NC	F-15E
	344th ARS	'SJ'	Seymour Johnson AFB, NC	KC-10A
	911th ARS	'SJ'	Seymour Johnson AFB, NC	KC-10A
23rd FW	74th FS	'EL'	England AFB, LA	A-10A
	76th FS	'EL'	England AFB, LA	A-10A
31st FW	307th FS	HS	Homestead AFB, FL	F-16C/D
	308th FS	'HS'	Homestead AFB, FL	F-16C/D
	309th FS	'HS'	Homestead AFB, FL	F-16C/D
33rd FW	58th FS	'EG'	Eglin AFB, FL	F-15C/D
	59th FS	'EG'	Eglin AFB, FL	F-15C/D
	60th FS	'EG'	Eglin AFB, FL	F-15C/D
56th FW	61st FS	'MC'	MacDill AFB, FL	F-16C/D
	62nd FS	'MC'	MacDill AFB, FL	F-16C/D
	63rd FS	'MC'	MacDill AFB, FL	F-16C/D
	72nd FS	'MC'	MacDill AFB, FL	F-16C/D
347th FW	68th FS	'MY'	Moody AFB, GA	F-16C/D
	69th FS	'MY'	Moody AFB, GA	F-16C/D
	70th FS	'MY'	Moody AFB, GA	F-16C/D
354th FW	353rd FS	'MB'	Myrtle Beach AFB, SC	A-10A
	355th FS	'MB'	Myrtle Beach AFB, SC	A-10A
	356th FS	'MB'	Myrtle Beach AFB, SC	A-10A
363rd FW	17th FS	'SW'	Shaw AFB, SC	F-16C/D
	19th FS	'SW'	Shaw AFB, SC	F-16C/D
	33rd FS	'SW'	Shaw AFB, SC	F-16C/D
507th ACW	21st FS	'SF'	Shaw AFB, SC	A-10A, OA-10A

12th Air Force
HQ Bergstrom AFB, TX (to move to Davis-Monthan AFB by March 1993 before Bergstrom AFB closes in September 1993)

27th FW	428th FS	'CC'	Cannon AFB, NM	F-111G (to F-111E)
	522nd FS	'CC'	Cannon AFB, NM	F-111D (to F-111F)
	523rd FS	'CC'	Cannon AFB, NM	F-111D (to F-111F)
	524th FS	'CC'	Cannon AFB, NM	F-111D (to F-111F)
35th FW	20th FW	'GA'	George AFB, CA	F-4E

Left column table (35th FW continued)

Wing	Squadron	Code	Base	Aircraft
35th FW (contd.)	561st FS	'WW'	George AFB, CA	F-4E/G
	562nd FS	'WW'	George AFB, CA	F-4E/G
49th FW	7th FS	'HO'	Holloman AFB, NM	F-117A
	8th FS	'HO'	Holloman AFB, NM	F-117A
	9th FS	'HO'	Holloman AFB, NM	F-117A, T-38A
	433rd FS	'HO'	Holloman AFB, NM	AT-38B
58th FW	310th FS	'LF'	Luke AFB, AZ	F-16C/D
	311th FS	'LF'	Luke AFB, AZ	F-16C/D
	314th FS	'LF'	Luke AFB, AZ	F-16C/D
	461st FS	'LF'	Luke AFB, AZ	F-15E
	550th FS	'LF'	Luke AFB, AZ	F-15E
67th RW	12th RS	'BA'	Bergstrom AFB, TX	RF-4C
355th FW	333rd FS	'NF'	Davis-Monthan AFB, AZ	OA-10A
	354th FS	'NF'	Davis-Monthan AFB, AZ	OA-10A
	357th FS	'DM'	Davis-Monthan AFB, AZ	A-10A
	358th FS	'DM'	Davis-Monthan AFB, AZ	A-10A
366th FW	389th FS?	'MO'	Mountain Home AFB, ID	F-15C
	390th ECS	'MO'	Mountain Home AFB, ID	EF-111A
	391st FS?	'MO'	Mountain Home AFB, ID	F-15E, F-16C
388th FW	4th FS	'HL'	Hill AFB, UT	F-16C/D
	34th FS	'HL'	Hill AFB, UT	F-16C/D
	421st FS	'HL'	Hill AFB, UT	F-16C/D
Inter American Air Forces Academy (IAAFA)	nil	nil	Homestead AFB, FL	GOA-37B GC-47D GC-130A/B, GF-5B, GT-33A

20th Air Force
HQ Vandenberg AFB, CA (all ICBM assets)

Wing	Squadron	Base	Missile
44th MW	60th MS	Ellsworth AFB, SD	LGM-30F
	61st MS	Ellsworth AFB, SD	LGM-30F
	62nd MS	Ellsworth AFB, SD	LGM-30F
90th MW	319th MS	F. E. Warren AFB, WY	LGM-30G
	320th MS	F. E. Warren AFB, WY	LGM-30G
	321st MS	F. E. Warren AFB, WY	LGM-30G
	400th MS	F. E. Warren AFB, WY	LGM-118A
91st MW	740th MS	Minot AFB, ND	LGM-30G
	741st MS	Minot AFB, ND	LGM-30G
	742nd MS	Minot AFB, ND	LGM-30G
321st MW	446th MS	Grand Forks AFB, ND	LGM-30G
	447th MS	Grand Forks AFB, ND	LGM-30G
	448th MS	Grand Forks AFB, ND	LGM-30G
341st MW	10th MS	Malmstrom AFB, MT	LGM-30F to G
	12th MS	Malmstrom AFB, MT	LGM-30F to G
	490th MS	Malmstrom AFB, MT	LGM-30F to G
	564th MS	Malmstrom AFB, MT	LGM-30G
351st MW	508th MS	Whiteman AFB, MO	LGM-30F
	509th MS	Whiteman AFB, MO	LGM-30F
	510th MS	Whiteman AFB, MO	LGM-30F

USAF Air Warfare Center
HQ Eglin AFB, FL

Unit	Squadron	Code	Base	Aircraft
AWC	4485th TS	'OT'	Eglin AFB, FL	A-10A, RF-4C, F-15B/C, F-16A/B/C/D
	det 5	'OT'	George AFB, CA	F-4G

USAF Fighter Weapons Center
HQ Nellis AFB, NV

Wing	Squadron	Code	Base	Aircraft
57th FW	422nd TES	'WA'	Nellis AFB, NV	A-10A, F-15C/D, F-15E, F-16C/D
	431st TES	'WA'	McClellan AFB, CA	F-111A/D/E/F/G, VC-25A
	A-10 FWS	'WA'	Nellis AFB, NV	A-10A
	F-15 FWS	'WA'	Nellis AFB, NV	F-15C/D
	F-15 FWS	'WA'	Nellis AFB, NV	F-15E
	F-16 FWS	'WA'	Nellis AFB, NV	F-16C/D
	4440th HS	'WA'	Indian Springs AAF, NV	UH-1N
	det 2	'WA'	Luke AFB, AZ	F-16C/D
	det 6	'WA'	Hill AFB, UT	F-16C/D

28th Air Division
HQ Tinker AFB, OK

Wing	Squadron	Code	Base	Aircraft
nil	7th ACCS	nil	Keesler AFB, MS	EC-130E
nil	41st ECS	nil	Davis-Monthan AFB, AZ	EC-130H
nil	8th TDCS	nil	Tinker AFB, OK	C-135E, EC-135K
552nd ACW	960th ACS	nil	NAS Keflavik, Iceland	E-3B/C
	963rd ACS	nil	Tinker AFB, OK	E-3B/C
	964th ACS	nil	Tinker AFB, OK	E-3B/C
	965th ACS	nil	Tinker AFB, OK	E-3B/C
	966th ACS	nil	Tinker AFB, OK	E-3B/C

Strategic Warfare Center

Wing	Base	Aircraft
99th Wg	Ellsworth AFB, SD	no aircraft assigned

AIR MOBILITY COMMAND (AMC)

Headquarters Air Mobility Command (AMC) Scott AFB, Illinois

Air Mobility Command (AMC) was formed 1 June 1992 to handle airlift and tanker operations to give the USAF its global 'reach'. Its first commander was General H. T. Johnson, who previously headed the Military Airlift Command and orchestrated the massive airlift during Operation Desert Shield. The AMC chief, like his MAC predecessor, has a dual role as he is also commander-in-chief of the unified United States Transportation Command (Transcom), which is responsible for air, sea and land deployment of assets abroad.

AMC is rapidly deleting the terms 'military' and 'tactical' from most of its nomenclature, including the names of its wings and squadrons. All former military and tactical airlift squadrons have been redesignated, in stages completed by April 1992, as airlift squadrons.

In its 21st and 22nd Air Forces, Air Mobility Command operates C-5 and C-141B strategic airlifters, to be joined by the C-17; C-130s for theater operations; and C-12, C-21 and other transports in the operational support airlift role. In its 15th Air Force, AMC operates the KC-135 tankers and KC-10 dual-role tanker/transports which support all long-range operations.

While airlift (a term in use only since the 1960s) is at the core of its operations, AMC's history is a rich potpourri with its origin in the founding of the Military Air Transportation Service (MATS) in 1948. This became the Military Airlift Command (MAC) in 1966, acquired tactical airlift (C-130) operations from TAC in 1974, lost its special-operations mission aircraft to AFSOC in 1990, and acquired tanker operations from SAC in 1992.

AMC's showcase is the 89th Airlift Wing at Andrews AFB, Maryland, which operates Presidential and other VIP transport aircraft including the Boeing VC-25A known as Air Force One. The 'real work' of the Command, as some see it, is the long-range transport and tanking function. Unlike other USAF commands, which spend most of their time practicing for possible war, AMC takes pride in flying every day the same 'real' mission it flies in wartime.

15th Air Force
HQ March AFB, CA (all tanker assets)

Wing	Squadron	Base	Aircraft
2nd Wg	32nd ARS	Barksdale AFB, LA	KC-10A
	71st ARS	Barksdale AFB, LA	KC-135A/Q
5th Wg	906th ARS	Minot AFB, ND	KC-135A
7th Wg	7th ARS	Carswell AFB, TX	KC-135A
19th Wg	99th ARS	Robins AFB, GA	KC-135, EC-135Y
	912th ARS	Robins AFB, GA	KC-135R
22nd Wg	6th ARS	March AFB, CA	KC-10A
	9th ARS	March AFB, CA	KC-10A
28th Wg	28th ARS	Ellsworth AFB, SD	KC-135R
42nd Wg	42nd ARS	Loring AFB, ME	KC-135R
	407th ARS	Loring AFB, ME	KC-135R
92nd Wg	43rd ARS	Fairchild AFB, WA	KC-135R
	92nd ARS	Fairchild AFB, WA	KC-135R
93rd Wg	93rd ARS	Castle AFB, CA	KC-135A/R
	924th ARS	Castle AFB, CA	KC-135A/R
96th Wg	917th ARS	Dyess AFB, TX	KC-135A
97th Wg	97th ARS	Eaker AFB, AR	KC-135A to inactivate in 1992
301st Wg	91st ARS	Malmstrom AFB, MT	KC-135R
305th Wg	70th ARS	Grissom AFB, IN	KC-135R, EC-135G/L
	305th ARS	Grissom AFB, IN	KC-135R
319th Wg	905th ARS	Grand Forks AFB, ND	KC-135R
340th Wg	11th ARS	Altus AFB, OK	KC-135R
	306th ARS	Altus AFB, OK	KC-135R
379th Wg	920th ARS	Wurtsmith AFB, MI	KC-135A
380th Wg	310th ARS	Plattsburgh AFB, NY	KC-135A/Q
	380th ARS	Plattsburgh AFB, NY	KC-135A/Q
384th Wg	384th ARS	McConnell AFB, KS	KC-135R
410th Wg	46th ARS	K. I. Sawyer AFB, MI	KC-135A
	307th ARS	K. I. Sawyer AFB, MI	KC-135A
416th Wg	41st ARS	Griffiss AFB, NY	KC-135R

21st Air Force
HQ McGuire AFB, NJ

Wing	Squadron	Base	Aircraft
89th AW	1st HS	Andrews AFB, MD	UH-1N
	1st AS	Andrews AFB, MD	C-9C, C-12A, C-20B/C, C-135B, C-137B/C, VC-25A
	det 1	Hickam AFB, HI	C-135C
317th AW	39th AS	Pope AFB, NC	C-130E
	40th AS	Pope AFB, NC	C-130E
	41st AS	Pope AFB, NC	C-130E
436th AW	3rd AS	Dover AFB, DE	C-5A/B
	9th AS	Dover AFB, DE	C-5A/B
437th AW	17th AS	Charleston AFB, SC	C-141B
	20th AS	Charleston AFB, SC	C-141B
	41st AS	Charleston AFB, SC	C-141B
	76th AS	Charleston AFB, SC	C-141B
438th AW	6th AS	McGuire AFB, NJ	C-141B
	18th AS	McGuire AFB, NJ	C-141B
	30th AS	McGuire AFB, NJ	C-141B
61st AG	310th AS	Howard AFB, Canal Zone	C-21A, C-22A, C-27A, C-130H, CASA C.212

22nd Air Force
HQ Travis AFB, CA

Wing	Squadron	Base	Aircraft
60th AW	7th AS	Travis AFB, CA	C-141B
	22nd AS	Travis AFB, CA	C-5A/B
	75th AS	Travis AFB, CA	C-5A/B
	86th AS	Travis AFB, CA	C-141B
62nd AW	4th AS	McChord AFB, WA	C-141B
	8th AS	McChord AFB, WA	C-141B
	36th AS	McChord AFB, WA	C-141B
63rd AW	14th AS	Norton AFB, CA	C-141B
	15th AS	Norton AFB, CA	C-141B
	53rd AS	Norton AFB, CA	C-141B
314th AW	16th AS	Little Rock AFB, AR	C-130E
	50th AS	Little Rock AFB, AR	C-130E
	61st AS	Little Rock AFB, AR	C-130E
	62nd AS	Little Rock AFB, AR	C-130E
375th AW	11th AAS	Scott AFB, IL	C-9A
	1375th AS	Scott AFB, IL	C-12F, C-21A
	1400th AS	Norton AFB, CA	C-12F, C-21A
	det 1	McClellan AFB, CA	C-21A
	det 2	Randolph AFB, TX	C-21A
	det 3	Nellis AFB, NV	C-12F

375th AW (contd.)	1401st AS			
	det 1	Offutt AFB, NE	C-21A	
	det 2	Wright-Patterson AFB, OH	C-12F, C-21A	
	det 3	Barksdale AFB, LA	C-21A	
	det 4	Peterson AFB, CO	C-21A	
	1402nd AS	Andrews AFB, MD	C-12F, C-21A	
	det 1	Langley AFB, VA	C-21A	
	det 2	Maxwell AFB, AL	C-21A	
	det 4	Eglin AFB, FL	C-21A	
443rd AW	56th AS	Altus AFB, OK	C-5B	
	57th AS	Altus AFB, OK	C-141B	
463rd AW	772nd AS	Dyess AFB, TX	C-130H	
	773rd AS	Dyess AFB, TX	C-130H	
542nd CTW	1550th FTS	Kirtland AFB, NM	MC-130E/H	
	1551st FTS	Kirtland AFB, NM	HC-130N/P, HH-3E, TH-53A, MH-53J, HH-60G	

Direct Reporting

US Military Training Mission		Dhahran AB, Saudi Arabia	C-12A
	Embassy Flight	Abidjan AP, Ivory Coast	C-12A
	Embassy Flight	Ankara AP, Turkey	C-12A
	Embassy Flight	Athens AP, Greece	C-12A
	Embassy Flight	Bangkok AP, Thailand	C-12A

Embassy Flight	Brasilia AP, Brazil	C-12A
Embassy Flight	Buenos Aires AP, Argentina	C-12A
Embassy Flight	Canberra AP, Australia	C-12A
Embassy Flight	Djarkarta AP, Indonesia	C-12A
Embassy Flight	Islamabad AP, Pakistan	C-12A/D
Embassy Flight	Khartoum AP, Sudan	C-12A
Embassy Flight	Kinshasa AP, Zaïre	C-12A
Embassy Flight	La Paz AP, Bolivia	C-12D
Embassy Flight	Madrid Barajas AP, Spain	C-12A
Embassy Flight	Manila AP, Philippines	C-12A
Embassy Flight	Mexico City AP, Mexico	C-12D
Embassy Flight	Mogadishu AP, Somalia	C-12D
Embassy Flight	Monrovia AP, Liberia	C-12D
Embassy Flight	Pretoria AP, South Africa	C-12A
Embassy Flight	Quito AP, Ecuador	C-12D
Embassy Flight	Rabat AP, Morocco	C-12A
Embassy Flight	Riyadh AP, Saudi Arabia	C-12A
Embassy Flight	Tegucigalpa AP, Honduras	C-12A

Air Rescue Service
HQ McClellan AFB, CA

36th RQS	Osan AB, RoK	HH-3E
37th RQS	F. E. Warren AFB, WY	UH-1N
det 2	Ellsworth AFB, SD	HH-1H
det 3	Grand Forks AFB, ND	HH-1H
det 4	Little Rock AFB, AR	HH-1H
det 5	Malmstrom AFB, MT	UH-1N?
det 7	Minot AFB, ND	HH-1H
det 8	Vandenberg AFB, CA	UH-1N
det 9	Whiteman AFB, MO	HH-1H
det 18	Plattsburgh AFB, NY	UH-1N
det 22	Mountain Home AFB, ID	UH-1N
det 24	Fairchild AFB, WA	UH-1N
41st RQS	Patrick AFB, FL	HH-60G
48th RQS	Holloman AFB, NM	HH-60G
		to be activated mid-1993
56th RQS	NAS Keflavik, Iceland	HH-3E
		to convert to HH-60G by early 1992
66th RQS	Nellis AFB, NV	HH-60G
71st RQS	Patrick AFB, FL	HC-130N/P
??th RQS	Misawa AB, Japan	HH-60G
		to form during 1992

Air Weather Service
HQ McClellan AFB, CA

55th WRS	McClellan AFB, CA	WC-135B

AIR FORCE SPECIAL OPERATIONS COMMAND (AFSOC)

Headquarters Air Force Special Operations Command (AFSOC) Hurlburt Field, FL

Air Force Special Operations Command (AFSOC) is the newest Command, as it was only established on 22 May 1990 when the forces of the 23rd Air Force, Military Airlift Command, were reorganized as a separate entity. The Command was created to develop the specialized role and to train forces in the methods of special operations. The AFSOC remit encompasses a host of duties including unconventional warfare, direct action against an enemy, special reconnaissance, counter-terrorism, combat rescue and foreign national defense. The Command is assigned the USAF Special Operations School at Hurlburt Field, which educates students from all four services, the Coast Guard, various government agencies and allied nations. The 1720th Special Tactics Group, also at Hurlburt Field, is responsible for numerous units located worldwide, the units being composed of small combat control teams and pararescue forces. AFSOC is the gaining Command for the AC-130As of the 711th SOS and CH-3Es of the 71st SOS AFRes, and the EC-130Es of the 193rd SOS, Pennsylvania ANG.

Three wings are directly assigned to AFSOC. The 1st SOW has headquarters and three squadrons at Hurlburt Field, along with another pair of squadrons at Eglin AFB. In Europe the 39th SOW is split with one squadron located in Germany and two others in the UK. These are due to move to RAF Alconbury by October 1992. AFSOC forces in the Pacific included the 1st and 17th SOSs, together with the parent wing. They were based at Clark AB, Philippines, but were relocated to Kadena following the spring 1991 eruption of Mount Pinatubo, which deposited ash and debris over the base. The removal of US forces from the Philippines was due to be completed by September 1992, and the move was implemented earlier than scheduled due to the eruption.

Air Force Special Operations Command

1st SOW	8th SOS	Hurlburt Field, FL	MC-130E
	9th SOS	Eglin AFB, FL	HC-130N/P
	16th SOS	Hurlburt Field, FL	AC-130H
	20th SOS	Hurlburt Field, FL	MH-53J
	55th SOS	Eglin AFB, FL	MH-60G
39th SOW	7th SOS	Rhein Main AB, Germany	MC-130E
	21st SOS	RAF Woodbridge, UK	MH-53J
	67th SOS	RAF Woodbridge, UK	HC-130N/P
353rd SOW	1st SOS	Kadena AB, Okinawa	MC-130E
	17th SOS	Kadena AB, Okinawa	HC-130N/P
	31st SOS	Kadena AB, Okinawa	MH-53J

AIR FORCE MATERIEL COMMAND (AFMC)

Headquarters Air Force Materiel Command (AFMC) Wright-Patterson AFB, Ohio

Air Force Materiel Command (AFMC) was formed 1 July 1992 through a merger of Air Force Logistics Command (AFLC) and Air Force Systems Command (AFSC), with General Ronald W. Yates, formerly AFSC chief, as its first commander. The command is responsible for developing, acquiring and sustaining USAF weapons systems. AFMC brings to a single command expertise in research, development, testing, technology and science, plus expertise in acquisition, logistics support and disposal.

In place of the numbered air forces which make up some Air Force Commands, AFMC consists entirely of Centers, some of which have acquired this designation only since 1 July 1992. Each is allocated a specific series of duties which, although employing a large number of personnel and a massive budget, has only a small quantity of aircraft.

The AFFTC (Air Force Flight Test Center) at Edwards AFB, California, evaluates and develops new USAF aircraft types, and has the B-2A, C-17A and AC-130U currently assigned. The Air Force Development Test Center (AFDTC) at Eglin AFB, Florida, conducts evaluation and enhancement of new and existing weapons with a fleet of fighter aircraft. The Aeronautical Systems Center (ASC), known as Aeronautical Systems Division (ASD) prior to 1 July 1992 and located at Wright-Patterson AFB, develops aircraft radar, avionics and communications systems with a small fleet of transport types.

AFMC's five Air Logistics Centers are each responsible for a variety of aircraft types which are processed at regular intervals for major overhaul and repainting.

The Aerospace Maintenance and Regeneration Center (AMARC) at Davis-Monthan AFB, New Mexico, stores and disposes of aircraft and associated aerospace systems.

Aeronautical Systems Center (ASC)
Wright-Patterson AFB, OH

4950th TW	4951st TS		Wright-Patterson AFB, OH	C-18A, EC-18B/D, NKC-135A, EC-135E, NC-141A, CT-39A, NT-39A, T-39B

Air Force Development Test Center (AFDTC)
Eglin AFB, FL

3246th TW	3247th TS	'ET'	Eglin AFB, FL	F-4D/E, F-15A/B/C/D/E, F-16A/B/C, F-111E, F-117A, UH-1N, T-38A

Air Force Flight Test Center (AFFTC)
Edwards AFB, CA

6510th TW	6510th TS	'ED'	Edwards AFB, CA	B-2A
	6511th TS	'ED'	Edwards AFB, CA	YF-22A

Unit	Sqn	Code	Base	Aircraft
6510th TW (contd.)	6512th TS	'ED'	Edwards AFB, CA	YA-7D, A-7K, OA-37B, NOA-37B, B-1B, C-23A, NF-4C, NF-4E, YF-4E, F-117A, UH-1N, T-38A
	6515th TS	'ED'	Edwards AFB, CA	F-15A, F-15E
	6516th TS	'ED'	Edwards AFB, CA	F-16A/B/C
	6517th TS	'ED'	Edwards AFB, CA	C-17A
	6518th TS	'ED'	Edwards AFB, CA	MC-130H, AC-130U
	6519th TS	'ED'	Edwards AFB, CA	B-52G/H
6545th TG	6514th TS		Hill AFB, UT	C-130B, DC-130A, HC-130H

6514th TS (contd.)			NC-130H, NCH-53A

Electronic Systems Center (ESC)
Hanscom AFB, MA

3245th ABW	Hanscom AFB, MA	no aircraft assigned

Other units

6585th TG	Holloman AFB, NM	QF-100D, QF-106A
Ogden ALC	Hill AFB, UT	F-16A
	Facility overhauls F-4s, F-16s	

Oklahoma City ALC		Tinker AFB, OK		Facility overhauls B-1Bs, B-52s and KC-135 models
Sacramento ALC	'SM'	McClellan AFB, CA	A-10A, F-111A/D/E, T-38A	Facility overhauls the A-10A and F-111
San Antonio ALC		Kelly AFB, TX		Facility overhauls the B-52 and C-5
Warner Robins ALC	'RG'	Robins AFB, GA	F-15A	Facility overhauls the C-130, C-141B and F-15
AM&RC		Davis-Monthan AFB, AZ		Aerospace Maintenance and Regeneration Center

AIR TRAINING COMMAND (ATC)

Headquarters Air Training Command (ATC) Randolph AFB, TX

Air Training Command (ATC) was formed on 15 April 1946 and has since that time recruited, trained and commissioned more than one million enlisted personnel and officers for the Air Force. Following basic training the Command trains personnel for every facet of Air Force operations from non-aviation duties such as catering and administration through technical trades and aircraft maintenance to aircrew.

Pilot training is conducted at seven locations in the southern states where students can learn to fly in uncrowded airspace with mostly perfect weather conditions. After the selection process and basic military training the student pilot completes three weeks of preliminary flight screening at either Hondo Airport (for those students attending Officer Training School at Lackland AFB) or at the Air Force Academy (for cadets studying at the Academy). The timetable for undergraduate pilots comprises around 500 hours of classroom lessons combined with 74 hours of flying training in the T-37B. At the completion of this portion of the syllabus the student transitions to the T-38A for a further 101 hours before graduating as a qualified pilot and being assigned to one of the major Commands for operational training. Navigators follow similar courses which are conducted at Mather AFB during a 28-week period flying the T-37B and T-43A. Navigator training was due to move to Beale AFB when Mather AFB closes but will instead relocate to Randolph AFB. The reduction in planned aircrew requirements will permit the 82nd FTW to deactivate in September 1992 with aircraft being redistributed prior to the base closing in September 1993.

The Air Force is introducing the T-1A Jayhawk which will enable the first stage of the Trainer Master Plan to be implemented. The plan involves Specialized Undergraduate Pilot Training (SUPT) which will tailor the trainee pilot towards either tanker/transport or bomber/fighter aircraft types. SUPT will involve all undergraduate pilots completing the T-37B course, before being streamlined to fly bombers/fighters with training being completed in the T-38 or tankers/transports with specialist training in the T-1A. The new trainer will provide students with familiarization of flight deck-configured aircraft.

Several Technical Training Centers instruct apprentices in a wide variety of maintenance trades. Since the closure of Chanute AFB, the primary center for technical training is now Sheppard AFB, which employs several dozen fixed-wing and rotary airframes. Sheppard conducts courses in aircraft and helicopter maintenance, civil engineering, and dozens of other non-aviation subjects. Lowry AFB trains students in avionics, logistics, munitions and space operations with the aid of a dozen airframes. Lowry is due to close in 1994 with duties being transferred to other Air Training Command bases.

Apart from conducting a limited pilot and navigator training role, the Air Force Academy operates a pair of UV-18Bs for parachute duties, while the 94th ATS has approximately nine TG-7A powered gliders.

Air Training Command (ATC)

Wing	Sqn	Code	Base	Aircraft
12th FTW	559th FTS	'RA'	Randolph AFB, TX	T-37B
	560th FTS	'RA'	Randolph AFB, TX	T-38A
14th FTW	37th FTS	nil	Columbus AFB, MS	T-37B
	50th FTS	'CM'	Columbus AFB, MS	T-38A
47th FTW	85th FTS	'XL'	Laughlin AFB, TX	T-37B
	86th FTS	'XL'	Laughlin AFB, TX	T-38A

Wing	Sqn	Code	Base	Aircraft
64th FTW	35th FTS		Reese AFB, TX	T-37B
	54th FTS		Reese AFB, TX	T-38A, T-1A
			tail code 'RE' allocated but not carried	
71st FTW	8th FTS	nil	Vance AFB, OK	T-37B
	25th FTS	'VN'	Vance AFB, OK	T-38A
80th FTW	88th FTS	nil	Sheppard AFB, TX	T-37B
	89th FTS	nil	Sheppard AFB, TX	T-37B
	90th FTS	'WF'	Sheppard AFB, TX	T-38A
82nd FTW	96th FTS		Williams AFB, AZ	T-37B
	97th FTS	'WL'	Williams AFB, AZ	T-38A
323rd FTW	454th FTS		Mather AFB, CA	T-37B
	455th FTS	'NT'	Mather AFB, CA	T-34A
Officer Training School			Hondo AP, TX	T-41A
	557th FTS		Air Force Academy, Colorado Springs, CO	UV-18B, T-41A/C
	94th ATS		Air Force Academy, Colorado Springs, CO	TG-7A
3300th TTW	Keesler TTC		Keesler AFB, MS	no aircraft
3400th TTW	Lowry TTC		Lowry AFB, CO	GA-7D, GA-10A, GB-1A, GB-52F, GF-4E, GF-15A, GF-16A/C, GF-111A
3700th TTW	Sheppard TTC		Sheppard AFB, TX	GYA-10A, GA-10A, GB-52D/F/G, GC-130A/B/D, GNKC-135A, GF-4C/D/E, GRF-4C, GYF-15A, GF-16C, GF-101B, GF-111A, GUH-1F, GCH-3C, GT-37A, GT-38A, GAT-38B
3250th TTW			Lackland AFB, TX	no aircraft

TTC = Technical Training Center

UNITED STATES AIR FORCES in EUROPE (USAFE)

Headquarters United States Air Forces in Europe (USAFE) Ramstein AB, Germany

United States Air Forces in Europe (USAFE) was formed on 15 August 1947, just five weeks before the Air Force became independent from the Army. Within one year of being established the Command was supporting the massive Berlin Airlift with hundreds of C-47 and C-54 freighters hauling everything necessary to sustain the population of West Berlin.

USAFE has predominantly been a tactical organization composed of fighter units located in France, the UK, West Germany, the Netherlands, Spain, Italy, Libya and French Morocco. The F-84E, F and G versions of the Thunderjet/Thunderstreak, and the F-86 Sabre, were the main types operated, along with the RF-84F and RB-57A for tactical reconnaissance and the RB-66B. The fighter types were gradually replaced by the F-100 Super Sabre, F-101 Voodoo and F-102 Delta Dagger, plus almost 150 F-105 Thunderchiefs. The Phantom entered USAFE service during the latter half of the 1960s and was joined by the F-111 in the early 1970s. The latter type remains current although it is scheduled to be withdrawn during 1992 and 1993, while the majority of Phantoms have been retired in favor of the F-15 and F-16. USAFE also operated its own C-130A theater airlifters and a small number of KB-29P and KB-50J tankers during the late 1950s and early 1960s.

For more than four decades USAFE had a common border with the former Warsaw Pact nations of East Germany and Czechoslovakia, and quite naturally the units ranged against one another were equipped with the most modern aircraft types available. However, the removal of Soviet influence and the collapse of the Warsaw Pact has enabled USAFE to make cutbacks in the number of squadrons assigned. The A-10A and F-4G began to be withdrawn during 1991 along with six squadrons of F-16Cs.

USAFE is composed of three numbered Air Forces, consisting of the 3rd AF controlling assets in the United Kingdom, the 17th AF overseeing operations in Germany and the Netherlands, and the 16th AF responsible for units stationed in the area adjacent to the Mediterranean. The 3rd AF is to reduce from four tactical wings to just one, while the 16th AF lost their only operational fighter unit during 1991 when the 401st TFW transferred its aircraft back to the USA. The 16th AF does operate a number of support bases in Italy, Greece and Turkey, with USAFE and stateside-based fighters regularly deploying for exercises. Within 17th AF the 50th TFW was deactivated during 1991 and its F-16Cs returned to the USA. The F-4G was retired in 1992 with additional F-16Cs assigned to the 52nd TFW, followed by one squadron of A-10As transferred to Spangdahlem from RAF Bentwaters at the end of 1992. The 32nd FG began upgrading with Multi-Stage Improvement Program (MSIP) F-15Cs at the end of 1991.

The deactivation of MAC, SAC and TAC during mid-1992 will see aircraft types from these Commands assigned to USAFE. These will include MAC C-130 and VIP types, SAC tankers and reconnaissance types, and possibly TAC E-3 Sentries, which will be assigned in some cases to composite or support wings.

3rd Air Force
HQ RAF Mildenhall, UK

20th FW*	42nd ECS	'UH'	RAF Upper Heyford, UK	EF-111A
	55th FS	'UH'	RAF Upper Heyford, UK	F-111E
	77th FS	'UH'	RAF Upper Heyford, UK	F-111E
	79th FS	'UH'	RAF Upper Heyford, UK	F-111E
48th FW	492nd FS	'LN'	RAF Lakenheath, UK	F-111F**
	493rd FS	'LN'	RAF Lakenheath, UK	F-111F*
	494th FS	'UN'	RAF Lakenheath, UK	F-111F**
81st TFW*	78th TFS	'WR'	RAF Woodbridge, UK	A-10A
	91st TFS	'WR'	RAF Woodbridge, UK	A-10A
	92nd TFS	'WR'	RAF Bentwaters, UK	A-10A
	510th TFS	'WR'	RAF Bentwaters, UK	A-10A
100th ARW			RAF Mildenhall, UK	KC-135R
313th TAG			RAF Mildenhall, UK	C-130E/H
				rotations from USA

* to deactivate
** to F-15E

16th Air Force
HQ Torrejon AB, Spain

40th TSW		Aviano AB, Italy	
401st TFW		Aviano AB, Italy	no aircraft assigned
HQ TUSLOG		Ankara AS, Turkey	

HQ TUSLOG (contd.)	39th TG	Incirlik AB, Turkey	
		tactical range support for rotational USAFE units	
	7217th ABG	Ankara AS, Turkey	
	7241st ABG	Izmir AS, Turkey	

17th Air Force
HQ Sembach AB, Germany

36th FW	22nd FS	'BT'	Bitburg AB, Germany	F-15C/D
	53rd FS	'BT'	Bitburg AB, Germany	F-15C/D
	525th FS	'BT'	Bitburg AB, Germany	F-15C/D
32nd FG	32nd FS	'CR'	Soesterberg AB, Netherlands	F-15C/D
52nd FW	23rd FS	'SP'	Spangdahlem AB, Germany	F-16C/D
	81st FS	'SP'	Spangdahlem AB, Germany	F-4G
	480th FS	'SP'	Spangdahlem AB, Germany	F-16C/D
86th FW	512th FS	'RS'	Ramstein AB, Germany	F-16C/D
	526th FS	'RS'	Ramstein AB, Germany	F-16C/D
435th AW	37th AS		Rhein Main AB, Germany	C-130E
	55th AAS		Rhein Main AB, Germany	C-9A
608th AG	58th AS		Ramstein AB, Germany	C-12F, C-20A, C-21A, C-135B, UH-1N, T-43A
HQ USECOM	7005th ABS		Stuttgart-Echterdingen AP, Germany	C-21A

PACIFIC AIR FORCES (PACAF)

Headquarters Pacific Air Forces (PACAF) Hickam AFB, HI

Pacific Air Forces (PACAF) was formed on 1 July 1957 when Far East Air Forces (FEAF) was renamed to encompass forces across the entire Pacific region rather than just those in the Asian part. FEAF itself was one of the oldest Commands, having been established on 30 December 1945 under the US Army Air Force, almost two years before the Air Force was separated from the Army.

FEAF and PACAF have had two periods of massive growth followed by a huge reduction of forces, the first being in 1950 when the Command was responsible for hosting large numbers of aircraft to repel the North Korean advance into South Korea. The successful outcome resulted in many of the units returning home to the USA, although some remained in South Korea and Japan as a deterrent. A dozen years later the Command was again embroiled in hostilities, as South Vietnam desperately fought the attention of the forces of the North Vietnamese and the Viet Cong. Huge numbers of aircraft were again flown across the Pacific for temporary assignment, with South Vietnam and neighbouring countries supporting combat operations. The protracted war, combined with an inconclusive outcome, saw the US agree to withdraw and virtually abandon the South Vietnamese to the inevitable. The US presence in South Vietnam and Thailand was eliminated completely, while that elsewhere in PACAF was returned to peacetime levels.

Throughout the remainder of the 1970s and 1980s the Command modernized, the F-4 Phantom (so long the backbone of the tactical community) being replaced by the 'teen' series of fighters such as the F-15C and F-16C. After many decades of operation from bases in the Philippines, the US was given notice to quit. In 1991, the explosion of the volcano at Mount Pinatubo pre-empted the run-down of aircraft at Clark AB. The 3rd TFW, with other units at Clark AB, had initially retired the majority of its F-4Es and F-4Gs to NAS Cubi Point, before relocating to Kadena AB, Okinawa, and to other locations in South Korea. The withdrawal of US forces from Clark AB was scheduled to have been completed by 16 September 1992, in any case. Of the two squadrons assigned to the wing, the 3rd TFS has deactivated while the 90th TFS moved to Elmendorf AFB, Alaska, to join the 3rd Wing and to equip with the F-15E.

On 9 August 1990 PACAF assumed the facilities and operations of units assigned to Alaskan Air Command when the latter was redesignated 11th Air Force. The realignment gives PACAF an enormous area of operations extending from the west coast of the Americas to the east coast of Africa, and from the Arctic to the Antarctic. At present there are four numbered Air Forces, with the 13th Air Force moving from Clark AB to Andersen AFB, Guam, but without aircraft assigned. The remaining three Air Forces have only a limited number of aircraft assigned, at levels nevertheless sufficient to maintain security of their respective areas of operation.

Tactical squadrons implemented changes to their designations during 1991, and are now identified as Fighter Wings/Fighter Squadrons, etc. PACAF has increased the number of aircraft assigned as those aircraft types which regularly deploy from the USA on temporary duty or are stationed in the region with other Commands have joined PACAF. This involves MAC C-130s and communications types, SAC tankers and TAC Sentries.

5th Air Force
HQ Yokota AB, Japan

18th Wg	12th FS	'ZZ'	Kadena AB, Okinawa	F-15C/D
	44th FS	'ZZ'	Kadena AB, Okinawa	F-15C/D
	67th FS	'ZZ'	Kadena AB, Okinawa	F-15C/D
	909th ARS	'ZZ'	Kadena AB, Okinawa	KC-135R
	961st ACS	'ZZ'	Kadena AB, Okinawa	E-3B/C
374th AW	20th AAS		Yokota AB, Japan	C-9A
	345th AS		Yokota AB, Japan	C-130E/H
	1403rd AS		Yokota AB, Japan	C-21A
432nd FW	13th FS	'MJ'	Misawa AB, Japan	F-16C/D
	14th FS	'MJ'	Misawa AB, Japan	F-16C/D
475th ABW			Yokota AB, Japan	UH-1N
603rd ASG	13th AS		Kadena AB, Okinawa	C-12F
624th ASG	1403rd AS det 1		Clark AB, Philippines	C-12F

7th Air Force
HQ Osan AB, RoK

8th FW	35th FS	'WP'	Kunsan AB, RoK	F-16C/D
	80th FS	'WP'	Kunsan AB, RoK	F-16C/D
51st FW	19th FS	'OS'	Osan AB, RoK	OA-10A
	36th FS	'OS'	Osan AB, RoK	F-16C/D
611th ASG	1403rd AS det 3		Osan AB, RoK	C-12F

11th Air Force
HQ Elmendorf AFB, AK

3rd Wg	43rd FS	'AK'	Elmendorf AFB, AK	F-15C/D
	54th FS	'AK'	Elmendorf AFB, AK	F-15C/D
	90th FS	'AK'	Elmendorf AFB, AK	F-15E
	962nd ACS	nil	Elmendorf AFB, AK	E-3B/C
343rd Wg	11th FS	'AK'	Eielson AFB, AK	OA-10A
	18th FS	'AK'	Eielson AFB, AK	F-16C/D
616th AG	17th AS det 1		Elmendorf AFB, AK	C-130H
			Elmendorf AFB, AK	C-12F
5073rd ABG	nil		Shemya AFB, AK	nil

13th Air Force
HQ Andersen AFB, Guam

633rd ABW		nil	Andersen AFB, Guam	nil

AIR FORCE RESERVE (AFRes)

The Air Force Reserve (AFRes) was established on 1 August 1968 when the Continental Air Command (CONAC) was renamed. At the time of its creation, the Reserve was composed exclusively of transport squadrons operating the C-119 Boxcar, C-123 Provider and C-124 Globemaster, along with five Air Rescue squadrons flying the HC-97G Stratofreighter and HU-16B Albatross. The AFRes, which was divided into Eastern, Central and Western Reserve Regions, set about modernizing its equipment with the introduction of the C-130A and B versions of the Hercules, and acquired a limited tactical capability with the F-105 Thunderchief and A-37B Dragonfly. Six wings introduced a radical new practice whereby AFRes units were assigned at front-line bases to crew aircraft from front-line units instead of their full-time colleagues. The benefits were twofold as it enabled Reservists to regularly fly the latest equipment, while at the same time enabling the Air Force to reduce the number of front-line aircrew. The units involved were given Associate status, and the success of the concept enabled the additional squadrons to be assigned to SAC KC-10As and one to MAC C-9As.

The Reserve has continued its modernization program, with the C-5A Galaxy and C-141B StarLifter joining the ranks in small numbers. The majority of early production Hercules have been superseded by later models, including many brand-new C-130H versions. A limited air refueling capability was added with three squadrons of KC-135Es, while the tactical element was upgraded to include the A-10A and the F-4D/E, with the F-16 recently replacing the Phantom.

AFRes is now organized into three numbered Air Forces, with the 4th and 14th predominantly equipped with airlift aircraft while the 10th AF is responsible for the tactical and refueling units. Like their ANG colleagues, AFRes aircraft operate along similar lines to the full-time forces, with the major Commands of AFSOC, ACC and AMC gaining the respective AFRes squadrons during mobilization.

Unlike the Air National Guard, which is organized on a state basis, the Air Force Reserve has the primary responsibility for providing the Air Force with immediately-available, combat-ready forces in time of war or national emergency. The Reserve has been mobilized on a number of occasions, most recently during Desert Shield/Storm when all three KC-135E, one A-10A and several Hercules squadrons were relocated to the Middle East. The intercontinental airlift squadrons flew hundreds of resupply missions between the USA and the Gulf region.

4th Air Force
HQ McClellan AFB, CA

Wing	Group	Squadron	Base	Aircraft
302nd AW	nil	731st AS	Peterson AFB, CO	C-130B
		to upgrade to C-130E in mid-1992		
	943rd AG	303rd AS	March AFB, CA	C-130B
349th AW (A)		301st AS (A)	Travis AFB, CA	C-5A/B
		312th AS (A)	Travis AFB, CA	C-5A/B
		708th AS (A)	Travis AFB, CA	C-141B
		710th AS (A)	Travis AFB, CA	C-141B
403rd AW	nil	815th AS	Keesler AFB, MS	C-130H, WC-130E/H
	934th AG	96th AS	Minneapolis-St Paul IAP, MN	C-130E
433rd AW	nil	68th AS	Kelly AFB, TX	C-5A
440th AW	nil	95th AS	Gen Mitchell Fd, Milwaukee, WI	C-130H
	927th AG	63rd AS	Selfridge ANGB, MI	C-130E
		to convert to 10 KC-135Rs late 1992 becoming 63rd ARS		
	928th AG	64th AS	Chicago-O'Hare IAP, IL	C-130H
445th AW (A)		728th AS (A)	Norton AFB, CA	C-141B
		729th AS (A)	Norton AFB, CA	C-141B
		730th AS (A)	Norton AFB, CA	C-141B

wing to lose its Associate status when it receives the C-141B from the 63rd AW when the latter inactivates and moves to March AFB in mid-1994

Wing	Group	Squadron	Base	Aircraft
446th AW (A)		97th AS (A)	McChord AFB, WA	C-141B
		313th AS (A)	McChord AFB, WA	C-141B
939th RQW	nil	71st SOS	Davis-Monthan AFB, AZ	CH/HH-3E
		to convert to HH-60G		
	nil	301st RQS	Homestead AFB, FL	HC-130/H/N/P, HH-3E
		to receive HH-60G		
	nil	304th RQS	Portland IAP, OR	HC-130H/P, HH-1H, HH-3E
		to exchange HH-3E for HH-60G mid-1992		
	nil	305th RQS	Selfridge ANGB, MI	HC-130H/N/P, HH-3E

HC-130s to transfer to 71st RQS (AMC) with HH-3E retired when unit deactivates mid-1992

Wing	Group	Squadron	Base	Aircraft
	919th SOG	711th SOS	Duke Field, FL	AC-130A

10th Air Force
HQ Bergstrom AFB, TX

Wing	Group	Squadron	Base	Aircraft
301st FW		457th FS 'TF'	Carswell AFB, TX	F-16C/D
		to remain at Carswell after base closes in 1993		
	924th FG	704th FS 'TX'	Bergstrom AFB, TX	F-16A/B
		to remain at Bergstrom after base closes in 1993		
419th FW	nil	466th FS 'HI'	Hill AFB, UT	F-16A/B
	507th FG	465th FS 'SH'	Tinker AFB, OK	F-16A/B
	944th FG	302nd FS 'LR'	Luke AFB, AZ	F-16C/D

Wing	Group	Squadron	Base	Aircraft
434th ARW	nil	72nd ARS	Grissom AFB, IN	KC-135E
	98th ARG (A)	78th ARS (A)	Barksdale AFB, LA	KC-10A
	916th ARG (A)	77th ARS (A)	Seymour Johnson AFB, NC	KC-10A
442nd FW		303rd TFS 'KC'	Richards Gebaur AFB, MO	A-10A

to add six OA-10As mid-1992 and move with parent unit to Whiteman AFB, MO, mid-1994, enabling Richards Gebaur to close in September 1994

Wing	Group	Squadron	Base	Aircraft
	930th FG	45th FS 'IN'	Grissom AFB, IN	A-10A

to convert from 18 A-10As to 10 KC-135Es late 1992, becoming the 45th ARS, joining the 434th ARW

Wing	Group	Squadron	Base	Aircraft
452nd ARW	nil	336th ARS	March AFB, CA	KC-135E
		to upgrade to 10 KC-135Rs late 1992		
	nil	79th ARS (A)	March AFB, CA	KC-10A
	940th ARG	314th ARS	Mather AFB, CA	KC-135E
		to move to McClellan AFB mid-1993		
482nd FW		93rd FS 'FM'	Homestead AFB, FL	F-16A/B
	906th FG	89th FS 'DO'	Wright-Patterson AFB, OH	F-16A/B
917th FW		46th FS 'BD'	Barksdale AFB, LA	A-10A
		47th FS 'BD'	Barksdale AFB, LA	A-10A
		to add 12 OA-10As in early 1933		
	926th FG	706th FS 'NO'	NAS New Orleans, LA	A-10A
		to convert to 18 F-16Cs late 1992		

14th Air Force
HQ Dobbins AFB, GA

Wing	Group	Squadron	Base	Aircraft
94th AW		700th AS	Dobbins AFB, GA	C-130H
	908th AG	357th AS	Maxwell AFB, AL	C-130H
	910th AG	757th AS	Youngstown MAP, OH	C-130H
315th AW (A)		300th AS (A)	Charleston AFB, SC	C-141B
		701st AS (A)	Charleston AFB, SC	C-141B
		707th AS (A)	Charleston AFB, SC	C-141B
439th AW		337th AS	Westover AFB, MA	C-5A
	911th AG	758th AS	Gtr Pittsburgh IAP, PA	C-130H
	914th AG	328th AS	Niagara Falls IAP, NY	C-130E
459th AW		756th AS	Andrews AFB, MD	C-141B
	913th AG	327th AS	NAS Willow Grove, PA	C-130E
	907th AG	356th AS	Rickenbacker ANGB, OH	C-130E

to convert to 10 C-141Bs and to move to Wright-Patterson AFB by 1994

Wing	Group	Squadron	Base	Aircraft
512th AW (A)		326th AS (A)	Dover AFB, DE	C-5A/B
		709th AS (A)	Dover AFB, DE	C-5A/B
514th AW (A)		335th AS (A)	McGuire AFB, NJ	C-141B
		702nd AS (A)	McGuire AFB, NJ	C-141B
		732nd AS (A)	McGuire AFB, NJ	C-141B
nil	932nd AAG (A)	73rd AAS (A)	Scott AFB, IL	C-9A

AIR NATIONAL GUARD (ANG)

The United States' history is steeped in the tradition of the volunteer willing to be called to arms to fight for his or her country during times of crisis. This dates from well before the emergence of the first flying machines, with militia organizing in 1775 and eventually winning independence. The National Guard was reorganized on clearly defined lines in January 1903 and, not surprisingly, soon included a number of aircraft which were supplied by private individuals. The National Guard continued to receive aircraft and many units were mobilized to active duty during World War II. After the war the Army was reduced in size to a peacetime level and the Guard took on an increased degree of importance as a ready reserve. The organization was to have been implemented in late 1945 but was delayed until May 1946.

The Air National Guard (ANG) was already an established component when the Air Force separated from the Army in September 1947. From that period onwards the ANG operated a variety of aircraft types to mirror that of the full-time Air Force, although all too frequently those assigned to the Guard were castoffs or elderly types 'handed down'. The Guard was active during the Korean War and in South Vietnam with units mobilized for periods of duty. The ongoing commitment in Southeast Asia by front-line units prevented the Guard from upgrading to more modern types, with the C-97 Stratofreighter, C-121 Constellation, C-124 Globemaster and the F-84 Thunderstreak remaining in service longer than planned as new equipment was supplied to the war zone.

The Guard was modernized during the 1970s and 1980s with aircraft types compatible with the increasingly important commitment to take on more of the everyday duties of the Air Force. This transfer of responsibilities included that of Air Defense of the continental US, leaving the front-line Air Force to concentrate on its global commitment. Likewise, the ANG undertook an increase in airlift and air refueling duties both internally and overseas. To perform these duties effectively the ANG received the latest types of aircraft, including some equipment purchased brand new.

The ANG is organized on a state-by-state basis with all 50, plus Puerto Rico and DC, assigned at least one unit. Funding is provided by the state and from central finances. Unlike the Air Force Reserve, which is basically a part-time version of the Air Force, the ANG is primarily organized for the benefit of the state in which it is located. The peacetime role enables units to operate in a much less rigid manner and allows them to support other states and the Air Force itself in a manner similar to the AFRes.

The future of the Air National Guard is assured as technologically-advanced, expensive aircraft types continue to be operated in smaller numbers by the regular Air Force while the ANG performs conventional duties. All Air National Guard units follow the guidelines laid down by their respective regular counterparts of AFSOC, PACAF, ACC and AMC. It is to these Commands that ANG squadrons would be assigned in times of national emergency or war. In the tradition of the ANG, personnel from several squadrons volunteered in 1990 for duty in the Gulf during Desert Shield with others mobilized by the time hostilities started. On 15 March 1992, the ANG redesignated its squadrons, dropping 'Tactical' and other prefixes.

Air National Guard (ANG)

Squadron	Group/Wing	Code	Base	Aircraft
101st FS	102nd FW		Otis ANGB, MA	F-15A/B, C-12J
102nd RQS	106th RQG		Suffolk County Apt, NY	HC-130N/P, HH-60G
103rd FS	111th FG	'PA'	NAS Willow Grove, PA	OA-10A, C-26A
104th FS	175th FG	'MD'	Glenn L. Martin State Apt, Baltimore, MD	A-10A
			to add six OA-10As late 1992	
105th AS	118th AW		Nashville Metro Apt, TN	C-130H
106th RS	117th RW	'BH'	Birmingham MAP, AL	RF-4C
107th FS	127th FW		Selfridge ANGB, MI	F-16A/B, C-130B
108th ARS	126th ARW		Chicago-O'Hare IAP, IL	KC-135E
109th AS	133rd FW		Minneapolis-St Paul IAP, MN	C-130E
110th FS	131st FW	'SL'	Lambert Fd, St Louis, MO	F-15A/B, C-12F
111th FS	147th FG		Ellington ANGB, TX	F-16A/B (ADF), C-26A
112th FS	180th FG	'OH'	Toledo Express Apt, OH	F-16C/D
113th FS	181st FG	'HF'	Hulman Fd, Terre Haute, IN	F-16C/D
114th FS	142nd FG		Kingsley Field, OR	F-16A/B (ADF)
115th AS	146th AW		NAS Point Mugu, CA	C-130E
116th ARS	141st ARW		Fairchild AFB, WA	KC-135E, C-12J
117th ARS	190th ARG		Forbes Field, Topeka, KS	KC-135E
118th FS	103rd FG	'CT'	Bradley ANGB, CT	A-10A, C-12F
			to convert to F-16C/D mid-1993	
119th FS	177th FG		Atlantic City IAP, NJ	F-16A/B (ADF)
120th FS det 1	140th FW	'CO'	Buckley ANGB, CO Buckley ANGB, CO	F-16C/D CT-43A
121st FS det 1	113th FW	'DC'	Andrews AFB, MD Andrews AFB, MD	F-16A/B C-21A, C-22B
122nd FS	159th FG		NAS New Orleans, LA	F-15A/B, C-130H
123rd FS	142nd FG		Portland IAP, OR	F-15A/B, C-26A
124th FS	132nd FW	'IA'	Des Moines MAP, IA	F-16C/D, C-12J
125th FS	138th FG	'OK'	Tulsa IAP, OK	A-7D/K
			to convert to F-16C/D mid-1993	
126th ARS	128th ARG		Gen Mitchell IAP, Milwaukee, WI	KC-135R
127th FS	184th FG		McConnell AFB, KS	F-16C/D
128th FS	116th FW		Dobbins AFB, GA	F-15A/B
129th RQS	129th RQG		NAS Moffett Field, CA	HC-130N/P, HH-60G
130th AS	130th AG		Yeager Apt, Charleston, WV	C-130H
131st FS	104th FG	'MA'	Barnes MAP, Westfield, MA	A-10A
			to convert to F-16C/D late 1992	
132nd ARS	101st ARW		Bangor IAP, ME	KC-135E
133rd ARS	157th ARG		Pease AFB, NH	KC-135E
134th FS	158th FG		Burlington IAP, VT	F-16A/B (ADF), C-12F
135th AS	135th AG		Glenn L. Martin State Apt, Baltimore, MD	C-130E
136th FS	107th FG		Niagara Falls IAP, NY	F-16A/B (ADF)
137th AS	105th AG		Stewart ANGB, NY	C-5A
138th FS	174th FW	'NY'	Hancock Fd, Syracuse, NY	F-16A/B
139th AS	109th AG		Schenectady County Apt, NY	C-130H, LC-130H, C-12J
141st ARS	108th ARW		McGuire AFB, NJ	KC-135E, C-26A
142nd AS	166th AG		Gtr Wilmington Apt, DE	C-130H
143rd AS	143rd AG		Quonset Point State Apt, Providence, RI	C-130E
144th AS	176th CG		Kulis ANGB, Anchorage, AK	C-130H
145th ARS	160th ARG		Rickenbacker ANGB, OH	KC-135R
146th FS	112th FG		Gtr Pittsburgh IAP, PA	KC-135E
147th ARS	171st ARW		Gtr Pittsburgh IAP, PA	KC-135E
148th FS	162nd FG		Tucson IAP, AZ	F-16A/B
149th FS	192nd FG	'VA'	Byrd IAP, Richmond, VA	F-16C/D, C-26A
150th ARS	170th ARG		McGuire AFB, NJ	KC-135E
151st ARS	134th ARG		McGhee Tyson Apt, Knoxville, TN	KC-135E
152nd FS	162nd FG	'AZ'	Tucson IAP, AZ	F-16A/B, C-130B
153rd RS	186th RG		Key Fd, Meridian, MS	RF-4C, C-26A
			to convert to KC-135E	
154th AS	189th AG		Little Rock AFB, AR	C-130E
155th AS	164th AG		Memphis IAP, TN	C-141B
156th AS	145th AG		Charlotte/Douglas IAP, NC	C-130B
157th FS	169th FG		McEntire ANGB, SC	F-16A/B, C-130H
158th AS	165th AG		Savannah IAP, GA	C-130H
159th FS	125th FG	'FL'	Jacksonville IAP, FL	F-16A/B (ADF), C-130H
160th FS	187th FG	'AL'	Dannelly Fd, Montgomery, AL	F-16A/B, C-130H
161st FS	184th FG		McConnell AFB, KS	F-16C/D, C-12J
162nd FS	178th FG	'OH'	Springfield-Beckley MAP, OH	A-7D/K
			to receive F-16C/D early 1993	
163rd FS	122nd FW	'FW'	Fort Wayne MAP, IN	F-16C/D, C-26A
164th AS	179th AG		Mansfield-Lahm Apt, OH	C-130H
165th AS	123rd AW		Standiford Fd, Louisville, KY	C-130B, C-12F
			to upgrade to C-130H in 1992	
166th FS	121st FW	'OH'	Rickenbacker ANGB, OH	A-7D/K, C-26A
			to convert to KC-135R in 1993 and move to Wright-Patterson AFB, OH, in 1994 enabling Rickenbacker to close in September 1994; to be redesignated 166th ARS, 121st ARW	
167th AS	167th AG		Shepherd Fd, Martinsburg, WV	C-130E
168th ARS	168th ARG		Eielson AFB, AK	KC-135D/E
169th FS	182nd FG	'IL'	Gtr Peoria Apt, IL	F-16A/B (ADF), C-26A
170th FS	183rd FG	'SI'	Capital Apt, Springfield, IL	F-16A/B
171st FS	191st FG		Selfridge ANGB, MI	F-16A/B (ADF)
172nd FS	110th FG	'BC'	W. K. Kellogg Apt, MI	OA-10A
173rd RS	155th RG		Lincoln MAP, NE	RF-4C, C-12F
174th FS	185th FG	'HA'	Sioux Gateway Apt, Sioux City, IA	F-16C/D
175th FS	114th FG	'SD'	Joe Foss Fd, Sioux Falls, SD	F-16C/D, C-12F
176th FS	128th FW	'WI'	Dane County RAP, Truax, WI	A-10A, C-130B
			to receive F-16C/D early 1993	
178th FS	119th FG		Hector Fd, Fargo, ND	F-16A/B (ADF), C-130B
179th FS	148th FG		Duluth IAP, MN	F-16A/B (ADF)
180th AS	139th AG		Rosecrans MAP, St Joseph, MO	C-130H
181st AS	136th AW		NAS Dallas, TX	C-130H
182nd FS	149th FG	'SA'	Kelly AFB, TX	F-16A/B
183rd AS	172nd AG		Allen C. Thompson Fd, Jackson, MS	C-141B
184th FS	188th FG	'FS'	Fort Smith MAP, AR	F-16A/B, C-12F
185th AS	137th AW		Will Rogers World Apt, Oklahoma City, OK	C-130H
186th FS	120th FG		Great Falls IAP, MT	F-16A/B (ADF), C-130B
187th AS	153rd AG		Cheyenne MAP, WY	C-130B
188th FS	150th FG		Kirtland AFB, NM	A-7D, C-130B
			to receive F-16C/D in 1992	
189th RS	124th RG		Boise Air Terminal, ID	RF-4C
190th FS	124th FG		Boise Air Terminal, ID	F-4G, C-26A
191st ARS	151st ARG		Salt Lake City IAP, UT	KC-135E
192nd FS	152nd FG		Reno-Cannon IAP, NV	F-4G, C-12J
193rd SOS	193rd SOG		Harrisburg IAP, Middletown, PA	EC-130E
194th FS	144th FW		Fresno Air Terminal, CA	F-16A/B (ADF), C-26A
195th FS	162nd FG	'AZ'	Tucson IAP, AZ	F-16A/B
196th RS	163rd RG		March AFB, CA	RF-4C
197th ARS	161st ARG		Sky Harbor IAP, Phoenix, AZ	KC-135E
198th FS	156th FG	'PR'	Muniz ANGB/ Puerto Rico IAP, San Juan, PR	A-7D, C-26A
			to receive F-16A/B late 1992	
199th FS	154th CG		Hickam AFB, HI	F-15A/B, C-130H
			to add four KC-135Rs early 1993	
210th RQS	176th CG		Kulis ANG, Anchorage, AK	HC-130H/N, HH-60G

Glossary

AAM	Air-to-Air Missile
AARB	Advanced Aerial Refueling Boom
ABCCC	Airborne Battlefield Command, Control and Communications
AC	Aircraft Commander
ACC	Air Combat Command
ACES	Advanced Concept Ejection Seat
ACM	Advanced Cruise Missile
ADF	Air Defense Fighter
AFB	Air Force Base
AFCS	Automated Flight Control System
AFLC	Air Force Logistics Command
AFMC	Air Force Materiel Command
AFRes	Air Force Reserve
AFSC	Air Force Systems Command
AFSOC	Air Force Sspecial Operations Command
AFTI	Advanced Fighter Technology Integration
AFV	Armored Fighting Vehicle
AGM	Air-to-Ground Missile
AIM	Air Intercept Missile
AIR	Air Inflatable Retard
ALCM	Air-Launched Cruise Missile
AMC	Air Mobility Command
AMP	Airlift Master Plan
ANG	Air National Guard
ANGB	Air National Guard Base
API	Armor Piercing/Incendiary
ASW	Anti-Submarine Warfare
ATB	Advanced Technology Bomber
ATC	Air Training Command
ATF	Advanced Tactical Fighter
AWACS	Airborne Warning And Control System
AWADS	All-Weather Airborne Delivery System
BAI	Battlefield Area Interdiction
BDU	Bomb, Dummy Unit
BLU	Bomb, Live Unit
BRU	Bomb Release Unit
BUFF	Big Ugly Fat Fucker
BVR	Beyond Visual Range
C³I	Command, Control, Communications and Intelligence
CAP	Combat Air Patrol
CAS	Close Air Support
CBR	Chemical, Biological, Radioactive
CBU	Cluster Bomb Unit
CFT	Conformal Fuel Tanks
CILOP	Conversion In Lieu Of Procurement
COIN	COunter Insurgency
Comint	Communications intelligence
CRT	Cathode Ray Tube
CSRL	Common Strategic Rotary Launcher
DLIR	Downward-Looking Infra-Red
DSO	Defensive Systems Operator
ECCM	Electronic Counter-CounterMeasures
ECM	Electronic CounterMeasures
EDSA	European Distribution System Aircraft
EFCS	Electronic Flight Control System
Elint	Electronic intelligence
EMP	ElectroMagnetic Pulse
EO	Electro-Optical
EVS	Electro-optical Viewing System
EW	Electronic Warfare
EWO	Electronic Warfare Officer
FAC	Forward Air Control
FBW	Fly By Wire
FFAR	Folding-Fin Aircraft Rocket

FLIR	Forward-Looking Infra-Red
FMS	Foreign Military Sales
FOL	Forward Operating Location
FOT&E	Follow-On Test and Evaluation
FSAT	Full-Scale Aerial Target
FSD	Full-Scale Development
FY	Fiscal Year
GAU	Aircraft Gun Unit
GBU	Guided Bomb Unit
GP	General Purpose
GPS	Global Positioning System
HARM	High-speed Anti-Radiation Missile
HF	High Frequency
HMMWV	High-Mobility Multi-purpose Wheeled Vehicle
HOTAS	Hands On Throttle And Stick
HUD	Head-Up Display
HVACAP	High-Value Asset Combat Air Patrol
ICBM	Inter-Continental Ballistic Missile
IFR	Instrument Flight Rules
IIR	Imaging Infra-Red
INS	Inertial Navigation System
IOC	Initial Operating Capability
IP	Instructor Pilot
IR	Infra-Red
JPATS	Joint Primary Aircraft Trainer System
J-STARS	Joint Surveillance Target Attack Radar System
JTIDS	Joint Tactical Information Distribution System
LANTIRN	Low-Altitude Navigation and Targeting, Infra-Red, for Night
LAPES	Low-Altitude Parachute Extraction System
LAU	LAuncher Unit
LF	Low Frequency
LGB	Laser-Guided Bomb
LLTV	Low Light Level TeleVision
LO	Low Observables
LOROP	LOng-Range Oblique Photography
LPI	Low Probability of Intercept
MAC	Military Airlift Command
MAR	Major Aircraft Review
MATS	Military Air Transport Service
MSIP	MultiStage Improvement Program
NCA	National Command Authority
NORAD	NORth American Air Defense
NTC	National Training Center
NVG	Night Vision Goggles
NWDS	Navigation and Weapon Delivery System
OCIP	Offensive Capability Improvement Program
OCU	Operational Capability Update
OCU	Operational Conversion Unit
ODR	Overland Downlook Radar
OSA	Operational Support Airlift
OSO	Offensive Systems Operator
OTH	Over The Horizon
PACAF	PACific Air Forces
PAVE	Precision Avionics Vectoring Equipment
PGM	Precision-Guided Munitions
PJ	Pararescue technician
PLZT	Polarized Lead Zirconium Titanate
R&D	Research and Development
RAF	Royal Air Force
RAM	Radar-Absorbent Material
RCS	Radar Cross Section
RFP	Request For Proposals
RN	Radar Navigator
RPV	Remotely Piloted Vehicle
RRITA	Rapid Response Intra-Theater Airlifter
RTU	Replacement Training Unit

SAC	Strategic Air Command
SAM	Special Air Mission
SAM	Surface-to-Air Missile
SAR	Search And Rescue
SAR	Synthetic Aperture Radar
SEAD	Suppression of Enemy Air Defenses
SHF	Super High Frequency
Sigint	Signals intelligence
SIOP	Single Integrated Operating Plan
SIP	Service Improvement Program
SLAR	Side-Looking Airborne Radar
SLEP	Service Life Extension Program
SRAM	Short-Range Attack Missiles
STOL	Short Take-Off and Landing
SUU	Suspension Underwing Unit
TAC	Tactical Air Command
TACAN	TACtical Air Navigation
TFX	Tactical Fighter, Experimental
TISL	Target Identification Set, Laser
TPS	Test Pilots School
TTTS	Tanker Transport Trainer System
UHF	Ultra-High Frequency
USAF	United States Air Force
USAFE	United States Air Forces in Europe
VFR	Visual Flight Rules
VHF	Very High Frequency
VLF	Very Low Frequency
WAFAR	Wrap-Around-Fin Aircraft Rocket

Index

Index

Picture acknowledgements

The publishers would like to thank the following organizations and individuals for supplying photographs for this book.

Front cover: James Benson, 416th Wing, Randy Jolly (three). **6:** Michael Pugh. **7:** Lockheed. **8:** Randy Jolly, Northrop. **9:** Lockheed, Randy Jolly (two). **10:** Graham Robson. **11:** Randy Jolly, David Donald, Michael Pugh. **12:** Randy Jolly (two). **13:** Randy Jolly. **14:** Randy Jolly. **15:** US Air Force (two). **16:** Randy Jolly. **17:** Randy Jolly. **18:** McDonnell Douglas, James Benson. **19:** Randy Jolly (two). **21:** Randy Jolly, James Benson. **22:** Grumman, David Donald. **23:** Randy Jolly (two). **24:** Richard Mullen. **25:** McDonnell Douglas, Lockheed. **26:** US Air Force (two). **27:** Peter R. Foster, US Air Force, James Benson. **28:** David Donald, US Air Force. **29:** US Air Force (two). **30:** Andy Thompson via Bob Archer. **31:** US Air Force, Vought. **32:** Randy Jolly. **33:** US Air Force. **34:** US Air Force. **35:** James Benson. **37:** Randy Jolly (three). **38:** David Donald, Randy Jolly. **40:** US Air Force. **41:** US Air Force (two), David Donald. **42:** US Air Force, Rockwell. **43:** Northrop (two). **44:** Northrop (two). **45:** US Air Force. **46:** US Air Force, David Donald (two). **47:** Lockheed. **48:** René J. Francillon. **49:** David Donald, Lockheed. **50:** René J. Francillon. **51:** Lockheed (two), David Donald. **53:** David Donald, James Benson. **55:** David Donald (two), James Benson, Robert S. Hopkins III. **56:** Robert S. Hopkins III, Jeff Wilson, James Benson. **57:** David Donald, James Benson. **58:** John Gourley, David Donald. **59:** Boeing, John Gourley. **60:** US Air Force (two). **62:** Peter R. Foster, US Air Force. **63:** US Air Force. **64:** US Air Force, David Donald. **65:** Robbie Shaw. **66:** US Air Force. **67:** Randy Jolly. **68:** Beech. **69:** Robbie Shaw, Beech. **70:** McDonnell Douglas. **71:** US Air Force (two), McDonnell Douglas. **72:** US Air Force. **73:** David Donald. **74:** Robert F. Dorr. **75:** David Donald. **76:** Boeing. **77:** Robert Archer. **78:** Chrysler. **79:** US Air Force. **81:** René J. Francillon, US Air Force, Peter R. Foster. **82:** US Air Force. **83:** US Air Force, James Benson. **84:** Randy Jolly. **85:** John Gourley, 475th WEG. **87:** US Air Force (two), Randy Jolly, Robert F. Dorr. **88:** Jim Rotramel, David Donald, Randy Jolly. **90:** James Benson. **91:** Lockheed. **92:** James Benson, US Air Force. **94:** Bob Shane via Robert F. Dorr, Lockheed. **95:** Robert F. Dorr. **96:** US Air Force, Peter R. Foster. **97:** G. Turner. **98:** McDonnell Douglas. **99:** Michael Pugh, Peter R. Foster. **100:** James Benson, Michael Pugh. **102:** McDonnell Douglas. **103:** McDonnell Douglas, David Donald, US Air Force. **105:** General Dynamics. **106:** James Benson, General Dynamics. **108:** General Dynamics, US Air Force. **109:** 174th FW, US Air Force (two), David Donald. **110:** Lockheed (two). **111:** Lockheed. **112:** Robert F. Dorr. **113:** US Air Force. **114:** US Air Force. **115:** Tom Kaminski, John Gourley, US Air Force. **116:** Richard Mullen. **117:** Robert Archer, Robbie Shaw. **118:** David Donald. **119:** Walter Wright/12th FTW, David Donald. **121:** Robert Archer, David Donald, Walter Wright/12th FTW. **123:** Robert F. Dorr. **124:** Jeff Rankin-Lowe. **125:** US Air Force. **126:** David Donald. **127:** Peter R. Foster. **128:** US Air Force, David Donald (two). **129:** US Air Force. **130:** Aermacchi/Lockheed, Pilatus, FMA, Grumman/Agusta. **131:** 475th WEG. **132:** 475th WEG, David Donald. **133:** 475th WEG, Richard Gennis. **134:** McDonnell Douglas. **135:** Randy Jolly (two), David Donald, Jim Rotramel. **136:** David Donald (six). **137:** David Donald, Jim Rotramel (two), Jeff Rankin-Lowe. **138:** Jim Rotramel (two), Randy Jolly, US Air Force. **139:** Richard Gennis, Randy Jolly (two), Jim

Rotramel. **140:** Randy Jolly (two). **141:** David Donald (two), US Air Force (two), Robert F. Dorr. **142:** US Air Force (four). **143:** David Donald, US Air Force. **144:** Randy Jolly, US Air Force (two), David Donald. **145:** McDonnell Douglas, Randy Jolly (two), Florida ANG. **146:** US Air Force. **147:** Lockheed. **149:** 27th FW, David Donald. **151:** Northrop. **153:** James Benson, US Air Force. **155:** US Air Force. **157:** Randy Jolly. **159:** David Donald. **161:** 63rd AW. **163:** McDonnell Douglas. **165:** McDonnell Douglas. **167:** McDonnell Douglas, US Air Force, David Donald. **172:** Paul Langshaw, Jeff Rankin-Lowe, Robert Archer, Peter Lewis, 3rd Wing. **173:** Jeff Rankin-Lowe, David Donald, 5th Wing, Robert S. Hopkins III, Randy Jolly, Chris Pocock. **174:** David Donald, Brian Rogers via Robert Archer (two), US Air Force. **175:** David Donald (two), Yves Debay, René J. Francillon. **176:** Randy Jolly, David Donald, US Air Force. **177:** 32nd FG, McDonnell Douglas, Randy Jolly, 36th FW. **178:** James Benson, David Donald (two), Robert Archer. **179:** Doug Remington via Robert Archer, David Donald (four), Paul Bennett, Kevin L. Patrick. **180:** Jeff Wilson (two), Gary Jennings, Joe Cupido, 60th AW. **181:** Robert Archer, David Donald (two), Doug Remington via Robert Archer, Jeff Rankin-Lowe. **182:** Doug Remington via Robert Archer, Robert Archer (three), Kevin L. Patrick. **183:** G. Turner, Lockheed (two), Joe Bruch via Robert Archer, Tom Ross. **184:** Rick Rizzo, Robert Archer. **185:** Robert Archer, Michael M. Anselmo, Michelle Hamilton, Jeff Rankin-Lowe. **186:** Jeff Rankin-Lowe, David Donald, Yves Debay. **187:** Robbie Shaw, Don Spering/AIR, General Dynamics, James Benson. **188:** Philip A. Tachauer, David Donald, General Dynamics. **189:** General Dynamics, Robert Archer, René J. Francillon. **190:** Grant Race, Jeff Rankin-Lowe, US Air Force, Michael Pugh. **191:** Jeff Rankin-Lowe, Peter Wilson, Robbie Shaw. **192:** David Donald, Randy Jolly, James Benson, Joe Cupido. **193:** General Dynamics, David Donald, Minnesota ANG. **194:** US Air Force, Michael M. Anselmo, Stan Morse, Robert Archer. **195:** Ben J. Ullings, James Benson, Robert Archer, Randy Jolly. **196:** McDonnell Douglas, David Donald, Michael M. Anselmo, Kevin L. Patrick. **197:** Robert Archer (two), Grant Race, Randy Jolly, Robert F. Dorr. **198:** Robert S. Hopkins III, Randy Jolly, Robert Archer, David Donald. **199:** Mark Hasara via Robert F. Dorr, Robert Archer (two), New Jersey ANG, Jeff Rankin-Lowe. **200:** David Donald, Robert Archer, Don Spering/AIR, General Dynamics. **201:** Jeff Rankin-Lowe, General Dynamics, Randy Jolly. **202:** Robert Archer, General Dynamics, Jeff Puzzullo, Randy Jolly. **203:** David Donald (four). **204:** David Donald, Peter R. Foster, Robert Archer, David Donald. **205:** Randy Jolly, James Benson (two), US Air Force, Robbie Shaw. **206:** Randy Jolly, Mark Hasara via Robert F. Dorr, James Benson, Robbie Shaw. **207:** Yves Debay, David Donald, Peter Lewis, Robert Archer, Randy Jolly. **208:** Robert Archer, David Donald, Jeff Rankin-Lowe, US Air Force, Peter R. Foster. **209:** Robert Archer, 435th AW, Graham Robson, David Donald (two). **210:** Randy Jolly (two), Lockheed, David Donald (two). **211:** Randy Jolly (two), via Robbie Shaw, Andy Thompson via Robert Archer, Richard Gennis. **212:** US Air Force, 28th AD, US Air Force, Wallace T. van Winkle. **213:** William J. Mondy, Jeff Wilson, David Donald. **214:** US Air Force (two), 924th FG, Randy Jolly, Lockheed via Robert Archer. **215:** 934th AG, David Donald, Robert Archer, Joe Cupido, General Dynamics, 3246th TW. **216:** Jeff Wilson, Jeff Rankin-Lowe, Martyn D. Swann, David Donald. **217:** McDonnell Douglas (two), Graham Robson, Jeff Puzzullo, René J. Francillon, General Dynamics, Georg Mader. **219:** Robert Archer (four). **Back cover:** Lockheed.